A World
of Love

LOVE, ELEANOR: Eleanor Roosevelt and Her Friends

DAG HAMMARSKJOLD: Custodian of the Brushfire Peace

ELEANOR ROOSEVELT: A Friend's Memoir

ELEANOR AND FRANKLIN

ELEANOR: The Years Alone

FROM THE DIARIES OF FELIX FRANKFURTER

ROOSEVELT AND CHURCHILL

HELEN AND TEACHER

A World of Love

Eleanor Roosevelt and Her Friends

1943–1962

Joseph P. Lash

Foreword by Franklin D. Roosevelt, Jr.

McGRAW-HILL BOOK COMPANY

New York   St. Louis   San Francisco   Bogotá   Guatemala
Hamburg   Lisbon   Madrid   Mexico   Montreal   Panama   Paris
San Juan   São Paulo   Tokyo   Toronto

First paperback edition, 1985
Published by arrangement with Doubleday & Company, Inc.

1 2 3 4 5 6 7 8 9 D O C D O C 8 7 6 5

ISBN 0-07-036487-7

LIBRARY OF CONGRESS CATALOGING IN PUBLICATION DATA

Lash, Joseph P., 1909–
 A world of love.
 Includes index.
 1. Roosevelt, Eleanor, 1884–1962—Correspondence.
2. Roosevelt, Franklin D. (Franklin Delano), 1882–
1945—Family. 3. Presidents—United States—Wives—
Correspondence. I. Title.
E807.1.R48L38   1985   973.917'092'4 [B]   85-13249
 ISBN 0-07-036487-7 (pbk.)

Contents

Foreword

AT THE CELEBRATION of my mother's seventieth birthday organized by the American Association for the United Nations, her last words were for her family. More than accomplishments, "I treasure the love of my children, the respect of my children, and I would never want my children or grandchildren to feel that I had failed them."

I wish I might be able to say the same in reverse. Whatever our failings, however, it has seemed appropriate to include a fair portion of my mother's letters to her sons and daughter among those to her friends. She had a special relationship to us, one that she did justice to in our adult lives in the midst of the hectic schedules that are so well reflected in these letters. She also treated us as friends, unwilling, she said, to make up our minds for us but willing always to work with any and all of us. I am glad that we gave her much happiness as well as difficulties.

It was characteristic that she allowed the AAUN to celebrate her seventieth birthday, "to commercialize it," she said, because she wanted to help the organization that sought to mobilize grass-roots support for the UN to clear itself of debt. Building a peaceful world through the UN was not the job of government officials alone, she insisted, but of "the peoples of the world, and it will be done only if they put their strength behind their representatives." So she worked in her final years for the AAUN, and it is timely to remind ourselves that she got "the most satisfaction" from her work in the UN. "There I was part of the second great experiment to bring countries together."

She was a person of seemingly contradictory yet connected positions. One should draw strength from the past, but one could do so only if one thought for oneself. Men and women should have equal rights, but the fact that they were different cannot be changed and it was fortunate for mankind that this was the case. She believed in God and was a faithful churchgoer, and she also believed "the Lord wants us to help ourselves and holds us responsible for our actions."

I am her son, yet it is more than kinship that impels me to say she was the most remarkable woman of the twentieth century.

Franklin D. Roosevelt, Jr.

Introduction: "Satellites" or "Pollinating Bees"

SINCE THE PUBLICATION of Volume I of *Love, Eleanor*, several batches of letters have been made available to me. Many of them are of such importance as documents of self-revelation that I have decided to backtrack and include them in an introductory chapter. I don't apologize for doing so. Eleanor Roosevelt belongs in the pantheon of great people who have helped mankind live according to its better nature. Many years ago a splendid exploration of the origins of Samuel Taylor Coleridge's poem "The Road to Xanadu" excited the literary world. Although Coleridge's poem numbered some fifty-five lines, few people felt that John Livingston Lowe's massive commentary was overwritten. Sometimes these two volumes of Eleanor Roosevelt's letters have seemed to me a comparable task of elucidation, and while I make no claims to a Lowes-like craftsmanship, Eleanor Roosevelt's personality warrants comparable treatment.

The first new archive that came my way was the result of Franklin Roosevelt Jr.'s discovery of a carton of letters, most of them written during the years 1928–1932 when he was at Groton School. His father was then Governor of New York. Unfortunately, there are few letters from him, but he always looms large in the letters "Fjr." (as his mother addressed him) received from her and his grandmother, Sara Delano Roosevelt. Eleanor by that time had made her own mark in politics, was assistant principal of Todhunter School, was co-owner of the Val-Kill furniture factory, and lent a willing hand to a hundred undertakings. A tall, energetic, vibrant woman, she was a model of composure and self-control, and one of her guiding principles was that she received the greatest satisfaction from doing things for other people.

In early July 1929 she was about to take her two youngest boys, Fjr., almost fifteen, and John, aged thirteen, to England and the Continent. Her closest friends at the time, women with whom she shared the Val-Kill cottage, Nancy Cook and Marion Dickerman, were also going. All were at a family dinner at the Big House and were talking about the impending trip, for which they were shipping over Eleanor's "Chevvy" as well as a Buick, when Mama objected that a Chevrolet driven by the Governor's wife was hardly a style of travel suited to the family of the Governor of New York. Fjr. followed up, saying, "Mom will probably land us in the first ditch." After assuring Mama she would take her grandsons through Europe in a manner appropriate to their station, Eleanor rose and fled from the room. Franklin, who sensed his wife's hurt, sternly ordered Fjr. to follow her and apologize. The horrified young man found his mother in tears.

Subsequently Eleanor wrote him. Her confession of vulnerability showed the depth of her pain as well as the fragility of the self-disciplined serenity that she thought she had achieved since the Lucy Mercer episode and Franklin's polio:

> Executive Mansion, Albany, N.Y.
> July 7, 1929
>
> Dearest Franklin jr—
>
> This is just to tell you as I promised what I have decided. I do not feel that I care to take any responsibility if anything should happen I would always feel responsible so I am cancelling shipment of the Chevrolet & asking the Automobile Club to have a car meet us in Liverpool. Luckily Marion paid me an unexpected $1,000 profit from the School & I can do it easily. I want you to understand that neither you nor Granny nor anyone is entirely responsible for the way I feel. All my life I have been physically afraid of doing anything myself & it took me years to get enough confidence to drive or to feel that I could hold any opinion, even against a nurse. For the last few years I have gained much in self-confidence & I have suddenly gone back & I imagine I'm too old now to pull out again. I'll do anything with anyone else but I won't do it myself any more.
>
> Much love dear to you & John.
>
> Devotedly
> Mother

The fear of retrogression stayed with her for many years, but by that fall (1929) she had regained the poise and balance she feared she had lost. The tour of the traditional sites in England and Ireland, of the battlefields on the Continent as well as of Chartres and the Pomery wine cellars, had been accompanied by constant roughhousing between the two boys so that she wrote her husband, "I think we will separate them for a while," but her letter to "Dearest Brother," as she also called Fjr., after he had returned to Groton in September, was full of a mother's love.

[E.R. to Fjr.:]   [September 1929]

    I am missing you a great deal for while occasionally when you & Johnny fought I wanted to beat you up this summer, still I loved being with you all the time & it isn't a bit pleasant to have you away. . . .

How many roles she had learned to fill by then is suggested by the crisp businesslike letter she sent Fjr. about his allowance, the sort of letter that was usually written at that time by a boy's father but which she wrote because Franklin was fully occupied as Governor.

[E.R. to Fjr.:]   [November 11, 1929]

    As to your allowance, I don't send it to Groton as you won't use it there. I put it in your account & when you come home you can decide what you need to buy and cash one check & pay for all your purchases. You will have Oct. 1st, Nov. 1st, Dec. 1st, $75 to count on. You pay for all your underclothes, pyjamas, shoes, socks, ties, handkerchiefs, presents & athletic supplies. I buy suits, coats, hats. Father pays all your school bills except athletic supplies & your travelling. Is that clear?

Her letter contained other family news because she had become a kind of family switchboard by which all kept informed about all. She had taken Elliott, after his rebellion against Groton, to try the Hun School in Princeton. Anna and Curt were moving into a house in Tarrytown. She herself would have an exhibition in Binghamton of furniture from the Val-Kill shop which Nancy Cook supervised, and, "Father will have very hard work this next month getting the Executive Budget ready for Jan. 1st. . . ."

An undated fragment of a letter to Fjr. spoke volumes about life with Mama at Hyde Park.

[E.R. to Fjr.:]   [No date]

    As far as possible I like things to move smoothly & that is why I am so little at Hyde Park. Scenes & disagreements make me sick & ashamed & I will do my best to avoid them in the future.

    Much, much love dear boy, may you be happy & successful in all you undertake & should the time come when I can help I will I hope to be able to be of use to you.

The hundreds of letters that Fjr. received and sent from his mother, grandmother, and girls present a genial picture of his life at Groton, which was still a shaping instrument for the country's WASP aristocracy, but they are not relevant to this book, so we leave them.

Another batch of letters I received from Harold Clark of Phoenix, Arizona. He had been a neighbor and friend of Esther Lape, and when she died he ended up with scores of letters Eleanor had written the suffrage-battle twosome—Esther, scholar, publicist, and student of public affairs, and her beloved Elizabeth Read, who was a lawyer at a time when women in the law were an exception. Both had become friends of Eleanor's when in 1921 she returned to New York from Washington and went to work for the League of Women Voters. The absence of hand-written letters to the two friends puzzled me when I worked on *Love, Eleanor,* and to have them turn up was a windfall. The more so as along with them came an unexpected dividend—a series of long, observant, tart letters to Esther and Elizabeth from Malvina ("Tommy") Thompson, Eleanor's secretary.

When I interviewed Esther Lape for *Eleanor and Franklin* she often said wistfully that she wished a book might be written about Tommy. I did not then realize that behind that wish were the scores of letters Tommy had written her about what her "boss" was up to. I also discovered the draft of an affectionate profile of Tommy that Lorena Hickok proposed to write, a somewhat odd enterprise in view of Tommy's sardonic views of Hick—and of most of us—voiced in these letters.

Tommy was born in the Bronx, daughter of a locomotive engineer who hailed from Vermont. She finished high school, taught herself stenography, worked for the Red Cross, and in 1928 came to work for Eleanor, who was heading up women's activities in Al Smith's presidential campaign. During the Albany years she worked half-time for Eleanor and full-time for Louis Howe, and at the end of 1932 Mrs. Roosevelt asked her to come to Washington as her personal secretary, the "most satisfying and exciting moment" in her career, she said. "I wouldn't want to change jobs with anyone in the world."

She was firm of chin, with a trace of Yankee severity in her face. "She could be a real critic," Eleanor said of her, but she was also hospitable to the people Mrs. Roosevelt liked, whatever her private judgments of them might be. "Everybody from the Queen of the Netherlands to Alice, the cook, told their problems to her."

She considered her boss the greatest person in the world and was suspicious of almost everyone else. The members of the Roosevelt family were exempt from her sarcasms. So were Esther and Elizabeth, to whom she was writing by the end of the thirties, "I do want you and Elizabeth to know how highly I prize your friendship, and that I count on it as one of the few tangible results of these past few years." The other exception was Edith Helm, widow of an admiral, Mrs. Roosevelt's social secretary as she had been of Mrs. Woodrow Wilson. Preparations for the 1941 Inauguration imposed a particular burden on Mrs. Helm, who—complained an even more overburdened Eleanor—met her at every turn with a question about arrangements. Tommy defended Mrs. Helm.*

---

* Most of Tommy's letters were addressed to Esther, although intended for both Esther and Elizabeth.

[Tommy to Esther Lape:] [No date]

Edith Helm threatens constantly to quit because she can't get much cooperation from Mrs. R. and I actually get sick at the thought of not having her here. I can't imagine working so amicably with anyone else. I think Mrs. R. would be sick too, at the thought of having to cope with someone new, but she is so busy and so tired, I think she doesn't realize that she gives Mrs. Helm short shrift. I also do not think that Mrs. R. realizes that Mrs. Helm is much older than either of us and therefore cannot stand too much pressure.

Apart from Esther and Elizabeth, Edith Helm and members of the Roosevelt family, Tommy saw Eleanor's close friends differently than her boss—not quite as parasites but as hangers-on—and her disparagements, if taken *cum grano salis*, form a spicy counterpoint to Eleanor's endearments. Little that Eleanor thought and felt escaped Tommy's alert eyes. Eleanor on her side was sure of Tommy's loyalty and noted often the contrast between Tommy's resolute rejection of the attentions of the ever-present lobbyists and Missy's responsiveness.*

By the end of the thirties, Tommy's references to Nancy Cook and Marion Dickerman were usually caustic. A magazine writer wanted to do an article about Mrs. Roosevelt and asked to interview the two women. "[B]oth Dickerman and Cook said they could not see her and did not wish to be interviewed on the subject of Mrs. R! They still want all the privileges however." She was angry about the Dickerman-Cook claims when it came to dividing the buildings at Hyde Park, claims which had "made Mrs. R. madder than a hatter. . . . The important thing is that she won't feel very happy at Hyde Park. I wish they could both get assignments in Russia or some other place sufficiently far away."

The references to Cook and Dickerman bristled.

[Tommy to Esther Lape:] [Mid-1940]

Miss Dickerman invited herself to stay here [the White House] during this conference on Children in a Democracy, and Mrs. R. of course agreed. However, Dickerman looked so doleful and woe-begone, I can't imagine why she wanted to come. Mrs. R. was very polite, but the ice around the edges was very apparent. If Dickerman's hide is thick enough to allow her to ask for these favors, I can't imagine why she can't put on a pleasant front. Mrs. Helm who knows very little about the Dickerman-Cook-Roosevelt situation, asked me what was wrong because she looked so sad. I know it is a play for sympathy from Mrs. R. but it apparently makes no impression.

* Marguerite LeHand, a charming and gracious woman had been Roosevelt's secretary and close companion since the early 1920s. Often she had been hostess at tea and dinner when Mrs. Roosevelt was away. She suffered a stroke in 1941, left Washington in 1942, and died in Massachusetts, her home, in the summer of 1944.

Tommy Corcoran made no play for Eleanor's sympathy, but the ebullient Irishman for a few years during Roosevelt's second term was among his closest advisers and thought it prudent to be agreeable to Eleanor. He sought her help in connection with the visit of the King and Queen of England in June 1939. Tommy described Corcoran's unsuccessful approach.

[Tommy to Esther Lape:]   [Mid-1939]
. . . However she had the King and Queen too heavily on her mind, and by the 23rd [Tommy thought they might go to the World's Fair] she expects to be deep into it and doesn't dare wait. She really has to keep her hand on things, because only last week Tommy Corcoran told her that a certain woman (wife of a bureau head) expected to be invited to the dinner or the musical after, and when she protested that the lists were strictly official, etc. he calmly threatened to go to F.D.R. Mrs. R. told him subsequently just what he could do and told F.D.R. that if Corcoran wanted to run the parties he could!

Malvina employed the editorial "we" in discussing the feelings in the President's entourage the day of his victory over Wendell Willkie in 1940 when F.D.R. was elected to a third term.

[Tommy to Esther Lape:]   [November 9, 1940]
We have been hearing all sorts of reports, authentic and otherwise that Mr. Willkie and his backers were planning on an appeasement policy if he had been elected and many people think he is still bent on putting over such a policy. We have also been told that the local priests in the various Catholic churches told their parishioners to vote against Mr. Roosevelt because of the strong communist leanings of Mrs. R. and the number of communists in government positions. As regards Mrs. R. it is all the American Youth Congress. Needless to say they have not sent any congratulatory messages to Mrs. R. I imagine they all hate the idea of having Mr. R. for another four years.
We also have had no congratulatory messages from the Cook and the Dickerman. They were not invited for Election night and were not at Hyde Park. . . .

She made a glancing reference to Earl Miller, the handsome ex-state trooper who was one of Eleanor's closest friends. Eleanor had gone to the wedding of a woman who was described as "one of Mr. Miller's ex-lady friends! I declined with thanks!"
F.D.R.'s third term brought another avalanche of mail.

[Tommy to Esther Lape:] [November 22, 1940]
. . . I have thought and thought of how to handle the mail and have not
arrived at any satisfactory solution. As long as Mrs. R. insists that every
letter must be answered and as many of them have to be answered by her
personally, because they are definite questions, I do not see what we can
do. . . . Mrs. R. tried answering by dictaphone but her voice didn't
register, and she does not know that when she becomes too expansive or
says things which I think are unwise, that I edit her answers.

It was Tommy who in 1932 on the campaign train had befriended Hick, who
was there for the Associated Press to cover Mrs. Roosevelt. After a talk with Hick,
Tommy had told Mrs. R. she could trust Hickok. The latter certainly considered
Tommy one of the few people around Eleanor who was a friend of hers too. By the
end of the thirties that no longer seems to have been the case. Eleanor had helped
Hick to get a job with the World's Fair and after that with the Democratic Na-
tional Committee. The party job required her to be in Washington, and Eleanor
suggested she stay at the White House and not try to maintain apartments both in
New York and Washington. Eleanor was briefly ill and Tommy wrote Esther and
Elizabeth—

[Tommy to Esther Lape and Elizabeth Read:] [No date]
. . . she needs us. She gives so much of herself quite apart from material
things to other people and gets so little (to my judgment) in return and I
feel helpless in the face of it. . . .
　　The fly in the ointment and there is always one—is that Hick gets
back from a four-months stay-away tomorrow and will probably put on a
show! If she does Elizabeth [a lawyer] may get an S.O.S. to keep me out
of Sing-Sing! I know I can depend on her.

The relationship of most of Eleanor's friends to her seemed to this author that
of pollinating bees to the most queenly of plants, and Eleanor herself wrote to
Esther, who had cautioned her against the benumbing effects of another four years
in the White House—

[E.R. to Esther Lape:] [December 19, 1940]
. . . I do not think I will ever become deadened because I live in other
people's lives. I must admit there are times when it weights me down
because I can't do some of the things I want.

But Tommy, to paraphrase a comment made on the relationship of Ford Maddox
Ford to Joseph Conrad, saw people like Hick as fat slugs upon the luxuriant lettuce.*

It galled Tommy that Hick stayed at the White House and constantly shared
her problems at the Democratic National Committee with Eleanor.

[Tommy to Esther Lape and Elizabeth Read:]   [Mid-1940]
     I think in the course of our lengthy conversation I said I knew Hickok
would have Mrs. R. doing all her work, and I was right. She brings all her
problems to Mrs. R. in person and Mrs. R. settles them. However, when
I talked to Ed Flynn whom I have known for years—he said he was going
to stand for no interference in his job as national chairman and that if
anyone built himself or herself up to the point where people thought he
or she had the most direct avenue to the P and Mrs. R. he would not
stand for it. I have no idea whether he was thinking about Hickok or not.
He did say that Jim Farley had some justification on his side because
others had more direct contact with the P. than Farley had. On Monday
I thought Hick looked a little the worse for liquid refreshment. She and
Mrs. Eliot Pratt share a room and she (Hick) told me it was too difficult
for her to get a bath so she had gone without one for three days. It is hard
to be reduced to sharing a bathroom with anyone—when one has become accustomed to the de luxe accommodations in the W.H.

A footnote in longhand: "Mr. Bernard Baruch sent me an old gold chain with
amethysts. I don't know why but it is very nice to have."

     Trude Pratt† and I began to figure in Tommy's wary comments to Esther.
Tommy accompanied Eleanor on a brief winter's holiday to Golden's Beach, Florida, in early 1941. Tommy's friend, Henry Osthagen, was there and Earl Miller. So
was Trude, and I joined them toward the end for three days.

[Tommy to Esther Lape:]   [Mid-1941]
     Mr. Miller did not like either of our guests. I went completely resigned
not to feel anything so I was calm and composed. . . . I think Mrs. R.
had some rest and relaxation. She spent many hours in the sun on the
beach and is quite tanned, but seems to need people around her and
things to do even on a vacation.

     I had assumed that I was in Tommy's good graces. She sought to ease my
unhappiness over Trude's decision not to see me again with accounts of her own

---

* *Group Portrait*, by Nicholas Delbanco.

† Trude Pratt, blond, amusing, and energetic, had left her native Germany in 1932, renouncing a
promising university career to marry Eliot D. Pratt. She and the author met in the course of work for
the International Student Service. She was in the course of obtaining a divorce, an anguished decision
that is reflected in these letters.

anguish over the breakup of her marriage. She sent me gay notes to keep up my spirits.

[Tommy to Joseph P. Lash:]   [Mid-1941]

You know Mark McCloskey and you also know Anna Louise Strong.*

Mrs. Roosevelt, who mixes her guests with complete abandon, invited both Mr. McCloskey and Mrs. Strong to lunch the same day.

Mrs. Strong did have a talk with Mrs. R. before lunch, and during lunch Mr. McCloskey talked without a pause about his work which is recreation in the army camps.

I later in the week met him at dinner and he asked me if he had talked too much. I reassured him and then he said: "I felt all the time that that mountain woman at my right was a bit awed at my audacity."

Said I: "Don't you know who that was? That was Anna Louise Strong, the No. 1 communist."

His jaw fell and I thought he was going to faint. He was sure Anna Louise was a woman from the Kentucky or Tennessee hills to whom Mrs. R. was being nice.

But Trude and I took too much of Mrs. Roosevelt's time and attention, "the love-birds," Tommy sarcastically captioned us in a note to Esther.

As Tommy became accustomed to speaking her mind and feelings to Esther and Elizabeth, complaints even about the amount of work Eleanor piled upon her began to surface.

[Tommy to Esther Lape:]   [July 22, 1941]

Just as an example of what we go through—on Saturday we had 55 people for a belated birthday party for Hall [E.R.'s brother]; 24 people (assorted) for a picnic lunch on Sunday; 17 Arthurdale Advisory Committee for lunch on Monday; and 30 people from the county to talk nutrition on Tuesday. I order the food and am consulted on all the crises. Mrs. R. will tell you quite sincerely that it is just a mere trifle to get food ready for that many. It is for her. All she does is the inviting!

In August 1941 Eleanor reluctantly gave up the 11th Street apartment in New York City that she rented from Esther and Elizabeth. "This is a very hard letter for me to write," Eleanor informed them and put the responsibility on Franklin, saying

---

* Mark McCloskey, former settlement-house worker in New York and regional director of the National Youth Administration. In 1942 he was with the Office of Defense, Health and Welfare Services.

    Anna Louise Strong, American Communist from the Pacific Northwest, married to a Russian with Comintern connections, indefatigable propagandist for Stalin's Russia, later jailed as a "notorious spy" by Stalin.

he wanted her to use the 65th Street house as long as Sara was alive and the two adjoining houses were not sold.

But in September Mama died. So did Hall. And to add to Eleanor's cares, she agreed to serve as codirector of the Office of Civilian Defense with Mayor Fiorella H. LaGuardia. Tommy's account of that anguished month contained the usual barbs against Eleanor's friends.

[Tommy to Esther Lape:]   [October 2, 1941]
   The time between Mrs. James Roosevelt's death and Hall's was very hectic. As you know Hall collapsed the night Mrs. R. died and was desperately ill until he died. Mrs. Roosevelt spent most of her time with him and from Saturday night until Friday night of last week, she did not have her clothes off except to change them. I don't know how she stood it—because the horrible noises coming from his room gave me cold chills, and she stayed in the room with him, except for the brief moments when she saw me. Zena [Raset, Hall's final companion] stayed with him night and day, and when he was practically raving, she was able to quiet him a little. He was unconscious most of the time—in fact all one could say was that his heart continued to beat. The final disintegration of his liver was too ghastly to talk about.
   Mrs. R. has been very brave about it, but little things she says and does make me know that she is really sad. Her columns were written under emotional stress, and she has cancelled several engagements—including the annual Gridiron Widows' Party and told me she had no heart for things like that. Thursday, Friday, and Saturday nights she spent reading old letters, digging out old photos of Hall and talking about their childhood. Certainly no one has had more grief and tragedy in her life—her mother, her father's whole history, her uncles and her brother, and the other things which you know. When we can think of this side of her life many things are understandable.

   . . .

   Mrs. R. is spending a full working day at the civilian defense office. We had planned that I would go there every morning but the two mornings I did go there I could do nothing but stand around. She has a civil service staff there, and we are trying to keep the work separate.

   . . .

   I imagine Mrs. R. is going to be irked many times by the slowness with which government people work, and I think she will have to push hard to get anything done. That is, until we have a war.

   . . .

   October and November are filled with jauntings back and forth, and the usual people are pulling at Mrs. R. I tried to talk to Joe Lash about weighing every request and reducing them to a minimum but he goes gaily on asking and dragging people in, and then he looks so smug and cat-eating-the-canaryish. However, when Mrs. R. so thoroughly spoils people, I suppose they can't be blamed for taking all they can get.

Hickok is still here—she can't pay rent and her income tax and her dentist bill—so she has cut out paying rent! The Treasury isn't as cooperative as the White House.

Elizabeth will be interested to know that one night when the Hickok was rather mellow, and ranting on about how she adored Mrs. R. etc. etc., she said that if anything happened to her, I was delegated to destroy all the letters which Mr. R. had written her. I accepted the assignment, but did not add that I had already made up my mind on that score. However, I do not think in the light of new friends, etc., that the letters to her are the greatest source of concern. I doubt if I could get my hands on all of them.

A note after Eleanor's fifty-seventh birthday—

[Tommy to Esther Lape:]   [October 14, 1941]

I know that Mrs. R. is weary beyond the limit of nervous endurance and that she was not too pleasant with anyone—Mrs. Morgenthau was on the verge of quitting this defense job. Mrs. R. seems to feel better this week and things are better. It would be easier to understand if the Tinys and Joes were treated the same way occasionally.

The President persuaded Mrs. R. to go down the River on the Potomac last Saturday and we all had a very pleasant time—he had a birthday cake and wine for a toast, but did nothing else birthdayish, and I think she had a good time in spite of not wanting anyone to mention her birthday.

November was crowded even for Mrs. Roosevelt as she tried to fulfill lecture engagements to which she had agreed before she took on the civilian defense job.

[Tommy to Esther Lape:]   [November 1941]

Someone must have said something to Mrs. R. about talking too much, etc., because she seems very sensitive about it and says she will not go to as many groups.

In January 1942 Eleanor planned a trip to the West Coast, chiefly in connection with civilian defense but also because it would give her a chance to see Anna. "She told me that she was not going to take me, that she was going to pay her own expenses and would not let me go on government transportation and does not want to pay my way." She described some of her boss's difficulties at OCD.

[Tommy to Esther Lape:]   [November 15, 1941]

Elinor Morgenthau thinks Mrs. R. is being very severely criticized about the whole civilian defense program; that some of the people in the office—old time government people—have her surrounded and hemmed in; that Mrs. R. is not forceful enough with them, and should be in the office to assert her authority. The govt. people want Mrs. R. to go out a lot to this place and the other—mostly their home towns—but this morning she said she thought she would send other people out and stay in the office.

In so many places the report comes back that people are not interested in civilian defense—the social services do not interest them, and it is difficult to convince them that there is any connection between well-fed children and national defense. Perhaps if Mrs. R. were to start on a floor-scrubbing project herself, or cooked and fed some school children with her own hands, it might become popular.

Mrs. R. has decided to do no more paid lectures until after this emergency is over. I think Anna and John had a lot to do with convincing her. . . . She will have to scratch gravel this year to pay the income tax.

The day after Pearl Harbor Tommy flew with her boss out to the West Coast.

[Tommy to Esther Lape:]   [December 16, 1941]

I think it was good psychologically for Mrs. R. to fly out, because for the first three days, people were rather nervous, but by Thursday and Friday everyone seemed to feel that the crisis was past and normal life was resumed. We went through a blackout in Los Angeles—it wasn't so bad. However, we did not have enemy planes overhead, so we could afford to be in good humor about it.

Did you read Walter Lippmann's crack at Mayor La Guardia and Mrs. R. for trying to do a big job with one hand, so to speak?

Mrs. R. is very much annoyed today with the Secret Service and indirectly with Henry Morgenthau because they insisted that she could not have 350 foreign students in the W.H. for tea. The party was held in the Labor Dept. auditorium. Also because the civilian defense council here does not want to have the usual, lighted community Christmas tree across the street in Lafayette Park because it is so close to the W.H. In exasperation, Mr. R. asked if they were going to take down the Wash. monument because an enemy could measure the distance between it and the W.H. She feels we should all be fatalistic, and was annoyed with Mrs. Helm for agreeing with the Secret Service. Mrs. Helm pointed out that we were in a war and under military rule and the best thing we could all do is to conform and bend to discipline.

I think Mrs. R. is overtired because she falls asleep night or day, when she is not concentrating on work. I don't think she has had enough sleep for weeks and weeks. . . .

. . .

The President looks amazingly well and is in good spirits. Perhaps knowing what he has to do is a relief. . . .

Out of all this experience of the last nine years and the slant I have gained on human nature, you and Elizabeth and Edith Helm stand out as the only real people it has been my privilege to call friends. . . .

In March, after Eleanor had resigned from OCD, an event that unfortunately Tommy did not record, Eleanor flew out to the West Coast to be with Anna, who had to check into the hospital for an operation. There had been many attacks in the newspapers on Eleanor. Usually she brushed off such criticisms, but now some seemed to get under her skin, as a letter Eleanor sent Esther from Seattle indicated.

[E.R. to Esther Lape:]   [March 1, 1942]
It was sweet to get your note & you & Elizabeth always help me so I love our times together.

Anna is having a transfusion this morning and then we'll spend the rest of the day with her except for 3–4 when I have to broadcast.

John says Pegler is after me again tomorrow & says I cannot share labor's viewpoint or be with the workers of the world because I've never been a worker. Somehow I know more about many people than he does & I do know what it is to work for a long day. I wish someone could tell him as I can't for I think it is a mistake to notice him too often! Fjr. was so upset by the Congressman's attack on him but I don't think any of these things would matter much if they didn't have a bad effect on the morale of people who believe all they see in the newspapers!

The operation was successful, and as Eleanor prepared to fly East she again wrote Esther.

[E.R. to Esther Lape:]   [March 4, 1942]
. . . I've really had a wonderfully *[sic]* rest & enjoyed John and the children but sitting round a hospital is a curiously tiring performance. It must be nerves and emotions! . . .

Tommy's letters to Esther had the usual slam at Hick.

[Tommy to Esther Lape:]   [December 16, 1941]
Our friend Hick is still here—the ushers call her "the enduring guest." She is worried for fear the gesture which Ed Flynn made to the Rep.

Natl. Committee will mean no work for her. She insists that it is impossible for a woman her age to get a job. I agree it is not easy to get a sinecure at any age unless you have someone like Mrs. R. do the spade work.

Earl Miller and I crossed Tommy's sights. Earl was in and out of the apartment at Washington Square that Eleanor had rented after Mama's death and the two adjoining houses on 65th Street were given to Hunter College. He was awaiting orders from the Navy, which had recalled him to active duty.

[Tommy to Esther Lape:]   [April 15, 1942]
     Apparently we have a steady boarder in one Lt. Miller and he is a noisy one. He came in late, some dame called him at 5 a.m. and he was up again at six a.m. and not quietly up either. Under Mrs. R.'s direction I arranged the "guest room" and he immediately rearranged it!
     The press was poisonous about the moving. Mrs. R. would not talk to them and would not pose for pictures, but they hung around all day and made disparaging remarks about the furniture. . . .

Earl still irked her two weeks later, as did some others.

[Tommy to Esther Lape:]   [April 23, 1942]
     Joe Lash goes into the army tomorrow morning, and perhaps we will settle down a bit. He has absorbed most of the time recently.
     Did I tell you that Mrs. R. invited Diana Hopkins and a friend to spend the summer with us? Harry very generously suggested that he pay part of a maid's wages and I suggested that he engage Mrs. Raset as sort of governess, because I did not relish the idea of having two children added to my responsibilities. He agreed and so did Mrs. Roosevelt and Mrs. Raset is all ready to come. Mrs. Roosevelt said she was going to look after them herself, but I know how long she would enjoy that.
     Lieut. Miller is staying at the apartment, and on my last visit, I spent three nights in town and some female telephoned him at the pleasant hour of 4 a.m. or thereabouts every night until I told her that I did not know what she did for a living, but I worked hard during the day and expected to be allowed to sleep during the night. I know I was disagreeable and when I told him he said I was perfectly right—that he did not want to be bothered.

Trude and I seem always to have disturbed Tommy, although when we saw her she was all cordiality and helpfulness.

[Tommy to Esther Lape:]   [May 7, 1942]

Joe Lash was inducted into the army as you probably read in the papers and was in Camp Dix only four days and then transferred to Miami where he will be for only 22 days. I am afraid Mrs. R. is seriously contemplating a visit to Miami with Mrs. Pratt and I hate to have her do it because of the publicity which is bound to ensue.

I am afraid Mrs. Roosevelt is going to have a dull summer with none of her satellites around her, and I am hoping she will have enough work to keep her busy.

Late that spring of 1942, after Eleanor's resignation from OCD, with her four boys all on active duty, as was Earl, and she had said good-bye to me, Tommy's picture of her boss when the world was not looking was of an unusually depressed woman.

[Tommy to Esther Lape:]   [No date, 1942]

Our work—the mail—has fallen off considerably and Mrs. Roosevelt has no writing ahead, so I do not know what we will do this summer to fill her time. I am urging her to start on the rest of her autobiography even if she puts it away for future editing and publishing. There is a great change in Mrs. R. and I do not know whether it is anxiety—suppressed anxiety for the boys or what it is. We practically never have any conversation. There is a frustration too at not having any specific work for the war, and the usual concentration on a couple of people—the Lash and the Pratt. As an example—yesterday we had nothing to do so I did not come to work, at her specific direction. During the morning I telephoned to find out if anything had come and could not speak to Mrs. R.—she was out somewhere. This morning I said I had tried to telephone and she said *"Why* would you want to speak to me?" That is so unlike her because on almost every other occasion, whether I was at home or she was off somewhere she has telephoned just to say hello in many cases. She hasn't asked me to do anything with her very much and I am not conscious of anything specific having changed her, so I really think it is the whole war situation. I, of course, am not going to be like Elinor Morgenthau and ask her what has happened because I like to think I have sense enough to realize that this period in history is not easy for any woman with four sons in the war, or one son.

A longhand note along the same lines begged Esther to be discreet in her letters to Tommy.

[Tommy to Esther Lape:]   [No date, 1942]

Don't write anything apropos of the above about E.R. because Mrs. R.

always opens your letters to me, feeling you have nothing to say that wouldn't interest her as well as myself. Very often she goes through the mail before I get to it!

Eleanor was still depressed:

So often she gives me the feeling that she is getting more & more "shut up" & I fear it is all disillusionment. We can't change our fundamental natures, I suppose, but she seems to cloak all new friends in all the virtures and attributes & usually finds they don't measure up.

She has suddenly decided not to go to the theatre in NYC any more, because one or two people have objected to the publicity! She loves the theatre so perhaps you could casually say you would like to go with her occasionally to change your trend of thought or anything you like (& I know you will handle it better than I could) so she will think she is doing something to please you. She said Saturday she was so "damn bored" with everything that that was one reason for not letting me go to H[yde] P[ark].

Tommy's insight into the disillusionment that can follow when someone overly idealizes her friends, as Eleanor tended to do, is not, in the author's view, wholly justified. People who out of warmth, compassion, and abundant energy endlessly give themselves to others are better off than more prudent natures who find intimate affection and benevolence a burden and encroachment. Eleanor always said "yes" to the challenges that confronted her, and if she sometimes erred there were others around to rein her in. She nurtured us all and she drew sustenance and strength from doing so. Yet she also considered Tommy's skepticism about the human animal, of which Eleanor was aware, even if not privy to these letters to Esther Lape, a sensible counterweight to her own tenderheartedness.

Eleanor recovered her spirits by July 1942 and again Tommy's letters to Esther complained about the intensity of her boss's absorption with people. Tommy did not share her boss's interest in people, including Harry Hopkins, although in his case her coolness mirrored Eleanor's.

[Tommy to Esther Lape:]   [July 21, 1942]

I imagine Mrs. R. told you about her reaction to the Hopkins family moving into the W.H.—bag and baggage. Harry has decided to keep Diana "home" this year and send her to day school. This is with no consultation with Mrs. R.—just a statement of his plans!

Did Mrs. R. tell you that the Dickerman has suddenly been seized with patriotic zeal? She wants the job of administering the office for the enlistment of women in the Navy for the third naval district. I doubt if she could get a job in a school—that whole Dalton* mess is pretty bad. However, she is 52 and the age limit for the Navy—men and women—is 50, so it is up to the President to waive her age. I doubt that he will do it. Evidently he must have said something to Harry Hopkins, because Harry talked to me about what pests they [Nancy Cook and Marion Dickerman] were, that it was a shame that the pool was attached to their house, etc. and couldn't the President order them off the property, and more of the same thing. I have never talked to him about them and I know Mrs. R. hasn't, so it must have come from the P. Of course, they sat in his lap when he and the Queen were at the pool and that may have annoyed him. They offered to "take the Dutch Royal family off Mrs. R's hands" for a meal. Last Sunday Mrs. R. had a picnic for the Hudson Shore Labor School people and they went swimming. Two or three of them dared to approach Miss Cook's terrace which runs right down to the pool, and asked for some water. She told them it was private property and if they wanted anything to go to Mrs. R.'s house! Unfortunately for them—they aren't royalty.

If Elizabeth feels like having a good laugh you might tell her that when Hick heard about the Hopkins living at the W.H. she said to one of the ushers "Why in Hell does *anyone* want to live in the W.H.?" This after two solid years of living there and not a symptom of moving. I told Mrs. R. this and she, of course, defended Hick as she always does when anyone is being rapped. Mrs. R. said she was sure Hick would move out if she could afford it. I gave up with just one remark—that her $5,000 a year must be stage money, because mine in good American dollars enabled me to keep the wolf just outside the front gate.

Dickerman and Cook did not have to worry about Queen Wilhelmina's reception at Hyde Park. "Perhaps we are becoming blasé on the subject of royalty," said Tommy. Later that summer she and Eleanor drove over to Westbrook to see Esther and Elizabeth.

[Tommy to Esther Lape:] [August 24, 1942]
I suggested to Mrs. R. that if the two lovers in whom she is so interested ever get to the point of marrying that she might want to give them my apartment at Hyde Park. She was quite shocked at the suggestion and turned it down! I thought perhaps she would be glad of a chance to get rid of me, and I could find another home. I know Westbrook would be my choice, if I could manage to live, especially if I ever seriously consider getting married to Henry who would want to live near the water.

Miller's feelings were hurt because Mrs. R. suggested that he find an

---

* The Dalton School in New York City had absorbed the Todhunter School, of which Marion Dickerman had been the principal and Eleanor Roosevelt had been a co-owner and teacher.

apartment and have his family live with him. He thought it was an invitation to get out and I am not sure it wasn't. . . . I imagine his wife is frightened to death of him and afraid of taking care of his baby. He has never asked Mrs. R. to be Godmother and I hope he remembers that I turned him down. I should be embarrassed to death if he proposes me at the last moment.

In the fall of 1942 the International Student Service, of which Trude became acting director after I went into the army, became chief sponsor of an International Student Assembly. It could not have been organized without E.R.'s support, and that meant Tommy's too.

[Tommy to Esther Lape:]   [August 30, 1942]
Next week will be hectic. The International Student Service has its youth assembly and every bed in the W.H. plus extra cots will be filled and innumerable people for meals.

Mrs. R. tried to interest people like Elmer Davis, Mr. MacLeish, etc. in the foreign delegations—Russian, British, Dutch & Chinese & they were all a bit shy—(shades of the Youth Congress). With the publicity which attended the arrival of the Russian delegates, Elmer Davis has taken heart & now wants to cooperate in routing them around the country!

We are both well. Mrs. R. vastly relieved that Jimmy did his duty as a Marine & suffered nothing more than a crushed finger.

"Did Mrs. Roosevelt tell you anything about the Student Assembly?" Tommy's next letter to Esther asked.

[Tommy to Esther Lape:]   [October 14, 1942]
I did nothing that whole week but work on the Assembly—Mrs. Pratt was given carte blanche to ask anyone she wished for meals and we never knew who or how many and the meals were all large—from 25 for breakfast up. The butlers worked hard because every night after the meetings, various people had to come back to talk. Without Mrs. R. and the W.H. I doubt that it would have been much of a success, but Mrs. R. is so generous she has been praising Mrs. Pratt for her wonderful organizing ability.

Tommy accompanied her boss on her state visit to England. The U.S. ambassador to London was John G. Winant, a man of Lincolnesque stature and mien who had been Republican Governor of New Hampshire and who was a good friend of Esther's, so much so that Tommy's letters to Esther reported his doings in detail when their paths crossed. He got on better with Anthony Eden than Winston Churchill. Esther and Tommy found this tall, quiet-spoken, lonely man appealing.

[Tommy to Esther Lape:]   [October 14, 1942]
This trip should be interesting and will probably be strenuous. Mrs. R. thinks she will just pay her respects to the K. and Q. and then be on her own. Harry Hopkins says she will have to do many other more or less social and official things—she will have to go to the Churchills, etc. Mr. Winant has arranged for someone in his office to receive telephone calls, open and sort mail, etc., and will lend us a typewriter. Harry Hopkins says Averill *[sic]* Harriman is closest to Churchill, can get things done and undone more quickly than Winant, etc. but I am fairly sure I shall deal more through Mr. Winant. I don't know him but neither do I know Mr. Harriman and I should think Mr. Winant would be fully capable of handling our situations and I am sure I will like him better.

We cannot take many clothes, so that problem is easily solved. I hope the snooty servants at Buckingham Palace, if the ones who were here are typical, will not sneer at my underclothes, etc., because I am not buying any trousseau! Let them sneer, says Elizabeth, I bet.

. . .

Mrs. Helm is having a fit because she is afraid I am going to break down. She broke down after her trip to Europe [with Mrs. Wilson in 1919] but she was gone from Dec. until May with one return trip home of 10 days, and she went to several countries and the most serious aspect of the whole thing, was that she was then, as now, a perfectionist and Mrs. Wilson stood much more on her dignity as the wife of the President than Mrs. R. does or will. Besides that was a time of triumph and a return to normal living—this must be different and much simpler. Besides that—if they think I am hopeless, I won't care and they can have any opinion they like of my social education!

I am not the type of person who gets outwardly excited over things—but I am, of course, excited over this chance to go. I would never have chosen to fly to Europe, but even at fifty I must keep up with progress, I suppose.

There was no time during the three weeks in England for Tommy to write to Esther and Elizabeth, although Eleanor managed longhand notes on Buckingham Palace letterheads to a few of us. On their return, Tommy's letter to Esther was filled with news of Winant.

[Tommy to Esther Lape:]   [November 26, 1942]
Mr. Winant could not have been nicer to Mrs. R. and to me. He is a grand person and is doing such a magnificent job over there. I do want to

tell you how the Biddles are trying to undermine him. Mr. B. is the ambitious one. I am sure they won't succeed because Mr. Winant has made such a place for himself. I think the British people would have spasms if he were to leave at this time.

I thought he was a bit in awe of Mrs. R. at first and even at the last I thought he was freer with me than with her. He seems lonely to me but perhaps I imagined that. He called me "Tommy" but I never got to the point of calling him by his first name, though when he telephoned me he always said "This is Gil." I told him you were my only outlet when I got confused in my mind about my job and life in general and that you were always such a comfort and so objective and understood that even my job had its ups and downs. He agreed that I could find no better person in the world to confide in and consult.

Both Tommy and Mrs. Roosevelt returned singing Winant's praises.

[Tommy to Esther Lape:]   [December 21, 1942]
I saw your letter to Mrs. R. about Mr. Winant going to India and I agree that he is a far better person than Phillips—he, in spite of his shyness and gentleness, has that something which inspires confidence. Phillips will always be polite and charming. However, I think the British would feel let down if Mr. Winant were to leave. He has such a fine basis on which to work with all of the British. I think I told you that the gossip is that Mrs. Biddle is trying to push him up and out and have Mr. Biddle made Ambassador. I have no way of knowing much about Biddle's ability —he is over polite and butters people much too liberally.

    . . .

Before I forget, I must tell you what Mr. Baruch told me. He gave me a draft on his bank for $500 for Christmas, saying he thought I would need it for my income tax, and could use it to more advantage than I could use more jewelry. Then he said he had been asked to send Missy a case or two of really good Scotch whisky for Christmas. That surprised me because I didn't think she was well enough to drink whiskey. Then he said that the money which he had given to the fund collected for Missy had not been used, so he wasn't giving any more to that until it was needed. That was a complete surprise to me because neither Mrs. R., Mrs. Helm nor I have been asked to contribute. We were asked two or three times to contribute funds for Margaret Durand. He always likes to talk about his "good deed."

Elizabeth was near death, and Eleanor went to spend the night with her and Esther.

[E.R. to Esther Lape:]   [December 19, 1942]

I know how much is in your heart & how empty life seems no matter how much you have to do. You must be so physically weary which adds immeasurably to the difficulty of facing any situation with oneself.

Among the British press clippings that Esther regularly sent Eleanor was one about Winant.

[E.R. to Esther Lape:]   [January 1, 1943]

I read the one about Mr. Winant at dinner to him and to Franklin and Mr. Winant seemed pleased. He stayed with us for several days and then went home for a few days. Franklin tells me he is getting him back again this week. Mr. Winant told me he would surely see you while he is here and I know that you will enjoy seeing him.

Tommy's letters did not usually deal with large matters of policy, but Esther always probed, eager to learn what Tommy's boss might be up to, even more perhaps than Tommy herself. Tommy's letters after Christmas did not disappoint.

[Tommy to Esther Lape:]   [January 4, 1943]

I was sorry Mrs. R. decided not to go to Maine for Mr. Bok [she did later that winter] but there has been an avalanche of letters about her constant travelling and several disagreeable newspaper articles & a question in a press conference as to how she justifies it etc. She has cancelled several engagements & lumped others in NYC together so as to avoid travel. She did not realize what she had arranged for herself until I made a list of engagements for Jan. & Feb. for the P. In black & white it appalled her—hence the changes. . . .

Mrs. R. is more than ever in a whirl—much pressure & no willingness to give time, uninterrupted, to anything. Perhaps it is concealed anxiety for her boys—I don't know, but she is hard to catch hold of for anything & is beginning to forget many details. She has been going to the Naval Hosp. for [X-] ray treatments for her shoulder—calcium deposit & arthritis.

. . .

You'll laugh when I tell you Hick admitted she had a real crush on Winant. If he were inclined to stray he'd certainly not be tempted.

Two weeks later Tommy wrote again, disturbed over the rising pressures from Negroes and the counterpressures from most of the white South, pressures that focused on Eleanor.

[Tommy to Esther Lape:]   [January 18, 1943]

I am sure that Mr. Winant will stop to see you—he was very positive when he talked to me. In answer to your question, I think he made a very real dent on Anthony Eden and a Mr. Law, son of Bonar Law and on Lloyd George's son, Willem, who is Fuel Administrator.* They told us of their planning for cooperation on China and in the Caribbean. There is probably no hope for Churchill—he was adamant when Mr. R. tried to insist that the first mistake was made in Manchuria and then the second in Spain. He rather lost his patience and said he was not going to change beliefs to which he had held for sixty-odd years. I liked Eden, he certainly isn't impressive looking, but as he may likely be the next P.M. I am glad that he is at least willing to talk seriously with a man like Winant.

I agree with you about your three points, but I get rather discouraged right here in our own country. Alice Huntington's stories about the aristocratic (?) southerners are appalling. They insist that the Klan will ride again (if the poll tax is lifted) and that the Klan of 1867 will look like a Sunday picnic. Their cheap labor is disappearing and they do not like it and are against anything which is a help to the Negro. I have heard what I thought were intelligent people talk about the Jews so that I shivered. Where do we begin at home and surely if we have these conditions here, how can we be a factor in urging, much less compelling, other peoples to remove discrimination?

Some of the stories circulated in the south about Mrs. R. (because of her fight against discrimination) are bad. All of the Congressmen who were defeated blame her. (I mean southern ones) and the latest story is that she has Negro blood and that is why she is so sympathetic! It doesn't help to have some of the government people—[Negro] rude and disagreeable even though one understands why.

I think Willkie's bid for the Negro vote and also for the vote of people who can't see any need for world cooperation is serious. . . . The Negro situation is the worst I think, and some of their leaders are not thinking in terms of consequence, only in terms of action.

A visit from Tiny† caused a wrathful explosion.

[Tommy to Esther Lape:]   [No date, 1943]

It is as I tell you. These people clamor all the time for attention, and Mrs. R. is too soft-hearted to say no to anything they ask. I do not know

---

* There was a closer relationship between Winant and Anthony Eden, the Foreign Secretary, than with Winston Churchill. Richard Law was the Parliamentary Under-Secretary of State for Foreign Affairs. He was the youngest son of Bonar Law, Tory Prime Minister in 1922.

† "Tiny" was Mayris Chaney, a professional dancer, who had been introduced to Mrs. Roosevelt by Earl Miller in the early thirties. Mrs. Roosevelt's employment of her to supervise children's physical fitness programs at the Office of Civilian Defense incensed congressional critics.

what the appeal is except that they make her feel they depend on her for their very existence—either financially or emotionally. When Tiny is here, she pays very little attention to her, and I can't imagine there could be any kind of conversation, except when Tiny unburdens her troubles and Mrs. R. seems to have a yen for listening to people's troubles—heart and otherwise. I am sure if Tiny were to go to the South Seas, it would mean nothing to Mrs. R. personally, and yet she will waste good time on such people. If she were my friend, I know Mrs. R. would raise her eyebrows at my choice. Incidentally, if she *were* my friend, I would meet her on dark corners! I am sure Mrs. R. knows that she is ruthless about using her for publicity and yet she doesn't mind. She is a very sly person —when she is with Mrs. R she is the simple, helpless female with no one in the world who loves her, etc. When she is on her own, she is hard-boiled and shows her claws—as she did to Mr. Crim when he thwarted her.

Our friend, Hick, is still holed in her [room] here and I imagine it will take dynamite to blast her out. She has been working since January 2nd or 3rd, has had two weekends—long ones and is taking all of next week off—starting tomorrow—to have four teeth extracted. How does she make a sinecure out of every job she has? How does she convince Mrs. R. that she is killing herself with work?

The sharpness of Tommy's comments may have taken Esther aback. We do not know because we do not have her letters to Tommy. But judging by Tommy's longhand comment, Esther may have remonstrated with Tommy.

[Tommy to Esther Lape:]   [February 11, 1943]
   I agree with you that fundamentally Mrs. R.'s values have not changed, and in cold retrospect some of the hurts seem very inconsequential & I know the Trudes & Hicks fill a temporary gap & I know her quality of defence of the attacked, often without logic—it is almost a reflex action. It is all superficial, otherwise she would be hurt when she is let down. I know I get weary & my perspective gets warped & it is only to you I unburden myself. I know you understand.

AUTHOR'S NOTE

In the preparation of this volume I had the experienced assistance of Ken McCormick and Carolyn Blakemore of Doubleday. In addition my wife, Trude, and son, Jonathan, continued to make invaluable suggestions, as did Merloyd Lawrence, whose helpfulness was an example of serendipity, the result of our association in the writing of *Helen and Teacher*. Larry Levine did some of the research.

Many of the letters published here are at the Franklin D. Roosevelt Library, directed by Dr. William Emerson. I am grateful to him and his staff for their unfailing cooperativeness.

Mrs. Roosevelt's letters to the late Dr. David Gurewitsch were made available to me by his wife, Edna. In addition she read the chapters in which she and her husband figured and made many valuable comments.

It was Franklin D. Roosevelt Jr.'s decision to publish the correspondence between his mother and her friends, including Lorena Hickok, that led to the publication of this volume and its predecessor, *Love, Eleanor*. One day, while I was editing these letters, he appeared with a carton filled with his mother's correspondence with him. These letters as well as the passage of time have enabled me to include a representative sampling of Mrs. Roosevelt's letters with most of her children. They also were her friends.

A World of Love

I

"When One Isn't Happy, It Is Hard Not to Live at High Speed"

THE WINTER AND SPRING of 1943 were the months of the visit of Madame Chiang Kai-shek to the United States, several weeks of which she spent at the White House. The tiny, ardent, but imperious woman became the symbol to the United States of the great Asiatic nation which it did not understand but was glad to have on the Allied side. "You'll have to ask someone else for real impressions of Madame Chiang," Tommy advised the curious Esther, for with Esther as well as Mrs. Roosevelt, the fact that Madame Chiang was a woman counted greatly.

[Tommy to Esther Lape:]   [February 11, 1943]
    I have only been allowed to see her at a distance! I think she is able and very lovely to look at, but she is a prima donna, temperamental and

admits that the Chinese people feel superior to *all* other people and that her hardest job is selling the white people to the Chinese!

Mrs. R. is quite impressed with her and argues against my opinion, although it is Mrs. R. who told me about the superiority complex. She has a niece with her who is a curious, rather neuter gender person, dresses like a boy, hat shoes, and all (Chinese) very small, aged 23, and a nephew who looks normal. Mrs. Helm and I think they are decidedly rude, and finding out anything about the Madame's plans is practically impossible.

Mrs. R. is talking seriously about going to China and says she thinks the P. may let her go. I should certainly hate to go if hired help such as I, would be untouchable. . . .

Mrs. R. does not have enough appreciation of the fact that she is first in the eyes of the world, the wife of the Pres. of the U.S. to resent them. For instance, when we dined with Queen Mary, the Queen put Mrs. R. on her left and the Princess Royal on her right, which I should think was a slight to the wife of the President. When I pointed that out, Mrs. R. was unimpressed. . . .

. . .

Mrs. R. said she thought we both needed a vacation, but that she was loath to go away and return to an accumulation of mail. I pointed out that if she would relinquish the mail to the people who have been working for us for ten years, they could handle it. Then she said that it was part of her war work and must continue! I suggested very seriously that she select someone whom she liked, younger and tougher than I, that I would be more than willing to do my best to transfer any knowledge I had, and continue to run the job from this end, letting the newer and younger person travel with her. This came up because she seemed disappointed, in fact even a bit annoyed, that I didn't want to go to Des Moines. I got the same refusal. I can't pick anyone, because if a new person is to travel with Mrs. R. it must be someone whom she really likes. I asked my doctor if he thought I was coming to the end of my hard working days and he insists that I have many years yet, especially as I do not seem to worry about anything.

Tommy did start out with Mrs. Roosevelt on the presidential train that stopped to enable the Roosevelts to visit Elliott's wife Ruth and their children in Texas but felt unwell and went back to Washington, and the train continued to Monterey for President Roosevelt's meeting with President Avila Camacho of Mexico.

[Tommy to Esther Lape:]   [April 1943]
Every letter or wire I had from Mrs. Roosevelt on this trip sounded as though it had been hectic, all of which made me feel worse about falling

out. Tiny was in San Francisco and pinch hitted for me on the telephone, although Mrs. R. admitted that she worried when Tiny answered the phone and did not like her technique. As usual Mrs. R. crowded so much into the days and evenings, she did not have a free second. I hope she had some peaceful hours with Anna, although I think Anna had some local things lined up. . . .

The President took Laura Delano, a Miss Suckley from Rhinebeck who is an off cousin of some degree, and Harry Hooker, and from what I could gather he spent all of his time with them, had two meals every day with them, and only once or twice had any of the others on the train at meals. Miss Delano picked up a five months' old Irish setter on the way —she needs a new blood line for her kennel. She had to get off at every stop—find a grass stop and wait for the biological functions which she then discussed in detail with anyone who would listen.

One night she was off the train and the secret service did not realize it until the train had started. They threw her on and threw the dog after her and were much annoyed. She is an imperious thing and gives orders to everyone. The secret service men, of course, are not supposed to wait on people and once or twice, refused either to put her coat back or go and get it. Miss Suckley is about fifty, rather mousy, and apparently a new friend. Evidently the P. likes women who are not too serious. Laura Delano is no fool, but she has the technique of so many women who appear to be just chatterers and Harry talks mostly about his health, mind over matter, exercise, rest, etc. Once or twice I heard him talking about taxes.

While I was keeping myself in bed, I asked the porter to find something for me to read and believe it or not, no one on the train had anything except the Sat. Eve. Post, Collier's and Esquire—not a single book, good or bad. Grace Tully and Steve Early played gin rummy all across the country.

Mr. Miller's wife and child are due to arrive today to spend a few days here. I hope I don't give the child a cold. He apparently has no idea of getting a place and having them with him and she insists she will not stay in Albany alone this winter and perhaps go to live with a cousin on Long Island. New style marriage! . . .

If it weren't for my devotion to Mrs. Roosevelt and my conceit that makes me think she needs me, I would be sorely tempted to stay home for a long while. This past week has made me think really seriously about finding someone to train as a substitute, but whenever I bring that subject up, Mrs. R. says she will wait until I can't work any longer and then decide. . . .

Tommy was with Mrs. Roosevelt on the West Coast when Trude reached her to say that I was being shipped overseas.*

At the end of April, along with nine others from weather forecasting school at Grand Rapids, I had been precipitately shipped overseas after G-2 allegedly had presented the President with taped proof of a "tryst" between Eleanor Roosevelt and myself. Eleanor Roosevelt's capacity for love was awesome, but it was a love she had learned to sublimate. I loved her in return, but physical love was for Trude, who, separated from her husband, had arranged to get a divorce in early summer, after which, with Eleanor's blessing, we were to have been married. Shipment overseas, as for many others, postponed but did not change our plans; if anything, we became more resolute that they should be realized.

I saw Eleanor in San Francisco just before my fellow weathermen and I boarded a Navy consolidated bomber for the flight to the South Pacific. She promised to watch over Trude and see as much of her as possible, to treat her, in fact, as one of her own children, and one of her first letters to me, after she had gotten an APO to which letters to me might be addressed, told me that Trude, her three children, and her brother were coming to Hyde Park.

[E.R. to Joseph P. Lash:]   [May 21, 1943]

If she prefers N.Y. we'll be there. The 14th is the night before she leaves for the West. Harry [Hooker] & she are dining with me & we are going to John Golden's prize soldier plays.† Then I'll see her off on the 15th. This sounds as though I were pushing myself on her a great deal but I do give her plenty of time without me & I don't think I've bothered her.

Tommy described to Esther her boss's reaction to the news that I was being shipped out.

[Tommy to Esther Lape:]   [April 26, 1943]

On Saturday we got word that Joe Lash was taken out of the weather forecasters' class in Grand Rapids, sent to Calif., and told he was to fly to his destination. I do not know whether I told you that the Army Intelligence has been sleuthing on him—checked on him and on us in the hotel in Chicago, read all of his mail, searched his belongings, etc. Mrs. R. protested through Harry Hopkins to the Army because her guests were being watched, etc. The Army assured Harry they had nothing on Joe

---

* Cf. *Love, Eleanor*, chapters xxii, xxiii. I had met Mrs. Roosevelt in 1936 as a leader of the American Student Union, a distant acquaintanceship that changed to friendship at the end of 1939, after she had attended hearings before the House Committee on Un-American Activities at which I had testified.
† *The Army Play by Play*—five one-actors written by enlisted men and acted by soldier casts. The five were finalists out of 115 plays submitted in a contest set up by John Golden, the producer. Sponsors of the plays which were shown on Broadway on June 15 were, in addition to John Golden, the Second Service Command.

and were calling off their sleuths. However, after Joe had been transferred to Grand Rapids for more advanced training, they continued, so we thought this was the pay-off for Mrs. R.'s annoyance. We wired Harry yesterday for news, then Joe called from San Francisco, but he did not know anything at all.

This morning after Mrs. R. left, Harry called and told me Joe was still in Grand Rapids. I told him Joe was here in Calif. and Harry insisted I was wrong, crazy, etc. However, when I told him Joe had called, he was inclined to believe that I knew Joe was here. Then he told me Joe was being flown to the South Pacific on Weds. of this week. I asked Harry if it was reprisal and he said no very emphatically and insisted that Joe and nine others were urgently needed.

We leave here tomorrow morning by plane for San F. so Mrs. R. can go out to the camp to see Joe, and leave for home late Wed. afternoon. Harry said he knew Joe was very happy to have a chance to get into the fight, etc. I said I agreed with him, etc. but I know Joe is very unhappy because Trude had promised to get a divorce and marry him this summer. The fortunes of war do not permit any long-term personal planning.

I do not know whether Mrs. R. in her obvious attention has brought this on Joe or not. I rather imagine the Army would resent any attempt at interference or any criticism, and I do not think it helps any of these enlisted men to get too much attention from high-up. . . .

The mystery remained of F.D.R.'s midnight summons to Counterintelligence reported in the previous volume and his alleged order that I be shipped to a dangerous combat post overseas. Tommy does not seem to have known about the episode, neither does Harry. Did it take place as Counterintelligence officer Col. John Bissell alleged, and if not, what exactly did take place?

A letter Eleanor sent Elinor Morgenthau from Los Angeles just before flying to San Francisco where she hoped to see me before shipment overseas did not hint at any midnight confrontation in the Oval Study between herself and F.D.R. as alleged in a Counterintelligence officer's account to an FBI friend. Instead she spoke almost harshly about the "army system" that placed persons like myself as well as veterans of the Lincoln Brigade under surveillance.

[E.R. to Elinor Morgenthau:]   [April 26, 1943]
I'm delighted the Spanish boys are getting some support but I don't think we can beat the army system. Joe's been hauled out in the middle of his course with nine others & at 24 hours notice orders from Washington have started them out here & overseas. I'm trying now to find out where & see him before I go home but they are not allowed to tell & I don't know if I can find out or see him if I do. I'm visiting hospitals at Corona & Long Beach today later. . . .

I am seeing Joe in San Francisco & then starting home. I hope your news of Bob is reassuring. . . . I'm just as worried as you are about gestapo & fascist methods, the line is hard to draw between necessary care & persecution.

If Eleanor knew more about my abrupt shipment overseas she did not tell me, and when occasionally I would pick up from a weather officer in the South Pacific a rumor that seemed to shed light, she advised me that it was best not to think about it.

In retrospect, June 1943 was about midpoint in the war. The Russians were pushing back the Nazi armies from Stalingrad; Japanese expansion was receding from its outermost limits in the Solomons and New Guinea; Allied air assaults on Sicily and Italy foreshadowed offensives there.

In Washington Prime Minister Churchill was a visitor, as was Madame Chiang Kai-shek. The latter wanted Eleanor to visit her in Chungking, but Franklin said no to Russia as well as to China. He had his own plans to meet with the Generalissimo and the Marshal and did not want Eleanor intruding on them. Even a trip to Australia and New Zealand, whose officials also had urged her to come, seemed doubtful to him "because of Congressional desires to visit in large numbers every front!"

Yet he understood his wife's yearning to be of use in the war effort. While he did not want her interfering with his own plans, he was ready to gratify her inner need to serve, which had turned their marriage into a partnership of mutual help after it had ceased to be one of shared passion and intimacy. Politics was his business, but he never ceased in private to pick her brains and, of greater consequence, to listen to the verdicts of her compassionate heart. So, cautiously, she began to prepare a trip to the South Pacific. "Pa now thinks I can go with C.R. [Smith, head of Air Transport Command] to the S. West Pacific about August 10th & I think I will go alone. I don't want to take up space unnecessarily & Tommy I know isn't keen about it. Trude feels she shouldn't leave the children & I don't think you [Anna] should. The chances are that I may not even see Joe tho' I shall of course try very hard."

She was right about Tommy's readiness to stay behind, although from Tommy's letter to Esther it was not clear whether she really did not want to go or was resigned to not going.

[Tommy to Esther Lape:]   [No date, 1943]

If she wants me to go and I feel I can be of any help, I will, of course, go, but as for any personal desire to go, I have none. . . . I am not especially tired. I think perhaps I am bored as we are not doing anything really interesting and I rarely have a chance to talk to Mrs. R. so I don't know what is going on in her mind. She keeps busy with people here [in the White House] and in NYC there is always Trude or Earl or someone else and when we are on a plane or a train she sleeps.

More persistently than most people at the top she advocated fighting the war in a way that would mean a better life for people afterward. Letters to children and friends ended with "the usual prayer for all of you," to which she added, "The world will have to be a *very* good world to make up for these years."

Her son James was hospitalized on the West Coast with malaria he had contracted as one of Major Carlson's Marine Raiders in the Pacific. "He is very urgent that I go traveling round in the Pacific! How do you feel? Would it be of any value & of any pleasure to the boys? Could I see anything of the boys?" she wrote me.

Eleanor's longhand letters to members of her family and to those of us who were close were chatty and ardent. She passed on the news of her children with the same naturalness and whimsy that she described an encounter between the Prime Minister and the Generalissimo's wife. She had a sense of the historic but also of the absurd, and the much-used exclamation point often served to underscore the latter. But absurd as the human condition often seemed to her, she sought to soften it with her love and graciousness.

"When one isn't happy it is hard not to live at high speed." So Eleanor sought to explain Trude's behavior to me after I had been shipped to the South Pacific. The words applied equally to her own way of life, for sadness never left her during the war. With four boys and her son-in-law John Boettiger on active service, the chances were not good that all would come through the war unscathed. So one worked, and the more one's energies were engaged the better it was.

She worried for Anna, her eldest, and the child to whom she felt the closest. Anna was trying as an "associate editor" of Hearst's *Post-Intelligencer* in Seattle to hold onto the paper while John was away. A V-letter came from John in North Africa, and Anna wrote her mother—

[Anna Boettiger to E.R.:]   [May 1943]
    Mummy, I think I'm really doing a good job of adjusting. I knock on wood as I say it! But, there is so darn much to do, & it really interests me —and, as I said, I am making it fun!

This brought an encomium from Eleanor, "I take my hat off to you young people of this generation & Trude & Anna I think will be as much heroes on the home front as you & John overseas."

John had volunteered and after a stint at the Military Government School in Charlottesville was commissioned as a captain, but he had arrived in Africa only to cool his heels waiting for a real assignment—a not uncommon experience in the ranks of the huge armies that were being pushed to the front everywhere.

His wife, meanwhile, found that the man whom Hearst had put in John's place was intent on remaining there and by August a disappointed John was writing in his diary, after he had received his first batch of letters from Anna: "I wept over them because they showed me clearly what a bastard I have been to come off on this chase and what a mare's nest I have left for her."

Despite wartime restrictions, Eleanor's social obligations remained breathtaking.

[E.R. to Joseph P. Lash:]   [May 20, 1943]
I went to a forum lunch of all the youth-serving agencies here today. Later we had 1/2 of the wives of the members of Congress for a movie & tea on the lawn & tonight I had a mixture of youth & age for dinner. The P.M. [Winston Churchill], his doctor & the very brilliant man who works out all the balances of production & shipment for him. Several Map Room people with their wives, the Aubrey Williams. . . .

Another day she reported about the William Phillipses. He and his wife were old friends, part of the group that had met every Sunday night during the Wilson administration. He had served as F.D.R.'s ambassador to Italy and was just back from India:

[E.R. to Joseph P. Lash:]   [May (?) 1943]
William Phillips dined here tonight & was interesting about India. He thinks the British viceroy is stupid & obstinate & he told the P.M. a change should be made & a gradual programme of their increasing freedom inaugurated at once. He says for them to say "if only the Indian leaders would get together we could do something" & then to throw them all in gaol where they can do nothing is absurd. Tonight we saw the Joe Davies film "Mission to Moscow." It is propaganda but I'm sure Davies told the truth as he saw it but I can't quite believe the trials were so simple & above board. . . . We had about 16 for dinner. Next week the Liberian President comes, & won't that be a funny dinner? I really wish it wasn't a stag party for I'd like to observe Senators Connally [from Texas] & Barkley [from Kentucky]—& one or two others!

Eleanor's knowledge that censors might scrutinize her letters to me did not keep her from telling a story about Madame Chiang and Churchill that involved a woman's vanity and high politics.

[E.R. to Joseph P. Lash:]   [May 18, 1943]
A curious little drama has been going on. The Chinese gentleman sent his lady a wire she didn't like so when I phoned to ask if she'd come down to lunch with these two gentlemen now here she said "no"—the one she had not met could come to her! He wouldn't go & I could see F. thought they might fight if left alone so the brother [T.V. Soong] was

sent for & wires buzzed & now I believe she is coming but it may be Friday or Monday!

Tommy had not shared her boss's enthusiasm for Madame Chiang, and early in May suggested to Esther, "I think Mrs. R. is weakening in her defense of Madame. She embarrasses Mrs. R. with her gifts—the latest is a jade ring set in diamonds." Tommy also described Madame Chiang's refusal to do a *pas de deux* with the Prime Minister: "I gathered from Harry Hopkins conversation that Madame C. wanted Churchill to go to see her and refused an invitation to come here to see him! Churchill evidently refused to go to see her."

Eleanor's letter to me about the Churchill-Chiang contretemps was also filled with news about herself.

[E.R. to Joseph P. Lash:]   [May 18, 1943]
I went this morning & had a permanent & cut my front hair very short for summer & I remind myself of you with your hair short!

From 5–9 p.m. I visited dormitories for government workers, one white & 3 colored & to my joy the colored are as nice as the white. . . .

Frances Perkins came to lunch & she was funny about [John L. Lewis] saying that he had such vanity that he never questioned his own complete rightness. Like someone who felt inspired by the Lord only he was his own Lord!

We heard today that John had arrived safely in Africa & I wired Anna. I'm asking the ladies in C.R.'s office & in the office of John's chief to lunch so I'll feel I have a little more personal touch since I'm probably going to send things often. . . .

We have the Senate ladies picnic tomorrow after Mr. C's speech to Congress. I'm going to listen on the radio because demands for seats are so great I thought no one who saw him as often as I did should go. I think I know pretty well what he is going to say. I wonder if you can pick such a speech up?*

. . .

You will be amused to hear that as a result of my "check up" I have a diet & am to lose at least 15 lbs. I mustn't eat more than 1,000 calories a day & it would be far easier not to eat at all! Won't it be wonderful if I really get even moderately thin again! . . .

If Eleanor had learned more about my abrupt shipment overseas she felt it was better that neither I nor Trude should know.

* My comment: "I hope to God I didn't hear him say the war might last four or five years more!"

[Joseph P. Lash to Trude W. Pratt:]   [May 12, 1943]

Today one of the men who was in the hospital when we left Gr. Rapids turned up. He had followed us a week afterwards and when he left there were still forecasters around at G.R. from the previous class to whom they were giving 15-day furloughs because they had no assignments for them. I wish I could stop thinking about the circumstances under which we came because the thing doesn't make sense, and doesn't help keep one cheerful. Certainly the work we are doing here does not explain the urgency with which we were all transported. We are, in fact, superfluous at present. . . .

Trude replied sympathetically—

[Trude W. Pratt to Joseph P. Lash:]   [May 22, 1943]

I think I understand, dearest, how much the extraordinary way of your being sent out there bothers you—I've been wondering ceaselessly—and barely smothering rebellions. . . . I feel so powerless. . . .

Both of us, however, were blessed with Eleanor's love. A package had gone off, Eleanor wrote me, but no letter "because I had no minute to write." My letters were beginning to arrive in eight or nine days, she reported.

[E.R. to Joseph P. Lash:]   [May 22, 1943]

I was visited this a.m. by the head of the American Legion Auxiliary, a very formidable looking lady & I'm glad I don't have to count on her sympathy & understanding of any human frailties. Betty [Winsor]* drove out with me to the Naval Hospital where I went for an X-ray treatment of my neck & arms. . . .

We drove out with F. to Shangri-La at two & had time for a good walk, which Falla & I took alone thro' woods as Betty had high heeled shoes on. It is a beautiful view from the porch where F. sits & the wild flowers in the woods & the fresh green was lovely & Falla & I both had a good time. Bill went fishing with the men but they had no luck. A man who shall be nameless tho' you may guess who he is since I told you long ago I did not think he liked me much & I dealt a good bit on my return from England with his setup, the initials are E.D. [Elmer Davis?] came down at six with his wife. F. gave her two of his cocktails & we had barely reached the table when it became clear that she was completely out of control. It was a really painful performance. I suffered for him at the time but also for her since she'll feel badly later. Why does a woman always

---

* Elliot Roosevelt's first wife. "Bill" was their son.

seem worse than a man, more unattractive I mean? I left with joy, as soon as I could! Betty, Bill & I were back here at ten p.m.

William Phillips came to lunch with F. after an hour with the P.M. & he said he was sure he got nothing over. All the P.M. did was walk the carpet & before William could finish a sentence he would say, "It would lead to a blood path *[sic]*. I cannot consent." Finally William said he managed to say "but I am only advocating that you continue the discussions" but he got nowhere. F. says Anthony Eden is more reasonable but I think he really likes the P.M. better and believes that he can manage him in the end.—We'll see!

Eleanor's letters—she insisted on calling them "scrawls"—mingled calendar, itinerary, diary, and commentary; yet even the most casual of encounters, when filtered through her personality, pulsed with the heartbeat of humanity. I discovered some Thomas Hardy paperbacks in the Tontouta weather station library in New Caledonia and wrote her and Trude after reading *Tess of the D'Urbervilles*, "He deals with a small segment of humanity, but deals with it truly." I was particularly struck by Hardy's view that "we usually have to go the long way round to discover there is a short way. And that seems to be true of Trude and myself. I wonder whether there was a short way and whether this will not be the best in the end." "Funny that you read 'Tess,'" she replied—

[E.R. to Joseph P. Lash:]   [May 30, 1943]
I saw it as a play when I was too young to understand it & must reread the book. I like Hardy, & my dear, I doubt if you & Trude could have travelled a shorter way. I do not know how you can nurture your love but I don't believe distance lessens love, not if you keep feeling the people you love are always with you & you do in thought to them. I think you are more constantly in Trude's thought & in mine than you were when we could be together by walking a short distance.

Hardy's comments about the local echoed with the overtones of human destiny. Eleanor's letters had the same quality. She wished I were around, she wrote me, and able to read for her the masses of material that poured in upon her. I discounted that as womanly flattery. Although grateful that she felt that way about me, I couldn't quite fathom why it should be so or what psychic alchemy made my reactions, and now Trude's, helpful to her.

She was full of Trude's plans to go to Reno in June and her own to go to the Pacific in August.

[E.R. to Joseph P. Lash:]   [May 23, 1943]
Trude looked white & tired when she arrived at 8:15 p.m. for dinner. . . . The answers have come in from the two ranches near Reno & she

will decide & write or wire at once. I will then write for a room for Anna
& myself on July 7th & will be with her for a week. She & Anna can ride
& do things together & it ought to be a help to both. She says she never
realized what it would be like to be without you & you poor dear are
probably missing her just as much as she misses you without being able to
talk about it much. She told me you sounded blue in your letter of the
14th & our cable had not yet reached you. How slow they were & when
will letters reach you I wonder or these packages we are sending. Dearest,
do write as you feel & don't try to hide your feelings.

Two things are the talk of the hour. Russia's dissolving the Comintern
which will take some ammunition away from Hearst, Patterson, Nye etc.
Dies announced that now his committee would soon be able to go out of
business which was a give away, wasn't it? It doesn't seem to help with
the Communists here much but at least they will be without Russian
money & perhaps they will feel the lack of a world movement back of
them & it will weaken them.

The next thing is Lewis's announcement that he will rejoin the A.F.L.
Green says he does not wish to jeopardize amity with the C.I.O. & he has
kept Hutcheson off the negotiating committee but I never trust Green to
be strong long. . . .

I'm going to try to spend every weekend in June at Hyde Park . . .
until some decision is made about the Pacific trip. I would hate to go
without Trude & yet I feel you & she should make the decision, with the
children it isn't easy to decide what is right. I wonder if it will be harder
for you to see me if Trude can't go?

She was sending a parcel that included the photographs I had requested.

[E.R. to Joseph P. Lash:]   [May 24, 1943]
The two I put in are proofs a good photographer took but she insists
on trying again. I think they are not flattering but they look like me!

Trude & I spent a nice hour together this a.m. & then I went to see
Elinor Morgenthau & caught the plane. The second batch of Congress
ladies were entertained & I had a talk at 5:30 with Elizabeth Christman
of the Woman's Trade Union League. Just the Britishers & Harry &
Louise for dinner.

I asked FDR about Lewis' move & he said "purely political, aimed to
destroy the C.I.O. & make the A.F. of L. Republican." Hutchinson *[sic]*
will be elected to replace Green & next year Lewis will go in. Hillman
who is wily is trying to get in the A.F. of L. ahead of Lewis & then
oppose his entry, but if he doesn't he'll stay out of both. He thinks if
C.I.O. can hold on long enough Lewis will make mistakes & the Interna-

tionals will desert & go to C.I.O. but he doubts if Murray will have the patience & the courage. I enclose Jim Carey's analysis as given me.

I agree with you that the Germans capitulation in Tunisia is heartening but I don't see such a rapid end after listening to F. However, they have to plan for the worst eventualities.

Do you have any training beside "weather," I mean exercise or shooting?

The next day Churchill and his retinue were off.

(Wednesday) Our guests left early at 8 a.m. & I have an idea they are bound for your part of the world so you may get a glimpse of them. I feel sorry that Trude hasn't been here during this visit but they've worked so hard there hasn't been much time to talk.

The omission of de Gaulle's & Le Clerc's name in Churchill's speech has stirred all the feeling I thought it would in the free French group & it was pretty petty I thought but F.D.R. is bitter about de Gaulle & I can't get across anything of the opposition point of view. . . .

My letters were straggling in: "I'm never quite sure what is and isn't censorable, and we never learn what has been censored so we don't improve by experience," I explained. My big news was that I was being transferred to Guadalcanal. "It's where I wanted to go if I were stationed in the South Pacific," I wrote guardedly. I described the "Base BarberShop" which together with a PX and an M.P. post, the tents, quonset huts, and planes constituted Tontouta Air Base. I played some poker, I confessed to Trude, and complained about the rains.

[Joseph P. Lash to Trude W. Pratt:]   [May 24, 1943]
    A muddy, rainy world in which your tent floor is soaked and you are grateful if the wind doesn't drive the rain into your blankets, where your pants are always soaking from your knees down, and your face streaming . . . and where, despite everything, everyone remains cheerful.

Eleanor sent me her itinerary through July. Presumably I would write her at the White House, but she wanted me to know where she was. Their guests were leaving, "tonight we dine en famille again. There is a question whether our Liberian guest arrives tomorrow on account of the weather so I may miss him." "Trude dearest," she prompted her—

[E.R. to Trude W. Pratt:]   [May 24, 1943]
    It has just come to me that if you've made your choice of a ranch we should send Joe a cable or he won't know your address in time. Could you

wire me tomorrow & I'll send a cable off at once & if you want to say
something special put it in the wire.

The last weekend in May, Trude, her three children, and her brother George
were with Eleanor at Hyde Park. The President, Harry, and Louise were in the big
house.

[E.R. to Joseph P. Lash:]   [May 30, 1943]
    I think these two days are doing Trude good. She will feel very sad
tomorrow when she says goodbye to the children & I am going to try to
persuade her to come to Washington since she has to see Nelson Rockefeller & we can return together Wednesday.
    After breakfast yesterday we all went to look at the horses & the kids
just got up & were led around. This morning we will go over & they will
really ride tho' Micky's will consist of being held on & led around on the
pony. The little girl with them is very nice & took them in for a very
short swim in the afternoon tho' the water is still really too cold. . . .
    Trude & Lt. Rush walked up to F's cottage & had tea with the Presi-
dent, the Crown Princess,* Mme. Ostgaard, & Tully. Harry Hopkins
went to meet Mrs. Hopkins & Diana who arrived at 6:17 with Tommy so
Diana will spend the day with us today. Tommy & I leave at 2 as I have
to go to speak at the Women's Service Club at 5 this p.m. & the Lt. goes
with us & on to Washington.
    Trude is going to ask Harry Hooker to represent her interests in the
divorce as the Pratt's lawyers insist she must have someone & I'm glad
for he will arrange for someone in Reno who is reliable.
    The March on Washington group have got out a leaflet called "Jim
Crow in the Army" which makes you weep & yet I imagine all of it is
true. What a lot we must do to make our war a real victory for democracy. Trude says you & she have more at stake in the war than others but
I get a feeling now & then that the stake for all of us is equally great if we
have any concern for the well-being of people as a whole. . .

Trude's letter reported what she had told Mrs. Roosevelt about the divorce
settlement.

[Trude W. Pratt to Joseph P. Lash:]   [May 28, 1943]
    In the meantime all the lawyer business is finished—only Harry
Hooker is to look it over for me. El & I spent the whole morning with his
lawyer who finally persuaded me that I too should have a lawyer. The
reason is that he was afraid I might some day feel I had been gypped

---

* Crown Princess Martha of Norway, who lived in exile in the United States and for whom the
President was chivalrously solicitous.

because I asked for so little and El has a good deal of money. I could not convince them that I know very well how much money El has but that I do not want any alimony.

Some things that weekend looked different to Tommy.

[Tommy to Esther Lape:]   [June 24, 1943]
    We have been here since last Friday but it has not been very peaceful. Mrs. R. asked Diana and Trude Pratt's little girl to stay for a week, and Earl and his wife and baby came. That filled the cottage. The big house was filled with Dutch royalty. . . .

Trude was sad about her talk with E.R. about her pending trip to Reno.

    . . . Mrs. R. said that the real source of strength was the family and that people who are driven to work as much by personal unhappiness or by belief in their work—are—with exceptions of course—never completely successful.

Diana and the Pratt children hit it off well at Hyde Park, and when no one at the big house called for the child Trude telephoned Louise Hopkins, who, Trude wrote, wanted "so obviously to leave her here (at the cottage) that I offered to bring her over tomorrow morning when the children go riding. You should have seen Diana's radiant face when she heard that she did not have to go back! . . . Diana and Vera sleep in the end room—Vera in her pyjama bottoms, Diana in the top because they 'want to wear the same things.'" Of the walk up the hill with Mrs. Roosevelt to the top cottage, Trude remarked, ". . . and as always I was puzzled why *he* seems to be so attracted. She [Crown Princess Martha] says nothing, just giggles and looks adoringly at *him.*" The next day Trude delivered Diana to Louise Hopkins: "When I told Louise that I was going to Reno, she said in a funny way, 'So you're actually going through with it!' which made me wonder about the kind of gossip that probably went around. I also remembered that Harry —a long time ago, said to me, 'You'll never go through with it. Women of your kind don't. They're too *nice.*'"
    The news that I was being moved to Guadalcanal greeted Eleanor on her arrival at the New York apartment.

[E.R. to Joseph P. Lash:]   [May 30, 1943]
    . . . So you too join the ranks of those who will remember the Island you are now on. I know it gives you a thrill & I only hope they let me go there. I think I go alone with C.R.* about Aug. 10th. Do you think there

* General C. R. Smith, creator of American Airlines and head of Air Transport Command. Mrs. Roosevelt was particularly fond of this tall Texan.

would be a chance of your getting somewhere for a few days if I asked,
should I not be able to go to you? Perhaps you won't want to however, it
might be special privilege, so I'll just have to get to that special Island
unless you write that you wouldn't want to see me without Trude! . . .
She is planning each little thing in the house with your wishes & comfort
in mind. One cannot shape destiny in some ways, but deep down, in big
things—I don't think any of us will be so changed by the end of the war
that we will not still belong to each other. There will be things to explain,
much to talk about, but all of us who bridge this time with love should be
more understanding than ever before. Take care of yourself Joe dear, for
Trude & I both need you pretty badly in the future. When you do get
mail dear it will be such a burden you will have [to] destroy my letters at
least or you won't be able to pack to come home!

I traveled from Noumea to Guadalcanal on a four-stacker destroyer along with
a fellow forecaster. I already considered myself one although the qualifying exam
would not take place until July. A fellow weatherman, Howard Beebe, and I were
"promptly inducted into the mysteries of 'atabrine' or quinine, the foxhole and
assigned to a tent," I wrote from Guadalcanal. My letters ceased temporarily, but
those from Eleanor were urgent and as detailed as ever—about her coming trip to
the Pacific, Trude's divorce, Earl, Elinor Morgenthau, Esther and Elizabeth.

[E.R. to Joseph P. Lash:]   [June 1, 1943]
    . . . It is getting really warm, we are eating on the porch & the
magnolia is in bloom & the honeysuckle along the steps smells very
sweet.
    Gov. Tom Dewey's aunt came to tea brought by a lady I had never
heard of who just said she'd like to have her see the W.H. Tommy said
she probably wanted to pick out the room she would some day occupy!
C.R.'s boss Gen. Harold L. George dined here & is going over the map &
he thinks I can go to Guadalcanal. Norman Davis was here too & he
wants me to go as a Red + representative which I may do. Uniforms
simplify travel & if I can do the job he wants done it will be an added
reason for going. . . .
    New York apt. 4 p.m. June 2nd. I flew over & went to see Elinor
Morgenthau who is still very uncomfortable & now I've deposited my
bags & going up to Lewis & Conger to look for some hot dishes which
Trude wants for her table in the new house. I hope I'll get what you like
since you will have to live with it! I've been longing for an answer to my
cable & yet I know it will be about two weeks in coming!
    Shad Polier* came to lunch but since Peyrouton is out & the rumor

* Shad Polier, a brilliant attorney, served with the Office of Price Administration until he went into the
Army. He was the son-in-law of Rabbi Stephen Wise and a leader of the American Jewish Congress. He

says that Nogues will soon be too, he had fewer reports to give me. FDR arrived very annoyed about Lewis & the strike. I wonder if one couldn't draft everyone & put them back to work! It is so serious to stop production & we will have such bitter anti-labor feeling & legislation. I'm unhappy about the whole situation.

She sent me a V-mail letter:

[E.R. to Joseph P. Lash:]   [June 2, 1943]
    This is an experiment to see if it reaches you sooner than the other letter I mailed from here today. After the meeting Trude & I walked, in spite of the heat which is great, to "Chez Jean" & had a good dinner & wished for your presence & thought of the last time we had been there together. Then I left her at home at 8 for an S.A. meeting & now I'm home & about ten o'clock Earl will drop in on his way back from a day off in Albany. Trude looks a little better but I hope the six weeks out west will make her over. . . .

Both she and Trude concluded that V-mail was no speedier than regular mail.

[E.R. to Joseph P. Lash:]   [June 5, 1943]
    . . . I shall be glad when I hear you have safely made your move & that mail has begun to reach you. I feel when things do get through you will be overwhelmed! I know I should not write so often but it seems impossible not to do so. You are so much a part of my life that I find myself constantly wanting to tell you about everything, big or small.
    Trude appeared at lunch on Thursday, bearing some lovely white peonies which she said were your favorite flower & they were to console me if I felt miserable after parting with a third wisdom tooth! I felt quite well so I just enjoyed them! I saw an Argentine woman in the p.m., a cripple, with a brilliant mind who has been advising the co-ordinator on publicity. If we've helped on the revolution she may have helped, anyway she was interesting and a kind of triumphant person. Then I saw Elinor Morgenthau, still miserable, and Mme. Chiang better, going to Canada the 15th & then to see us & then home. In the evening I spoke at a student nurses forum in Brooklyn. Yesterday Tommy & I went out on a 9 o'clock train to Westbrook & spent the day with Esther & Elizabeth & I think the latter is failing rapidly. I barely got home when Henry Morgenthau called to ask if I would come up to the hospital as Elinor had to have

brought to Mrs. Roosevelt information about the anti-Jewish decrees of the Vichy Government and Marcel Peyrouton's part in promulgating them as Minister of the Interior. Darlan had made Peyrouton Governor-General of Algeria, but the resultant uproar obliged him to resign and join the Free French Army, which he had just done.

another operation. Her trouble was due to a clot & they had to remove it. I dashed up & was there till 11 p.m. I hope now all will go well with her. . . .

Later. Trude came & she had a horrid time too at the dentist but looked well in spite of that. She tells me what you wrote about political reactions to so little news was removed from her letter so we're still in the dark. Try to tell us in terms which won't frighten the censor! I imagine it is good for you to think only in big terms & without the disturbance of annoying arguments. . . .

By the way did you lose your sweater, socks, etc.? You may not need them but I've started another sweater since they take me so long. You [word indecipherable] it when it is finished & we'll knit you more socks very quickly if you want them. Did you lose any of the things you really cared about besides clothes.

The rain & mud sound bad but I've had even more graphic descriptions than yours! Watch out for malaria where you are now.*

Saturday p.m. late. The coal strike is called off by Lewis but until the War Labor Board makes a decision & the miners accept it nothing is very certain. I think tho' it is good for the country to have Lewis give in. I wrote one column on it which seemed to me to hit the fundamental question. If you ever have time or inclination to go thro' those that the office mails you, you'll come across it & I'd like to know if you approved. . . .

I've just finished a book 'Is Germany Incurable?' by Brickner. Not being a psychiatrist it seemed to me long in spots but it is interesting if you skip judiciously! I'll send it to you when Elinor has read it. . . .

Soon after she transferred her activities to Hyde Park she and Tommy went up to Westbrook to see Esther and Elizabeth. Afterward Eleanor wrote Esther about her joy in seeing them even though Elizabeth, "Lizzie," as she called her, was too frail to be much of a participant.

[E.R. to Esther Lape:]   [June 6, 1943]
I finished Dr. Brickner's book on Germany *[Is Germany Incurable?]* on the way home & decided that tho' interesting one cannot treat a whole people in that way. I really think that France is as bad as Germany in some ways & the Dr. doesn't really satisfy me.

I was unsure what Eleanor really thought about Brickner's basic thesis that the Germans as a people were paranoid and that a very long period of reeducating was essential. I detected a reserved kind of sympathy. Trude also wrote about Brickner.

* "The mud is like molasses," I had explained.

She had been to a luncheon organized by the American Friends of German Freedom and our friend Paul Hagen. There several influential thinkers including Brickner addressed themselves to his thesis. "It was so bad that Paulus [Tillich] who sat at the speakers' table jumped up and spoke furiously for about 5 minutes really condemning all the speakers. . . . Paulus made the only realistic statement, that whatever the causes, without social security all education will prove wasted."

Trude went down to Washington as Mrs. Roosevelt had urged and listened to the President address the United Nations food conference. He stressed that food production, industrial production, and buying power had to be viewed together.

[Trude W. Pratt to Joseph P. Lash:]   [June 5, 1943]
    He was in an excellent mood, joked and told stories at dinner. He seemed to be more amused by me than Louise but then I had not heard the stories before. [Judge Samuel I.] Rosenman [an old and trusted aide of Roosevelt, whom he served as policy adviser, speech writer, and editor of his public papers and addresses] was there, still weak from his long illness. The President called him "his chief gossip" and that did not go down well. He then asked me whether I had known it—and I said no, but it was good to know it. And that too was not too well received.

Eleanor in a V-mail letter that she typed also spoke of Trude's arrival: "We were with F.D.R. and Harry and Louise for dinner." It was a small episode but significant. F.D.R.'s friendliness and warmth toward Trude was not the demeanor of a man who had just placed the man she loved and intended to marry on some "hit" list. Even more, Mrs. Roosevelt, who loathed double-dealing and dishonesty and had a deep sense of dignity, would never have placed Trude next to the President, not to mention inviting her to the White House, had the scene described by Counterintelligence of the confrontation between President and First Lady ever taken place.*

"Trude felt so badly that a letter from her did not reach you first," Eleanor wrote from the White House.

[E.R. to Joseph P. Lash:]   [June 8, 1943]
    She used V. mail, I did not so I deserve to trail along behind everyone else. It is over a week since I cabled Trude's address knowing it would

* In *Love, Eleanor* I reproduced the FBI document that reported agent G. C. Burton's conversation with a high Counterintelligence officer. According to the latter, CIC had bugged my visit with Mrs. Roosevelt at the Blackstone Hotel in Chicago. The tape that CIC made on that occasion and that allegedly showed an affair between Mrs. Roosevelt and myself so angered the President when it was played to him that it caused him to summon Mrs. Roosevelt to the Oval Room for an angry confrontation, to order General Arnold to have me on my way to an exposed combat post within ten hours, to disband Counterintelligence, and to block the CIC officer's promotion. (Chapter XXII, *Love, Eleanor.*) Subsequent scholarship has cast doubt on Burton's story. The tape has vanished, and these letters demonstrate the falsity of an "affair" between Mrs. Roosevelt and myself.

give you her plans. Now I know I'll go to your part of the world between August 10th & 15th. No decision can be made about islands I stop at but I'll stop at everyone I possibly can go to. If I can't go to you I'll try to arrange for you to come to me, that is if you want me to. I ought to get an answer to the letter in which I asked you how you'd feel before so many more weeks go by. Trude & I talked about the plaguing question of whether separations & experiences such as you go through now, must change people fundamentally. Your friend Lewis scared her, saying she couldn't expect you to return at all the same. I told her much of what I wrote you, that we all change because of experiences but not in fundamental things. Great love, which keeps people in one's mind & heart all the time, can I think increase your understanding & devotion in spite of being apart. You suffer more because you miss people more but if it is worth loving at all it is the only real & enduring way to love.

I'm doing some typing every day now because I must be my own secretary on the trip west & the later one in August. . . .

I hate to see this anti-strike bill go through. It isn't all bad but much of it is bad. It will take some time to adjust I think & labor should be strong & united or it will do much harm. If Lewis hadn't behaved as he has it need never have passed.

I'll keep sending books & Tommy has some socks for you.

I miss you very much. I'd give so much to have you walk in. I'd like to hold your hand & feel you near, but I wouldn't have much to say for I feel very tired in my mind or perhaps I should say my heart. I'll be alright tomorrow! I love you very much & you are never far from my thoughts & may God bring you back to us safely as soon as possible.

[E.R. to Joseph P. Lash:] [June 11, 1943]
I called Trude & read her your cable & she said life seemed better.

. . .

This has been a busy week with the President of Paraguay here on Wed. He seemed nice & is a good soldier I'm told. The Cuban has again postponed, the government is too shaky! I spoke at the Old Soldiers Home Wed. night while the bigwigs had a stag dinner & then I took the midnight to N.Y. & found David & Maude in the apartment having arrived on Wed. night. We had a grand reunion & then Irwin Ross joined us for breakfast. He's writing an article on LaGuardia & I urged him to see a few more people before his views become rigid.

I went to see Elinor Morgenthau who gets well very slowly. Next Mme. Chiang who *looks* very well & goes to Canada this week. At 12:30 Trude & her four Germans came to talk of their pamphlet. Maude was much interested but overcome by their optimism. She thinks European chaos is inevitable & their plans impossible. I went at 3:30 to dedicate the garden & visit their club & at 4:30 Trude, Justine Polier & I met at the Biltmore over a cocktail. Justine told me she wanted to leave the bench & work on something which she felt contributed more to the problems of today. I think she & Trude might work something out together. They would make a wonderful team, wouldn't they? . . .

Ickes has fined the miners & when I asked F.D.R. why this morning he said he knew nothing about it! It seems unwise to me.

I'm taking Diana up tonight so I must go to the train. Bless you dear boy. When I hear from you I want more than ever to hear your voice & see you & hold your hand. I miss you & love you very dearly.

E.R.

Anna's having a bad time but I'll tell you about it some other time.

Eleanor's call to Trude from Washington about the cable produced a quick note. "A thousand cheers—and hallelujah! At least you get my letters now—and you know my address for the next six weeks. . . . It has been very interesting to watch people's reactions when I told them that I was going out west. Most people seemed to expect it and to understand."

Anna's difficulties at the *Post-Intelligencer* mounted.

[E.R. to Anna Boettiger:]   [June 12, 1943]
. . . I think you are having a dreadful time & I think all of the men [of the Hearst management] have been pretty two-faced with you & John all these years. . . . Well, you are a wonder, if you succeed it will be wonderful & if you have to give it up it won't be a failure, just a strategic retreat!

I know just what you mean about John's letters. Somehow, they can't give you a warm close feeling when they have to be so guarded. . . .

Not a word from Elliott or Fjr. & I do hope all is well.

Margaret Fayerweather, the old Albany neighbor who bored everyone in the Roosevelt household except Eleanor, made her annual visit. Her three children were grown; and in writing about her to Elinor, Eleanor showed how little ready she was for retirement.

[E.R. to Elinor Morgenthau:]   ["Friday night"]
She stays at home & runs the place & feels it all rather useless. I suppose a time comes to us all when we feel it is our preparation for leaving the world but I'm glad I don't feel it yet, don't you?

Eleanor was at Hyde Park on Saturday for Trude's birthday. Trude sent me a long letter about the Nazi beheading of seventeen Munich students and professors who had called on the German people to overthrow Hitler. "[I]t must mean something," she wrote carefully, but Mrs. R. did not encourage her to hope for an early end to the war. Though "the OWI says we should always write cheerful letters to soldiers," Trude said, she could not deceive me or herself; instead she talked about her thirty-fifth birthday the next day. "There is so much I hope for from the next year. And it all starts and ends with you coming home to me so that we finally start a life which is the only right and useful one for us—a life together."

Eleanor also wrote.

[E.R. to Joseph P. Lash:]   [June 12, 1943]

This is just a line because you are so much in my thoughts that I can't go to bed without talking to you a little! George is in your room & I love to have him but oh! how I wish you were there, that room seems to belong to you & only to you! Trude, George & Lenore, the Russian [delegate to the United States Student Assembly, an outgrowth of the International Student Service], Tommy & I came up at 9:20 & we went swimming at once & it felt wonderful to be in the sun & after lunch to walk the woods & be free. I brought your letters up from N.Y. & put them with your other papers & both Tommy & Trude know where they are in case anything should happen to me. I hope Trude will come up & be here in August & Sept. It will be a comfort to Tommy & good for Trude. I've thought of something I want to talk over with you when we have a chance in the future.

All the men on the paper have told Anna that they agree with Mr. Hearst & want to publish his colored stories, but so far she has kept them out & she hopes to put up a good fight. I'm cheering her on but I confess I believe it is pretty hopeless.

We are going to see if we can send you a regular cable tomorrow so you will know how much you are in our hearts & minds. It is so hard for Trude & I wonder sometimes how you stand it. Have you built a wall around your thoughts & just force yourself not to think of certain things? Sometimes I think that is what you must do for you have to be so bottled up. . . .

Sunday, June 13th. I woke Trude with a kiss from you this morning & gave her your present at breakfast. Before lunch we four* had a walk, Tommy refusing to go & saying her muscles ached from yesterday! We went the short turn up over the hill that is the new road to the right & I told Trude that I remembered walking that with you when you were waiting for her none too happily one day! She said those days she hoped were over forever & she could think of nothing which would disturb you both again in that way. A swim & we lay in the sun a while & now we've

---

* Mrs. Roosevelt, Trude, her brother George, and his girl.

had her birthday cake & I enclose to you with the hope it will take you all
the luck it might bring me, the horseshoe in my piece of angel cake. . . .

Trude described her birthday gifts: "How do you expect me to smoke less
when I have the prospect that everytime I open my cigarette case—your picture
looks at me? I found it on my breakfast table this morning. It is a wonderful case
and will go with me wherever I go. Mrs. R. gave me a broiler, which I wanted very
much, because one can cook right at table with it, and I think we will have fun
when you come home. I got Chinese pajamas—so I can match you, and 2 dinner
bells, one for you and one for me, and useful things like a sewing kit."

Troubled by my silence, Eleanor cautioned me against leaping to alarmist
conclusions about Trude.

[E.R. to Joseph P. Lash:]   [June 14, 1943]
   It seems endless since a line has come from you & in both cases they
were V-mail & said little. I think you may have been in transit & thus I
hope the cable indicated your safe arrival. Then I wonder if you have
been through one of the old black & uncertain moods. Whether letters &
changes in Trude's plans have had anything to do with it. I hope you
never write hastily. It is too far for misunderstandings & I assure you that
she is living on her future life with you. She came to dine & go to the
play tonight in the white chiffon dress which always makes me think of
you. The soldier plays were good & she was the most beautiful person
there. She & George & Peter join us at breakfast & all the meetings are
over with Harry Hooker & Eliot & his lawyers. He will sign tomorrow
night & leave Wed. & I'll call her to say goodbye that morning. . . . I
love you very much.

Eliot signed the papers: "At least he knows that the reasons for our failure did
not start in 1942 and had been there for many years." So Trude wrote me from the
Palmer House in Chicago, enroute to Nevada. At the White House Eleanor found
a V-mail letter from me sent from Guadalcanal and replied—

[E.R. to Joseph P. Lash:]   [June 15, 1943]
   F.D.R. told me your present place of abode had not been so comfortable the last few days. My heart sinks & I pray for your continued health
& safety & I shall not tell Trude.*
   . . .
   I shall think of you & your exams in early July and be wishing you all
possible luck. I loved your story of the garden & I hope nothing destroys
it. Man's desire for beauty & order should have some encouragement!

* "Our fox holes were not dug for fun and there have been some dramatic shows," I wrote Trude.

I'm enclosing the stub to show that your present to Trude was paid for. She seemed to like it very much & I told her I had carried out your orders as nearly as I could. I also enclose a little account of the plays we went to last night. They really were good!

Ruth is here & I got a letter from Elliott tonight saying his plane crash had given him a bump on the end of his spine & as it continued to hurt he was having an x-ray. I imagine he's broken the little tail, we all have left over from our monkey ancestors! . . .

Eleanor now wrote both to Trude and to me. Her letter to Trude showed how much Trude had come to mean to her.

[E.R. to Trude W. Pratt:]   [June 16, 1943]
I'm so sorry you had such a time over your Chicago to Reno reservation & do hope they got you something. . . .

These days have been hard & you've been anxious about Joe. I'm glad you got word from him at last before you left.

Tomorrow afternoon I go to N.Y. & I'll see Elinor Morgenthau who is better, & Earl will dine with me but I look forward to it much less than when I'm going to see you. You've come to mean so much in my life & then when I'm with you Joe seems closer too! . . .

"Such excitement today!" she wrote me that same evening—

[E.R. to Joseph P. Lash:]   [June 16, 1943]
I called Trude & said goodbye about 9:15 a.m. & then went out for an hour & returned for a press conference & after that Mrs. Kerr & a woman judge from Dallas came in. . . .

Jan Struther is here, much younger & more charming than I had thought. You remember she wrote "Mrs. Miniver?" Her husband is a prisoner in Italy & she has her two children here & one boy training in England.

Mr. Baruch came to tea & gave me the four books everyone should read, The Bible, Plutarch's "Lives" & 2 I had never heard of which he is sending me & which I'll send on in a month or two to you.

Tonight I gave the Capitol page boys their diplomas. The only Senators there were Burton of Ohio who spoke, Green of R.I. & one Congressman. Not much of a show of interest.

Green, Murray, Harrison, Tobin all came to lunch today to discuss the Women's Trade Union League. Incidentally the anti-strike bill came up & they are very much excited. I wish it would bring them all together. If I were FDR I wouldn't sign it but I'm not enough of a politician to judge the temper of the country.

I feel even lonelier with Trude speeding away & yet I'm so glad she is off & all papers are signed & settled & she feels at rest about everything. Two more big dates ahead, the day she gets her divorce & the day you two are married.

In one of the packages Mrs. R. sent me via C.R., Trude had placed a pair of green garters. Chivalry required that I wear them even though, apart from their hue, they seemed a little incongruous with the shorts and muddy shoes we usually wore.

[Joseph P. Lash to Trude W. Pratt:]   [June 23, 1943]
I never told you about the reception your bright green garters received out here. . . . This evening we were on the way down to the movie, clothed only in shorts, shoes and socks when Chip suddenly exclaimed, "I'll go no further if Lash is going to wear those garters. I'll endure them in the tent, but I'll be damned if I defend Lash against the Marines when they catch sight of them." The outcry was unanimous, so I had to doff them, darling.

Usually I lamented that I was unable to talk about "the great events going on hereabouts," but when they were reported over the radio, the censor relaxed:

You will have read—it came over the radio from Frisco yesterday—of the great air battle in which the Japs lost 84 planes. It is something to see a plane hit and go down. Its movement is slow and tranquil—a spiral, something like a leaf lazily floating to the earth. . . .

A typed V-mail letter from E.R. told of the newspaper reports of air battles over Guadalcanal. They were dangerous but more so in imagination than they seemed to me in reality. Sitting on the rim of a foxhole with others after the Henderson Field sirens sounded, with the big night sky sliced by searchlight beams and tracer bullets and occasional toylike planes lazily tumbling earthward, which we assumed were Japanese, it all appeared like a diverting spectacle.
"I forgot to tell you," E.R. wrote me—

[E.R. to Joseph P. Lash:]   [June 17, 1943]
that your last V-mail letter came just as you had written it and not transcribed. I am now practising [sic] my typing every night since I must be my own secretary in the near future for a time at least. There is news in the evening papers about the air battle of June 12th over your island. I shall await mail sent after that date with great anxiety. . . . I saw Elinor Morgenthau this afternoon and I am glad to say she seems at last to be on the road to recovery. . . . Earl dined with me tonight and now has

gone to bed and it is only ten o'clock so I am shortly going to bed to read the last New Republics and if they have good articles I'll send them on to you. It is really wonderful not to have a basket of mail that must be finished before I feel I have a right to do anything else, but then tomorrow Tommy will bring me twice as much to do, so one never does really escape. This is a stupid letter but I needed to talk with you and you are very much in my thoughts.

She dashed up to see Elinor Morgenthau, then took the train to Hyde Park.

[E.R. to Joseph P. Lash:]   [June 18, 1943]
. . . & tomorrow a hectic week end begins! Queen Wilhelmina & staff arrive in a.m., the soldier plays in the late afternoon. Sometimes I wish I could be two people. I saw Wilhelmina's announcement that the Empire would be a Federation of Sovereign States after the war. That is coming on some for the old girl!

After the uncertainties of travel without a reservation, Trude arrived at the Tumbling DW Ranch in Franktown, Nevada. "A letter from you was waiting for me. The whole feeling of loneliness was gone." There were snow-capped mountains, rivers rushing through canyons, a modern ranch house and good horses. The only complication was the presence of Mrs. Dorothy Backer,* who was there with two children and a mademoiselle.

E.R.'s letters to Trude were filled with the doings of Trude's daughter Vera, who joined Diana Hopkins for a week at the cottage.

[E.R. to Trude W. Pratt:]   [June 21, 1943]
We miss you very much & it was wonderful to get your letter. I began this yesterday but wrote only four words so now it is 6:30 a.m. on the 22nd. I've had a busy weekend but most of it has not been bad. Vera seems well & she & Diana rode yesterday & it has been so hot that they have had two swims every day. They are staying till Thursday & going to N.Y. by train & Georgie will put Vera on her train for New Milford & Mable will take Diana to Washington.

Chicago must have been bad & I am sorry but your wire saying you had arrived & it was beautiful was a relief. Anna found the balance you hope for out there but you have the added trial of Joe far away & the uncertainty of the future. Physical well being helps the mind however & I hope you will relax for a bit & sleep & eat & exercise when you feel like it but not think too much about your problems at first. You will see

* Mrs. Dorothy Schiff Backer, publisher of the New York *Post.*

straighter later on & the balance which will take you through this & whatever must be later on should be something from within. . . .

The Queen leaves at 11 a.m. this morning. I'm going over to breakfast at the cottage & then I'll bring the kids back to ride & go to the station. Mme. Chiang & 2 nieces & a nephew come at one for a picnic lunch at the cottage. F.D.R. may come over as he doesn't go down till tonight but the strike & race riots in Detroit are giving him a bad time. Too bad domestic troubles have to occur when the war in itself is a big job. You will be a little remote from the news for a time & it may be as well for it can be disturbing. . . .

All my love to you dear. I am looking forward so much to the 7th. Not having you near leaves a strangely empty hole in my life. You & Joe seem so much really "my own" that I must guard against being too possessive just as I do with Anna!

Write as often as you can without it's being a burden! Devotedly.

A long letter to me added some details of her Hyde Park life.

[E.R. to Joseph P. Lash:]   [June 20, 1943]
I thought you'd like the text that I enclose of the W.L.B. [War Labor Board] decision. I'm upset about all the things happening to labor & yet I think they have to a large extent brought it on themselves. The split in their own ranks, the slowness to clean up in the unions that needed to be cleaned from within, John L. Lewis & poor public relations always spell disaster.

. . .

Earl & Simone & the baby arrived this morning & the baby is sweet & absorbs all Tommy's attention. I stayed at the cottage in a bathing suit most of the morning & afternoon but had to come here to the Big House for lunch & dinner & am sleeping here tonight. I regret my porch, however, for my room is hot. Queen Wilhelmina has not changed at all. She has the same people with her & tonight F.D.R. talked all evening with her & the P.M. van Kleffens. F.D.R. said tonight that he regretted our attitude on Spain & Ethiopia but the action on Spain was a request from the League of Nations.

The soldiers plays went even better here last night than in N.Y. & everyone enjoyed them. The contingent of soldiers appreciated them most & they loved taking Corps., Sgts. & Lts. to task & making them as ridiculous as possible. . . .

Goodnight dear. I'll finish tomorrow. I was driving thro' the woods late this p.m. & you know how lovely & mysterious they look & I thought of you & how safe we were & how we could enjoy beauty without fear &

how you must always watch & wonder where danger lurks. My love is always with you dear.

Monday a.m. I just drove over to the cottage for breakfast. It is beautiful but it is going to be hot. I was right behind the jeep changing guards & the boys stationed in the woods will be well prepared for your part of the world. They say the mosquitoes are very bad & you will probably say they haven't begun to find out about them! Have you had more of the kind of training we talked about the night before you left? I should think it would be necessary.

Vera & Diana are ready for breakfast & want to ride & then I must devote my morning to the Queen. . . .

She was full of Vera's reactions in her next letters to the two of us.

[E.R. to Trude W. Pratt:]   [June 23, 1943]
The child looks well. At first she seemed in a shell but she has had a good time with Earl & Simone & loves their baby, just sits by him & adores! Tonight we celebrated Simone's birthday & their wedding anniversary & Vera seemed quite natural and outgoing. I wish she were staying but we must have her in early August when you get back. . . .

I mailed you a package of my clothes today so I would not have too much on the plane. In fact several packages may appear & just keep! I'm reading Laski's book & will bring for you.

At last Elinor Morgenthau seems better, which is a great relief, since we were all worried yesterday, but the fever broke last night & the crisis of whatever she has had seems over.

Diana & Vera leave tomorrow & Tommy & I take Earl & Simone & baby home, meet Henry [Osthagen] in Albany & bring him back in the evening. I did a lot of housecleaning today & started to rearrange my books & put some in the playroom & I hope to finish Friday. . . .

Much the same news went to me, but some items were added.

[E.R. to Joseph P. Lash:]   [June 23, 1943]
. . . I like to know your living conditions but of course you tell me less of the daily dangers than I get from F. who tells me that scarcely a day goes by that you are not visited by the enemy.

I will do my best to avoid the "propaganda" feeling on the part of the boys. I got my Red + uniforms Monday so I guess final plans will be made next week. Elliott wrote me such a depressed letter that I almost wished I was going to China so I could see him. No letter from Fjr since he sailed seven weeks ago to Ethel or to me but F. says he'll be in the "deep blue sea" for some weeks still. . . .

After the first letter from me that had greeted her arrival at Tumbling DW, Trude became anxious over my silence, but then letters began to arrive more regularly. "I knew you were getting desperate," Eleanor wrote her from Hyde Park—

[E.R. to Trude W. Pratt:]   [June 25, 1943]
& of course Joe must have too & I am so happy for both that this bad time is over though until the war is over we will have to do a lot of living on faith & hope. I sense in Joe greater security in himself & I'm happy about his letters. . . .

I'm counting the days too till I see you. I never am bored with people I love. It is just being near them one craves & I've been missing you enough to know that that is all I want. The other things are just added joy, talk, exchange of ideas, reading together, not essential, but all things to be thankful for.—I'm always more afraid of boring you & Joe, because you are clearer & so much younger but I've almost got over that & begin to take it for granted that you love me as I love you! . . .

An influx of letters from me brought a remonstrance: "How could you think I would not know where you were when we agreed on the descriptions & I had a long training with Jimmy! You certainly must be a good sailor to stand a destroyer, it is the worst motion there is. Of course the sweater is useless but I didn't know your destination when I sent it!" She knew where I was and constantly kept after the President for the latest bulletins.

[E.R. to Joseph P. Lash:]   [June 24, 1943]
A grand wire just came from Trude saying she had a long letter from you in which you said you had most of the mail. It was good news for F. had just been telling me of two events in which on this very day considerable mail went to feed the fishes in your vicinity, and I began to feel that was why ours did not get to you. I also forgot to number yesterday's letter so this is 35. Our Dutch royalty left this morning and we went to the Hyde Park station to see her off. They are so nice but so dull, perhaps you are a better ruler if you are dull. Mme. Chiang came at twelve thirty for a picnic on the lawn by the porch, she brought two nieces one just arrived to study law, a sister of the little one who looks like a boy but quite feminine. Thursday they will go to Washington and then on. I still like Mme. very much and F. said today that she had a brilliant mind. By the way, it looks improbable that tourists will be allowed to visit the place many boys will remember this summer, so don't forget to answer my question about special privileges. . . . Elinor Morgenthau seems more seriously ill tonight than at any time, and I cannot help being very anxious. She seems to have some kind of infection and the sulfa drugs don't

seem to help. I offered to go down tomorrow to see her but Henry says she is to have a transfusion and it would only tire her more. They are such a close family that I hate to think of her Bob unable to get home and see her. I only hope he does not know how ill she is. Goodnight dear boy, I feel a bit gloomy about domestic affairs tonight. Detroit riots are bad reading. Strikes seem to point to the need for government operation of the mines which I do not dread but many will, the one bright spot is that F. is still considering his action on a bill I did dread to see him approve.

She was scheduled to spend the weekend on Long Island with Hick, with whom she still kept in touch, infrequently but with great candor. "I've been at the big house & Royalty is a strain even when it is as simple & stodgy as the Dutch Queen!"

A long letter went off to me after her stay with Hick.

[E.R. to Joseph P. Lash:] [June 27, 1943]

We are having our 16th really hot day & yesterday morning I left HP & spent an hour with Elinor Morgenthau in the hospital (she is better, but weak & discouraged & still running a low temperature) & then on a crowded noon train journey to Mastic L.I. to spend 24 hrs. with Hick. It was a journey undertaken for friendships sake & I think she wanted me to tell her country neighbors about Great Britain & the war. I did it but it was so hot & yet I enjoyed it & seeing Hick in the one place she really enjoys but it was hot!

I got back here at 7:30 to find an envelope from Washington & your letter written on the 13th & postmarked the 14th so I know you came thro' one hot time safely. Jimmy & Romaine are here & we had dinner together & it was so good to see him. He looks thin & was soaking because of the heat but he's nearly over the malaria. He goes back to the hospital the 19th for 5 days of tests & then hopes to get to work somewhere. He told me some things that reassured me about your abode as far as you are concerned. He is also willing to talk to F.D.R. about going to your Island as he feels I should go. He gave me some advice as to how to see things & what to look at & will give me more. He told me how to guard against what you fear as far as possible. He says everyone is propaganda shy! . . .

I am glad you want to see me even tho' Trude can't go. . . .

I am interested in all you say about a year's service at 18. I've been tending to some of the same reasoning. James said he gave a weekly lecture on world affairs & tried to make his boys think as citizens not as soldiers but he thinks no one else in Marine Corps or Navy is interested.

The citizenship end looks very important to one just now. Congress passed the anti-strike bill *at once* over FDR veto. . . .

I'll certainly try to send the seeds for vegetables but I'll have to try to find out what might grow in your climate & include some simple directions for planting. James tells me they won't suffer from drought & he tells me to take a little electric iron along & leave it with you as it is the only way of drying one's clothes!

Seeing James & hearing him talk seemed to bring your world nearer . . .

It made Tommy angry that Mrs. Roosevelt had to visit Hick on Long Island, a visit that she made—

[Tommy to Esther Lape:]   [June 24, 1943]
much against her will but I imagine the pressure was too great to resist. . . . I said cattily about Hick, that of course she *never* sees Mrs. R so of course Mrs. R. has to go out there. It is just a conceit that makes Hick want her to come. . . .

The meager news reports from Guadalcanal seemed awful to both Eleanor and Trude. "You certainly are making news now, and my heart misses many beats many moments of the day and night when I try to imagine how big a raid must be in which 77 enemy planes are shot down," Trude wrote me. Eleanor sought to reassure her.

[E.R. to Trude W. Pratt:]   [June 28, 1943]
I knew your heart would be standing still daily but till I talked to Jimmie last night I had nothing reassuring to say but he tells me that only those servicing machines are in danger, the other are safe underground from all but a direct hit & the chance of that is 1,000 to one, so we can go on saying our prayers but you can feel more assurance for his safety I think.

I hope you got my letter with the checks, & since then other letters & wires for I know these are hard weeks. You are going about things well in building a routine day & I hope I'll have the courage to ride up & down the precipices, but since I found I could wear my riding clothes & sent them out I probably will!

The heat has been awful for days & when you say your fingers are cold, I know I should pity you & instead I envy you! We drip all day! I didn't mind at H.P. but going down to L.I. was a test of friendship. The night there was grand & cool however but the day & the train trips bad as to weather. I enjoyed the time with Hick nevertheless!

I had a letter from Joe written the 13th the day after the big attack but of course he never mentioned it. His letter was full of the future & he said until your letters came he had not been able to think of the future but he had spent hours over your sketch of the house & all you told him about the rooms & he felt so happy. . . . Where do you suppose Dorothy Backer learned so much? I imagine she is genuine in her offer but Joe would have to make good & the Post pays notoriously low salaries.

I am afraid anything can happen in the race situation. Detroit shld never have happened but when Congress behaves as it does, why should others be calmer? Did your paper have the text of the President's veto, if not I'll bring it for I thought it good all except his suggestion on the change in the draft law which I don't think shld be tied up with it! I think every locality must try to handle its own situation & I hope men of good will may predominate . . .

Elinor Morgenthau has flebitis *[sic]* in the other leg, have you ever known such persistent bad luck . . .

Tomorrow I go to see Elinor again & we then fly to Washington about noon. Tommy went down today or she would send love. I've got Benet's last poem & will bring it to read aloud. Much, much love.

Trude joined the others at the ranch for a trip to Carson City, which was ten miles away, and to its gaming tables. She lost $14 "very simply and quickly" and swore that it would be "the first and last time." The cost of a divorce was high, it seemed to her, for it included the cost of the railroad tickets, $10 a day at the ranch, $300 for a local lawyer. "I wrote you that El balked at the last moment, and did not—as is customary—pay for the divorce. He said it was the principle, not the money. He did not want a divorce, and if I wanted it I could pay. Which is quite understandable."

Eleanor prepared to join her at the ranch.

[E.R. to Trude W. Pratt:]   [July 1, 1943]

Everyone felt I should not stop in Detroit next Monday so I leave from *here* (N.Y.) Tuesday evening United Air Lines. If all goes well I leave Chicago at 10 p.m. & arrive in Reno at 9:30 a.m. This will be the last letter to reach you I think before I appear. I'll be so glad to see you. I think I shall hug you to death. It is very lonely without you, even tho' I think you are in my thoughts all the time. I like your presence & the feeling that you are somewhere near far better than I like my thoughts.

I got your wire about the radio so I imagine you get news.

This will be a busy weekend with both the big house & the cottage full but there are more people than I enjoy having around! Sara & Kate are coming & Jimmy & Romaine come Sunday, the Grays will be there & Mara & Richard Miles & his young aviator friend. The Norwegians don't give me much excitement but they are nice to look at! Eve Curie comes to lunch tomorrow to say goodbye. She is joining de Gaulle's women's army. Somehow I don't see her drilling but she'll probably be good!

A heart full of love to you dear. Till the 7th!

Eleanor sensed Trude's anxiety about her children. It was an additional reason to spend a week with her at the ranch. She also had begun to look forward to her meeting with me. "How will we meet, must I be formal or may I kiss you? Your censors must know we at least know each other! Has anyone said anything to you? . . . F.D.R. said tonight you'd had two active times last week & I can't get over a catch in my throat." Trude was sending me Charles Beard's *Rise of American Civilization* and she was sending Eve Curie's book. "There is much that I want to talk over with you in the field of home affairs but it must wait. We are certainly going thro' a period of reaction which is at its height in Congress. I'm glad Chester Davis is out & I hope Marvin Jones will do better."

"Lippman *[sic]* is right, the home scene is discouraging," her next letter to me said.

[E.R. to Joseph P. Lash:]   [July 1, 1943]

I feel sure Wallace is right about Jesse Jones, but whether it is wise to bring it out in the open is another question. I thought F. was negligent in his timing for sending up his veto on the anti-strike bill & he tells me it was presented in the early afternoon on Lucas (the floor leader's) advice to Jimmy Byrnes. F. added it was bad judgment from both [of] them, but there is no use crying over spilt milk. One wonders if it was accidental bad judgment or deliberately done. It is almost cold here & very beautiful & green & quiet. The sunset during supper was lovely. I ache to have you here when things are nice & I enjoy them. . . .

Friday night July 2d. A wonderful letter from Trude today, part of which I am enclosing. I'm sure she writes you all & more than she would ever write to me, but the fact that she does write me certain things shows I think that they are going deep & if you ever need reassurance, which I hope you never will again, it may be well for you to reread her words to me.

I met FDR & all the Norwegians this a.m. . . . We swam & lay in the sun awhile this morning, then Eve Curie came to lunch. She says she must do some manual work & be near the soldiers & therefore she is joining de Gaulle's women's army & asking to drive trucks or ambulances. When they go back to France she must be able to face people doing actual hard work.

Margaret Fayerweather came too & Tommy & I had the usual run in as to whether being worthy made up for being unattractive! We all lunched at the big house but we had supper here. Tomorrow they all come here to picnic at noon.

This evening we have been reading poetry aloud & talking till 11:30 p.m. & all evening I felt you & Trude should be with us. When talk is good I miss your contribution & I like to read things when I can look to see if you are enjoying them! . . .

Franklin vetoes the "inflation bill" & he expects to have it repassed over his veto. I asked if he thought our lack of leadership & discipline in Congress came about because we'd been in power too long & he said "perhaps, we certainly have no control." I think the country has forgotten we ever lived through the 30's!

Eleanor seemed to know exactly what to say to a lonely man 9,000 miles away. If I had not already loved Trude with a completeness that admitted little increase, Eleanor's letters from Tumbling DW Ranch a few days later would have caused me to fall in love with her all over again.

[E.R. to Joseph P. Lash:]   [July 7, 1943]

Trude looks beautiful! Brown & healthy & thin around the waist, her weight is 138 lbs so she has lost 10 lbs & I hope she'll stay around 140 lbs. but she looks & feels in good shape. Walking & riding have been good for her! I was so glad to see her running towards me when I got off the plane. The Woods were there but I had eyes only for her & I kept thinking "if only Joe could see her." These weeks have done her good physically & mentally & emotionally. She found she could help Dorothy Backer & that gave her confidence. She understands better all you have been through these last years & she is much better able to cope with problems of household & children.

The close relationship between Eleanor and Trude, where each read many of my letters to the other and often spoke for the other in writing to me, since I was the object of this common solicitude, never was felt by me as intrusive in the intimacy between Trude and myself. Perhaps I was too smug and self-centered, although it always mystified me that I elicited these strong feelings from two remarkable women. But more to the point was Eleanor's care not to interfere or be meddlesome. She had a sixth sense in that regard. I have written elsewhere that for her there was "no love but borrowed love," referring to her satisfaction in furthering the romances of close friends. As these letters show, she went to great lengths to advance the cause of true love, but behind it, also, was the sadness of an unfulfilled personal life.

Eleanor's letter of July 7th went on:

My room is next to hers & we sat on the porch & we read all your letters to me since she had left which I had brought out for her & she let me read some of yours to her but she saved one to discuss this evening where you talked of future work, the Villager, New School, etc. I don't think one can decide now, but Trude can keep her eyes & ears open & I will also & I feel when the time comes many openings may be there.

I was thrilled to find a letter here written June 18th. . . . That one sounded tired & I know just how emotionally exhausting that climate is from Jimmy. Don't grow careless about your health or anything else. We do read the headlines & Trude tells me she wakes & can almost hear the bombs drop & can't go to sleep, so I tell her all I can to reassure her but I confess I'm not so good at not worrying myself in spite of all my good advice. Your shifts sound long & with all the moving it must have put an extra strain on all of you. Both Trude & I understand about the censor & we know much that you cannot write.

After supper we went off for a walk, the air was soft, the light on the mountains beautiful, a young moon with a brilliant evening star & we talked of you & of her & we both of us long for you & want you near so much that it is a relief to be together & talk about you. I read and reread your letters & wait for the day when you can tell us all the things you cannot write. After our walk we sat in my room & talked till Trude went to write to you & I am undressed & am now writing. Having had to sit in Cleveland last night from 8:30–2:30 a.m. & then in Chicago airport from 3:30–4:30 a.m. & not getting here till 4:30 this afternoon makes me surmise that I shall sleep well tonight! If I wake we will take an early walk & eat our breakfast in the sun on the porch.

I thought I might escape the press but N.Y. found out & telephoned so I'll see them tomorrow morning & I hope keep Trude's name out of the interview. I'm going to try to ride & Trude says you will have to learn! She showed me all the colors for the house tonight & I think it will be lovely. I tried to get a kodak to bring out to take snap shots but one can't buy either kodaks or film. I sent you one taken of us at Mr. Golden's soldier play.

Also one of me taken with James & Romaine taken in the W.H. grounds. They'll probably be long in reaching you but I can't do anything else & if they are a bother anytime destroy for anything you like I can get again & these are just for you to enjoy now.

By the way would you like for Trude & me together to do something for your whole squadron or your mess for Xmas? I could send you table decorations, fruit cakes & little bags for each one with odds & ends if you'd give us an idea of numbers & things you'd all like.

It was just as well Anna had not joined them. As Eleanor wrote her from the ranch—

[E.R. to Anna Boettiger:]   [July 8, 1943]
. . . I had a press conference this morning as they heard I was here and it was as well for a rumour was about that you were here getting a divorce and if I had not scotched that John might have had a disagreeable shock in Africa. I carefully said that I had stopped for a few days rest and was not visiting anyone in particular.

I'll be with you soon now. I'll have some interesting things to tell you about Jimmie & Rommie. Every [day] I live I become more convinced that the human animal is the most interesting study in the world. There is never anything predictable about people when you know them. . . .

She typed a letter to Elinor—

[E.R. to Elinor Morgenthau:]   [July 8, 1943]
This is being done for practice! . . . I hope you continue to improve. Don't force yourself but get up to the country as soon as you feel really strong enough for the trip. . . .

At the end of her stay at Tumbling DW in response to a wire that Elinor sent her—

[E.R. to Elinor Morgenthau:]   [July 11, 1943]
Please give Bob my warm congratulations. It is unusual for a reserve [officer] to be made executive officer on a destroyer and you and Henry must be very proud of him.

It is wonderful here but not having taken any exercise in ages you may be able to guess what riding, walking, and gardening has done to every muscle in my body. Yesterday we took a mountain ride, about an hour and a half of climbing up to a beautiful upland pasture, there we picnicked among sheep and cattle and rode down late in the afternoon. I wouldn't have missed it for the views were wonderful but I had to walk my horse most of the way home even when we reached the floor of our own valley, and everyone else would have been ready to canter!

I'm deluged with invitations and people just must talk to me and have letters, telling them to see me from Bill Donovan who I feel quite sure hardly knows that I exist to you and Henry whom I feel sure would wire me direct, therefore I have been adamant and only been caught a few times.

I've talked a good bit to Mrs. Backer, and for the first time I feel I know her a little and I like her more than I ever have before. I feel very sorry for her however, she is not adaptable to an outdoor life and still seems to be seeking some inner security.

She continued to be lyrical about Trude.

[E.R. to Joseph P. Lash:]   [July 9, 1943]

There are many things which should make you happy if you could be here with us. First, Trude is well. She skips from sheer physical well-being! Then you are so much a part of her that though every man here admires her & could be led on she has an armor which seems to say "I belong to my man." She has grown in herself. She is sure what life means for her & it is wrapped up in you. It has made her wonderful with others. She is understanding, thinks of little things to do for them & seems about as different from the usual run as can be. She's a big person & the sheer force of her personality & its sweetness carries to everyone from the maids to the most sophisticated. Dorothy Backer, who is a person too, seems weak & ineffectual & uncertain besides Trude.

You are the source of this strength & the certainty of her love. It is wonderful to be with her. We stood looking at the stars last night & she turned to me & said "I wonder what they look like in the S. West Pacific" & I just had been thinking "I wonder what stars Joe sees." The uncertainty of when you are to be home & be married is hard to bear but there is a certainty about the ultimate happiness which helps.

We walk together morning & evening & we've ridden twice tho' I gave them a poor time today because the muscles of my back ache so much I couldn't bear a canter. We tried twice & I had to stop. I fear being old it may take me longer to get accustomed to using certain new muscles & then losing fat is putting a strain on them too. I hope I'll be at least 20 lbs. lighter if I get out to your part of the world & we meet! Here in this wonderful exhilarating air I think of you & your awful climate & hard work & long to get you home & have a peaceful world again.

. . .

We're discussing what to send you for Xmas, decorations for your mess? Would you like little bags for all the boys in your tent & fruit cake & candy? We'll have to get it off in Sept. & I may not be here then. I am sorry I haven't sent more tobacco. Trude says we don't take your one passion seriously* so I'll send some at once & bring you some if I go & a new Dunhill pipe. James advises a new watch because he says they wear out so fast! With this offensive I don't know what FDR & the military will finally feel about my going. Of course I must not add to anyone's cares & I won't go if I have to have fighter plane protection anywhere because James says that every place [Secretary] Knox went to was bombed the next day.

* Sir Walter Raleigh smoking tobacco.

My weather group, which had been stationed on what was called "Pagoda Hill" near Henderson Field and which, along with the Navy and Marine fliers, messed at the "Hotel de Gink," now moved several miles to be closer to the headquarters of the Thirteenth Air Force. Howard Beebe, who also had been part of the Grand Rapids group, and I took and passed the forecaster's exam. I would be part of a small group making forecasts for bomber missions, I informed them. Eleanor answered on the portable typewriter she intended to take with her to the South Pacific.

[E.R. to Joseph P. Lash:]   [July 11, 1943]

Wonder of wonders, two letters forwarded from Washington arrived from you yesterday. . . . Trude had several too, and it is fun reading them together. . . .

I am glad you liked those columns you mentioned. I will have more courage when F.D.R. is no longer in the W.H. if I am still writing a column. I'm enclosing the column I am filing the day I leave here. It is the most I have thought F. would be willing to have me say. He feels he must not irritate the southern leaders as he needs their votes for essential war bills. I am not sure that they could be much worse than they are. The rest of the country seems to me sadly in need of leadership on labor questions and race relations. It seems to me inevitable that there will be some feeling between those men who have served overseas and those who were not able to go. You ought to have consideration, and you will have learned much. You know the big city [and] have now met and come to understand the men from rural areas, in fact, I think that will be an asset to you in the future. . . .

I think Tommy sent you a pair of socks but I'll tell her you can get all you need. She sent you a cap for under your helmet too but you don't have to wear it. She has been meaning to write and I think she will while I am away and she has a few minutes to call her own. I have the sweater well started but I can't think that you will want it for the present, which is just as well for it won't be finished for a while.

I had a nice letter from Elliott yesterday and he says they have been very busy. I have an idea the attack was hurried because of the German offensive against Russia. I wish Elliott might come back for a visit on Ruth's account more than on his. He has been gone a year on this tour of duty and he had one previous trip to Africa and a long time in the North so it all adds up to a long separation. None of the girls seem to me to be meeting their separations as well as Trude and Anna. I think it is because they care primarily about themselves and their own concerns and can never see the cause as something bigger than their individual difficulties. . . .

She recalled to Hick their trip together to Yellowstone in 1933.

[E.R. to Lorena Hickok:]   [July 9, 1943]
What fun we had tho' I realize I was brutal in Yosemite.
I've had two rides & am as stiff as an old lady my age would be which
is very stiff indeed. Tomorrow we go on a riding picnic up into the
mountains & I rejoice because we will have to walk!

The week at Tumbling DW drew to an end.

[E.R. to Joseph P. Lash:]   [July 12–13, 1943]
. . . Trude feels she made so many mistakes & that you paid for them &
she probably did but in the future your lives will gain from them I think.
She suffers in spite of her happiness but she must "keep young for you"
& as Mlle. said as we rode in today "she is full of energy but always doing
for others." There will be times when [you] undoubtedly will want to
spank her but will always love her! We had a picnic lunch today with Sara
Ann, Mlle. & Florence & found a lovely spot by the brook. Trude rode
the most difficult horse. . . . Now I've tucked Trude away after listening to the 11 p.m. broadcast which told of much activity in your part of
the world. With you out there & Elliott & Franklin on the other side,
there really isn't much peace these days & I say with Jan Struther "God
keep us tired." Goodnight dear boy, I'll finish tomorrow.
July 13th. I doubt if you can read what I wrote last night, but I'll send
it, you can look upon it as a cross word puzzle! I was weary last night and
it makes my hand writing even worse than usual. We watched Trude
garden from six-thirty to eight o'clock this morning, and Mlle. and I gave
her a little help when the work was easy enough for us to do. The others
have been working again since breakfast but I had to do some writing.
Trude and I have had our coffee and toast on our own porch every
morning and it seems the nicest meal of the day. I shall miss that hour. I
am glad Trude is going with me today even for these few hours of
change, and I know the rest of the time will pass quickly, but I shall be so
happy when I meet her in New York.
Joe, dear, I dream sometimes that a miracle will bring you home to us
before we expect you. If only you might be sent to O.C.S. it just doesn't
seem right for you and Trude to have to wait so long.

Tommy, normally blunt-spoken, was ambiguous about her boss's stay with
Trude at Franktown, Nevada.

[Tommy to Esther Lape:]   [July 9, 1943]
I have had three or four letters from Mrs. R. stating that she has had a

good time, loved the country around Franktown. Some of the columnists
(Winchell in particular) said that Mrs. R. was out there with Anna who
was getting a divorce. Mrs. R. had to deny it emphatically. The letters do
not say whether she really enjoyed the week or just endured it. At the
moment she is with Anna and I know she is enjoying that. . . .

In Mrs. R.'s absence Nancy Cook had annoyed Tommy. Eleanor had invited
the Military Police unit to use the swimming pool in front of Nancy and Marion's
cottage. It was "like Coney Island," complained Nancy. Since Mrs. R. paid all the
upkeep of the pool, retorted Tommy, she had a right to invite whomever she
wished to use it. "No response to that," added the loyal Tommy.

Eleanor went from Reno to San Francisco. Trude accompanied her for a day:
"I would have hated being here alone & thinking of the last time. Now we can talk
of the next time!" On the train to Seattle she dashed off a farewell note to Trude.

[E.R. to Trude W. Pratt:]   [July 14, 1943]
    I can't tell you how I hated to say goodbye today, nor how much I miss
you. Being with you has been a great happiness for me & I am so grateful
that you wanted me.
    I'm weary tonight. I find the hospitals exhausting & my feet would
hardly walk at the end but I hope the boys got some feeling from it that
their Com.-in-Chief is interested by proxy! They are so gallant & what a
fight they have before them! God grant that we make a good enough
world to compensate for their sacrifices . . .

"Remember you asked," she went on the next day, "if I would be bored?
Well, I never thought of it which is the best proof that I never was, and I [hope]
you never were either. I missed our lovely morning breakfast, you know we must
manage now and then to go off places just you and Joe and I where we can have
breakfast and a view and peace and quiet together!"

She now began to have the sense with Trude that she had long had with Anna
of an almost lyrical intimacy, a parallel she drew when Anna in Seattle read her
John's letters or it was just as "Trude read yours."

[E.R. to Joseph P. Lash:]   [July 15, 1943]
    It was hard to say goodbye to Trude yesterday at the hospital because I
knew she hated to go back to her life at the ranch. Happiness for you two
should not be far off if there is such a thing as a law of compensation for
you have both suffered to attain it. Trude has grown more beautiful I
think, her expression is so lovely, and something inside seems to shine as
I was never conscious of it before. It was wonderful to have her the extra
day and night in San Francisco, and to take her to the hospital was grand
because just looking at her must have given the boys more pleasure than

anything I could say to them. I went on to the second hospital, when Trude went to the plane, and the Admiral said what a lovely person she was with which I agreed strange to say. By five I reached Johnny's house to see the kids but I was nearly dead. I did my best to be an appreciative Grandmother but there is something not only physically exhausting but emotionally draining in these hospital visits!

I reached here at long past midnight but Anna was at the airport and she had been working all evening. She looks very thin, but is making a wonderful effort to meet what is almost an intolerable situation. She said rather wistfully that after the war she was never going to work with people she neither liked nor trusted again, but for the present she was accomplishing some things and not using John's savings, she was keeping the family going and taking care of the place and if possible she was going to stick it out. I only hope she can stand it, but we like fights, it may really pull her through!

We went to an interesting meeting this morning on a second Alaska highway which this part of the country wants built. The military road now built leads into the midwest and this coast feels it does not help them commercially nor is it enough to do the military job alone. Much of what these men talked of was based on a report of the N.R.P.B. [National Resources Planning Board] and Anna says they all wanted it abolished as wasteful but primarily because it was a New Deal Agency!

Now we are sitting on the lawn and Anna is reading John's letters as Trude reads yours. I'm sure all these past weeks writing must have been very hard for you but I'm so glad whenever I see your handwriting. As soon as I get home I will write you definitely what my plans are. If we do see each other soon I hope there is more than a fuzz on your head or I shall not recognize you.

She went with Anna on a boat that belonged to a friend of Anna's. "It was very comfortable, & Mrs. D. cooked wonderful meals & the weather was good. The moon was enormous only I didn't feel sentimental. Today we saw Mts. Baker & Rainier clearly & believe me that is a rare & very impressive sight but I think I only like being in very close quarters with people when I love them very much. I would go off with Anna & John or with you & Trude anywhere & live anyway we had to live & be happy but there are no other people I can think of with whom I enjoy it!" Trude meanwhile, back at Tumbling DW was spending a morning in bed, which pleased Eleanor.

[E. R. to Joseph P. Lash:]   [July 17, 1943]
She says she was glad she went to San Francisco but the hospitals took it out of her as they do with me. Both she & Anna feel the challenge of the men, if they can smile you must, but it isn't easy for either one! . . .

No letters have come thro' from you since the one postmarked July 1st. I realize I am spoiled but I read the news with my heart & my throat & when several days bring no mail I worry & I fume inwardly & tell myself how silly it is & go right on doing it.

It took mail from Guadalcanal about three weeks to reach the United States. I was not allowed to talk about the clashes with the Japanese that took place in the Solomons, but I was struck "by the paucity of the Jap forces employed against us, especially in the air. . . . they are husbanding their forces in the hope that war weariness will set in after a victory in Europe. . . ." Although a weatherman, I welcomed assignments that carried an element of risk, and as soon as I passed my qualifying exam as a forecaster I put myself down for flight duty. A chance came to do some "weather reconnaissance in a Black Cat and it was my turn so I was out for nine hours." I put that in nonchalantly, but I was very pleased to be earning "flying pay." Mostly my letters were about domestic concerns. I had named the house Trude had rented on 11th Street "For Keeps," and the baby we would have when I returned "Spinoza," and Trude had become "dearest wife to be." My weather mates and I were temporarily quartered in a Quonset hut but in a coconut grove, and seated outside the hut smoking a cigar I moralized in doggerel:

> *You say, my darling, OWI decrees*
> *That only gay letters be sent overseas. . . .*

I sent a copy to Eleanor, who received it in Seattle.

[E.R. to Joseph P. Lash:]   [July 18, 1943]

    Please never feel anything is too trivial to write or that we mind the repetition of little things. We get the big things in the news and are not slow in imagining your part in all we hear about. I sometimes hear little extra news but if it worries me I don't pass it on to Trude otherwise you may be sure that I tell her anything I hear which I think would be of any interest.

    I like your verse, and I am glad that you realize the loneliness is a two way street. Of course we know that you are in danger and undergoing hardships we can't even bear to think about for you, but things happen to people inside which have nothing to do with physical hardships. I see it happening to Anna. She has relaxed and gained two lbs. since I've been here but she won't be the same inside when the war is over. Perhaps she will be finer. Trude is different too, more understanding, more thoughtful, finer. I remember one night when you were very discouraged and you said "Yes, I know all her faults but I love her just the same even when I'm not sure that we will ever be happy." Now I am quite sure you will be happy if neither of you tries to keep anything from the other.

Rover* may leave between August 10th and 15th, and it is nice you can still enjoy seeing her even if the Pup can't be along and I know that is going to be very hard for all concerned. Of course war situations may change all plans, but I will try to tell you definitely in the cable we will send the day Trude gets back to New York. . . .

She now wrote Trude regularly.

[E.R. to Trude W. Pratt:]   [July 18, 1943]
Your grand long letter came yesterday, rather book & all & I was so happy to hear you were being sensible & staying in bed for the morning. I think several mornings would do you good. I've never said much but you should build up your muscles down there & make sure you have no tears otherwise when you want to have a baby you may find unexpected care, which you would hate, is required!
I was especially *happy* that you felt as I did about our time together & I was so glad you could come to San Francisco. Anna & I have talked much about you & Joe & she understands well what you have gone through & are going thro'. She sends you her love & hopes sometime she can really see more of you & Joe because she said in Washington she first began to feel Joe was opening up to her a little!
My aches are nearly all gone but I know when I get home I must really do it gradually & not let myself stay so soft. We've been busy but not physically. . . .
I wake at six & think of you gardening & now somehow I live on the thought of August 3d.

She sympathized with Trude's restlessness during her last weeks at the ranch: "Such a warm welcome will be awaiting you in New York on the 3d. I made the discovery long ago that very few people made a great deal of difference to me, but that those few mattered enormously. I live surrounded by people and my thoughts are always with the few that matter whether they are near or far."
On her flight east she pecked away on her portable.

[E.R. to Joseph P. Lash:]   [July 21, 1943]
I got a cryptic message from Elliott yesterday which I think may mean he will be in Washington tomorrow, in which case I will go right to Washington, stay for a few days and then go to Hyde Park and stay for good. James will be back on active duty next week. He is going on a mission not far from where I have just been. . . .
I am feeling very sad over the handling of a situation which arose

* "Rover" was the code name given Mrs. Roosevelt during her 1942 trip to Britain. "Pup" was a reference to Tommy.

between EW* and Commerce. I have not been able to ask F. about it but I have a hunch advice was taken which was not good. I trust W. and he is a real person with convictions whereas J. seems to me just a selfish business man.

Trude writes these last weeks are hard, but she is keeping busy all day and spends her evenings writing to you so I know she will be alright though I will be glad when I meet her ten days from now in New York. . . .

Mrs. Roosevelt's trip to the Southwest Pacific still was unsettled, Tommy thought, as her boss returned from Seattle.

[Tommy to Esther Lape:]   [July 20, 1943]
She says the first thing will be to settle definitely on the long trip with the P[resident]. I imagine he will give in unless it upsets war plans—I don't know what she'll do if she doesn't go. There aren't enough interests here.

Back in the east she went to see Elinor Morgenthau, who "goes home to-morrow." Earl came to dinner.

[E.R. to Joseph P. Lash:]   [July 23, 1943]
[Elliott] looks well & is much thinner. He has much of interest to say & being with Ruth seems to be very happy for both. I hope he gets a few days in Texas as both seem to want it very much. I think he loves his work & in some ways is more mature but I would not like to tackle any social questions with him. We called Anna as he knew John was in Sicily & had seen him, & we also called James as I doubt they will meet so it gave me a chance to talk to both A. & J. too which was nice.

F. is preparing a speech on the State of the Nation & I wonder what he will say. He doesn't know yet when he will give it & I wonder if you can hear it.

I'm going out to the hospital tomorrow for a last check-up & final shots but F. hasn't had time to talk to me yet so I am not sure yet of plans.

I shouldn't be writing you tonight because for no reason I am low in mind. I think it is the Washington atmosphere, one breathes more easily elsewhere!

* The row was between the Board of Economic Warfare, headed by Vice President Henry A. Wallace, and Jesse H. Jones of Texas, who headed the Department of Commerce and several federal lending groups. The two men and the agencies they headed were feuding. On the surface the controversy was a typical bureaucratic one, but the two men also symbolized different approaches to fighting the war and winning the peace. The public exchanges between the two men angered Roosevelt, who ordered them to cease public recriminations. Mrs. Roosevelt sided with Wallace, who had been 100 percent for the New Deal, while Jesse Jones was a leading conservative.

I'd better go to bed but I love you & you know my optimism will bob up tomorrow!

Her next letter was typed at what a later President dubbed "Camp David" and which she called "F.D.R.'s Shangri-La."

[E.R. to Joseph P. Lash:]   [July 25, 1943]
    Yesterday was a red letter day, three letters from you, written on the 5th, 8th and a V-Mail sent the 10th. Such riches I had a wonderful time reading and re-reading. Then Trude sent an extract from a letter in which you gave your reasons for "the paucity of Japanese forces" and you will be amused to know that some of what you say is in F's next speech, a first draft of which I read last night, and in talking he said practically all that you say.
    I have not won my battle yet to go unrestricted when I rove. It is put on fear of impeding war movements, but Dr. MacIntire is most anxious that I should see his hospital and has promised to speak to F. for me. I expect in any case I must go since many think it important. I doubt if I will dare ask for you to come out if I can't go in for I would fear to bring disfavor on you, and perhaps be the cause of your not getting home as soon as you otherwise might. This trip will be attacked as a political gesture, and I am so uncertain whether or not I am doing the right thing that I will start with a heavy heart. Well, enough of my doubts, I'll go because other people think I should, and if I see you that will be a joy, and if I don't I'll try to do a good job on seeing the women's work and where I do see our soldiers I'll try to make them feel that F. really wants to know about them.
    I talked over the W[allace] and J[ones] episode with F. He said he almost took similar action when two other, a little less important burst into the press a while back but they apologized to each other publicly, this he felt was so bad it could not be ignored. He said among other things that W. was no leader which is the only thing made me still feel that some influences were at work. I said he was the only articulate new dealer and few would now feel the desire to fight, and F. became a little bitter about the inability of progressives to mobilize practically, so to-day I pinned him down as to what person he had talked to and who could therefore be consulted as to his attitudes and policies. Of course there was no one and I only hope it may lead to his appointing someone and talking to them not only on policies but on organizing for some tangible accomplishment. Sam [Rosenman] told me to-day that in his speech he was telling about the programme for education and after war employment to be carried out for the soldiers. He can only present it to congress

however, and unless the people want it and make their desires known to Congress it will not go through.

I'm glad that you are happy in the army, and glad too that what I sense in Trude, is getting to you in her letters. My only fear for your futures lies in your danger, once you are safe I feel that you two have every chance for as good a life together as one can have on this earth. Both of you are probably richer people because of all you have suffered. Take care of yourself for her sake. You must be desperately tired with disturbed nights and so much work and the enervating climatic conditions. The mosquitoes alone would wear one out in ordinary circumstances. . . .

We came out here last night as F. is doing his speech. Sam and Bob S.* are here. Elliott and Ruth and I walked through the woods to the pool and I had a swim. Elliott just lay in the sun and said he had not come home to exercise. I sense in him a let down now that his responsibilities are not immediate. He came by way of England and the northern route so was flying a mission over S[icily] less than a week ago. All of you will have to realize that when you return it will take months perhaps before you can overcome the sustained period of strain you have endured.

James is off again Wednesday but this time to the north, it will be active but the climate should be easier on him. Bobby Morgenthau is to be executive officer on a destroyer, we think in F. jr.'s squadron, and since he has been given two more weeks leave because his ship isn't in I hope F. jr. will be in in two weeks. I had Schaffer take Mrs. Morgenthau home on Saturday because I felt the big government car would tire her less. It will take a long time for her to get well I fear as she still has one badly swollen leg.

Elliott is going off soon, and hopes to get some free time in Texas and I hope he will come to New York or Hyde Park before he leaves. Our social philosophies are miles apart but he has grown and he is very intelligent, and very able I think. It is curious how difficult it is even for me at my age to remember what not to say!

In a separate envelope I am sending you airmail some clippings and a copy of Wallace's speech at Detroit which I think very good.

Jimmy Wechsler came to lunch yesterday and he is now head of [PM's] Washington bureau since Ken Crawford has gone to News Week. It appears he got discouraged always having to fight. Jimmy was going to Detroit to cover Wallace and find out all he could about the race riot situation.

Dear boy, I must stop. I love you very dearly and think of you constantly.

* Playwright Robert E. Sherwood, who had joined the inner team of F.D.R.'s speech writers.

"Just back from Shangri-La," she wrote at the top of a letter to Trude from the White House.

[E.R. to Trude W. Pratt:]   [July 25, 1943]

I'm not sure yet whether I go to the S. West Pacific. I will have to decide by tomorrow night & if I go I leave N.Y. on the 16th & San Francisco about the 18th. The chances are I will not see Joe & I've written him that. I doubt if I can get F. to let me go to Guadalcanal because he insists there may be too much activity. I have asked him to leave the decision to the men on the spot but if I can't go I will not dare to ask that Joe be flown anywhere else, because it might bring him dislike & retard his final coming home leave. Well, I'll decide by Tuesday!

We went up to Shangri-La yesterday in time for dinner & Falla & I took a walk before breakfast. Later Elliott & Ruth & I walked up to the pool & I swam. I sense in Elliott a let down & weariness which I think all these men will have when their war duties are over. He & I have such different philosophies that I have to remember to talk carefully! The Army is very down on de Gaulle & after listening to a report from Murphy last night I ended by feeling very confused. If you believe him & Elliott de Gaulle is a fascist & just personally ambitious & no one else is much better. Giraud's virtue is that he is first a soldier, tho' he may well be fascist too he has no political aspirations!

Dr. Tillich seems to me a little arbitrary in his manner of writing! I'll send what he has written to the V.P. By the way I asked FDR about Wallace-Jones affair. He said he was forced to do it & would have done it before with Patterson & Jeffers if they had not publicly apologized to each other. F. was bitter I thought about Wallace developing no leadership & the general inability of the liberals to show any strength in Congress & insisted that he gave more time to domestic affairs than to the war. When I asked him today to whom he talked enough so one cld go to them & get authentic information as to policies & ways of work he acknowledged that there is no one! The V.P. is making a speech in Detroit tonight which I've read & think very good on the whole. I sent it to Joe, but some paper will carry it tomorrow & if P.M. doesn't I'll cut it out somewhere & send it to you. Jimmy Wechsler came to lunch yesterday & he told me he was now acting head of the Washington Bureau & he went to Detroit to cover Wallace & to try to find out present conditions on the race question. . . .

Her thoughts were now focused on her trip to the South Pacific.

[E.R. to Joseph P. Lash:]   [July 27, 1943]

Last night I had a final talk with F. & I told him that I felt a certain

Island was such a symbol to so many people that it would do more harm than good to go & not go there. Nurses, WACs, Red ✚ workers were there & so he promised to leave it to Ad. Halsey with the understanding that there must be no interference in military plans. He is talking to Arnold today & if it would be better to start a few days earlier I will, tho' one of our most frequent visitors from overseas, this time with a wife & daughter may appear & that may make an earlier date difficult. There will be no word until Rover reaches a continent, so we may not meet, but again about 5 days after leaving I might drop from the skies! I'll put in the cable the leaving date from S.F. & I'll send you addresses & you will know that whatever happens I want to go wherever you are & I want to see you & I love you.

We are still all excitement over Mussolini's fall & the possibilities. The great panjamdrum (is that how you spell it?) told me if things began to crack he might go to the place from which you will remember that I brought back the apartment plans.*

Dr. Eagleton in the most apologetic & mysterious note you ever read asked me to see a young man who is a scientist & appeared this morning. He was convincing & rather frightening & we must have peace in the future I think. I'll tell you more about it some day. I sent him to F.†

She reassured Trude about the increasing safety of Guadalcanal.

[E.R. to Trude W. Pratt:]   [July 27, 1943]

As of yesterday I hear that the past ten days they have had no bombing on Guadalcanal so the boys may have had a little rest but it was too late to help with the exam. It will be wonderful to have you read parts of Joe's letters & talk them over. I never could understand why Joe feared being an embarrassment to those he loved. They shared his views & were vulnerable in other ways so why he felt that way was incomprehensible, after he was assured that the joy he brought by his friendship & that he received from them compensated to both for any disagreeables! I've often felt that the President's wife brought her friends more drawbacks than pleasures & still worry as to whether I don't offer too much & put those I love in the difficult position of not wanting to hurt me by refusing but yet not feeling it wise to accept. Sometimes I forget & decide to be natural & then again I repent & decide I will think of others & not indulge myself! Therefore I should understand Joe but I always get annoyed with him. . . . F.D.R. speaks on the radio tomorrow night & I

---

* When Mrs. Roosevelt returned from London in 1942 she brought the apartment layout where the President and she would stay if and when they came.

† Mrs. Roosevelt learned about the atom bomb from a young physicist who spoke for several of the key figures in the Manhattan Project.

think the speech is good. Sat. 6 of them breakfast & lunch at the cottage & he goes on to Lake Huron for ten days of fishing. He said much what Joe wrote about Japan so I read it to him & he said it was a good analysis.

"Here we are, Trude dearest, back at H.P. & it is peaceful & very nice," she wrote later the same day. A piece from Neil Vanderbilt's magazine in Reno was not meant to be "unkindly," she suspected, but one "must always be on guard. . . . Well, dear, long ago I decided the things that are not true never really hurt!"

A V-mail I had written only ten days earlier told of my assignment to assist Captain Liese as a forecaster for the "strike" missions of the Thirteenth Air Force. "Of course such responsibility must frighten anyone but you will take it," she wrote, "& I'm sure you will do it as well as can be done." My letters had not made her anxious, but "I sensed the weariness & I knew from Jimmy much you did not tell. . . ."

[E.R. to Joseph P. Lash:] [July 28, 1943]

Well, F. told me today he had talked with Gen. A[rnold]'s assistant & final decisions are made. Whether I get to your Island is to be left as I asked to those on the spot. If no activities impede I am to go & I will have 2 or 3 opportunities as I move about. He thought I should go which seemed to satisfy F. I'll let you know how & where a letter can reach me in Noumea & in New Zealand & Australia. I will be taking a longish route out but I am surprised at the rapidity with which such distances can be covered. I am concerned that they give me time enough on each landing to see all I really should see. . . .

I've seen those Quonset huts & I don't think I would like them, tho' the scenery about you & the early morning hours sound nice. Do you think I'll have a chance to spend them with you? I'm wondering if I'll really see you if I make your Island.

Louise & Hildur* came up this afternoon in time for a swim & dinner. We talked after listening to F's speech which they evidently liked. I'd read it & the radio was behaving badly—so it was difficult to evaluate its effectiveness. I hope the men in the armed forces heard it for it stated the Administration's plans for them in the postwar period but frankly said Congress would have to cooperate. Russia came in for commendation & China was promised more materials. I'll cut it out tomorrow & mail it to you. The girls go back to N.Y. tomorrow morning & Louise must be in readiness to go to England this weekend but of course she may not get off. . . . Just this minute the telephone rang & it was a wire from Trude saying she just listened to the speech & thought it wonderful! that she missed me & there were only 6 more days! . . .

* Louise Morley and Hildur Coon had been active in the International Student Service.

I did 4 columns today. I must leave ten or twelve behind in case filing is not possible even after I reach a spot where I am announced.

Hick had appealed to Eleanor while she was in Seattle for help in taking the women's organization in New York away from Jim Farley. The latter, despite his break with F.D.R., had kept his hold on the state party. The national committee-woman from New York, Mrs. Good, complained Hick, was reluctant to move; "Mrs. Good & most people in this world are chicken-hearted." Eleanor immediately fired back, "[B]ut I advise you not to build a woman's organization without telling Jim. He would be justified in feeling hurt but if you tell him & then go your own way he will feel you have kept him informed & I don't think he will fight you."

She caught up with Hick's news in Washington and afterward wrote crisply about the inclusion of women in delegations to international preparatory conferences:

[E.R. to Lorena Hickok:]   [July 26, 1943]
    I talked to F.D.R. & he wants to make a statement but not for the News Reels so I called Ellen Woodward & asked her to send over suggestions. I finally told F. how I felt about the Wallace-Jones affair & he said he felt it had to be done but his reasons haven't convinced me. How did you like Wallace's Detroit speech?
    It has been grand to see Elliott & yet I'll be glad to get to H.P. I don't like Washington. Too big for me I guess, I like provincialism! We are at Shangri-La for twenty-four hours & F. is writing a speech, pretty good. . . .

Yet the speech did not wholly please her: "Here is the speech," she wrote me, "it is good but somehow not quite satisfactory. Why? I think because I wanted something specific on cost of living, wages, etc. He tells me that will come as soon as Marvin Jones has settled his programme." Trude had gone to Lake Tahoe and in order to be up for the sunrise had stayed up all night. I had better tell Trude to take care of herself, she advised me. The impulse to give her muscles a workout was again upon her, spurred by her experience at Tumbling DW. She went to the stables at Hyde Park "to get a horse & *walked* three times around the field. To-morrow I'll try trotting if it is dry enough." With Tommy she had done two columns, "one timeless for future use when I am 'lost.' "
    A bad fright over Fjr. on a destroyer in Sicilian waters led her to speculate about her feelings toward her children and how she felt about Trude and me.

[E.R. to Joseph P. Lash:]   [August 1, 1943]
    I had a bad scare Friday night. I called F. & he started right in with 'Frankie is all right.' My heart sank & I said 'what happened?' Their ships

on the north Sicilian coast were divebombed by Germans. F. had heard late Thursday night but forgot to call me or Ethel. The ships fought off the attack but they had six near hits & their destroyer was pretty badly off & just made port for repairs with five killed & six wounded. I know Frankie's been ashore since & is o.k. but I know he'll feel very badly about the men & the one officer is the Lt. j.g. who is injured but so far I've been able to get no details for the families, all of whom are trying to get information from Ethel. I called her & we were cut off so she nearly had heart failure till we were connected. Of course one expects these things but when they happen it is none the less a shock & one realizes more vividly how dear the people one really loves are. You seem like one of my children sometimes & then again like that rare thing a child with whom one has a deep understanding & friendship & for whom one has a deep respect as a mature person. Anna is the only one of my own children I have that relationship with & so I cherish it with you & I hope you feel it too & I think Trude & I are perhaps going to be able to develop it as time goes on. To have three young people one felt really deeply tied to, if they feel the same way, is really more than anyone should expect from life!

F. was here yesterday morning & with 4 men [one was Winston Churchill] went off to fish in Lake Huron & won't go back to Washington till the 8th or 10th. Last night I went to the N.Y. City Sanitation Dept. workers recreation camp on Lake Whaley. They made over "el" cars & they are nice! I showed my film & talked & they seemed to like it. Today Walter Reuther with his wife came up with Jim Loeb for the day & I have longed for you. That young man has imagination. He wants the President to include some 2d line leaders like himself with the big boys & he wants some real Labor-Management com., the first in Willow Run. I'll tell you that story when we meet, if all goes well that might be in 3 or 4 weeks! F. is completely reassured so I hope since I have 3 opportunities to go fr. yr. first stop [New Caledonia] to your present one that no military operations will block me all 3 times.

Despite—or perhaps because of—tensions in Harlem, she got off at the 125th Street Station on the way down from Hyde Park.

[E.R. to Joseph P. Lash:]   [August 2, 1943]
We had a near race riot in Harlem last night but I don't think it will get bad. A white policeman tried to arrest a colored prostitute in a hotel they had been watching. A colored soldier hit the policeman on the head with a club & the policeman fired & hit him in the shoulder. Then the colored people just rioted among themselves, killed each other &

wounded each other & many arrests were made before order was restored. One more sad chapter added!

Earl was in and out and later returned with Simone and their baby. Trude, her
divorce granted, was flying east. As happened often to civilians, she was put off the
plane in Salt Lake City, "but I can't ask for White House priority [and] she may
have to come part way by train. She was upset, but when I told her the kids were
coming Friday & the story in the 'News' wasn't really bad, she felt better. I'll send
the story to you & I think when they questioned Eliot he answered well."*

The actress and future congresswoman, Helen Gahagan Douglas, and Helen
Ferris of the Junior Literary Guild, of which Eleanor was one of the judges, came
to lunch. "Helen [Douglas] goes home tomorrow. She & Melvyn have gone
through so many trials which you & Trude have coped with & will have to cope
with, even the slighting 'Mrs. Roosevelt's protege' is held against him as against
you! I think we'll all survive." She was unable to get Trude onto a plane before she
reached Chicago, but arranged to have two of Trude's children, Vera and Mickey,
at Hyde Park for her arrival "no matter how she comes!"

Before leaving for the South Pacific she went to see Cousin Susie [Mrs. Henry
Parish, at whose 76th Street house Eleanor had married Franklin] in Orange.
Maude joined her.

[E.R. to Joseph P. Lash:]   [August 4, 1943]
    I wonder if we must all grow self-centered as we grow older? Do we all
lose our sense of proportion? If so I count on you and Trude to take me
out and drown me. Earl and Simone and the baby are here, but he has
only twenty four hours, so goes back tomorrow afternoon. Ten days from
tomorrow I will if all goes as planned be leaving in the morning from
New York. So many rumours have come in my mail lately of curious tales
which supposedly have been circulated among your companions that I
confess to wondering how many will be believing them. If I had said or
written any of the things which I have been told have been circulated as
coming from me I should not blame anyone for being indignant.

A V-mail reported she had gone out to the airport to meet Trude.

[E.R. to Joseph P. Lash:]   [August 4, 1943]
    In spite of three nights practically without sleep, she looked radiant &

---

* *The Daily News*, August 2, 1943:

. . . .

[Eliot] Pratt was at the farm yesterday. He said his wife and Joe Lash had been friends for years and
he thought Joe was a 'definite contender' to succeed him.

"No doubt that is how your wife acquired many of her radical notions," the interviewer suggested.

"Well, I don't know about that," he said chuckling. "Quite probably it was the other way around."

seemed so happy & free. Even Maude who saw her for a minute at the elevator as I was walking her home said to me how much better she looked & how buoyant she seemed. . . . I gave her all the letters I had saved for her to read & she had letters here from you so she was happy & we composed a radio to go off tomorrow & I hope the answer returns before I leave but I fear it won't. . . .

The next day they were at Hyde Park.

[E.R. to Joseph P. Lash:]   [August 6, 1943]
Trude has been writing you a book so this is just a line not to tell you details but to give an outsider's impression for what it is worth! The children seemed to fling themselves on Trude. There was great excitement in her & a little *apprehension* before they arrived, but they were the first off the bus & at once all was perfect. . . . Trude is happy, the house looks nice, she has busy days ahead. People she cares about are welcoming her back. You wrote her a perfect letter. Sometimes I have been afraid that with you away, if hurts came she might find them hard to bear alone but you have provided her with an armor. Great love between two people is perhaps all one needs, but it exists so rarely & when it does & when they cannot be together, I cannot help being resentful at a fate that divides you. What makes both of you wonderful, I guess, is your sense of willingly sacrificing yourselves in the greater effort of your generation. I hope you will see some measure of improvement in the whole social structure so that all you have endured will be repaired.

She was not yet sixty yet already was beginning to think of withdrawal as the young took over.

[E.R. to Joseph P. Lash:]   [August 8, 1943]
. . . I know you trust me & love me as I do you & I certainly hope we can do many things together in the future but you must not forget that you & Trude must be the ones to *do* in the future, my participation with all you young things will be more as a background & a place of refuge to rest & recuperate!

It has been wonderful to have Trude & Mickey & Vera but today has been hard for them. The children were conscious of the approaching separation & it is hard for Trude. She will be busy with the house & it is not so long now till they come back to her & she says it is far easier than Reno. . . .

I am so glad you have gained the strength & confidence you felt you lacked & above all I'm glad you will never feel unworthy of being my friend. That feeling on your part or on anyone's part not only seems funny to me but always has made me start to look for what was wrong in me that gave anyone that feeling! You will never really lose your own interests, it is too deep in you to think in world terms, & Trude has it too much to let you slip. . . .

She came back from Westbrook and a night with Esther and Elizabeth. "It really is like old times to have a whole evening of talk," she thanked Esther. ". . . Harry & Louise are going to move to their own house but no one seems to have hard feelings though P. doesn't like their going." She went to Harlem to a school children's meeting "& lastly Nehru's nieces who are to study here at Wellesley. We shouldn't despair of what we may accomplish when they seem full of hope!" She picked up Trude and they went to dinner with Harry Hooker at the Chez Jean restaurant.

[E.R. to Joseph P. Lash:]   [August 10, 1943]
    These last few days at home are busy for me & having the Churchills won't make it easier but somehow I'll get off! I'm so afraid I won't do a good job but if I get to see you, it will be worth going anyway. I'll feel guilty too that I have what would mean so much to Trude & to you. She lives on your letters & the last came so fast. I think you two are very happy & I love you both! I'm so sorry about the poison ivy or poison oak. You have a very bad case. Wash with yellow soap & disinfectant if you ever know you are *near* it again, sometimes one is more sensitive to it even after a bad case. . . .

Two days before she was to leave she was entertaining the Prime Minister at Hyde Park. "As you know we are never idle here," she wrote Hick. "But a Prime Minister can keep one busy! Mrs. Churchill didn't come yesterday but Mary is here & a nice child. We had a picnic out on our picnic grounds & we swam twice & I played deck tennis till I am weary. . . ." She dashed off a V-mail to me.

[E.R. to Joseph P. Lash:]   [August 13, 1943]
    I was happy that you told me what Trude wrote about my arrival in Reno. I'm always afraid that others are not sharing my own pleasure but feel they must be polite and though I have nearly overcome the feeling with you, and now with Trude, too, still reassurance is always pleasant. Tommy & I are both happy that you like the idea of using the playroom as a cottage, and while I am gone she and Henry hope to get Trude here and make some drawings. . . . A well-known and frequent guest [Churchill] tonight read us letters from Germans taken from airmen who have been brought down in the last few weeks. Many of them described raids

in April and said they could stand no more. One woman begged her boy in Tunisia to be careful and when he felt he could do no more to let himself be taken prisoner. They were sad and encouraging from our point of view.

As Eleanor's departure date approached, Tommy began to regret her too easy acquiescence in Eleanor's decision to leave her behind.

[Tommy to Esther Lape:]   [August (?) 1943]
   As the time approaches for her to leave, I get a very queer feeling in my tummy—I hate to see her go. She said last night that she knew she would regret many times not having taken me, but thought it good discipline for her to do things for herself. . . . I feel today that I could not possibly organize myself for such a trip, and yet I know if I had planned all along to go, I would be stimulated and able to work.

A visit to Elinor and a final note to her old friend:

   I wish I could think of something which would make you stop worrying about me. There really is no danger or I assure you I would not be going and I only hope you will all be wishing me luck in doing a good job!

"Heres the itinerary but it may vary," she wrote Esther and Elizabeth. "I could not get a map. Tommy will send you the diary."
"The P. was very sweet to her as she left," Tommy reported to Esther.

[Tommy to Esther Lape:]   [No date]
   She left all her jewelry—engagement ring, pearls, etc. with instructions as to their disposal in case anything happened. Of course, I realize that anything can happen to us at any time, but it gave me a queer feeling, especially as she did not leave them home when she went to Great Britain.
       . . .
   Tiny is getting married to the band leader with whom she has been in love—he is only 30 and she must be at least 38. The wedding is today in San Francisco so that Mrs. R. can be there. . . .

Eleanor sent a quick note to Trude from Johnnie's in San Francisco.

[E.R. to Trude W. Pratt:]   [August 17, 1943]
   I hated to leave you yesterday feeling so miserably & with so much still to go through. Besides I know how hard it is to see me go where I may

see Joe, when you & Joe are the ones you [who] ought to be together. I wish so you could be in my pocket!

I leave at ten tonight, the trip out was smooth. No other woman on the plane. This is just to say I love you & will do all I can to bring Joe a picture in words of you & his home.

II

"This Trip May Have Been Worth While"

E LEANOR'S TRIP to the South Pacific has often been described. It is retold here because the letters she managed to dash off were so revealing of her inner personality. The letters were between herself, friends and family, and especially her devoted secretary, Malvina Thompson, who remained at the White House, sent her the news she cared about, and made copies of the typed diary she sent back to go to F.D.R., her children, and a few close friends.

In some notes that she prepared after F.D.R.'s death in connection with the writing of *This I Remember,* she said that among the war memories that stood out most vividly in her mind was "the day that he [F.D.R.] told me he thought it would be useful for me to go to Australia, New Zealand, and the islands in the southwest Pacific." She then added:

. . . the take off at night from the San Francisco air field was a dramatic moment and I confess a rather lonely one. The first landing on a little coral atoll in the Pacific Ocean would have been an interesting experience at any time, but the uncertainty of whether the officers and men would find my visit agreeable or just a bore made it a rather trying experience at the start.

A letter to "Tommy dearest" from San Francisco, gave Tommy the news of her movements before take off.

[E.R. to Tommy:] [August 17, 1943]

I hated to say goodbye yesterday but I am sure it is best to take this trip alone and we will go together to China! Please have a good time and rest while I am gone and give as good a time as you can to all the people you know I would like to do it for if I was home! In copying this as a diary leave out all personal parts to you. Use your own judgment about dates or anything else while I am gone. Remember also that if you think anyone should be hired or fired you have my entire confidence and I want you to act as you think wise.

A V-mail note to me—

[E.R. to Joseph P. Lash:] [August 17, 1943]

This is just a test of speed. Trude & Tommy saw me off yesterday afternoon & went to dinner together. Poor Trude was sad & suffering from her teeth. She slept after lunch & didn't finish her letter to you, but she will mail it & I have other things.

Tiny was married here today as I could be here & I do hope she will be happy. He seems a kind and gentle person.

I covered the house with Trude yesterday & I hope I know all the details. There is no doubt it is a lovely house & I think suited to you two & the kids & the kind of life you will enjoy. . . . I am at Johnny's & leave tonight.

Her next letter, begun August 18, covered the long leg to Honolulu. "I slept in that much scorned red flannel lining to my Red Cross coat as it grew fairly cold." In Honolulu, in Brigadier General Ryan's house, she "did my exercises to get the kinks out," had breakfast, and was on her way to Wallis and Christmas Islands, where she inspected the hospital, spoke to several small infantry and artillery detachments, greeted some natives "of whom there are only nine on the island," signed "short snorter bills." She thought "the men here have been glad to have me come, but of course it is hard to tell since we are a polite people. I did think Col. Rustin, the highest ranking man who is about to leave, was not very pleased at first, but he seems more friendly, I think."

En route to Bora Bora, her plane stopped at Penryhn Island in the Cook group. The officer in charge told her she was the first white woman he had seen since he had left the States ten months before. There were colored troops in the area, "and there seems to be no trouble anywhere out here between white and colored." There were 700 Navy men on Bora Bora and about 2,500 Army. "A very interesting discussion started by one man asking if F. was going to run again, then the ice was broken, and the concern about post war jobs was discussed at length."

It eased her mind to realize that the men welcomed her presence. "The men do talk and I think doing this is worth while, though I sign endless autographs." At the next island, Attatuka, "the Colonel, regular Army, Mass. Republican, and snobby was not pleased to see me. I'm sure he would sleep with a Maori woman but he told me he does not believe in mixed marriages, and he would like some Army nurses because some of the younger officers want to marry some of the native girls."

A letter from Tommy that Eleanor thought must have been written August 22 or 23 gave her the news Tommy thought her boss wanted to have: she had paid all the bills and deposited the Syndicate check as well as some checks from her literary agent, George Bye. She had not paid the Abercrombie bill for Red Cross uniforms because she did not know whether Mrs. Roosevelt or the Red Cross would pay it. Nelly Johanssen, a Hyde Park neighbor, was canning peaches but they cost more than store peaches in glass jars. She had supper with Elinor Morgenthau. Everyone was sending Tommy letters for her and she was sending them out into space. Esther was having an expert make out Eleanor's tax returns—the job that the ailing Elizabeth used to do. "The much heralded 'simplified' form is far worse than ever —at least to my feeble mind." Two of the black women who worked for Mrs. Roosevelt, Alice and Georgie, were sunning themselves out at the pool "much to Nancy's [Cook] annoyance. . . . I just shrugged my shoulders when she complained." She was inundated with invitations from the Byes, Carlins, John Golden. "Henry [Osthagen] comes today—Trude tomorrow if her mouth permits."

Eleanor's stopover in Samoa represented the kind of visit she dreaded. The Marine general in charge did everything for her comfort but kept her away from the men. "I was not favorably impressed." The hospital held 700 patients and was well-equipped, "but I heard one thing that troubled me. There is no wine or beer for the men so last night four men died from drinking distilled shellac." At the end of that entry she directed Tommy to weed out "what ought to go to Norman Davis [Red Cross] without cutting it out from the diary where you think it will be of interest to F. or others." She asked after Tommy's sister Muriel and the latter's daughter Eleanor. "You do so much for my friends that I wish I could just be there to do something for Muriel and Eleanor. I miss you and yet I think you would not have enjoyed this trip and you would have found it hard."

From the Fijis her plane *Our Eleanor*, as the crew had christened the large craft, flew to Noumea in New Caledonia, headquarters for the South Pacific forces led by Admiral Halsey and General Harmon. She began a letter to Jimmy, relieved, as she explained to Tommy, that "the news from the Aleutians continues so good that I hope he will be in San Diego when I get back." At Suva in the Fijis, which was the headquarters of the British High Commissioner of the West Pacific, she visited several hospitals and also was treated to a bit of ceremony. American GIs who had relieved the marines at Guadalcanal were resting there: "You tell these boys that you hope they will get home soon and they cheer. They are plenty hard boiled but as far as I can tell my being here is giving them a kick. Soon we will be in Noumea and then I will see Admiral Halsey and know my plans for which everyone is clamoring."

But in Noumea she added a very discouraged postscript in longhand.

[E.R. to Tommy:]   [August 26, 1943]

At night—I doubt if I can get to Guadalcanal & have just written Trude & am making a package for Joe writing him. I'm sorry as seeing all these masses of boys who seem pleased just to see me as a stranger makes me realize it might have meant something to Joe. Ad. Halsey says to go on to New Zealand & Australia & when I come back I can go to Espiritu Santo & he will try then to get me to Guadalcanal but he sounded so doubtful that I am discouraged & really sorry that I came. I simply will never face another hospital at home & while I'll write the column I don't think I'll bother to talk of anything but the Red ✚ when I come home. I'm going to feel ashamed to have been so near by & yet not to have gone there & want to forget about it as soon as possible. I've sent the packages to Rose Franken's boy.

The Ad. has a dinner tonight. There's a full programme laid out for tomorrow as weather forecasts are bad & we don't leave till the next day for New Zealand. This will go off tomorrow. Love.

ER

A more indignant letter went to Franklin.

[E.R. to F.D.R.:]   [August 26, 1943]

All well & nothing eventful. I go to New Zealand tomorrow because they expected bad weather today. On the 2d to Australia. Ad. Halsey seems very nervous about me, the others I can see think I could safely go to Guadalcanal. He says on my return I may go to Espiritu Santo & he will then decide, conditions may be more favorable. I realize final responsibility is his but I feel more strongly than ever I should go & I doubt if I ever go to another hospital at home if I don't for I know more clearly than ever what it means to the men. Malaria is as bad as the enemy & causes more casualties! Gen. MacArthur is in New Guinea & Gen. Eichelberger will take charge of me. I sidestepped being an official guest of the Gov. but will spend one night at the Gov. General's. I won't get near any dangerous spots in Australia either. In some ways I wish I had not come on this trip. I think the trouble I give far outweighs the momentary interest it may give the boys to see me. I do think when I tell them I bring a message from you to them, they like it but anyone else could have done it as well & caused less commotion! Much love & I hope you take care of yourself. I hope also the Quebec conference has gone as you wished. Take a little rest now & then.

> Devotedly
> ER

Her letter to Hick was more guarded. Absent was the note of exasperation and complaint.

[E.R. to Lorena Hickok:]   [August 25, 1943]

The trip has been interesting & quite easy for me but I'm glad I did not bring Tommy since 6:30–7 is our usual breakfast hour & you know how she loves getting up early. I'm in good health but I have no zest for travel any more, however, if it does any good I'll be satisfied. I can't judge at all whether it will accomplish what FDR hoped for or not.

Here from Ad. Halsey down there is a deep hatred of the Japs & I think that makes the fighting easier. Most of them think the Japs will fight a long time, only Ad. Halsey hopes they will crack suddenly.

She was more open about her feelings in her letter to me saying she might not be able to get to Guadalcanal.

[E.R. to Joseph P. Lash:]   [August 25, 1943]

It has been decided that I should do New Zealand & Australia first & they will see on my return if my wish can be accomplished but they are not encouraging. If I see you it will be a surprise & a joy, if not my personal disappointment will be great but I think I'll be even sadder because I feel it will have a bad effect at home on boys & their families. I had a hunch I should not come & I feel it more strongly than ever. It seemed to me from the start a terrible chore with the chance of seeing you the one pleasant & happy personal thing but chore or not I must do the best I can with the whole job & forget there are any personal feelings where I am concerned!

"If Tommy shows you the daily schedule I've been sending home you'll see why the column is all I get written," she advised Hick from Auckland—

[E.R. to Lorena Hickok:]   [September 1, 1943]

Well, the trip is nearly half over. The people here are kind & they like F.D.R. & our marines have won all their hearts, so they are very nice to me. I make so many speeches daily that I'll soon be talked out but

George Durno is a help telling me what goes well & the reverse as he watches & overhears remarks in the crowd.

These boys break your heart, but they're so young & so tired. Malaria is almost as bad as bullets. They are hardly out of hospitals before they are at Red Cross Clubs & dances & they laugh at everything. I take my hat off to this young generation & I hope we won't let them down. I've talked to every kind of group from Maoris to hospital patients, high ranking officers & the people of New Zealand.

She still was downcast in New Zealand.

[E.R. to Tommy:]   [September (?) 1943]
The round is much the same daily, hospitals, Red Cross clubs, camps, factories, etc. I did the important broadcast tonight so that is behind me. Tomorrow night we leave and go to receive a Maori welcome. Then another night by train to Auckland. The same round there. . . . as I have no word from anyone I wonder if they are keeping you [Tommy] informed as to my whereabouts? Be sure to arrange for my trip across to Washington or New York via James if he is home. I feel a hundred years away as though I were moving in a different and totally unattached world. I don't like it much. It is a pity to be doing this when the zest for new things is so largely gone. It is terribly depressing too I guess though one isn't conscious of it at the time.

It cheered her up to add messages via Tommy to her friends:

Must go to bed. Give my love to Trude, to Maude if by chance she did not get off, to Elinor, to Anna and to the boys if you send them any news. Please tell Esther and Elizabeth I think of them very often, and the same to Hick and Earl. I can of course hear nothing from Joe so if Trude has any news let me know how he is. Incidentally I am in the best of health and my feet are not bothering me at all.

And yet, as so often in her life, her inner discontents and her conviction that she was not doing as good a job as she felt she should were concealed by an outer poise and performance that left her associates awed and speechless. Maj. George Durno, a former newspaperman who had covered the White House, had been assigned to her by Air Transport Command. He sent Tommy a note:

For your information, Mrs. R literally took New Zealand by storm. . . . She did a magnificent job, saying the right thing at the right time and doing a hundred and one little things that endeared her to the people. Personally, when this tour is over I am going to return to one of

the convalescent officers' retreats we have visited and catch my breath—
or something.

Before she left Auckland she scrawled another note to Franklin again making
the point that everyone assured her that Guadalcanal was safe.

[E.R. to F.D.R.:]

Your message reached me this morning & I was happy to hear that
Elliott was still there & hope he is enjoying the children & that the heat
is not too much for them. I'm glad that you are satisfied with the Quebec
conference & I'm also glad that so far reaction to my trip has been
favorable.

The people here are very kind & our Marines have certainly made a
grand impression. Lots of people ask about Jimmy & his men in hospital
speak of him with such warmth, one boy with his arm off told me "they
don't come any better than Jimmy"—

Tell Mr. Churchill the German letters have been listened to with great
interest & are a great encouragement. All these men ask if I've been to
Guadalcanal & say now it's safe & I should go so I hope Ad. Halsey
permits it on my return.

I hope you are allright. Tell Dr. MacIntire his hospitals are tops—not
for publication, they are better than the army. The Red ✚ is doing a swell
job but needs more personnel badly & they must work out a better basis
for cooperation with the Navy & Marine Corps.

The schedules are strenuous but so far I'm getting by nicely, tho' I
speak so often I expect to run dry soon!

Ask Tommy to send me a message with all the news. Much love.

She sent a cable to the President via Navy communications:

> MANY THANKS FOR MESSAGE.
> GOOD LUCK AND LOVE TO ELLIOTT WHEN HE GOES.
> TELL TOMMY ALL WELL.
> LOVE, E.R.

A note to Tommy told her of the radio message from F.D.R. in which he had
said "the reaction to my trip was favorable, but he never reads the unfavorable
people so I'm anxious to hear from you. I wonder if I ever will." She might later
have regretted her footnote to this letter. "Tell FDR Gen. Pat Hurley made a great
hit down here." The bulk of the note dealt with her approaching move on to
Australia.

[E.R. to Tommy:]   [September 1, 1943]

Every minute of every day is filled & every evening but I'm fine &

nearly half the time is behind me. I dread Australia & then there are so many speeches that I know I'll be talked out. George Durno tells me if he thinks things are well received or not & that has been helpful. Not having you to watch audiences is a drawback. The mail is heavy & will all go back to you & you can have all letters for me to sign on return.

She still hoped to get to Guadalcanal as she wrote me from Auckland.

[E.R. to Joseph P. Lash:]   [September (?) 1943]
    It seems funny to be nearer to you & yet to feel much further away than at home & not to be sure that I can get any word to you & to know that there is no way I can hear from you. I just hope you are well dear boy. This is just to tell you that if I can get to you at all which will depend on what Ad. Halsey says, it will be between Sept. 17th & 21st. Try to be round those days so if I get there you can be found as I rather think they will only let me spend a few hours & they will want me to do certain things while there. If I leave these parts without seeing you I will find some way of letting you know. I will be about a week on return trip & once landed in San Francisco I can write regularly & I hope hear regularly again & I will send you a cable as soon as I see Trude. I miss you very much & being cut off like this has been very hard—I've not had a word from home either—The schedules are hard but I hope I do a good job. Like fighting the war this type of trip isn't worth doing unless the job accomplished is good.
    The people are friendly & our Marines have been taken into the homes & made a grand reputation for themselves. There is friction between the Marines & the New Zealand soldiers on account of the Americans having more money & better manners with the ladies!
    All my love to you dear boy,

    Three installments of Eleanor's diary reached Tommy. She sent the first copy to F.D.R. "I think these first installment diaries are grand," he noted in a memorandum. "Don't forget to let me see the rest of them."
    En route from New Zealand to Australia Eleanor began to allow herself to feel she was doing an acceptable job. "Well, six days in New Zealand are over," she wrote Tommy, "and I think it went well." Tommy should pick out a few representative letters from those she was sending back "and give to F.D.R. to read so he can have a general idea of the way it went." She had one personal complaint: "If I get no word from you in Australia I shall know that I am to go without news on this trip." On the more general level, "I dread Australia for thirteen days but they will come to an end. Even the British trips can't touch these schedules."
    In Canberra she had the first letter from Tommy with its welcome budget of news. "I must go to bed since with the change in time it is now nineteen and a half

hours since I got up!" A second newsy letter from Tommy did not catch up with her for several days but it contained the information she wanted. Maude and David had gotten off for Ireland; how they kept within the weight limit with all the boxes, packages, and bags, Tommy did not understand. She had dinner with Elinor M. and had invited Simone and the baby to come to Hyde Park for the weekend, but Simone felt it was "too much of a chore." Simone stayed away but Earl was about. "Because Earl and I were affectionate with each other, John G[olden] accused me of being in love with Earl and Earl was really embarrassed!"

A note about press reports of E.R.'s trip: "There still is nothing unfavorable in the press or in the mail about the trip. Pegler is still fighting with Jim Carey [of the CIO] and the Ladies H.J. in his column and yesterday he took a crack at the P. because of the Four Freedoms."

Hick had moved out of the White House temporarily to Chevy Chase where Judge Marion Harron lived because, she told Tommy, "the W.H. was not attractive without you." Trude was still having trouble with her teeth. Tommy thought she might have the rugs put down and the curtains up at 29, but decided they would only accumulate dirt and should wait. A postscript showed her anxiety for her boss: "I don't know what you'll decide after this trip. I am convinced I can't be independent of you & your presence."

After two days in Canberra, Eleanor wrote Franklin—

[E.R. to F.D.R.:]   [September 5, 1943]
    My 'being social & polite day' is over. At nine this a.m. we leave for Melbourne. Yesterday was busy and wearying, however. I like Mr. Curtin very much & I hope you will ask him to come to the U.S. again. I think he would come & his coming could not but help be salutary for our labor people. They have a curious situation here with the Seamen's Union. They have a strike because the seamen want to force the engineers & non-com's into their union or leave them without representation on the arbitration com.. Lord & Lady Gowrie are very nice & have been most kind. The rivalry between states here complicates life very much. I saw Bob Patterson, Knudsen, etc. my last evening in N.Z. & he told me to see Port Moresby if I could since there was no danger there but gave such a wonderful impression of activity. He seemed pleased with what he had seen & Knudsen saw the need of more planes. Of course I see & hear nothing of military things but the Red ✚ must make some changes. Time enough when I get home to report however & easier to talk about than to write.
    Evatt told me last night he was satisfied & happy with the way the commitments you had made to him were being carried out.
    The Australian gov. people, which is all I've seen so far, seem very happy that I came & they understand it is only a friendly gesture but like it. From now on I'll get more of an idea of the people. This country is

still in a [word indecipherable] state. The boys have married so many
Australian girls that I should have looked up on getting them into the
U.S.A. before coming as I'm deluged with letters on the subject!

Last night both the Chinese & Russian representatives pressed me to
know when I was going to visit their countries so hurry up with your
meetings Sir!

Truth to tell, however, I very much doubt that these trips have any real
value & they certainly put our high ranking officials to much trouble &
travail of spirit! Incidentally the Johnsons have been very kind.

Her vexation with the higher brass in Australia was not softened by the knowledge that she surely had of MacArthur's pomp and swagger. She again unburdened
herself to Franklin the next day.

[E.R. to F.D.R.:]   [September 6, 1943]
Word came last night from Gen. McArthur that it would require too
many high ranking officers to escort me in Port Moresby & he cld. not
spare them at this time when a push is on. This is the kind of thing that
seems to me silly. I'd rather a sergeant & I'd see & hear more but I must
have a general & I'm so scared I can't speak & he wouldn't tell me
anything anyway. Generals Eichelberger & Byers & Ad. Jones are dears
but I'd much rather be unimpeded. The papers here complain that I see
none of the plain people, neither do I really see any of the plain soldiers. I
have an M.P. escort everywhere that would do you credit. I have all the
pomp & restriction & none of the power! I'm coming home this time &
go in a factory!

The weather is fine, the days full, & I feel fine & I'm not doing
anything which couldn't be better done by Mr. Allen of the Red ✚ who
could go see their people near the battle front & should come out here
now.

I grow fatter daily since we eat at every turn—

The absence of mail made the restrictions on her movements the more gall-
ing: "Dearest Tommy, No news & no mail & all goes smoothly, busily & dully here.
Much love, E.R."

Her letter to Tommy from Sydney outlined an itinerary on the way home that
would enable her to see Jimmy if he was in San Diego.

[E.R. to Tommy:]   [September 7, 1943]
Please tell the St. Francis in San Francisco to keep a room for me when
the Air Transport notify them. Also let me have Tiny's married name &
phone & address in L.A. I can only remember "Hershey" [it was Mrs.
Hershey Martin] & if I go there I want to see her. Let me know about

James & arrange for return trip either from S.F. to S.D. & then home from L.A. & only one night & day in S.D. or straight home from S.F. I won't go to Anna but I'll phone her. I think I shall be anxious to get back to H.P. but if F. is in Washington I'll go there for two days & hold a press conference.

All goes well & the Australian broadcast is done. I have a feeling that after tomorrow the schedule will be lighter & since I don't go to Port Moresby I may get off sooner to Noumea. I will only spend two days there if I am not allowed to go to Guadalcanal & 2 or 3 days in Honolulu. FDR apparently cabled suggesting I shouldn't do so much so you might tell him if I wasn't busy I'd go crazy or go home tomorrow. Admiral Jones wanted me to spend a day at his cottage by the sea & I explained that when I got home I would rest but I had no right to do so while here. Wherever I go I have M.P.'s & Generals & Admirals & it surely is something awful to live up to! No mail here from home & of course I can have no word from Joe as I might as well be on a desert island. The war news at least is good.

> Much love to you dear.
> E.R.

I heard today of the horrible accident to the Congressional & will be happier when I'm sure that no one we know was on it.

A letter to Hick from Sydney underscored the ubiquity of the military brass and pomp.

[E.R. to Lorena Hickok:] [September 7, 1943]
I don't write because literally the column is all I do & there is nothing else to record. It is a boring trip with a long schedule of doing similar things daily. Everyone is cordial & to be visited by the wife of the President of the U.S. is flattering. So they are kind! I'm surrounded by Generals & Admirals & M.P.'s wherever I go & you know how that would please me. I'll be glad to be home but not in Washington. I'll need a long dose of the cottage & N.Y. City to forget this pomp & ceremony!

I hope all is well with you. I heard the Congressional was wrecked today & 150 killed & only hope no one we know was on it. Railroads must be wearing out.

She almost trilled with delight when toward the end of her travels in Australia several of Tommy's letters caught up with her.

[E.R. to Tommy:] [September 10, 1943]
Three letters from you yesterday & two today really have made my life

much more bearable. I do miss you very much but you shouldn't be anxious. They treat me like a frail flower & won't let me approach any danger. This royalty business is painful but I don't know how to avoid it & I think besides feeling cut off from those I love the difficulty of knowing whether all the trouble people have taken is justified by the results is too difficult for me to evaluate. If I see Joe the personal effort will be more worth while but if I don't I doubt whether from the public viewpoint the Congressional group now here couldn't do just as good a job!

I'm horrified at Abercrombie's bill for I thought Red ✚ uniforms were cheap. I pay it, so send a check. They should be used for years to make them worth it! I had thought $250 would cover everything.

Thank Gen. McCloy for word about Jimmy. If you think Anna really needs me of course I'll go home that way but I'll just spend a night & a day & go on the next afternoon. I gather James won't be back.

I feel a desire to get home, New York & H.P. *not* Washington tho' of course I'll go there if FDR is still there but I gather from the papers he may be meeting Stalin. . . .

Italy is good news but of course not the end! When do the Hopkins' move?

I'm so very glad you don't like being independent of me for I don't like being independent of you even tho' I think it probably was well for you not to come on this trip. (I'm sure you would have hated it as much as I have)! Much, much love dear & thanks again for writing. I just read & reread your letters & feel quite close to you for a time at least!

Devotedly,
E.R.

I'm glad Esther is getting an expert on taxes. I hope Edith Helm was well & enjoyed her trip & you had a good time with her. I wish you could stop John Golden giving me the piano. I'd rather have Earl's in the future for purely sentimental reasons & I hate the wasting of money. I'd much rather he would give the money to U.S.S.A. [United States Student Assembly]. I don't use the apartment enough to warrant such expense.

I have Tiny's address & phone number from her.

E.R.

Tommy might complain to Esther about her boss's preoccupation with many of the people around her, of whom Tommy did not think too highly. She grumbled about the hecticness of the pace that Mrs. Roosevelt maintained, but she counseled Edith Helm, E.R.'s very dignified social secretary and one of the few people Tommy exempted from suspicions of sycophancy, that she must learn to adapt to Mrs. R.'s ways or not return to the White House. "I told her," she wrote Esther, "she can't change ER—that ER is completely bored by the W.H. & H.P. & if she [Edith] comes back she must accept that fact & not let it upset her."

This writer does not know whether the reception or dispatch of letters gave Eleanor the greater pleasure. In any case she knew that the flow of information and tenderness was a two-way affair. She sent me a final note from Australia.

[E.R. to Joseph P. Lash:] [September 10, 1943]
On the 14th I return to Noumea & then I will know whether I am to be allowed to get to you. This has been a hard trip because I wanted so much to see you & I had to see so many others. I have learned a lot but for the honor of the U.S.A. I must be treated like royalty which is exhausting & every one is kind & yet you know you are consuming valuable time. I only hope the results are sufficiently good on all sides to warrant the disruption of so many people's lives! I can't go to Port Moresby they say, hence my earlier return. Should be with you between 15th & 17th, otherwise don't expect me. I'll be heartbroken but I will have done all I can. I hope that poison rash cleared up. I've seen some bad skin infections & I certainly have a respect for malaria! Dear boy. I love you.

A wonderful letter from Trude yesterday but you have later news.

Her letter to Hick was a good summary of her travels in Australia.

[E.R. to Lorena Hickok:] [September 12, 1943]
. . . Australia is an undeveloped country & I doubt if many people at home have any idea of transportation difficulties. The terrain in which those boys fight is also unfamiliar to us & unbelievably difficult. I do camps, hospitals, Red ✚ services day & evening & see men who have either been in to New Guinea & come out with a shadow on their faces but a grim hatred of the Japs or new men going in to something they knew nothing about or are ill prepared for unless they have special training at home. There have been, of course in each big city some official entertainments but I only have one of those still left to do. At dinner tomorrow night in Brisbane given by Mrs. MacArthur. I've only done 2 radio talks which I prepared, one in New Zealand & one in Australia. There have been several "few words" daily to my varied audiences. I begin to think the job has been a good one as far as these countries are concerned but for our own men I know F. should have insisted that I go to New Guinea & Guadalcanal or not sent me.

I have lots of information for the Red ✚. George Durno has felt responsible for me & I think he is satisfied. He has been very kind & nice.

I didn't take the trip for pleasure & I haven't enjoyed it, but I am very well & it hasn't been at all tiring.

My love to you dear. I think of you & your love for travel & wonder if you would have enjoyed it.

MacArthur's unwillingness to allow her to go to Port Moresby rankled, as she indicated in a last letter to Franklin from Australia.

[E.R. to F.D.R.:]   [September 13, 1943]

Nothing to report except that I am well & have been wrapped in "protection" so I shall breathe again when I get home! I've had so many Generals & Admirals & M.P.'s to protect me that I remind myself of you. I'm sorry not to fly to Port Moresby, it would have pleased the men & they can't understand it. They all say, "but it is quite safe Mrs. Roosevelt & you ought to see the field we've made!" The news looks encouraging & I hope the time is shortened for these boys, they do want to get home!

George Durno has been very nice & felt very responsible & I think he's satisfied with the impression made in New Zealand & Australia. I wonder if James will be back, if not I'll go to Anna for a night on my way home. I wonder too if you'll be in Washington or Hyde Park or off to see Stalin! If you are in Washington it might be as well to go there for a day or two to sign mail & have a press conference, see Norman Davis & find out what he and the O.W.I. might like me to do & then I'd like to go to N.Y. & H.P. for a time. I'd like to tell Dr. Mac too that his hospitals are uniformly good.

I lunch with the Gov. Gen. of Queensland today & dine with Mrs. MacArthur. Leave early tomorrow.

Hope all goes well & don't forget Tommy will hear from Johnny when he & his family arrive. It should be the 18th or 19th I think. I wonder what you know of Jimmy, Elliott & Fjr.?

She flew from Brisbane to Noumea. Her pencil was busy enroute to Brisbane telling Tommy "It's been mostly Red ✚ Army & Navy the last few days. . . . The boys last night all asked if I wasn't coming to New Guinea & I feel more strongly than ever about these restrictions. You needn't worry, I've never been so hedged about with restrictions in my life. It makes me want to do something reckless when I get home, like making munitions!"

In Noumea she received the welcome news that she would be allowed to fly to Guadalcanal.

[E.R. to Tommy:]   [September 14, 1943]

. . . I feel happy tonight for we are going to Guadalcanal. We leave tomorrow here, then Effate [*sic*], a big hospital, & Espiritu Santo for the night & the 17th to Guadalcanal. Not having heard one word from Joe in 6 weeks & having no word from you or Trude here I realize he may no longer be there but I hope for the best & shall be more glad than I can say if I see him.

I left the Australians friendly & happy I think. For the rest I only hope it was a good job. I know I should have gone to New Guinea.

On George Durno's urging, she wired F.D.R. to ask whether the plane *Our Eleanor* that had carried her through the trip could take her to Washington. Tommy should let her know which child on the West Coast seemed to need her most as she could spend the night either in San Francisco, Seattle, or San Diego. "Come to think of it I guess I better spend one night in S.F. & see Sisty & get home the 24th."

She reached Guadalcanal at dawn and spent a hectic day there* that included a visit to my weather detachment as well as a look at my corner of a tent that I shared with several bunk mates so she might tell Trude. In the notes she prepared for the writing of *This I Remember* she said: "The most exciting time [in the Pacific] was the landing on Guadalcanal after a three hour bomber flight in the dark, because Guadalcanal to me was a symbol of the war in the southwest Pacific with all the suffering and hardships our boys had gone through. . . ." The next day she wrote me from Espiritu Santo and enclosed some snapshots taken of her with Admiral Halsey and General Howard.

[E.R. to Joseph P. Lash:]   [September 18, 1943]

I thought these might amuse you & remind you of the lady in uniform! How I hated to have you leave last night. When the war is over I hope I never have to be long away from you. It was so wonderful to be with you, the whole trip now seems to me to be worthwhile. It is bad to be so personal but I care first for those few people I love deeply & then for the rest of the world I fear. I've worked hard today however. We were up at 3:45 & left the field at 5 were here at 9:20. I've been to three hospitals, a big navy recreation field & talked to a lot of boys in this last place & in hospitals & now I've taken a shower & I'm clean & Ad. Fitch has a party to which I must go. Two Senators have just arrived, Brewster of Maine & Mead of New York.

I will spend the night of the 19th at Wallis & 20th at Canton or Christmas or perhaps get to Honolulu. I'll radio from there to Tommy to tell Trude I saw you. I think over every minute we had together & I'm glad I saw where you live & work. We have a comparison now for other places!

---

* Cf. *Eleanor and Franklin*, pp. 688–90.

I have to show my film (the Eng. one) & tell about it here so you see I'm not idle.

> I love you dearly, bless you—
> E.R.

She sent me a quick note from Honolulu.

[E.R. to Joseph P. Lash:]   [September 19, 1943]

I've just regained the day I lost on the way down! I sent you a letter from Wallis & I hope it gets to you [it didn't] but it didn't seem to me a very efficient island. Last night we were at Christmas again & the only thing I did of any importance was to get up at 6 to go to see a boy who'd been badly hurt in an overturned tank. I did get him to smile by promising to see his mother & tell her about him. She lives in Astoria, L.I. It was a six hour flight over here & I had my hair washed & sent everything to be cleaned & washed & then had an enormous press conference. Your boy from Yank was here & so pleased to hear I'd seen you & said he had a letter from you. He agrees with you as he'd heard the story under a different form so I'll write "Yank" in N.Y. I think I'll ask that they print the column.*

I finished reading the report on postwar planning & it is worth your reading so I will send together with some pamphlets (if I can get them) as soon as I get home. I finished the body of your sweater today & got a start on sleeves! I also radioed Tommy to tell Trude I had seen you & you were well & in good spirits.

I dined with the Gov. tonight & they had a nice Hawaiian group to sing in the garden afterwards but I could hardly keep awake. It was nice just the same & I kept wondering if someday you & Trude & I might come & really enjoy it! Nothing is really happy to me just now & that is why I am better when I'm busy.

I must go to bed for at 6:30 I must be up! This hotel is taken over by the Navy as a rest area for sub crews & I want to see if I can get some boys to eat with me at breakfast. We start out at 8 & never get back till 6 & dine out at 7! They do arrange pretty steep days & I always have to do the column at night! I leave here Wed. night. All my love dear boy.

A final note to Tommy from Honolulu: "It was wonderful seeing Joe & I'm so glad I didn't miss Guadalcanal. . . . I'm anxious to know so many things about the kids, Earl (the wretch hasn't written me once) & Hick—Trude I long to see to tell her about Joe. (I hope her teeth are all done & she is better.) . . .

---

* A malicious story described Mrs. Roosevelt as believing overseas service had made soldiers so savage we should be kept in the Pacific even after the war ended for a period of "re-education."

"I begin to think even in its effect on the men this trip may have been worthwhile."

She had covered seventeen islands, New Zealand, and Australia and her companions estimated she had seen about 400,000 men in the camps and hospitals. "I got to Guadalcanal," she wrote Hick on the plane homeward bound, "which was a satisfaction & I didn't get to New Guinea. I still can't tell whether the trip was worthwhile where the men were concerned but I hope it was."

On the plane home she wrote brief notes for speeches and reminders to herself of matters to take up with various people, F.D.R. first of all—

FDR: Should there not be a call on men like those now in the War Production Board whom you decide are qualified to remain thro transition period for patriotic reasons. Their jobs being held for them?

FDR: Isn't resumption of peacetime industry largely dependent on bank loan policy & possible guarantee by the govt. in same way as was done for conversion to war industry?

Also undertaking to help other nations undertake needed work where some men as supervisors would be needed from here.

For FDR: I do not like General. . . . Hospital Wallis not comfortable enough after such long establishment. (Dr. MacIntire.) Men not chief concern anywhere. Officers have too much, men too little (Guadalcanal). Army hospitals generally not as well equipped as Navy. More permanence in Navy set up.

For FDR: French natives poorly cared for—Wallis, Noumea. Plans for services in post war to be announced now as legislation is passed.

There were chits for Norman Davis of the Red Cross to ask "if he wants any speeches in or out of uniform. Get all reports together I've sent home but without names. . . . Uniforms—Shoes." Another chit to remind herself to ask OWI "if it wants any speeches." A chit headed "Mabel," her maid: "Have all uniforms cleaned & put away. Blacks never worn but take to Hyde Park for use." And for Tommy: "Tell women at Red + striped shirts much better than plain material. Will she tell manufacturer?"

A cable went to F.D.R. on the 21st:

BEST I CAN DO IS REACH SF NOON THURSDAY PACIFIC COAST TIME. TRANSPORT PLANE WOULD NOT ORDINARILY GO TO NY BUT CAN GO WITH YOUR PERMISSION AND ARRIVE EARLY FRIDAY. OTHERWISE WILL YOU GET ME THURSDAY RESERVATION AND PRIORITY ON COMMERCIAL PLANE AROUND 4 PM FROM SF PREFERABLY UNITED. SHOULD ARRIVE THAT WAY NY BY 3 NEXT AFTERNOON. ASK JAMES MEET ME THERE AND WILL SEE HIM OFF MEET YOU IN WASH. NEXT DAY OR GO TO NY TO SEE JOHN IF HE LEAVING IMMEDIATELY LOVE

To Tommy she cabled:

FIND OUT FROM FDR WHAT HE DECIDES. WIRE ME ST. FRANCIS SISTY'S
SCHOOL. WILL PHONE ANNA. MUST SEE JAMES AND JOHN IF HE LEAVING
IMMEDIATELY. MEET ME NY FRIDAY LOVE ER.

THE PRESIDENT TO MRS. ROOSEVELT AM ASKING ARNOLD ABOUT PLANE.
JIMMIE NOT ABLE BE IN SF ON TIME. JOHNNIE HAS LEFT FOR HIS SHIP.
HOPE YOU COME WASHINGTON WHERE I ARRIVE SAT MORNING OR HP IF
YOU GET TO NY EARLY FRIDAY.

A later message from F.D.R.:

ARRANGEMENTS HAVE BEEN MADE FOR YOU TO CONTINUE ON TO NEW
YORK ON PRESENT PLANE.

She dashed off a line to me from the St. Francis in San Francisco when she
briefly deplaned there on Thursday, September 22.

[E.R. to Joseph P. Lash:]   [September 22, 1943]
    I must send a line from the place where I hope Trude will be meeting
you someday in the not too distant future. I got a letter from her here &
I've sent her a wire to come in tomorrow morning to the apartment. I am
going on through because Jimmy is in N.Y. & wants to see me there
tomorrow & leaves in the evening. I felt he might be off again & I shld
not miss him. I had Sisty for lunch & she is happy in school & the
headmistress likes her. FDR is in H.P but goes to Washington tomorrow
night so I'll see James off & go to Washington Sat. a.m.
    I had a press conference here & learned that Pegler had written a
vicious column but if the reaction from the boys is good he won't matter.
I won't forget to send clippings but you write me honestly how the boys
felt on your island. . . .

    Her friends were jubilant on her return. Tommy had called her the previous
day, Hick wrote. " 'I talked to her!' she said. 'I talked to her. I was crying, & I
couldn't think of anything to say.' Dear Tommy! I felt like crying too! What a
relief!" And from the less demonstrative Esther: "I suppose we would have seemed
pretty feeble to you, to have suffered jitters until you landed at San Francisco—but
that is what some of us have done. We are weaker than you thought us!"
    A letter to me commenting on Trude's looks added that "Tommy is really
happy to have me back & it is nice to get back & find all so glad to see you, it
makes me feel important!"

III

Fear Transformed into Courage

ELEANOR'S RETURN from the South Pacific was accompanied by the onset of a depression severe enough to be evident to the people around her. Was it due to her sense that the young men and women she had seen throughout the South and Southwest Pacific were winning the war but that the peace which justified their sacrifices was being lost?

A speech that Quentin Reynolds, the war correspondent who had just returned from Italy, was making to Republican audiences mirrored her own feelings.

[E.R. to Joseph P. Lash:]   [November 30, 1943]
    The gist is: I came back from months on fighting fronts, proud of our achievements. We've got the best army, marines & navy & flyers in the world, the best equipped & fed & paid services, the people back home must feel great to have accomplished this. To my surprise I find discouragement, sour faces. My Wall St. friends wail over taxes, my sporting friends over liquor & gas, farmers clamor for higher prices, labor for higher wages, so I can't figure out who's doing this wonderful job at home that makes this marvellous job possible overseas & I'm forced to conclude it's the Administration & that man Roosevelt.

The disparity Eleanor saw between the attitude of the men on the fighting fronts and the "old Adam" asserting itself on the home front certainly had much to do with her sadness. But there was more to it than that. "I long to see you & have news of you," she wrote Hick on her homeward flight. "I've felt very cut off from those I love on this trip because we moved around so much it was hard to get mail." Just as Antaeus in Greek mythology needed the touch of the earth to grow stronger, so she needed her family and friends from whom she had been cut off.

After a stop in San Francisco to catch a glimpse of Sisty, she returned to Washington by way of New York City in order to see James, who was off on a Marine mission in the Pacific, and Trude, to whom she delivered a letter from me.

[E.R. to Joseph P. Lash:]   [September (?) 1943]
    Your darling came today at noon & stayed for lunch & I gave her your letter & I told her of our time together. She is thinner & her teeth are much better but she still has a long session [with the dentist] & then I hope she will put on a little weight. Her face is too pointed. It makes her look young but not husky enough to suit me. I was so glad to see her, except for you I've never been so glad to see anyone & I held her close for myself as well as for you.

    Jimmy had met her that morning at the plane "& stayed with me till noon . . . & came back at four & I took him to the 6:20 plane. . . . He'll be under Nimitz I guess when they make their next push. Earl came over for dinner & now I end my day with this line to you."
    She had wired Hick that she wanted to see her at the White House when she arrived there. "I came back & had lunch with F.D.R. & he asked after you & seemed much interested in the whole trip," she wrote me. She knew how avid I was for tidbits from the White House, second only to news about Trude. "The Hopkins move about Oct. 25th. He seems very miserable to me. Averill [sic] Harriman was here for lunch & is going as Ambassador to Russia! . . ."
    She expanded on these White House items in her next letter.

[E.R. to Joseph P. Lash:]   [September 26, 1943]
    Last night I had a long talk with Louise Hopkins & they move to their own house about Oct. 20th. Harry looks very badly but they say it is not a return of the old trouble. . . . The Averill [sic] Harrimans were here too & he's going as Ambassador to Russia. In London I think Winant helped him & I hope he'll do well. Perhaps it is bad to have known people since their *early* youth!
    I find a real personal split between Hull & Welles. F. says W. is no more really liberal than H. but speaks more often, more clearly & never showed his speeches to his superior. Everyone needled both until the

break came & now Stettinius, because Russia likes him, takes W's place.
I only hope he is good enough.

A long letter to Anna, who after John's departure was finding her position on
the Seattle *Post-Intelligencer* increasingly unpleasant, described Eleanor's first days
at home as well as Franklin's coolness to John's suggestion that Anna be given an
assignment not far from him.

[E.R. to Anna Boettiger:]   [September 27, 1943]

Anna darling, Your letter, enclosing John's came this morning & I
think you have done the right thing & I will write him. If he gets
assigned somewhere possible for you to join him then we can ask Pa for a
little special influence & you'll have to turn the kids over to me for a time
but Pa would do nothing about bringing John home or getting him to a
place where you could join him.

I had a nice time with Jimmy on Friday & saw him off in the late
afternoon. He doesn't think they'll go off for 6 weeks or so. He'll probably be with the Nimitz group in the middle Pacific area & Nimitz told
me those plans would mature between 6 & 8 weeks from when I was
there & they will dovetail with moves made by Halsey & McArthur
areas. . . .

I'm glad you like the Guadalcanal cemetery column. It was a moving
sight. Joe was fine, tho' atabrine makes everyone a bit yellow. He is a staff
sergeant now, & has passed the army board out there as a candidate for
officers training school but they are shutting down & the S.W. Pacific
has a small quota so he may never be sent home for the school. Of course
he longs to come home & get married but like many others he must wait
& pray & work! I loved seeing him & he was glad to see me I know & we
spent 3 hours together tho' they were a bit divided!

I thought Sisty looked well & was doing well. She'll gain in self confidence & then she won't bother Buzz so much.

I doubt if it would do much good to have anyone talk to Harry or Pa
about the trip but I find Mr. Patterson [Assistant Secretary of War] told
Mr. Baruch I did a wonderful job & that will help. Pa asked me more
questions than I expected & actually came over to lunch with me Saturday & spent two hours!

I am still weary but slowly getting rested. Tommy & I go to N.Y.
tomorrow & to H.P. Thursday to write my Red ✚ report. Much love
darling, *Mother.*

Mama's domineering ways had caused Eleanor and Franklin deliberately to
hold off from trying to run their children's lives. Franklin, immersed in affairs of
state, with the world at war, was able to do little for them anyway except to have

them present at historic moments. Usually they turned to Eleanor with their domestic problems, certain of an affectionate if often unhappy advocate of their cause
with their father. The other children felt she was partial to Elliott. I thought she
felt closest to Anna and John and vested special hope in Franklin. He was executive
officer of the destroyer *Mayrant,* and she sent me a vivid account by Quentin
Reynolds of his handling of his ship when it was bombed with heavy casualties and
damage by Nazi Stukas off Sicily. "I'm enclosing a letter Quentin Reynolds wrote
me about Fjr. because you've always thought he had qualities of leadership & these
are proofs of that."

Back in New York she and Trude went to see my mother and two of my
sisters. One of the latter brought in her baby, "a marvellous boy, but you & Trude
will have a marvellous one too someday & it will be different because you two are
different." At Hyde Park another old friend, Elinor Morgenthau, came to spend
the night, "her first visit since her illness & her legs are still swollen." At Eleanor's
cottage she slept on the porch. Trude and Eleanor went across the Hudson River to
visit Wiltwyck Training School for delinquent boys. It was the beginning of a
lifelong commitment to Wiltwyck.

[E.R. to Joseph P. Lash:]   [October 2, 1943]
   When I see places like that I long to be Marshall Field or his Foundation! It wouldn't take much to make it an ideal place & those poor little
boys make your heart ache. I want primarily to get at the things which
are fundamental, the social evils which create families such as those
children come from.

She sent me a column by Westbrook Pegler, who was syndicated by the King
Features Syndicate. He sought to portray her trip to the South Pacific as a waste of
taxpayers' money, a needless diversion of air power, and a cover-up of her desire to
see me. "Having established this deception, she swooped down to Lash & publicly
kissed him," one column said. Another put it, "she reached up and kissed Joe
Lash." She also sent me snapshots that "a very fresh young sergeant" had taken of
her and Trude and added, "a little less pleasant but entirely to be expected is
Westbrook Pegler's piece. I hope you won't mind the world of Pegler's & I.N.S.'s
readers knowing that I kissed you!"

When criticism became particularly intense she sometimes wondered whether
she should not withdraw from public life but always concluded that was what her
attackers wanted. As a child she had been timorous and fearful and now made it a
rule to stand up to critics; but she was always aware of them.

"How I wish we did not have to have a campaign this year," she wrote me
after a few days at home. "I'm going to be the main point of attack I fear & I never
was good at being wary!" She went on to talk about Henry Morgenthau's "bold tax
bill" and the "violent" attacks the Southern Democrats as well as Republicans were
making on it, and summed up, "Paying for this war is not easy."

"Mrs. R is in a much better frame of mind than her letters led me to expect," Tommy faithfully reported to Esther.

[Tommy to Esther Lape:]   [October 3, 1943]
In one letter she said she couldn't bear to speak or write about the trip, but since she has returned she has accepted many invitations and agreed to write articles for the *Ladies Home Journal* etc.

Tommy was miffed with Maude Gray, Eleanor's aunt, who had returned to Dublin with her husband David, who was U.S. minister there:

Maude wrote Mrs. R from Ireland that she must pay more attention to me,—make more fuss over me than Earl, Trude, etc.! I could slay her— why doesn't she mind her own business! I tried to remember complaining to her and I can't—I guess it's because I don't "scintillate" all the time the way she does and because I often retire to my own sitting room to read or work!

At Guadalcanal Eleanor had seemed to me very weary and I had written Trude in some alarm. In a birthday letter to Eleanor I begged her to slow down. The advice she gave everyone else she wouldn't hear for herself.

[E.R. to Joseph P. Lash:]   [October 9, 1943]
You mustn't worry about my health. It is fine. I really am rested from the trip. It was tiring. The schedules were long & I found the emotional strain great but that was good for it will make me work harder here at home. The days (& nights) before I got to you had been very busy but I wouldn't have had one second less with you, in fact I wish I hadn't let you go home at all tho' of course I know it would have been wrong for I couldn't have done the next day's job too well! It was a long one too on Espiritu! Seeing you made the whole trip worthwhile for me. I just can't help being a very "personal" person I fear.

Just before Eleanor's fifty-ninth birthday Princess Juliana and her children were at Hyde Park. So was F.D.R. "She is sweet and simple," Eleanor wrote after Juliana's departure, "& I hope enjoyed herself. I took her down to tea with the Morgenthaus yesterday but I don't find her easy to talk with."
A new regional weather officer in the South Pacific, Colonel Peterson, in- spected our operations on Guadalcanal. My abrupt shipment overseas still puzzled me. I wrote Trude and Eleanor—

[Joseph P. Lash to E.R.:]   [October 17, 1943]
He was the one who issued the statement at Bolling field [in Washing-

ton, D.C.] when the newspapers attacked me for having a "soft berth" and also was the one who urged me to stay in forecasting school when I wanted to go into foreign service last year. . . . He told me our coming out here had been a "snafu" deal from beginning to end. One, that we were supposed to be the top ten in the class & to have been qualified immediately as forecasters, (2) that we were not supposed to go overseas for some months after we left school! . . .

Eleanor's cryptic comment on this news may have concealed a greater knowledge of what had happened than she had conveyed to me, though it hardly reflected the kind of drama that was alleged in the G-2 files: "That whole story of the mistake in shipping you out seems so odd! No use in speculating on it however."

An earlier letter that Hyde Park weekend describing F.D.R.'s warmth toward Trude also seemed to belie the G-2 account in the files. "Trude has had some chances to talk with F.D.R. & was pleased at the way he spoke to her of you. Before dinner tonight she read him a part of your letter that I had asked Tommy to type for him—what you said about the Fair & the Comintern & he asked for it to keep which I hope will please you & I think pleased her."

Trude wrote me in considerable length about that weekend.

[Trude W. Pratt to Joseph P. Lash:]   [October 9, 1943]
The Pres. greeted me with a big grin—and whispered "Well, my child, I heard a special island in the S.W. Pacific is doing alright." "Yes, Mr. President," I said and beamed back at him. "I am happy for the two of you and tell Joe that we'll try to finish this business as fast as we can."

And then we talked for a good part of the evening. Mrs. R. changed the table order (she told me afterwards) so I sat at the Pres. left—Juliana at his right. He said he was having great difficulties with S[talin]—and remarked that in Russia public pressure was even stronger than here, though he had to take it into consideration much more in his policy. But in August the man could not come because of pressure at home though he had promised definitely to come! He did not dare to be away for two weeks—not because of the Army either! That rather startling fact is, of course, completely unknown. He said that Litvinoff told him 10 years ago: Russia in 1929 was at zero—where capital solvency is concerned, USA at a hundred. This suit of clothes would not have belonged to me then—nothing did. Now I own it, I also own a Dacha,—we have arrived at 20, you have sunk to 80. When we have come up to 40 and you down to 60—we shall easily be able to do business.

The Morgenthaus, Hick, Harry Hooker, Betty Roosevelt, Tommy, and Tully were there for Eleanor's birthday. "It was a good party," Trude wrote me afterward. "The Boss was very gay and almost raucous and Mrs. R. in the end seemed to enjoy it too. She looked very slim and beautiful in a marvellous long black dress."

But very worrisome was Trude's account in the previous day's letter of Eleanor's mood.

[Trude W. Pratt to Joseph P. Lash:]　　　　　　[October 10, 1943]
. . . Tommy wanted to talk. She is worried about Mrs. R.—and I feel uneasy too. Mrs. R. is strange, often sits and looks absentmindedly into space, and then realized that she had not heard a word. It's worrying and I feel helpless, but at the same time seems more natural than her apparent freshness and restless activity of the last few weeks. As long as she had to keep going—her iron will carried her through in spite of her deep horror at what she saw and the great sadness at the continuing bloodshed and dying. And the happenings here since her return have not contributed to make her feel that everything possible is being done to prevent any future wars.—I'm only guessing—and trying to make myself feel less worried, and if Tommy knew I am writing about it she would be upset— and so would Mrs. R.—as she has brushed aside any questions concerning her. But this afternoon even the Pres. said something after he had in the presence of Juliana tried to get Mrs. R. to invite Juliana to Washington— and only met complete lack of response. There may be more than that to this particular incident. I know Mrs. R. has felt strongly about—and against—the continuing influx of royalty—and the absence of any large number of Americans. . . .

I ventured another explanation of Eleanor's sadness.

[Joseph P. Lash to Trude W. Pratt:]　　　　　　[Oct. 28, 1943]
Part of it as you say is a terrible sorrow, made more acute by what she saw in hospitals out here, that we may be losing the peace. But I think another and larger part of it has to do with a great inner loneliness. You can help a great deal there, for the only people who can help dispel that kind of loneliness are those to whom she is bound by ties of affection and Mrs. R. loves you.

Eleanor's sadness was real. It was not simply the conjecture of the people around her. Perhaps it related to her birthday, a date freighted with tragic memories of her father and brother, as well as her incessant questions about the uselessness, as she saw it, of much of what she did. Unusual was her willingness to write me about it—perhaps because she sensed that Trude might be doing so.

[E.R. to Joseph P. Lash:]　　　　　　[December 13, 1943]
On Sunday I got moody, & it worried her [Trude] mostly I think I was

annoyed because I couldn't get any time to be quiet & work but had the house full at the big house, but in addition I guess my heart is never too light these days & when one comes to celebrations one thinks more of those who can't be there. I so hope you & Trude & Anna & John can be with me in the future, happily & often, & that I'll know the others are well & happy wherever they are.

Who can be sure of the causes of her melancholy? Just as love of friends and concern for Franklin helped her perform prodigious services for the country, so her sadness was a spur to work and vision. She had felt strongly about getting to Guadalcanal and New Guinea because there the young GIs were nearest to danger, and their loneliness and hardship determined her to work harder at home and to win the peace.

Too often, Santayana wrote in his essay on Dante, we are kept from "feeling great things greatly, for want of a power to assimilate them to the little things which we feel keenly and sincerely." She had that power. Her language was prose, her moods prosaically characterized as "depressions," but she had a mind that was "poetic in its intuitions." The cares that filled her letters—America's treatment of its blacks and other minorities, including the Nisei, the travails of the poor, the rights of the trade unions, equality of sacrifice, America's responsibilities in the world—were almost prophetic in the way they became dominant themes at the end of the century. The shortfalls of human nature, although always a grief, also were a challenge. "Show me a hero," said F. Scott Fitzgerald, "and I'll write you a tragedy."

An early bond between Eleanor and me had been her discovery that, although I was a child of the twentieth century, I knew the poetry of Arthur Hugh Clough, one of the Victorians on whom she had been raised. I never wearied of reciting the first lines of his philosophical lament. It was rooted in an existential sadness similar to Eleanor's:

> *To spend uncounted years of pain,*
> *Again, again, and yet again,*
> *In working out in heart and brain*
> *The problem of our being here. . . .*

Trude's friend, the theologian-philosopher Paul Tillich, who later married us, sent me a reprint of his paper "The Conception of Man in Existential Philosophy," and his inscription seemed to me to describe Eleanor's sadness, except that he used the word *Angst:*

Man flees forever from his own *Angst.* In doing so he is driven from one courageous action to another, transforming *Angst* (dread) into fear and overcoming fear by courage.

Basically it was Eleanor's belief in God that helped her to overcome the contradictions of human existence, as Tillich saw man's existential situation. For him *"Angst* is the situation of the isolated individual fearing the abyss of nothingness and the threat of annihilation all around him."

For Eleanor the mystery that surpasseth understanding was embodied in her father's prayer book, which still remained at her bedside table. A copy of *The Robe* she had sent me caught up with me on Guadalcanal. "It is built around Christ's robe," I wrote Trude, "which the Roman legionaries who crucified him are supposed to have thrown dice for at the foot of the Cross, but the fate of the robe becomes incidental to the narrative of the way the teachings of Jesus took hold in the countryside, developed into legend and founded a Church."

"It is a great story," Eleanor wrote me—

[E.R. to Joseph P. Lash:]   [October 13, 1943]
. . . & the greatest of all the underground revolutions but we've allowed churches & doctrines & priests to separate us from the reality which is as real today as it ever was. It is a way of life, which is true democracy. I'm glad you are reading the New Testament, aside from everything else it is beautiful as literature. Much of it is wonderful to read aloud. Try it sometime.

She was a faithful parishioner of the St. James Episcopal Church in Hyde Park, but outward conformity belied an inner spiritual freedom. "I still don't feel any urge to 'belong' to a specified religious group," she commented on Hendrick Van Loon's joining the Unitarians, "perhaps because supposedly I've always been an Episcopalian tho' I never did a thing that really conformed!"

With time hanging heavy on my hands on Guadalcanal I started a garden with the aid of seeds Eleanor obtained from the Department of Agriculture. I also began the draft of a book on what one soldier thought. I sent it to Trude, who showed it to Eleanor. She sent it to her agent, George Bye, and met with publishers, all of whom decided it didn't tell a story but stated the program of a liberal in GI clothing. But there were compensations.

[E.R. to Joseph P. Lash:]   [November 11, 1943]
    She [Trude] sent me your article "What is in it for me?" I like it very much & am going to try it on F.D.R. tonight. She thinks it is too much of a speech & fears that Christ should not be spoken of in the same breath with Henry Wallace. That doesn't bother me, perhaps because Christ to me is a man (divine or not, what matters?) who fought a fight in his day almost single handed, but everyone who takes up the fight is of the same kind. Only a very liberal paper or magazine would print it however!

The article received greater tribute than publication, which it never achieved. Eleanor read it to Franklin. "He was interested but said 'It would get by as a speech, but there is too much emphasis on certain things. It needs rewriting, give me a copy I'd like to try my hand at rewriting.' So, dear, if you find your ideas on 'What's in it for me' scattered thro' F.D.R.'s next speeches I hope you won't mind because it wld be hard to find a magazine liberal enough to print it, tho' we'll try!"

Everyone, it seemed, wanted her to speak on her return from the Pacific. But her movements were restricted as congressional and press critics of the President's policies sought to make her a scapegoat for their own furies and frustrations:*

[E.R. to Joseph P. Lash:]   [October 23, 1943]
    The outcry in Congress is so great that F.D.R. feels I should not use Government transportation or even go on any far trips for a while so I'm trying to speak nearby & I'll try to get some chances on the air. Later I'm sure he'll say go ahead again but just now it seems he wants a little peace. I guess the tax bill is on his mind! He has a cold but I don't think it's bad.

There were other restrictions, all of which she complied with meticulously. She wrote in a letter that went to all her friends, "As you probably know it is not going to be possible this year for any of us to have turkey for Thanksgiving and probably not for Christmas. I am sorry that this means that I will not be able to send you a turkey as I have done in the past."

Her movements were limited, but she was busier than usual. "Three days gone by," she wrote me in early November, "& I have not written but when I tell you that the days have been so filled that I've sat at my desk till 3:30 a.m. you will forgive me." She spoke at the CIO convention in Philadelphia, "the delegates seemed full of life & energy. There is strength in a gathering like that." In New York she did a broadcast, talked with Marshall Field about some racial work, spent an hour with Cousin Susie, and had the ebullient Broadway producer John Golden come for her there "& I enjoyed the quaint combination! I gave out the 5,000,000,000 /sic/ theatre ticket for him & said polite words to all the producers & got home just in time for dinner." She took Trude, Harry Hooker, Tommy, and the Lou Harrises—he was home on leave—to *Othello*. "[Paul] Robeson is moving in it because the lines might be said by him today! The character is never convincing & all of a piece however to me." She did a recording for the Army, and at a meeting of civilian employees in the Adjutant General's office "I tried to simplify my

---

* In February, Congressman Dies in the House had attacked thirty-nine government employees as "irresponsible, unrepresentative, crackpot, radical bureaucrats" and urged Congress to refuse to appropriate their salaries. The House did so in the form of a "rider" to a vital war appropriations bill. The rider denied salaries to Goodwin B. Watson and William E. Dodd, Jr. of the Federal Communications Commission, and Robert Morss Lovett, Governor of the Virgin Islands. The President, while forced to sign the bill, condemned the rider as a bill of attainder. In 1946 the Supreme Court unanimously overturned the House's action.

thoughts on the future for them. Soon I must sit down & try to write it out & then I'll send it to you."

Gaily she described an accidental encounter with her cousin Alice Longworth. She

came up in the train this morning & had to sit with us as the train was full & I enjoyed her. She is a vivid & amusing creature no matter how unkind at times! She remarked that no matter "how much we differed politically there was always a tribal feeling between us"! Her candidate for President is Bricker!

Despite Edith Helm's complaints to Tommy about the difficulties of working with Mrs. Roosevelt, she was back on the job "and we still do not see eye to eye on what is important," Tommy wrote Esther.

[Tommy to Esther Lape:]   [October 28, 1943]
I have accomplished one thing with her [E.H.]—and that is to write memos to Mrs. R. and not interrupt her every five minutes. I do that and in one sitting Mrs. R. can answer the day's questions, but I haven't yet convinced Mrs. Helm that that is easier, so Mrs. R. gets innumerable small memos which annoy her. The answer is that Mrs. Helm is a perfectionist and I am far from being one. My desk is the talk of Washington because of its untidiness—hers is a sample of what the efficient secretary should have! However as long as it doesn't bother Mrs. Roosevelt, I am not worrying. . . .

The Hopkins family is moving out soon. Mrs. Hopkins has a French governness for Diana! . . .

Never far from Eleanor's mind those months was worry over her children. "James is off again," one letter announced, and in the next she sent parts of letters from Fjr and John Boettiger, who were in the Italian campaign: "This question of the treatment of those we conquer hits them with the Italians. . . . I'm sure we have to face realities & economic decisions are most important for people must have security to want peace."

The last was a staple of her thinking.

[E.R. to Joseph P. Lash:]   [October 28, 1943]
Tonight the Lehmans & Sayres came to dine to get a chance to tell F. some of their troubles. The Relief Com. meeting is on the 9th & they feel no one is fighting for them or telling the country about their needs. They should lay in stores of food, clothing, seeds, farm machinery & they fight here with local demands. Now 44 nations will have to agree to take

their quotas. It looks like our first test on working together & we are not even sure what our own Congress & our own agencies will do.

She did not agree that fulfillment of America's responsibilities for relief and rehabilitation abroad meant scanting needs at home. She reported a long discussion with F.D.R.:

[E.R. to Joseph P. Lash:]   [Nov. 1, 1943]
    The picnic in the playroom seemed to put F.D.R. in a good mood & we got a better discussion on the cost of living & the R.R. men & miners' demands. He will not concede however that to most people especially in the lower income brackets, the cost of living is really measured by the cost of food. He agrees that food has gone up, but insists that the price is offset by stable rents & better prices in other things.*

She liked people who accepted power yet thought adventurously. She had the Henry Wallaces to dinner and wrote me afterward—

[E.R. to Joseph P. Lash:]   [Oct. 17, 1943]
    The V.P. and Mrs. spent the evening with me alone & I was interested to learn many things. One thing, he thinks Jesse J[ones] will have much postwar power & be a major factor in deciding whether our economy shall be one of scarcity or expansion. He looks upon possible victory of the opposition party with grave apprehension because he fears the control will be in the hands of those who want a few to have the real power. He also pointed out that if the war comes to an end in '45 & we only had a production level such as we had in '40 because of demobilization of an army of 12,000,000 & the increase of those normally coming to the work market because of their age we would have 19,000,000 unemployed, so we must have an economy of plenty at home & a rising in standards abroad.

She did not think it worthwhile to tell me of their political talk, or perhaps awareness of the censors' eyes kept her from talking about Wallace's possibilities in '44. Trude wrote me that Ed Flynn at lunch had described Wallace as a drag on the ticket. Trude was for Wallace nonetheless.†

* He ordered seizure of the coal mines at the end of October. "Coal must be mined. The enemy does not wait," he said. At the end of December, when the railroad unions threatened to walk off their jobs, he ordered the Government to operate the railroads.
† Wallace's account of that evening as he described it in his diary: "October 17, 1943. At the White House Mrs. Wallace and I ate with Mrs. Roosevelt and Miss Thompson. When Miss Thompson had left and the three of us were alone, Mrs. Roosevelt spoke very frankly. She said the children were all strongly against a fourth term for the President, they had not been very keen for the third term but were all very strongly against a fourth term. I said that some newspaper surveys indicated that if the war with

A month later the Wallaces had her to dinner. "I dined last night with the Wallaces & had an interesting talk with him. He wanted me to know he was loyal to the President & felt he was helping by 'giving the liberals a shoulder to cry on.'"*

Eleanor did not tell the Vice President, whose renomination she favored, what she told Trude. "The V.P. thinks the Pres. will have to run again. . . . She [Eleanor] told me of a conversation with Eddie Flynn. . . . He thinks the Democrats will have no money while the Republicans will of course roll in it. Therefore [the President] will have to have as running mate some one like [Sam] Rayburn who will bring in some money."

Although she looked to Wallace for liberal leadership in the future, without design or ambition she was herself emerging as the nation's conscience.

[E.R. to Joseph P. Lash:]   [November 11, 1943]
I had a little talk on the domestic situation & the future which cheered me. F. said he knew we were at a low point at home, he knew liberals were discouraged but it was better to have it so now than later. He had to deal with realities & get all that was needed for war purposes & immediate postwar needs by keeping conservatives with him. If he had to run, & he hoped he wouldn't have to, he'd put in a fighting nat. chairman & make a liberal campaign & clean out a lot of people playing with the Republicans whom he couldn't do without till certain things were lined

---

Germany were over by next summer, the probabilities were that the President could not win. She said she realized that if the war with both Japan and Germany were over, the President could not win, but she had not heard about surveys on the basis of what the situation would be in case only Germany were defeated. She asked very practically what would be done about it. I was amazed when she said that she thought if I were nominated, I could win. Of course I said nothing in reply. She said that the difficulty would be to get me nominated, that, of course, she and the President would be for me as the logical one to carry out the policies of the President. She assumed, however, that the Southerners would be dead against accepting me. I made no comment whatever except to say I felt the forces behind the Republican Party were such that it would be very dangerous for the Republicans to win in 1944. . . ."

* ". . . At the dinner for Mrs. Roosevelt, I talked to her at some length on the future of liberalism in the Democratic Party. She agreed completely that the Democratic Party must be a liberal party. She then said she had been talking about the matter to the President. The President told her that so far as he personally had been concerned, it had been necessary for him to refrain from furnishing liberal leadership until the Democratic primaries were over in the southern states. He did not want a third party put in the field in the South. . . .

"Referring back to the conversation I had had with her the last time I was at the White House, I told her I was completely loyal to the President. She indicated that she did not think he ought to run for a fourth term if there was no chance of his winning and she was sure his political judgment was good enough that he would not run if there was any likelihood of his losing. She mentioned again as she had before, the fact that the children did not want him to run. . . .

"I told Mrs. Roosevelt I thought the three big distracting forces in the Democratic Party at present were: one—the big interests; two—the bigoted Catholics; three—the venomous Roosevelt haters.

"I put on some Red Russian army songs for Mrs. Roosevelt and also some Russian rural songs. She seemed to like both. Also I put on several Spanish records. Mrs. Roosevelt put in most of her time knitting a sweater, which was nearly completed and which was very well done. Apparently she has rather an unusual facility as a knitter. . . ."

up.—He also remarked that internationally he had to deal with many prima donnas & at home they were almost as bad.

She was always pressing Franklin to go further because better than anyone else she appreciated the pressures on the President from the other side. Whatever her personal hurt because of his inability to offer her warmth and intimacy, she appreciated his leadership. "I don't think F. will need any courage from me!" a letter to me remarked at the time.

The same letter spoke about "F's food message on the subsidies. It seems to me clear & persuasive & I wish every citizen will read it, which they won't. The Farm Bureau carries a page against subsidies which I'll send you tomorrow after I've shown it to F." A few days later there was an exultant note in her account of the first United Nations conference about postwar problems:

[E.R. to Joseph P. Lash:]   [November 9, 1943]
   Today in the East Room with the flags of 44 nations as a background 44 United Nations representatives signed up to try & feed & clothe & house & rehabilitate the world. It was impressive & F's short speech clear & good so they begin their meetings in Atlantic City tomorrow & human nature will reassert itself & each will strive for some personal advantage but I feel in the end something great may have begun today.

Roosevelt's food message, the longest he had ever sent to Congress, over 10,000 words, pleased her. It reflected her own thinking and her many discussions with the President. He had posed the government's basic dilemma. The demands on America's food supplies were greater than ever because its people were eating better than ever. Nine million men and women in the armed services had to be fed. Food shipments to our allies had not diminished; Russia, in fact, in the first six months of 1943 had received one-third of all Lend-Lease food tonnage, and now food had to be sent to the newly liberated areas. To get farmers to produce more, there had to be the inducement of adequate prices, but if prices rose, workers would press for higher wages. Without subsidies or equalization payments to farmers the whole stabilization program would unravel. Mrs. Roosevelt was pleased, Trude wrote me, that the President's message embodied so much of her own thinking. "She was also very happy about the food message and found in it, she said, much of what she had always advocated, but what she always thought had never been accepted."

Eleanor was pleased, too, that another facet of postwar planning would be in the hands of Bernard Baruch.

[E.R. to Joseph P. Lash:]   [November (?) 1943]
   FDR told me Baruch would be in charge of credit for demobilization & of the uses to which the plants should be put & the first meeting was

held today. I'm glad for he has always felt we could have full employment & he has imagination. He has asked to come to see me tomorrow & I'm quite interested to hear his plans.

She had more personal news:

. . . Also a lady from Santo Domingo who is heading up the women's Pan-American organization came to see me & it looks as though in Feb. F.D.R. might want me to go around the Caribbean & to Uruguay, Brazil, Venezuela, Colombia, & Panama if the S.Am. women want a meeting. I think it might be well to hold a few meetings with them because they should help in the rehabilitation period—Elinor Morgenthau, Tommy and I dined with Mrs. Helm & came home fairly early.

Eleanor took everyone to see *Sons of Fun,* which Trude described as "a less funny, less good, much longer 'Hellzapoppin.' " Mrs. Helm had thought the President's wife should not go, but Eleanor decided "it was funny & not too bawdy!"

Judge Rosenman talked with her about the reorganization of plant facilities "so as to make conditions better for women." She had an hour's "real talk" with Baruch "on war demobilization in industry of which he is in charge. I wish I had his clear mind. . . . [T]he gist is that the answer to many questions is quick conversion & that is the first problem & is all to be planned *before* the war ends."

"Yesterday morning," another letter began—

[E.R. to Joseph P. Lash:]   [November 13, 1943]
I spent more than an hour with Sam Rosenman & Mrs. Kerr & in the afternoon another hour with Miss Lenroot & Miss Goodykoontz & I think we are going to get the child care centers, foster care, recreation for older children, shopping, etc. going where industry really needs the women. Why Sam is bringing me in on all this I don't know but I'm glad if I can be helpful. He sent me over a survey of the understanding that farmers have of subsidies which is astonishing. Only 14% knew what the meaning of the word was!

She and Hick "talked politics," which usually meant at that moment the desire of the Democratic women to have women included in the U.S. representation on postwar agencies and conferences. Hick "suspected it was she [Eleanor] who had accomplished the appointment of women as delegates or alternates" to the postwar organizational conferences. "Hick dear," a terse memo said at the beginning of 1944, "FDR wants 15 or 20 women who might serve as alternates or advisers on these technical committees or to Mr. Acheson."*

* Dean Acheson, an Assistant Secretary of State, was working on postwar economic plans.

The phase of the war that Churchill called "Closing the Ring" had begun. American forces established a beachhead on Bougainville in the Solomons; Marines, Jimmy among them, invaded the Gilbert Islands. The Germans had evacuated Sicily, Mussolini had fallen, and Italy had surrendered. The Russians, having recaptured Kharkov and Kiev, were cleaning out the Ukraine. Hull led a U.S. delegation to the tripartite foreign ministers conference in Moscow and returned to Washington just in time to report to F.D.R., who was leaving on the USS *Iowa* for meetings in Cairo and Teheran.

In scarcely veiled language Eleanor wrote me about these events.

[E.R. to Joseph P. Lash:]   [Nov. 11, 1943]

Well, it is about 9:30 p.m. & I've just seen several people off. They meet first a gentleman who travels from an opposite direction almost as far as they do & then they travel a bit further themselves & meet a gentleman who feels he cannot be away too long from his fighting forces, who continue to do well. Mr. H. has returned enthusiastic about all the Russians & so are such conservatives as Jimmy Dunn of State Dept. who was along. Mr. Hull says they are like your country cousins come to town, a little slow but well worthwhile & he is convinced they will make no separate peace & that we must & can cooperate in the future. They tell a good story. The British were telling Stalin that Churchill hates the Germans as much as the Russians do. "Yes, but he doesn't like fighting them as much." The comparison in casualties is horrible, they lose almost daily as many as we've lost in that area in the whole period of the war.

F. is insisting that Fjr. join him which will be interesting but I'm afraid it won't be good for Fjr. not to carry through with his ship till he gets her home. However, I see F's point, that Elliott can't be with him all the time & he needs Fjr. . . . I'm glad to say he plans a food speech on radio on his return which is badly needed for the message will never be read by the farmers. Then I hope he'll make a speech on the Ed. message (to provide educational and training benefits for veterans) if Congress has done nothing.

   ·   I had people for lunch today, among them Anna Rosenberg who has now been discovered by Mr. Baruch & they have a mutual admiration society.

Although a staunch advocate of women's rights, she did not feel that to be equal with men meant to be identical with them. A letter about Trude's health and needs reflected Eleanor's views of womanhood and its fulfillment.

[E.R. to Joseph P. Lash:]   [November 13, 1943]

She is better & has gained a little but how she hates to eat fattening things. Trude is very much a woman Joe, & with you away she feels unfulfilled. She'll bloom when you come home & having a baby will give Trude more inner satisfaction than any other form of creative work. In the meantime there are more strains on her which can't be lifted & are only alleviated somewhat by good physical care. She will say things to me like "Life with Joe will be the most wonderful life in the world, without him I cannot contemplate it" & sometimes I feel that she only really lives now when she is writing to you. All I can do for her is try to make her take more food & more rest because she must be well for you! I use the same plea on Anna who has just had a bout with the "flu."

She made it impossible, nor did her friends wish, to keep their troubles as well as joys secret from her. Earl "came in & has just left to go back to the station. He gets on so badly with Simone & as usual both are a bit to blame but it will be sadder for him if things don't work out. Perhaps both will learn however with the years!"

She went to Westbrook to see Esther and Elizabeth ". . . & I am sorry to say Elizabeth slept most of the time & seems much worse." Afterward she wrote Esther—

[E.R. to Esther Lape:]   [November 16, 1943]
    I struck a graduating class of Coast Guard boys going down & not only signed all their certificates but practically lectured & argued all the way to N.Y. while they blocked the aisles & draped themselves all over the nearby seats!
    Today has been a busy day but I like N.Y. & the apartment—so much better than Washington!

She dined with Elinor Morgenthau. "Bobby Morgenthau left today. He went to dinner & the play last night with his mother & me & while dinner was excellent I could have wished for a better play!" She met Trude, who dropped her at Madison Square Garden to speak at the War Fund meeting. "I sat with Gov. Smith on one side of me & Archbishop Spellman the other most of the evening!"

"This has been a funny day," her next letter to me from New York began, "starting with some Zionist ladies who were sad because I felt I could not take up the question of the future of Palestine & proceeding thro' several other visitors & Eddie Flynn for lunch & then going with John Golden to see the movie of his 5 soldier plays, the U.S.O. in Harlem, a short speech for the Business & Professional Women & home to dine! What days! The world would go on as well if I sat & read a book I'm sure!"

But back in Washington there was a real challenge, the kind she enjoyed. Her guest was the youthful Walter Reuther of the United Automobile Workers. He had not yet achieved the union's presidency but was author of the "Reuther Plan," which dealt with the large issues of postwar industrial conversion and full production. He saw labor's problems in a large context and that attracted her. The attraction was mutual. She said she would put him in touch with Bernard Baruch, and Reuther accompanied her to the Walter Reed Hospital so that he might hear her talk about the South Pacific. "No word yet of the travellers," she wrote on her return to the White House, "but I hope to hear tomorrow. . . . The White House seems big & empty but I'm going to be too busy to feel lonely! Now I'm going to bed to read a manuscript for the Junior Literary Guild."

She planned a quick trip to Boston to spend the day with Johnny and Anne and for the commissioning of the large aircraft carrier *Wasp*, to which Johnny was assigned. Thanksgiving without men (and turkey) was subdued ". . . & at lunch we had some good American burgundy & drank to the success of the travellers on their present mission & just at that moment Tommy called from Washington to say a message had come from them to say all was going well & also that the Marine Corps wanted me to know Jimmy came thro' the Gilbert Islands fight alright."

The spartan dinners on the home front made my letter about the heaping plate on Guadalcanal in retrospect seem a little thick-skinned, but for Eleanor and Trude the home front should not have done less.

[Joseph P. Lash to Trude W. Pratt:]   [November 27, 1943]
    Thanksgiving dinner was a great triumph for the QM dept. Our mess trays were simply heaped with food—a sizeable portion of turkey, cranberry sauce, vegetables galore, pumpkin pie & ice cream. Some of the boys had talked speculatively about going thru the mess line twice but were so chock full they simply sank into their sacks. I topped it off with the last of your fragrant cigars.

With Tommy, Eleanor went up the Hudson to visit Earl and Simone in Loudonville outside Albany "& it was the pleasantest day I have spent with that little family & gave me hope things might be happier some day, tho' Earl has less idea of enjoying a baby & building a relationship with him than any human being I've ever seen. . . ."

"Dearest ER," I wrote her on the subject of nomenclature, "I still don't like this salutation. It in no way conveys how often I think of you & how deeply I cherish your friendship," but it was better than "Dearest Mrs. Roosevelt" or my short-lived use of "Dear Aunt Eleanor." She sought to make it easier. "Perhaps someday you & Trude & the children will find some nickname you all like. I'd like it better for I hate any of you to call me or write me as Mrs. R." Anna was about to arrive with her children and that was a great anticipation, and, she added, "I don't know yet when our important travellers may return. Interesting things should come from their travels & I'll send you all I can."

Her exchange of letters with Franklin during these travels showed the cordiality and mutual helpfulness—everything but passionate love and intimacy—that existed between the two. Their children brought them together, but there, too, there were tensions—for example, over whether Fjr. should accompany his father or stay with his damaged ship. The most telling sign of a basic reserve was Franklin's unwillingness to have her along at his meetings with Chiang, Churchill, and Stalin. No women would be there, he told her. It hurt, especially after she learned of Madame Chiang's presence in Cairo and Churchill's daughter, Sarah. "There is another thing," Trude wrote me. "Mrs. R. wanted very much to go. But the Boss just put his foot down. Absolutely no women.—But Mme. Chiang was there. . . ."

Anna also had wanted to go with "Pa," and Eleanor had pressed her case with him and afterward had written Anna—

[E.R. to Anna Boettiger:] [November 6, 1943]
Pa's up at Shangri-La, trying to get a last rest & a visit with Martha & some others & he's off I think for Norfolk & goes over on the Iowa, Capt. MacCrae's new boat. I'll read him your desire but I fear all females are out! . . .

The President, Hopkins, Marshall, King, Arnold, and Leahy embarked on the USS *Iowa* at Hampton Roads. F.D.R. sent her a last-minute warm note:

Friday—p.m.
Dearest Babs,
A pouch goes to the White House in a few minutes & early tomorrow morning we will be off. Everything is very comfortable & I have with me lots of work & detective stories & we brought a dozen good movies. I hope we will be secret for a good long time. It is a perfect day but cold— I expect to get lots of sleep till we get to the Nile! At that point I will disguise myself as Moses in the Bullrushes and draw inspiration from the Sphinx.
I hope you will get a fairly quiet time, but I fear Christmas preparations will be a bit rushing.
I will write you by pouch about the 25th & it should get to you by the 26th.
Ever so much love—I wish you could be on the trip with me.
Devotedly
F

She replied immediately.

Nov. 16th

Dearest Franklin,

It was nice to get your Friday note & tomorrow you should be at your first destination. I'll be glad to know of your arrival for the radio people practically said you were on your way to Cairo.

I've been very busy, doing one or two speeches a day & last night I was sandwiched between Al Smith & Archbishop Spellman!

I hope the Sphinx is a help for I think you will need all the inspiration you can get!

I'm going up the 24th to the exercises at the commissioning of Johnnie's ship. I'll see Missy too.

I go back to Washington Thursday but will be here next Monday for the dedication of 47 & 49. In fact I shuttle back & forth a lot because I'm doing so much I didn't intend to do!

A letter from Anna says she is green with envy that she can't be with you & see her John. Do have him with you all you can, also Elliott. Take care of yourself.

Much love
E.R.

On the corner she wrote, "My love to Fjr. Elliott & John."

He wanted to stay in touch but at arms length. He wrote her from aboard the *Iowa* on November 18:

Dearest Babs:

All goes well and a very comfortable trip so far. Weather good and warm enough to sit with only a sweater as an extra, over an old pair of trousers and a fishing shirt. I don't dare write the route but we should see Africa by tomorrow night and land Saturday morning.

All our crowd are getting a real rest, mostly reading—though I have had 2 staff meetings. It looks as if I'll be away a little longer than I thought.

It is a relief to have no newspapers! I am going to start a one page paper. It will pay and print only news that really has some relative importance!

Take good care of yourself. Love to Anna and the chicks and loads to you.

Devotedly
F

On November 20th she wrote again:

Dearest Franklin,

A note from Anna says John wrote tonight he might go to London after Rome fell & she's afraid you will miss him. Do try not to let that happen.

I got back last evening. Your room is being painted & the White House seems very deserted but should be very clean when you return.

I haven't seen either Louise or Diana but I asked for them tell Harry & was told they were very well. I'll try to see before I leave tomorrow night to go back to N.Y. I'll be back here Tuesday just for the day & then go to see John's ship commissioned.

Michael Hare came in today from Honolulu & brought messages from Jimmy. I'll be glad when we get some word from you. Love to the boys & you.

E.R.

The *Iowa* arrived at Oran in North Africa on November 20 and from there F.D.R. flew to Tunis on the *Sacred Cow.*

Tunis
Nov. 21, 1943

Dearest Babs,

We landed safely yesterday and came through to Tunis where I am safely ensconced in a very nice villa overlooking the sea and just beyond the ruins of Carthage. Elliott and F. Jr. met me when we left the ship— and are well, tho' F. Jr. has the trouble he wrote of. He finally decided he had best go back with the ship and I think he is right to want to see her safely to Charleston. He and I will probably get back about the same time.

This p.m. I reviewed Elliott's whole outfit. He is in top command of all the Reconnaissance Air—U.S.-Brit.-So. African and N. Zealand—5,000 men and 250 planes. He flies to Italy tomorrow and joins me in Cairo. By the way all this is secret. The press will say nothing for 5 or 6 days after it happens.

Cairo—Nov. 26th. The 1st meetings are in full swing. The Generalissimo and Mme. Chiang are here. Things have gone *pretty* well. We all have villas way out of town and about 1/4 mile apart. I've visited the pyramids and been fortified by the Sphinx. I'll give free transportation to any Senator or Congressman who will go over and look at her for a long time.

Last night I had a very nice Thanksgiving dinner. Elliott and John B. arrived in the a.m. and J. is o.k. I will keep them both with me from now on—also Winston and his daughter Sarah and A. Eden and old Lord Leathers and Tommy Thompson and my personal staff—19 in all.

We are off on the next leg tomorrow. All well but awful busy. Harry is standing it all right.

Ever so much love.

> Devotedly
> F.

She had not yet received this letter but wrote him en route to Boston on November 23:

Dearest Franklin,

All goes well here. I had a grand letter from Fjr. today & I hope you find him better. Of course he knew nothing of your trip when he wrote.

I was glad to hear that you were safely at your journey's end & hope all goes well.

I'll go to see Missy tomorrow morning & attend the ceremonies for the commissioning of Johnny's ship. Wed. Nov. 24th back in N.Y.

The ceremonies went off very well today & the ship is a big one. I liked the Captain & Executive Officer & met Johnny's superior officer who said nice things about him. Johnny himself seems more enthusiastic than I have ever seen him. The children came in to lunch & were well. Anne got an earache just before I left & was spending the night in town in case it had to be opened.

The rumors that Elliott was shot down over Germany gave us some bad hours but apparently was just a rumor. Missy seemed well today & talked a little more.

Tell Harry Louise looks well & they were all still in the W.H. but she hopes to get in before you get back.

> Much love
> E.R.

Will you see the enclosed get to Fjr. & Elliott?

F.D.R.'s letter of November 18 reached her only on December 2. Her reproach to Franklin because of the presence of women at Cairo and Teheran while he had kept her away was bantering but definite:

I've been amused that Mme. C. & Sara Churchill were in the party. I wish you had let me fly out! I'm sure I would have enjoyed seeing Mme. C. more than you did, tho' all the pictures show her in animated conversation with you & he wears a rather puzzled look as Winston chews his cigar.

I wish I knew about the children & who is with you & when you get home. Does the trip being "a little longer" mean many days or what? Might John B. come home with you? as well as Fjr? I have to be away the 12th–14th so hope you don't arrive then for I want to meet you!

A long letter to me in the South Pacific touched many bases though it began, "Nothing of great interest to you has happened today." It then went on—

[E.R. to Joseph P. Lash:]   [December 3, 1943]
. . . tho' I talked over negro housing in the Dist. with Pauline Redmond Coggs & Mrs. McGuire I think if you were here you would be horrified as I was at the conditions now existing. New public buildings, new military roads have been built on condemned land, mostly lived in by negroes. They are ousted and no place is provided so now 10 families live in one family houses! Then we deplore the high rate of tuberculosis and syphilis. What hypocrites we are!

Only a day & two nights now before Anna & the children arrive. I only hope John B. could be here & then if you & Trude & the kids were coming too my joy would be complete.

You know for a long time holidays haven't been days of joy for me & I've never been quite sure why I felt as I did, but, when this war is over, if you all come home safely, even if I can't be with you, I think I'll be happy because these years are over. I'll write some more tomorrow, so goodnight & my love goes out to you.

Dec. 4th. A busy day! I went to the blood donor place at 9 & then at 10 began my Spanish lessons again. . . .

A letter came from the travellers & by now they must be on the way home. I am relieved to find that John B. & Elliott went with the chief & Fjr. insisted he had to bring his ship home & after meeting the travellers in Tunis was allowed to return & travel homeward under his own power. I knew he ought to do that & I'm so glad he did. He missed much that must be historically interesting but I think he'll have more inner satisfaction if he gets ship & the men home safely. I'm keeping my fingers crossed for him. . . .

P.S. I forgot to tell you how I wish the boys would deluge their Congressmen & Senators with protests on the failure of the bill to allow the soldiers a vote. State by state it will never be possible. It is a combination of Rep. who fear the vote for F.D.R. & Dem. who fear the poll tax wld be circumvented.

How strongly she felt about Fjr.'s coming home with his damaged ship was evident in her next letter to Franklin:

Dec. 5th

Dearest Franklin,

Your letter begun the 21st & ended the 25th arrived yesterday & I was so glad to hear you had seen all the boys. It must have been hard for both you & Fjr. to decide he should return on his ship. I wish I knew when both of you would arrive! It is grand that Elliott & John could be with you for Thanksgiving & you sound as tho' you had had a good party.

I'm sorry things only went *pretty* well with Chiang. I wonder if he, Mme. or Winston made trouble. The questions are so delicate that the Sphinx must be a relief & quite understandable after you try to solve the present.

I loved your quip about the Congressmen & the 1-page paper. The latter would have few readers I fear! I think Congress's failure to pass anything to simplify the soldiers voting results in great resentment, at least I hope so.

I imagine you now have been to Malta & Italy & are on the homeward trek. The announcement from Germany yesterday of a secret force to be used to destroy in great & unprecedented ways has made one young scientist jittery again & he is calling me on the phone this morning but what can I do?

I'm just off to meet Anna & the chicks & will finish later.

Later. All have arrived & had breakfast & seem well & are happy that you saw John & will have late news of him.

Much love
E.R.

"Between the 16th & 18th we ought to welcome various strangers home," she wrote me.

[E.R. to Joseph P. Lash:]   [December 5, 1943]

Fjr. met the travellers in Tunis & blandly F. wrote me it seemed wiser for Fjr to return with his own ship! I'm glad Fjr had the sense of responsibility & that F. respected it. Of course I should never get excited for things always turn out this way!

A last letter from Franklin:

En Route Tunis to Dakar
Dec. 9th, 1943

Dearest Babs

Homeward bound. Tell nobody but I *hope* to get to W. the 16th or 17th. I am now on a 12 hour plane trip which I hate. But on the whole it has been a real success. I said goodbye to John B. yesterday p.m. in Sicily.

He went to Cairo and Teheran with me and is in good shape. Elliott saw me off at 6 this morning in Tunis and is moving his whole outfit to Italy. I suppose Fjr. will get in about the time I do. Lots to tell you about and lots and lots of love.

Devotedly
F.

Eleanor's affection for people flowed into many channels. At the moment one was her intense feelings about the GIs' right to vote and the opportunities they should have on demobilization. Another was her insistence on a voice for women in the postwar agencies. And perhaps most emphatically, her opposition to America's treatment of the Negro.

[E.R. to Joseph P. Lash:]   [December (?) 1943]
   I saw Lillian Smith from Georgia this a.m. She edits 'South Today' & because she is a Southerner has done some wonderful things in race relations but now they are after her & the FBI is looking into her as a communist! I don't know what I can do but I telephoned Mr. Biddle [the Attorney General]. I just read a pamphlet on Liberia & our record is even worse than I thought. I wish I had a few nice things to tell you, these will come when F. comes home. Meanwhile the little Spanish boy sits before me right in front of your picture & insists on marching on!

As unremitting as was her concern for the disadvantaged, there was a mother's fierce affection in her constant references to her children. She saw their flaws clearly, more so than those of her friends, but that did not make her less ready to help them out of the difficulties into which they often got themselves. Like many other mothers, she often asked herself where she and Franklin had gone wrong in bringing them up. At the moment it was Elliott who wrote her from overseas about his troubles with his wife Ruth. She is "upset, more upset than I've seen her," Trude wrote me. "Ruth wants a divorce right away and Elliott told Jimmy he hoped he would crash. She's upset because she feels she did not start Elliott out in life right. Maybe it is true, I don't know. . . . [H]as he [Trude's son Peter] if he should go wrong a right to reproach me as Elliott reproaches Mrs. R? What a shortsighted, tormented and pitiful person he must be! She seems the only one who can help because he can never seriously doubt her love."
   Elliott's letter "disturbs & depresses me greatly," Eleanor wrote me.

[E.R. to Joseph P. Lash:]   [Dec. 10, 1943]
   I wonder why you who so easily might have an attitude of self-pity never have it & my boys so often behave as tho' their Father's life had ruined theirs. It isn't true but makes a good excuse for every kind of weakness. Anna & I held an indignation meeting but it hasn't helped me

much to write the letter I must write. God give me wisdom & understanding that is a prayer I guess I should never forget. . . .

Another blow, although expected, was the death of Elizabeth Read:

[E.R. to Joseph P. Lash:] [Dec. 13, 1943]
    I feel sad about Elizabeth, but like Louis she went so far away in her
mind two or three years ago that I find I haven't the sense of sharp loss it
would have been if she had died a few years ago. I feel terribly for Esther
for she will feel she has lost a child she gave her such constant care &
devotion. Strangely enough when I said goodbye last time I was there,
she looked at me so intently that I felt she thought she was saying
goodbye & had to shake myself free of the thought.

She wrote Esther—

[E.R. to Esther Lape:] [December 14, 1943]
    What can I say, life without Lizzie will be almost impossible to face.
She loved you so dearly & you gave each other so much. I would have
liked to go up tomorrow just to hug you though I know Miss Phillips is
right & you would probably be better alone with Lizzie, since your sister
& Miss Phillips can do all the chores. You do know both Tommy & I
wanted to do anything we could & we'll be there on Wednesday, so you'll
know we are standing by even if you don't see us.
    Ever since I first knew Lizzie I've loved & admired & respected her. I
will miss thinking of, when we next meet what I'll tell her & ask her, but
she's been part of my life so long that I'll never forget her & life will
always be richer because of her friendship. I want to do anything I can to
make life more bearable for you & if you can bear to be with people I
hope you will come & stay as long as you can as soon as you want.
    I love you very much & I wish my arms could be around you.

When Trude saw Eleanor in New York, she was grave and pensive over
Elizabeth's death, said Trude, "not as utterly depressed and sad as on Sunday, nor
yesterday, when she talked of Elliott and Ruth." "Yesterday was a hard day,"
Eleanor wrote me—

[E.R. to Joseph P. Lash:] [December 15, 1943]
not so much because of Elizabeth's death. So much of her was gone
before & I knew it was a release but because I could help Esther so little.
I remember how I felt when my first baby Franklin died at eight months
& I think Esther feels in some ways the same kind of loss of someone to
care for who was helpless & needed her. I didn't get over it for a long

time but I indulged in some pretty wrong thinking & I wish I could help Esther to avoid that but somehow I'm not quite close enough. We've always been good friends & enjoyed being together & talked freely, but one has to love deeply to help anyone in the really bad moments of life.

A few weeks later she wrote me again about the relationship of the two women, and no anatomist of love could have delineated it more delicately.

[E.R. to Joseph P. Lash:]   [January 6, 1944]
Queer when one evaluates human relationships how few go very deep. I spent last night & until after lunch today in Westbrook with Esther Lape. I spoke in their movie theatre last night & to the school children today so I justified my trip since they raised over $1,500 for the Red Cross. It is my feeling about Elizabeth which I have been thinking about. Between Esther & herself there was a deep relationship, built over 30 yrs & she was unselfishly devoted to Esther. Each had interests & friends of their own but Elizabeth always subordinated anything to Esther's interests tho' she had the stronger character & tho' less brilliant, she had better judgment & in some ways a better mind than Esther's. Their lives were in all but the physical relationship, like the best kind of marriage & I think Elizabeth built it. I missed her presence & while I am fond of Esther & enjoy her it is Elizabeth one would talk to & be sure of understanding. Even with me it was a real relationship & I can see why Esther is lost without her.

Whatever Eleanor's irritations with Franklin, she shared the excitement and anticipation of his return to Washington. She, Anna, and two of the latter's children, Eleanor and Curtis, as she now called Sisty and Buzz, met Franklin and drove home with him. "He looks well & as tho' he'd enjoyed himself. On the whole he said all went well. . . . He feels badly because they promised the Chinese something & at Teheran Mr. C. said he did not remember agreeing to it & went back on it. To my surprise F. seemed really annoyed."
Trude was staying with her the day of the President's return and was at dinner the first night, so Mrs. R. left it to Trude to tell me about it, but did say—

[E.R. to Joseph P. Lash:]   [December 18, 1943]
. . . I was more interested in Fjr's growth & sense of responsibility. [He had brought the *Mayrant* into Charleston.] He is older & more stable I think but that doesn't mean he can't kick up a lot of excitement in the future! . . .
Sunday, Dec. 19th. My impression grows that FDR liked & got on well with both Stalin & Chiang. He says on military strategy he compromised on two minor points with the British. Their high command is deter-

mined to take the Dodecanese Islands instead of concentrating on a
strong Burma campaign. This upset F. who thought Chiang & Dicky
Mountbatten had virtually been promised the Burma campaign first but
Churchill said he had not understood it that way.—F. feels the D's
[Dodecanese] took up German troops & kept them where they could do
no harm but in the main he said they had agreed. I don't know what the
second compromise was. I've got nothing out of him on postwar except
as Trude will have told you they seem to think in terms of breaking up
the German Reich.

Trude's letter about dinner in the family dining room was almost an essay on
F.D.R. at Cairo and Teheran:

[Trude W. Pratt to Joseph P. Lash:]   [Dec. 19, 1943]
. . . But back to Friday. When I wrote you the short letter I had had
only a glimpse of the President and had not seen Franklin Jr. at all but I
saw them both at dinner. Franklin shocked me, he looked old and drawn
and much more of a person than I had remembered him. Much more
like his mother's son. His story which he told in his father's study after
dinner was a very terrible one, he told it only after much urging—and
had a hard time to seem casual, but told it with modesty and an impersonal voice, if there is such a quality. It's the story of a ship, and men
dying in live steam and officers getting paralyzed with fear.—I think
Franklin will be o.k. He brought a beautiful bracelet, a tiny filigree one
for Ethel,* and was so happy she liked it. I think he must love her, he
looked at her that way, and almost cried when she proposed a toast to the
"two beloved Franklins."
        . . . Now I'll tell you exactly what happened. I was told to come to
the study for cocktails, and when I came across the hall from the blue
room there was the boss [the President] and Mrs. R. and Franklin, and
Franklin grinned and said, good to see you and took both my hands—and
the boss said, good evening Trude my child, you've grown too thin, there
is too little left of you, you used to be a big girl, now you're only a whisp
—what's the matter—and I said—too many people are too far away—
but it's good to see you home again. He said "I must look after you and
feed you up" and he kept on all dinner trying to make me eat—and
saying things that made the food stick. . . .

The Christmas season took over. Two months earlier Eleanor had set aside an
evening for her private celebration with Hick, who afterward took the train to

* Mrs. Franklin D. Roosevelt, Jr. (Ethel Du Pont).

spend the holidays at her cottage in Moriches, Long Island. "Home," Hick wrote, "and what a wonderful word that is!" The next night Eleanor had her annual party with Earl. "He was very sweet & seemed to have a happy evening." Then she celebrated with Trude and her children at the house on West 11th Street that Trude had rented after her divorce:

> from 4 o'clock on she was here. We trimmed the tree . . . put red candles on . . . played the Marion Anderson records and Mrs. R very quietly and beautifully told the kids the Christmas story. . . .
> after dinner Mrs. R and I rushed upstairs and distributed the presents. . . . Then we lit the tree, the candles all over the room—put on Holy Night. . . .

Eleanor made a quick trip to Washington for dinner with Tommy and Henry Osthagen at Tommy's apartment. She talked with Elinor Morgenthau.

Trude, having put her children on the train to spend the holidays with their father in New Milford, went up to Hyde Park. On Christmas Eve the President broadcast from the library to the millions of American troops all over the world.

On Guadalcanal my own little weather detachment celebrated our own Christmas, this one made festive by red and green streamers and a small tree we had cut in the jungle. There was a stocking and card for each man that Mrs. Roosevelt had sent. "The table was magnificent," I wrote Trude, the tree even had an "angel," one of the seminude dress models Trude had sent me. There were bottles of scotch and bourbon grouped at the base of the tree by Major Buechler, and the whole place was lit up by bayberry candles that Eleanor also had sent us. "Everyone was very pleased. Then the Major opened up the 'bar' and soon the place was filled with shouts, the clinking of metal cups as we wished one another Merry Christmas. . . . The party was over in fact by 9 p.m.; none of us is in a condition for long drinking bouts."

At Hyde Park after the President's broadcast, a group of M.P.s from the Military Police battalion that guarded the estate carolled the President and after dinner there was a party for them and their comrades and the President addressed them extemporaneously. At midnight Eleanor and Trude went to church. "I had not been to Catholic Church since 1927—this was just like it. . . . I could not have gone to Communion for any price—though Mrs. R did—and perhaps wanted me to."

After my reading of *The Robe*, which had been "an eye opener" on Christianity's beginnings, I had read *The Apostle*, by Sholem Asch, which, I wrote Eleanor, "went a long way towards making me feel Christianity was part of my heritage as a Jew." Eleanor was interested that I described myself as belonging to no organized religious group.

[E.R. to Joseph P. Lash:]   [December 23, 1943]

Of course Christ started the movement which all men of good will have followed ever since. The Jews who rejected him were the theologians of their days & the privileged ones, the very type of people you, in your day fight. Christ was a Jew & is part of your heritage & I think one of the men to be proudest of in your history. Those who follow him can believe in the brotherhood of man, no matter how they differ in other ways.

"We missed you today," she wrote me on Christmas.

[E.R. to Joseph P. Lash:]   [December 25, 1943]

The nicest time was a walk Trude & Harry took down towards the river thro' the woods. It was wonderful having Trude here but the kids kept her up talking so she has had no rest which grieves me. Fjr. worried her by telling her his love affairs, just after she had taken much trouble talking to Ethel & felt she was helping the latter a little. Of course I'm not much good to talk to about these things because I know Fjr loves to talk, if he's sincere he'll do what he means to do & the less said the better & if he isn't the less said the better. I guess one of the sad things in life is that rarely do a man & woman fall *equally* in love with each other & even more rarely do they so live their lives that they continue to be lovers at times & still develop & enjoy the constant companionship of married life. I imagine that the really great number of men & women who are faithful to each other not only in deed but in thought are so more often because of a lack of opportunity for romance elsewhere rather than because they've learned the secret of "the one & only great love." A cynic you will say!

Some cynic! She flew up to New York so as to be present for Bob Morgenthau's wedding. "Elinor dearest," she had written her when informed of Bob and Martha Pattridge's impending marriage—

I wanted to write even though I had talked to you. Having the first child marry is an event & a wrench. I am so very happy that you love the girl.

Her own sons' marital problems would not have dispirited her so had she not felt that faithfulness was an achievable relationship. "I think I am depressed about Elliott & Fjr. in their emotional difficulties which Trude has doubtless told you about more than I have. I say a prayer of thanksgiving for those of you who seem to have the capacity for deep feeling & constancy." She grouped Anna and her husband, who was overseas with Military Government, with Trude and me.

[E.R. to Joseph P. Lash:]   [December 29, 1943]
    She & Anna seem to have been getting to know each other a little &
they have had some good talks. I hope they help each other for both are
struggling so valiantly through the dark period. Holidays are bad times &
Sis whispered to me at Xmas dinner "don't make a sentimental toast or I
shall cry." I assured her I wouldn't but didn't add that I most certainly
would cry too—for her & for John & for Trude & you.

At the New Year's eve party F.D.R. turned up in a wrapper because he had a
"touch of the flu" and gave the toast to the United States of America. "It was a
small party, just the Morgenthaus (Joan & Henry III home), Tommy, Miss Suckley
& Bishop Atwood. . . . On this day or rather night dear boy I want to tell you
again how much being close to you & Trude mean to me. . . . I'm grateful
beyond words that you are my friend & care for me." And to Trude she wrote—

[E.R. to Trude W. Pratt:]   [December 31, 1943]
    It is my custom to write a little line on New Year's eve to those I love. I
like to tell them all over again how much their "closeness" means to me,
how much seeing them & being able to do little things for their pleasure
or comfort adds to my joy in life. I always feel that in you & Joe I shall
see much accomplished that I dream of now as a mere future possibility. . . .

A New Year's Eve wish for Anna—

[E.R. to Anna Boettiger:]   New Year's Eve
    This is just a little line for you to carry thro' the coming year. I know
how empty life seems, how purposeless & how deeply lonely. The contrast between great companionship & the present blank is what makes it
so hard to bear.
    I can hope & pray that the coming year will bring your John back &
you know that both of you are never out of my mind & heart. God bless
& keep you both & give you health & strength for this ordeal.
    All my love, admiration & devotion to you dearest one.

                                                        Mother

IV

What Democracy Meant to Her

THE IMPENDING INVASION of Europe shadowed the first six months of 1944. Eleanor knew D-Day was coming; indeed, who did not? "It runs thro' my mind like a never ending refrain 'when will it end, when will it end,' " she wrote me. The dread of the lists of "killed in action," the wounded, and the missing was always with her. "I can smile & shake hands & go right on thinking about something else!" and anxiety over the casualties marched hand in hand with hope in the future, especially in the young people in the services. "I must say neither business nor the public inspire me with much confidence but the young returning soldier does. Last night, to meet John Hersey who wrote 'A Bell for Adano' I asked 3 boys returned & studying at George Washington . . . & 15 assorted Sergeants, Corporals, & privates from Walter Reed who had asked questions last Thursday." She hoped Hersey had gotten the material he wanted for his article for *Life*.

[E.R. to Joseph P. Lash:]   [April 27, 1944]

Today I went back to the discussion group at Walter Reed & the amputation ward asked if I wld go up to them. Joe, they wring your heart but most of them are so cheerful. The great number here are from Italy, a kid of 19 seemed the worst to me till I came to a boy who has been there a year & the wounds won't heal. I've got to get him here for he looks as tho' he hated the world. "I'd like to go & get drunk" he said & I answered "Well, at least I'll give you a drink."—What adjustments they make! Both Lawson & Robinson offered their wives divorces at once—It seems hard for men to understand that any decent woman doesn't just love a man's "outside." It is what he is in mind & heart & soul that matters. The gallant cheerfulness is what gets you most for you realize what the nights must be.

Conscience made cowards of some; for her it constantly posed the question: What can I do to keep it all from being in vain? She pushed for women to be represented on the U.S. delegations to conferences on postwar arrangements. "I've been sitting in for 2 days with a group of women discussing how women can be got into policy making positions. . . ." She noted that at the Packard and Cadillac plants 50 percent of the work force were women, and though Winston Churchill in March received what she described as "a swell vote on confidence," she added—

[E.R. to Joseph P. Lash:]   [March 30, 1944]
but I cld wish he hadn't opposed equal pay for women teachers. I get home to find they were sending only men (very good men) to the International Conference in London on education & the delegation was leaving tomorrow. I've got one woman added but wasn't it stupid?

She still was not a convert to the Equal Rights Amendment. She had in the past opposed it, agreeing with the Women's Trade Union League that the manufacturers and employers favored it as a way of removing from the books the laws that protected women.
She wrote me in early February—

[E.R. to Joseph P. Lash:]   [February 8, 1944]
    Then I had the proponents & opponents of the Equal Suffrage Amendment fight it out for my benefit from three to four-thirty. There were no new arguments on either side so I remained where I had been convinced that we'd better wait for an amendment till all labor laws are farther along before we do away with those we have that are a protection to women.

Despite this statement that she was standing fast on the Equal Rights Amendment, she sent a memorandum to F.D.R. the next day, "May be time for a change." He replied immediately, "I do not think it is a vital necessity in the next platform but if it is put in I will not weep about it!"
    As usual, we had exchanged valentines. Mine was written on a B-24 enroute to Truk from Guadalcanal, a long, tedious journey from which I sent a weather forecast so the bombers would know whether to come up or not:

For St. Valentine's Day
Written on "The Little Flower" a B-24 of these parts

So steady the progression of this plane
You could think it part of the celestial chain;
Immense playground of planet and star
Of this too man seeks to be Tsar.

Here between two waist gunners I sit
Who on the Equator are trying to spit.
Which is one purpose a bomber can dispense,
Who knows which one makes more sense.

. . .

She had written me at the beginning of the year—

[E.R. to Joseph P. Lash:]   [January 9, 1944]
I keep talking to F. about your chances of getting home & he said
today you might be called home to teach on Pacific conditions. I know he
won't ask but if he even suggests I'd be encouraged!

On St. Valentine's Day she wrote—

[E.R. to Joseph P. Lash:]   [February 14, 1944]
I understand so well how hard it must be for you & Trude to keep even
a semblance of cheerfulness as the days & weeks drag on. I often have to
look at your little Spanish boy to remind myself how long whole peoples
wait for the fulfillment of such simple desires & we are so soon impatient.

I was becoming reconciled to the likelihood of a long stay in the South Pacific,
but when the regional weather officer visited our station on Guadalcanal I asked
whether as military activity moved north I might be assigned to the Army orientation program. He and the colonel in command both felt I was the man best
qualified for the assignment. Perhaps they should send me back to the states for the
Army's Orientation School at Washington and Lee, I suggested.

[Joseph P. Lash to E.R.:]   [March 2, 1944]
They do not know, however, whether they have the right, because we
are such a small detachment to send back a man. But the Captain promised to investigate the matter again and discuss it with the Colonel. It
will in the end be up to USAfispa but the Colonel will back me to the
limit. And that was very cheering news. You see, I never give up hope!

"I wish you would try to be shifted to the orientation work," Eleanor wrote me after I spoke of its expansion and my desire to do so.

[E.R. to Joseph P. Lash:]   [February 13, 1944]
    You could do it so well & tho' there might be obstacles put in your way, with good recommendations from your officers they might be overcome. No harm in trying anyway.

Trude stayed with her at the White House and had to rush back to New York.

[E.R. to Trude W. Pratt:]   [February 23, 1944]
    Anna says she's sorry you didn't come to say goodbye but she'll see you next week & so will Anne. How nice we'll have you all that weekend. F.D.R. is pleased too & says he'll have a big party & stay up till 9:30! Every other night he's going to bed at 9—

There was an affectionate rebuke for me because of lingering "male supremacy" sentiments. I had written—

[Joseph P. Lash to E.R.:]   [May 19, 1944]
    I hope Trude will be able to work in the campaign. Her heart is set on it and she will do a good job. I wonder though whether Trude is good at working with other women. She is a man's woman and other ladies resent that, and Trude has an almost masculine (male conceit on my part) intelligence which makes her impatient with female fripperies. Anyway she should be careful if she goes to work in the Women's Division.

She berated me for saying that Trude was—

[E.R. to Joseph P. Lash:]   [June 3, 1944]
"a man's woman" & has a masculine intelligence. You males are so conceited! Women don't need masculine intelligence, feminine brains can work along with you & often give you a helping hand. I hope she is a male's woman but that won't keep her from being a woman's woman too! *Some* women may be jealous of her but *some* men are jealous of other men, & I've known men who in their way had as many "fripperies" as women! Besides one can't always live on a high intellectual level, & you wouldn't like it if any of us lived there constantly! Now you are forgiven & I hope Trude works wherever she gets the best job!

A few weeks later, as she listened to the Republican convention, she returned to the matter of "masculine" minds.

[E.R. to Joseph P. Lash:]   [June 27, 1944]
   I shall wait till you get home to argue the historical fact that women's minds are inferior to the "masculine intelligence" but someday I hope to show you where the female of the species is at least on a par in a purely feminine way. Had you heard Claire Luce at the Republican convention tonight I think you would have agreed that she was more effective than Gov. Warren, Rep. Joe Martin, or Mr. Herbert Hoover.

"White supremacy" attitudes bothered her even more than those of the male as she contemplated the future.

[E.R. to Joseph P. Lash:]   [January 14, 1944]
   I've got a novel now *[Strange Fruit]* by Lillian Smith of "South Today." It is horrible & yet true but I dread the publication for her. The South will find it hard to take but she gets her points over & I think it will be read even in the South & there surreptitiously!

[E.R. to Joseph P. Lash:]   [January 16, 1944]
   I went to a meeting last night of the Washington group (white & colored) that are trying to work out better race relations & heard Pauline Redmond explain how hard it was to reassure the young colored people about the future & keep them steady & I must say I worry about the future. . . . It really is discouraging because the Christian spirit seems so unChristlike!

And after she had finished Lillian Smith's book, she worried even more. "[T]he South will kill her. She has revealed what one never mentions." Eleanor fought for black rights, but she also urged moderation. She addressed a Friends meeting together with the black president of Howard University, Dr. Mordecai Johnson.

[E.R. to Joseph P. Lash:]   [February 26, 1944]
   His speech was very dramatic & moving & he felt it deeply but I'm not sure it is wise to talk as he did. He arraigned all the Allied nations except Russia, for their treatment of their colonial people & ended with us at home. It was a passionate statement of the wrongs in the war but pointed to none of the gains, which are there tho' they are small & I thought he left the black man so little hope that it was a damaging presentation rather than a helpful one.

She admired the wounded veterans whom she talked with, their courage, cheerfulness, and stamina, and those qualities mattered more than their points of view, but at times she had misgivings about the latter, qualifying her enthusiasm about the young with the realization that their views were shaped by the same conservative forces that seemed to be slowing down the nation at home. She heard George Biddle, the younger artist brother of Francis Biddle, the Attorney General—

[E.R. to Joseph P. Lash:]   [January 18, 1944]
. . . and I want to tell you about it because his concerns are largely mine. He has lived with the men in Italy, up at the front, in Naples, in Sicily, in Africa. He's a painter & they treated him as one of themselves. He says they are so kind, they feed the mules their sugar, back of the lines you never see one without an Italian baby which he's feeding. They don't know what they are fighting for. They want to be home, but they're going to win because once in, you win. They have no conviction about Democracy, such as a young Russian, or Nazi or even a Britisher has about his particular type of life. The sad part is that the boys represent what they have known at home & we are no better. We won't think through what we mean by Democracy & face the problems that our theories bring us, those in the field of economics & race relations. We won't even accept the fact that our sacred "free enterprise" has to be controlled & planned if the boys are to have jobs! Will the younger generation have the wisdom to bring the changes without a revolution?

Such radical views did not endear her to the conservatives. Westbrook Pegler attacked her regularly. He published a column, she informed me, that did not mention her, but clearly was a dig at what he called her "greed." She took a trip around U.S. outposts and garrisons in the Caribbean, going as far as Belem in Brazil, and afterward read the accumulated clippings. They were, she said, "violently anti-E.R. In the midst of accusations that I am the most disliked woman in the country they cry out because I am invited to make so many speeches & I wrote so much!"

1944 also was a presidential election year. She assumed Franklin would run again. He had had a bout with the "flu" at the end of 1943. At the end of March a young heart specialist, Dr. Howard G. Bruenn, diagnosed "hypertensive heart disease." Whether she was told of it is not wholly clear. In any case, she was not happy about Franklin's general condition. A note at the end of January that reported F.D.R. as saying he felt better added, "but I don't think he longs to get back & fight."

Her resistance to his running again had abated compared to her blunt statements in 1939 and 1940, but she still looked at the significance of another victory by him with a rare openness of mind.

[E.R. to Joseph P. Lash:]   [July 25, 1944]
I argued with Jimmy & left him in a better frame of mind I hope but

still unconvinced that the Republicans might do a better job than the Democrats! We need a new party of course, but I don't think we can risk it now. Of course if F. runs & it isn't clearcut what the people elected him to do so that both Republicans and Democrats know it beyond question I think he will be in a "hellish" situation.

The issue of reelection without a mandate that Congress recognized came up sharply at the end of February when the President vetoed a tax bill that ignored his recommendations and that he called "not a tax bill but a tax relief bill providing relief not for the needy but for the greedy." The harsh language caused as loyal a legislator as Alben Barkley of Kentucky, the Senate majority leader, to announce his intention to resign as leader on the ground that the President had assailed his integrity as well as that of other members of Congress. "F. was indignant over the tax bill," Eleanor wrote me, "& he has annoyed Congress by the 'apt' phrase on relief. Those phrases are tempting but I'm not sure of their wisdom. The facts however are pretty devastating." Roosevelt placated Barkley with a wire from Hyde Park, and Barkley's Democratic colleagues immediately reelected him, as Roosevelt had urged.

[E.R. to Joseph P. Lash:]   [February 23, 1944]
    F.D.R. used too apt a phrase & they have overridden his veto. I called him at Hyde Park & he is quite calm over it. Says the people needed to know the situation. Barclay *[sic]* will now be elected unanimously & have greater strength & also more responsibility. I think F.D.R. is more philo-sophical daily. He knows he will only be reelected if they can't find anyone else & I really think he doesn't care except he means to say & do as he thinks right at home. He is also fighting the British now at every turn & perhaps he's getting a bit weary but he'll go on as long as the people want him. The whole Congressional picture is discouraging from the point of view of self-government but it will pass & the war goes well!

At Franklin's request she agreed to tour American outposts in the Caribbean in early March, accompanied this time by Tommy. "I asked E.R. whether she was taking me on this trip," Tommy reported to Esther, "because I said I would have liked to go on the other and she said no, it was because she did not want to go alone and she did not want anyone else."
She did not want to go, Tommy said.

[Tommy to Esther Lape:]   [March (?) 1944]
    There seems to be a real weariness on E.R.'s part which was not apparent before and a pessimism about the future and earning ability, etc. We are apparently going to the Caribbean but with reluctance. I

thought she was anxious to go but she says she is only going at F.D.R.'s request and there is no enthusiasm.

Her letter to me was full of her hesitations. It "may be a wise thing to do tho' I hesitate about it but F. thinks it useful so Sat. we are off. Tommy is no more enthusiastic than I am. . . ." This was a different kind of trip from the one she had made to the South Pacific "because primarily it is inspecting bases & making everyone feel they are doing a very important job. . . ." It was as hot and monotonous as Guadalcanal had seemed to her. "I'm glad you are not in this area [she was then flying from Belem to Natal] for I'm sure you would hate it!" The trip did not seem as "worthwhile" as that to the Pacific. "The boys are anxious to go home or move to a fighting area."

She heard the same tale about her wanting to hold all men in quarantine before returning home from overseas that I had told her about on Guadalcanal: "I said every boy should wear a red or white armband & be held in a camp for 6 months after the war! Lucky they are not for or against FDR because of me!"

The class divisions in Brazil hit her hard. "In this country there are the very rich & the very poor but no middle class. There is so much to do that it is hard to know where you would begin. The people are likeable however & I think Mme. Vargas has done good work for young people."

Tommy's being along had made the trip more agreeable. Her tart commentaries had been a help "& it makes the mechanical part of the trip so much easier & she is fun with her penetrating comments!" Back at the White House at the end of March she summed up the trip's usefulness: "I think I brought F. back some useful information & the diplomats were well pleased. I think some boys liked it & some didn't but I've seen more of another war picture."

She met Earl several times before she left for the Caribbean, Elinor Morgenthau even more frequently, for the period had begun when Elinor was in and out of the hospital with heart and circulation problems. She was much on Eleanor's mind. "What fun our spree was," Eleanor wrote her as she departed, and she used an expression that occurred often in recounting her doings with Elinor: "We always do have fun together. I am anxious to hear about your cardiograph. You shouldn't be fainting on the roadside." Her long letter to Elinor was descriptive and meaty.

[E.R. to Elinor Morgenthau:]   Tuesday, March 14th [1944]
    We fly so high that pens leak so forgive this pencil. We've had wonderful weather & this is such a comfortable & easy trip that I doubt if I'm going to be able to lose the 5 lbs. I hoped to shed! I am chiefly impressed with the jungle we have subdued & the building we have done. Now things are being curtailed everywhere but should the need arise everything is ready. The men are homesick & I don't wonder but they've done a grand job. So far the hospitals seem adequate but dreary. Malaria control has done wonders at field & shore stations. Zandry Field in Dutch

Guiana seemed to me the dreariest spot, right in the jungle and 30 miles from Paramaribo. The climate here is humid but so far nights have been fairly cool.

I've talked with a great many boys, our own are slowly moving out, & the Puerto Rican boys who move in seem to do well with good leadership & they show great physical improvement with adequate food. Having everything interpreted is hard but French was a help with the Brazilian officials last night.

I don't think much of either Red **+** or the U.S.O. in this area. U.S.O. has good facilities but I have only once been really impressed by a woman. She was a Puerto Rican in Caguas & most of the men seem nondescript.

I'll be glad to get home but Tommy thinks the trip is going well & that the Army & Navy officers are glad that I came. I'm never sure & only time will tell.

A gay letter from the Panama Canal toward the end of her trip—

[E.R. to Trude W. Pratt:]   [March 23, 1944]
In a few minutes we start out for the day & it is now 7:45 so you see even your children don't get you up much earlier than the Army! It is hot & muggy in the day time but cool at night. The Canal impresses me as a great feat but I can't see why the Nazis or the Japs haven't put it out of commission. So little would do it & it must mean that the defense has been really very good. We do a great variety of things, ending up last night with a concert for the Navy Relief Society in the Opera House at which a really wonderful pianist appeared & he is a sailor! This Army & Navy has anything & everything you want!

At the outset of the trip Hick had written her that the visit to the Caribbean, which began with a stay in Puerto Rico, was almost ten years to the day since Hick had accompanied her to that island. "Can you believe it was *ten* years ago?" Then, as if answering an unspoken question on why they had drifted apart emotionally while remaining the closest of friends, "Yet so much has happened and we are both older and, in my case, I hope wiser. Well—it was a beautiful trip, dear. But I wish I had been more mature, more stable." Eleanor sent Hick several letters but did not comment on Hick's self-reproaches. She stayed at La Forteleza with the Tugwells. He was now married to Grace. "Rex's manner is his real enemy. I think he has done a grand job & some people recognize it but he antagonizes many."

Tommy's evaluation of the trip to Esther on her return was affirmative.

[Tommy to Esther Lape:]   [April (?) 1944]
The trip was very interesting and Mrs. R. did really bring a lot of

interest and excitement to the soldiers, sailors, etc. I suspected that most of the top officers were not so sure they wanted to have Mrs. R., but after her visit in each place, they all agreed that it had been well worth while. . . .

Everyone seems to think that the trip did Mrs. R. a lot of good, that she is better than when she left and is in better spirits. She was very much worried about Ruth's divorce action and discouraged because the last time she saw Ruth, Ruth promised to wait until the end of the year. Then came a note saying she was instituting proceedings at once. Mrs. R. is more concerned about the children than anything else. . . .

A competitive syndicate wants to take Mrs. R.'s column when her present contract expires in Dec. and is willing to make a much better financial arrangement. I am getting their proposition in writing and shall present it to the present syndicate. We might as well be Shylocks, and get the best we can out of it. Apparently the new syndicate doesn't care whether we stay in the W.H. or move out next January.

On their return to Washington Eleanor found F.D.R. ailing again.

"He hasn't been well & he's now having a thorough check-up. When the tests are all made we hope he will go to Guantanamo for 2 weeks. Harry Hopkins was operated on today, nothing malignant found & the Mayo doctors think he will be better." The next day she wrote more about F.D.R.'s illness. He "is not well but more will be known by Monday & I think we can keep him in good health but he'll have to be more careful. I think the constant tension must tell & tho' he has said nothing, I think he's been upset by Elliott & Ruth."

Elliott and Ruth's decision to divorce depressed her deeply.

[E.R. to Joseph P. Lash:]   [March 2, 1944]
    I must just begin a letter to you to ease my own heart. It has been a hard day. Ruth wrote announcing that she had heard from Elliott & in ten days would send him papers to sign & file for her divorce. I had hoped they would wait till after the war & I am sick at heart & grieve for the children. I said goodbye to Johnny, when his ship leaves they go straight to the Pacific so I guess it was goodbye till the end of the war. I'm sorry for Anne & the kids & life hasn't seemed very rosy to me. . . . You said I was strong, well, I feel remarkably weak tonight. My "tummy" has felt queer all day & I'd like a shoulder to cry on! Since there isn't one handy, I probably will go to bed & be saner about it all tomorrow.

When I sought to comfort her, her answer, which arrived a month later, said simply, "I did write you a depressed letter & it is always easier to tell you how I feel than to tell anyone else. I don't know just why but it makes me feel better!"

She was constantly growing, and the stages of her growth after the estrangement with Franklin at the time of the Lucy Mercer affair were marked by her relationships. There had been Nancy Cook and Marion Dickerman, Earl and Hick, and now I was the one to whom she confessed I was a shoulder on which to lean. I was the "other" who, by the alchemy of psychic relationships, becomes the person who excites and encourages growth and intimacy. But it was only partially satisfactory. In her courtship days, when one after another of her debutante friends were wed, she had called young Franklin's attention to the words of the vows that were exchanged during the Episcopal service. They were prescriptive for her. To fall in love and marry meant to lose oneself in the other. In *Anna Karenina* the happiness that Levin and Dolly find in marriage might have described her own expectations.

She was helping Trude find a paying job, but "she mustn't get too tied up for you want a wife & mother as well as a co-worker. That is what she wants to be anyway & it does not allow one to do a full time outside job," she wrote me. I did not then fully understand the poignancy of her advice to me about my relationship with Trude.

[E.R. to Joseph P. Lash:]   [January 21, 1944]
    There is one thing I've always wanted to say to you. When you do come home & get engulfed in work, will you stop long enough now & then even if Trude is working with you to make her feel she is *first* in your life even more important than saving the world? Every woman wants to be first to someone sometime in her life & the desire is the explanation for many strange things women do, if only men understood it!

There was the nub of her alienation from Franklin. James said his father probably loved Lucy but that did not exclude love for his mother. That may have been the case, but Franklin did not give her the sense of intimacy and sharing for which she hungered. After the Lucy Mercer romance she never again had the feeling that she came first with him.

In the spring F.D.R. underwent the series of tests that were administered by Dr. Howard G. Bruenn, who had been newly brought in by Dr. (Admiral) McIntire. She saw all the doctors to learn the results of the tests. Whatever she learned she kept to herself. "F.D.R. is not off & won't go till Sat. at the earliest. He begins to be better however but it is slow." He did not go to Guantanamo but to "a place belonging to Mr. Baruch in South Carolina & he may stay 3 weeks or even four but on his return should be fine again." She did not write what the tests had shown nor what she had been told of the nature of F.D.R.'s illness. It had been late in March when Dr. Bruenn had been called in by Admiral McIntire, and for the first time F.D.R.'s illness was diagnosed as "hypertension, hypertensive heart disease, cardiac failure (left ventricular) and acute bronchitis." Anna later said that even if her mother had been told F.D.R. had hypertension it would have meant little to her, and Eleanor always denied that he had ever had a heart attack. Nor did she know that Baruch's plantation was not far from Mrs. Rutherfurd's place in Aiken, North

Carolina, and that Lucy was one of Franklin's guests. He was in his sixties and crippled and it was, said his son James, "a very real friendship and they shared the memory of a romance when both were young."

F.D.R.'s illness troubled and worried her, so did her children, especially Elliott and Ruth, and "Frankie is always a problem." She was severe with the latter but in many respects thought herself and Franklin's public career responsible for many of their vulnerabilities. The son of editor William Allen White came to dinner: "He rejoiced my soul expounding his theory on a Society for the Sons of Famous Fathers, motto, 'You are following in your Father's Footsteps.' Vice President Jesus Christ."

Franklin's illness imposed new duties on her. For a few weeks at the beginning of the year she thought that John Boettiger wanted Anna to come to London to be near him.

[E.R. to Joseph P. Lash:] [January 3, 1944]
. . . John I know will want her to get to England. Can I take care of the children satisfactorily? Not without giving up many other things, perhaps I should. Just for the minute I'm a bit stumped by the [word indecipherable] of decisions that I may have to make. Oh, well, if I keep from thinking selfishly they'll probably come out all right.

She did not have to solve that particular claim on her energies. John not only was ordered home but remained on duty in the States, and Anna gave up their house in Seattle to settle at the White House. She did so at her father's request—only, she later told me, after clearing it with her mother.

Eleanor no more than her husband was theoretically minded, but her intellectual curiosity was insatiable. She found Baruch's large views stimulating. "Smart girl," he commented when she indicated her distrust of a certain administration figure. Eleanor appreciated such a comment from that wily old man. "His report on reconversion is nearly ready & every move he's taking makes sense." Later that year when she was at Hyde Park she wrote that "Walter Reuther & Jim Carey came yesterday & stayed overnight. . . . I find Reuther always stimulating & Jim is always a dear. . . ." The next day she went on, "All of us felt Walter Reuther's quality. He is simple but sure of himself. . . ." Her active mind never stopped weaving projects. "I think I've been getting something started which may spur industry to plan with labor on work for disabled veterans & with the Veterans Bureau on the type of training needed. I got Jim Carey & Mr. Wilson of the G.E. who is the Exchairman of the W.P.B. to see 2 men, one a disabled officer today." Another train of thought was started by David Lilienthal, the head of TVA:

[E.R. to Joseph P. Lash:] [May 25, 1944]
I was reading Lilienthal this afternoon & I think the TVA story is interesting because of the vistas it opens for us & the other nations. The

world holds so many possibilities for people to have comfort & happiness that I pray our statesmen have wisdom or perhaps I should say that the majority have wisdom. They did give the FEPC a substantial appropriation even tho' the Southerners were solidly opposed!

With much to learn and much to do, she wrote almost weekly to all of her boys and helped Franklin where he allowed her to, adapting to his schedule and necessities. He spent more time at Hyde Park the winter of 1944, and that meant Eleanor also spent more time at the big house. She wrote in February when she and Trude drove over to the cottage to get some country clothes: "I always feel a little homesick when I go there & we are staying here & yet I think I will have to stay here a good deal off & on so I might as well get to like it!" She came back to her resistance to the big house in May. "I really must live in the big house this year whenever I can," she wrote me and voiced her pleasure that Trude would spend the summer at Hyde Park.

[E.R. to Joseph P. Lash:]   [May 19, 1944]
    I want to be at the cottage so I'm having everything I need in both places & then I can flit easily back & forth. My heart is in the cottage. I'll never like this big house but suddenly F. is more dependent, the children & grandchildren look upon this as home & the cottage is just mine, so I must try to keep this "lived in" & really pleasant! Never from choice would I live here however & never alone.

In June when she left Washington to make Hyde Park her summer headquarters she emphasized anew her negative feelings toward the big house:

[E.R. to Joseph P. Lash:]   [June ?, 1944]
    I've unpacked a little & have some photographs where I can enjoy them & feel at home but really living here is hard for me—I've made Mama's room pleasant & I can work in it & not feel her presence in the room but over here there is no getting away from the bigness of the house & the multitudes of people. F. has a diet, the Crown Princess [Martha of Norway] another & running this house is no joke! I'll be glad to be in the cottage next weekend.

F.D.R. in April had been convalescing at Hobcaw, Baruch's plantation in South Carolina. Eleanor herself flew down for a day at the end of April along with the Curtins of Australia.

[E.R. to Joseph P. Lash:]   [April 24, 1944]
    The Pres. looks better to me but I think he suspects the doctors don't know what is the matter so he worries & he told us he still had no "pep."

Dr. McIntire assures me he is confident the doctors do know & he is getting better.

F.D.R. remained at Hobcaw, she wrote at the end of April: "F.D.R. sounds better & is going to stay away all this coming week." Her letters were equally buoyant about Harry Hopkins. He had been ill and then checked into the Mayo Clinic. She had his daughter Diana in for a swim at the White House and his wife Louise for tea. "Harry is doing well & in two weeks they [he and Louise] will probably meet in Hot Springs, Va. & after a time there he hopes to come back to work."

On F.D.R.'s attitude toward a fourth term—

[E.R. to Joseph P. Lash:]   [May 1, 1944]
I think the conservative trend is evident throughout the country. I don't know what F. will decide but if he thinks he is needed I'm sure he'll make the fight & if he loses I shan't be as sorry as I would be if he didn't accept the responsibility when he felt he should. He will undoubtedly if he runs have an opposition Congress but he had that in Albany & it is not as hard to handle as a majority that won't stay with you! When the opposition has the majority, they have to accept responsibility & the Executive can appeal to the people.

As the war moved north of Guadalcanal I had volunteered for weather service on Green Island, a coral speck at the northern end of the Solomons. For a few weeks bulldozers rumbled day and night replacing jungle growths with air strips, and cloudbursts mired everything and everyone in seas of coral and mud. Life was a misery. Gradually a little fresh food appeared, a mess hall was built, tents were stabilized, existence became bearable. We "bitched" for the benefit of the home folks—they must never be allowed to forget how "grim" life was here—but I sometimes wondered whether the soldiers in World War I hadn't had it worse in the trenches. The few weathermen who were on flying status went out two or three times a week either to take a look at nearby Rabaul and radio back the weather or on the daylong flight across the Equator to Truk.

[Joseph P. Lash to E.R.:]
Our little weather unit has been assigned a small, stubby navy bomber in which we scout out possible targets for the weather. I went out on the first flight. I had seen my fill of the weather over the target but still we kept drawing closer. Finally the pilot turned and yelled "let's go home." I beamed but became even more apprehensive when he didn't turn the plane. A few moments later he yelled again and this time urgently, "Let's go home." Only then did I realize it was up to me to decide when we went home. We scooted out of there fast!

I usually was scared stiff on these missions, but they were preferable to an existence without adventure or risk.

Eleanor, who understood the desire to be tested and the taste for risk for herself, found it difficult to see others, especially those close to her, in danger. She cautioned me gently about flying. When she heard the news of Bob Morgenthau's ship being sunk from under him, she immediately called Elinor and followed with a note.

[E.R. to Elinor Morgenthau:]   Saturday
    I know you must be proud of all the wonderful things that have been said & written about Bob but also your heart must have stood still in reading it all. I congratulate you & Henry but I hope you will not have to go through such anxiety again.

A long letter from Eleanor crossed one of mine that had described in semiveiled terms life at APO 293 [Green Island].

[E.R. to Joseph P. Lash:]   [April 27, 1944]
    I was so glad that at last two letters had reached you & I feel sure the flow will be fairly normal from now on! This letter from you of April 19th with its information as to no fighting etc. led me to discover that the "map room" had given me wrong information on your A.P.O. after much protesting & promise of secrecy. I now know, & only one other person will know when I reach N.Y. on Saturday, where you are!
    I hope those showers materialize. You know some people are affected by distilled water & get dysentery, prickly heat, etc. I hope the well will help you.
    You know FDR has always said we progressed only from crisis to crisis & all you say is true. Those who think ahead & foresee will meet the need when it comes. Trude & I talk about a research institute very often. Between you the job could be superbly set up and carried through. I must say neither business nor the public inspire me with much confidence but the young returning soldier does. . . . The gallant cheerfulness is what gets you most for you realize what the night must be.
    . . . A letter from Adm. Halsey today says the war in his area is over & he's evidently very anxious to move on. I saw Gen. Eichelberger & his troops made a landing today.
    The President-elect of Costa Rica, his wife & son were here for tea. His Sec. of State is a man of 24! His son is at school in Los Angeles. I like him & think there are possibilities in him but he might be very ruthless too.
    Bobby Morgenthau was saved but his ship, 50 men & 3 officers were lost. He has now had his baptism of horror. Henry Jr. is gone bound for

the emerald isle first. I get all tight when I think of each & every one of you & I feel as tho' I could not stand another day & here you face another year—Gosh but we are homesick for you!

Joe, dearest, I must go to bed, but first I must add that I found your notes on Fromm's "Escape from Freedom"* very interesting. I want to talk to you about freedom. One can be free within the law & one can get over the "particle of dust" feeling by being oneself to the utmost & yet being related to the great upward struggles, all that one loves, human beings, nature, ideals, kinship with God & man add to the sense of relatedness. There is a point beyond which one cannot explain or think thro; one can only feel & believe—You won't believe that for 20 years perhaps!

Your thinking along these lines is growing clearer & more interesting. Christ was a great psychiatrist. He said we had to be like little children because he knew just thinking alone never solved the riddle which at some time preoccupies us all.

When I received Eleanor's letter, I wondered at an "inward center" that enabled her as almost a postscript to her letter to describe an approach to life with the simplicity and illumination that characterize all great statements. She wrote with such assurance and dispatch because all that happened, all whom she dealt with, were fuel for her ever-active imagination and intellect. Her constant sense of wonderment and curiosity also reflected a childlike self-questioning. "I'd like to talk long & peacefully & uninterruptedly with you," she had written Trude before leaving for the Caribbean, "& in the future with both you and Joe about some of the things which are the roots of our motivation. I'm so often conscious of falling short in that facing of ourselves & putting into practice what one accepts intellectually."

She confronted the contradictions between the democratic ideal and the American reality more honestly than any of us—in the first instance in regard to America's treatment of the Negro, as well as women and Jews, and above all the poor and exploited. The contradiction and the challenge it posed to her personally was an ever-recurring theme in her letters.

There was also a tough-minded side of her nature that enabled her to look unblinkingly at the grimmest necessities imposed by her desire to see the war won as quickly as possible. One weekend that spring she and Anna had argued with John Boettiger, now a major, over the policy of bombing Europe's cities.

---

* As a result of reading Fromm's *Escape from Freedom* I had become increasingly preoccupied with the problem of "What is Man?" I had written her: "Did the conceptions of the good and the beautiful vary from culture to culture or were there permanent and absolute values? Justice Holmes in his letters to Pollock remarks that more and more he was becoming persuaded that 'the sacredness of human life is a municipal ideal having validity only in the jurisdiction.' Perhaps all we can ever hope to achieve is a system of 'municipal' ideals which will make life tolerable and pleasant."

[E.R. to Joseph P. Lash:]   [April 27, 1944]

He's been reading reports on bombings & feels that we are building up
such a hate in Europe by our raids, he fears that the Germans have
evacuated Rome & established themselves outside & that we may still
bomb Rome & get a blast from the Pope. Of course all these things are
true & yet I think in the main we try to bomb cities & areas which will
prevent production & that is the only way we can prevent the loss of
many of our men. If we had a convention & both sides lived up to it &
no one used airplanes that would be different but if stopped they would
go on & think it showed our weakness & thus the war would be prolonged.—Am I wrong? Have I become hard-hearted? How do you look at
it? The Quakers and pacifists deluge me with literature along John's line
of thought.

Another letter along the same lines indicated little sympathy for conscientious
objectors.

[E.R. to Joseph P. Lash:]   [July 2, 1944]

The Quakers aren't happy over my views on C.O.'s so I've asked them
if they would not be happier to have me stay away from their meeting in
Antioch!

She sounded almost disappointed when she described her appearance at Antioch. She had been to Dayton and saw a "jet" plane—

[E.R. to Joseph P. Lash:]   [July 12, 1944]

& it flies at 450 miles an hour. Also a helicopter that settles & rises on a
tiny area. Then I spoke twice at Antioch & had questions each time.
Largely Quakers & "Brethren" (does that mean Mennonites?) but no
one asked me about C.O.'s.

Her tough-mindedness flashed again when Trude and I passed on the doubts
of some of our friends in Americans for German Freedom about the demand for
"unconditional surrender" put forward by Roosevelt and Churchill at Casablanca.
As the President would say a few weeks later at a press conference in Honolulu:

Q. And the goal with Japan is still unconditional surrender? The President: Still is with everybody. There has been a good deal of complaint
among some of the nice, high-minded people about unconditional surrender, that if we changed the term "unconditional surrender," the Germans might surrender more quickly.

Mr. Churchill and I have made no modification of the terms of unconditional surrender.

Eleanor's letter to me two weeks before reflected her own view.

[E.R. to Joseph P. Lash:] [July 12, 1944]

I doubt if "unconditional" surrender to us or even to the British is keeping the Germans fighting. I think they know that we will be decent but they know what their actions in conquered countries will bring them & I doubt if we can save them & that is what will keep them fighting as long as they can I fear. I think the President hesitates to get down to details. They all agreed on broad principles at Teheran but he knows there will be many points of dispute when details have to be set down & he wants as little to divide the Allies as possible until the war is won. There are disadvantages to this theory but I think he believes this is the safest course to follow.

She supported the President's position on unconditional surrender, but she was receptive to arguments from Trude and me against the division of Germany. Trude was in close touch with a Council for German Democracy that was headed by Paul Tillich and Paul Hagen. She sent Eleanor a proposed Council manifesto that Trude wanted to sign and that was strong on denazification but, as Trude wrote me, urged "no division of Germany nor destruction of its productive apparatus."

"I read the statement carefully," Eleanor replied to her, "& I cannot see why you should not sign it. Everything in it seems reasonable to me."

All that winter and spring of 1944 Eleanor had been conducting an inner soliloquy, using her friends as foils, about her attitude toward Franklin's running again. Suddenly at the end of April she wrote me, "Perhaps we will have left Washington when you return, will that be a disappointment to you?" It might have reflected her customary wariness about taking elections for granted. It might have reflected a sudden sense of Franklin's mortality.

I replied qualifiedly.

[Joseph P. Lash to E.R.:] [May 11, 1944]

Politically, yes, in one way, because as I wrote you, I believe we can achieve an orderly demobilization in the framework of full employment, and a decent peace, only under the President's leadership. . . . But in another way, still speaking in political terms, I would not be disappointed at all (were the issues not so crucial). . . . I think going into the opposition might be a healthy thing for us. . . . Personally I would not be disappointed. Of course the opportunity to be present on historical occasions has great fascination for me, as has the White House with its historical associations, but it has meant at the same time a gradual loss of all privacy. . . . It would be nice for a change to help you move, for instance, without it becoming a political event of front-page importance! I think we shall be able to have more fun as private citizens. . . .

"It was just about what I thought you'd say," was her comment.

The intensified bombings in Europe, including those of the Pas de Calais area, a possible invasion sector, and the dire warnings in the German press foreshadowed the imminence of D-Day.

[E.R. to Joseph P. Lash:]   [April 30, 1944]

We all feel the invasion must come soon in Europe & I confess to dreading it though I'll be relieved when it is over & the long fight has begun. I pray that our advance may be as rapid as the Germans but I fear that is impossible.

She was asked to prepare a radio speech for D-Day "& I can't think of what I want to say. I only know I don't want to say any of the things they suggested!" Then on June 5th she wrote: "F says there may be some news tomorrow & results will be uncertain for 30 or 40 days & I feel as though I couldn't bear it. To be nearly sixty & still rebel at uncertainty is ridiculous isn't it?"

The next day—

[E.R. to Joseph P. Lash:]   [June 6, 1944]

Well, Joe, dear, the first day of invasion is over, the last dispatch F. just read says that over a 60-mile front in Normandy we have cleared 10 miles. All has gone according to schedule tho' it was rough at the start & we have lost 1 destroyer, 1 mine sweeper, & 1 L.C.T. with how much loss of life we don't know. There is less tension but F keeps us all a bit undecided by saying that he doesn't know what he will do & when he hears Hitler is ready to surrender he will go to England at once & then in the next breath that he may go to Honolulu & the Aleutians! He feels very well again & looks well.

She hung on the radio, devoured the papers, and thought of nothing but the war. A letter to Trude apologized for not going to Hyde Park that weekend: "I feel cheated not to have the weekend at H.P. with you but I can see it was better to stay here." She did not explain why. She sent Trude and me each a copy of the President's D-Day prayer signed by him.* "They are having a hard time at the center of our line but if the weather improves things will go better.

"I spent the morning at Forest Glen [Hospital] & the afternoon at Walter Reed. Dorothy Thompson & her husband were here last night & we gave a dinner for the Polish Prime Minister & so go the days."

* It had been drafted by Anna and John.

A letter to me about Dorothy Thompson was more pointed.

[E.R. to Joseph P. Lash:]   [June 9, 1944]
Dorothy Thompson & her husband Mr. Kopf were here Wed. night & I like him. He's a Bohemian & he's changed her, she is happy & gentler & simpler. She came to see F.D.R. however, not me, so I'm glad she saw him!

The middle of June she transferred her activities to Hyde Park. "My last two days in Washington were very busy & I got on F's train last night with the Norwegians, a bit breathless & very weary!" There was a domestic note.

[E.R. to Joseph P. Lash:]   [June 21, 1944]
All last evening I wrestled with Earl & Simone! I use that word for mental not physical activity & believe me it was most active. I hope you & Trude never tie your dear selves up in such knots of misunderstandings & trivialities!

A paragraph crisply reported news that later made books.

[E.R. to Joseph P. Lash:]   [June 19, 1944]
Churchill announces he thinks things will go faster than we realize & I hope he is right. FDR told me tonight our air carriers fought the Japs & downed 300 of their planes off Saipan. One battleship hit but not disabled & the carriers o.k. but many of the young aviators must be gone. I can hardly bear it & I know Johnny will suffer. DeGaulle's beginning to make himself unpopular & perhaps in the end FDR will have the majority with him on his attitude towards him. F. tells me all the leaders are against Wallace but he thinks the people are largely for him & my hunch is that he's going to back him. . . .

On June 25th she wrote me:

The news this afternoon is very good & cheered us all. When Stalin says he feels the collapse of Germany is at hand I feel it must be in the offing. I cannot believe that Japan will go on long after that. . . . Oh! What a relief & joy it would be to know you would not have to await a rotation policy!

There was a cryptic reference to what I later realized was the development of the atomic bomb. Some of the physicists like Szilard and Fermi had approached her with their worries:

Dr. Lowen, the young N.Y. University professor who was so worried about the German secret discoveries has asked to see me again, so after doing a little household shopping I'm awaiting him here. We now have the discovery I'm told which he feared Germany would have first but I gather no one wants to use it for its destructive power is so great that no one knows where it might stop.

There was good news from Italy. Not only had Rome been liberated but Marshal Badoglio and his cabinet had resigned and would be succeeded by a cabinet representative of the anti-Fascist parties. The news pleased Eleanor.

[E.R. to Joseph P. Lash:]   [June 11, 1944]

Well, if you were here you would like the way things are going politically in Italy. I'm beginning to think I ought to be more patient for in the end FDR does seem to get pretty much what we want. The papers complain that we could have had it long ago, but who knows?

V

"I Wish I Were Free"

HE WAR was always with her, but events during the summer and fall of 1944 also were quickened by the presidential campaign, and especially by Vice President Henry Wallace's efforts to remain on the Democratic ticket as the President's running mate.

She supported Wallace, did her best to help him, although her letters to her closest friends usually contained the qualification "but he's not a good politician." She saw the Vice President just before his trip to Siberia and China, and wrote afterward, "He is keen about it but I don't think he grows in political wisdom however & that grieves me." Trude, who was at Hyde Park a good deal that late spring and summer, wrote me in early May, "The Boss would like Wallace as running mate but does not think he can get him renominated! Who will it be? Byrnes, Rayburn, Barkley, or Truman?"

The name Truman bobbed up in the letters of another of Eleanor's friends, Hick. She worked at the Democratic National Committee as full-time executive secretary of the Women's Division and continued to live at the White House. As early as March 1944 Hick alerted Eleanor to the push for Truman. She wrote her in the Caribbean—

[Lorena Hickok to E.R.:]   [March 23, 1944]
There's quite a boom on for Senator Truman for vice-president—un-

doubtedly inspired by Hannegan becoming Chairman of the National Committee. Personally, I very much prefer Truman to Sam Rayburn, who, I think is one of the weakest men in politics.

Eleanor tried to figure out Franklin's attitude. She sensed he was uncomfortable with Wallace, but he usually put it to her in terms of the opposition he heard from the party's political leaders because of Wallace's alleged drawbacks. "F. tells me," she wrote on June 19, "all the leaders are against Wallace but he thinks the people are largely for him & my hunch is that he's going to back him." She did not write of Franklin's White House dinner with such party chiefs as Ed Flynn, Frank Walker, Mayor Kelly, and Hannegan, at which Anna and John also were present, and at which Franklin accepted the organization view that someone other than Wallace was needed.

But Roosevelt's attitude seemed ambiguous and he moved cautiously. According to Wallace's diary, Roosevelt's dinner with the political leaders took place on July 11, a few days before the opening of the Democratic convention in Chicago. Roosevelt talked with Wallace both before and after that dinner, reported that the leaders felt he would be a burden on the ticket, but did not ask him to withdraw, saying, according to Wallace's notes, that he would send a letter to the convention "that he thought a lot of me, and that if he were a delegate to the convention he would vote for me. He would also go on to say that he did not wish in any way to dictate to the convention." Wallace's entry in his diary ends:

> When I was leaving I said to the President, "Well, I am looking ahead with pleasure to the results of next week no matter what the outcome." As I shook hands with him he drew me close and turned on his full smile and a very hearty handclasp, saying "While I cannot put it just that way in public, I hope it will be the same old team."

Was the President engaged in a charade in order to hold on to his labor and liberal supporters? Wallace later felt he had been taken in, and assumed that Eleanor always acted at Franklin's bidding.

Eleanor may have heard about Franklin's meeting with the party leaders from Anna, if not from the President himself. Of all the women about Roosevelt at the time, the President felt easiest with his daughter. Trude wrote me in mid-June, ". . . and Tommy told me that he still does not want to see many people, has lunch with Anna every day and clings to Anna and Mrs. R." Trude amended that a little later: "One thing struck me yesterday. Several times when we spoke of political possibilities and what the Boss might think about them—Mrs. R. said, 'Anna is the only one who knows about that.' " So Anna may have filled her in.

Eleanor's letters from Hyde Park were conflicted between her impulse to be loyally self-effacing and her desire to exert an influence on public events in her own right. She wrote Hick, who was on her way out to Chicago—

[E.R. to Lorena Hickok:] [July 7, 1944]

The days go by with plenty of people coming & going & the constant occupation that young people bring but no sense of participation in great events. I know the platform & candidates have to pussyfoot to keep a party together that ought to split apart!

Elliott is on the way to matrimony again but I've had not one word from him anymore than I had from Ruth about her marriage. . . .

F. is going westward & I will go as far as the coast and fly back so it shouldn't take more than seven days. This is secret so don't mention it. I shouldn't leave at all with the house & cottage to run & so many children.

"I dread another campaign," she wrote Hick a few days later as she prepared to board the presidential special, "& even more another 4 years in Washington but since he's running for the good of the country I hope he wins."

"I wrote a column on Wallace," she wrote me from Chicago, "but F. says I must hold it till after the convention. I wish I were free!"

Trude, who drove with the President and Mrs. Roosevelt and Tommy over to Highland in order to board the presidential train, wrote me—

[Trude W. Pratt to Joseph P. Lash:] [July 14, 1944]

It seems decided that the President will ask for Wallace but not get him. His *advisers* have convinced him that any firmer stand would be disastrous. I still am not convinced. Labor is firmly for Wallace, so are the Negroes.

"I hated to leave you the other day," Eleanor wrote Trude from the train—

[E.R. to Trude W. Pratt:] [July 16, 1944]

& I don't know that I'm being very useful on this trip as there is nothing to do. We make no stops except service stops. F.D.R. sleeps, eats, works & all I do is sit through long meals which are sometimes interesting & sometimes very dull. . . . Tommy and I played some gin rummy yesterday & I am a bit ahead, outside of that I've made a few observations from the window which you will eventually read in the column!

She was for Wallace even as she sensed that F.D.R. was distancing himself from the Vice President.

[E.R. to Joseph P. Lash:] [July 16, 1944]

The fight in the convention is over the V.P. nomination & F has written the chairman that he wants Wallace, or he may have put it even more carefully than that since I haven't seen the letter which comes out tomorrow. I can't tell but I'm not happy about it. I am no politician but I think he could have had Wallace & been as strong as he will be if they put a conservative on the ticket. Hannegan came on board in Chicago & F. said afterwards that Jimmy Byrnes seemed to be gaining strength, which from my point of view is deplorable. I am reading, preparing to write a review, Wallace's "Democracy Reborn." It is just a collection of his speeches but as I reread them carefully I find them very impressive & I think the man has grown to be a statesman but it is doubtless true as F. says that he is no politician.

I find myself contemplating the possibility of F's defeat with apprehension for the country, but from my own point of view four more years of the White House life is almost more than I can bear. I am very conscious of age & the short time in which I have to live as I like & I know that it is such selfish thinking that one has no right even to let it be in one's mind.

She was even blunter to Hick about her feeling that Franklin could have won with Wallace.

[E.R. to Lorena Hickok:]   [July 16, 1944]
. . . Mr. Hannegan came to see F. at the Chicago station & I gathered after he left that a conservative would be the next V.P. I'm sorry because I think it is bad politics not to stick to Wallace as well as disloyal but I never would be any good in politics! One of my troubles would be ever getting excited about anything but that is just a sign of old age, & I hope you are able to live through these next few days.

Although she insisted she was no politician, she had a sixth-sense feeling for political possibilities and how they should mesh with longer-range goals. "I'm soaked in the convention," she had written me at the end of June in reference to the Republican gathering that nominated Dewey and Bricker.

[E.R. to Joseph P. Lash:]   [June 27, 1944]
I listened to all the speeches but Hoover's & I feel they have worked themselves into a hopeful frame of mind. I'm not as cynical on all governments as your New Zealanders* but I have a curious feeling tonight. Too many promises were made to the soldier, the farmer, the worker, the business man. We would return to a constitutional government; we would restore to Congress & the States their rights under the Constitution, free enterprise wld give us jobs, & revised taxation would lighten our burdens! All promises & no performance. We'll promise too, in our con-

---

* After logging 100 hours of flying time, I had been given a week's rest leave in Auckland, New Zealand.

vention & how little any of us really know what we can do after the war. All one should say is: "Build a character that can meet new conditions without fear, develop the power to think things thro' & face facts & recognize the interdependence among men."

I wonder why we can't all be humble & less bombastic?

But when I indicated unhappiness over both major parties she replied firmly that talk about party realignment should not cut across or thwart the election campaign.

[E.R. to Joseph P. Lash:]   [July 3, 1944]
I'm interested in your idea of writing an essay "In Search of a Party," & we were discussing the question the other day. I am not that kind of democrat our Southern "white supremacy" group represents & yet with labor as it is which labor party would one join A.L.P. or the Hillman P.A.C.? No party would probably meet one's desires all the time & yet organization is the only way to have strength & some party discipline is essential.

She saw the basic issue clearly and cautioned the President and his friends:

[E.R. to Joseph P. Lash:]   [July 9, 1944]
. . . the Dewey-Bricker ticket is not going to be a pushover. It is part of the fight of the future between power for big moneyed interests & govt. control & more interest on the part of the people in their govt.

That was why she was so strongly for Wallace's renomination. Franklin's letter on Wallace, when she saw it, seemed to her—

[E.R. to Joseph P. Lash:]   [July 18, 1944]
pretty lukewarm. He told Hannegan he would accept Douglas or Truman but it looks like Byrnes. All the military on the train, the high-ups at least, & Elmer Davis think Byrnes would be marvellous. I was surprised to hear Davis agree & began to understand some of his assistants who have always puzzled me.

There has been a horrible explosion in San Francisco Bay with hundreds of men killed. Our casualties at Saipan also horrify me & yet I guess that is what has brought about Tojo's fall. F. says from there bombing Japan will be easy. By the way around early September I may go on another trip to a place I visited before but this time at the start I'll be an adjunct. The plans are not all made as yet.*

* This was a veiled reference to London where evidently she was to accompany the President. But the defeat of Hitler took longer than sometimes seemed likely in early summer.

She saw James and Romaine and Anne in San Diego and then took them all back to the train to see F.D.R. She went with James to see Colonel Carlson at the Naval Hospital, for the leader of the Marine Raiders had been wounded at Saipan.

[E.R. to Joseph P. Lash:]   [July 20, 1944]
    Well, we listened to all the convention speeches last night & the whole thing seems more alive because of the V.P. contest. All the speeches were too long. I'm gradually learning the value of brevity. Louis Howe used to say, "Begin with something startling, say what you have to say & sit down." He was right. F. thinks he tried not to be a dictator & is pained at some of the reactions. As a matter of fact most people want to be told, they don't want to decide for themselves. They like to be able to blame someone afterwards if they make a wrong decision! Wallace is fighting. He spoke on the air briefly last night & it was nice but not inspiring.

Roosevelt was irked by columnist and old friend Ernest Lindley's reaction to his "pro-Wallace" letter. "F. felt," Eleanor wrote Hick, "that he, F., didn't want to be a dictator. Hard position when you don't want to be a dictator but you want your own way. I still hope for Wallace." She left Franklin in San Diego, where he and his military aides boarded the heavy cruiser USS *Baltimore* for a journey across the Pacific to confer with General MacArthur and Admiral Nimitz and other commanders. "I'm sick about the whole business," Eleanor confessed to Hick on her return to Hyde Park, "but of course not surprised. I don't know myself what F. wanted but I know he thought Wallace couldn't be nominated & told him so."
    "I was sorry about Wallace & wish F. had been willing to 'dictate' a little! Truman is good I imagine but the bosses were for him so I'm suspicious!" she told Hick. "We were gloomy tonight about the Wallace defeat," Trude wrote me after talks with Eleanor at Hyde Park. "The truth is the Boss did not want Wallace, thought himself that he was a mystic and dreamer. And, says Mrs. R., he never felt at ease with Wallace after he had treated him so unfairly in the W-Jesse Jones fight."*
    Despite Eleanor's disappointment over the Wallace defeat, her letter to me defended the President against the resentful and angry charges of some labor leaders and liberals.

[E.R. to Joseph P. Lash:]   [July 29, 1944]
    I think the liberals as led & symbolized by Wallace & the labor groups as represented by the P.A.C. learned some bitter lessons in Chicago. I am constantly surprised that I do not get angry anymore at the bosses but just greatly annoyed with the other groups who are so slow to understand how things operate! You have to have the delegates to win in a conven-

* See Chapter I.

At the opening of *The Army, Play by Play,* 1943. John Golden on Mrs. Roosevelt's left, Fiorello La Guardia behind Golden. Old friend and lawyer Harry Hooker to E.R.'s right and next to him Trude Pratt. (Courtesy Franklin D. Roosevelt Library.)

Eleanor Roosevelt in 1943. Among the few photos of herself that she liked.

Eleanor Roosevelt in the South Pacific, Admiral William F. Halsey on her left. "Guadalcanal is no place for you," he first told her, and then later relented. "I was ashamed of my original surliness. She alone had accomplished more than any other person, or any group of civilians, who had passed through my area." (Courtesy Franklin D. Roosevelt Library.)

Eleanor Roosevelt addressing group of patients on Guadalcanal during her 1943 trip to South Pacific. (Courtesy Franklin D. Roosevelt Library.)

E.R. with Elinor Morgenthau at the "Army at War" Art Exhibition. (Courtesy Franklin D. Roosevelt Library. With permission of Cosmo-Sileo.)

As Franklin's surrogate at the 1945 Inaugural dinner. She is shaking hands with Henry Wallace, who she had hoped would be renominated as Vice President. (Courtesy Franklin D. Roosevelt Library/Thomas McAvoy, *Life* magazine © 1945, Time Inc.)

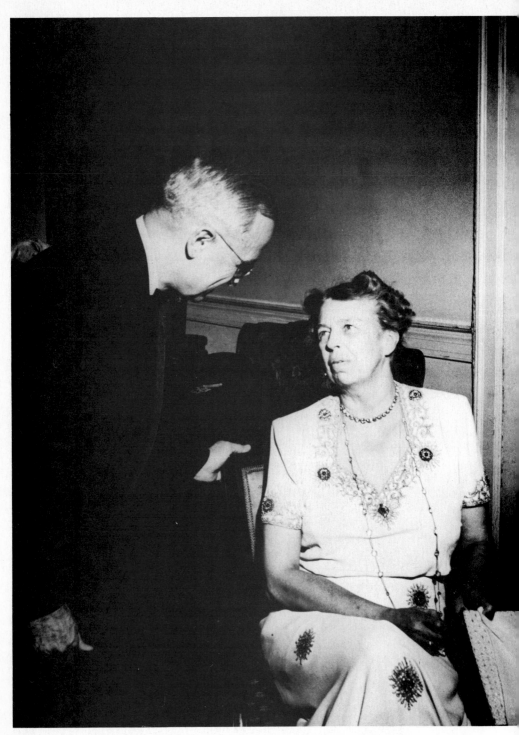

With Vice President-elect Harry Truman at the Inaugural dinner. "I am told that Senator Truman is a good man," she had written in the summer. "I hope so for the good of the country." (Courtesy Franklin D. Roosevelt Library/Thomas McAvoy, *Life* magazine © Time Inc.)

In the Rose Garden at Hyde Park, April 15, 1945. (Bettmann Archives)

Broadcasting on V-E Day, May 8, 1945. A woman of sorrows. (Courtesy Franklin D. Roosevelt Library. With permission of UPI. Bettmann Archive.)

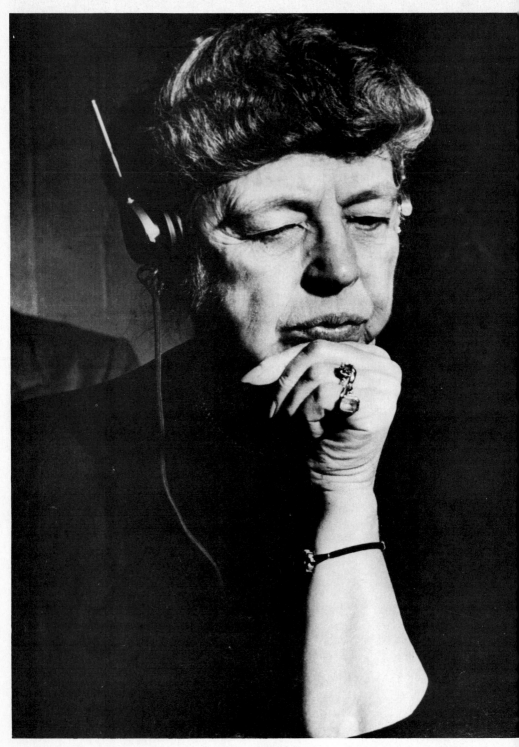

At Lake Success during a meeting of the United Nations Human Rights Commission. (Courtesy Franklin D. Roosevelt Library. With permission of Agence France-Presse.)

At the 1947 UN General Assembly. Secretary of State George Marshall at her left and Ambassador Warren Austin, head of the delegation. John Foster Dulles at her right. (Courtesy Franklin D. Roosevelt Library.)

E.R. with Fala by the pond behind her Val-Kill cottage. (Courtesy Franklin D. Roosevelt Library.)

A 1949 photograph. (Courtesy Franklin D. Roosevelt Library. With permission of N.Y. *Herald Tribune*.)

Esther Lape. They were friends from 1921 on. "I don't think she ever stopped loving someone she loved," Esther said of Eleanor's feeling for Franklin.

tion & you have to control the machinery to elect the delegates. Many Wallace followers feel FDR double-crossed Wallace. He did not. The people around him convinced him that he should dictate his choice of V.P. to this convention in the interests of party unity & Wallace was not going to add strength to the ticket because the average person considered him starry-eyed. (This is where I think they were wrong: it wasn't the average person but the *conservative & politician.*) F. had Sam & Ickes meet & tell Wallace & they saw him, showed him the letter & Wallace said that he wanted to make the fight but wanted no more than that from F. (I felt that the letter was not strong enough.) Hannegan then wrote F. asking if Wallace could not be nominated wld he accept Truman or Douglas. F. wrote that he would & added that he thought either one would strengthen the ticket. He had not said that in the letter to Wallace & that gave the bosses the chance to say Truman was really his choice. Then in Chicago on the train Hannegan told him, FDR, Byrnes wld be nominated. F. felt he wld lose votes as Wallace wld, tho different ones & told Hannegan & Byrnes if the latter withdrew making a statement that he did so in deference to the President's wishes. Wallace behaved wonderfully & he has come out a man of greater stature & I think may develop into the person to unify labor & independent forces tho' it is early yet to know.

Coming home to Hyde Park meant sleeping at the big house even though Franklin was in the Pacific. Anna's children were with her and domiciled there, and preferable though her cottage was, family obligations came first, except when she went over to the cottage to work with Tommy, chat with Trude, and swim in the pool. She went up to Boston to attend Marguerite LeHand's (Missy's) funeral nearby. Bedridden and speechless after her stroke, Missy had kept going, watched over by her relatives, until her death. Eleanor was glad to get a letter off to me from the Statler in Boston—

[E.R. to Joseph P. Lash:]   [August 2, 1944]
since I thought I'd have time to write at the apartment last night but Tommy wanted to talk. Living in the big house means that. I do my work with Tommy but I'm not over there when she is free to talk. Trude spends hours when she should be writing or sleeping trying to make up for my absence but nevertheless Tommy doesn't like my change of abode! I miss being at the cottage too & running the big house with its servants & children & guests is quite a chore but I've never let such things bother me & since I know it must be as long as F. wants to live there I've made up my mind to make it as pleasant & easy as possible. It took quite a while to reach this philosophy however so I can't blame Tommy!

Miss LeHand died early Monday morning so I am here for the funeral. Her death must have been a release & I'm glad F. is away for he would have felt he had to come & these journeys are always depressing. I fly back & speak at Dubinsky's Labor Party dinner & visit the C.I.O. War Relief work rooms this p.m. & see Hick who wants to tell me about the convention from her point of view.

I dread this campaign. I feel that no one can do much, the lines are already drawn. Dewey will talk. F. will travel & talk some but the people know now what they want I think. I don't know how it will turn out. If F. loses I'll be personally glad, but worried for the world! Four more years would seem a long time!

There were difficulties for Trude at Hyde Park. Her children were resented by the Roosevelt grandchildren, and that had to be straightened out. Trude voiced another discontent in a letter to me at the end of her summer at Hyde Park.

[Trude W. Pratt to Joseph P. Lash:]   [September 17, 1944]
Real friendship is terribly difficult to establish and to maintain and I don't think Mrs. R. has any real friends—or not many. She is either a mother to people or a mother confessor—or a teacher, or protector. And in return they want to own her.—But I can't be her child, and I don't need protection—and I am not tempted to give up my own identity. But I want very much to be her friend, and I now think we can be friends.

Hick was one of the possessive ones whom Trude had in mind. Hick returned to New York from Chicago to set up headquarters for the women at the Biltmore, the location of the Democratic National Committee. Hick wrote Eleanor of her run-in with the chairman, Robert Hannegan.

[Lorena Hickok to E.R.:]   [No date]
I finally got the rooms I wanted at the Biltmore, but Mr. Hannegan phoned Mrs. Tillett [the head of the Women's Division] and complained because I kicked up such a fuss. I told her I didn't care—that I was annoyed with Mr. Hannegan. She seemed a bit shocked. I'll do no more fighting from now on. She can get things for herself, in her own way. But I'm convinced that the only way to keep Mr. Hannegan under control is to get tough with him every now and then. Not to mention Mr. Pauley!

Eleanor sought to cool Hick's combativeness. "Do let Mrs. Tillett do the fighting, she ought to do it!" Partly Eleanor worried about Hick's health, but there was more to it than that. "Someone has suggested to me that Mrs. Tillett would be aided by a conference with the President and I'll try to get it arranged while in Washington next week," she wrote Hick.

Eleanor sent Trude in to headquarters to talk with Hick where she might work again as she had in the 1940 campaign. Hick gave her research to do. It did not go smoothly. "Hick vetoes everything I suggest and spends her time telling me everything is taken care of. . . . But, you know, even though I expected it, Hick's continuous references to Mrs. R—her never-ending stories at every-so-slight opportunity—amaze me. It is probably very healthy for me to see it, because the danger always exists that I might sometimes say, 'Mrs. R. thinks this or that'—and I shall certainly be less apt to now." Hick proved too much to take and, when Doris Byrne, the head of the Women's Division of the New York state organization, asked Trude to become her assistant, she accepted. ". . . I decided it would be a little better if I could work further away from Hick . . . there will not be any jealousy downstairs,—and one can really work."

"Your difficulties with Hick are the kind we will always encounter," I cautioned Trude. ". . . I would like to see you secretary of the Women's Division, but you won't have any chance if you allow yourself to be provoked into open war by Hick."

FDR returned from the Pacific. Absence and distance enabled those closest to him who before had seen him daily to sense a certain deterioration in his condition.

[E.R. to Joseph P. Lash:]   [Aug. 18, 1944]
    FDR seems to have enjoyed his trip thoroughly but he does look older
& he has to accept certain limitations which I think he feels are the price
of finishing his job. He rests after lunch but he does not mind people for
meals now. He talks very little but I feel he is optimistic . . .

A few days later, Eleanor again referred to FDR's looks.

[E.R. to Joseph P. Lash:]   [Aug. 23, 1944]
    He still complains of getting tired too quickly & he looks older. Whatever he had last spring took a toll but I guess he still feels his experience
& equipment will help him do a better job than Mr. Dewey. . . .

Trude also was troubled, and from 9,000 miles away I tried to assuage her worries.

[Joseph P. Lash to Trude W. Pratt:]   [September 6, 1944]
    You speak of how the President looks. I don't trust the photographs
that are appearing because I know the Republican press is trying to build
up a picture of him as an irritable old man. But it would be extraordinary
if his face did not show the marks of the last twelve years. What interested me in the photographs that I have seen lately, however, were the
way the President seemed to look more and more like the old Mrs.
Roosevelt as I remembered her. Have you had the same impression?

Among the people Eleanor invited to Hyde Park that summer to use the cottage and the pool were two veterans who had lost their legs overseas. Watching these young men swim in the pool despite their amputated legs caused Eleanor to burst forth, as she often did—

[E.R. to Joseph P. Lash:] [August 26, 1944]
If we don't make this a more decent world to live in, I don't see how we can look these boys in the eyes. They are going to fight their handicaps all their lives & what for, if the world is the same cruel, stupid place.

There was little she could do, she feared, but despite such self-deprecation, her ability to seek out and face the realities of human suffering and courage and to always ask of herself "what can I do?" was itself a measure of her sense of fellowship with all human beings.

Franklin had telephoned her in mid-August to say that "Uncle J. could not come so W.C. is coming to Canada & we will go there about Sept. 12th but I need only be there about three days." She and Tommy had gone up to Albany by train to spend a day with Earl and Simone. "Both told me things were much better & they were happier so I feel happier."

Events of world consequence alternated in her letters with news of family and friends.

[E.R. to Joseph P. Lash:] [Sept. 4, 1944]
. . . We are getting so near Germany that the War Dept. is sitting up nights over the plans for occupation. It looks as though the Germans really preferred the Americans & British to reach their soil before or at least at about the same time as the Russians. I have an idea that this Canadian meeting will not be all smooth sailing since many things put aside in the past must now be settled.

Sisty and Buzz had left in mid-August—"it is going to be lonely without them"—and after Labor Day, when Trude and her children prepared to say goodbye, she wrote, "I feel sad tonight. Seeing the children & Trude packing today really brought to an end what has been for me a happy time." She took Trude to the train and the next day together with Tommy was in Westbrook, Connecticut.

[E.R. to Joseph P. Lash:] [September 6, 1944]
Esther is an interesting person to be with, even tho' her activities are circumscribed she lives so much with ideas & reads the news of the world from so many sources that she has some of Louis's ability to gauge public trends.

She went with Franklin to Quebec for the conferences with Churchill. Mrs. Churchill was with the latter. Because Eleanor knew it gave her friends pleasure, she wrote them, using the Citadel's regal letterheads. There was not much for the women to do, but the President summoned Henry Morgenthau, Jr., the Secretary of the Treasury, to come and present his ideas on the treatment of Germany's economy.

[E.R. to Joseph P. Lash:]   [September 11, 1944]
I hope for the sake of these negotiations & the future that F. is elected & continues vigorous in action till the major trends are established. I talked to him & to Henry M. & I'm interested to find how much F. knows & keeps to himself even from people like Henry M. & yet he lets them all talk. I told Trude that Henry told me how thoughts were running on Germany but I'm not sure F. has made up his mind. I think he asks some of the questions Trude once asked. The more speeches Dewey makes the less I trust him & that is not partisanship for I can be pretty objective! . . .
I'm going back Thursday to dine with Fjr as he leaves Friday for your part of the world & is likely to be gone till the war ends. He looked well when I saw him last Friday in town.
I went to the Artists Com. for Roosevelt Friday a.m. & they are the first active group I've seen. . . . The rest of the day I spent with Cousin Susie & it was sad & very funny in spots. She discovered what she calls "the middle class" this summer at the Inn in Buck Hills Falls & was surprised that she liked them but even more surprised that they were against F.D.R.

A relaxed note went to Trude.

[E.R. to Trude W. Pratt:]   [September 12, 1944]
The ladies have no duties so I'm being lazy & luxurious. I have breakfast in bed but it doesn't appeal to me much except it is a good time to read! Tommy & I did two columns this a.m. but outside of that & a big dinner to which she came last night I've not been able to see much of her since I must do things with the other "ladies"!

She lamented to Elinor, "It seems such a waste of time. The ladies' duties are all social & it would be boring except for the meals with a few people when the P.M. & F. are entertaining. I like Mrs. Churchill & Princess Alice but I don't grow intimate quickly." The Churchill party was coming to Hyde Park from Quebec, she informed Elinor, and added, "Will you & Henry come to dinner Sunday night at 7:45?" A letter to Hick was in the same vein except for a perceptive comment on the complexity of the problems that suddenly confronted Roosevelt and Churchill:

"I don't know what work goes on here but we talk much at meals. These people are all nice people & in some ways that is discouraging because they've not found the answers. How can we hope that they'll find them in the future."

In the meantime, as the summer ended and autumn began, there had been a major change in my own life in the army. The war had quieted down in the South Pacific as U.S. and Anzac forces moved farther north. With little to do, morale became a major problem. Orientation or Information and Education classes on "why we fight" and the like began to be emphasized. Such classes and lectures were supposed to be handled by officers but they were delighted to pass them on to enlisted men. Suddenly I found myself in August 1944 lecturing and teaching. It was duck soup for me and was noted by the regional headquarters of the Seventeenth Weather Squadron, whose detachments covered the South Pacific. I was transferred to Noumea in New Caledonia, the headquarters base of the Seventeenth, and put to work to prepare an orientation manual for weathermen. I ran into old friends there and they reminded me that there was an I&E School at Washington and Lee and that the South Pacific had a quota for each class. Within a few weeks I had, with the help of Morale Services of Base Command, completed the handbook and it was sent out to weather detachments all over the South Pacific. I also had found out more about the school at Lexington. "Can you send me some Roosevelt buttons?" I asked Trude and shortly afterward sent some auspicious news.

[Joseph P. Lash to Trude W. Pratt:]   [August 30, 1944]
. . . I am fearful of raising your hopes but we finally located the channel thru which applications for Washington and Lee are submitted. Lt. Gershman went down to have a talk with the Lt. Col. who assigns the quotas out to subordinate units and who apparently has the final say on who goes. He talked to the Colonel about me & the Colonel thought I could go on the next quota! So Lt. McEneny, our Personnel Officer, quickly drafted an official letter requesting that I be sent. It was a swell letter and was signed by the C.O.

I was close to hysteria at the prospect. So was Trude, who shared the news with Eleanor, who wrote me from Quebec.

[E.R. to Joseph P. Lash:]   [September 8, 1944]
. . . You do write good letters, but the news that you might get back to the "School" & on the Nov. quota is a great excitement to us. You & Trude must not count on it too much but of course we all do & I'm keeping my fingers crossed and praying. Trude & I talk sensibly to each other about it & then hug each other & know we don't mean what we say.

The developments came fast. That same day I was writing home:

> I went around to talk with Lt. Col. Shreve, who is the head of Morale Services, and who is really the final arbiter here in the matter of who returns to school. He told me he had approved my application, and that now it was only a matter of the theater's getting its next quota.

A week later:

> I saw Colonel Shreve today and he told me the quota had come through for the November class and I was on the quota . . . and he feels pretty confident that I will be sent to OCS from Washington and Lee.

"She looks transfigured at the thought," Eleanor wrote me, "& I hope so much you two will not be disappointed."

[E.R. to Joseph P. Lash:]   [September 14, 1944]
     The Negro situation in the Army, &, therefore, in the homes of the Negro soldiers seems to be bad. I don't see how we can escape a decision on the treatment of Negroes everywhere when the war is over & whether we can do it without bloodshed is a moot question. Half my mail is on this subject.

The weekend of the 16th Trude was at Hyde Park as was Hick. "Of course Trude & I talked of little else but your chances of returning & we even planned the wedding as we walked through the woods. When you two are married I shall feel that one of my great desires has come to pass!"

Hick, in advance of her visit, had sent Eleanor a long letter on leaving the Democratic Committee. If F.D.R. won she might stay until April to break in a new person, but a "long rest," she thought, might prolong her life "by several years. . . . I know I'd not be interested in staying with the Democratic National Committee if there should be formed a new liberal party with people like you and Henry Wallace and Helen Gahagan [Douglas] leading it."

For Eleanor it was a busy weekend at Hyde Park. There was the President's household to run as well as her own cottage. Sometimes it seemed to get too much for her and writing appeared to help. She lamented she had little time to read Sumner Welles's book written after he had left the State Department, *A Time for Decision.*

[E.R. to Joseph P. Lash:]   [September 18, 1944]
     . . . my time slips away in such useless ways. Today for instance I've just been a glorified housekeeper! My household however changed every hour

& I just gave all the orders & then I had to change them all! These are
the days when the resentment at the tyranny of people & things grows on
me until if I were not a well-disciplined person I would go out & howl
like a dog!

The Churchills & party came at 11, Harry Hopkins at 12, the Duke of
Windsor at 12:15. After lunch I dashed to the cottage & did one column,
returned at 3:30 changed all the orders given at 12:30 & walked with
Mrs. Churchill for an hour & a half ending up at F's cottage for tea,
worked again from 6–7:15, dashed home and had Henry & Elinor Morgenthau & the Lytle Hulls for dinner. Now the mail is done & my spirit
is calm & I can enjoy writing you. I do not agree with Mr. Churchill on
Spain & he insists on bringing it up at every meal. He talks picturesquely
but I'm almost tempted to say stupidly at times. Table talk has been
interesting however. Evidently he expects us all to meet before long at
the Hague, the paratroops having landed in Holland. I'll be glad when
Holland is freed. Princess Juliana has gone to England & her goodbye
letter was very sweet. There was almost a note of regret in it.

They, the Churchills, leave tomorrow night. I will go to Washington
returning on Sunday next. I go with Elinor Morgenthau, leaving in the
late afternoon, to Oswego, to visit the refugee camp. I have a feeling I
am going to find it very sad. Telling oneself that people might be worse
off isn't much good.

Her next letter to me was full of the Oswego visit and the campaign.

[E.R. to Joseph P. Lash:]   [Sept. 21, 1944]
I got home from Oswego & the refugee camp late last night. It was an
interesting day, heartwarming because the people were so evidently
happy to be free from fear but pathetic beyond words because they were
such good people. Educated, professionals & merchants I gathered for
the most part, the one man had a chain of motion picture theaters & had
written scripts in Hollywood, another was an opera singer with a beautiful trained voice. About 400 of the 982 came from JugoSlavia & look like
exceptional people. There are 14 nationalities represented & 4 religions,
50 Catholics, 10 Greek Orthodox, 10 Protestant & the rest Jewish. The
attempt to make the partitioned off barracks like homes is heart-breaking.
I cannot help wishing that those who want to stay might stay. The
Oswego people seem to have welcomed them & there is appreciation
apparently that they have much to contribute to the community. . . .

The campaign seems not to move. I think all at the top are new &
inexperienced & no plans were prepared. I would be troubled but I feel
that people have made up their minds & don't want to bother with
meetings. How they will vote I don't know but campaign activity will

have little effect now I think. Mr. Dewey's train progresses. At first I heard the crowds were small, now I don't know much about the coast. His speeches could & should be answered but the papers print only his speeches. Tonight Wallace spoke at Md. Sqr. Our static was bad but the papers should carry his speech. Saturday night F. makes his first speech. Rumors fly & organized whispering campaigns flourish as usual: "the President is very ill," "we are getting a divorce," I have said "all para-troopers are beasts & will have to be reeducated to civilized living" etc. etc. You are familiar with it all.

Trude is now working for Doris Byrne and I hope she can do something. . . .

It was a difficult time for Tommy. The summer, she told Esther, had gotten her down.

[Tommy to Esther Lape:]   [September (?) 1944]
. . . Perhaps I am jealous, although I have no real reason to be—none of these people threaten my job or my personal life. I know E.R. well enough to know that she gets bored with people after a while and I fully realize that I am an old subject. As soon as Trude and Joe get organized and settled that will lessen, I am sure.

I was amused at Harry Hooker the other day. E.R. has asked him to get a transcript of Joe's divorce, etc., so they won't have to waste time when he gets back in getting married, and he was telling me all he had to do. In the course of his conversation, he said that Trude was one of the most beautiful women, etc., and had the best mind *for a woman* of anyone he knew and that he could not understand what she saw in Joe. He knew that E.R.'s interest was because Joe had been kicked around, etc. Harry is such a bellwether and tells everything that is said to him, I wonder how he would like it if I repeated his snooty remarks about Joe. Mrs. Kermit Roosevelt was lyrical about Trude, her brilliance, her hard work, her charm, her tact, etc. Hick also put in a plug for her, even though she was the one who fixed it so that Trude would work for the state committee and not the national. I must have looked surprised because later Hick said she had told Mrs. R. those things about Trude because "Gosh, Tommy, there isn't much I can do to make her happy."

Tommy realized that she was letting off steam against the "hypocrites and fabricators," as she put it in another part of the letter, but after the election she intended to make it plain to Mrs. Roosevelt that, devoted as she was to her, if she wanted to get someone else, "I am unwilling to stay on and become an obligation or a duty."

During Hick's visit she had evidently strongly urged Eleanor to speak up on the matters she felt keenly about and not to worry about the impact on Franklin's campaign. Eleanor's letter saying she loved having Hick at Hyde Park urged Hick to leave the Democratic National Committee sooner rather than later. She again expounded her credo of political loyalty and service to Franklin.

[E.R. to Lorena Hickok:]   [September 21, 1944]
     Don't worry, dear, I don't think I could help fighting for the things I believe in as long as I live. There really isn't any use in making the campaign harder for F. however. When it is over I can go right ahead.

An affectionate note from Hick sent to arrive on Eleanor's birthday avoided wishing her a "happy" and asked instead for "a *contented* birthday. You are still my favorite person in the world." In passing, Hick asked whether Eleanor had been surprised by the sudden death of Willkie, who was admired by independents and with whom the President secretly was seeking a postelection entente. Eleanor answered stoically. "Yes, dear, I thought about Wilkie *[sic]* but why should we be surprised? There is a destiny you know. FDR seems to be going strong now. He is going to make more speeches." Her general attitude was that one did the best one could, but should never be surprised by fate's interventions. Her own life with Franklin was as good an example as any. She had entered the White House filled with foreboding that the real Eleanor would disappear, yet every poll, the mail, the demands on her from every side, showed that the country was beginning to realize what a rare person there was at its center. The more she fled the limelight, the more it shone upon her and the nation liked what it saw.

     For several weeks my moods in New Caledonia had oscillated between intense expectancy over the prospect of getting home and dread that G-2, which so far as I could make out had left me severely alone overseas, would reawaken and at the last moment cancel my orders. Despite misgivings that I might be tempting fate, I wrote Trude that a "Nov. 8th" wedding was fine, "altho I shall be back east by the last week in October." I agreed with her that a small ceremony attended by "Mrs. R., Tommy, my family, the children and whomever else you want" to be followed by a reception later was "wonderful" and added the practical note, "You should reserve a room in Lexington" [Va.] where the Information and Education School was located.

     Finally—

[Joseph P. Lash to Trude W. Pratt:]   [September 25, 1944]
     This morning as I sat at my desk a telephone call came from Base Command. "Sergeant Lash?" "This is he." "Sergeant, what will your furlough address be in the States? We have to write it in the order." I gulped hard and told him "245 West 11th Street." "That's all, thanks."

I let out a yowl that startled everyone in headquarters, but not until I was on the boat did I feel secure. The experience with Counterintelligence was taking its toll. However much I tried to bury my anxieties I would henceforth face the problem whether my response to people and situations did not reflect terrors and demons whose power varied inversely with the distance at which I kept them at bay.

I sent Eleanor a birthday letter just before boarding the troopship SS *General Morton* for the return trip to the States.

[Joseph P. Lash to E.R.:]   [October 1, 1944]

I mentioned to you that I had been invited to speak before a Signal Corps outfit, which I did on Friday. Afterwards the Sergeant in charge of the program told me that they had thought of inviting me to speak on the subject of "Eleanor Roosevelt," but in view of the election had decided against it.

And as he told me this I said to myself—that is a subject on which I very much would have liked to have spoken, and what would I have said? How you had made the ornamental office of First Lady into an expression of American democracy's concern with all the people; how you had transformed the White House from a symbol of remoteness and officialdom into one of warm friendliness and hospitality; that you had done all these things not for political gain or prestige but because of the promptings of your great heart. And that it was that heart of yours which had aligned you with all the forces and movements in America that were battling the age-old battle to give men and women a chance for a decent life; that the same warm love which caused you to befriend an unfortunate family or a luckless person caused you to help an oppressed minority, a trade union, a youth organization. That none of these things were done without a struggle, a struggle against tradition and custom, against family sometimes, and class, and against your own shyness and lack of preparation for public life. And that as the political passions of the times subsided, you would loom ever larger in the hearts and imaginations of the American people and that your life would be held up as an example to all.

VI

No "Dresden Doll"

ELEANOR'S REPLY to my birthday forecast awaited me when the "snortin' *Morton*" berthed at San Francisco. The latter was the troop transport that had taken us back from the Pacific. Humility and self-effacement were in her letter, but she did not wholly rebuff my assertion of the way she had loomed ever larger in the public mind.

> [E.R. to Joseph P. Lash:]   [October 22, 1944]
> Your birthday letter will always be dear to me. You say such nice things & I know you think them, & if I don't deserve them still I love you to think them.

The '44 campaign was in its final days. She did not campaign in the sense of soliciting support for Franklin's candidacy, but her presence, almost as powerfully as Franklin's, magnetized a gathering. Her messages about the need to win the peace were listened to intently. The three key campaign issues, she told a press conference, were: winning the war, setting the foundations for a lasting peace, and assuring jobs for all afterward.

Behind her exhortations was an urgency that was fed by her visits to the war wounded:

> [E.R. to Joseph P. Lash:]   [Oct. 2, 1944]
> I went to Mitchell Field & spent hours & came home exhausted. One whole ward of boys paralyzed won't ever walk again. How can it ever be made worthwhile to them & they are such wonderful looking kids. . . .

To portray the effect of her presence at campaign rallies is to risk the charge, as William James said when he wrote about the saintly, of sanctimoniousness. The worldly saw her as manipulative. They credited her only with a superior ability to conceal her drives. It was not their absence that marked her character. What counted was the self-mastery and discipline that had enabled her to convert ambition, jealousy, physical love into service to others. Her closest friends criticized each other, sometimes maliciously. When she heard, she did not join in. The jealousies among Eleanor's friends were as powerful as they were among Franklin's, but she was never harsh or malign herself. The "discretion" of her heart, one literate friend wrote, constituted a "selflessness" that left her vulnerable to all sorts of claims and requests. It frightened her friends for her. It mystified the ideologues.

The chairman of the Democratic National Committee, Robert Hannegan, treated her with diffidence. He was Truman's man, and while after the convention she supported Truman, her hopes for the future were pinned on Henry Wallace. Her loyalty to Wallace, as well as her patent distaste for political "bosses," were enough to make Hannegan uneasy. Even more, he feared her active espousal of the Negro cause. So he kept his distance. But she was often at headquarters in New York, popping in on the Women's Division to chat with Hick and with Trude over at the State Committee.

"Trude is making a name for herself at Democratic headquarters," she had written me just as I left New Caledonia, "but she is working so hard I will be glad she has to spend several days meeting you!" A cool note about the national chairman: "Hannegan came in tonight to ask me to speak on the air on registration & I told him to ask FDR."

"Whatever you do about getting married is all right with me," her letter of welcome said on my arrival in the States. It was a few days before the election, and Trude and I worried lest we become an election issue that was used against the President.

[E.R. to Joseph P. Lash:]   [October 22, 1944]
Trude & I have talked over the wedding. The Poliers* scared her by saying Brownell the Rep. chairman was desperate & would stop at nothing & you would be used to show we had brought you home to marry her. I would not care nor be troubled for the world loves a romance but it would hurt you.

Eleanor was generous and impulsive. Trude and I, however, decided on caution. I kept out of sight until election day, when we went up the Hudson to stay at the big house and to listen to the returns. Election day in Dutchess County was bright with the golds and maroons of the foliage. A walk along Hyde Park's roads, the leaves crackling underfoot, gave life zest. As we hiked Hyde Park's paths with

---

* Judge Justine Wise and Shad Polier.

Eleanor, we argued the importance of her asserting a more forthright position of leadership in the country. Millions of people were voting for her as well as for the President, and she had a responsibility even if her name was not on the ballot. Eleanor made the customary protestations, but she listened—to Trude and to me as well as to others.

My bedroom on the second floor at the big house was connected to another with which it shared a bathroom. Admiral Leahy, the chief of staff, was lodged in the other room. That weather-beaten tar was a little startled to collide with a T-Sgt. at the wash basin, but all was civility. Late election day afternoon everyone gathered in the library and the President toasted Trude and me. We were to be married the next day. There was evidently more to that scene than I then realized or than Eleanor told me and which I only began to sense in 1978 when the FOIPA [Freedom of Information and Privacy Act] papers disclosed the President's hand in having me shipped overseas in April 1943.

At midnight the torchlight parade of Hyde Park neighbors, joined this time by three busloads of Vassar girls, arrived outside the big house. The President was wheeled out. Eleanor wore a flowing black dinner dress, and Anna leaned on the back of his chair. It was too early to make any statement, the President said, "But it looks like I'll be coming up from Washington again for another four years." Afterward Eleanor beckoned into the big hall for snacks the scores of radio and press correspondents and photographers who had been shivering outside. At about 3 a.m. Dewey conceded. She told the women who covered her that she viewed the four years ahead as probably the most difficult years "the world has ever seen" since they involved "winning the war, making the peace and rebuilding the world."

The day after the President's reelection Eleanor and Tommy attended our wedding at 245 West 11th Street, the brownstone Trude had rented. Trude's children were there and my mother. Trude's friend Kaete Hoerlin, whose first husband, one of Germany's leading music critics, had been shot by the Nazis, asked Sascha Schneider to provide the wedding music. Trude was dressed in a pearl-embroidered sea-green dress. I was in my GI best.

It was a simple ceremony, and Eleanor was happy in our happiness. Paul Tillich, who married us, spoke of the "blessings" Trude and I had received from our parents and went on:

> And blessing, beyond this, has been given to you: Both of you have received and are receiving the blessing of your great friend, the First Lady of this country, with whom we share today *her* joy as she shares *your* joy; whose presence expresses for you the warming, protecting and blessing power of friendship. . . . Friendship is given; it cannot be demanded. It is a blessing, it cannot be forced. And what is true of friendship is even more true of love. . . .

He touched delicately on our former marriages that had ended in divorces:

> Both of you have experienced the limits of human will, the fragmentary nature of creation. . . . A strong will and a straight decision can do much, they cannot do all; and they cannot do the best. The best in our time, as in the time to come is the blessing given to us by God and man.

Back at Hyde Park the next day Eleanor wrote Trude—

[E.R. to Trude W. Lash:]   [November 9, 1944]

> You and Joe were very sweet to let me share your evening after the wedding & I am very grateful & love you both very much.
> Tell Joe, I've thought a great deal about what he said & when we have time we must talk some more about it because doing what he suggests implies some great changes & I'm not sure I am able to undertake them. In any case there may be no immediate trip for F.D.R.

Eleanor regarded us as a threesome. It was a relationship that all three of us welcomed and not a response to her need to escape loneliness.

The President had been hoping for a German collapse, in which case he and Mrs. Roosevelt would immediately fly to London, Paris, and to what had been the front. I had been urging her to subordinate herself to the President's needs and, whatever the rebuffs and lack of intimacy, to be available to him.

She went to Washington with the President. At her news conference on arrival she was asked whether she was glad for another four years. She answered slowly, for no question occupied her more.

> I suppose that besides being years of heavy responsibility the next four years will also be years of great opportunity, and suppose everyone should be glad for opportunity even if not for responsibility.

Had Communism been an issue, the press wanted to know, and that elicited an expression of her basic political philosophy:

> I think the number of Communists in this country is so small that only one thing would ever make it a danger—the kind of knowledge that would make people feel democracy could not meet their needs.

Had she been one of the issues? "That was one of the phonies," she replied. People knew she had no "real power, or influence about vital issues. Those aren't the things that people make decisions about. But the election showed that the people as a whole believed even a woman has a right to do what she believes is the right thing."

Strictly speaking, she was correct in saying she had no real power in the sense that the obligations and responsibilities of the presidential office are defined in the Constitution and the statute books. She knew it was the only position acceptable to Franklin; equally, public expectations of a spouse's role in the White House wavered and were unfathomable. But did she really believe she had no influence? In the *Ladies Home Journal* that November she asserted defiantly that she preferred a life of service to the role of "Dresden doll . . . when the world is rocking on its foundations." She asked rhetorically: Should the President's wife "be blind, deaf and dumb?" She had learned from Aunty Bye* "not to be bothered by what people say as long as you are sure that you are doing what seems right to you, but be sure you face yourself honestly."

She felt the obligations of leadership. She talked with the President and Harry Hopkins about the next four years, and Hopkins recorded what she said:†

> Mrs. Roosevelt urged the President very strongly to keep in the forefront of his mind the domestic situation because she felt there was a real danger of his losing American public opinion in his foreign policy if he failed to follow through on the domestic implications of his campaign promises. She particularly hoped the President would not go to Great Britain or France and receive great demonstrations abroad for the present, believing that would not set too well with the American people.
>
> She impressed on both of us that we must not be satisfied with merely making campaign pledges; the President being under moral obligation to see his domestic reforms through, particularly the organizing of our domestic life in such a way as to give everybody a job. She emphasized that this was an overwhelming task and she hoped neither the President nor I thought it was settled in any way by making speeches.

The unique function that Eleanor performed for her husband, Robert Sherwood commented upon this Hopkins memo, was "as the keeper of and constant spokesman for her husband's conscience."

In his diaries, Henry Wallace recorded a talk with Eleanor the day the Roosevelts returned to Washington. She had asked him to come to see her:‡

> When I saw Mrs. Roosevelt, she told me that the liberals looked on me as the outstanding symbol of liberalism in the United States. She said that any program they worked up ought to be passed on by me. She said she was going out to the CIO convention on November 20 and she wanted to know whether I would head up a greatly broadened PAC. She felt that Sidney Hillman was not suitable for heading up such a broad

---

* Mrs. Sheffield Cowles, sister of Theodore Roosevelt and Eleanor's father, Elliott.
† *Roosevelt and Hopkins*, by Robert E. Sherwood (New York, 1948), p. 831.
‡ *The Price of Vision*, edited by John Morton Blum (Boston, 1973), pp. 390–391.

liberal organization. She said furthermore that even though I had a position in the government, she thought I could go in on such an organization. She said she knew I could not answer offhand such a matter. Later in the day I called her up and told her the first thing that occurred to me was that whatever was done should have the complete and enthusiastic blessing of Sidney Hillman. Second, I told her that I felt the only way any liberalism could express itself on a national basis was through the Democratic Party and I felt it would be damaging to the Democratic Party and to the liberalism boys if I should take the position she suggested. In brief, I turned down the proposition flatly but nicely. I can't help but wondering, however, to what extent her husband is up to his usual maneuvering tricks.

In one respect, if not more, Wallace was wrong: to assume she was acting on behalf of the President. Wallace had been wounded deeply by Roosevelt's embracing him just before the convention, from which he had concluded that the President supported his renomination. He was wary of the White House, and that included Eleanor as well as the President. But she was trying to use her powers for the public good, not as a messenger of Franklin's. On election day Esther had written her from Salt Meadow, and her advice was much like that of Trude and myself.

[Esther Lape to E.R.:]   "Election Day Afternoon"
I would like to take a few minutes out of the quiet of a lovely sunny afternoon—a golden broadside of light coming into the western window of my room—to say how much I hope the next four years will be gracious and lively and *new* years, and not just more of the same.

Of the outcome of this election I cannot feel the slightest doubt—you are in for it. And it is better for all of us that you should be. And I believe that it will be better for you also. I hope that you will take time to think out the best ways to make available—in the places and the persons best able to use it—the tremendously increased powers that are so peculiarly now yours. It sometimes seems to me that no human being ever had so much chance to use power, both personally and impersonally, for stimulus and for grace and for beauty and for persuasion and enlightenment. How to use it most effectively does involve selection and decisions not required of most of the rest of us.

Eleanor replied twice to this letter. One reply was a note dated November 16 that Tommy typed out on the basis of some lines Eleanor had penned on the margins of Esther's letter:

I know I have a responsibility in these next years, but I feel inadequate and still find it hard to make a decision. I fill my time to overflowing now and always wonder how much I accomplish.

But the day before she had written a longhand letter to Esther that dwelt on her relations to Franklin.

[E.R. to Esther Lape:]   [November 15, 1944]
. . . Thanks for your letter dear. You spoke of a selective job & that is the hardest thing for me to do, since I've always done what came to hand & now when I should plan it is very difficult. Maybe I'd do the most useful job if I just became a "good wife" & waited on F.D.R. Anna has been doing all of it that Margaret Suckley does not do but she can't go on doing it. If I did I'd lose value in some ways because I'd no longer have outside contacts. I'd hate it but I'd soon get accustomed to it. It is funny how hard it is to be honest with yourself & not be swayed by your own wishes, isn't it?

Tommy seems pretty well & loved being with you. She stayed in Washington this weekend. Joe & Trude are married & I hope they are always as happy as they now are. Much Love dear & bless you,

                                        E.R.

The responsibilities of being a "good wife" worked on her conscience. Four days later she wrote Esther again.

[E.R. to Esther Lape:]   [November 19, 1944]
Your letter and the past week has given me much to think about & sometime we will talk over these things. I find it hard to know sometime whether I am being honest with myself so much of life is play acting, it becomes so natural!

One thing I know you are wrong about. There is no fundamental love to draw on, just respect & affection. There is little or no surface friction. On my part there is often a great weariness & a sense of futility in life but a life-long discipline in a sense of obligation & a healthy interest in people keeps me going. I guess that is plenty to go on for one's aging years! I'll be a fairly good handmaiden & with all the others to help I think FDR's sense of a place in history will keep him on a forward going path. He'll know it has to be that way & he is really very well I think.

Your towels are ordered but they will not be ready for Xmas so they will come as an "out of date" birthday gift. Tommy & I have got something for you together which we hope you will enjoy & it will arrive for Xmas.

I look forward to seeing you soon & in the meantime,

Much, much love

E.R.

She was more reticent in her reply to Hick, perhaps because she had had a talk with her. Hick had listened to the returns at Belle Roosevelt's and wrote her on November 10—

[Lorena Hickok to E.R.:]

Well—are you glad the darned old campaign is over? I'll bet you are. And so am I! It was, beyond any doubt, the meanest campaign since 1928—and I think it was meaner than that one. . . . Darling, I don't like to think about the next four years for you. Rotten luck—but, my God, we couldn't let that little man with the mustache be President! Not *now*.

"There are lots of things I don't like to think about just now, but I guess the answers will come as we go along," Eleanor answered. Franklin was going at the end of the month to Warm Springs for two weeks, taking Laura and Margaret Suckley with him "so I won't have to go."

It suited the President to go without her because Mrs. Rutherfurd, who wintered at Aiken, was again one of his visitors. Perhaps, too, Eleanor's "powers," as Esther called them, were too much for Franklin, strong man though he was. He did not want Eleanor too close. Wallace noted a talk with Henry Morgenthau about the new State Department appointments, whose conservative nature had alarmed liberals. Wallace told Morgenthau he had informed the President he wanted to be appointed Secretary of Commerce in the new cabinet.*

He [Morgenthau] said he was going to be seeing Mrs. Roosevelt. He asked me if Mrs. Roosevelt knew what I wanted. I said no. I hadn't told her. He said Mrs. Roosevelt was very, very strong for me. When he told me this I couldn't help but think that this would make me weaker with the President because I have the feeling that at the present time he fights everything she is for. I didn't care to say this to Henry Morgenthau, however. Morgenthau said he was exceedingly anxious for me to be in the cabinet because he felt otherwise the forces of reaction were in serious danger of taking over the President.

Tommy's unsentimental bulletin to Esther about our marriage and the party three days later positively sizzled.

* *The Price of Vision*, p. 402.

[Tommy to Esther Lape:]   [November 19, 1944]

You probably know that Joe Lash and Trude Pratt were married, all bets to the contrary! It was a very simple affair, the actual ceremony, but the following Saturday they had a large reception to which I did not go because I preferred to stay in Washington, but to which all the big shots, Baruch, Golden, etc., went. Baruch gave $250.* I don't know what Golden gave. I am waiting to see Golden say a few "amusing" words about his going because he has sounded off to me on every occasion about that bleached so and so! Baruch, too, is a hypocrite because last year before Mrs. R. left for the s.west Pacific she asked him to write a character letter for Joe to use in applying to officers candidate school. After she was well on her way he asked me "who" the young man was, that he had not heard the name, and when I told him, he said he never wrote that kind of letter and as far as I know, he never did. Anna made some crack to him about going to the reception when he was here last week and he said, "There is so little I can do to please your mother. I felt I ought to go." I went to the ceremony, but at least I have never "sounded off" to anyone like Baruch or Golden and I have a job to protect, at least I like to protect the atmosphere.

Tommy's missive was full of her boss's activities:

Mrs. R. is, as usual, seeing all sorts of people and keeping busy so I actually see little of her, so I write memos instead of trying to ask questions.

She too, was enlisted in the campaign to narrow the focus of Eleanor's activities to the more meaningful ones:

Two other people, Louis Weiss, a lawyer, and Doris Fleeson, the newspaper woman, spoke to me about Mrs. R's activities and spreading herself too thin, etc. I suggested they talk to her and not to me, but they are all shy. . . .

All of which leads me to wishing that Mrs. R. would slow down—she never gets enough time off her feet but she seems to be fine from all outward appearances.

She will be alone at Hyde Park with the P. for over Thanksgiving. Elliott is here but is not going to H.P. and neither is Anna. Then the P. goes to Warm Springs for a week or so and Mrs. R. is not going. He is taking Miss Suckley and Miss Delano.

* I'm mystified by the $250 contribution and have no idea what it was given for—unless for one of the organizations that Eleanor and Trude always were helping.

Directly after our wedding reception, Trude and I took the train to Lexington, Virginia, where I attended the four-week Information and Education school at Washington and Lee. Trude was able to get a room at the Robert E. Lee Hotel, "a cat walk around a bed," she wrote Mrs. R., but our joy in being wed made up for all discomforts. I found eight hours of classroom work unusually burdensome, and Trude discovered that the telephone and writing pad scarcely filled the hours when we were not together, but these were minor drawbacks. "A food package just arrived from you," she wrote Mrs. R. "It will be great fun to prepare 'snacks' for Joe when he arrives home after a tiring day. We miss you. We both are sure that after the war we shall have to live close to you."

Virginia celebrated its Thanksgiving a few days after the national holiday and, since I did not feel I could afford to leave Lexington, Eleanor offered to come down to share Virginia's Thanksgiving with us. "It was grand to hear your two voices this morning & know you both were so happy & that Joe has the chance for O.C.S.," she wrote Trude. I had written discouraging her visit, but she had not yet received my letter.

[Joseph P. Lash to E.R.:]   [November 17, 1944]

Right now I have really good prospects for being sent to OCS. I made the top grade of "superior" in the first examination and everyone acknowledges my qualifications for this type of work. But I am afraid that none of this will count unless I manage to preserve some measure of anonymity. I hope very much that you will agree with this reasoning and not mark me down for a scared rabbit.

My circumspection hurt Eleanor. She had gone to Chicago to speak at the CIO convention and attend a meeting of the Rosenwald Fund. Trude went to New York to spend Thanksgiving with the children. She immediately sensed a reserve in Mrs. R.'s voice when she spoke with her after her return from Chicago.

[Joseph P. Lash to E.R.:]   [November 23, 1944]

Trude told me over the phone that you had returned to Washington and I have been hoping against hope that you would call me. I would call you, but you see I need forgiveness badly because I feel I have been disloyal in the matter of the Thanksgiving party. My instincts were against my writing you as I did, but it seemed like the "reasonable" thing to do at the time. I know now I was wrong. One does not temper love with expediency. I am sorry for the pain I must have caused you.

Even before this letter arrived, Eleanor, who was in New York, sought to reassure me and conceal her hurt at having been excluded.

[E.R. to Joseph P. Lash:]   [November 23, 1944]
Your letter reached me after I got back from Chicago but I understood
from the telephone talk. I had thought something of the kind might
occur but it will be so wonderful if you can stay in this country & go to
O.C.S. that I think you should do everything with that end in view. It
was grand to see Trude yesterday so happy & to feel in your letter the
same joy. God bless you both! I persuaded Trude to tell you that I really
don't want you to drive up on the 2d [my birthday]. The weather may
become bad & that road can be dangerous driving in sleet and snow. You
would be tired on Monday, the powers that be would not like your
leaving & it isn't worth the risk for a few hours. If you were not coming
later that would be different but you can come the 13th & Franklin &
Anna will both be there then & I want you especially to see them. I love
seeing you, but it would be spoiled by anxiety & fear, for I would feel so
guilty if anything went wrong. Please therefore, do not come till the
13th. Mickey* will have a perfectly happy time with his friends on his
birthday here. The trip to Washington for them can be any time.
When does the next OCS start? I'm on my way up to Hyde Park after
returning to Washington at noon yesterday to attend a dinner last night.
We leave H.P. Sat. night so Trude is coming down on the 7:30 Sunday. It
will be fun to have her & won't you be glad to have her back! These few
days without her have surely made you feel more than ever how much
you want to be here & not thousands of miles away.
Mrs. [Adele] Levy asked fondly for you both when I saw her in Chicago.
I love you very, very much Joe dearest, & I'll greet you with far greater
happiness on the 13th than on the 2d!

Despite her reassurances I knew she had been hurt. "I still do not feel right
about the Thanksgiving Party, but that is not your fault," I replied. "You have
made it as easy as possible for my conscience." Later events and relationships
would supersede the whole episode in my memory, but a letter of Tommy's to
Esther, which came into my hands in 1982, revived it anew.

[Tommy to Esther Lape:]   [November 25, 1944]
Mrs. R. planned to spend Virginia's Thanksgiving on the 30th with
Trude and Joe at Lexington, Va., and Joe wrote that he felt her presence
would jeopardize his chances for O.C.S. and of course Mrs. R.'s feelings
were hurt as you know they can be. Trude was smart enough to sense this
and so they wrote an appeasing letter—to wit—that no one should weigh
love against expediency, etc. but the weighing was already done and

* Trude's youngest child, Roger Sherman Pratt.

nothing would make E.R. go now. These brilliant people don't seem to be able to understand E.R. If the whole thing had been put on the basis of wanting her no matter the cost, she wouldn't have gone.

Hick meanwhile had announced that she was returning to Washington but would stay with Marion Herron in her new apartment, at least for the weekend. Also she had told Mrs. Tillett, her boss, that her deadline for leaving the Democratic National Committee was April 1. Eleanor immediately invited Hick and Marion to come to supper at the White House when she returned to Washington on the 26th. "I promised to go to a dinner at 5:30 p.m. for colored wounded men & I can't disappoint them. . . . Your room is empty and ready whenever you come." Eleanor had seen Representative Mary Norton of New Jersey, another of Hick's close friends. "She & I want you to go to the doctor & live up to whatever is subscribed *[sic]*. . . . I'll go with you if you want, to Tommy's doctor" in Washington.

Hick was stubborn. "I promised Mary that I'd start looking for a job, but I don't *think* I promised her that I'd go to a doctor. . . . It isn't good for people to know all about their blood pressure all the time. And it's damned depressing." She did not want to stay with the Democratic National Committee:

> I'm awfully tired of Mr. Hannegan and Mr. Pauley—especially Mr. P. If Ed Pauley doesn't blow up in our faces one of these days, I'll be surprised. And, anyway, I think we are now witnessing the twilight of the Democratic Party. The Democratic Party didn't elect the President—this year nor four years ago. He did it himself. . . . The only job in politics I'd be interested in would be with the New York State Committee, setting up a good liberal women's organization upstate.

She had to renege on the invitation for the 26th, Eleanor wrote Hick. F.D.R. was returning to the White House "& all the world with him. . . . I may have to put you a little while upstairs in Diana's room which has a bath and is light and airy because Elliott may come back again and Harry Hooker is ill here with 3 trained nurses so the big corner rooms have to be in use."

Another letter to me sought to allay my feeling that I had acted disloyally.

[E.R. to Joseph P. Lash:]   Sunday [Date ?]

I found your little note & I'm sorry dear but it never occurred to me you'd feel this way. We are meant to use our brains & it was & is obvious common sense not to do anything prejudicial to your chances. I was not hurt in the least. It would have been the same if you'd been Fjr. or John. It would be a sad state of affairs if you couldn't tell me or I couldn't tell you what I honestly thought on any situation. The trip up here seems to me unwise as I wrote you & even more so now when your time may be limited & everything may count for or against you in final decisions. I'll wait for you with open arms on the 13th.

I still trust in miracles & I'm glad Trude goes back to you today. A world of love.

E.R.

I'm sending to "For Keeps"* 5 vols. of the Encyclopaedia of Social Sciences for your birthday. Five more to follow at Xmas & 5 for Easter. Next year will start on the Britannica! These are your real birthday gift tho' you won't get them till late.

My officers at I. and E. school continued to be enthusiastic about my work, yet also cautioned me that hitches might arise to keep me out of OCS. I began to prepare Trude and myself psychologically that shortly after the course ended I probably would be on the way again to the Pacific. I entreated Eleanor to make sure that we would have some "real time together" after the 13th when school ended and before I had to entrain to San Francisco. She replied immediately.

[E.R. to Joseph P. Lash:]   [November 27, 1944]
Your Saturday letter came today & I hasten to say that one day would seem very little to me & I will spend all the time I can in N.Y. between the 15th & the date of your departure.

We just have to be resigned to four more years of being careful & I hate it more than you & Trude do but it is part of the price one pays. In my own case there seems to me to be so few compensations but most people wouldn't feel the same way about it & I'm just queer I know!

I'm glad you'll have no more lonely times & what fun you & Trude will have on your birthday. Some day I'm going to join in on some of it again & this year I'll be with you in thought & spirit.

I saw Mrs. Morgenthau today & she will go home from the hospital Wed. Harry Hooker asked after you both & loved Trude's letter. He goes on well.

Anna goes to N.Y. tomorrow to stay in the apartment till Thursday & see some friends. F.D.R. & party left today for Warm Springs. Sec. Hull has resigned & Mr. Stettinius takes his place.

I shall stay here till the 6th when I go to N.Y. stopping in Philadelphia to speak at a meeting for Molly Yard. I'll be back the morning of the 9th as Elliott said he would be back the 8th & I figure he will perhaps arrive the 10th or 11th!

I hope O.C.S. goes through tho' what you would do in Transportation I can't imagine but the school might wangle you back I suppose.

Don't let your conscience bother you my dear. You have only one duty

---

* So we had named the house at 245 West 11th Street.

—to enjoy your wife & savour to the full every moment you have to-gether! Bless you both, give her a hug for me. I love you both very dearly & I'm longing to be with you both when the right time comes.

School instructors encountered Trude on the street in Lexington and assured her my "case" looked good for going to OCS, but one could never be sure. Trude kept Eleanor informed both about my grades and also about fears expressed by some of our friends in Lexington that G-2 might step in and veto my application, whatever the school's Board of Officers decided. "FDR spoke to Pa Watson before leaving today," Eleanor informed Trude. "I'm keeping my fingers crossed." We concluded she had communicated our apprehensions about a G-2 veto to the President and that he had asked General Watson to keep an eye on the matter.

We would pass through Washington on the 13th on our way to New York and she asked us for a list of friends in Washington we would like to see.

[E.R. to Trude W. Lash:]   [November 29, 1944]
I look forward more than I can say to the 13th & hope we can have a *real* party. I was tempted to see if I could go to Staunton by a Sunday a.m. train, carry lunch for 3 & return in p.m. & get you to drive over but I didn't even look up trains for I knew it was wrong to think I cld be anonymous & it might be rainy & cold & very unpleasant so impatiently I wait for the 13th!

I am very depressed tonight. Elliott called me from Beverly Hills, Cal. to say he was going to be married on Sat. He says he has known the girl, Fay Emerson, by name, some time. He told me when here however, he did not mean to marry till he was home, had a job, etc. & I fear it is just another of his quick actions because of loneliness. I've certainly not suc-ceeded in giving my children much sense of backing. I called FDR & told him & he took it calmly. I tried to get Anna in N.Y. but she was out. He didn't ask me to come out & said he did not know if he was bringing her East. I have a curious kind of numb & dreary feeling.

Elinor Morgenthau is home & after talking to 30 students on politics from 8–9 this evening I went to see her as she was alone for the night. I got home at 10:30 & have just finished the mail & must go to bed since it is one a.m. The day was busy.

You can't think how happy you & Joe make me. Just be as happy as can be! Ever so much love to you both.

                                        E.R.

I think of you as I wake & as I go to sleep & often in between!

Eleanor's letters to Franklin while he was at Warm Springs were spaced be-tween several telephone calls. His replies were cordial, businesslike, and brief. The impersonal message she transmitted from Madame Genevieve Tabouis, the redoubtable French journalist, brought this reply from Tommy, who signed herself "Secretary to Mrs. Roosevelt":

> Mrs. Roosevelt has word from the President in which he says:
> "I am putting in a word for the extending of Madame Tabouis' contract. I have had no word from her." Mrs. Roosevelt suggests you write the President.

Eleanor had appended a longhand note to her letter to Franklin about Madame Tabouis.

[E.R. to F.D.R.:]   [December 4, 1944]
   This has been a very full & busy day & tomorrow is much the same. Wednesday I am going to New York & will return on Saturday. I gather from the paper that Elliott and his new wife may appear next week. I have no great enthusiasm. Much love.
                                                           E.R.

There was more about Elliott in her letter the next day, although it was chiefly about James and her unhappiness over the State Department appointments that had been announced subsequent to Hull's resignation.

                                                   December 5, 1944
Dearest Franklin,
   The enclosed memo on the cameo might interest you. I'd like to get it if you want it. I also send the first page of a letter, one of many which has come breathing faith & admiration & since I am such a pest I thought this might compensate a little!
   I talked to James tonight back in San Diego & probably to be there a couple of months. Perhaps he & Romaine could come for Inauguration. What do you think? He says Faye Emerson is pretty & aggressive & he thinks is just out for what she can get.
   I will have to have $1,000 for Xmas money. There is not enough for Xmas cash in the house account. Will you ask Tully to send it as I have to get all envelopes written & filled.
   You haven't made me any happier over the State Dept. Now if Clayton brings down Leon Fraser as one paper suggested it will be perfect!
   Had a war-recreation conference in East Room all day & a party here tonight for 55 of M.P.'s, 20 from Walter Reed & 20 from Bethesda.
   I go to N.Y. tomorrow & return Saturday. Anna has a cold but I hope will be better tomorrow as she went to bed early tonight.

Much love dear. I hope the back is better & you can swim at last.

Devotedly,

E.R.

A letter to Trude the same day expressed more bluntly her dissatisfaction with the State Department reorganization.

[E.R. to Trude W. Lash:]   [December 5, 1944]

I'm feeling much upset over the State Dept. It is reorganized but for the worse I fear. I know FDR will feel my protests are based on ignorance & that the need for harmony to put over his peace setup is all important but I am suspicious of this whole bunch.

I hope Joe's paper & exams are wonderful & I long to hear if the [OCS] board has met & yet I hate to hear for fear of bad news! I pray it will be good & if I know nothing when I get home from N.Y. Sat. I'll call you both about 7 p.m.

I asked everyone for drinks on the 14th & I added Tommy & Henry & Elinor & Henry Morgenthau. . . .

She did not let up on the State Department's reorganization. She knew she was being a "pest," as she had put it. She may have suspected what Wallace noted in his diary—that whatever she was for Franklin almost automatically opposed. "Dearest Franklin," she wrote the following day, as her conscience drove her on to tell him what she long had realized others would not—

[E.R. to F.D.R.:]   [December 6, 1944]

I like the statement on Sforza and our attitude toward the other governments very much indeed. But, are we going to use any real pressure on Winston? I'm afraid words will not have much effect.

All of the newspapers which were agin you and all the people who were agin you in the election are now loudly praising the State Department set-up. It does make me nervous but perhaps it is all right if you can make them all behave like reformed characters so the rest of us who have been doubting Thomases will have to take our hats off to them.

Anna heard that John may be home any day since his work is finished. That really is exciting. Harry Hooker says he feels like a new man. Perhaps several weeks in bed is what we all need to improve our dispositions! Marquis Childs wrote a very nice column about the way you always retire and think through your problems rather carefully and then come back ready for action. Ernest Lindley wrote a column completely upholding all your State Department today. So!

[And in longhand:] Much love, I'll be back in Washington on Sat.

Devotedly
E.R.

Another newsy letter began on an affectionately cautionary note.

[E.R. to F.D.R.:]   [December 12, 1944]

Dr. Mac says you leave Saturday, stop at New River & arrive Monday & I'm glad as I want to see you before you begin to look weary!

A wire from Elliott says he & the new wife will also arrive Monday & I dread it.

I go to N.Y. Tuesday the 19th & return Wed. at midnight. We are having the office party the 21st at 11 unless you prefer to have it alone the 23rd & the house tree on the 21st at 4. I go to N.Y. the 22d & to H.P. the 23d. Ethel & the children will probably come up the 23d & we will look for you & Anna etc. on the a.m. of 24th.

John looks very well & is very grand as a Colonel. Joe & Trude come tomorrow for the night. He passed all exams tops Trude was told today but they don't know yet what he will be able to do. I'm going to N.Y. for Sat. on the chance that he leaves Monday but I'll be back here Sunday.

The grapevine says Henry Wallace wrote you he'd like to go into Commerce. Is it true?

A nice Xmas card from Johnny, looking back longingly to last year. Elizabeth Rathbone's young Joel is missing in Germany as of Nov. 22d. He's barely 19 & she's struggled to bring him up, but then I do nothing but read about broken hearts every night.

Ernest Lindley's columns shld please you, have you been seeing them? He says the State Dept. appointees are well balanced. Stettinius had a big off the record press conference in N.Y. Friday evening & I think they liked him.

Much love,
E.R.

The four-week course at I and E school ended, and on the 13th we were in Washington, where Eleanor, with Tommy's help, had invited many of our friends. But admission to OCS still was unsettled. As often during the war, Trude's and my feelings gyrated crazily between hopes for another four months in this country at OCS and dread that on December 23 I would have to report to a port of embarkation in California as my orders specified. I had become so pessimistic that Eleanor at our request had asked the White House ushers to get Trude reservations on the transcontinental "Streamliner." "I am sure Mr. West knows the magic word," Tommy assured us.

Eleanor rarely was busier than that Christmas season. Tommy had tried to persuade her to use the war emergency to pare down her Christmas list, but Eleanor would not let anyone go. And when Tommy protested that U.S. Post Office warnings to "mail early" were not the same as the laws of the Medes and Persians, she was equally unsuccessful.

The value of human relationships was paramount. They were the key to happiness that was symbolized by Maeterlinck's *Blue Bird,* as she noted in her Christmas letter to Esther.

[E.R. to Esther Lape:]   [December 13, 1944]
    . . . I've been thinking so much of you & Lizzie today & wondering if in any way we can still give to those we love when they go ahead.* So many women must be longing to do it these days. Perhaps when we are happy in ourselves & think happily of those we love it is a gift to them a la Bluebird! I never think of you without thinking of Lizzie also.

She had her Christmas party with Hick. "Tonight was very nice, dear," the latter wrote, "and I love you for your generous thought about my vacation. But I can't let you do it. . . . A happy Christmas to you, dearest. No one in the world deserves it more."

She celebrated Christmas with Trude and me and the children in New York before going to Hyde Park for family festivities. A note to Hick, who had gone to her cottage on Long Island—

[E.R. to Lorena Hickok:]   [December 21, 1944]
    I hope this will reach you before Xmas. I shall think of you in the little house & hope that the day will be very happy. . . . Let me know about the doctor. I really want to hear all details & I hope you have all the necessary tests. . . .
    Elliott's new wife is pretty, quiet & hard, I guess. She seems capable but I don't think she is more than a passing house guest! I hope I've behaved well!

Hick went for tests and reported, "Were you *ever* right? It seems I have a blood sugar count of 272, which is pretty high, considering the fact that normal is under 100." The doctor had placed her on a sugar-free diet. She thanked Eleanor for her many Christmas presents, "There is no one else in the world like you."

"Your report from the doctor did not surprise me," Eleanor commented after she had returned to the White House, "& I'm glad you are facing it at last & doing the necessary things. . . . It was nice at H.P. but very busy as always at Xmas & it

* Elizabeth Read had died a year earlier.

has been busy ever since. I'm going to take some time to read in N.Y. That is one of my most ardent resolutions but the first few days don't seem to provide it!"

She invited Trude and me to the White House for New Year's Eve. I was on my way to Camp Lee at Petersburg, not Fort McDowell on the coast. The President had overruled G-2, which I assumed had been blocking the school's effort to send me to OCS. A direct order went from him to the Army that I was to be admitted to the next class unless G-2 had something against my record in the service.

New Year's Eve was somewhat muted because the outcome of the Battle of the Bulge was still uncertain and because of the President's evident frailty. As Trude and I went up to him after the toasts to wish him a happy New Year he expressed his pleasure that I was going to OCS and wished me well.

What had happened was described by Assistant Secretary of War John J. McCloy in a letter dated May 22, 1945 to the House Military Affairs Subcommittee that was investigating the commissioning of alleged Communists. The school had rated me "superior," his letter said, but in Washington the Information and Education Division, while it "did not find him lacking in loyalty, it was of the opinion that he did not conform to the type of individual desired by it for orientation work.

"On the same day that such consideration was being given (Dec. 29, 1944) the division received instructions that the Commander-in-Chief desired telegraphic orders to be dispatched sending Lash to Officers Candidate School unless there were objections other than objections arising from his civilian activities.

"The military record of Lash being unexceptionable, the President's order was forthwith complied with and Lash was ordered to the Quartermaster Corps officers school."

At Camp Lee, I marked time until the new class should begin in mid-January. "I am in a casual company," I wrote Eleanor, ". . . all types of details are coming my way! This morning I cleaned out the barracks. This afternoon I policed up the area. And I also have the job of keeping the fires in the stoves going."

My address now was, I wrote Trude and Eleanor:

Candidate Joseph Lash 32326519

VII

"One Can't Live in Fear, Can One?"

ROOSEVELT'S FOURTH INAUGURAL was, as Helen Keller, who attended it, said, an "austere ceremony." He did not want it on the "Hill," he told his son James, but on the lawn outside the White House. Its plainness conformed not only to the severities of the war but to the limitations on his energy. Afterward, he saw the few people he wanted to see in the Green Room —members of the family, Princess Martha, a few officials whom Anna brought in to him—while Eleanor deputized. Joined by other members of the family from time to time, she shook their hands and made them feel welcome. All admired the way she enabled the President to husband his energies. That had been their way ever since polio had stricken him and Louis Howe had told her she would have to serve as his proxy in the Democratic Party and public life.

She had sent friends her Inaugural schedule so they should know when and where she might be reached. On the day before the Inauguration, "we have a lunch & reception for Democratic workers but I could come to the telephone. From 4–6 I'll be out at the Democratic Club & at 7:30 I'll go to the Electors dinner but I should be home by 11 p.m." On Saturday, Inauguration Day, she was busier: "10:30–11 religious service, 12 Inauguration, then lunch which will mean receiving till 3. I begin again at 5 & should be home all evening."

Anna and John Boettiger, James, and Elliott were there; Fjr. and Johnny, who were in the Pacific, were represented by their wives. Thirteen grandchildren were also in the house. Franklin wanted all with him, but it was she mainly who had seen to it that it was done, just as it was she who had written him in Warm Springs in early December that if he wanted James at the Inauguration he should ask for him.

She wrote me the day after the Inauguration, partly because she sensed how disappointed I was not to be able to leave Camp Lee the first week of OCS, but also to unburden herself over her worries about Franklin's flagging energies and her inability to be helpful where it really counted because he no longer had the patience to hear her out. Eleven days earlier she had written me—

[E.R. to Joseph P. Lash:]   [January 11, 1945]
The other evening when we were quiet I asked him about the State Dept. appointments. It boils down to having, for various reasons, followed the line of least resistance because he feels he gets enough direct information from ambassadors & others to make up his own mind on policy.

I did not realize it then, but behind the depression she referred to in her January 21 letter was not only worry about Franklin's weariness but also unhappiness because he did not want her at Yalta. Since Sarah Churchill was going, he thought Anna would be a help and comfort, but Eleanor's presence would only complicate matters because everyone would feel they had to pay attention to her. She may have suspected, although I do not think she did, that Anna was pleased to give her father the pretext for not taking Eleanor with him to Yalta, for Anna told Bernard Asbell, who edited the letters between Eleanor and Anna, and who asked her, "Do you think your mother was hurt?"—*

"Yes, I'm pretty sure she was," Mrs. Halsted [Anna] replied. "Of course, I was so terribly anxious to go that this wasn't half the embarrassment that it was to have those papers thrown at me, when he said, 'Sis, you handle these.' " She was referring to various papers that Mrs. Roosevelt gave to the President for perusal that he passed along to Anna.

"I wanted desperately to go, you see," Mrs. Halsted continued. "But I also knew that if mother went I couldn't go. The other thing was that Averell Harriman and Churchill were bringing their daughters, and there would be no wives. So I just fell in with this, just blocked it out for my own purposes very selfishly."

* Asbell, Bernard, *Mother & Daughter* (New York, 1982), pp. 181–82.

Eleanor probably did not know of Anna's complicity, but she was aware of Franklin's rebuff after she had offered to accompany him to Yalta and that contributed to her depression.

[E.R. to Joseph P. Lash:] [January 21, 1945]

I realize this may never reach you since you have a new address & I don't know it, but I hope they may trace you & I want to tell you what a wonderful job Trude did on Friday & Saturday. Her new hat was wonderful & she did a wonderful political job by just being her sweet & thoughtful self.

We missed you very much & the ceremonies were simple & impressive.

I have been worried about personal things & I am tired & so very depressed tonight. The next years seem impossible to live through but by tomorrow morning that will be different. I saw Jimmy & Romaine off tonight & hoped I helped straighten out some things for them. He won't go off for another month or six weeks. F.D.R. & Anna go tomorrow night & I'm not really happy about this trip but one can't live in fear, can one? . . .

The President was absent from Washington five weeks. Before he left he sent to the Senate his nomination of Henry Wallace to be Secretary of Commerce and to head the Reconstruction Finance Corporation, both jobs that had been filled by Jesse Jones. The latter had been politically disloyal to the President in the election and had made himself the symbol of conservative resistance to the liberalism represented by Wallace. The President also nominated another fearless opponent of the conservatives, Aubrey Williams, Hopkins's former deputy, to head the Rural Electrification Administration. Both men became the targets of the Dixiecrat coalition in the Senate. Eleanor did not wish to tax Franklin's strength, but if no one else was able to speak up to him, she felt an obligation to do so, especially as he had placed his support of Wallace on the basis of repayment of a political debt rather than on Wallace's qualifications for the two posts. "Dearest Franklin," she wrote him in longhand in a letter that went by diplomatic pouch—

[E.R. to F.D.R.:] [January 26, 1945]

The Jones-Wallace fight is on. Of course Jones has behaved horribly & your letter when published was hard on Wallace. I know you wrote it hoping to make Jones feel better but I guess he's the kind of dog you should have ousted the day after election & given him the reasons. He would not have published that letter! Elliott's nomination [he was on the list to be promoted to Major General] so far seems to have brought little adverse comment & his record was published which was good. I hope it goes through quickly for Elliott's sake!

I had two very busy days in N.Y. & returned Thursday morning. The children all seem very well & Anne may go up to New York tomorrow with friends for the weekend.

People like Oscar Ewing are telling newspapermen that "Henry is a nice fellow, but he shouldn't have R.F.C." So tomorrow I'm going to call Mr. Hannegan & ask what he & the Com. are doing to back Wallace & at the same time I shall speak about McKittrick. The statements made by Jones & Wallace I hope you read because Jones is looking backward & Wallace forward. Even if they take R.F.C. from Commerce you still appoint the head so if you choose someone Wallace wants to work with you still control the situation, don't you? They can't reject too many people! I rather like these quarrels because in the questioning the men reveal themselves rather more than they know!

I'll be here till Monday & away that night to go to the dinner for Wallace & then here till the children leave. The *1st* to *9th* Tommy & I will be at the apartment in N.Y.

I think of you & Anna & hope all goes well. John & Johnny keep each other company & the other children keep Johnny busy. Give Anna all my love & the same to you.

I thought Churchill's speech hardly helped your meeting!

A week later from New York she wrote him again.

[E.R. to F.D.R.:]   [Feb. 2, 1945]
Your message came through to Barkley but we wish you had added a little word for Wallace. We assume that you take it for granted we know you believe Wallace will help you do the job, but a little reassurance would be helpful!

I'm enclosing a note from Jerome Davis which you might like to give Mr. Churchill when he's offering that award for a plan on India! Nehru's sister, Mme. Pandit came to lunch. She thinks there may be less blood-shed than Mr. C. fears. She says Gandhi is revered but can no longer be the leader.

A cable to him to urge stronger support for Wallace had gone through the Map Room. He did not answer her directly. Presumably his message to Alben Barkley, the Senate majority leader, was the result. He sent her a cordial but brief note from Malta, which he and his party had reached aboard the USS *Quincy* and where he had rendezvoused with Churchill.

Dearest Babs, [February 2, 1945]

Got in safely. Lots of sleep but need still more! Anna is fine and she also is getting a rest and looks very well.

It's been a good voyage. When your wire came I had to wait for we were under "radio silence"—a submarine near us! But it seems to be a good result today.

I have been all over this interesting place this p.m. The Prime is here and will leave tonight on the next leg of the trip. I hope for news of the Senate confirmation of Elliott.

Will write from "there" in a couple of days.

Lots of love.

She reported to Maude Gray, "I heard Sat. that all was well and proceeding according to schedule with our travellers." She gave her aunt the family news, said Elinor Morgenthau was coming to stay in New York and both nights they were going to the theater, and she closed, "We are busily engaged working for Wallace but the fight is really one that goes deeper than a particular political post & will go on for some time I think."

There were cabled messages to Roosevelt from Sam Rosenman, who was in London, about the Wallace situation. To James Byrnes, whom he had persuaded to leave the Supreme Court to handle domestic affairs for him and who was in the party that accompanied him to Yalta, the President appeared unresponsive to such messages and handed them on to him with "little indication of personal interest." That may have been the case, or Byrnes may have misunderstood the periods of apathy that now regularly descended upon him. When James had said good-bye to his father before returning to the Philippines, he looked "awful," James later wrote. "At times the old zestfulness was there, but often—particularly when he let down his guard—he seemed thousands of miles away."

In the end, Wallace was confirmed as Secretary of Commerce but not given the R.F.C. to administer. Eleanor's next letter to Franklin was silent on the subject.

[E.R. to F.D.R.:] [Feb. 9, 1945]

Tommy and I got back today & I did have a good time in N.Y. Lt. Conrad came to lunch & brought the orchids which he said you told him to get me. Many thanks dear but I rather doubt his truth since you wouldn't order orchids & so I suggest you don't forget to pay him!

Those were curious sentences. Were the orchids meant for St. Valentine's Day, Lt. Conrad assuming that the President would have sent them had he been there? Was she being ironic or roguish, wishing despite herself he might have done so?

She sent Valentines to a few of the people she cared about. Hick, just about to leave for Georgia for a rest, replied, "Thanks so much for the sweet Valentine I found here last night. One of the sweetest things about you is the way you never forget anniversaries. I love it." Eleanor's letter to Franklin continued:

> I thought you'd like the enclosed column. I talked to John on the telephone & he is out for dinner but I've just said goodnight to Johnny who looks fine & seems pleased that Trude's two children are coming for the weekend.
>
> It does seem that Germany must soon stop fighting & I do hope so. I hope too that your conference isn't too difficult. I was glad to get word from Anna that Harry saw Elliott in Paris & he was well. His promotion hasn't yet gone through but it will I think.
>
> Much much love.

Two days later the Big Three ended their conference with a joint communiqué, and Franklin wrote her in his usual cordial voice—that of lifelong companion and easy gallant—from aboard the USS *Catoctin,* Vice Admiral Kent's flagship, which had been anchored at Sevastopol in the Black Sea serving as a communications link.

> February 12, 1945
>
> Dearest Babs:
>
> We have wound up the conference—successfully I think and this is just a line to tell you that we are off for the Suez Canal and then home but I doubt if we get back till the 28th. I am a bit exhausted but really all right.
>
> I do hope all goes well. It has been grand hearing from you and I expect another pouch tomorrow.
>
> Ever so much love.
>
> Devotedly
> F.

She applauded his accomplishments at Yalta but continued to worry about Wallace.

> February 13, 1945
>
> Dearest Franklin,
>
> We seem to be almost united as a country in approval of the results of the conference. I think you must be very well satisfied & your diplomatic abilities must have been colossal! Jonathan [Daniels] is happy. John is happy, all the world looks smiling! I think having the first U.N. meeting in San Francisco is a stroke of genius. At last will Marshal Stalin leave his own country or won't you three have to be on hand?

You must feel a great let up in strain & satisfaction & I hate to think that you must return to the petty partisan struggle here. I had Mr. and Mrs. Wallace to lunch on Sunday. He says Vandenburg is lining up the question on purely party lines & it will depend on how much you really want to bring pressure. They tell me Jones still goes to his office. He's not a sensitive person, is he! Aubrey was accused of all the crimes by McKellar, so you will have to fight for him too. His seems to be a miniature fight but similar to the one on Wallace.

They are afraid he might build liberal farmers thro' R.E.A. [Rural Electrification Administration]. Oh! well, I guess we are as prejudiced our way as they are their way. I wish I knew what you really thought & really wanted. I've explained your letter to Jones & wondered if I was doing some wishful thinking & Mary Norton asked me the other day if you really wanted Wallace.

I have a sense of relief that Elliott is confirmed & now the attacks on him will die down but Anna will be the next victim until I do something awful!

Much love, dear, congratulations & I hope you enjoy the return trip & that it is placid & uneventful so you get a rest. Tommy & I will be in N.Y. till the 18th & then I'm there from the 22d to 24th so I hope you arrive when I am home.

Devotedly
E.R.

Trude after the election continued to work in New York for the Democratic State Committee under Doris Byrne, who was in charge of the Women's Division. Someone had leaked to the *Herald Tribune* that the wife of "the Joe Lash" was working there. Eleanor's letter to me was chiefly concerned with Trude's troubles and what she considered a loving wife's role to be.

[E.R. to Joseph P. Lash:]   [Feb. 18, 1945]

It was wonderful to hear your voice this morning & the thought that you were here a week ago seems incredible.

I am anxious to hear what Colonel Shreve has to offer & hope it is something that will interest you but keep you here for a time at least.

It seems to me that until you & Trude are together she will not settle down to a more contented & normal way of life. The times we live in make all you young people feel a great sense of responsibility but when you can carry the public responsibility & Trude can contribute to it by giving you & the children the kind of home you all need & the inspiration & work in her leisure hours, she will be a more serene & healthier person. I will try to keep her in bed Tuesday morning!

The travellers won't return till the 28th or 1st but Anna's letters sound as tho' they are satisfied. I think they must have convinced Stalin of their good faith & that is a great step. The sniping & criticism will now begin! The Wallace & Williams fights should about be over by then! McKellar in the hearings brought down the house by insisting that N.Y.A. [the National Youth Administration] had supported "symphonies" a communistic word which he did not understand!

The same day Franklin was writing her from the USS *Quincy*, which was en route to Algiers from Alexandria.

February 18, 1945

Dearest Babs:

Headed in the right direction—homeward!

A *fantastic* week. King of Egypt, ditto of Arabia and the Emperor of Ethiopia! Anna is fine and at the moment is ashore in Algiers. Give John and Johnnie my love. I hope to come to Washington when you say you were going to be there—one of those 8 days.

Devotedly
F.D.R.

He said nothing about Wallace or Williams and that was not accidental. They were part of his job and he did not want her in it, except on his terms. Communications were erratic. "Dearest Franklin," she wrote him on the 20th—

[E.R. to F.D.R.:]   [February 20, 1945]

Your note of the 12th has just come. I can well imagine that you are tired & I only hope the trip home will give you a chance to let down & rest though I suppose you will have to be preparing a report to the Congress & the nation, I grieve to say I fear some domestic problems await you. It looks as though Wallace had the votes if you convince the Democrats you really believe in him & need him. Aubrey is being questioned by the Com. tomorrow on his belief in the Divinity of Christ which I thought was against the Bill of Rights! His vote is more doubtful. Both fights are merely symbolic of the bigger one "Are we to be liberal or conservative" & I guess Sen. Bailey of N. Carolina & Sen. Ball are two good examples. I wouldn't attach such importance to it only I wonder if we'll be much good in any world organization if we don't fight this question through at home.

Usually we have the Cabinet dinner on March 4th. It wld be hard to get food for a formal dinner this year & it is a Sunday. If you are having the Service that a.m. or p.m. in the East Room why not have tea or a buffet lunch or supper right after it? If you will radio your desires we will make the arrangements. If you are wanting to do nothing we will do nothing, only it can't be done on March 1st for the 4th.

Get all the rest you can.

Trude had been to Washington to speak on a panel and discussed affairs at the Democratic State Committee with Eleanor. I had in the meanwhile written her about the hostile *Herald Tribune** story, saying: "It is important for Trude and me to remember that this type of attack, while it is in terms of personalities, is part and parcel of the 'big fight' that is going on in the party and the country."

[E.R. to Joseph P. Lash:]   [February 20, 1945]

This is just to say thank you for the letter & to tell you that I put Trude on the 4 p.m. train for N.Y. I met her last night & we had fun together talking but she still looks tired. She did a grand job on the panel. She spoke more clearly & better than anyone & looked lovely. She feels Doris distrusts her & that they will have to talk it out when Doris returns. I think [Vincent] Dailey likes Trude or he wouldn't have bothered with the press. I think Doris is shrewd enough to get over her jealousy, for Trude will be very valuable to her. I think things are coming out well but I see Fitzpatrick [chairman of the New York State Democratic organization] Sat. & will try to discover who gave the story out. True, you can work outside the party but I don't want you forced out. Of course it is all part of the big fight & as we win on other fronts it will be easier for you. It looks as though Wallace had a margin of 11 votes. Aubrey is much closer.

The travellers may now arrive on the 27th or 28th. I'm sorry about the deGaulle business. Caffrey, Winant, & Kirk all came to see F.D.R. Wasn't the description of Ibn Saud's tent on the destroyer deck a strange meeting of East & West? . . .†

Hick accepted Eleanor's invitation to stay at the apartment at 29 Washington Square in New York: "Since I am going off the payroll March 1st, I guess it's time for me to ease up on hotel living." Eleanor sent a few friends a speech she planned to deliver in New York in a broadcast for the National Democratic Forum on postwar themes, including the need for full employment and dealing with famine

---

* The *Herald Tribune* reported Trude's presence at the Democratic State Committee as an assistant to Doris Byrne, vice-chairman of the committee and head of its women's activities. The reporter dwelt heavily on her marriage to me and my radical past.

† Jefferson Caffrey was Ambassador to France, John G. Winant to Great Britain, Alexander Kirk to Italy. Caffrey brought word that General deGaulle had declined the President's invitation to meet him in Algiers. Ibn Saud, the spiritual leader of the Arabs as well as the ruler of Saudi Arabia, whom Harry Hopkins described as "a man of austere dignity," along with a large group of retainers, all in burnooses and kaffiyehs, came on board the USS *Quincy* in Great Bitter Lake, transferring from the destroyer which had drawn alongside. To Roosevelt's request that he admit more Jews into Palestine, Ibn Saud gave a blunt "no."

and underdevelopment abroad. She rarely wrote out speeches in advance. That she did so this time indicated that she considered it important. She seemed to be accepting what her friends had long been urging—that many people cared about her views.

[E.R. to Lorena Hickok:]   [February 20, 1945]
I thought you might like to read this broadcast which I make at the Nat. Dem. Club in N.Y. on Sat. at 1 p.m.

Today has been busy. Went & had my hair done at 9. Had the last Arthurdale Com. meeting at 11 but decided to meet if need be again. Had a buffet lunch for 75 & Mrs. Tillett gave her panel on Dumbarton Oaks. It was good but too long. Appointments & tea guests from 4 on & Grace Greene, Fannie Hurst & Michael Hare for the night. The Fulbrights came to dine & we went to the Phil. Symphony. It was lovely & worth the late work which I have just concluded. Quite a day tomorrow too!

"I think the speech is superb—one of the best you've ever done," Hick observed from Georgia. ". . . I hope you will give serious thought to a book on the subject," I urged, and her answer was soft: "Books take time to write Joe dear, but I'll put that speech away till summer or the train trip across the continent!"

A previous letter had described the President's return on February 28.

[E.R. to Joseph P. Lash:]   [February 28, 1945]
The travellers returned this morning & the President looks ruddy & well & rested. Gen. Watson's death on the 20th at sea was a strain & shock, but easier I think for F.D.R. than for Anna. F. seems resigned & philosophic. He says he felt well all the time & he feels evidently that all went well. He liked Stalin better & felt they got on better than before. He says his one complete failure was with Ibn Saud on Palestine but says F. "he's 75 & has been wounded 9 times. It will be easier to deal with the son who comes to power." I believe there are 49 sons! He does not seem upset over de Gaulle. We do go out to open the San Francisco conference.

Anna had a bad cold & her little Johnny has an abscess in his throat. Penicillin is doing wonders however. Franklin wants to go to H.P. Sat. night so I will go & take a Sunday eve. train to N.Y. where we will be Monday & Tuesday & come back here on the midnight.

Trude did so well on Monday & looked so lovely that everyone spoke of her. She has such a happy time with you. Oh! if only the breakthro' at Cologne meant a real weakening of German resistance. I want the war to end for many reasons but my most "personal" reason centers around you

two. Every night I pray that years of close & happy companionship lie
ahead for you two dear people.

An equally long letter went to Hick.

[E.R. to Lorena Hickok:] [February 28, 1945]
It was good to get your long letter of the 23rd & I was relieved that
you liked the speech. It went well when I made it! . . .
FDR & Anna returned this morning. He looks well & says he is well
pleased. Tomorrow he broadcasts from Congress at 12:30 & it is rebroad-
cast at night. Sis has a dreadful cold which I hope will soon pass. It was a
tragedy to have Pa Watson die & yet he had been so ill & I think for him
it was probably not a bad way to go. The Arlington services today in the
pouring rain were dreary & tomorrow at 9 a.m. I go to a "mass." Belle
[Roosevelt] is here & Clochette has had a baby boy & all is well & I think
Belle is getting a rest. She will probably still be here when you arrive at
least I hope so.
Little Johnny has had a bad sore throat which was no way to greet
Anna but he is glad to have her home!
I quite understand your feeling about visiting & I think I'm worse than
you are but it is a sign of age & we must not let it grow on us or we will
be elderly spinsterly hermits!

Hick wrote from Georgia and returned north the next day so we do not have
Eleanor's comment, if she made any, on Hick's worry that her hostess, a widow,
was too wrapped up in her only son, an ensign, and embarrassed him by making too
much of a fuss over him. Hick had added:

What a ghastly thing it is to put all one's emotional eggs in one basket!
It's much better not to have any emotional eggs though a lot of people
would not agree with that statement. The boy is a nice youngster. . . .

Eleanor had found a more rewarding solution to this problem than Hick. Her
mother-in-law's life might have been better, Eleanor firmly believed, had she not
sought to dominate her and Franklin's lives. Though intimate relations with people
were the stuff and substance of her own life, she had learned how to be involved
with people without trying to possess them.
She accompanied Franklin to the Capitol, where he spoke to the nation and
Congress about Yalta. He excused himself for not putting on his leg braces and sat
while he addressed them. "Here is a copy of F's speech," she wrote me, "tho' he ad
libbed so much that the papers put in special 'boxes'!"

[E.R. to Joseph P. Lash:] [March 3, 1945]

It was grand to have your letter, tho' I don't expect you to write dear when you are so busy. . . . How I would hate to make out those "buddy sheets"!

I haven't had a chance for a real talk with Trude so I did not know of your decision. I think there is no question but that you both will be able to work politically. Trude finds it hard. Human nature has such depths but then it rises too! Most of the time it is petty & that Trude finds very hard but as far as our relationship goes, till we leave the White House it will always be a stumbling block, or rather, a mixture of good & bad for you. We can minimize the harm it brings you by care & we will. After we are out, we will be forgotten overnight & then on a purely personal basis we can have good times & I hope I can be useful & helpful but from the public standpoint you will be surprised how quickly back numbers sink into oblivion! . . .

The President is thin but looks well & he plans to be away a good bit. We leave tonight for H.P. & he gets back Wed. a.m. I'll be in N.Y. Monday & Tuesday & return Wed. a.m. too. Then he plans to go to Warm Springs March 27th or 28th & stay till about April 15th. We leave for San Francisco April 20th & return the 30th or May 1st. Then he says in about ten days we leave for London, Holland & the front but this last is not certain. I doubt if I do any travelling alone unless I continue on this trip to other places which he does not cover. He said he wld only be gone if we went for 4 weeks.

. . .

Mr. Golden has been here for 2 nights & he's tearing one play to pieces & starting on another. It is an exciting business! The Congressional ladies come to tea in force!

Hick left the White House, scrawling a farewell note.

[Lorena Hickok to E.R.:] [March 21, 1945]

The goodbyes have all been said, and presently I shall be on my way out of Washington with two orchids pinned to my shoulder—and wishing that I could live up to the nice things that have been said to me these last few days. With you as an example I tried awfully hard to do a good job, and most of the time, I think I honestly did give the Women's Division the best that was in me. But many times I was irritable and impatient and intolerant. One of the qualities I loved most in you is your tolerance, and yet I can be so intolerant if people do not live up to my standards—which have been mostly set by you.

It's all very mixed up and inconsistent and makes me very much dissatisfied with myself. And also makes me feel awkward and inadequate when people say nice things to me—even though I love to hear them and even though, especially now, they mean a lot to me.

I wish I had the words to tell you how grateful I am for your many kindnesses these past four years—and especially for letting me stay here four years. It did two wonderful things—kept me near you and made it possible for me to hang on to my house, which is infinitely precious to me. I shall miss you. Yet I shall feel that you are near. After all these years, we could never drift very far apart. You are a very wonderful friend, my dear.

Eleanor returned to the White House on March 22 and immediately replied.

[E.R. to Lorena Hickok:]   [March 22, 1945]
I got home this a.m. to find you gone & only your sweet note which made me sad. It has been nice knowing you near & having you coming & going. True we won't drift apart but seeing each other casually will be more difficult & as long as I'm here & so busy I'm not going to be much good to my friends.

I'll look forward to H.P. this summer & by autumn you will be in N.Y. now & then!

Tommy & I had a nice trip but they were busy days & I'll tell you a secret age does tell. . . . I really must stop this night travel!

Tommy as usual was vinegary in writing to Esther. She had accompanied Mrs. Roosevelt to North Carolina, where Eleanor spoke for Josephus Daniels, F.D.R.'s mentor at the Navy during World War I.

[Tommy to Esther Lape:]   [March 22, 1945]
You will be amused to learn that Miss Hickok, now that she is retired and living down on Long Island, is going to write a biography—dealing with E.R.'s relationship with her mother-in-law, the causes of the restlessness, etc. She plans to give it to Anna to keep until the right time! True to my resolution, I said nothing, but it seems like great temerity to me. Who really knows both sides of the story of the relationship between "Mama" and E.R? Who really knows what motivates a human being and certainly Hick knows only one side of E.R.—admittedly a side which I do not know.

The one question I long to ask E.R. is "do you realize that all of these so-called intimate friends exploit their relationship constantly and give nothing in return?" I don't dare and shouldn't. But there isn't one of this inner circle who does not use everything possible.

I shall never write a line. I made that promise to Elizabeth [Read] and it is an easy one to keep and I know how much it meant to her to know I was completely honest, but if I did, and was honest, I would be most unpopular!

Tommy's letter also told Esther, evidently in reply to Esther's wanting Mrs. Roosevelt to speak, "Mrs. Roosevelt says she can't be in New York for the meeting on May 3rd." She went on:

> The last trip to North Carolina was to Greensboro to speak at three colleges. The two days were not very strenuous, at least I wasn't tired, but E.R. looked and acted so weary. One or two people who have known her for some time thought she looked much older and much more worn and were concerned. She took a nap both afternoons before dinner which is unusual for her.

I had written her of my concern about the three-week field trip "on the hill" with which the OCS course ended and which was said to be pretty strenuous. She replied—

[E.R. to Joseph P. Lash:]   [Mar. 7, 1945]
    That 3 week stretch on bivouac sounds long & hard for both of you & so remember any time you want to come here you are welcome.
    I'll tell Franklin what you say about the reaction to Yalta.
    I think the report was good & made in such a conciliatory manner. I think de Gaulle is our one stumbling block.
    Jimmy has flown out with his amphibious unit to the S.W. Pacific. Johnny is on Ad. Clark's ship doing a coordinating supply job which is an experience but he says is interesting. Fjr. seems to have been very busy & one of his officers telephoned from Arkansas this morning & sounded very enthusiastic.
    There is a little book by Pearl Buck I'm saving for you when you come!

A long letter from Hyde Park sympathized with my aches and pains but made it clear that I was expected to master all tasks at school.

[E.R. to Joseph P. Lash:]   [March 26, 1945]
    . . . I've thought of you as platoon leader & all your anxieties on your military work. I can only wish you luck but I have great faith in your ability to overcome all obstacles.
    Trude wrote me a discouraged note too. All people who want to do good work & drive at it, have the same experience. One thing which you both will have to learn I imagine is that part of "your work" is in living. Just the way you live has perhaps more influence than the "work" you do. Trude can't make over the State Com. in a few months, no matter how

much she puts into it. It will have an influence though & in the long run it will count. . . .

Tommy was indignant to find Hick in the Washington Square apartment the weekend that Mrs. Roosevelt was in Hyde Park and wondered whether her telephone conversation with Esther had been overheard.

[Tommy to Esther Lape:]   [March 27, 1945]
    Hick, who to my surprise, was spending the weekend at the apartment, left me word that a Connecticut call came in after I had left yesterday. Was it you?
    When I talked to you Sunday night I thought I had the place to myself and was completely surprised on Monday morning to have Georgie tell me that Miss Hickok would have breakfast with me! She came in very late on Sunday and I did not hear her. . . .
    The Syndicate signed E.R. up for another five years until December 1950! I wanted to ask for a better break but E.R. wouldn't let me. This is good, I think, because if we leave D.C. in 1949, in January we have two full years to test out the column when out of the W.H. 1950 seems a long way off except when you realize that we have been writing this column since January 1936. I feel with more time and attention, it can be worth while after we leave Washington, but it can't be tossed off in fifteen minutes.

Tommy may have been distressed to find Hick in the "29" apartment, but that was not her boss's reaction when she went through New York on the way from Hyde Park to the White House.

[E.R. to Lorena Hickok:]   [March 27, 1945]
    It was grand to find your letter here & Tommy said you really seemed in good spirits in spite of your blood sugar. Do take care & rest enough so you won't have to have insulin.
    Of course come back the 19th or 20th & stay as long as you want. In fact if you call Georgie come in any time, she will always know if anyone else is coming.
    The two days in Hyde Park were very good for FDR & I think he'll enjoy the next two if the weather stays good. Everything is just beginning to grow & I wanted to stay right on! I did a lot of reading & Tommy & I have to go up for a long weekend in May and do some necessary chores in the big house & then I'll have to spend a few days in town to get what is needed.
    Today is a horribly busy day here & tomorrow is equally bad in Wash-

ington. I have to go out & talk at a Walter Reed forum in the morning &
I always hope to do well for them.

The midpoint of the course at OCS had passed and I was not among those
"washed out," but my platoon leader cautioned me that I was not "up to par" on
my military. I decided I could not afford to dash to Washington on the weekend, as
I had planned, and instead practiced my "command" voice. It distressed Eleanor
but not as badly as Thanksgiving. Trude, too, who was expecting a baby, decided to
stay in New York instead of meeting me in Washington.

[E.R. to Joseph P. Lash:]   [March 28, 1945]

There is no use my pretending I'm not very sad that you & Trude can't
be here the 7th but long ago I learned to weigh the relative importance
of things & it is all important that you devote yourself to your job.
Failures are not in your line! I'm glad however, that you did go up to see
the children. I think to Vera it will mean something of value.

When your job here is done, it may be possible to meet. I'll be gone
with F. to the coast from April 20th to May 1st or 2d but I won't be busy
in May & for the greater part of the time will be able to adjust my plans
if an occasion comes when we can be together.

It was good to see Trude last evening & I'm glad she has come to see
she must let up a bit. She tires easily & she should stay rested. I'm sorry
she has to take a house for the children,* but it is no doubt the wisest
plan. I told her to use H.P. or the apt. for herself whenever it was
convenient. After you know your next move your plans will all be easier
to make. Don't let her travel much or do much from June 1st on. The
last 2 months one feels clumsy & heavy & "waiting" is about all one is
good for!

I've been on the go all day! Two hours at Walter Reed this morning &
one hour with the men from the reconditioning camp at Camp Meade
from 1:30 to 2:30. At 3:30 a lady to talk about the programs for "Christians & Jews" 4–5 two new Ambassadors & 5 a woman to talk about a
dental programme in the Mass. schools! Mrs. Fayerweather arrived to
stay a week & we went to the Farmers Union dinner for Aubrey Williams. What will the papers say tomorrow?

Now the mail is done & I can grieve a little & be sorry for myself
because you can't come & yet I'm so deeply thankful you are in this
country & some day we'll all be free to be together again.

The war news is good so we should not complain!

---

* In Martha's Vineyard. She felt life was too artificial for the children at Hyde Park.

Margaret Fayerweather was an elderly and somewhat long-winded friend from Albany days. She visited Eleanor every spring. Even Eleanor occasionally admitted she might be a bit tedious, but the loneliness of the White House for her was ever-present and the visit meant so much to Margaret that Eleanor had her back year after year. History is indebted to her diary for some impressions of the President during what turned out to be his last day at the White House on his way to Warm Springs. The President seemed "terribly thin and worn and gray" and his hands shook and when Margaret asked Eleanor about these signs of ebbing strength Eleanor added, "He no longer wants to drive his own car at Hyde Park—lets her drive, which he never did before, and lets her [Eleanor] mix the cocktails if Colonel Boettiger is not present." But Eleanor also cited Franklin's unreadiness to retire, his plans after the White House years to help straighten out the Middle East and Asia and asked her friend, "Does *that* sound tired to you, Margaret? *I'm* all ready to sit back. *He's* still looking forward to more work."

Franklin's condition worried her, Eleanor wrote her aunt, Maude Gray, in Ireland. It was not indifference or insensitivity that caused her to think of his ups as well as his downs:

[E.R. to Maude Gray:]   [April 1, 1945]
. . . Mrs. Fayerweather is here for her week's holiday too so we are quite a household & you can imagine that none of them find Mrs. Fayer-weather very thrilling but I like her & enjoy having her! . . .

FDR with whom I talked today seems settled in Warm Springs & the rest will do him good. He should gain weight but he hates his food. I say a prayer daily that he may be able to carry on till we have peace & our feet are set in the right direction.

Wallace could carry on but no one else in our party & few Republicans. Ball seems to be the best. Elliott cables that he hopes the end will come soon in Germany. The boys in the Pacific are not so optimistic. All three are there now & I suppose in this battle. I can't help worrying about them all, they've been in so long, will their luck hold.

"We've had a busy time," she wrote Hick on Easter Sunday, which found Washington abloom.

[E.R. to Lorena Hickok:]   [April 1, 1945]
I left FDR at H.P. on Tuesday a.m. & put in a busy day in N.Y. speaking far too often! Got in here Wednesday a.m. & so did Mrs. Fayerweather. She is here for a week & I enjoy having her but she bores all the others! FDR arrived Thursday a.m. & left in the p.m. for Warm Springs & Laura with her dog, Margaret Suckley with Falla made up a happy party. . . .

"I talked to Franklin last night," she wrote me the next day, "& he sounded weary but the weather doesn't sound as nice there as here.

[E.R. to Joseph P. Lash:]   [April 2, 1945]

This secret agreement at Yalta sounds to me very improbable but I do know F. murmured that Molotoff was interpreting certain things differently from the way they had been understood. Of course I don't know what happened & can't ask over the telephone but I just don't think FDR would be stupid enough to make secret agreements.

It looks today as though the war was moving fast everywhere & I hold my breath & hope. Wouldn't it be wonderful if you never had to leave again? That is wishful thinking isn't it? . . .

Elinor Morgenthau had shown a growing frailty. Then on April 5 very bad news came about Elinor, who was in Florida.

[E.R. to Elinor Morgenthau:]   [April 5, 1945]

Henry telephoned me that you had a slight heart attack & if that is so do be as good as Harry Hooker was & be still & rest. Complete rest is the only answer & tho' I know how you will hate it, for the sake of all of us who love you do please do just what they tell you to do. . . .

All the news is good so I hope you will not have to worry about Henry much longer. I know that in spite of the brave front that you put up there is constant anxiety in your heart & the long strain wears on your physical condition. All the operations have taken their toll & the mental anxiety when you cannot be active is always harder to bear. Henry has the satisfaction of the accomplishments in his work but I know that you've grieved that your physical strength did not permit you to do more. You are so important to us all that now you must just rest & get well & then perhaps we can all have a quiet summer in the country! I'll promise to hoard my gas & come & stay.

Hick informed her that Mary Norton* wanted to go to the San Francisco founding conference of the United Nations, but the members of the House Foreign Affairs Committee—all men—all wanted to go. Mary deserved to be a delegate and Hick would love to accompany her. Eleanor hedged her reply.

[E.R. to Lorena Hickok:]   [Apr. 5, 1945]

I think they are swamped with people for S.F. but I agree that Mary should go if any Congresswoman goes & I'll tell FDR. I'll write her as soon as I get back on the 13th.

* Democrat, New Jersey, and head of the House Labor Committee.

She told Hick about Johnnie Boettiger's infected throat, Elinor Morgenthau's heart attack, and the news that the ship of Willard Roosevelt, Belle's son, had been badly damaged:

> All these secrets weigh me down! I just pray Willard is safe. Ethel spent 2 hrs with me at noon today & at last my bad FDRjr is writing but he began a letter to her Dec. 15th & mailed it Feb. 1st! I could wring his neck & at times hers too!

Trude was another patient, coming down with a siege of asthma. That had its compensations for me as I went charging up to New York for the weekend. Eleanor wrote afterward—

[E.R. to Joseph P. Lash:]   [April 6, 1945]
> I can't tell you what a happy two days these have been. Somehow when we three are together I feel content & at peace & entirely sure. I love you, don't worry, I'll watch Trude carefully.

A long letter went from Hyde Park to Franklin. She did not know it would be the last she would send him.

April 8, 1945

Dearest Franklin,

I was so weary last night that I went to bed at 9:30 & when you got me it was 10 our time & I was half asleep! We've worked from 9–5 with a half hour off for lunch both days & then gone to see Betty after a bath! Every case & barrel in the cellar is unpacked. I'll have to rearrange much of the china & glass when Anna [McGowan] has cleaned & cleared off some shelves in the store room. It is all put away now & there are some things in the smoking room & in your den for you to decide what shall be done with them. We ache from our unwonted exercise but we've had fun too! In May I'll finish the job.

As I told you I saw Ethel in town on Friday & I think she'd be very pleased if you asked her to come along & bring Joe (Franklin III) to San Francisco. Alice could take care of him & go along as the nurse would have to say with Chris. I said nothing to her so you do whatever you feel like.

I forgot to tell you that Elinor Morgenthau had a serious heart attack at Daytona & Henry has been terribly worried. I think Elinor can't stand the war strain & trying not to show it has had an effect on her circulation.

I am anxious about Belle's Willard & shall be relieved when Ad.

Brown lets me know something definite. I just hope nothing happens as Belle has had so much.

I haven't felt sleepy tonight so I've written James, Elliott, & Frankie, Elinor Morgenthau, Rommie & Sisty & now I must go to bed as we leave in the morning & go up to New Hampshire tomorrow night & I'll be in Washington Wed. eve.

Poor little Johnny was brave but had a horrid time & Anna & John are having a dreadful strain. We had a talk tonight & she'll call me in N.Y. tomorrow.

Give my love to Laura & Margaret & I'm glad they'll be along on the trip to San Francisco. Much love to you dear. I'm so glad you are going. You sounded cheerful for the first time last night & I hope you'll weigh 170 lbs when you return.

Devotedly
E.R.

Four days later she was called out of a meeting in Washington and asked by an upset Steve Early, the President's press secretary, to return at once to the White House. When she arrived he and Admiral McIntyre gave her the news that deep in her heart she had dreaded for many months and never more so than when she had gotten into the car and sat with clenched hands during the short drive. The President was dead, they told her. Her cable to her sons read: HE DID HIS JOB TO THE END AS HE WOULD WANT YOU TO DO.

VIII

End of a Period in History

A S HAD HAPPENED so often in Eleanor's life together with Franklin, personal hurt over his behavior toward her was subordinated to the duty she felt she owed him, the children, the country. So it now was in his death. At Warm Springs, to which she flew after Harry S Truman was sworn in, to accompany Franklin's body back to the White House, she learned from Cousin Polly [Laura Delano] that Lucy Mercer Rutherfurd had been there when Franklin died and that she had been to the White House for dinners at which Anna had been hostess.

To the world she presented a figure of grave dignity as she sought to ensure that the departure from Warm Springs, the funeral train, the slow parade through the streets of Washington, and the services in the East Room were as Franklin would have wished. But privately she summoned Anna to her room at the White House and in a controlled voice told her, whom she considered a beloved, intimate friend as well as daughter, that she felt betrayed. The episode passed. Her relations with Anna, so far as those around them knew, continued on the old companionable basis, but for a long time Anna felt that a certain reserve always shadowed her mother's feelings toward her. The world learned of this only many years later from Anna. Eleanor did not tell anyone but performed her duties with the self-effacement and self-command that had always characterized her relationship to Franklin and that had had the paradoxical result of making the nation more conscious than ever of her presence at his side.

Eleanor, through Tommy, thoughtfully suggested to Trude, who was expecting a baby, that she not come to Washington but go to the big house at Hyde Park and wait there. She also persuaded Hick, who hated funerals, not to come at all. And Esther came to the Hyde Park interment from Connecticut: "Not a guard that did not have my name on the list. Nothing was too small for her to arrange." Elinor Morgenthau was in the hospital in Florida after her heart attack, and Tommy wired me at OCS: AFTER CONSULTATION IT WAS DECIDED WISER FOR YOU NOT COME.

"It's not frightening to be here alone it is reassuring," Trude wrote from the big house. "The house is quiet and really calm. . . . There are soldiers and much activity outside but I can hear nothing inside. . . . Don't you think that the main lines of the peace are really firm?" After Trude left the funeral train at Penn Station in New York following the President's interment at Hyde Park, she described the solemn rites:

[Trude W. Lash to Joseph P. Lash:]   [April 15, 1945]
The funeral was very beautiful. The day was gloriously snappy, very sunny and blue, white lilacs were in bloom—and early in the morning there was a mist over the Hudson,—the birds were singing. And when the West Point cadets were lining up in their scarlet capes and the marines—and the band walked slowly down the hill, and then the hearse with 6 black draped horses and 7 scarlet-bridled ones—it did not look like April 1945—but rather like a timeless symbol of dignified ceremony.

Soon the cannons were booming, then the music started, getting louder as the cortege wound up the hill (how on earth did they have enough breath to climb and blow the brass instruments!)—then the caisson came to a rolling stop outside of the hedge. You heard the coffin grate as it was lifted off the caisson—a simple coffin draped with a flag—old Mr. Anthony [the local minister] quavered the Episcopal service—there were rifle shots—and then it was all over. Fala barked once after each shot—a child whimpered, it didn't really cry—and then it was all over.

On the funeral train back to Washington Eleanor was in one car, President Truman in another. Trude made some notes at the end of that extraordinary day.

April 15, 1945
Jimmy Byrnes seems to be the one who, of all the men who have cooperated closely with the President, will be among the intimates of President Truman. It was very obvious at the funeral at Hyde Park, that he wanted it understood that he belongs to the new era. The Roosevelt family followed the President's coffin and the Trumans followed them, a

few steps behind. Mr. and Mrs. Truman and their daughter were accompanied only by the President's military aid—and Byrnes. He never left Truman's side and after the funeral went immediately back with the President and his family—in their car to the train, while all the other officials stayed for a while.

I heard afterwards from Mrs. Roosevelt that Byrnes had been extremely difficult about the arrangements concerning the funeral. He told her to ride in the same car with the new President which she refused to do. He protested vigorously because he was supposed to ride in the car with the Congressional leaders while the Roosevelt daughters-in-law were with Mrs. R. He proved himself to be "a very small human being, indeed." (Mrs. R.) Some of the cabinet officers seemed completely stunned. Henry Morgenthau arrived early at the house. He refused to refer to Truman as the "President" and told me of his despair at the idea of his successor. He apparently has been shown very clearly that he will not be wanted. Nor has he any desire to stay. The same is true of Miss Perkins. Truman's friends say openly that Biddle will be replaced by Fulton, that Morgenthau will go immediately, that Byrnes will take Stettinius's place,—and that Hannegan and Pauley will be in the cabinet.

Sam Rosenman has handed in his resignation, so has Jonathan Daniels. They are sure that they will be accepted.

Harry Hopkins had a long talk with Truman and reported to Mrs. R. afterwards. Truman said that he felt very competent as far as the army and the conduct of the war was concerned, that he knew his way around on the domestic scene but that he is completely lost in the field of international policy. He asked Harry to help him (he did not offer him a job), but Harry feels that he would not know where to begin—and does not see much hope for cooperation.

Mrs. R. offered Truman her and Anna's help—as far as personalities are concerned, and T. gratefully accepted the offer. At least he said he would ask for her help.

Mrs. Truman will have a number of meetings with Mrs. R. and will be introduced to the newspaper women at a tea on Thursday.

For the time being Truman will keep Grace Tully—and Monty the driver. Mrs. R. told me that she would tell T. what she thinks of people (like Hannegan, Pauley, etc.) but that she will tell him only once,—after that the responsibility will be his.

Mrs. R. confirmed my impression (after her talk with T.) that he had asked Stalin to send Molotoff to San Francisco, *after* he had received a message from Stalin which opened the door for such a request.

Elliott (I don't know who else of the R. children) is afraid that Mrs. R's liberal friends will lead her into unwise actions. He gave me a long speech about the duties of those "who are really close to her." "She must be silent," he said, and "must not let the liberals own her." Tommy supported him very strongly. (I did not take any of it seriously.)

Weariness overtook Eleanor on the trip back to the White House from Hyde Park, but between a sense of envelopment in a dream and talk with her son James, whose flight home from the Pacific ended in his catching up with the train at Penn Station, the journey passed more quickly than she expected.

Back at the White House Eleanor began to write again. Her first longhand letter was dated April 15. It may have been the only one so dated and went to Gen. George C. Marshall. Later there were longhand letters to others. One to me she dated "Sunday night," although it was already Monday.

[E.R. to Joseph P. Lash:]   [April 15–16, 1945]

I have wanted you sadly. I'm sure you know that but for reasons I will some day explain I knew it was better not & when this last training bit is over then we will have real time together. Now I can plan to be with you & Trude & I think I will not do you harm! I am going to need you very, very much. The services were very beautiful here & at Hyde Park and as Franklin would have wished I'm sure. Perhaps his going will unite the nation & achieve his objectives better than had he lived.

It was wonderful to find Trude at H.P. & have her come down with me to New York.—Now my time must be given to the children & the settling of all the business & getting out of the White House Friday afternoon.

                                                E.R.

[E.R. to Lorena Hickok:]   [April 16, 1945]

I loved hearing your voice at Warm Springs & I've felt you near in thought every day. When the busy weeks are over, the business settled & the children are busy with their own lives again you will come & be with me a while, won't you? Be sure to go to the apartment when you wish as I'll only be there this Sat. & Sunday & there is room anyway.

I'm too weary to do more than say I love you.

[E.R. to Elinor Morgenthau:]   [April 16, 1945]

Your telegram was so like you. I knew you would want to come to me & I wish you could have been here but there has been so much to do & so many to think about that I've had little time to think. . . .

Readjusting is not so hard physically but mentally. I realize I counted much on Franklin's greater wisdom & it leaves one without much sense of backing. Having James & Elliott & Anna & John is wonderful, though & all the "wives" are here too. Wills & business are a bit hard to concentrate on but one must & I have my work for the summer cut out at Hyde Park.

Please thank Edith Lehman for her sweet note. I was glad to know you were progressing. Be careful. I love you much.

Sometime on Monday the mail was brought to her and she quickly penned second notes to Hick and to me. Letters were a way of staying in touch with reality. There was regret for what might have been and rarely was in her life with Franklin —the union of souls described in the Episcopal marriage vows that they had exchanged. As she freely acknowledged what Franklin had meant to the world, she gently insisted on remembering that theirs had been a flawed partnership. That became clear in later notes to Hick and to me.

The news of the President's death had evoked from Hick a tribute to his leadership and her confidence in Eleanor's future.

[Lorena Hickok to E.R.:] [April 13, 1945]
. . . I never realized what implicit faith I had in him until now—since he has gone. I still think, God help me, that Truman will make a better president right now than Henry would have made. At least, at the business of getting along with Congress. But I also have an uneasy wondering if *he* will get along with Congress by letting *Congress* run *him*. Also, I don't like his closeness to Hannegan. You will infer—and your inference will be correct—that I haven't much use for Mr. Hannegan. One thing I think I never fully appreciated before was that one never had to worry about the President letting *anybody* run *him*.

Dear, last night I wrote you a pretty dazed and incoherent letter which I am tearing up. It was wonderful and reassuring to hear your voice this morning. No use burdening you with *my* bewilderment and terror. After all, I guess I only feel like millions of other people in the world. And they'll all be telling you! You are like that—people instinctively turn to you for comfort, even when *you* are in trouble yourself. And I guess I'm like all the rest.

For you and your future I have no worries at all—although I *do* hope you will take at least a few weeks off this Spring and Summer to rest. You will find your place—a very active and important place, I feel sure—and fill it superbly. I'd like to hope it may be something in which I can help you if only indirectly, from the sidelines. In a way, you know, you are going to be more your own agent, freer to act, than you ever were before.

Eleanor's second letter to Hick, despite its brevity, said a great deal.

[E.R. to Lorena Hickok:] [April 16, 1945]
. . . I don't wonder you felt panicky, we all did, I think. . . .

Life is so busy that I have no time to think! I was offered two jobs today one paid and one unpaid but I'm not deciding on anything till later in the summer! Much love dear & thanks

E.R.

Mrs. Truman toured the W.H. this morning & I liked her.

Her second letter to me that day spoke of her sense of bereavement.

[E.R. to Joseph P. Lash:]   [April 16, 1945]

Your letter of Saturday came today & it warmed my heart. I know you would do anything to help but somehow I am very calm. Only a bit keyed up because there is so much to do & to think about! I don't need much sleep luckily but some day I want to sleep twelve hours.

I count on you & Trude for much happiness & don't ever lets be sad about anything as long as we can be together! I want to cling to those I love because I find that mentally I counted so much on Franklin I feel a bit bereft. Anna & John & the boys & their wives have all been sweet but the business that must be gone through is a bit appalling. . . .

Before she left the White House, a long letter went to Maude about Franklin's death at Warm Springs. It was silent about the presence of Mrs. Rutherfurd there.

[E.R. to Maude Gray:]   [April 17, 1945]

This may be the last time that I can write by pouch as I leave here Friday so I want to tell you about Franklin. He had grown older & seemed tired but we were at H.P. & he seemed better only too thin. He went to Warm Springs & seemed to enjoy it & had two lazy weeks with only Laura & Margaret Suckley to stimulate him. He was sitting on the porch when he complained of a headache & slumped in his chair. They carried him to bed in a few minutes he was unconscious & never regained consciousness though he lived two hours. I flew down with Steve & Dr. Mac. We started back the next morning. It was a shock but I'm so glad he had no pain & no long illness. I believe his objectives for peace may be more fully attained because hatred seems temporarily gone.

The work before me is heavy & I'm going to be in the cottage at H.P. working in the big house till it is in order & all belongings appraised divided & stored till the end of the war. Then the children will have homes again. . . .

Much, much love you both & I hope soon the war will end in Europe. A kiss to you dear,

E.R.

"Mary Norton wanted to send me to the conference in S.F. & I had to be firm with her," she explained to Hick, who was a confidante of Mary's. "It is better for me to do no job of that kind. Sticking to my own is enough just now. . . . Anna is nigh dead."

A diaristic letter went to Hick on Thursday.

[E.R. to Lorena Hickok:] [April 19, 1945]

The Trumans have just been to lunch & nearly all that I can do is done. The upstairs looks desolate & I will be glad to leave tomorrow. It is empty & without purpose to be here now.

I've asked Helen [Gahagan Douglas] & Mary Norton to come in on their way to Congress & say goodbye tomorrow & the Cabinet comes at 11. At 3 the top secretaries Steve, Dr. Mac. etc., at 3:30 office forces, at 4:30 household, garage etc. at 5:30. I leave for the 6 p.m. train & so endeth a period. Franklin's death ended a period in history & now in its wake for lots of us who lived in his shadow [new] periods come & we have to start again under our own momentum & wonder what we can achieve. I hope you & I will be working together but as I don't intend to take on anything new till all the business of the Estate is over, you may be at new work before I am.

I may be a bit weary when I get home tomorrow but I'm so glad you will be at the apartment. Tommy will probably be more weary than I am!

A final note from the White House to me—

[E.R. to Joseph P. Lash:] [April 19, 1945]

This is the last evening & I have a great sense of relief. I never did like to be where I no longer belonged but the Trumans have been very nice. The upstairs looks desolate with all the things gone that make a home. The really hard thing will be disentangling things at H.P. & getting appraisals made & the children's choices etc. I am going to reduce my possessions during my life!

Requests are pouring in on Mr. Carlin from other countries for my column so Sat. a.m. he is coming to talk with me about it.

Of course it is curiosity as to how I handle this period & will soon wear off. I'll see Trude Sat. a.m. & I hope we can lunch together.

I am weary & yet I cannot rest. When do you think that will cease?

The note to Esther from Hyde Park carefully distinguished the shocked sense of being plunged into a new world that she felt after Franklin's death from "loneliness," which had been with her for many years.

[E.R. to Esther Lape:]   [April 25, 1945]

You have an understanding heart dear but you should know it is more shock & a sense of unreality than loneliness. I think we had all come to think of him as able to carry the world's problems & now we must carry them ourselves.

The things to be done are dull as you knew they would be but they are my job for the children's sake & for the sake of FDR's wishes. It is mostly physical work & it makes mental work harder but I'll get into the way of it soon. . . . Tommy is being grand but you should see the mail!

Many of Eleanor's friends began to busy themselves with planning a role for her now that Franklin was dead. People did not realize, or were unwilling to accept, that she was a strong, independent person. While friendships helped her to define her opinions and stake out her own life, she was determined to be in command of the latter. A letter to Hick about Mary Norton's frailty—Eleanor hoped it was not because of a bad heart—had the explanatory comment: "We can't lose any more liberals." She considered herself a liberal, and it amused her when politically conservative friends like Harry Hooker and John Golden undertook to plan her life: "Everyone has been so kind," she wrote me, "& a few have been very funny. Remind me to tell you about a self constituted brain trust which proposes to order my life in the future!"

She had firm opinions of her own about what was happening:

[E.R. to Joseph P. Lash:]   [April 25, 1945]

I telegraphed Mr. Stettinius in San Francisco & had such a nice wire back. I hope he is successful. I listened to the opening on the radio & Stettinius has strength & feeling in his voice. President Truman hasn't a good radio voice which somewhat spoils his sensible utterances.

She spoke jestingly about those who would plan her life for her:

[E.R. to Lorena Hickok:]   [April 30, 1945]

Harry Hooker came to supper last night & he's had a letter from John Golden so that Committee is really being formed!

In New York she went out to do her first marketing "thinking I had better acquaint myself with stamps & prices etc. The first time in 2 years. I've actually been to market & enjoyed it." She had to live things to really know them. She did not wish to be cut off by pomp and position from life's realities. She had long looked forward to the period when she and Franklin would be out of the White House and laughingly had often predicted that she at least would soon be forgotten.

"The story is over," she told reporters. At the same time she groped for a job to do.

Even during the exhaustion and shock of the first weeks after Franklin's death, her mind kept track of the larger movement of events:

> I've been hoping all day for news of the final surrender in Europe. I can't help feeling the Japs won't keep on long alone. It would seem so much to their interest not to force us to annihilate them.
>
> I went to the christening of the new supercarrier this morning & I think Franklin wld like to have such a noble ship bear his name.

She summed up the nation's reaction to Franklin's death in a letter to Maude at the end of the month that showed her ability to transcend any sense of personal injury in a just evaluation of Franklin's leadership.

[E.R. to Maude Gray:] [April 29, 1945]

> I should have written long ago but since the 12th we have been very busy & I am only just beginning not to feel too weary to think. We knew of course Franklin had aged & no longer felt very strong but everyone including himself felt that with care he could carry through these four years. He wanted to see a good peace made but perhaps a better one will come through his death. The upsurge of love & realization of how much they had depended on him & left to him has I think made many people feel that they want to see his objectives succeed where before they were critical on many points & might have been apathetic or really obstructionist. One feels in the San Francisco conference that a strong hand is missing. I am sad that he could not see the end of his long work which he has carried so magnificently but I am thankful he had no pain & no long illness in which he would have watched others not doing as he would have done.
>
> I want to try to carry out his wishes as far as we can where his material possessions are concerned & I want to do as much as I can for the children.

She owed it to her children and to Franklin's memory to spend the first months after his death settling the estate. At the same time her interest in world events never flagged.

"V.E. day was a curious day," she wrote Maude—

[E.R. to Maude Gray:] [May 9, 1945]

> I was sad Franklin could not have announced it & yet I felt no desire to celebrate. I won't feel any lifting of the burden I imagine till the Japs are through. They seem to want to fight till the bitter end! Some celebra-

tion went on in Times Square but the City as a whole was quiet. We may have more gas but I surmise not much more!

Although she had declined Mary Norton's suggestion that she attend the UN founding conference in San Francisco, she followed developments there closely and not uncritically. U.S. sponsorship of the presence at San Francisco of Argentina, which had played the Nazi game until the very end of the war, seemed wrong:

> I don't like this Argentine business, do you? One should show that one has really shed fascism before one enters the United Nations it seems to me.

Hick had sent her a letter from a Jewish friend in praise of F.D.R.

[E.R. to Lorena Hickok:]   [May 5, 1945]
  Your friend was a bit fulsome but many others seem to have felt the same *personal* loss. It is touching & very wonderful. I hope he knows it! . . .
  I think all is going well with Johnnie [Boettiger] now but I'll be glad when all the kids & the dogs are settled with me & Anna can relax a bit. She looks strained. Business complications & work on "things" will be keeping me busy till June 15th but then I hope to be fairly well enough. When you come in you'll find I have new dining room furniture as I gave Elliott the set from 65th St. This table fits the room better & I hope you will like the combination. I picked each thing up separately. Mr. Baruch is giving me the chairs & sideboard!
  Have you seen that little "Pocket Books" memorial to FDR? It was done in a week—costs .25 has some inaccuracies but on the whole is very good I think.

In a later letter, E.R. seems to be breaking away from the tyranny of "things" and duty.

[E.R. to Trude W. Lash:]   [No date]
  I think I'll come down on the 24th of May to dine with you & Joe may be home on furlough. If so would you like to go & hear Henry Wallace at the New School, we could go together? I'll only stay the night. . . .
  I'm glad you like my columns, they are more fun to do now that I am freer.

My perennial problems with G-2 involved her again—to an extent I did not realize until years later when I read several entries in the Stimson diaries made at the time of the President's death.* I had thought after the President's order that I was to be admitted to Officer Candidates School that my troubles with G-2 were over. I had not fully understood Tommy's telegram to me at Camp Lee the day after the President's death which said that, after consulting others, it was felt I had better not ask for permission to go up to Washington for the services. Later, especially after Assistant Secretary McCloy's letter to the House subcommittee investigating the commissioning of alleged Communists, I had learned a little more. At the end of May Eleanor received a chatty letter from Elinor and after a happy reply that began, "I could hardly believe it was your handwriting & I am so glad you feel able to write again," she added casually, "I had Joe & Trude dine with me tonight & he has his commission & looks well. Walter Trohan wrote a nasty story but tho' he doesn't yet know what they'll do with him, he is an officer!"

I was aware at the time that a last-minute effort had been made to deny me a commission. I knew too that I had not been given an Information and Education assignment but attached instead to a training battalion at Camp Lee. Eleanor did not tell me what had gone on behind the scenes. I found out more when I consulted the Stimson diaries in the 1970s in connection with a projected book on Roosevelt and Churchill. I then learned from Stimson's April 1945 entries how General Marshall had deposited on his desk a file of G-2 papers which questioned my Americanism and urged that I not be commissioned. The allegations worried Stimson, especially after he received a note from the President in Warm Springs asking him to see Colonel Boettiger. What the colonel said I do not know, but Stimson's final entry about the matter read:

> April 30, 1945—I called in Colonel John Boettiger and finally got an opportunity to tell him what I had done in regard to the case of Sergeant Lash. I read my letter to him in order that he could tell Mrs. Roosevelt what I had done. He expressed his gratitude for my action.

In June 1971 I learned from Professor Forrest Pogue, who was at work on his definitive biography of General Marshall, that the general had been an "unwilling recipient" of the G-2 material, which, in addition to attesting to my "un-American activities" during the thirties, concluded—and the words are my paraphrase of what Professor Pogue told me—that I was "influencing Mrs. Roosevelt in a leftward direction." The episode had been a great embarrassment to Stimson and Marshall, said Professor Pogue. Neither wanted to back G-2, nor did they feel "after April 12 in a mood to deny Mrs. Roosevelt anything that she cared about deeply."

On June 1, after I had joined a basic training battalion at Camp Lee, I received the following from Eleanor—

* Stimsom Diaries, Yale University, April 3, 4, 5, 11, 12, 30, 1945. Interviews with Professor Forrest Pogue, June 4, 1971, Nov. 4, 1973, April 1981.

[E.R. to Joseph P. Lash:]   [June 1, 1945]
   Darling, I hate not to be planning to see you but unless you get
ordered away in which case I'll try to go somewhere if it is only for a
glimpse of you, I feel probably the powers that be will be less stirred if I
stay away! How glad I will be when the war is over. In civil life we won't
have to worry about my doing you harm I hope!

   Of Eleanor's help in this matter there is no question, but the perils in this
friendship left me with the feeling that I was an object of special scrutiny, a feeling
which would never leave me.
   The organization of Eleanor's household without the assistance that the
White House had afforded her produced mishaps she explained to Anna.

[E.R. to Anna Boettiger:]   [May 19, 1945]
   I took [hired] a colored ex-service man last Monday & last night he
took i.e. stole my car & drove it to Goshen with 3 girls & 2 other men, all
drunk, & they smashed up & 4 were killed & he & 1 man are in the
hospital still unconscious! I thought I was being kind but next time I'll
bond him! I'm insured but that won't restore people to life or keep him
out of jail if he recovers. He was just a bad boy but it will give a bad name
to all the colored soldiers. I'm trying to get another to emphasize that it
is an individual who went wrong & not a group but I haven't heard of
anyone yet!

   Relations with Anna were back on an even keel:

Anna dearest,   [May 15, 1945]
   The Roosevelt Home Club of Hyde Park sent representatives to see
me today & they want to hold a Memorial Service on the 30th of May at
the grave. They will make it short & it is to be at 10 a.m. starting with a
short prayer by Mr. Anthony, two hymns by the choir & a short 15
minute speech by some one who knew Father well. They want me to get
some one from Washington or from N.Y.
   I wonder if you could find out whether Frank Walker might like to
come if you think he would speak interestingly enough seeing that the
people have to stand the whole time & also that there will be a number
of children representing each school. Perhaps Jonathan Daniels or Felix
Frankfurter or Henry Morgenthau might be good. Please ask anyone you
think would do & tell him that I will be delighted to have him spend the
night before at the cottage. . . .

   So began the tradition of inviting an associate of Franklin's to speak at the
Memorial Day services at the grave. She preferred to have one of the children do

the inviting; if they did not succeed, she took it on herself, always supplementing the bid to speak with an invitation to spend the preceding night with her at the cottage.

She began to turn outward again.

[E.R. to Lorena Hickok:] [June 1, 1945]

I worked hard & had a lot of people at H.P. between Monday & Thursday! The service on Memorial Day was touching & Frank Walker's speech was moving. Yesterday I spoke at a small Democratic women's lunch here at Mrs. Lasker's. I find any gathering of that kind however rather trying still. Perhaps I feel subconsciously I shouldn't be there! The Wiltwyck School meeting was better but I didn't have to speak. . . . Frances Perkins comes tomorrow & I'm most anxious to hear her plans.

A letter to Maude contained details with a period flavor.

[E.R. to Maude Gray:] [June 1, 1945]

No dear I don't want the black dress. I have plenty & when the warm weather comes if it ever does, I'm going to wear white with a black belt in the country.

She was not content to thank people through her column for the letters that poured in after Franklin's death. She wanted each letter answered, she wrote Trude.

[E.R. to Trude W. Lash:] [June 5, 1945]

Tommy sends her love & I think we've solved the problem of help on the mail for her this summer. Dorothy Dow wants extra work to do at home & Tommy will send it to her & I'll pay her for her time. Sheila Linaka will come Sunday & do the filing which Tommy hates so we are set I hope till we settle on a real job next winter. I may take a tiny office rather than go in with a magazine. I've asked George Bye up next week to talk it over.

"It looks as though this evening I might really read a book," her letter to Trude ended, and followed with another sign of a return to more normal ways of feeling, "I hope to do an article on the way to Washington Thursday." Her talk with Frances Perkins troubled her. "There is much in the political field that worries me but I doubt if I can be of much help." The next day she was cheerier: "I'm glad Truman came out for FEPC. I wrote Hannegan a letter & sent the President a copy on general observations of policy & if I get any answer I'll let you know."

Elinor Morgenthau's return to Washington in early June overlapped her own second trip there. "There is one advantage to having you in bed," she wrote Elinor afterward. "You are always there when I am free." She saw President Truman on this trip, and her calendar was as crowded with appointments those few days as her White House schedules had been.

[E.R. to Lorena Hickok:]   [June 11, 1945]

I saw Mary [Norton] in Washington & had a good talk. Helen [Gahagan Douglas] was held on the floor & when she came I was in the tub & couldn't see her. I felt sad but will write her. Friday in Washington was hectic but I saw Elinor who was better. I also really saw a little of Anna & John but in rather a hectic way. Perhaps if you have to say goodbye that is a good thing however.

Elliott & Faye, Scoop [Faye's son] & a housekeeper all came up with me Sat. p.m. & both of them went to N.Y. today & Elliott to Washington. Faye returns tonight & starts to put her house* in order tomorrow & I hope they will be settled there on Saturday when the other children arrive. The youngest & his nurse will stay with me all summer & I'm glad as I think a little quiet is better for a three yr. old.

Have you got a phone yet?

I lunched with Mr. Truman in Washington & I didn't feel queer in the house it all seemed so different. His family is gone, the house is bare & stiff & he's the loneliest man I ever saw. He's not accustomed to night work or reading & contemplation & he doesn't like it. He's not at ease & no one else is. I am so sorry for him & he tries so hard.

I think Frankie may arrive any day. He is just waiting for his relief in Guam & July 1st he reports to the War College in Newport, R.I. I hope he has time to come up with Ethel for 2 days so he can see what I chose & make other choices for himself.

Jimmy is now at sea on the way to an operation. Johnny still seems to be out there.

Elliott hopes in a few weeks to be out of the army. Somehow my family keeps me stirred up even when I am quiet! Pegler is about to attack some old business deal of Elliott's in 1939 & asked his comments & I advised no reply. It is really an attack on FDR & that part is not true & the rest is only partly true but why deny or explain?

With F.D.R. just recently dead, his political enemies sought to get at him through his family. Elliott offered a particularly juicy target. As his brother James later wrote: "Elliott fell in with some millionaires in Texas [in the thirties] who promised him a fortune in radio, used his name and left him deep in debt. Against his best interests father wound up asking Jesse Jones to bail Elliott out and Jesse

* This was F.D.R.'s cottage on the hill behind Eleanor's. The newspapers called this his "dream house." Elliott's decision to live at Hyde Park comforted Eleanor, and she bent over backward to make him and his family feel welcome.

arranged a $2-million loan which saved Elliott's skin." Elliott always reminded Eleanor of his namesake, her father, and the other children felt she indulged him. They felt this even more strongly when he and Faye settled at Hyde Park, even though Elliott's presence made it easier for their mother to continue to live there. "That young man certainly got himself in a mess," she wrote Elinor, "but I blame Jesse Jones a bit too—that does not excuse Elliott's negligence however."

He might have been negligent, but he and his hearty family gave Hyde Park a liveliness and gaiety that her companionable nature welcomed, even as she lamented a lack of quiet in which to think. She wrote Elinor—

[E.R. to Elinor Morgenthau:]   "Sunday" [June (?) 1945]
I would have written you earlier in the week but all four grandchildren [Elliott's & Faye's] stayed with me while Faye worked in N.Y. & Elliott was in Washington & believe me I was busy. I have two horses in my stable very gentle & easily handled by children but Chandler [Elliott's daughter] couldn't make hers go ten feet from the stable without turning back! Finally Elliott yesterday fought him for a 1/2 hr. & came in exhausted! In the afternoon we took all the children to Laura's for a swim & supper & I came down on a late evening train to meet Joe & Trude today. They spent till 3 p.m. when he left to go back to camp & tomorrow Trude will take her children to Martha's Vineyard returning when the doctor decides she should.

Frankie is home & I tried to see him but he had to go to Newport at once so I wait to hear when I can get a glimpse of him. He sounded weary from the trip but so happy to be home when we talked on the telephone.

I'm sorry you won't be up for a little while but if you don't come soon I shall run down to Washington for a few hours with you for I'm getting anxious to see you. Grace Tully comes this Thursday for a few days to finish the papers in F's study. I'm all done in the house & wish Congress would hurry up so that Mr. Ickes could take it over.

Hyde Park might be hot but still it was better than her city apartment.

[E.R. to Lorena Hickok:]   [June 19, 1945]
I spent Sunday with Esther—a lonely soul but I think she stimulates her emotions too much. Sometimes it is better not to live emotionally even if you become some what cabbage like! I stayed till after supper & didn't get home till nearly one a.m. . . . I'm rather glad I can't be here for Eisenhower festivities but I sent him a wire yesterday for FDR would have enjoyed his homecoming.

Hick's ailments and lack of a job made Eleanor jittery. She spoke about it to Mary Norton, who promptly arranged to put Hick on her payroll. "I'm so glad you are going to do Mary's work for her," Eleanor wrote Hick—

[E.R. to Lorena Hickok:]   [June 20, 1945]
   She said she needed the help badly & it is the kind of work you will enjoy. With that as a background I think you could get work from others & live in the country which would be good for you & which you would enjoy. I know I will have jobs which you can do from time to time. How about the telephone?
   I'm so glad you like those columns but the Communist one* which I thought clear seems to be in the process of being used by some as material *against* Russia! What can't some people do! Pegler told someone it was such a good column he was sure I had not written it!
   . . . I like that "gal" [Faye] very much! Elliott gets home tomorrow & I'll know more about his troubles. Anna & John & family are in Seattle & very happy & not worried yet about work!

> Much much love
> E.R.

Tommy is overworked & I can't get her to try to get a Secretary.

A note to me about Pegler—

[E.R. to Joseph P. Lash:]   [June 20, 1945]
   You may be amused to hear that Pegler tried to find out if I had been paid highly for the articles I once wrote for Woman's Day, the A & P magazine, but he found there was nothing wrong there! Pegler & O'Donnell must be afraid that Franklin's memory may interfere with their plans. I am not worried about Anna & John but Elliott's mixup troubles me for him. Jimmy Doolittle called & asked him to go & he will leave in early Sept. for the Pacific. Nothing yet from Frankie.

Henry Morgenthau, Jr., no Nobelist as an economist but courageous and a Roosevelt confidante, had thought his days numbered as Secretary of the Treasury from the moment of F.D.R.'s death. Increasingly excluded from vital international economic decisions, he handed his resignation to Truman at the beginning of July.
   "When Henry called me tonight," Eleanor wrote Elinor, "I felt he was relieved & I hope you too are not unhappy at having the Washington days come to a

---

* American Communists, acting on the basis of an article by French Communist leader Jacques Duclos, written it was assumed at the behest of Moscow, had deposed Earl Browder, portraying his collaboration with the New Deal as a collaboration with capitalism and declaring American "imperialism" again to be the enemy. Eleanor's column said the action had "added fire to the general fear of Communism as an international force."

close." "He feels it is to be too 'political' a set up & I think he's worried about Elinor & glad to be free," she explained to Trude. "Evidently the rumours & Byrnes's appointment [as Secretary of State] were too much."

A day with Edward J. Flynn, who had accompanied F.D.R. to Yalta and then gone on to Moscow: ". . . he was very interesting about his time in Russia," she wrote me. "He told His Holiness the church should change their tactics & stop attacking the Soviet." She was hostess to a "wild household." Martha Gellhorn* was there, "hurting" because of what she had seen in Germany, and Grace Tully. At last Fjr. was coming, but she would have to take him off "and talk hard as we walk Fala in the woods. Children overrun the place all day & we have a picnic lunch daily since 4 or 6 are always here from the top cottage. Aren't you glad to be in bed? . . . I can't leave here Tuesday or Wednesday so I will make it later on, even the following week will find you still there I expect."

There was no lilt in her response to Eisenhower after his visit to the grave: "Yesterday Gen. Eisenhower came to H.P. & I took the children over to meet him but I don't think even the older ones were impressed." She worried about Elliott, she wrote Elinor.

[E.R. to Elinor Morgenthau:]   [July 23, 1945]
[He] is so restless & now that the air force won't keep him he wants to try to get in the Canadian air force & go to the Pacific. He won't go to an airfield in this country which I can understand but I'd rather he came out & faced civilian life. It would be hard but some day it has to be done!

Elliott was interested in settling at Hyde Park, and Eleanor encouraged him to do so. He had ambitious plans—this time to farm and develop most of the 1,000 acres that F.D.R. had owned, as well as live in the top cottage. F.D.R.'s trustees were prepared to sell them to her. She wrote her son James, who was one of the trustees.

[E.R. to James Roosevelt:]   [June 27, 1945]
If you were to decide to sell I would not try to live in this cottage because I know quite well that unless the place is run as a whole and my expenses at the cottage are paid as part of the expenses of the place out of the income coming in from the estate, I could not afford it. I do not expect to put on that income the cost of my apartment in town or any of my other expenses.

I am not interested in the income from the trustees except as it puts this place in order for whichever one of the children desires to use it in the future. If it is Elliott, then I think it will be fine if he can be the one to run it and if during the the next few years he can enter into some

* She was in the process of a divorce from Ernest Hemingway, but if she told Mrs. Roosevelt, the latter did not talk about it.

arrangement by which he has an option to buy it . . . I am perfectly willing to put whatever comes from the estate into this place as long as whatever the cottage costs me is paid by that income. If it can not be, it simply would not make any difference to me as I would not live here. . . .

There was information about the family and an expression of horror over the amount of money the executors had put "into marble for the grave but I suppose you all decided together . . ." A solid paragraph of political news voiced her opinions, as was her wont, quite crisply.

I think President Truman is doing extremely well. I also think that Mr. Stettinius brought the San Francisco Conference to a very successful conclusion. I suppose now that Mr. Byrnes will become Secretary of State and Mr. Stettinius will go to London and Heaven knows what will happen to Winant. I have heard it rumored that he might be sent to Paris which might or might not be good. I hate Jimmy Byrnes going in because with all his ability, I think he is primarily interested in Jimmy Byrnes but after all, Father used him and I imagine that President Truman will feel that his past association will make working together easier.

The three-page, single-spaced letter which Tommy typed had a postscript in longhand that ended, "You won't be so snooty about sheets etc. when you have a house! Bless you, gratefully & devotedly—Mother."

Elliott wanted to borrow the money to buy the place but Eleanor insisted that she try to rent it from the trustees. Anna, who was back living on Mercer Island in Washington state, supported her mother. If there were profits on the rental operation she was willing to have Elliott keep them rather than divide them among all the children. Eleanor had to buy, she informed Anna.

[E.R. to Anna Boettiger:] [August 4, 1945]

The trustees met. They decided to accept no offer of rental on the place but to sell *now*. I lay awake all night thinking about it & then decided I would put all my personal capital in & buy it. It will probably cost more than I have but they will accept a mortgage for the balance since I have to pay 4% & otherwise they can make no investments bringing in more than 3%. It is as broad as it is long. Till I die I get all income so am just without any principal. Having bought it I can then sell to a child (Elliott if he makes the money) or dispose of it as I wish at any time. If they sold now there would be no place for grandchildren or any of the children to come if they happened to want to visit me. Father's tree planting would be ruined & his cottage dismantled. I don't want the job of running it but it seemed wrong to shirk it. Elliott wants to help &

still says when he can he wants to take over. If he doesn't in the end & I live a few years someone of my grandchildren may. I shall go at it slowly & try to run it as a business & in time it may produce a small income. I can't even put off tenants now under O.P.A. regulations. . . .

The job offers began to increase. Trips to Russia and to China tempted her. She thought hard about Sidney Hillman's desire to have her head the National Citizens Political Action Committee affiliated with the CIO-PAC. Once she had tried to persuade Henry Wallace to take over the NCPAC and to broaden its base, but Communist influence in the organization made her uneasy, although anxiety over Democratic Party policies under Hannegan and Pauley confirmed the need of a liberal ginger group. She exempted Truman from her criticism. "I don't wonder the papers confuse," she wrote Trude after her visit to Washington in June, "but I think Truman is trying to follow FDR's policies & yet win more friends in Congress & among Republican leaders. He may succeed & if he does more power to him. He is shrewd but when he has to formulate policies it will be hard."

She consulted her friends about the NCPAC offer. All stressed that administrative lines had to be precise and her authority recognized, especially in view of some of the shadowy Communist influences at work in the organization. "Your analysis of the N.C.P.A.C. position is clear & right I think," she wrote me. "I'm going to meet with a small committee on the 17th I think in the afternoon & talk it over. I shall ask just what you have suggested."

[E.R. to Joseph P. Lash:]   [July 18, 1945]
   The meeting with the N.C.P.A.C. last night left me torn in my mind.
I don't know how useful I will be to them. I have an aversion to taking on
responsibility except individually & this is a big one. On the other hand,
it seems to be the one group that has organized nationally & can sway
political parties & they need to be swayed.

In the end she turned Hillman down, using the same argument Henry Wallace had used with her in December, when he turned aside her proposal that he head the organization—that it would "alienate" the Democratic Party.

That left her still groping for a job to do, especially as the powers that be indicated that it might be wise to postpone any trip to Russia until the spring of 1946 and as in China the Generalissimo's troubles began to mount. She took a small office in midtown New York and employed Hick to help with articles and speeches. "I don't think I'd hide you were doing research and digests for me," she advised Hick. "It'll come out & they'll think I'm trying to hide something! Don't talk about it unnecessarily but be truthful."

She worried about Tommy, who was unwilling to take a vacation or employ an assistant and understandably began to slow down. "Tommy left today for 4 days vacation," she informed Elinor, "& she acted as tho' she were being sent to the stake!" Eleanor watched over Trude and Marie Morgan, whose husband, her Aunt Pussie's son, was in the Pacific. Both Trude and Marie were in the last weeks of pregnancies, and were in and out of her apartment on Washington Square, where Trude was staying when labor pains began.

[E.R. to Elinor Morgenthau:]   [September 1, 1945]
     At 6:30 a.m. yesterday Trude appeared & she was having pains every 10 minutes. At 7:30 we were in the hospital & a fine boy weighing 8 lbs. 6 oz. was born at 11:15 last night. It was a very hard time for Trude but both she & the baby are fine today & Joe arrived just after the baby did last night so all are very happy & then I can begin & see some of the numerous people I've set aside till after these hospital visits were over.

The next day was V-J Day. "Isn't it wonderful to be in a world where peace has come?" she wrote Hick. "I find that many are worried however. President Truman called me last night & spoke almost at once of the dreadful problems ahead. I hope he speaks with confidence however for the people need it in spite of their rejoicing."

[E.R. to Lorena Hickok:]   [September 1, 1945]
     At 5 a.m. the next morning I was waked to take her [Marie] to the hospital so you may have helped to bring on that long delayed infant! Anyway it is a boy weighed at 8 lbs. 13 oz. & arrived quickly. We were at the hospital at 6 a.m. & at 11:15 a.m. it was born.
     Today I brought Trude & her baby home from the hospital & all goes well. They will be moved by the middle of the month I'm sure but my room is empty in any case so you can come when you want. . . .
     Yes, I'd like to wring Churchill's neck but our Lend-Lease performance seems to me bad manners which may have serious consequences. I tried to get Sam Rosenman to tell him how I was feeling today but didn't succeed.
     I'm going to H.P. tomorrow p.m. to meet De Gaulle Sunday a.m. at Franklin's grave. I'll return Sunday p.m. to meet May Craig here.

"I told your mother she better advertise that she births boy babies only!" Tommy reported to James. They had rented an office in midtown and she had her own apartment at "29." "It is nice to have life more or less on the verge of settling down."
     Hick, noting that she was now fifty-two, and that was four years older than Eleanor had been when they first met, recalled how old Eleanor had felt when she reached fifty: "Tell me—do you still feel like an old lady?" "My dear," replied Eleanor, who was almost sixty-one, "I feel more of an old lady than at fifty but I've learned to hide it better! I have more limitations but I know them & accept them!"

The visit of May Craig, a newspaper columnist who had toured the western battlefields and seen some of the concentration camps, like that of Martha Gellhorn and another columnist, Doris Fleeson, had been a wrenching affair. "May's description of Dachau made me feel ill," she wrote to Anna.

[E.R. to Anna Boettiger:]   [August 27, 1945]
. . . My column circulation has been going up steadily until now. I'm getting $300 or $400 more every month than I did in the W.H. I'm glad you & John think they are good. Someone took a test of readability & I came out [undecipherable] but the reason isn't so flattering. Lippman *[sic]* & Krock require a college education to understand. A 5th grader can read me, so more people read me! Geo. Carlin is delighted but it is a rather doubtful compliment!

"The columns are always better when I'm stirred up but I can't be that way all the time," she advised Hick. And sometimes that which stirred her she thought better to ignore publicly.

[E.R. to Anna Boettiger:]   [September 13, 1945]
Pegler wrote one fairly decent column on Jimmy but today he attacks Pa openly & I would love to answer so it is taking much self control to keep quiet. Read it if you get a chance & remember how snidely he insinuates vast millions & no thought for others in his employ. They are all receiving full wages & will be pensioned as Pa expected but it is best to say nothing. . . .

For a few months the attacks on F.D.R. had been absent, but there was a steady drumbeat of criticism against other members of the family.

[E.R. to Joseph P. Lash:]   [July 13, 1945]
Randolph Paul [formerly a high Treasury official and now a lawyer with Paul, Weiss, Wharton] told Elliott the Rep. Natl. Com. had started the attack on him & were going to investigate my income tax & Jimmy's. There is nothing in mine but they can, they think make enough look badly in Jimmy's to keep the waters muddied till the 1946 campaign! I rather look forward to being investigated, I can say so much I couldn't in the past!

The war was over and her letters were full of the men returning and her boys looking for jobs. All summer she had written her columns and her magazine page "If You Ask Me." Now she began to prepare a few lectures in the late autumn. Hick helped with material.

[E.R. to Lorena Hickok:]   [September 26, 1945]

I've been dreadful about writing but I've been too busy to put pen to paper! The stuff you sent me was wonderful & will fill a need not only for the speech I used it for but for many other occasions. The L.H.J. questions don't come in till between the 1st & 5th but when you get back I've a load of reading for you to do. Wire when you will come to the apartment. Fjr & Johnny are in my spare room tonight & tomorrow but after that I expect no one & look forward to you but the boys do surprise me now that they are looking for jobs. Also they show more interest in not paying hotel bills!

I'm glad Mary [Norton] is going abroad but a little worried too. There is so much unrest now & they will try to break labor & I hate to see friends of labor leave responsible positions. . . .

All the boys are looking for jobs but John is the most serious I think! Fjr still flits from idea to idea!

I had been put out of Information and Education and ended my army career as Assistant Receipt and Storage Issue Officer at Fort Oglethorpe, Georgia. When the Army announced its point system for determining the order in which men were separated from the service, I turned out to be among those with the highest number of points on the post, our son Jonathan's birth two days before V-J day having given me an extra twelve points. So I was among the first out.

Eleanor had been sending me a $50 check monthly to supplement my army pay. She should no longer do so, I wrote, as I had accepted a job, and she answered—

[E.R. to Joseph P. Lash:]   [No date]

Please keep this last check. You won't begin to earn till Nov. 1st & it will help my income tax since I pay it as a salary to Trude! I hate to stop because of the sense of pleasure & "belonging" it gives me!

Along with the good, I brought you plenty of bad I feel but in the long run the good will outweigh the bad I hope. You & Trude together can surmount any difficulties I am sure. Of course I'll turn to you both probably too much! Johnny will always be close to my heart.

Ever present was the question of the work she should undertake as her main job. She had agreed to teach again, she wrote Hick.

[E.R. to Lorena Hickok:]   [October 14, 1945]

Every Wed. evening I give a half hour lecture at the Women's Trade Union League Class in Current Events—20 minutes review of the week, 10 minutes a special subject interpreted. Then they have 1/2 hour of questions. Will *you* take any papers you think essential, bill me, clip significant things or items of interest, list & send me.

Have you anything new on housing? I'll send you latest reports I have & you can add anything not in material you gave me last summer. Won't have to have this till November. . . .

We've been much upset since Marie Morgan called up yesterday a.m. to say the War Dept. had wired Forbes died on the transport coming home. She came right down here & my heart aches for her & one can do nothing, only watch a young thing suffer! Strange world!

Anna and John came east, the letter went on.

Sis went all over the big house & kept saying "It is the last time we'll see it this way" & I think it was very hard for her. Natomah her old pony will have to be shot too & I could see she was sad but the poor horse can't eat hay or grass anymore.

She continued to use the word "hectic" to describe the schedules she set herself. At the beginning of November she thought the load was easing:

[E.R. to Lorena Hickok:]   [November 8, 1945]
    Life continues to be hectic but much less so & I see daylight ahead. I won't be satisfied however till Tommy tells me she has nothing to do, then I will feel I've achieved a victory.

    The material for last Wed. lecture was a great success. . . . My first lecture on city housing is Monday night.

"Jimmy dearest," she wrote him on the West Coast—

[E.R. to James Roosevelt:]   [November 12, 1945]
What wonderful news! We have all been rejoicing with you & I am especially glad to have another James Roosevelt in the family. I know Father would have been pleased. The baby is so big & must be strong too. I hope both he & Rommie continue to do well. I've written her a little note . . .

She reported other family news and said she hoped to see Jimmy's house in January, when she planned to be on the West Coast. She still was groping for a job to do.

Anna and John, after their trip to Hyde Park and Washington, returned to the West Coast in search of a newspaper to run. They had to start with a shopping weekly and were upset, especially Anna, because of the scarcity of letters from Eleanor. She had written no letters, Eleanor replied.

[E.R. to Anna Boettiger:]   [December 5, 1945]

How could you think anything was wrong between us & I would not tell you? I've thought of you daily & rejoiced that we had the time together but life has been literally so busy that I've gone to bed between 2 & 4 a.m. when I couldn't stay awake any longer & I've written *no* letters!

Thanksgiving was nice at H.P. but busy. The whole Committee on choosing H.P. for U.N.O. hd'qt's visited me in a.m. . . . .

A telephone call from President Truman changed her plans completely. It gave her the job she longed for, although her first reaction, as it had been through much of her life, was to protest her unfitness for it. Fjr. was with her at her Washington Square apartment when President Truman called and he heard his mother remonstrate that she knew nothing of foreign affairs or parliamentary procedure. But the President had insisted, she told Franklin Jr. when she returned to the table. He wanted her to serve on the U.S. delegation to the first United Nations Assembly in London. She had to do it, her son urged her, as did the rest of us.

It had not been an impulsive gesture by the President. He had told Byrnes he wanted him to find an appointment for Mrs. Roosevelt in the field of foreign affairs because, like Henry Wallace's, her support was indispensable to him. Byrnes promptly placed her name at the top of the list of those whom he wanted at the General Assembly, noting that because of her husband's interest in the success of the UN she might accept. Truman had immediately telephoned her. Only the racist Senator Theodore G. Bilbo of Mississippi opposed her confirmation by the Senate.

But she never took anything for granted in politics. The incessant attacks upon her, the resignation that had been forced upon her at the Office of Civilian Defense, added to her wariness. A few days after Truman telephoned she wrote Hick—

[E.R. to Lorena Hickok:]

Please bring me Clare's [Luce] speech.* I have not seen it. I'm not a bit worried. I was explaining not attacking as every man there knew. It was Hearst papers largely. I don't care whether I'm confirmed or not. Life is pleasant & less busy as is. I'm not looking for more work!

---

* Clare Boothe Luce, Republican Congresswoman from Connecticut, reproached Mrs. Roosevelt in the House of Representatives for having made a speech critical of Madame Chiang Kai-shek. Madame Chiang was "two different people," Mrs. Roosevelt said, one who talked persuasively about democracy, the other who "hasn't any idea how to live it." Mrs. Luce described Mrs. Roosevelt as "one of the world's noble women," but recited Madame Chiang's record as proof that she knew how to live as well as talk democracy. In private letters, however, Mrs. Luce felt warmly about Mrs. Roosevelt's achievements as a woman.

But she did care, not for herself, she kept insisting, but for Franklin's sake. She thought President Truman was wise to think her presence in London might serve to remind delegates of Franklin's great hopes for the new organization.

[E.R. to Anna Boettiger:]   [December 20, 1945]

All my plans are changed & I leave on the 30th of Dec. by boat for England. I'm leaving Tommy here, she isn't well . . . [Ambassador] Winant will find me someone there. I'm going to write the column but nothing that the press is not in on where the conference is concerned but I think there will always be personal things which can be made interesting. I won't be seeing you therefore dear for a while. . . . They say we'll be gone from 3–6 weeks!

You will be relieved to hear that I had a physical check up & for my age I'm a remarkably healthy specimen!

. . .

Much much love darling. Say prayers that I'm really useful on this job for I feel very inadequate.

She boarded the *Queen Elizabeth* on December 30. "My cabin is comfortable & everyone most kind," her farewell note to Elinor read. "I hate to leave but if I can do something worthwhile it will be worth the effort."

Everyone was "most solicitous" for her, she wrote Trude and me. "I hope all goes well these next weeks for you at home & for me abroad since it is your lives & Jonathan's that will be affected most. . . . I can't say it is fun going alone but I know it is better for Tommy & it is only for a few weeks!"

She had made a will, she wrote Anna. "I am comfortable & tho' the responsibility seems great I'll do my best & trust in God."

IX

Wonderful to Be Free

S HE WAS sixty-one at the beginning of 1946. Like many people at that age, she might have been content with a ceremonial role as a delegate to the first UN General Assembly in London. Two colleagues, Republican delegates Senator Arthur Vandenberg and John Foster Dulles, were distressed that she had been selected and did their best to relegate her to window-dressing roles. She herself had begun to speak of her readiness to retire to a rocking chair at Hyde Park, but that was jest and contrary to her spirited temperament. She had turned down Sidney Hillman's invitation to head the National Citizens Political Action Committee because "I did not feel I could control the committee's policies," scarcely the statement of someone who wanted to shun responsibilities. Since World War I she had sought out only the jobs that meant real work and taxed her abilities. Even the pressures in the White House to become a "Dresden doll" had not kept her down. She had emerged from those years as the New Deal's conscience. The experience, nevertheless, had left her with a sense of unfulfillment. She had served as an instrument of Franklin's purposes, not her own, and she came to describe the years after his death as "on my own."

The calendar of these years remained as crowded as it had always been, but now she more easily acknowledged the pleasure all this gave her. Virginia Woolf's voluminous diaries have been described as full of "the rush and glory and the agony and never getting used to any of it." Similarly, Eleanor Roosevelt's letters to her children and friends and her Assembly diary are her record of the new people she came to know, the new scenes she participated in, her joy in people's company, and her freshness and wonder at mankind's progress, slow though it might seem to be, and her wish to help shape it.

Her singular personality, at once so dominant yet intuitive and sympathetic, constantly put forth new growth. She spurred herself to make friends of people who helped her self-definition, and she had learned to suppress any initial impulse to say "no" to a new experience even if it meant danger. According to Virginia Woolf's final diaries, when some people taxed her with taking needless risks in writing although she had been so successful with the old narrative forms, she flung back—and the words might well have been Eleanor's after Franklin's death—"I will not be 'famous,' 'great.' I will go on adventuring, changing, opening my mind & my eyes, refusing to be stamped & stereotyped. . . ."* That was the spirit in which Eleanor embarked on her new role as a member of the first delegation.

As soon as she boarded the *Queen Elizabeth* she began a diary that she sent to Tommy to copy and send around. Although its first entry lamented an inability to remember names, a sign she suspected of oncoming old age, she welcomed the new United Nations world into which she plunged. She mastered the heaps of documents that were delivered to her stateroom, and sought to plumb their real meanings in talks with advisers and other delegates. She made a broadcast for NBC to the United States and held a ninety-minute press conference in which she placed one remark off the record. In terms of her personal development it was the most significant:

> For the first time in my life I can say just what I want. For your information it is wonderful to be free.

One of her first shipboard letters went to Elinor Morgenthau, whose frailty worried her. She wrote candidly to her old friend about the panjandrums on the delegation, who might not have appreciated her realistic eye.

[E.R. to Elinor Morgenthau:]   [January 3, 1946]

The basket from Charles has been a joy and your thought as usual warmed my heart. I was rather gloomy starting out alone but I am sure it was the wise thing to do. Everyone has been very kind and I was very glad of the pills Henry took so much trouble to get me. The first two days were pretty rough but just two pills set me on the right path and I never have felt ill again. I don't like sea trips, however, and if it can be done I shall fly home.

I find the importance of the Senators a bit trying, Gee! but they are touchy. If they say anything and the speaker doesn't stop and listen they

---

* I am indebted to Robert Kiely's review of vol. 4 of *The Diary of Virginia Woolf* for pointing up this aspect of Woolf's final entries (New York *Times Book Review*, July 11, 1982).

are all upset. I have committed no sins so far at least I know of none, but believe me I am watching my step. I have worked hard, going to every meeting I could make and seeing as many of the bright young men as I can on the side. Mr. Pasvolsky [chief State Department adviser on the UN Charter], if that is the way you spell his name, is for me an interesting study, and he strikes me as a pretty smooth article. I wish I knew what Henry thinks of him. Our ships news is very meager so I know little of what is going on in the world.

I hope you take care of yourself and I shall write when I can. Mr. Stettinius told us he hoped we could be done in three weeks, so I hope.

A world of love dearest,
E.R.

The letter to Elinor was typed; so was the letter she sent Trude from London. The letterhead read "United States Representative to the United Nations."

[E.R. to Trude W. Lash:]   [January 6, 1946]

You and Joe will get many letters written on scraps of paper from now on but I thought you would like just once to see one of the perquisites which go with being a delegate. Tommy will I hope have sent you the diary of the trip. I truly learned a good bit and worked hard on the trip. I talked with many of the young state dept. boys. They have a plan for international trade and commerce all worked out but it seems to me to have no foundation since nowhere do they propose a world survey of resources. They say Russia would not stand for it, but each country could do their own and as confidence grew perhaps they would see the value of an exchange of knowledge. Without it I see no hope of making raw materials more accessible on a more equitable basis. I met a few of the South American delegates and the head of the Canadian delegation on the ship. My old friend Hadow from the British Embassy was on board. He is familiar with every step of the way since he was at San Francisco and translated the Charter into Spanish.

Louise Morley [she worked with Trude and me at International Student Service] was sent over from the Embassy to help me on arrival. She has been very good about showing me how to get to the necessary places. We went for supper to the Embassy canteen, which is a godsend since we get army food which is really good. I showed her all the pictures of the baby and she thinks him very beautiful though no picture of course can convey all his charm. She still hopes Peter [Cochrane, her husband] may be home in the spring. We lunched together again today but I doubt if I can see her again until Wednesday. I shall stop with Janet Murrow's package on Tuesday on the way to the closing of the Red Cross Rainbow Corner. I wish it was not closing though of course we have fewer men here. They do come over on leave from France and Germany and I think they need the Red Cross badly.

I have a nice girl to do personal things every morning from nine to eleven. I leave her at ten and go to the office but she will do notes and leave for me to sign. The lady I have in the office is white-haired but seems capable. I went to look at my office on the way back from lunch today so I would know where to go without asking tomorrow. It is very nice with good light for both me and my secretary. I'm really sorry Tommy isn't here to enjoy the luxury. I have a double room, bath and sitting room at Claridge's and it is warm beyond belief, perhaps because it is warm and almost sunny out today!

I telephoned Maude this morning and I hope she and David will come here soon. David can stay with a friend in his flat and Maude says she will be glad to share my room since no other would probably be available and I may not be able to go to Ireland when this conference is over. I am still waiting to hear from Mr. Stettinius whether they would like me to go to Germany or not. The LaRue Browns* are coming in to tea in a few minutes and tonight I dine with Mr. and Mrs. Adlai Stevenson. He has headed our work on the temporary commission since Mr. Stettinius had to go home and I hope to learn something about the people on the other delegations who are still not even names with which I am familiar.

How I wish I could see you and Joe and Jonathan this minute. You all seem very far away, and I don't like it very much, but if something worth while is done it will be worth it.

She worked hard, and her weariness began to show in a laboriously typed letter to Hick.

[E.R. to Lorena Hickok:]   [January 9, 1946]
This is just a little note to go in Tommy's letter as I hope she is giving you my news. Bill Chaplin was on the boat coming over and I did a broadcast for him and expect to do another few words on Sunday the 13th.

I hope your time with Helen [Gahagan Douglas] goes well. Wish you would get Tommy to give you anything she can to read and brief for me so there won't be a mass of printed material to go through on my return. I'm reading so much technical stuff here that I'm getting a disciplined mind again.

It is dark here by four. If you want [to] read anytime you have to turn

---

* LaRue Brown, a Harvard classmate of F.D.R.'s and active in his behalf in Massachusetts politics. His wife, Dorothy, was a daughter of George W. Kirchway, who had been dean of Columbia Law School when F.D.R. was there and a co-worker with Eleanor in the early years of the League of Women Voters.

on the lights. These are tough people, they would have to be to stand their climate.

"The work is hard," a letter to me commented—

[E.R. to Joseph P. Lash:]   [January 10, 1946]
& I should have someone familiar with my interests & people connected with them. I am getting thro' but I have of course to explain everything.

The opening today was impressive but my column will tell you about it. I did a bit on a broadcast tonight too & I'll do another Sunday night & on the 17th the Albert Hall speech will I think be broadcast.

. . .

The strikes must be very bad at home & they look very wrong from here. I feel the Pres. should call in labor & management & tell them what this means to the world & find some solution.

Because she wrote late and got up early she worried that she kept Maude awake. Her physical stamina made her rather proud, she told Anna, who had gone into the hospital for tests.

[E.R. to Anna Boettiger:]   [January 11, 1946]
. . . You are less rugged than your Ma. The old lady holds up very well under the load of work here & believe me it is formidable! Tommy will send you the copies of my diary letters which I try to send when I can't say all in my column. It is bad not having Tommy or someone who knows the people with me & overworking new secretaries seems inevitable but I am managing tho' some of the letters I sign make me smile. They sound like Senators or State Dept. officials.

My contribution to this meeting beyond the fact that I am Pa's widow & by my presence seem to remind them all of him is very insignificant. Perhaps when we get to work on our Com. I shall feel that there is more I can do. I've got on well with the delegation & I don't think they've tried to hide anything as yet!

January 13 was a Sunday. That meant time for personal letters. She had been assigned to Committee 3, the Economic and Social Committee. The men had put her there on the assumption that it was a "safe spot" where she would not do "much harm," she later concluded. At the time she willingly accepted it.

[E.R. to Elinor Morgenthau:]   [January 13, 1946]
Yes, I think my assignment to a committee was the natural one. We have only met once to elect a chairman & plenary sessions with speeches & voting will go on into this week. Then our Com. work will begin & I

think that will be most interesting. In the big sessions only Byrnes speaks
& I confess to boredom but I go & sit for fear something will come up &
I won't be on hand!

"You know I don't like sitting & doing nothing," her diary note that day said.
"Remember in getting someone," she cautioned Tommy—

[E.R. to Tommy:]   [January 13, 1946]
that we will be away a great deal, or at least I will. I want to do some
lectures & go to the west coast soon. Next if the session [UN, 2nd part] is
not held till the summer I will go to Russia in the early or late summer,
which ever fits in best with Elliott's summer plans, as I do want to go to
Campo with them & be at Hyde Park when the children are there. . . .

Writing to Trude, who had confessed to a sense of "what's the use" in the
face of some office difficulties, she urged her own philosophy of keeping at it.

[E.R. to Trude W. Lash:]   [January 13, 1946]
. . . & some day you will see the fruits of your labors. The people here
heighten my belief in people. They stand outside to see the delegates,
rain doesn't keep them away. They look shabby but they hope & if they
can surely we can too. . . .
   The delegation won't *follow* me dear but I think they won't like to
propose anything they think I would not approve of! Thus they want to
keep to organizations & I go along on that. The next part is when subjects that are difficult come up.
   I wish you could have watched the Russians' faces when New Zealand
apparently opposed G.B.'s choice of Canada for the Security Council.
They would feel such behavior among their satellites showed weakness &
it is going to take time to realize that when you are sure on fundamentals
you can differ on non-essentials. G.B. had told the Dominions to decide
& they could not agree. S. Africa & Canada chose Canada. N.Z. & India
& Australia wanted Australia. We had told Gr. Br. we'd vote for Canada
& we did but Australia won!

"Oratory ended yesterday and Committee work begins tomorrow," a postscript to Elinor announced. When Tommy from New York cautioned her boss that
she was doing too much and eating too little, she insisted she felt in splendid form.
Even when she lost her voice, which she did just before her address to the august
Pilgrims Dinner, she did not slow down. Leadership was ingrained in her, veiled
and controlled though it had been while Franklin was alive. Her judgments were
compassionate, but there was no mistaking the sense of governance and authority

with which she viewed the UN scene. A crisp paragraph to Elinor Morgenthau shrewdly appraised the other members of the delegation, all men.

> [E.R. to Elinor Morgenthau:] [January 20, 1946]
> Vandenburg *[sic]* is smart & hard to get along with and does not say what he feels. Byrnes is much too small for the job & when all is said and done Stettinius is more courageous and honest but might be more easily fooled since Byrnes is smarter but can never give any inspiration. I think Connolly *[sic]* is nicer than I thought but he has no real sensitivity and is always the Senator from Texas. J. Foster Dulles I like not at all. Frank Walker is staunch and true and competent. Sol Bloom is able and petty and vain and yet in ways I like him, ex-Sen. Townsend (74) is honest, plain and I like him but not very brilliant.

Equally unsentimental was her evaluation of the difficulties and the time it would take to root the new UN in mankind's thinking.

> There are too many old League [of Nations] people here and too many elderly public men. Young blood is badly needed but the men who would now be in public life and around 40–60 were killed in the last war. One is actually conscious of the loss of a generation when canvassing Europe for the Secretary General. People keep writing urging the establishment of a world government, why our own Congress wouldn't stand for doing away with the veto power and Russia is back in Daniel Boone's days so why should she! It will take years of working together and creating confidence before anything beyond what this structure sets up can be attempted. I wish everyone wld. make this work first.

She said the same to me in a comment about pleas that she stand for world government.

> [E.R. to Joseph P. Lash:] [January 20, 1946]
> . . . We will have to crawl together, running will be out of the question until all of us have gained far more confidence in each other than we have now. I can't even get Byrnes to agree that we might do better if he talked at one time to Bevin, Gromyko, Bidault [France] and Koo [China] on the Secretary General.

The "elderly" diplomats made her uneasy:

> They are accustomed to diplomatic ways, secrecy appeals to them, and this will only succeed if everyone says what they really think. I think perhaps the biggest job to be done is to make the people at home feel this

is their machinery which they must use to build peace, but they will have
to keep it oiled and make it run.

A drive that Sunday to Windsor, where she was shown Napoleon's letter of
surrender after Waterloo as well as some original drawings by Leonardo and Dürer,
brought forth the familiar lament that a life in the library might be more agreeable.
"I begin to think we all hurried too much in life." But the leisurely life did not
comport with her zest for experience, nor the exercise of a sense of command that
repeatedly came through her diary notations about America's role in the world:

> I watch our delegation with grave concern. Secy. Byrnes seems to me
> to be afraid to decide on what he thinks is right and stand on it. I am
> going to try to tell him tactfully that everyone has to get the things they
> need from us and that is our ace in the hole. We could lead but we don't.
> We shift to conciliate and trail either Gr. Britain or Russia and at times I
> am sure a feeling that we had convictions and would fight for them would
> be reassuring to them.

A note to Hick reflected her constant worry about Tommy.

[E.R. to Lorena Hickok:]   [January 22, 1946]
   I was glad to get your letter & to know you were to be in town this
week & with Tommy. I feel much happier about her & I hope you do go
up to Hyde Park for the week end. I'm glad you think she feels better &
is catching up with the work. I loved all you told me about Fala too. I
miss him & I'm glad he's happy.

She went on to talk about the difficulties of working with the Russians as well
as persuading the other members of the delegation to her point of view. The role
that she saw for the United States reflected her own struggles as an individual not
to become the pale echo of a formidable mother-in-law and a power-loving husband. To hold her family together she had learned to cloak firmness of position in
gentleness of manner and made both more acceptable by a readiness to take on
added responsibilities. She now urged the same on the United States delegation.

[E.R. to Lorena Hickok:]   [January 22, 1946]
   This is turning out to be an interesting experience tho' not very excit-
ing. The next session will be the one where debates really occur. The
Russians are hard to work with because everything has to be decided in
Moscow but I think a little frank firmness on our part would help. Byrnes
is a curious study, when I come home I'm going to give you thumbnail

sketches of my playmates that I don't dare put on paper. I have one priceless letter from the Sec. for the archives.*

I'm going to Germany before I come home but a week after the close should see me in N.Y. I shall try to go to Maude Feb. 2d for Sunday & I think Gen. Ridgeway will take me.

We had a funny meeting this evening. At seven p.m. they voted to stay & finish their business, then Noel Baker got up evidently prepared for a major speech & the chairman asked to reconsider & meet tomorrow a.m. & we all got away! Funny things go on but I'm getting to know delegates from many places & I think I will grow more useful.

Goodnight dear, much, much love & write me how Tommy really is.

> Devotedly
> E.R.

She alerted Trude that she had a plan to use her as her aide at the meetings of a nuclear group to establish a Human Rights Commission.

[E.R. to Trude W. Lash:]   [January 22, 1946]

I'm sure it is hard for you to go on working now but you wouldn't be happy without a job for a long time. I have an idea for a short one for you & I want to talk to you about it.

The Russians are very nice as individuals but hard to work with because every step must be reported back to Moscow. We were very stupid over the election of President of the Assembly & I'll tell you about it on my return. Now there is an impasse on Refugees & I have a priceless letter to show you from Byrnes! We have the same situation looming on specialized agencies (ILO) & while in order to get organized we may avoid collisions now it will come in the next part unless some of us talk honestly with the Russians. They have to know we mean what we say but don't say it because we either fear or hate them.

I do have to work hard but it agrees with me tho' sometimes I'm sleepy when I shouldn't be! . . .

She went to the Byelorussian dinner, which that delegation appreciated. "I tasted Vodka and *don't* like it." The same diary note for Tommy asked:

> January 17, 1946
> How is Elliott's book coming and has any part gone to the publishers?
> He promised to send me typed copy to read but it hasn't come.

* Letter not found, but she distrusted Byrnes as a self-seeker.

She wanted to be helpful to Elliott. His decision to settle at Hyde Park had made it more possible for her to remain there. His accounts, moreover, of "Pa's" disagreements with Churchill had impressed her. Elliott had become aware of those frictions while accompanying his father to several of the wartime conferences. Although she knew that Elliott was headstrong, not given to nuances and with a tendency to overdramatize, she also worried over Churchill's influence upon Truman and did not discourage Elliott from writing.* She would surely be home by the end of February, she wrote us—

[E.R. to the Lashes:]   [January 27, 1946]
. . . & have time to catch up & get my thoughts straightened out. I ought also to go for a few hours to Washington to see the President but I see that he goes on a cruise Feb. 11th. It seems to me he is being too attentive to Churchill. I fear Winston will make him believe certain things which just aren't so.

She expressed the same fears to Elinor.

[E.R. to Elinor Morgenthau:]   [January 27, 1946]
It looks to me as tho' the President was running into Churchill's company too much and I am a bit nervous. FDR could cope with Churchill but he might fool someone not cognizant of world affairs.

"I'm not so convinced that Great Britain and ourselves must line up to keep the Russians in hand," her diary entry that day commented. "I think we must be fair and stand for what we believe is right and let them either or both, side with us. We have had that leadership and we must recapture it." She made her views known to a few members of the delegation. "I had a long talk this evening with Ben Cohen and Mr. Sandifer, my State Dept. adviser. I took the chance to say some things that I hope will go back to both the President and the Secretary."

She was canceling most things on her return home "as I want to write what articles I can before it fades from my mind," she wrote Trude, who had counseled her to pay more attention to such requirements as food.

[E.R. to Trude W. Lash:]   [January 29, 1946]
Don't worry about me. I'm eating plenty & it is very fattening. I certainly have not lost weight! The work is heavy & the social schedule is worse but everyone thinks I look well & I feel perfectly well. . . .
I've just had a cable from Louise Hopkins about Harry. She says he is failing fast & I am very sorry. They had so little happiness together. I sent her a cable.

* *As He Saw It* appeared in 1946.

Tommy's daily bulletin kept her abreast of the goings-on in her household and among her friends. "The mail is picking up," Tommy's letter at the end of January said—

[Tommy to E.R.:]   [January 29, 1946]
but we are right up to date with it.

Earl didn't come in Monday night as he had said he would, and I called him yesterday. He stayed over and came down Monday on an early train. He said Simone was pleasant but very distant. A man across the street offered $40,000 for Earl's place. His friend Pete had offered him $25,000 and I told him that was too low according to present prices. Earl thinks he may sell it because it costs so much to keep it up and take care of the children. He will move Simone and the children to his little house and not have any home himself. He was complaining about the grocery bill which was about $85. I told him you had one from Mack and Frey for $75. and a much larger one in NYC and that the cost of food was high. . . .

Tommy's detailed accounting of Earl's efforts to sell his house in Loudonville outside of Albany and his grumblings about housekeeping bills reflected her awareness of her boss's absorption in such details about her friends' lives. Mack and Frey were quality grocers in Poughkeepsie which Eleanor patronized.

Tommy's teeth bothered her, and the dentist prescribed major work. Eleanor worried about that and was grateful to Hick when she stayed with Tommy, choosing not to remember, if she knew, that Tommy was not overly enthusiastic about Hick.

[E.R. to Lorena Hickok:]   [January 29, 1946]
It was grand to get your letter this morning & I'm glad you are there with Tommy this week. I hope all goes well but I hate the ordeal for her. My rooms seem to be too full!

. . .

The Sec[urity] Council settled on a Sec. General today. I think progress is being made here & I think the Russians want to get along. All the news & some observations are in my diary to Tommy.

I feel sad that Harry had to die. He & Louise had so little time to be happy together. I hope a real relationship exists between Louise & Diana.

I'm not bored or tired but I begin to want to be home & to be impatient!

The Morgenthaus sent Eleanor a cable on F.D.R.'s birthday. They had been members of the Cuff Links Club, a group that had worked closely with F.D.R. and celebrated his birthdays.

[E.R. to the Morgenthaus:]   [February 3, 1946]
I was glad to get the telegram on the 30th from you and Henry. What kind, thoughtful friends you *always* are! I thought of our old reunions, but they would have little meaning with Franklin gone, since he held that curious and rather divergent group together because of their various associations with him at different periods and only a few were in all the periods! You and Henry and I have long and unbroken associations which are good to think about when you are far away! . . .

   . . .

There is so much oratory in our committee as well as in the Plenary Sessions that I think we all need in school to learn the art of condensing our thoughts! Mr. Bloom made a great hit with his UNRRA speech and got some nations to make tangible pledges and all spoke highly of him and he went home yesterday feeling a hero. He has his foibles and he hated not being a delegate but I think he did a good job. He's a funny mixture of emotionalism and hardness which comes from fighting your way up I guess but starting with a good heart.

I went to the service for the delegates in St. Paul's today and it was very impressive with Attlee reading the lesson and Spring-Rice's really lovely hymn to his country sung. Tonight Mr. Stettinius dines with me alone and I hope to get a little of his reactions. He doesn't seem to pal around much and I gather the Senators don't feel too close to him.

For the last two days I lost my voice but it is much better today and I hope will be all right tomorrow. I have no cold so it is weariness or a little catarrh which the climate encourages.

Much, much love.

E.R.

Tommy says you are studying Russian. My hat is off to you and I wish I had done it years ago.

As the session drew to a close, work intensified and the people streamed in, including the women delegates who numbered so few they squeezed into a single room. The loss of her voice worried her, she wrote me—

[E.R. to Joseph P. Lash:]   [February 3, 1946]
since I may have to talk in committee meeting in the morning & I'm speaking at a big dinner given by the "Pilgrims" in the evening. They tell me it is important & the first woman they've had in 40 yrs so perhaps its fright has removed my voice!

   . . .

Eventually the Security Council will have Argentina brought before them but they seem to have enough to keep them busy for the moment.

That Vishinsky & Bevin came thro' the first session on Greece & spoke their minds so plainly was good I think. Much is out in the open but Stettinius dined alone with me tonight & left at nine to see Bevin. Some way must be devised where neither will lose face & Greece will hold a free election, or as free as possible. The Greeks want the British to keep order because they fear the Russians *within* Greece would cause civil war before the elections. Then they want the British out but they want Russian armies out of Bulgaria & Yugoslavia & the standing armies of those countries reduced. We send food & clothing to Yugoslavia but they have an army of 300,000 men, so the peaceful pursuits are not getting much attention. They (the Yugoslavs) say if the armies outside their borders were freed to return as peasants & the officers were all declared war criminals or just became exiles then they wouldn't need so many soldiers at home. There you have just one simple little European problem! The Philippine delegate came to see me today & I feel very sorry for them & I think they are our direct economic responsibility.

I felt sad over Harry Hopkins death & people here felt they had lost a real friend. Today I see in the Times from N.Y. that Mr. Mac Duffie died on the 30th, Franklin's birthday. Even tho' I did dismiss him for drinking I was fond of him & I'm sorry for poor old Lizzie.*

We are having a little problem with drink in the military part of our delegation but now they are getting down to work I hope they will straighten out.

Jay Krane lunched with Senator Townsend & me today & went to the service at St. Paul Cathedral for the delegates. It was impressive but I wondered how the delegate from Saudi Arabia who sat in front of me with his flowing robes felt about it. Mr. Attlee read the lesson, he's not a very impressive man but he read very well. The choir sang Spring-Rice's poem which I like so I enclose it, thinking you & Trude might be interested to see it. I enclose also 2 little medals which were sent me & I thought might interest the kids.

The final days of the Assembly were devoted to finding a compromise resolution about the repatriation of refugees on which East and West could agree. The Soviet bloc insisted on forced repatriation of the million refugees in the displaced-persons camps. Since the majority of the refugees were political opponents of the Communist regimes that had come to power, return would have meant almost certain imprisonment, probably death. Her diary on February 8 read:

We defeated the Russians on the three points we disagreed on, they were all fundamental and I'm afraid while I was brief I was clear in my

---

* Both had been on the household staff at the White House. He had been the President's valet.

opposition. Wise Mr. Sandifer of the State Department seemed pleased but whispered "The Russians won't like that."

She sought to be firm on principle without being provocative in behavior. A week before the session ended she wrote in her diary:

February 6, 1946

. . . I think we cannot agree. I will tell any of you who are interested what I have learned in these meetings. It is a liberal education in backgrounds and personalities but one thing stands out. Since the Civil War we have had no political or religious refugees fleeing our country and we forget to take it into account. No Europeans or South American forgets it for a minute. Next it seems to take years of stability to make you look beyond your own situation and consider there are human rights that operate for those who think in a way that you think wrong!

"It isn't just that we don't trust the Russians," she wrote Trude after Committee III had voted for the Western version of the resolution on refugees. "We often don't understand what motivates them. They think only about concrete situations which face them & understand little or nothing about anyone else." She sent her last letter before she boarded an army plane to Frankfurt. It described her debate with Vishinsky in the plenary session of the Assembly.

[E.R. to Joseph P. Lash:] [February 13, 1946]

Yesterday we fought the whole battle over again in the Assembly on refugees which we had fought in committee & we won again hands down. This time Mr. Vishinsky & I fought it out evidently the Russians don't let any but delegates speak in the Assembly! The Russians are tenacious fighters but when we finally finished voting at 1 a.m. last night I shook hands & said I admired their fighting qualities & I hoped some day on that kind of a question we would be on the same side & they were cordiality itself!

Also you will be amused that when Mr. Dulles said goodbye to me this morning he said "I feel I must tell you that when you were appointed I thought it terrible & now I think your work here has been fine!"

So—against odds the women inch forward, but I'm rather old to be carrying on the fight. . . .

X

Eleanor and Her Children

ELEANOR RETURNED from London in the late winter of 1946 a figure of world stature, "the hardest working delegate," some termed her, whose capacity for disciplined work was recognized by diplomats and politicians. They found inspiration and balm in her presence. There was no quarrel when the State Department asked her to serve as the U.S. expert on the preparatory commission to draft a human rights declaration. Her firm but unprovocative handling of Andrei Vishinsky—"Mrs. F.D.R. Bests Reds in the U.N.O. Clash," the papers said of her debate with the sharp-tongued, prosecutorial chairman of the Soviet delegation over the forced repatriation of refugees—made her the logical choice for the position. So, tall, black-garbed, energetic, she made her way to Hunter College in the Bronx where the preparatory meetings were to be held. She was elected chairman of the "nuclear" human rights group by acclamation. Her public career on her own was launched.

"It has been hectic since I got back," she wrote Anna, who with John had settled in the west and were trying to transform a local shopping paper in Phoenix, Arizona, into a daily newspaper. "Everyone wants to see me, the mail is enormous & all the boys are in & out." Although she continued to avow a readiness to retire to a life of dignified obscurity, she relished life at the center, the more so as the United Nations was central to her hopes for the future of mankind.

The organization of her private life was beset with greater difficulties than her public work. Tommy's devotion was unflagging, but ill health plus mountains of work and Tommy's reluctance to employ assistants caused her problems. She was a blessing but also a burden. Earl, after endless squabbles in which Eleanor often tried to act as peacemaker, was estranged from Simone, his wife. Hick needed work and suffered from high blood sugar. Elinor Morgenthau's frailty ever since her heart attack was always on Eleanor's mind. I had come out of the army and needed her support in my work at the Union for Democratic Action. Trude, who acted as secretary of the Nuclear Human Rights Commission at Hunter College, found the conflicting currents of marriage, motherhood, and career difficult to negotiate. Esther still lived in the shadow of Elizabeth's death and longed for the consolations of Eleanor's visits.

Everyone wanted something, and she was glad to be of help. All took second place, however, to her children's needs after the war. The latter turned to her, each with questions of where to live, what to do, how they shared in F.D.R.'s legacy. She willingly shouldered the responsibility, even though her advice was often disregarded. In addition, she had her own private life and household to organize. That meant decisions about her apartment on Washington Square, the neglected house in Campobello, and, above all, how to continue Hyde Park as the center of the Roosevelt clan and her own activities.

On April 12, 1946, President Truman came to Hyde Park for the first anniversary of his predecessor's death. She wrote Anna afterward—

[E.R. to Anna Boettiger:]   [April 15, 1946]
I'm glad you liked what I said at the ceremonies. It all seemed dignified & simple. Just the President & I went out to the grave & he laid his wreath & no other flowers but those from the greenhouse were there. Later the diplomats placed wreaths. Today I took a spray of lilies over from the family. . . .

. . . Last Sat. 700 visited the house & the papers say several thousands came on Sunday but no admissions were charged that day to Dutchess Co. people. The crowds are almost reverent as tho' they really cared deeply. . . . Very quiet & no laughter. . . .

A letter to James and Romaine on their wedding anniversary included a small check and the additional news that—

[E.R. to the James Roosevelts:]   [April 14, 1946]
I've decided not to go to Russia. The heat & tension over Iran I fear would make it hard for them to trust me & let me write freely & see things—Tommy is not well & she worries if I go off so I think I'll get her well & try to go on with my autobiography! Any time you come I shall await you with open arms!

Two weeks later she wrote James again, a six-page longhand letter. Part of it dealt with the executors' handling of the estate, adding that she planned to go to "Campo" in the summer. "You will not sell to anyone else without letting me know." James was living in California and she suggested delicately that he not consider running for office in New York, which she knew attracted Franklin Jr's ambitions, perhaps Elliott's too.

[E.R. to James Roosevelt:]   [April 29, 1946]
Also I forgot to tell you that I never saw the stupid clipping about my disapproval of your political activities but a reporter asked me about it when I was speaking in Hartford & I told him it was silly that you were all grown & I wouldn't interfere or disapprove of any political activity any of you might engage in. I gathered you were running for office in N.Y. which seemed to me impossible but later Sidney Hillman told me he hoped you would!

Her efforts to help Anna and John were second only to those for Elliott and Faye, the chief difference perhaps being that Anna and John were in Arizona while Elliott and Faye settled at Hyde Park. There were frequent family conclaves that sometimes turned into angry exchanges over the films that were to be made of F.D.R.'s life, the books that were to be written, who was to have precedence in the political careers that were to be launched. Again her other children felt that she was partial to Elliott. His project-filled presence at Hyde Park made it less lonely and more manageable. "I will be very glad to have you here to supervise some of the men on the place," she had written him in California right after F.D.R.'s death. "They are getting me down & I cannot keep track of what everybody ought to be doing & I know I am not doing the right thing."

To encourage Elliott in his decision to settle at Hyde Park she had gone into partnership with him and together they were purchasing some 825 acres of farm-lands, woods, and buildings from the F.D.R. estate. She had put up most of the money. Elliott began a large dairy operation and took over F.D.R.'s top cottage as a home for himself and Faye. Eleanor abetted him, hoping the responsibilities of management as well as her own helpfulness might restrain his wilder impulses. She had sought at first to rent the land from the executors, but they said they had to sell to the highest bidder, which is what Fjr. wanted her to allow them to do. "I have to buy the Hyde Park land because when it came to selling it all at once I could not bear not to try to hold it in the hope that some child would want to run it some day. I'm sure that is what Father wanted," she wrote Anna.

After one strife-ridden family reunion, the children turned to her imploringly. She should act as arbiter. She doubted their amenability to her advice, but their bickering was almost unbearable. Afterward she wrote each of them that she was willing to act as clearinghouse but not to make decisions for them.

The memorandum she sent them read:

FDR.Jr.

Summing up this discussion:

We have agreed we are not going to be governed by any majority decision.

We are to be guided as to our methods and get the opinions of the others.

We have agreed to recognize the right of each individual to act according to his beliefs.

We have agreed to submit ideas or plans to mother and to decide by her decision, as to wisdom, methods, etc. If it is o.k. with her, it is o.k. with us.

It is my understanding that this is a meeting in which we agree to arrange for a biographical picture to be produced not sooner than ten years from now, research to be done and agreement on rights, etc. We agreed we should agree on biographical picture now to preclude any other arrangements which might hurt the biographical picture. We agreed to seek professional advice. (Mother to see John Golden for advice).

Mrs. Roosevelt:

I have agreed that when any member of the family decided to undertake anything that affects the other members of the family or has any connection with Father and the family, he will tell me about it and give me an idea of what it is to be, and I will then send it to the other members of the family so they can know about it and not find it out through other sources.

I am perfectly willing to lay down with you the methods by which we will keep each other informed and have opportunity to get each other's information. I am not willing to make decisions for anyone of you. You will all have to make up your own minds as to what you want to do. I am willing to ask for advice, and to get advice to the best of my ability. I am willing to work with any or all of you.

Out of this discussion, I feel that Anna's letter was a good letter to write. It is good to have her point of view. I understand well the point of view that both Elliott and Jimmy have. Jimmy can not go back on his contract with Mr. Kennedy and Elliott can not go back on his contract to edit Father's letters. In the future, we should all get professional advice on what we do to find out whether it will hurt the biographical picture.

I want you to agree that you will never say anything derogatory about each other or make any kind of remarks that can be so construed, and you will never allow people in your presence to say anything which will reflect on the integrity and character of the family.

Elliott's brothers and sister loved yet distrusted him. They resented what they considered their mother's closeness to him and discounted her protestations that she was available to those who needed her most. They particularly resented his putting himself forth as the interpreter of their father's relationships with Churchill and Stalin. Eleanor encouraged him to do so at a time when she was voicing her own uneasiness over President Truman's seemingly uncritical acceptance of the British statesman's views. When Elliott described "Pa's" disagreements with Churchill as he had heard them at dinners alone with F.D.R. or at bedtime, she seconded his desire to make a book out of them and wrote its introduction. The book seemed to her to accord with much that F.D.R. had said to her about British imperialism as well as his constant concern that Stalin might think that he and Churchill were ganging up on him.

At the time the book appeared, an increasingly paranoid Stalin was seeking to protect the Communist camp from the outside world by isolating it, a position that he justified by proclaiming anew that the world was divided into "two camps." His propagandists eagerly made use of Elliott's book to pin the blame on the United States and Britain for the breakup of the unity of the Big Three. Although at the UN she was finding that the Russians interpreted every effort to be conciliatory as weakness, she defended Elliott's publication of his father's views. She knew, however, from her own talks with Franklin that others might have drawn different conclusions, as indeed Anna, James, and Fjr. were doing. Amity was preserved at Hyde Park only by staying off difficult subjects. She hated the contentiousness among her children but was careful not to seem to be siding against Elliott.

The sons were six-footers, mettlesome and attractive. James had started to build an organization in California with the aim of running for governor. In New York, Fjr. was considered the golden boy of American politics and the Democratic Party people there, except Edward Flynn, who advised him to move slowly, were anxious to run him for office. She tried to restrain him. As Durward Sandifer, her State Department adviser at the London Assembly, reported to Irene, his wife:

> She said she had called him in and said, "Now Frankie I've seldom asked you to promise anything or insisted upon your doing what I told you to do. But, I want you to promise that for five years you will not go into politics. You must have a long enough period of discipline that you will know your own views and have settled convictions. If you do not know your own mind and have convictions of your own to guide you, you will be of no use to the country in politics." "Frankie promised," she said.

Much as she worried about Elliott, Anna and John's efforts to resettle themselves were an almost equal preoccupation. After her return from London, she went west on a lecture trip, intending to combine it, as she always had before the war, with visits to children and grandchildren. But Anna and John had gone east in what became a continuing search for newsprint. "If we miss meeting in the East I shall feel very sad," she wrote Anna—

[E.R. to Anna Boettiger:]   [No date]
for I don't see much chance again for a long time.

    What an idiot I was to come west to see you all! In the future I'm going to stay home & wait for you all to come & see me. I'm getting too old for this travelling anyway & I wouldn't go to Russia if everyone didn't seem to feel it might be useful just now & the same will hold good later of China I fear but then, believe me my travel days are over. I hated the trip out here & am still dead so the time really has come to stop! . . .

She never got to China, and her trip to Russia, on the advice of President Truman, was postponed, and took place only in 1957, when she no longer was on the delegation. Instead, that summer she began to work on the second volume of her autobiography and traveled to Campobello, a return that was made easier because Elliott, Faye, and their children were there. "The air would do you all good!" she advised Anna.

[E.R. to Anna Boettiger:]   [July 31, 1946]
    Elliott & Faye & the children have been here a week & they love it. They want if we can work it out to go shares on putting it in order & then run it like a family club. . . . All family could come at cost. Fred Adams says there is no sale value so I hope we can get all land etc. for $1500 & Elliott will go shares. . . .

The other children grumbled, but were it not for Elliott's interest in Campobello, the house there might have been abandoned as Mama's next door had been.

[E.R. to Joseph P. Lash:]   [July 30, 1946]
. . . Elliott & I have decided we want if we can to keep this house. It is unbelieveably beautiful here & remote from the world! The sunset tonight was marvellous & we had a nice picnic with the Bernards on Penguin Island. . . .

She described even grander plans to James:

[E.R. to James Roosevelt:]   [July 31, 1946]
. . . Elliott will go shares with me. We will run like a club [,] offer Auntie Maude rooms in lower wing & hope that any of the family who ever want to come here will do so. All paying costs while here.—Tommy loves it here & I think I'll try to come up for a month or six weeks in

summer. We would each have our own table in the dining room & so be together when we wished & alone when we wished. I hope it works out.

. . . I don't want Father on any stage for years, done by any one. Back shots I would stand for, no more—A documentary really good with Father only as he himself made a speech which they have, I would not mind but no one acting him.

All summer she fretted she might have to go to Geneva in August for a session of the Human Rights Commission and was relieved, she wrote Trude on Martha's Vineyard, that she did not have to go until the close of the UN Assembly in November.

Our decision to go to the Vineyard had been a wrench to her as it was to us. She wanted us at Hyde Park, but Trude's children were not happy there and the Roosevelt children in many little ways made it plain to us they too did not want us there. We did not complain to Eleanor; she had problems enough. Tommy had to have a gallstones operation, and, as Eleanor wrote Trude, Anna and John might have to close the *Arizona Times*, as they called the paper they were trying to turn into a daily.

[E.R. to Trude W. Lash:] [August 3, 1946]
Anna & John are on their way tomorrow to try & get paper. . . . If they don't get it, they say they must close & that spells financial disaster for them but they found no interest in Washington in a liberal paper which was not part of a chain!

Elliott appears before the Brewster Com. in Washington tomorrow tho' I should think they had all the information they needed!

Faye is at Dennis. . . .

In mid-August she compounded her personal troubles by dozing off and hitting another car while driving to New York. She was badly shaken, but sought to make light of the accident after making certain the driver of the other car was unharmed. "I must have become drowsier than I realized," she later wrote. Her eyes were blackened and her two front teeth broken off. "Now I shall have two lovely porcelain ones, which will look far better than the rather protruding large teeth which most Roosevelts have."

"I'm improving in appearance daily & have thought myself into a better frame of mind," she wrote Hick a week later, adding, "I still look odd but much better." The accident seemed symptomatic of her difficulties in getting her private life to run smoothly. She made light of her car accident in a letter to James, and sought diplomatically to reassure him about Elliott's forthcoming book, *As He Saw It.*

[E.R. to James Roosevelt:]   Sept. 7th [1946]
. . . I'm wonderfully recovered & the car will be repaired they say as
soon as they can get new parts.

Elliott says to tell you that in the book he explained that all conversations were not exact words but approximately the gist. *Look* in the con-
densation left out that explanation. The book is much better than the
articles I think. . . .

Though her duties as a delegate to the second General Assembly went more
easily, including a second debate with Andrei Vishinsky, privately she debated
whether to give up her apartment in Washington Square. "It will be better for me
to really settle in H.P.," she wrote Anna, "& just keep a double room & bath in
Tommy's apartment where any of us can stay but only in relays. . . ."

She visited her Cousin Susie, she wrote Anna a few days before her own sixty-
second birthday.

[E.R. to Anna Boettiger:]   [October 6, 1946]
[She] has been miserable. She feels I was most inconsiderate to have an
accident & Henry [Mrs. Parish's husband] didn't consider her when he
committed suicide & between us we've given her another nervous break-
down! Poor Henry. . . .

She made light of her own aches and pains: "I'm well, my ailments when I'm
conscious of them are largely because of my age! Tommy is better too," she wrote
Anna.

"Is it possible for you & Joe to plan to come up on the 11th [October] Friday
for my birthday & stay the weekend?" she asked Trude. We went and she continued to treat us as members of her family, but circumstances were pushing us apart.
I had gone to work for the Union for Democratic Action, Trude for the Citizens'
Committee for Children. Eleanor's main focus of public activity was the United
Nations. Our four children needed their own family center, their own "turf," as a
later generation would dub it. Eleanor respected our wishes, but they made us less
helpful to her. "Nov. 8th is your wedding anniversary," she wrote Trude. "Would
you care to have me stay in town & have a little buffet supper for you here that
night or would you rather go to H.P.?" We went to Hyde Park but we could tell by
little signs that we were failing her. She returned the latchkey to our house on 11th
Street, and we returned the key to her Washington Square apartment. None of us
had used them, but they had seemed to symbolize the closeness of our relationship.

Trude and I understood and sympathized with Eleanor's preoccupation with
her children's problems and, in view of their attitude, felt helpless to help her.
Sometimes it seemed that the best we could do for her was to withdraw so that she
should not have to worry about us. Nothing was said. On the surface she was as
concerned as before with our lives and we with hers, but we no longer were the

"other" to whom she wanted to turn on morning's waking. When we went to Martha's Vineyard the summer of 1946 instead of staying with her at Hyde Park, she realized we were doing so in part not to be in her way. She and Trude telephoned each other every morning around breakfast time, calls that continued all through Eleanor's life. She talked with us, as she knitted away, about her children and her problems with Tommy, who did not want an assistant yet was unable to keep up with the calls and mail and manuscripts to be typed. "Somehow you will manage & everyone will have a good time," she wrote Trude at the Vineyard. "You are a miracle worker & Joe must be too! I have unbounded respect & admiration for you both!" But she did not try to stop us. It made life easier that we did not compete with her children for her solicitude. They came first, and it was an unspoken condition of our continued closeness that we recognized that.

"I have been working harder than ever with the UN," she wrote Jimmy—

[E.R. to James Roosevelt:] [November 15, 1946]
. . . I leave the house at 8:30 every morning & I am having all the members of my committee—committee #3, in groups of ten or twelve meet here in the evenings so that we can get to know each other & have informal discussions. I give them beer, whiskey, grape juice & cheese & crackers, so the evening has some air of being a party & not all business. . . . The number of words which can be uttered on any subject appals me. . . . I do think we are making progress but it is slow.
. . .

Everyone tells me what a grand job you did during the campaign & what excellent speeches you made. Were you much surprised at the outcome? No one had much hope in New York State, although I thought Gov. Lehman had a better chance than any of the others. Eddie Flynn was quite reconciled before hand & felt that the Democrats had been in too long.

"Jimmy arrives tomorrow & will stay here & Fjr. & Ethel, Elliott & Faye will all be here for dinner," she informed Hick as she expressed the hope that "1947 will be a good year" for all of us, but she knew that feelings about Elliott ran pretty high among her other children. Matters still had to be settled with the trustees of F.D.R.'s estate about the purchase of additional land at Hyde Park. She had written Anna in October—

[E.R. to Anna Boettiger:] [October 9, 1946]
I'm afraid Mr. Koons [lawyer for the F.D.R. estate] is not wrong & the property will have to be advertised. I think the best way to safeguard the situation you fear is to let Elliott buy outright as he can put a clause in sale that if he has to sell or wants to any time the other members of the family shall be given a chance to buy. Neither he or I would want to lease

& if it is sold to outsiders I shall not live there & told Mr. Koons, thinking some people might buy wanting to be my neighbor.

She was talking about the Moses Smith farm, which abutted the entrance to her own fields at Hyde Park. She and Elliott intended to use it, she explained to Anna—

[E.R. to Anna Boettiger:]   [February 19, 1947]
for cows & chickens & a two family house that needs immediate work. No milk house & we must have one, small & built out of cinder blocks with a concrete floor for it has to be clean as we will sell cream & use skim milk for pigs & chickens. Mr. Koons told me yesterday that even tho' the Trustees have agreed to sell to me it won't be sure till the Surrogate & the grandchildren's guardian approve. The consent may not be obtained until July & I must move the farmer & our cows & the chickens & pigs out of the old farm as soon as possible. Incidentally to carry itself I must get a "big" start by April 1st. We can put the fields in cultivation anyway & Elliott is going up today to start getting estimates. . . .

A few days earlier she had written to all her children except Elliott about F.D.R.'s early letters:

February 16, 1947
As you know, Elliott & I have been going through endless boxes of old letters & we find letters going back to Father's childhood. We have decided that a very fascinating book, showing the development, with photostatic copies of the letters in many cases, could be done with a minimum of story written around the letters very much in the way I did my Father's letters.

Elliott will do the work and he will take the advance, but on the book we would like to write a foreword which all the children will sign, stating that we felt that this book would be not only historically interesting, but a satisfaction to many of the people who had been fond of Father, as they could see his development through his own letters.

If you are satisfied with the work when it is done and will sign the letter, we will make it a family project and anything over and above the advance would be divided equally among us.

Will you let me know how you feel?

The other children were not happy over the prospect of Elliott's editorship nor of his "interpretations," as it was put, of their father's childhood. Eleanor's support of his partnership with Harry Brandt, a New York owner of movie theaters, in the production of a documentary about F.D.R.'s life left them equally uneasy. I tried to get a showing for the benefit of Americans for Democratic Action, the organization of former New Dealers and independents that had been launched at the beginning of 1947 with Eleanor's blessing. Elliott stopped that, and Trude wrote Eleanor, who had started west, a distressed letter. She replied from San Francisco:

[E.R. to Trude W. Lash:]   [March 10, 1947]
    I was glad to get your letter today though March 1st seems long ago! I knew quite well what had happened over the "preview." I understand Harry Brandt well, better than you or Elliott do. He thought he'd give Joe something for nothing & Elliott's objection surprised him. He tried to get Elliott to put anything which was made on this film with him back into a company to produce some pictures on John Paul Jones based on material Elliott found in the Library. I think I stopped it for Harry B. can afford to lose money & Elliott can't.
    I love you & Joe & trust & believe in you & no one means more to me. I've worked so hard this winter & been worried about my way of life & so I've missed seeing all I'd like to of you & Joe & the children but I hope things will settle down a bit for you as well as for me & from now on we can be more together.
    Dear child, I know you & Joe wouldn't exploit me & I don't need protecting! I am doing things in endorsing this film & financing the place & farm & helping Elliott with a book of his Father's letters that may cause criticism but I surmise Elliott has to be established and encouraged & become more secure. Jimmy needs more money to give his wife the security she demands & if I can help without doing anything I think wrong, the criticism doesn't bother me. The only reason I worried about the Simone & Earl trouble was because I knew it would bother the children who seemed to have trouble enough. The sooner I can live in dignified obscurity at H.P. the happier I will be! . . .

The *Arizona Times*, for which Anna and John had built a plant and which had appeared three times a week, was about to become a daily. That coincided with a crisis in the relationship between Anna and John. Funding difficulties were compounded by an inability to get paper. John lost confidence in himself and in their ability to succeed. Anna emerged as the stronger one, willing against his advice to pledge her future inheritance in her father's estate as additional collateral, a "gamble," she wrote John, that she was willing to take in order to save their marriage.
    Eleanor scheduled a second lecture trip to the West Coast mainly because it could be dovetailed with visits to the children and grandchildren, especially Anna and John. On her way west she stopped to see Curtis, who was at military school. "Buzz is nearly as tall as I am but he looks like Curtis Dall [Anna's first husband]!

That must be a trial for Anna." On the West Coast she spent a day at Reed College, where Buzz's sister was enrolled. The contrast in attitudes amused her: "He seems able & independent & very conscious of his responsibilities to the family & its budget & very annoyed with Sisty because she doesn't see things as he does. A common failing with us all, isn't it?" she wrote me.

Tommy was with her, the first trip Tommy felt able to take. "Tommy and I have been wanting to tell you & John what a wonderful job you have been doing with Sis & Buzz." She wrote Hick that the lecture in Chico, California, was a sellout, but when she discovered that Anna and John had gone east in their continuing search for newsprint, she again questioned the usefulness of such continental treks.

[E.R. to Anna Boettiger:]   [March 8, 1947]
. . . I am furious at being here when you are in N.Y. I believe I'll just stay home after this year & let all of you come to me! These trips are an effort, their value is problematical, & I don't make anything except expenses out of them! I imagine one reaches more people by writing & I can do that at home!

But the trip west gave her a chance to see Tiny (Mrs. Hershey Martin) and her baby, as well as her children, Jimmy & Romaine and Anne and Johnny, and their children. She would not easily give up such travels.

[E.R. to Trude W. Lash:]   [March 15, 1947]
. . . James & Romaine & I talked long last night. Romaine seems more interested in public affairs & Anne less. The new babies are beautiful & all the children fine & well.

She was back at Hyde Park in time for a memorial ceremony on April 12. "Please tell Henry how well I thought everything went on the 12th," she wrote Elinor. "It was lovely & I hope a simple ceremony then will be a tradition." She thanked Elinor for the flowers she had been sending all winter. "You are the most thoughtful, generous friend & I am deeply grateful for your affection."

"On April 1st from 6 p.m. on," she wrote James in California, "I've asked the boys Fjr. & Elliott to come for the evening & talk out all our problems. Anna & John will try to be here also & if that works out it will be fine. Will you get Johnny's ideas pretty clearly as he will be the only one not here." It was another family conclave in which she tried to get her children to agree on the motion picture that might be done based on F.D.R.'s life as well as on Elliott's editing of his letters. "Each one of us has a distinct point of view and feelings on this subject," another letter to James asserted, "and I think the sooner a meeting of minds is achieved, the better the family unity." It was a vain hope, the children agreed after her death, but not because she did not try.

She needed the affection and understanding of her friends that spring. "All is well with me tho' my personal problems have been a bit overpowering," she wrote Hick. "Anna & John go back Friday & will I hope have their financing done & everything else moves on to development." A week later she declined a Morgenthau invitation to go with them to Bermuda.

[E.R. to Elinor Morgenthau:]   [April 23, 1947]
    The lovely spring blossoms are a joy & as I was starting to write & thank you your note about Bermuda came. You & Henry are very generous & dear friends & I would love to go with you & would gladly pay my own way but unfortunately May 23rd I go to Chicago for a Rosenwald fund meeting & then I make three belated speaking dates in the middle west. If I am well I must keep them so I'll be gone from the 23rd–29th. June 9th for two weeks I'll have to be at Lake Success for five days each week & so I think I'd better be home in between. Life doesn't run so smoothly yet that I can run out on Elliott. I appreciate your wanting me more than I can say.

She was determined to stay put at Hyde Park, but when James called to say he needed her in Los Angeles for the Democratic State Committee dinner, she went. Scarcely back east, she had to arbitrate between Elliott and Franklin. The annual convention of the American Veterans Committee was due to be held in New York City. Franklin, who was the leader of the anti-Communist caucus in the AVC and with whom I was working closely, received a call from Elliott that he had been approached by the left to run for the AVC chairmanship. He was considering it seriously, he said, even though he had taken no part in AVC affairs. "Both F. and his mother," I noted in my diary, "talked to him Friday evening. Mike Straight talked to him early Saturday morning & told him that he would lose—& that finally ended it." My note added, "Mrs. R. did speak to Elliott after talking with Franklin & urged him not to run—but her attitude is one of support for Elliott & absolute neutrality as between him and F."
    Trude and I went to Martha's Vineyard for the summer. Eleanor wrote us from Hyde Park.

[E.R. to the Lashes:]   [July 11, 1947]
    I've missed you all ever since you have been gone. I feel cheated to have been here so little. In one's old age one should be stationary & leisurely so as to savour life & enjoy one's friends. This period must soon begin for me!
    Your neighbors [on the Vineyard] sound fascinating as a combination & I'm glad you have some you'll enjoy talking with as well as the ones you will argue with.

It sounds as tho' housekeeping would be easier for Trude. Jonathan will soon get accustomed to the surf. He is full of courage!

I wish I could stop over with you even for a day but not this summer. I fear I'll have to go to Geneva if not to Lake Success. Either way I'll only have a week at home!

The Sandifers were at Hyde Park that weekend. "The plans for the annual trip to Campobello pervaded the atmosphere. . . ." Before Eleanor and Elliott left, however, they went to Washington on July 14, Bastille Day, to receive the Medaille Militaire awarded to President Roosevelt posthumously by France. Irene Sandifer recorded:

Mrs. Roosevelt rode with us [the Sandifers] to New York and then she, Elliott, Chandler, Elliott Jr. and Mr. and Mrs. Morgenthau flew to Washington. The award was made at the French Embassy by the French Ambassador, Henri Bonnet. Among those present were President Truman, many members of the Roosevelt Cabinet and agencies, and the Justices of the Supreme Court and Cabinet members and Robert Sherwood.

The next day she was off again to Campobello, this time with four of Elliott's children, Tommy, two of Elliott's dogs, and Fala. They spent the night at Ogunquit, Maine, and saw Faye in *State of the Union.* Tommy and I are getting too old for such excitement," she wrote of the lively trip up—

[E.R. to Joseph P. Lash:] [July 19, 1947]

but it was fun too. Faye is excellent in the play & she doesn't have to act because the play expresses what she would feel naturally! She arrives here tomorrow for a week with three friends so she can help Elliott decide a lot of questions. I'm shedding all this responsibility as fast as I can, you see!

A fond letter to Anna—

[E.R. to Anna Boettiger:] [July 19, 1947]

. . . It was a caravan, truck & station wagon & my car. The children moved from car to car, Fala stayed with me. . . .

I still don't know whether I go to Switzerland on Aug. 23d for a session of the Human Rights Commission but I have been asked to serve on the Assembly again & await Senatorial confirmation. . . .

. . . I've revised for the last time I hope the nine chapters of the book & tomorrow I start dictating new stuff. . . .

One is so far away here that wars & rumors of war seem to recede into the background & yet I am really discouraged over Russia's attitude on the Marshall Plan & find it hard to understand. Elliott feels they think we won't come through but even that makes no sense to me for they are furnishing the reasons why we shouldn't. . . .

Elliott had received an advance of $10,000 against royalties, no mean sum at the time, to edit the book of his father's childhood letters, and as they left for Campobello, he was sending the other children Eleanor's proposed foreword and his own footnotes.

Anna's reply bristled with questions to Elliott: "Will Jimmy and Franklin and Johnny and I have a chance to see the 'brief historical and biographical notes' as well as the 'short commentaries before each section'. . . . If each of them—the five children and mother—received 10% of the royalties what happened to the other 40%?"

Mrs. Roosevelt chided Anna for her distrustful letter to Elliott, but her own letter did not allay their suspicions.

[E.R. to Anna Boettiger:]   [July 28, 1947]

Elliott gave me your letter to him to read & I hardly think you realize what a critical & almost hostile letter it sounded like. The "notes & historical data" are identifications of places & people, the research has been considerable to identify & put in order. The publishers paid him an advance ($10,000) but Elliott says it has already cost him more. We none of us know how they will sell. I suggested originally that they be published. I only divided the mail in the boxes (I still have a number to do). I hope you have received from time to time letters from yourself to Father, to me or Granny. Father's letters I gave Elliott, he did the reading, sorting, etc. & all the work. At the beginning I suggested that all of us sign the foreword & each of us (outside of Elliott) receive 10% of net profit after advance as I liked to feel that we all had some share in the enterprise. When I found you were all unwilling or reluctant to sign I told Elliott to call the whole plan off but he persisted in the 10% idea. You must know that by the time letters are in galley proof there is no time for extensive changes & I can think of none that you could make since these are matters of fact which we have had enough trouble in finding. They occurred before you were born & when Father was not yet in political life. This volume ends with college.

Elliott has already put all his earnings of the past year & the money borrowed from E.K. [a rich Californian who gave business advice and lent money to several of them] into the farm. After Oct. if you come East I hope you will come up to see what has been done. He will have more of an investment than I have in it & while we will be partners he will own the major share. There are plenty of building sites for children or grandchildren should they ever want them. I hope it will be the one place where there are roots for a family needs that I think.

Good luck to you & John on this trip. A great deal of love to him & a special hug to you.

Elliott's letter to Anna, written the next day, listed the costs of the book, assured her that he was "not riding a free gravy train as your letter implies," wished, as Eleanor had, that Anna and John's trip to Norway in their hunt for newsprint would be successful. "It seems outrageous that you can't get paper here," Eleanor wrote them. Anna was not wholly placated, as Eleanor's next letter indicated.

[E.R. to Anna Boettiger:]   [August 20, 1947]
Elliott says you will get complete page proofs on the letters very soon. Please read fast & send James & tell him to send Johnnie & have him return to Fjr. Research has all been to verify facts & explain allusions. For instance who was "old rubber boots"? Elliott did not mean any other members of the family should have done the work on the "letters," obviously only one person could. Three of you are too far away & Fjr. is too busy. . . .

Elliott was assisted by a student from nearby Bard College, James Rosenau. He was a gifted young man, and his research, as reviewers recognized, was a model of scholarship and fairness. Fears about editorial misinterpretation abated, although suspicion and resentment of Elliott's financial share in the project remained.

General Marshall had succeeded Byrnes as Secretary of State. Eleanor found working with him during the 1947 General Assembly very satisfactory and relished telling about the moment in plenary when he asked her to go over to another member of the delegation, John Foster Dulles, and calm him down. Dulles was spluttering over some abusive Soviet remarks. "I like Marshall to work with," she confided to Anna. The latter and John were en route to Norway. "I shall pray that you get your newsprint. It does not seem to me that the Norwegians show much gratitude for all Pa's devotion to their Royal family in exile." Her loyalty to her children knew few bounds and she rarely asked for gratitude, but her pique here reflected a slight dig at F.D.R.'s solicitude for Princess Martha.

Anna's marriage with John was breaking up. "He's not built to enjoy that kind of risk when it is someone else's money he's gambling with," Anna wrote her mother, as their paper suffered heavy losses, adding ". . . I can't write any more— I'm really feeling too low." Eleanor tried to hold the marriage together: "I've written John a note because I feel if he can get to feel he can succeed, your battle is more than half won." Her letter to Anna at the end of October, amid the General Assembly's importunate demands, was full of sympathy. "I love you darling, & think you the finest, most loyal human being I've ever known." Anna urged her husband to seek psychiatric help, which he refused, to go away for a while and to leave the running of the paper to her. They separated at the beginning of December, and Anna learned that he had been seeing another woman.

"We are off to H.P.," Eleanor wrote Hick at the end of November, "& Tommy seems to feel so much better that I'm thankful & hopeful for the future." The impending trip to Geneva weighed upon her.

[E.R. to Lorena Hickok:]   [November 25, 1947]
  I am not happy to go but chores have to be done & perhaps I won't have the chance to do many more & then I'll be sorry so I give myself a good lecture & try to be interested & hopeful about the business.

Then out of the blue a mysterious, unexpected attraction transformed her life. David Gurewitsch, an old friend from Trude's Freiburg days and her physician, who had met Eleanor at Trude's, came to the latter with a plea for help. His own illness had been diagnosed as tuberculosis. He had been told to go to Davos, Switzerland, for a sanatorium cure, but was unable to get airplane passage. Would Trude help? She spoke with Eleanor, who secured a seat for him on the same plane she would take to Geneva.

A comment to Hick might have reflected her readiness for a new friendship.

[E.R. to Lorena Hickok:]   [December 8, 1947]
  As we grow older I think we have to enjoy each happiness that comes our way for we know our time with those we love is running out.

XI

A New Friend

ELIZABETH BARRETT BROWNING'S *Sonnets from the Portuguese* speak of how Robert Browning burst upon her reclusive life. It had been shadowed by "melancholy years" when a voice said:

> *'Guess now who holds thee?'—'Death,' I said, But, then*
> *The silver answer rang,—'Not Death, but Love.'*

Eleanor was sixty-three when her quenchless desire to love and be loved settled on David Gurewitsch. Her letters to David lack the passionate intensity of the first to Hick, but they were love letters. She was fifteen years older and a figure now in history, which made even more remarkable her ability to shake free of convention and upbringing to love a younger man. He was forty-five.

Perhaps the attraction was fated. In 1917, when America's entry into the First World War brought high-ranking Allied missions to Washington, that of the British was headed by the former Prime Minister and then Foreign Secretary, Arthur Balfour. He was a tall man of languid grace and cultivation, and Eleanor had found him "charming in the way that a good many Englishmen are and very few of our own men." So she had written her mother-in-law after sitting next to Balfour at dinner. David had some of the same quality of taking women seriously. He held a woman's hand in his own, looked at her intently, kissed her hand, and began a conversation that instinctively and intuitively conveyed the feeling that he understood and cared. He was slim, elegant, and smiled shyly. The brief encounter in Trude's room in 1945 had left traces. After the President's death when Eleanor was back in New York, she had her medical records sent to him but, in good health, saw him rarely until Trude came to her with the plea that he needed transportation. She wrote Trude and me from the Hotel Beau Rivage in Geneva.

[E.R. to the Lashes:]   [December 5, 1947]
Dr. Gurewitsch stood the trip well. We all got to know each other well & I think he enjoyed it. Abba* & I saw him off by train from here for Davos & he telephoned me that the trip was not bad & that he had found a good room awaiting him & the mountains were lovely & he was sure his decision was a wise one. The doctors had not yet seen him.

Her readiness to trust and confide in David reflected itself in her note to Anna. The latter had been trying to persuade John Boettiger to seek help from a psychiatrist.

[E.R. to Anna Boettiger:]   [December 2, 1947]
Dr. Gurewitsch who came on the plane with me as he has to stay in Davos for a while told me of a fine psychiatric clinic in Kansas City. He says all kinds of people go there for nerves & it is no stigma. I told him of John as a "case" & he said he should have a doctor's help, it might shorten the period of mental depression.

The meeting of the Human Rights Commission, for which she was in Geneva, was pivotal. Its UN-appointed director, John P. Humphrey of Canada, had drafted a bill of rights for mankind. This document had been reworked by Dr. René Cassin, the eminent and loquacious French jurist. It now had to be adopted by the Commission and forwarded to the member nations and considered, if the UN's timetable were kept, by the General Assembly in Paris at the end of 1948. As chairman, Eleanor pushed the delegates like "a slave driver," as one of them complained. The draft was finally approved 13–4, when Eleanor, whose heart was set on getting home for Christmas, obtained a vote. As she and James Hendrick, her gentle State Department adviser, left the chamber at the end of the meetings, he prompted her, "Now you can take your slide." So Eleanor, in a gesture of youthful exuberance, ran and slid, ran and slid again, along the marbled floors of the Palais des Nations.

Behind the scenes recorded by history, the "coupling of two souls," as Ben Jonson called the act of falling in love, had proceeded. It is recorded in the letters she sent him. Most of his, unfortunately, are missing, as are accounts of the telephone calls they exchanged.

* Abba Schwartz, a graduate of Harvard Law School, served in the Navy on the Murmansk run during the war. At its end he became U.S. representative on the Intergovernmental Committee on Refugees and later, in the Kennedy years, Assistant Secretary of State for Security and Consular Affairs.

Geneva
Dec. 4th, 1947

Dear David,

What a joy to hear your voice this morning.

I start the day happier.

This is just a line to tell you that I go Saturday afternoon to the dinner of the Conseil d'États in Bern and stay with the American Minister overnight so I will not be here til Sunday evening. Please do not call Sunday for I would be broken hearted to miss hearing your voice!

George Wenzel* comes Saturday and will lunch with me and have dinner Sunday evening and I'll find out if it would give his mother pleasure to see me the following Sunday. Otherwise I am here every morning til 9 and I shall be so glad to hear your voice.

Good luck with the doctors and my love.

E.R.

Elinor Hendrick, Jim's wife, helped as her secretary in Geneva, but personal letters she wrote in longhand and on the 8th letters went to Hick, Trude, and David. "The work is fantastically hard & long hours but I'm bearing up well," she assured Hick. ". . . A week & 2 days & I'll be starting for home." She had dined with Trude's brother, George Wenzel. "We tried to work out a trip to see your Mother but I can't be away except on Sunday & it can't be done." A long letter went to David.

Geneva, December 8 [1947]

David dear,

I found your letter on my return from Bern last evening. Your mother's letter shows her love for you and her great faith and I return it as you may want to keep it. When one has complete trust it often removes the sense of a burden of personal responsibility—but few of us reach that point of feeling a sure and close guidance. You need not translate German, I can't read script anymore but I still understand the language fairly well.

Writing on your back must be hard and though I love your letters don't tire yourself ever for I will understand. I fear you are in for difficulties about your treatment which may make it hard for you. I confess to feeling selfishly glad that you find yourself so American! I want you so much to look forward to home and work across the Atlantic.

George Wenzel had dinner and spent the evening Sunday night. We have tried to plan how I could go next Sunday to see his mother but we must work all Saturday and it does not seem possible. So I gave him my

* Trude's brother.

packages for his mother and I can report to Trude that he thinks her well and in good spirits and he will spend Xmas with her. George looks older and not quite happy but was dear and sweet as always.

We worked till 7 p.m. and then I went to dine at International House and to speak at the university to students. I only spoke for 20 minutes and then they asked questions for an hour. There were many Americans there and we talked together as they went out. I wonder if these young people will help understanding at home.

I liked the Swiss I met at Bern and I plied them with questions so I've written several columns on all I've learned about various phases of life here. They are self centered though and they rarely ask questions back!

Elinor Hendrick says she sent you some of what she thinks are "queer" letters and I only hope they amuse you.

Tommy writes she feels better day by day and is staying in Hyde Park through part of this week which pleases me as I'm sure it is better for her.

I would like to go and see you before I leave but I know it is best for you to pursue the even tenor of your care without outside intrusion just now, but I shall plan on March or April. I hope I'll hear your voice again several times before I leave at 4:15 a.m. on the 18th. Isn't that a horrible time to go and I'm sure we won't actually get off! I shall miss you.

May your strength grow and with it our friendship. I'm grateful that you wanted to come across with me for it gave us a chance we might never have had otherwise. My thoughts turn to you often.

Affly.

E.R.

David helped her replace a vaccination certificate that she had mislaid.

[E.R. to David Gurewitsch:]   [n.d.]

Many thanks David dear for getting off my vaccination certificate so promptly. Mrs. Hendrick took it today with my ticket and so I can leave. Somehow I shall not like leaving and feeling so far away. It has been so good to talk to you and feel not far away—don't tear up any more letters for I am going to want to hear whenever you can write and feel that I am not really far away from your thoughts at least. Do plan to come home soon enough to take a holiday with us at Hyde Park or Campobello and bring your little girl. Sometimes little girls get on well with old ladies and there will be some children about!

Tommy writes they were snowed in last week in Hyde Park and I begin to look forward to that in January and February!

We work harder every day but I think something will be done. My love to you.

E.R.

David protested that he did not want to press his presence and problems on her and she answered that he must have reacted to her own inner insecurity.

December 13th night [1947]

David dear,

It was a joy to get your letter and I could almost see the scene around you. How cold the mountains can look and how still a snowy winter landscape can be. Being so quiet is hard but I think you will get quiet inside in time, and it will give you time to think and you will be a deeper person for this enforced discipline and turning inward. I like the still nights, sleeping out on my balcony at home, with only the stars to look at just because it gives one a feeling of taking in. You have given out so much you must need it very much and in the future you should get snatches of it more often.

Don't ever worry about being a nuisance. I've always liked you and been drawn to you since we first met and the trip just made me sure that we could be friends. I never want to burden my young friends and with all my outward assurance, I still have some of my old shyness and insecurity left when it comes to close relationships and that is probably what makes you feel shy. I've really taken you into my heart however, so there need never be a question of bother again. You can know that anything I can do will always be a pleasure for me and being with you is a joy—

I have nothing to report but more hard work. I drive hard and when I get home I will be tired! The men on the Commission will be also! I do not think the Arabs will defy the U.N. if we show firmness.

Can I do anything when I get home for you as regards your little girl?

I sent you the "Roosevelt Era" and a box of candy someone sent me because I do not need to grow fatter!

George Wenzel is here again this weekend and he and Abba dined with us when we got home from the session at 9:15. Tomorrow they spend the day. My love and thoughts are always with you.

E.R.

She worried over Anna's problems with John and the paper.

[E.R. to Anna Boettiger:]   Dec. 14 [1947]

. . . You are a wonder to carry all this & I take my hat off to your courage. It is doubly hard because of the emotional strain I know you must be under where John is concerned & I hope he can get some good psychiatric help & come back more quickly than now seems probable. Nevertheless, the next few months in which success or failure will be assured rest on your shoulders. You have the ability & the courage to meet it & I am deep in respect & admiration for you. . . .

A fuller letter went to James and Romaine that same day. Her tart observations about her son Johnny's converting to Republicanism showed the importance she attached to loyalty in politics.

Sunday, Dec 14th
Geneva

Dearest Jimmy & Romaine,

I feel far away but I think of you all so often & hope these last weeks are not too trying for you Rommie dear.

The people here report Pauley* not in too happy a position about speculation in commodities. Quite o.k. for a business man I suppose but not so good for a government official. The rich in this little country have a wonderful way of beating the high income taxes! They just bargain with the government & threaten to move if the taxes they offer to pay are not accepted! I've learned a lot about all phases of life here though I've had little time for anything but Commission meetings.

I think we'll send an interesting document to the Governments for comment. I've driven myself & members of the Commission very hard & I think the men will be as glad as I will be when it is over!

I expect to leave at 4:15 a.m. on the 18th by T.W.A. & hope not to have the delays we had on the way over.

I do hope Anna is finally set, she has so much courage & the strain of carrying this burden alone must be great. Fjr. says Johnny is now a Republican & won't divulge the sources of his financing but says he has plenty. Somehow I feel he has shed his family & identified himself with Anne & her family. That might be wise & necessary but he might need some of us in the future but then I guess he feels he can count on us! He wired me of his decision but beyond that I've heard nothing from him.

I saw Louella Parsons† at a dinner in N.Y. before I left & she told me how much she loved you & how hard she was trying to help you get into the Roman Catholic Church. If you were over here you might be interested in the political activity they engage in against the Communists. There are 2 Ambassadors to the Vatican on the Commission & it has been interesting to hear them talk, but I say nothing. Both have urged my coming to Rome.

There is little "news" in the Swiss papers but some of them have really well written articles. The cost of living is high for heat, clothes, etc. but food is plentiful & good & not too expensive, rents are controlled & bread rationed, milk is scarce & they import. Ordinary coal is $40.50. a

---

* Edwin W. Pauley was a California oil man and power in the conservative wing of the Democratic Party, an appointee of Roosevelt's, a friend of Truman's. Mrs. Roosevelt was deeply suspicious of "the Pauley crowd," as she termed it.
† A Hollywood newspaper columnist whose gossip about the movie world was widely read.

ton & anthracite up to $50. & all hard to get so houses are very cold. The standard of living is high, wages almost as high as at home & it is a conservative, self centered, complacent nation in the midst of misery!

I must stop & do some studying of documents for tomorrow.

A world of love to you both & to the children.

Devotedly
Mother

Geneva
Dec. 14th

Trude dearest,

. . . George is here again & he has seen your Mother. She is well & has your package which I brought & she is getting your packages & all goes well. George & Abba spent some time in the session & returned with us for dinner here. We got here about 9:15 p.m. & they left at midnight. They spend tomorrow with us & if the weather is good we hope to go to Chamonix. We would have had meetings but we could not use the building! I think the results won't be too bad but the work has been very hard. Tommy tells me the World Telegram doesn't print my columns & there is no news of the meetings in the papers which is natural tho' there are reporters here for the U.P. & N.Y. Times. . . . My dear love to Joe & a big hug for you,

E.R.

Geneva
December 15th [1947]

David dear,

Just a line to thank you for the pills and your letter. I stayed in yesterday as a result of your good advice and got through today, even the talk tonight went well. My cold is in my head and not over yet but I hope will clear up before I fly—

I am encouraged about the work. I think a good working paper will go to the Governments for comment.

I find the Swiss are 1 of 16 countries in the Marshall Plan but very anxious. It shall cost them nothing!

All my advisors are lawyers or I would be lost! Common sense is valuable now and then, I find however!

I'm glad you just do whatever you think is good for you. I believe each person is different.

It was grand to talk to you and I love your letters—I'm sending you a little package when I leave, just things to keep you warm, but I hope the shawl which I have used for many years and found comforting will bring you warmth and comfort too. Anyway when you use it just feel my affection about you—

I'll cable when I get home. Send the book to H.P. when you have finished it. I'll be there most of the time. I will write often and remember to ask me for anything you want. I hate to leave you and be beyond the reach of your voice but I will look forward to a visit in the Spring. Bless you dear and my thoughts will never be far away—

My love to you.

E.R.

New York 11 New York
December 18th [1947]

Dear David,

I talked to you only a short time ago and I will surely do so again before I leave but I'll mail this as I leave for the airport so it will reach you as I am on the way.

I've been thinking about this meeting here, at first it seemed sad to me to go into that beautiful building* built with love and hope by nations who thought they had found the way to peace and understanding. Now I think it gives me encouragement and I wish more meetings could be held here for when you see the present activity you realize that perhaps man's spirit, his striving, is indestructible, it is set back but it does not die and so there is a reason why each one of us should do our best in our own small corner. Do you think I'm too optimistic?

I think we could do better with the Russians, too, in spite of just having read Marshall's statement at the Pilgrim's dinner and Molotov's interpretation of the failure of the conference.† Our own early days should help us to understanding. They feel the Western powers agree together *first* on a plan and they are not brought in till all is settled. That we could change as a first step.

Don't get too interested in your patients and work too hard. Please get well as fast as you can. Will you be able to go on slow walks with me when I come in late March or early April? I love the postcard with the view from your window and I like to know what beauty you look out on—

By the way, the fur foot muff in the package I sent you is from Mrs. Hendrick—I don't know how you will use it but it might keep your hands warm!

A letter from Trude makes me feel she is tired. I am going to try to get her to come to me for a week when Xmas is over—No, I have done my

---

* Palais des Nations.

† Molotov blamed the failure of the four-power Council of Foreign Ministers on the three Western delegations' acting in concert. Secretary of State Marshall, in his address to the Pilgrims, an organization to promote Anglo-American friendship, saluted the "fraternal relations" of the Western powers.

Xmas shopping before I left and nearly all plans and orders are given so Xmas should be no strain, just pleasure. Next year perhaps you will spend Xmas with us? I like to have people I love around me!

My cold is nearly gone, just a little stuffiness left and I feel a great weight off my shoulders with no U.N. work till May before me! You will be hearing from me often because it is easy to write when I am peacefully at H.P. where I love to be!

My thoughts and love go to you,

E.R.

New York 11 New York
December 20 [1947]

David dear,

I sent you a cable last night and I must send a line for I know how long even Air Mail takes.

. . .

I've just talked to Joe and Trude and all the family is well and I shall come down Tuesday and be with them at 6 o'clock for their Xmas celebration. On New Year's Eve they will bring Jonathan and stay over the weekend which will give them a rest I hope!

Elliott and Faye are selling Xmas trees madly and tonight they will dine with me and I will hear all about the farm!

While my hair is being washed this morning I'm going to read Marshall's speech and tomorrow I'll write you a long letter for there are thoughts on many subjects turning round and round in my head! Just know this takes you my constant thought and love—Your book is ordered —Christmas morning I'll try to telephone you between 9 and 10 but of course the connection may be bad.

Devotedly

E.R.

Hyde Park
December 22d 1947

David dear,

I've just arranged to call you Xmas day but I'm so late in making the arrangements that I had to make it 10 a.m. which I fear is a little late for you. Next time I'll start arranging earlier!

No snow here but clear and cold and a little ice just forming on the pond. The nights on the porch are wonderful with the stars looking so bright and near.

I have almost caught up on mail. There are as usual endless things people want me to do but I'm just refusing. This afternoon I go to Wiltwyck to read the Dickens "Xmas Carol" to the boys and Josh White with his little boy is coming up to sing to them and I give them all ice cream and cake so I hope it will be a happy party.

The telephone co. has just called back to say the hour is still not set so I may talk to you Xmas eve, whenever it is I shall be happy!

I'm enclosing Marshall's speech for fear you may not see it. I think only raising the economic level in the USSR will bring them to the point where they can consider the individual and not the mass only. There is where we are short sighted in not starting to do business. Things of the spirit must wait till the physical needs of . . . . . are met. The Ukrainian said to me "Yes, I heard it said in the U.S. men have freedom to starve!"

It spoiled me to be able to talk with you! Now I think of so much I would like to be able to sit down before the fire and talk out with you. . . .

My love and thoughts go to you and may the New Year bring you happiness which now you cannot even imagine possible. Bless you.

E.R.

Who was David Gurewitsch? He was born in 1902. His parents were Russian. His father, a philosopher of mystic bent, Jewish, had just completed a book of metaphysics which dealt with "the spirit and nothingness." Two months before David's birth, at the age of twenty-six, he walked into the waters or allowed himself to be engulfed in a Swiss lake. A friendly reviewer of his book, *Contribution to the Foundation of the Synthesis of Being*, characterized it as a "voluntary death." He had finished his life's work, David later said of his handsome, bearded father. His mother, a tiny woman of great will, took her two boys (David's brother Valdi was one year older) back to Vitebsk, Russia, and left them there to go to London to become a doctor with psychic healing gifts. She returned at the time of the Russian Revolution and the three went to Berlin, where she practiced medicine and undertook to translate her husband's work into German.

David turned into a handsome youth, and his pleasing ways brought him into contact with Germany's infant movie industry. His name began to be linked with some of its stars. He tried his hand at farming and in the ceramics business, but he wanted more out of life and began medical studies in Berlin. He went to Freiburg in 1929 to complete the prerequisites to study at Basel's medical school. He needed Latin and was directed to Trude Wenzel for help. He received his M.D. from Basel and did his internship in its hospital. But Hitler had come to power and, being a young Zionist, he chose to go to Jerusalem as a doctor in the infant Hadassah Hospital. Armed with letters from Jerusalem he went to the United States in 1934 to study pathology at the Mt. Sinai Hospital in New York City.

On shipboard he met Nemone Balfour of the aristocratic Scots family of that name and a niece of Montague Norman. She was a large-boned, handsome, cultivated, headstrong woman who had studied voice in Vienna for four years and was on the way to the United States to do a low-keyed concert tour. David, who was stateless and traveled on a Nansen passport, found Nemone's patent rootedness in British upper-class life especially attractive. They fell in love. Nemone returned to England believing they were getting married. He returned to Paris of a different mind. So he later told their daughter, Grania. But Nemone's family caused difficulties about her marrying him. "One is English," she was told. "One isn't Jewish. One doesn't work." The Balfours were landed gentry, either Presbyterians or Church of England. Their home in Scotland included a chapel. Nemone's mother insisted that David be baptized. He refused. Her father's friend, the Archbishop of Canterbury, undertook to speak with David, and, said Grania, "my father passed. He wasn't after my mother's money. He had ideals. They were married in the stone chapel." On David's side, his mother, having learned that David had indeed promised to marry Nemone, sternly instructed him, "Gentlemen do not walk out on such pledges."

They decided to settle in the United States. When David learned that Nemone had been subject to depressions since she was twelve is unclear, nor whether he knew at the time of their marriage that she had been seriously depressed after disappointment in Vienna with her singing career. In 1940 Grania was born. In 1947, when David was on his way to Davos, the Alpine sojourn was a therapeutic necessity but also a separation from Nemone.

On New Year's Day Eleanor telephoned the absent children. She had the Lashes with her. She adjured Hick by letter, "May we see each other often. . . ." And to David in Davos she cabled, "Good wishes for the New Year. Affectionate thoughts."

XII

David Gurewitsch

SOON AFTER Eleanor returned to New York she invited David's wife Nemone and their seven-year-old daughter Grania to Hyde Park. They were unable to come before the end of January, and when they did come the visit may have been a little strained, not because of the little girl but because David had told Eleanor of the tensions in his marriage with Nemone. With Eleanor's enormous need to take on the problems of the people she cared about, and careful though she was not to seem to be siding with him, she shared his perplexity whether he should make another attempt with Nemone or gently bring their marriage to an end. David had portrayed Nemone to her as wanting the separation that coincided with the "cure" at Davos. Nemone and others said the initiative was David's.

Who is to judge in these matters? Eleanor's interest was in David. Whatever he wanted, she was ready to support. Her letters to him vibrated with the delighted discovery that she still could love and communication with him had a special sweetness.

The day after New Year's she wrote about the event's special character at Hyde Park.

Jan. 2d [1948]

David dear,

I'm enclosing Wallace's speech and I wonder how you will feel about it. It seems to me incredibly naive and just wishful thinking with no facing of the realities of the world situation, but it will have an emotional appeal for who in the world does not long for "peace, abundance and security?"

Trude and Joe and Jonathan arrived safely on New Year's eve and Elliott and Faye had many friends up here and some of the neighbors came for a late supper and to see the New Year in. We have two traditional toasts—to "The U.S.A." and to "all those we love who are not with us." I thought of the many who have gone on to "things we know not of" and of the many I would have liked to have with us and I thought especially this year of you in gratitude that I knew you better and in hope that our friendship would deepen and strengthen with the years.

It is snowing again and very beautiful but those who travel will find it hard for all trains are off schedule and no planes operate!

My love to you.

E.R.

She had sent David copies of her autobiography, *This Is My Story,* some manuscript chapters of the book on which she was working, *This I Remember,* and Wallace's speech.*

David's reply dwelt on Eleanor's childhood as reflected in *This Is My Story.*

[David Gurewitsch to E.R.:] [January 11, 1948]

. . . If one considers how many "mistakes" were made with you, and what a difficult youth you have had and compares it with the result, in which balance and absence of neurosis are so prominent, one begins to wonder. In how many people the greatest protection and psychology do not prevent weakness and neurotic trends, yes they even seem to breed it.

What did Eleanor make of this? She had achieved one of the most arresting self-analyses in history, conquering depression, withdrawal, and unhappiness and converting them into serenity and altruism without the benefit of psychoanalysis. Indeed, she felt that turning to analysis was a way of escaping rather than facing up to one's problems. Yet part of David's fascination for her was his knowledge of psychiatry, and it was he who had suggested that John Boettiger, whose case she had described without identifying the person, might well benefit from a stay at Menninger's, a suggestion that she had passed on to Anna.

The rest of his letter may have referred to Nemone. He concluded his comment on how people coped with unhappy childhoods, saying, "It may be of course

* Henry Wallace at the end of 1947 in a nationwide radio address announced his candidacy for President in 1948 on the ticket of the Progressive Citizens of America (PCA), which earlier in December had urged him to run. The Democrats, he said, had become a party of "war and depression. . . . There is no real fight between Truman and a Republican." It required a "new party to fight these war makers. . . . We have assembled a Gideon's army—small in number, powerful in conviction, ready for action."

a question of constitutional makeup which will resist or succumb regardless of approach."

He shared her views of the Wallace announcement. He had liked Wallace's letter to Truman in 1946 urging a friendlier policy toward Russia, but "The present speech sounds cheap and demagogical." His letter ended "thank you for Nemone's and Grania's invitation. I hope you like the little girl."

She plied the absent David with gifts and with evaluations of the great with whom she had to deal.

Val-Kill Cottage
Jan. 20th [1948]

David dear,

I am so glad you enjoy the autobiography and please don't send it back. It is a gift to you if you like it well enough to want to keep it. . . .

I have finished revising all I have written on the 2d volume and the copying is being started. The carbon copy will go to you and please return it with comments and criticisms since it will not go finally to the publisher till March.

I promised you what inside gossip I gathered in Washington last week. The newspaper girls are discouraging, no one has any stature according to them and a truly disinterested statesman doesn't exist. Marshall is encouraging, without bitterness. He feels England played a perfidious role in the London conference but finally came up to scratch and he still believes Europe can be saved in spite of this being an election year and Congress being very stupid. Mr. Baruch's testimony yesterday was magnificent and I hope the Democrats accept it as their blueprint for domestic and foreign action. I'll enclose it. The President is still well meaning but such a little man!

I got back to N.Y. on Friday the 16th and then had to fly to Raleigh, N.C. and back on the 17th for Mr. [Josephus] Daniels funeral. He was such a good friend and I am so fond of Jonathan that I wanted to go.

. . .

"Haply I think on thee," the poet wrote to his lover, and Eleanor's letters to David eased the burden of trying to hold together the marriage between Anna and John. "John left this afternoon," she wrote Anna from Hyde Park. "I only hope what I said was right." She was a partisan of John's but intensely loyal to Anna.

Val-Kill Cottage
February 1st

David dear,

. . .

It was wonderful to hear your voice today but I wish you could have seen your little girl's face. She looked so completely happy. . . .

I am sorry you have Nemone's worries just now. I do not think

Nemone will have a depression. She looks well. She is troubled I am sure but she does not know me well enough to talk about it and then she knows that I am first your friend. As a rule one loves people with all their faults included! I knew the story and I grieve for you both but try not to do something which will hurt you and not be lasting. The child will suffer and she needs security. She would be happy if you were here with her I think. . . . I wish I could help in some way dear David but no one can make decisions of this kind but the people concerned and tho' I'd like to be near you just to hold your hand I know I could do nothing that would be helpful. Nevertheless I look forward to April. I think Tommy and I can get to wherever you are April 18th and 19th. Do you think you can get a room nearby?

The first chapters of the new manuscript are going to you or may have gone if Tommy got the stamps. . . .

David dear, don't worry too much about others, think of yourself and Grania and Nemone only if you think life for you *all* can be lived as *you* must live it, because you are you, then make your decisions for that which you feel will bring happiness and contentment and pray! We can't ever be sure to be wise but we must be ourselves and live as we feel is right for us. What a mixed up sentence but perhaps you'll understand!

My love to you.

E.R.

David's regimen at Davos began to ease, and his letter to her was filled with the anticipations of her visit in April. She was coming to London at the beginning of April for Britain's unveiling of a statue to Franklin in Grosvenor Square. As she wrote to Anna: "We sail on the *Queen Elizabeth* March 27th at noon & Claridge's Hotel will be our abode till April 15. Then 15th–17th Zurich & see Dr. Gurewitsch, 17th–19th Brussels to speak night of 17th, 19th–21st Holland with Juliana & 21st back to London. Sail 22d. . . ."

He looked forward to her visit, David replied to her February 1 letter, "But only for 2 days it seems a very long trip indeed. You could not stay a little longer?" Perhaps he might save her part of her journey. "Could I not come to the Dolder* overlooking Zurich? . . . I am longing to see you and to be close to you. Please if you can do it, add a little more time. It takes a little time to break down shyness and all kinds of barriers." He added a page of comments on the drafts of chapters she had sent him from *This I Remember*. One page of such comments he had torn up, he said, and as if overcome by the temerity of the page he was sending, added, "Now I feel like tearing this page as well." He signed "Your David."

Anna's troubles with John and the paper weighed heavily. "I'm sorry he [John] felt we were not interested," she wrote Anna "but I can't talk to him. I can't know

* A famous Swiss hostelry.

so many things & it will be better in the long run if we haven't said things we might regret." Eleanor still hoped the marriage might be repaired, but if Anna made a success of the paper that John had abandoned she prayed that John in time would understand "that you couldn't quit. . . . I hope you can both accept it & go on for the sake of your own happy companionship which means much as one grows older & for Johnny's security."

David had his problems, too, but she found release in writing him. "But if the while I think on thee, dear friend,/All losses are restored and sorrows end," the Bard had written.

Val-Kill Cottage
February 25th [1948]

David dear,

Your two sheets of the 16th and 19th came today and you amuse me the way you tear things up. Your criticism of the chapter is right but this can't be like the other book. I'll talk it over with you and you will get more chapters soon to fill in the gap up to the one I sent you on the 1940 Convention. This book will be interesting chiefly because of the little lights it may throw on Franklin. I did mature over the years but as you yourself say the first book just gave a picture of me and when it ended as a person I was pretty well set!

I am afraid I can't stay longer. . . . If you want to come to Zurich that will be wonderful but don't do anything not good for you or which might upset you or hold you back. Somehow I want you home surely by next Xmas. . . . I hope it will be a hotel! David, don't be shy with me and set up barriers. I feel very close to you and now that I've seen Grania I know more about you. I'm old enough to be your mother but sometimes older friends can be useful particularly over the rough spots that come in all lives.

. . .

Politics look bleak here and I can't help feeling we are being governed by fear and I hate it. I go to Washington next week for two days but I've written all I feel on Palestine to the President so I don't think I can do anything more by seeing him—

. . .

Affly,
E.R.

The reference to Palestine was to her running battle with President Truman and Secretary of State Marshall over the U.S. failure to back the Palestine partition plan that had been adopted by the General Assembly and for which the United States had voted. She was outraged by the U.S. embargo on arms, which in effect favored the neighboring Arab states that were threatening to nullify the UN resolution by armed invasion. Alarmed by Arab threats, the United States backed away from an international police force and proposed a temporary trusteeship to replace the British mandate. She told Truman and Marshall she was ready to resign from the U.S. delegation.

It was a turbulent spring. The "coup" referred to in her next letter to David was the brutal seizure of power in Czechoslovakia by the Communists, a move justified by Henry Wallace as a Communist effort to forestall a right-wing coup allegedly encouraged by U.S. Ambassador Steinhardt. Three days after her letter to David, Czech Foreign Minister Jan Masaryk was found dead on the sidewalk below his apartment, a suicide or a victim of defenestration.

Val-Kill Cottage
March 7th 1948

David dear,

How horrible of them to pull a wisdom tooth out without an anaesthetic. That is cruelty I think! I'm glad you felt better afterwards but it must have been agony.

By now you know that I will be in Zurich on April 15th if all goes well. . . . I don't think there need be publicity or to-do! It would just mean more time to see you and talk and as I wrote you I can't make it longer because I have to speak in Brussels the night of the 17th. The 19th–21st I'll be in Holland with Juliana and sail the 22nd. I wish I could be longer with you but the Human Rights drafting committee begins May 2d and I must do some preparation and some personal business.

Selfishly I wish you could leave Davos in July and rest over here till Sept. Perhaps go with us to Campobello if sea air is good for you and then come here for a little while till you are ready to work. You will know better when you hear what the doctors here think after seeing your Xrays. . . .

I had a note from Nemone on my return from Washington this week and she sounds cheerful. I hope I can see Grania again before leaving if not I'll telephone and get the latest news for you.

. . .

Washington was a discouraging atmosphere and I was glad only to spend two days! I think we act on our fears so much nowadays that no one feels secure or gets a lift about anything they do. I think the country relied on Franklin so long that they are looking for a "father" to cast all their worries upon!

Wallace is going to pull a big vote and elect reactionaries to all offices I think. The last "coup" seems to give none of his non-communist liberals any worry and of course the communists are jubilant. I fear Italy comes next and then what happens in Greece and Palestine? We have shown no courage on Palestine and I fear the weakening of the U.N. Heavens!

Here I talk of "fears" like everyone else and I really feel we should be making an effort to find some more positive approach to all these problems!
. . .

I am looking forward to seeing you David. It is the one personal and entirely happy time that I count on during this trip! My love to you.

E.R.

Can you read my scrawls?

Val-Kill Cottage
March 18th

David dear,
It seemed a long time since I had heard so I was both relieved and happy to hear today. I thought you might have had trouble with the tooth.
. . . If you come home in early Sept. I shall be here to greet you even if I have to go later to the U.N. Assembly. I only hope that in talking over your personal situation I may be of some help. It is hard to tell whether accumulated experience can be of any value but just talking to someone else frankly is sometimes a help. At least I am glad your emotions are no longer involved so as to make you unhappy for that would retard your recovery.

The political situation is most disturbing and I have been deeply worried. I wrote both the Secretary and the President somewhat along the lines you suggest. It seems to me someone must sit down *now* with Stalin. Since Truman is not strong enough alone, he should take a delegation of strong people. I think I dread people's fears more than anything in the world. It leads to stupidity and cruelty. The Russians behave badly but so do we. I'll bring you some of the letters on this subject as I think they will interest you from the psychological point of view—Palestine is the result of our fears. I will tell you all the behind the scenes stories when we meet. Some of them seem to me incredible. We will have I fear a reactionary President and I don't envy him his job.

I've been a good deal in and out of N.Y. and I've been speaking too often so the book gets on slowly but I'll bring you some more chapters. . . .

E.R.

Tommy, although going with her to London, was slowing down. Eleanor's responsibilities at the UN, even though she enjoyed her duties as a member of the U.S. delegation, were relentless. There were rumors of her differences with President Truman and Secretary of State Marshall over Palestine. Her unhappiness with the drift toward war was better known. Marshall thought it wise to send "Chip" Bohlen to New York to reassure her about U.S. policy toward Russia. She was so busy with long letters to the President and Secretary of State that, except to David and Anna, she wrote little. The Sunday before she sailed she had Nemone and Grania at Hyde Park so that she might be able to report to David when she saw him in Zurich. She lunched with Cousin Susie and Elinor Morgenthau, and the night before she sailed her engagement book read: "7:30 Elliott and Faye, Fjr. & Ethel, Trude & Joe dine."

There is a difference between the outsiders' perceptions of the public and private lives of the people in the headlines. Her emotional life that stormy spring focused on David and Anna. But center stage in the public view in 1948 was the Democratic effort to prevent Truman's nomination. Two of Eleanor's sons, Elliott and Franklin Jr., were deeply involved in the effort to draft General Eisenhower, an effort not unmixed with brotherly rivalries. Among the Roosevelt children there was no sense of precedence in running for public office as Joseph Kennedy had established among his sons. Franklin Jr. was preparing to issue a statement urging General Eisenhower to make himself available to a Democratic draft. He consulted many of his father's associates. "You're exactly like your father," Ed Flynn told him. "Louis and I had to hold your father back. . . . Your father's friends don't think it's so good." Baruch's comment was similar: "You remind me of your father. When he felt this way there was only one thing to do—to let him have his head and go." But just before Franklin issued his statement, Elliott stole a march on him and issued his own "draft Ike" declaration. James would be heard from later. But what the press wanted to know was where Eleanor Roosevelt stood.

So long as she remained on the U.S. delegation, she declared in "My Day," released while she was on shipboard, she worked under the President and Secretary of State and cooperated with their policies.

> I am not trying to do anything whatsoever in the way of party politics. My sons, as a rule, tell me what they are going to do, but they are grown men and I decided long ago that once children were grown they must be allowed to lead their own lives. If they feel it right to take a stand of any kind, they must abide by the results of their own decisions. I do not interfere with them now that they are grown to man's estate.
>
> They did not always agree with their father, and, when they did not agree, they said [so] in no uncertain terms. He always preferred to leave them entirely free. The most that I can expect or that I desire of them is to be told of their intentions as a matter of courtesy, but I do not expect or desire to control their consciences or their actions.

She had arranged to see Hick before she left for London because she was anxious to encourage her to collaborate with Tommy on a book about her. She wrote encouragingly from the *Queen Elizabeth*—

[E.R. to Lorena Hickok:]   [March 30, 1948]
  I'm thrilled that you've begun to write & that you find it easy. You &

Tommy can have much material ready & I'd rather have you two dissect me than anyone else in the world & I'll feel so much more secure feeling that you both have a little security! I may be flattering myself but I think it will be saleable.

We are most luxurious & Tommy is a good sailor too, much better than I am really. I never *want* to do anything or to be nice to anyone on shipboard & about all I can manage is 2 meals a day! . . .

. . . Have dictated some of the revision on book to Tommy & part of a column to have ready for the day we land & many "thank you" notes, otherwise I've slept an endless amount! Coming by boat was a concession to our hosts the Pilgrims & the British Government! I like flying better because it is over more quickly! . . .

But to Trude she confessed, ". . . there are too many people one knows on board so there is no time for rest or work besides I don't work well on ships so very little is done on the book."

After the ceremonies in Grosvenor Square at which Britain's statue to Franklin was unveiled, she went to Windsor Castle: "Thanks for your letter & the clippings," she wrote Hick on castle stationery. "I was pursued across the ocean by telephone from newspapers which I refused to answer. . . . Harry [Hooker, the President's representative] has enjoyed all the formalities, being met on the steamer by the Mayor and Mayoress with the gold mace in attendance was a thrill to him." Tommy was staying with Lady Reading while her boss was at Windsor. "I have had a bad time sorting people out without Tommy! I sat by the Duke of Wellington & Duke of Edinburgh (Elizabeth's husband). All the historic names are a bit bewildering. Queen Mary is 81 & as spry & interested as when I saw her nearly 6 yrs. ago."

She found a note from Anna at Claridge's and immediately replied:

London
April 6th, [1948]

Anna darling,

. . . I'm sorry if James was upset. Fjr. said he'd called him. Elliott only answered an invitation to join the Wallace forces & did not give out his letter till he found the N.Y. Post had it in garbled form. It was pure coincidence that they both came out together.

Mr. Charles Bohlen is still in Russia, at least he came to see me for General Marshall the day before I sailed. . . .

Perhaps I can manage the trip for both Sis & Van but don't say anything as one, I may not be in the Assembly, & two, I might not have the money . . .

She saw several Allenswood schoolmates, lunched with Churchill, and spoke to the Pilgrims' Dinner. She spent a good deal of time with Lady Reading, who had headed the British women's voluntary services during the war. A cheery, plain-spoken, and well-informed woman, she had become a close friend. Finally on Thursday, April 15, she was driven to the airport for her flight to Zurich and two days' stay with David. "This has been a strenuous trip," she wrote Anna after a stopover in Belgium and a visit with Queen Juliana and Prince Bernhard of Holland, "the only relaxed time was in Zurich & I was glad to find David Gurewitsch practically well." Wherever she went, the welcome had been warm. "What friends Father made everywhere for the United States. It ought to bring tangible results to us in the future if we are wise. . . ."

Eleanor's visit exhilarated David.* Whatever the reasons, he had been "chosen" by this extraordinary woman. His heart literally sang.

[David Gurewitsch to E.R.:]   [n.d.]
    You have been in Zurich. I got your wonderful letter from Brussels and you reached me from the boat. You are on the high seas, recovering, I hope, from all the to-do and I am back on my back, but quite differently, peacefully and comfortably. Like everything connected with you, also Zurich was a surprise. It was so much more than I had anticipated. It was more intense and more intimate, it has brought you closer. I did not know that just accepting, taking, without another return except for gratitude and warmth could be as simple. You have done nothing but giving and I nothing but accepting and still I am not ashamed, not even shy about it, just grateful and much closer.

There had been much discussion about Nemone, and evidently he had decided to seek a divorce:

    Nemone has answered, summarizing what I essentially knew: her feeling of being forelorn, her worry about Grania, her feeling that nothing was gained for her by leaving me. But also stating that she would stand

---

* Interview with David Gurewitsch, May 31, 1970. "She came to Zurich with Tommy. I was to reserve two rooms for Miss Thompson so she could preserve anonymity. But in the airport as the airplane was coming down it was announced over the loudspeakers that Mrs. R. was arriving. As I was trying to park the car I had rented, I was told, 'you can't park here.' I replied, 'It was for an arriving passenger, Miss Thompson'. Oh, said the guard, 'You mean Mrs. Roosevelt. There are six cars waiting for her from the Swiss Foreign Ministry, the U.S. Consulate, etc.' It was the first time that I saw her in action. A little girl presented her with flowers, red, white and blue. She managed to dispose of all of them and drive away with me without hurting anybody. She did all the formalities required of her, yet without hurting anybody."

Subsequently, December 7, 1971, David told me more about the stay at the Dolder, a Noël Coward story. "I got three rooms in the Dolder, a big hotel. All the main rooms face a golf course, each with a balcony. Three rooms—for myself, Tommy and Mrs. R. I walk out to the balcony just to look at the view and at that moment on the very next balcony to mine, somebody walks out, and the person who walks out is my girl friend. I knew nothing about it and there is a connecting door between the two rooms, Mrs. R. on the other side. That lady had a husband with whom she was staying in that room. It took some maneuvering. Mrs. R. always knew about [my] affairs. Nothing escaped her."

by the decisions taken without further discussion, if I felt this to be the
best course to take. . . .

He would see Nemone and Grania and then they would go to England. He intended to ask Nemone to appoint a lawyer

so that things can be made ready while we are both in Europe. I shall ask
her to stay with Grania until I return and then go to Nevada.

Eleanor's letter from Brussels is lost, but she began a long letter the day she
boarded the *Queen Elizabeth* and she posted it on landing in New York on the
27th.

Cunard White Star
R.M.S. Queen Elizabeth
April 22d

David dear,

    I'll begin this tonight because I want to say certain things and if I wait
I may forget but I won't mail it till I land as I may find a letter saying you
are back at the Sanatorium. Your voice told me all your disappointment
this morning and I don't wonder for I had made up my mind as you had;
all was well. Perhaps we expected too much but David don't go back and
be miserable for I feel that would be worse for you. I'm glad Zurich did
not make you feel tired but I'm sure it did tire you. However, perhaps it
was as well to be warned for you will be careful till you are sure all is well
now. . . .

    Both in Belgium and in Holland I felt there was great fear of Russia
tho' they talk about it less and are not jittery as we are. I've come to the
conclusion that the royalties of little countries in Europe are rather pathetic—lonely and sad—and I think I even include British royalties in
that feeling! I had to spend an hour and a half with Queen Mother
Elizabeth in Brussels and she is pathetic and yet she has many artistic
gifts and one would hope for a fuller and more satisfying life for her.
Juliana's baby can see just a little in one eye and she is such a sweet,
pretty and happy little thing. It must make Juliana very sad.

   . . .

    Somehow the thought of you back at the Sanatorium worries me for I
don't feel the doctor there can help using you and leaning on you and
that must sap your strength. I'm selfish but I want you home soon.
Switzerland is a long way off when you would like to drop in and talk
once in a while: Goodnight David dear, bless you and take care of yourself for you are a very precious person.

    April 24th—I think you would be interested in a small T.B. hospital for students who were in the resistance movement which I visited with Juliana in Holland. . . .

April 27th—I doubt as I read this over whether you can read it but I send it as you will know I thought about you! Joe and Trude were here for dinner as we docked and reached home by 4 P.M. Plenty of headaches in the way of home problems await me but it is better to be home to handle them. Trude wanted to hear just how you were. My love to you and bless you.

E.R.

Her calendar the day the boat docked simply read "Home." She did not go to Hyde Park but stayed at her Washington Square apartment to see Elinor and Cousin Susie and then went down to Washington where, in addition to government officials, she saw Anna. The latter had decided to give up the paper in Phoenix and move to Los Angeles with Buzz and Johnny. Elliott, who was serving as his mother's representative in radio and television, had interested the American Broadcasting Company in an "Eleanor and Anna" program which would be produced by friends of Anna. "She gets *all* the pay," Eleanor explained to Maude, "& it will help her pay her debts."

At the beginning of May she was in Hyde Park. As she wrote David:

29 Washington Square West
May 3d

David dear,

It was good to get your letter today and to hear your voice yesterday. Grania's little face is always a joy to watch when she talks to you. She does long to see you and so I am glad she will go to you for I know you too long to see her. I hope Nemone will not upset you, don't let her go into a depression. She looks well now. . . . Your plans all sound good and sensible, the only thing I fear is an inevitable emotion which you can scarcely escape being with Nemone. Intellectual discussions are one thing but emotions are another! Just don't get hurt. You will have to explain to Grania too and that won't be easy because she is so young. She has a right to be told however, and having a responsibility for you will give her more security.

. . .

The Human Rights Commission opened today and our Supreme Court decided the Courts could *not* uphold restrictive covenants on housing. That is a big step forward in Human Rights. I loved getting home to the country, to Elliott and my little dogs. Anna was here and I saw her and I think she is working out her paper and her personal problems. . . .

I'm so glad my visit made you feel closer to me, why should you talk of shyness in acceptance of love, that just shouldn't exist for older people should be able to give for otherwise they would have learned little from living! My thoughts and warm love to you.

E.R.

May 6th

David dear,

I am trying to get Nemone and Grania passages back on or about Sept. 15th on the Cunard Line and think I will succeed. . . .

The work on the H.R. drafting committee is very difficult because it really requires legal training and I have none and at this point every word and phrase in the Covenant is weighted for its legal meaning.

Joe and Trude came to dine tonight and Joe is trying to decide what he wants to do and I don't believe it is an easy time for him.

Politically things are not much clearer. I dined with Mr. Baruch and he is as confused as I am. The situation in Palestine is still baffling and the [tension] between Russia and ourselves [is] uppermost in the minds of all people. I'm ashamed not to be able to decide what I think we should do but all ways seem equally bad!

   . . .

Devotedly,
E.R.

Some events in her life were not reported. Elinor Morgenthau had had to check into the hospital again, and despite the demands of her UN schedule at Lake Success Eleanor went to see her. "Earl for day & night," her calendar read for May 9.

29 Washington Square West
May 11th

Dearest David,

Your dear letter of May 3d was a great pleasure but I had to laugh over your having to decipher some parts of the letter from the states again. I know how badly it was written and you should do as my children do, send it back with the parts you can't read marked!

   . . .

I am having a party this next Friday evening for the members of the Human Rights drafting Com. and Nemone has agreed to come and sing for a little while. I know they will enjoy her.

I can't help thinking how happy you and Grania will be together. I wish I could look down from a cloud and see you both but I worry a little about how you will manage Nemone and yourself. It isn't an easy situation. By that time I hope however Dr. Maurer* will have proved correct and you will be physically stronger. . . .

I work all day at U.N. and a good deal at night but I am well. We will be on the job I fear till June 20th. I may get off from the 19th–24th if the drafting committee is through and the full Commission doesn't meet until the 24th. I would love a really long weekend as we have an office to put in order in Hyde Park.

Joe and Trude came to dine tonight and Joe and T. went to a lecture at the New School given by young Eugene O'Neill on Franklin. It was good but he said F.D.R. was less of a leader between 1936 and 1940 than before or than after Pearl Harbor. That he could have prevented war but didn't realize the threat and I don't think that is true. . . .

I must go to bed but I love writing you, my thoughts go to you often but time is a most precious commodity which I lack most for the things I want to do most!

All my love and don't worry about clinging too much to me. I rather imagine you had few opportunities to relax and lean on anyone, things have been the other way around usually and it will do you good to cling a little!

Devotedly,
E.R.

Even she was surprised by her own loquacity when the next day she wrote him another long letter.

29 Washington Square West
May 12th

David dear,

I enclose the note about Nemone and Grania's return passage. . . .

Of course what you are doing is right and sensible and I don't want you to lose time and I want you to take every precaution. I think I dreaded the return to an institution and its atmosphere and feared you would not be as happy and that might be harmful. I wish I could be taking care of you! I'm sure I do it better than I preside over the Human Rights drafting committee! Today was the first day that I began to understand some of the legal points we are now dealing with and when I am not clear myself I cannot make it clear for others! I am not a lawyer and four have to sit behind me to guide me and they all see different pitfalls in every phrase and I am sometimes in a complete daze! I leave at 9:40 A.M. We get to Lake Success and work at 10:30 and I get my lectures in the car. I preside till 1, lunch with inquiring souls, preside from 2:30 to

* He was Director of the Davis TB Sanatorium.

5:30 or 6 and then drive back. If I go out the column and mail await my return and the night is all too short—I'm hoping we can get a long weekend before the full Commission meets on the 24th. I rather think it will last till June 20th. I've decided not to go to Campobello this year but to finish the book.

Tommy seems fine. I think the trip did her good—

I have had only three letters from you, one must have been lost. I love them, but don't let writing to me become a burden. I understand that you must find it difficult at times—I am happy to have a photograph and it is on the desk before me as I write. It is good to look at you, though I wish you were really here. . . . Don't worry about my being imposed on. There are always people, more or less interesting, and I am accustomed to it. I love having Grania and she is getting accustomed to me and to Hyde Park. One cannot rush a child but I want her to feel she belongs as a friend. . . .

She recounted the difficulties of Jimmy and his wife, adding,

I think I can help but it is a complicated situation but in a big family that is sure to happen. The children have often thought that I did not do the right things for them but when things go wrong they usually bring them to me! I would feel I had really failed if they didn't. . . .

E.R.

She loved David, but was it the mighty and beguiling passion that poets describe when they speak of "natural love"? For if the latter has one aim, it is the happiness that comes from fulfillment. And her next letter to David still was filled with doubt about the importance of happiness:

29 Washington Square West
May 20th, 1948

David dearest,

Two letters from you and I feel very happy for your news seems good and I begin to feel you are really well again when you say you feel well. Of course you must take all the tests and be sure and be quiet and very careful. When will Grania and Nemone go to you and where will you be, in Klosters? Grania will be anxious till she gets to you. I doubt if I can see them again before they leave but I will telephone.

Dr. Maurer annoys me because you always have to consider him, but if the two question marks are happily answered by July 10th I shall bless him! As you look at me from the little Kodak, you look so much better, I believe in my heart too that you are well—I love looking at my little picture and it goes with me wherever I go! . . . Happiness, I don't think

I could answer you about, it is a relative thing and not very important perhaps?

I think you are right about the Russians, they will I think come to terms. They should not be strengthened till there is much better real understanding than there is at present. No, I don't think Gen. Marshall will go on after this year but he might go to Paris and that might be important. Now I worry about Palestine but the Frenchman M. Parodi* told me he thought the Jews could hold the ground against the Arabs because the latter are so divided. Please mark and send me Kinsey's book. I had heard of it but have had no time to read it or anything else since the Human Rights drafting commission began May 3d. The full Commission begins its session next Monday, May 24th and I hope to be through June 18th but might well not get through till the 25th!

. . .

E.R.

A letter from David told her that the sanatorium's director left him alone, that his balcony was "peaceful and beautiful" and the Alpine spring vivifying. The sanatorium was still worried about some tuberculosis bacilli that had shown up in some tests and he might have to stay at Davos longer than he anticipated. "That interferes with staying in Klosters with Nemone and Grania. It may be easier not to be under the same roof with Nemone. . . . Do you think it wiser to live apart? It may be easier to discuss things, to find the right mood if we were together. On the other hand it will also be apt to cause more tensions." Would she not have more peace writing in Campobello? "People can get less at you." His letter ended on a vain injunction, *"Please* do not overwork. My love to Trude and Joe. I have written to Trude long ago. But I know that she never answers letters."

> 29 Washington Square West
> May 26th

Dearest David,

Your letter of the 20th came and I read it with such pleasure. None of my fears for you at Schatzalp seem to be materializing and so far no bad news on tests and I hope and pray they will soon be over and the results will all be negative.

I think it is as well that you will not be in the hotel with Nemone. She came to tea with me yesterday. . . .

I was free yesterday and this morning because our stupid Consuls in the Ukraine and Byelorussia didn't grant the visas to the delegates from those countries and the U.S.S.R. demanded we wait for them. We are retaliating because the Russians have acted similarly to us but we were all

---

* Alexandre Parodi was the Permanent Representative of France at the United Nations.

wrong to hold up delegates to the U.N. It gave the Russians a good point on which to attack us and now they are delaying on everything. Some members have to leave by June 15th and I don't see how we are to do our work!

. . .

Yes, Campobello would be cooler and quieter if the house wasn't filled with workmen and children. If I moved 8 children and supervised the work it would not be so, so I decided not to go. Once I have everything organized at H.P. it will run smoothly and if I find Tommy suffers from the heat I can take her away for a few days here and there. We will work every morning from 10–1 on the book and I should finish in a month. Faye's play is a success and she may not be home except Sundays and I cannot leave Elliott with all the children to look after.

Henry Morgenthau brought a Mrs. Meyersson from Palestine to breakfast last Tuesday. A woman of great strength and calm and for me she symbolizes the best spirit of Palestine. Evidently at last we mean to follow through on a policy of aid to the Jewish state. The British role seems to me quite stupid, no more greedy and self interested than ours has been, but at last we seem to be doing better. Private citizens must be interested David dear, and I think you are a good politician. If all of us are not interested in a democracy, we will lose our freedom! . . .

. . .

E.R.

She dined with Hick and Pauli Murray, the latter a black woman, a graduate of Hunter College, with whom she had become friends at a camp for the unemployed in the Bear Mountains in the thirties. "Justice Douglas for day," her book read on May 30 when the Justice had been the speaker at the Memorial Day remembrance of F.D.R. at Hyde Park. Maude and David came to stay for several weeks on their way home from Sarasota to Portland. Anna and Buzz came. A solicitous note to David:

29 Washington Square West
June 7th, 1948

David dearest,

I have been negligent and your dear letters which came today made me realize how the time had slipped by since last I wrote.

Grania and Nemone will be with you by the time this reaches you. Don't let the discussions upset you and set you back. It will be hard to explain to Grania but she will understand later if not now. Nemone should not get tense and upset and I think she can control herself unless she feels there is something to be gained by becoming uncontrolled.

. . . When you are back, I think it would be wise to do whatever will make your life easier and I would try to plan a little less hectic life. I know you love your work but even what one loves may wear one out! Let me know as you hear from the guinea pigs!

The work goes on but we adjourn the 18th. I'll be in a bit here and there during the next 2 weeks and then just stay at Hyde Park and close the apartment on June 25th. I must work hard on the book and I look forward to being in one place and having all the children around tho' I shall have to make a rule about uninterrupted morning hours for work!

I think a good declaration on Human Rights will come out of this meeting but no finished covenant—

E.R.

Her next note advised David that if he should return to the United States while she was at the United Nations: "Remember the cottage here is yours and it is bright and quiet and cheerful. I know I could get a maid."

29 Washington Square West
Tuesday, June 15th, 1948

Dearest David,

Grania and Nemone have been at the chalet several days and I hope the strain of both joy and pain is lessening a little. I think your talks with Grania will not be difficult but your fears for Nemone and your sense of responsibility may make the days or hours with her difficult. I pray you will not get too upset and that you can enjoy Grania.

I am glad your Xrays were good and I hope you will follow the normal doctor's advice. . . . It would be fun to spend what hours I could manage to get free being with you. I might even come a day or two early to have a little real holiday with you!

We will end at the U.N. this Friday and next week I close this apartment for 2 months I hope. I am not satisfied with our work on the Commission but the declaration is quite good I think. I will send you a copy when all is complete. I lunch with the Russians on Thursday. They come to H.P. to lunch with me on Sat. I like them and we get on well but how hard it is for us to understand each other! . . .

Last weekend I was overwhelmed by people about 14 for every meal but now I expect to be quieter and more restful!

. . .

David dear, bless you and take care of yourself, this is a dull letter but I am getting tired, so I will just send my love and very constant thoughts to you.

Goodnight.
E.R.

She sent him a copy of the French-U.S. resolution in which the Human Rights Commission on June 17 approved the Declaration of Human Rights and forwarded it for consideration by the Assembly. The work had been hard, but she thrived on getting this job of her own done. She closed the apartment in Washington Square and had the members of the Commission to Hyde Park for a picnic.

She thought to touch base with all her children on the West Coast when she flew out to Phoenix for the wedding of Anna's daughter, her first grandchild, Eleanor ("Sisty"):

> 29 Washington Square, West
> June 19, 1948

Dearest Jimmy:

[The first three paragraphs were typed by Tommy, the remainder in E.R.'s script.]

If Sistie decides to get married during the first week in July, I shall try to fly out to Phoenix and I thought I would come on to Los Angeles to see you and Johnny and all of the grandchildren.

Please tell me quite honestly whether you want me to come or whether you think it might be too much of a trial for Rommie to have to see me. If I come, I will only be there for one day with you and one with Johnny and a glimpse of Tiny and then fly right back.

Tommy thinks you were serious when you said that the New York delegation was considering nominating me on the first ballot. I can't believe you are and of course, I would be very much opposed to it.

I've just heard Johnny is coming East & your note said you might be here in July so I think I'll just go to Phoenix & home.

Much love darling, I'll come to N.Y. to see you but would rather have you here for a night!

> Much love
> Mother

We'll leave morning July 6th & be home late July 8th.

She described to David her summer life at Hyde Park. There were many children and many guests with forays to see the Morgenthaus, Esther, Mrs. Lewis Thompson, a redoubtable reformer and Republican who hailed originally from Staatsburgh, just north of Hyde Park. There was also work on her book.

> Redbank, New Jersey
> July 1st, 1948

Dearest David,

It seems a long while since there has been any news of you and I hope it means that all your strength is going into enjoying Grania and not too much into the inevitable tensions and heartaches that must come I fear between you and Nemone.

. . .

. . . Work on the book goes forward now in spite of many guests and many children on the place to whom, with the elders, I furnish a picnic lunch out by the swimming pool daily. Everyone seems happy and content.

The Republican ticket is a strong one and I feel Eisenhower will not be drafted and I don't think Truman can win against it. I feel sure he will be nominated, however. I expect a fair foreign policy from the Republicans if they win, tho' the progressives will have to fight the reactionaries. In domestic things I expect reaction as far as they dare.

My thoughts and love go to you daily.

E.R.

What do you think of Yugoslavia?*

David left Davos for good in July, looking forward, he wrote Eleanor, "to the south side of the Alps . . . quieted in my inside . . . more sure of myself . . . grown up. I have found you during this time—and I adore you. I see you and sit with you in the Dolder room and feel your strength and your humanity and you sit at my bed here and your warmth and friendship is deep inside me, with complete confidence and so much happiness. Your existence has changed much in my life."

He loved her but she understood she was not first in his life, and that the condition of being allowed to love him, as in the case of Earl and myself, was to befriend and draw in the women to whom he was and would be romantically attracted. She was prepared to pay the price.

---

* On July 1, 1948, Tito was denounced by the Cominform for his pursuit of nationalist aims and deviation from Soviet policy. On July 11, the New York *Sunday Worker* published a Cominform order to the world's Communist parties to model their organizational methods and rules on those of the Soviet Party. The Yugoslav paper *Borba* and Milovan Djilas, then Tito's comrade-in-arms, declared Yugoslavia wanted no break—only to be treated as an equal. Tito would successfully resist Stalin's pressure and become the first Communist-bloc leader to reach a friendly relationship with Western governments.

XIII

---

*Coping with
People's Fears*

DAVID WAS ENTHUSIASTIC about the draft Declaration of Human
Rights that Eleanor had sent him and was sure now that she would come
to Paris for the fall General Assembly for its adoption. "And probably it
can be put through the Assembly—one of the few things which can. Would you
have to go with a Republican victory? Nobody can do it, but you."

She was going to Paris for the Assembly, she explained to Anna on her return
from Sisty's wedding, and could take Buzz, although—

[E.R. to Anna Boettiger:]   [July 15, 1948]
he can have no job. . . . I am a delegate & we sail Sept. 13th. . . .

 Tommy & I loved being with you & the wedding was lovely & Sis will
always have a wonderful day to look back on. How you went through all
the strain I do not know. . . . I love & admire you darling but get a job
& a salary & have less responsibility. I hate to suggest it but I wish you'd
come East where in little ways we might make life easier now & then.
Elliott would love it as much as I did.

A cheerful note from David—

[David Gurewitsch to E.R.:]　　　　　　　　　　[July 20, 1948]

Only a line of my thoughts and of my love. I am so happy to be out of this Sanatorium. I landed in a little inn on the lake, the weather is warm, it is real summer around me—for the first time this year, but it is cool, as it is high. Tomorrow I shall go over the Bernina Pass into Italy. . . .

He was moving around the Italian Dolomites, seeking to get accustomed to life away from the sanatorium. At the end of August, after tests and a further checkup in Zurich, he intended to go to London to be with Nemone and Grania till September 9.

[David Gurewitsch to E.R.:]　　　　　　　　　　[August (?) 1948]

On the 20th I shall come over to Paris, of course—for dinner at the Crillon. I do not think you have to worry about my beginnings in N.Y.

I think that I have acquired a little more sense about balancing my various trends. I do not know yet when Nemone will leave. But it is quite possible that I shall still find her at home. News from her are good. She continues to sound happy and not tense. . . .

Trude and I had been with Eleanor at Hyde Park over the Independence Day weekend and then drove to Martha's Vineyard for the summer. I had been working very closely with Franklin. Trude was associate director of the Citizens' Committee for Children, of which Eleanor was a stalwart member. Eleanor was satisfied that our marriage was working and, perhaps with a sense of relief, appreciated that we did not present another problem. But she was aware, too, that I was having trouble finding a firm footing in postwar politics.

After the initial flurry over the "draft Eisenhower" movement abated, primarily because of the general's unavailability, Fjr. and I spent many hours assessing the many bids to run for Congress that he received from the various political leaders in New York. I considered myself, and Fjr. appeared to agree, his closest adviser. But the intensification of Cold War tensions and the rise in public hostility to people like myself who had either been Communists or associated with Communists made political activity difficult. Friends in the various movements in which I was active— the American Veterans Committee, Americans for Democratic Action, Young Democrats—despite their faith in my intellectual independence and respect for my relationship with the Roosevelts, began to fear they might be tarred with the same brush that was being used to smear me.

I recall one searing episode. It was typical. Some of the abler young men and women in New York County had banded together under the leadership of Joseph Broderick, a partner in Sullivan and Cromwell and a Navy veteran, to challenge Tammany. A handful of us went down to see Mayor O'Dwyer at City Hall. Just before we went in, Joe took me aside and asked embarrassedly if I thought my presence in the delegation would focus the newspaper stories on me and my radical past instead of on the group and what it was trying to accomplish. He and the others would stand by me, but they left it up to me. There was such a danger, and I left.

What happened at City Hall was happening in a less explicit way elsewhere. I resigned as the ADA's New York secretary. I began to take courses at the Russian Institute at Columbia only to be brought up short by a friend, Saul Padover, who had worked for Harold Ickes. He greatly doubted that any college, certainly no government agency, would dare use me, however high the grades I might score.

I worried about earning my share of the household expenses. A diary note about a discussion with Fjr. reads:

> When F. was sick in the hospital we had a long talk about our working relationship. F. wanted me to work for him these spring months & pay my expenses. I told him, however, that was not the political relationship I wanted with him. I would do the work but no pay! He wrote Mrs. R. calling me stuffy. I've been writing speeches and answering some of his correspondence. I find, however, I'm writing speeches for non-political audiences where he gets a fee. He said something about divvying up with me, but has let the matter drop. I could use the money.

The Democratic convention was meeting in Philadelphia. Franklin was going. I wanted to, but I had become gun-shy about running the journalistic gauntlet on such occasions and I decided to stay on the Vineyard. I began to feel I was trapped. I don't have the letter I wrote Eleanor from the Vineyard at the time,* but I received the following reply from Eleanor at Hyde Park.

July 23rd.

Joe dearest,

I have thought much of your letter because it is the first time you have spoken to me of your plans & thoughts. Don't let people get under your skin. You are wise to rest & you have taken no holiday since the war. Enjoy this summer & don't let other people poison it for you.

I hope the W.C.B.S. plan goes through but I wonder why you don't tie up with political work and teaching in some of the labor groups? That I would think you would find interesting, there is a future in it & you ought not to find it hard to get in with some union. Mike Straight might well give you a regular editorial position. He needs to reorganize! I do feel next autumn you must go to work & earn all you can for I think Trude

---

* When Mrs. Roosevelt died, her daughter Anna went through some letters she kept close by. They included many of those I had sent her. Anna returned them to me but some were missing. And only a handful of David's letters to Mrs. Roosevelt survived her sifting.

should work less & there may come a time when you will feel she should not work at all on a regular job.

The Democrats will lose I think this year but I agree with you that things should be easier to reorganize as the position now shapes up. I am still worried as to where the leadership is coming from.

All goes well here. I drove over yesterday with Elliott to New Bedford to get Chandler who spent a week on Nantucket. I hated to be so near & not see you. I'm glad Johnny still talks of the pool. Elliott has a proposed site he wants you to consider so we must go over it when next you are here.

Did I tell you & Trude that I have been officially notified as a member of the delegation but I've not been ratified by the Senate! Tommy & I sail Sept. 13th but you will be back after Labor Day, won't you?

Love to Trude & Johnny & to you dear boy, & good luck to your decisions.

E.R.

The Sandifers—he was her main State Department adviser—were with her at Hyde Park about this time. They stayed in the stone cottage by the pool. Mrs. Roosevelt had bought out the "lifetime rights" to the cottage that Nancy Cook and Marion Dickerman had been given and they had moved away. Elliott's children were with her, Chandler, Tony, and David, and Faye's son, Scoop. Fjr.'s youngest, Chris, with a nurse was there as were the children of Eleanor's niece, Hall's daughter, Ellie. So was Mrs. Forbes-Morgan, a distant kinswoman, and her two children, Barbara and Forbes. Eleanor loved having them there and, though furiously at work completing *This I Remember*, was always ready to take charge personally of a birthday party. Elliott, wrote Mrs. Sandifer, was "the great favorite of the children. He played with them in the pool and delighted Ellie's boys when he bought them Texan boots." Nothing illustrates better Eleanor's powers of concentration than her ability to work on her autobiography amid the clamors of her noisy household.

Eleanor took the Sandifers with her to Fishkill to dine with the Morgenthaus, "the most delicious food," wrote Irene Sandifer, "broiled chicken, green beans, corn on the cob, with a first course of soured creamed herring served with small potatoes. This was new to us." The chief subject of conversation were the political conventions and the impending race between Truman and Thomas E. Dewey and the universal expectation that Dewey would win. "Mrs. Roosevelt's discussion about the election, her repeated statements that this would be her last Assembly, that she would not serve under Dewey, that she was sure he had promised the position on the Human Rights Commission to Martha Taft—all indicated to me that she was truly sorry to see what she thought was the end of her service. In saying she would not serve she was really preparing herself to accept what she thought was going to be inevitable. Probably she could not have served under a

Republican administration, because even under Truman she more than once was about to offer her resignation because she did not agree with the President's policy."

Val-Kill Cottage
July 30th, 1948

David dearest,

It was nice to feel you were free and moving around where you will find lovely and familiar country and I hope enough casual and interesting people to keep you amused. Don't overdo, it would be easy to be too ambitious at first.

I saw Mr. Baruch last night, back from a short visit to England, Holland, Greece. He says Churchill is worried about war but his (Mr. B's) feeling is like yours that it will not come now. He feels it need not come at all if only we are wise but that is a good deal to expect of us, isn't it? We are so inexperienced in this new world role—

I do not feel we will have war now so I look forward to our meeting in Paris on Sept. 20th, I hope. It will be wonderful to see you well and I hope carefree. Have you your return passage for October 14th? If not I might be able to help from this end so let me know. We sail Sept. 13th on the "America." Trude did not go abroad but now plans that the whole family will go next summer. She and Joe and Jonathan (and George on weekends) are at Martha's Vineyard and the other children get there in August. They all sound happy though Joe is still troubled because nothing seems really interesting to do except politics and he had made up his mind that there is no opening for him there at present.

My Anna has sold the paper, losing all she put in but it is better in so many ways than she had thought that I am relieved for her.

Our children here flourish and I find Franklin Jr's little boy Chris an interesting study but I wish I could shed his English governess!

I've been trying to read Kinsey on the American male but so many children are not conducive to reading and what time I have goes into the book which now goes forward fast—

I know the country you are in and wish I could fly over and join you! My thoughts do in any case often and often and my love goes too.

E.R.

More than a half dozen grandchildren as well as the marital problems of her sons and daughter, Tommy's ailments, and the publisher's pressure to finish *This I Remember* made paying attention to the problems of her friends more difficult than usual. But there was always a thought for David.

Hyde Park
August 5th, 1948

Dearest David,

Your vacation sounds wonderful and the Italian Dolomites will be beautiful. We crossed the Bernina Pass and drove thro' the Dolomites and stayed at various places years ago, so I can picture the scenes you will enjoy.

I hope the Zurich tests will be completely reassuring for you and I hope you don't have to go to Dr. Maurer and the Schatzalp again. The man must be cruel and self centered.

It will be hard for your Mother. If she is "guided" in all she thinks she will find it hard to let you make your own decisions and you will find it hard to tell her and to stand against her. It is very good that Nemone is taking it all so well and you and Grania will have a happy time before they sail.

I suppose you have read about all the spy excitement caused by a Miss Bently an ex-communist spy herself who is now accusing everyone else? They are staged, I think, to take people's mind off the very little which the Congress is willing to do at this Special Session and to discredit the New Deal, since Dewey still runs against F.D.R.!

I hope the book will be ready before I leave and I'll bring the manuscript if we have no galley proof.

I am still surrounded by problems among the younger generation but I imagine the state of the world and its confusion is bound to reflect itself in individual confusion. I hope we do not have war. When I do get back, you and Grania will come often for weekends, won't you please?

This is a dull letter and I'm sorry but I think I'm tired or rather a little drained, so this will take you my devotion and love and I'll go to bed! Always affly.

E.R.

She saw Hick a few times that summer. Hick helped assemble material for *This I Remember* and asked questions to stimulate her memory. She also suggested ideas that might wind up in Eleanor's column, in lectures, or on the radio and television, which was then in its infancy. E.R. in turn obtained regular work for her old friend at the Democratic State Committee.

Another letter from David on the idylls of the Southern Alps, this one dated "Bergamo, August 8th, 1948":

Dearest Mrs. R.,

Only a line from this beautiful town. I am sitting on the old piazza of the Cita Alta, there is an Italian sun. . . . It is a relief to see the combination of gentleness and prettiness in so many girls. One just cannot help liking the Italians. They are so endearing. . . . I am sorry that Trude did not go for this so long delayed trip. Again more tension to be stored up inside her. My presence and my participation in sightseeing is being claimed.

. . .

My love again and again

Your
David

Her answer was that of the altruist in love. David's happiness made her happy.

Val-Kill Cottage
August 16th

Dearest David,

Your letter from the park in Bergamo sounded happy and carefree as though you had companionship you enjoyed but were relaxed and happy and it made me happy! The Italians are nice people and one cannot help liking them. They are not very good fighters but I always enjoy Italy, its beauty and charm obscure any dirt or poverty!

. . .

Please write me about the lab checks and tests in Zurich and I hope you do not see Dr. Maurer.

Trude and Joe seem to be having a happy time at the Vineyard and she sounds rested—They are all planning to go abroad next year and I hope these plans materialize. Anna is moving by Sept. 1st to Los Angeles as she hopes to have a job there. It is not settled yet and she might have to come East if she gets no job there but she wants to stay there so I hope she gets the job. It is a suggested radio program with me, 5 days a week 11 minutes divided (5 to me). She would be editor of a woman's little trade magazine in connection with it—She would get *all* pay which would be my contribution towards helping her to pay her debts. I can record twice a week which wouldn't be much work and I would only furnish ideas and edit what they write so I think once this book is done I can do it without too much strain.

. . .

My little Grandson Chris will go home with his father (Franklin Jr.) on Wednesday. I got the governess to leave Sat. a.m. and she returns this afternoon. We have not had a single crying spell since she left. I think I know what the child needs, he has gained 4 lbs. and has had no boils and is much calmer but he needs his parents not servants!

I am through 1942 in the book so I hope to finish. All my love and thoughts go to you.

E.R.

Not only was she doing a radio program with Anna but the latter's brother John was looking for an apartment for her in Los Angeles. The whole family rallied around Anna, and Eleanor wrote sympathetically: ". . . I knew what a let down you would go through as the tension eased. Giving up great hopes & going thro' great emotional upheavals take it out of one too. . . . I'll write Curtis [Buzz] next week & send him money for the trip & if you let me know what his tuxedo costs I'll pay for it. . . ."

The Morgenthaus and their son Bob came to Hyde Park to dine and to exchange intelligence, as they had so often done in the past. She wanted Trude and me to use the stone cottage vacated by Cook and Dickerman, and followed with a note about the possible purchase of a house near Val-Kill.

Val Kill Cottage
August 13th

Dearest Joe,

What a nice long letter & I am glad the suggestion about the unions seemed to open possibilities to you. The idea of your editing an anthology called 'The Soviet Idea' seems to me wonderful & I do hope it materializes.*

. . .

The cost of living is certainly fantastic & that is the one thing that might defeat Dewey if it can be clearly pinned on the Republicans.

May Craig is coming up next Thursday to see me about Miss Bentley & the spy hearings. It seems wicked to me to smear Currie & Hiss.

Frankie telephoned me he'd cooked you a good meal on the boat. He comes up Tuesday for his birthday dinner as Ethel will be away & he takes Chris home on Wed. I hope he finds his child improved in many ways. At least he's learned to swim like a fish!

We are up to 1942 on the book & I'm just going over the diary I kept in G.B. on the trip that autumn. It was voluminous!

It will soon be Jonathan's birthday so give him a kiss for me. Why don't you take the lower floor of the stone cottage when Marie [Morgan] goes back to N.Y. & use it week ends? . . .

The President wants to see me so I go down on Wedn. 18th for 2 hours. A chore but not too much for him to ask! He wanted to send me to Holland for the jubileee & the coronation but I said I couldn't go.

I can well understand why you love the Vineyard & that is really why I feel you should not buy here yet but stay in some of our vast space! I miss you very much & look forward to seeing you later Labor Day before I leave on the 13th. . . .

E.R.

* It didn't.

Val-Kill Cottage
August 16th.

Dearest Joe & Trude,
    The enclosed property describes a house & land on top of hill opposite
the Thackrey's & adjoining our land. It is for sale & might be had for
$12,000 & Elliott wld be prepared to buy or rent most of the farm land
for $4,000.00—I doubt if you would consider it but I send it even tho' he
is sending it to some friends as I was sure you wouldn't want to buy.
    How are you all? All goes well with us & Fjr. comes up tomorrow for
his birthday & takes Chris home Wednesday. We will miss Chris & I
think he has improved too—
    Much love to you two dear ones,

                                                              E.R.

Family anxieties were unending that summer. As she prepared for the Paris
UN Assembly, where she would play a leading part, word came from Anna that
Buzz, whom Eleanor planned to take with her to the Assembly, had come down
with a mild case of polio. Eleanor's letter to Anna was upbeat. "You remember how
badly Father's hands & arms were affected & they were normal very quickly. A
prayer is in my heart for you and for him all the time." It was a moment to be
strong, she urged her daughter—

[E.R. to Anna Boettiger:]   [August 28, 1948]
    Perhaps when things like this happen which seem just too much to
bear, we are being given a lesson in values. There is no use in trying to
teach the weak but the strong are worth training. When a child is ill you
know that the other losses were of little importance, his life & happiness
are all that counts. You work to repay money losses to others because you
have a sense of integrity & responsibility. You work for some future
security so as not to be a burden on the young but you learn that the
satisfactions that come are in doing the work well & in making those you
love happy. You are one of the strong people of the world & I love you
dearly & grieve that you have this added burden. . . .

A woman of contradictions. She wanted her children to be self-reliant and
independent and her letter to Anna almost sounded Nietzschean in the distinction
it drew between the strong and the weak, yet at other times she stressed that she
loved people for their weaknesses as well as their strengths. A sympathetic letter
came from David, whose very helplessness on the way to Davos had appealed to her
nurturing instincts.

[David Gurewitsch to E.R.:]   [n.d.]
    I had new Xrays and another checkup. The development is according

to plan but the wisdom of my stays in towns is being questioned though it is admitted that it is not the air which counts, but a still strict routine of rest during the day. Not because I am ill, but because it produces more safety for a firm scar. . . .

His letter crossed Eleanor's with its report about Curtis's polio.

Val-Kill Cottage
August 26th, 1948

Dearest David,

I am glad you have had the further consultations for it will make you careful in England. If you find the shortages and climate upset you, why not go back to the mountains for a month and come through to Paris on your way to the steamer? I'll have to work hard from the moment of arrival I'm sure, so our time together would have to be subordinated to the work and I don't want you to struggle to be in Paris September 20th though I confess I look forward to seeing you more than I can say. I would rather you were careful however and did what is best for you. . . .

Why not plan to take weekends off this winter? I can let you and Grania have 2 rooms here whether I am home or not! I could not arrange it till I get home however.

I am very troubled today because Anna's boy Curtis who is to go abroad with me if he is able is said to be a mild case of polio—They've taken him to the hospital and 5 days must pass before we know the worst. I'm worried for him but to pile this on top of everything else makes me tremble for her. There seem to be periods in life when one wonders how one is to live through. . . .

I saw both the Secretary of State and the President on a flying visit to Washington the other day—They are putting considerable responsibility on me in this session—Dulles has suggested that we point out that all our troubles are rooted in a disregard for the rights and freedoms of the individual and go after the USSR, not thank heavens, claiming perfection but saying that under our system we are trying to achieve these rights and freedoms and succeeding better than most. They want me to make an opening speech to set the keynote outside the Assembly and I am trying to plan it now—I feel as you do, there cannot be a war but strength and not appeasement will prevent it—

The school teacher's case is sad and not good for the USSR over here—*

---

* The cause célèbre caused by the Soviet kidnapping of O. S. Kosenkina, a tutor to children of the Soviet UN delegation, who had defected. Rather than return to the USSR, she jumped from a third-floor window of the Soviet consulate in New York.

The Congressional Com. however seems to me to be doing more harm than good.*

I'm trying hard to finish my book so I'm not taking a vacation but I'll rest on the steamer and read a great deal!

Whenever I see you I shall be happy but take care of yourself!

My thoughts and my love go to you.

E.R.

P.S. We are having the warmest weather of the summe!

Since polio came within David's domain as a doctor, his sympathetic letter meant a great deal to her.

London
29.8.48

My dearest Mrs. Roosevelt,

I just was told about something like infantile paralysis in Anna's boy in the papers two days ago. I sent you a telegram. I just hope that if it should be true, that he is a mild case and that he will be entirely well, like the majority. That I am not there to help just at such a moment! . . .

A week in London. Now it is time to get out in the country. I shall go in 2 days with Grania. Nemone is well and obviously happier without me. I just do not feel like writing about myself. My thoughts are so much with you. How much there was of weariness and trouble for you since you stepped into the plane in Zurich! My love goes to you and my prayers and my thoughts.

Your David

Two days later he wrote again.

9.1.48

My dearest Mrs. R.

Your letter came today, yesterday I had your telegram. It was 4 days later and it was still a mild case. Most cases, specially the mild ones, have shown the worst by then. But the waiting in these first days, the watching of the devastating progress from hour to hour, from day to day is the one aspect of my association with this disease, which I can hardly bear. Poor Anna, and on top of all the rest of it! By now it is all clear. What muscles are affected, and to what extent? . . .

And it seems so wise that you with your balance between idealism and reality, have been chose for this big keynote address. A general outline of our objectives is so badly needed. I remember your wonderful London speech on the freedom of the individual. We need so badly a platform

---

* The House Committee on Un-American Activities.

simply expressed, demonstratively produced. Another big job on your shoulders. You are the only one, besides General Marshall who has the ear of the world, but you are much better qualified to do it. It makes one happy to think that you are working on it. The book will probably have to await completion under the circumstances!

. . .

Your
David

His letter from London arrived quickly, and she answered just as promptly, acknowledging—and it was a measure of her confidence in him—the many worries she had to carry.

Val-Kill Cottage
Sept. 2d, 1948

Dearest David,

Your dear letter of the 29th was here when I came home from N.Y. late this afternoon. I loved your telegram too, it was a mild case and tonight Anna called me to say the quarantine was over (California State law is 2 weeks) and Buzz has had no temperature since he reached the Naval hospital at Colorado 10 days ago. . . . Anna sounded so relieved, like a new person, and it seemed to me a miracle that we should be so lucky. My heart was so heavy and now it is light again—

You are right, since I left you in Zurich the problems, mostly psychological ones, have been rather heavy on me. I'll tell you all about them in Paris and you can tell me whether I've been wise or wrong in handling my large and complicated family!

. . .

You will laugh I had a wonderful time today doing Xmas shopping! I was afraid I might be late in getting home.

The book is really almost done and I hope to get the first draft in though Tommy may not find it possible.

. . .

I am really getting excited at the thought of seeing you soon, it will be a real joy for me! Bless you dear for all your thoughts and concern for us and many many thanks.

Affly and devotedly.

E.R.

Eleanor embarked on the SS *America* for Paris on September 13. The General Assembly was being held abroad because the United States was in the final weeks of the presidential campaign. The major business before the Assembly was final action on the Declaration of Human Rights that had been sent forward by her commission. It was also a moment of high tension in East-West affairs. Stalin had imposed the Berlin blockade, and that had created a sense of Soviet readiness to provoke war. After consulting Secretary of State Marshall she had accepted René Cassin's invitation to address the Sorbonne in the opening days of the Assembly. Her speech would highlight the basic issue dividing East from West. When Andrei Vishinsky at the beginning of the Assembly delivered a fire-and-brimstone attack on the West, Mrs. Roosevelt, according to Durward Sandifer, her adviser, in a letter to his wife, "said it left her with a sense of complete futility and hopelessness."

That was her inner feeling, but outwardly, as she spoke to the notables of Western Europe gathered in the amphitheater of the Sorbonne a few days later, she was unruffled, her gravity mixed with smiles, the French in which she spoke a legacy from her days with Mlle. Souvestre. "She did a perfect job," Sandifer exulted to his wife. "She extemporized in the beginning and Dorothy [Fosdick] said it was just right. Once she got a big laugh when she interpolated that having raised a large family she thought she was a master of patience, but she never really knew what patience was until she came into contact with the Russians in the Human Rights Commission."

Eleanor credited the success of the speech to the suppleness of the French language, which, she said, lent itself to saying difficult things. In her column she confessed "that speaking at the Sorbonne seemed to me altogether too great an honor for a woman who never had earned a degree after four years' work in college. I was nervous and apprehensive. . . ." But she was pleased with her performance. To Anna she wrote, "The Sorbonne speech is done & went well. Buzz went tho' he could understand nothing. . . ."

David had arrived in Paris on the 20th as planned. She managed several evenings with him, and Sandifer was startled by her energy.

[Durward Sandifer to Irene Sandifer:]   [September (?) 1948]
    Mrs. Roosevelt is quite a different person from what she was in London. She has been around and likes negotiating and wants to be kept busy all the time. I'm really going to be on the job eighteen hours a day keeping all her time lined up and getting my preparatory work done in between times. She even wants to have an idle hour. For the first time I feel she is driven by some inner compulsion that will never let her come to rest. . . .

A note to Trude sounded more relaxed than Sandifer made her appear.

                                        Hotel Crillon
                                        Sept. 27th 1948
Trude dearest,
    Your cable came, & I answered rather unsatisfactorily as none of us

knows when we can return! I hated to miss Joe that last day but goodbyes are always sad. . . .

We are comfortable here tho' the first days were chilly & the houses seem to hold ancient chills so both Tommy & Buzz have had bad colds. . . .

Mr. [John] Golden is here & goes home Friday so he will tell you about us. Dr. Gurewitsch also came from London so he looked Buzz over for me & also Tommy. He has gone to the country till Friday but we all went to several rive gauche restaurants for dinner together & had a good time.

Buzz is taking French lessons from a wisp of a lady in whose home I used to spend my student holidays. These people are finding it hard to live! She told me pay for a lesson was 120 frs & one gets in regular legal exchange 300 frs to $1.00 & prices for food are about what they are at home!

Work is hard & I must run but I will write soon again. . . .

E.R.

David fascinated her. His psychological insight, his tact, his responsiveness to her affection and solicitude, and his help with Tommy and Buzz made her grateful. Here was companionship, and she grasped it avidly. There was a precedent in her family. Her great aunt, Corinne Robinson, her father's younger sister and a poet whose poems Eleanor loved to recite, had stirred old New York by one friendship in particular. "She did have an admirer, Mr. Charles Munn, with whom she went on one or two trips abroad after my grandfather died," recalled her grandson, Joseph Alsop. "These greatly agitated old-fashioned New York, but neither my grandmother nor my mother paid any attention to it. Mr. Munn was exceedingly rich, very old-maidish, but I should certainly say without hesitation, certainly not my grandmother's lover. I believe, however, he asked her to marry him after my grandfather's death."

One poignant story about David's youth would have entwined him about her heart. For her, Paris was full of memories of Souvestre and of her father. David had his own. He was born two months after his father had died in a Swiss lake. When he was about twelve years old, in Berlin, he would fantasize as he saw men on street corners, "Are you my father?" As the poet said, "But if the while I think on thee, dear friend,/All losses are restored and sorrows end." So as the two exchanged recollections of unhappy childhood years, each became more reconciled to the present.

"Dearest Joe," she wrote me from the Crillon, October 4, 1948:

It was wonderful to get your letter of the 24th with Trude's little addition. What a monkey Jonathan is! He will keep you & Trude busy but I predict he will manage Mickey in the long run.

What you are studying is almost a new science & I think may prove very interesting. . . . Frances Perkins telephoned me last night from Washington asking for a letter endorsing Truman by name. She said Drew Pearson was saying that I was for Dewey. She made the point that we needed as big a Democratic vote as possible even tho' we were defeated, so I've written & sent her a letter to the President. If it ever sees the light of day I hope you will approve.

. . .

I confess to be worried by all that goes on here, much of it I know nothing about but hear in round about ways. In Committee III we've passed one item & the Russians beaten on an amendment still accepted the whole convention which was an unheard of thing for them & very encouraging but in Human Rights we are still arguing procedure!

. . .

David Gurewitsch is here, goes to some sessions & gives us much of his time evenings & on days when I can be free & at other times sees his friends & seems to have a good time. I hope he won't overwork when he goes home. . . .

I must go to bed so my love to you both. Please keep on missing me for I miss you both & long to get back to you.

> Devotedly
> E.R.

An affectionate letter to Hick dwelt on Truman's effort to arrange something with Stalin:

[E.R. to Lorena Hickok:]   [October 13, 1948]
From this distance the campaign doesn't seem to be going well & this last Vinson* thing created a sensation with accusations of by-passing U.N. etc. in papers outside of the USSR & thus jubilant over our lack of unity. Dulles & Marshall are both back & the latter goes to Greece & Rome this weekend.

The celebration of Mrs. Roosevelt's birthday on October 11 required infinite forbearance from her friends. She did not want it to be remembered, yet was aware if a child or friend did not; at the same time she rebuffed any gift that required money. Nor did ritualistic observances please her. A small dinner with people she loved, in this case David, Buzz, and Tommy, an exchange of toasts, an exchange of cables and letters with a handful of people in the United States, she seemed to accept. All knew, however, that they worked against her ever-present conviction of the vanity of the human condition.

Poor Sandifer, her adviser, was determined that the delegation should have a

* In October President Truman wanted to send Chief Justice Vinson to Moscow for talks with Stalin. Widely criticized as an election stunt, the idea was dropped.

chance to show its love for her. She had made a "big fuss" over his birthday, as his wife Irene wrote in *Mrs. Roosevelt as We Knew Her,* when they were at Hyde Park. His letter from Paris described the delegation's party with champagne and a birthday cake inscribed "Joyeux Anniversaire GA Del." Forty members of the delegation attended.

[Durward Sandifer to Irene Sandifer:]   [October 11, 1948]
    Mr. [Benjamin] Cohen* gave a very touching toast, and I made a little speech presenting the [signed] testimonial. I said we would have made it a surprise but that Miss Thompson advised not, and we, knowing Mrs. Roosevelt's habits and schedule were bound to agree—we had however, made the fatal mistake of not inviting the Chairman of Committee III. We had been advised that Mrs. Roosevelt did not like fanfare for her birthday. However, I knew from report and experience that other people's birthdays were great occasions in the Roosevelt household, with cakes and never more than twenty-one candles. In Paris candles were hard to get so we had thought twenty-one bottles of champagne would be a good substitute and generate more light than the candles. Then I read the document with the space for each signature. . . . You will be happy to know that as I handed her the testimonial she proposed a toast [between the two of us] "to our absent ones." Wasn't that wonderful and also characteristic. . . . Seven or eight of us stayed for a while and chatted and ended with Porter McKeever† singing *Auld Lang Syne,* holding hands in a circle. Mrs. Roosevelt asked which attendants on her floor of the hotel had children and asked that the remaining cake be divided between them.

Her report to Anna on Buzz's condition omitted any reference to the birthday party. "I have a letter from big John [Boettiger] for my birthday. I feel sorry for him & for you darling. He may not be able to help what has happened to him."
    She sent thank-you letters to Trude and me for our birthday cables. They were separate because each of us had our requests—Trude for help with Wiltwyck School and I for a date on which she might address the ADA. It was characteristic of how we regarded her that our birthday cables also asked for help, and she preferred the request to the birthday present. She wrote Trude—

[E.R. to Trude W. Lash:]   [October 16, 1948]
    . . . It must be a desperate time at home but it is baffling here too. The Russians attack furiously in every committee. They seem to want to see nothing accomplished until one wonders whether they should be barred

* Noted New Dealer whose name was graven indelibly on the minds of the thirties as the partner of Thomas L. Corcoran.
† Press officer of the U.S. delegation.

from contacts until they want them enough to try to cooperate. We get no further in Com. 3 because they use each point to say things which need only be said in Com. once! We've spent more times listening to attacks & counter-attacks than in work which we are supposed to be here to do!

Abba Schwartz dined with me last week & he goes to Palestine shortly. . . .

David Gurewitsch went off to meet the steamer & sail for home this morning. Do call him up for I think he rather dreads the re-adjustment back to work. New York seems like a big place when you have been far away & practically alone for a year! I have loved having him here & it has been a relief to me when I was worried about Tommy & Buzz. We've done some pleasant things, all of us, like the opera & Versailles & Fontainebleu & lots of little restaurants for dinner & last night a play at the Comédie Française.

Tommy seems as well as usual again but I know what I can't let her do. . . .

Next week hard work begins with night meetings & I shall do little else.

The letter to me said that Henry Morgenthau had indeed gotten in for dinner and gone off to Palestine with Buzz.

[E.R. to Joseph P. Lash:]   [October 16, 1948]

. . . Ben Cohen was here & we had a frank talk on the Palestine situation. I find myself frustrated at times. The world in which I move is devious & I don't understand it very well.

   . . .

I have not liked such Post editorials as have been sent me & I think Ted Thackrey* has shown little judgment. Truman's last move on Vinson & the resulting publicity have been very bad. . . .

A week later there were letters to Anna, to Trude and me, and to David. She was ready to sign a radio contract together with Anna for two years.

[E.R. to Anna Boettiger:]   [October 25, 1948]

. . . The big name business I'm uncertain about as Churchill† might do something awful so I'm going to suggest Mrs. Pandit for the first or Nehru her brother, who will be here any day, then Marshall & Dulles. . . .

I don't think I can send you $200 a month unless you need it badly but

---

* He supported Henry Wallace, while his wife, the owner of the paper, in a parallel column supported Dewey.

† Anna's backers wanted Mrs. R. to get Churchill for the first broadcast.

tell me if you do because I can manage it. Expenses run high here & I don't know how much I'm making while I'm here. . . .

I'm glad big John is in a better frame of mind & doing better. . . .

I spent Sat. & Sunday in Stuttgart, Germany. Human misery is widespread over here. . . .

Her letter to Trude expanded on her German experience, along with a few personal admonitions.

[E.R. to Trude W. Lash:]   [October 25, 1948]

. . . I don't think your efforts at abandoning duty for pleasure sound very successful! . . . I'm sorry you had a cold & I fear 1 a.m. Wiltwyck meetings lead to it. I honestly think it is more important for you to stay well than to be a rock which keeps Wiltwyck going. Someone else should do that. . . .

The weather is still beautiful here & it was wonderful on Sunday in Stuttgart. I still find ruined cities hard to take & when you see the struggle the Germans now have you feel a beast not to forget what you know is just as bad if not worse elsewhere, especially when you feel that some of the women & children before you are scarcely to blame. I'm sorrier for the German refugees even than for the displaced persons of other nationalities & currency reform has hit the welfare funds & relief funds of cities & states. The human misery of the world is very apparent when you visit Germany & the camps. I did feel the attitude of people was better & much improved since '46. Notably I was received with much less hostility than I expected and the League of Women Doctors of Stuttgart having asked me, the Berlin women are now begging me to go there.

The Committee still crawls but today was a little better! Tell Joe I'll write him soon, give him my love & a hug to Jonathan & love to the others.

She gave additional details in her letter to David. It began and ended with her solicitude and love for him.

Hotel Crillon, Paris
October 25th, 1948

David dearest,

It was an unexpected joy to get your letter from the steamer this morning. Believe me I have thought of you daily since you left but with a special little prayer since the 21st. I am so glad the trip was relaxing and you arrived in a calm frame of mind. That will help, and try to hold on to it no matter what happens around you. I went to Stuttgart Saturday morning and I was favorably impressed by the women doctors who had invited me. They are conscious of all their needs and conditions are bad but for the first time they do not fly away from all responsibility. I expected a cold reception since Franklin and I were not especially liked during the Hitler regime but to my surprise the restored State Theatre was full with no seats vacant in the 3 top tiers and though my speech was honest they received it warmly. I spoke in German, bad German, but everyone seemed to understand and I found I could understand them fairly well. . . .

The Jewish D.P. camp was magnificent in spirit and all the camps are better organized with better shops for training than in '46 when I was there before. I hope we get the people out soon though. The worst problems are the Germans from occupied territories. Many of them want to emigrate for they feel they are not wanted. The conditions were worse in one of their camps than anywhere else.

The Bill of Rights moves a bit faster and I think we will leave in early December. You know how much I want to be on the same side of the ocean with you. I'm glad you love me and I love you dearly and send you my devoted thoughts.

E.R.

A letter to me drew a vivid picture of Secretary Marshall.

Hotel Crillon
Oct. 26th, 1948

Dearest Joe,

. . .

I wish you had been here this evening to go with me to a little restaurant on the left bank where I took General Marshall & Mrs. Marshall for dinner. I like him so much & he is a strong person but I fear very tired. Last Sunday he went back to places where he had fought near & houses he had lived in during World War I & was saddened to find poverty & hardship where there had been ease & plenty. I came back from Germany too with a weight of human misery on my heart so our reports this morning to the delegates had been none too cheerful. Russia's attitude is discouraging & Marshall I think believes it is a case of our staying & outbluffing your adversary but the stake of war is such a high one that the game cannot be played lightheartedly.

. . .

John Gunther* told me a nice little story on Farley. They met in

---

* American journalist and writer, best known for his series of "Inside" books. He had recently published *Inside U.S.A.* (1947).

Prague & J.G. said he'd been in Trieste whereupon Farley bent on selling Coca-cola said "I think I'll drop down to Trieste & see Tito, business doesn't seem very good round here!"

. . .

Devotedly,
E.R.

The Truman-Dewey race was coming to an end, and her letter to Hick, who was working at the Democratic State Committee, dwelt on that.

Hotel Crillon, Paris
Nov. 1st

Hick dearest,

It was wonderful to get your letter of the 25th & I was proud to hear of what you had done with the women. That was a swell idea of yours & I hope you get credit. Ed Flynn telephoned me that he had some hopes in N.Y. State & asked me to make a short broadcast which I did rather against my better judgment!

Barclay* [sic] certainly hasn't been much help. He is not colorful & has got little popular appeal. Truman has done much by himself in the campaign in spite of a few mistakes. Dewey will win I think but should Truman win the work of keeping him up to his progressive statements will be quite a task!

. . .

Tommy feels much better but it is cold in the hotels here & I'll be glad now when we start for home, as I don't feel we are doing much.

Buzz is back from Israel & had a wonderfully interesting time & we are proud of all the nice things everyone has said about him.

Tommy sends love & so does

Your ever devoted
E.R.

A letter to me told of her reaction to the surprise results of the election. She must have written to others, but those letters have disappeared.

Hotel Crillon, Paris
Nov. 5th

Dearest Joe,

A thousand thanks for your letter & for the wire. It is rather nice to be an American when the people so evidently take their democracy seriously & do their own thinking as they did in this election. I did not have

* Alben W. Barkley of Kentucky, majority leader of the Senate, Vice President under Truman 1949–1953.

enough faith in them! Dewey just wasn't big enough & I think they felt more sincerity if not ability in Truman.

I do feel however that those among us who want the Democratic party to stay a progressive party will have to try to remind the members of Congress that they were elected on that basis & our labor groups & liberals [merit] some consideration. The President is so easily fooled in spite of his good intentions. I am going through a very difficult time with the delegation on its true position & future position on Palestine & am much upset by some of the things that go on. The interchange of letters between the Secretary and myself would be funny if it were not tragic, for he as well as the President is fooled. I hope & pray Mr. Lovett goes for I think he is a dangerous person in the State Department.*

I'll certainly read your articles with interest & your analysis interests me & I lean toward a firm but unprovocative policy toward the USSR. They are furious with me & I enclose an excerpt from their press which you & Trude can laugh over.

. . .

I am glad you are seeing Fjr. occasionally & letting him talk. Of course he is to blame in part but Ethel cannot make him into a different kind of person & expect the best in him to develop. I worry about all these children & wonder what has happened to the women of today. Rommie is taking a long rest at home with her mother & leaving Jimmy to run the house, the children & his work. Heaven knows where that will lead!

My love to Trude & Johnny & a world to you.

E.R.

The two "Johns," Masterson and Reddy, who were producing the "Mother and Daughter" radio program, came to Paris to do recordings with Mrs. Roosevelt. ". . . they are pleased. I hope the programme sells soon," she wrote Anna. She had been to London with Buzz and Tommy. "Buzz seems to love London & being with Lady Reading. He says she reminds him of Granny. The most secure part of his life perhaps?" She explained to Trude her perspective on living in the same world as the Russians.

---

* The State Department led by Secretary Marshall opposed the White House and the President and favored going ahead with the peace plan of the assassinated Count Folke Bernadotte. It would have transferred the Negev, which was assigned to Israel under the UN's partition resolution, to Transjordan. Mrs. Roosevelt was the chief opponent of Secretary Marshall, to whom she was personally devoted, at delegation meetings on this issue.

Robert A. Lovett, a banker with Wall Street connections, was Under Secretary of State. He had been a leading advocate within the Department of abandonment of the UN's partition resolution. He and Mrs. Roosevelt also had locked horns over whether to protect human rights by covenant, which she favored, as well as by declaration, which she had been instrumental in piloting through the Human Rights Commission.

Hotel Crillon
Nov. 17th, 1948

Dearest Trude,

I was so happy to get your letter & delighted that Joe arranged a surprise party for your anniversary. You sound as though you had really had fun & I think that is important.

It is sad, dear, but I think it will take a long time to get real understanding with the USSR government. It will be the result of long & patient work. Their government & representatives think differently from the way we do. Even in private conversation they see things differently. They will have to reach a higher standard of living & not be afraid to let others in & their own out before we can hope for a change.

The Palestine situation fills our delegation meetings & I begin to hope we won't come out so badly thanks to the President's last stand by wire. Ben Cohen & I plug along in spite of feeling sorry for the Secretary who fears the breaking up of a united front in Europe. I lunched with some french government officials who are upset at our Ruhr policy & I agree with them & not with the U.S. & U.K. so I always seem on opposite sides from Bohlen, Ross (Lovett's man) in our delegation meetings. I only fear the things they don't bring up however as when we know we can do a little!

Sen. Austin went home last night to have an operation. I fear he has not the health & quickness any more to command respect & give confidence but he is a fine man of integrity & I like him. If Mr. Jessup* could take his place I think everybody would be happy.

Sunday Time has flown & I've been busy so excuse the break! Now the Secretary has gone home. I lunched with him yesterday & told him some things I felt I must say on Palestine before he left. If things go as he *says* I believe all will be well but I've made some amazing discoveries & I have a deep distrust of Bohlen & Ross.† Ben Cohen is stronger than I [can be] but both of us suffer from not knowing all that goes on between the Department & Dean Rusk who is the representative here.

. . .

It must be wonderful to see people take hold at home & plan for accomplishments. I hope we can keep the President & his political advisers really moving on liberal lines. Morris Ernst‡ I would find as hard to accept as Lovett or Forrestal but in a different way.

. . .

* Philip Jessup, American jurist and expert on international law. He negotiated with the Russians to end the Berlin blockade and later served on the World Court in the Hague.
† Charles "Chip" Bohlen advised General Marshall on U.S.-USSR affairs. Jack Ross was a political officer in the U.S. delegation.
‡ Morris Ernst, a lawyer with Greenbaum Wolff & Ernst, had done chores for F.D.R. Mrs. Roosevelt did not particularly like him.

When you saw David he probably told you about his personal affairs. The world is full of unhappy people which makes me realize how much one should enjoy every moment of happiness!

Your estimate of what happens to girls like Romaine & Ethel is a wise analysis no doubt but I think it is lack of honesty with oneself & lack of real intelligence which keeps them from understanding & accepting life as it is in the long run. . . .

All my love
E.R.

"Our working hours are getting bad as they do at the end of the Assembly but yesterday, Sunday, was a fairly quiet day," she informed Anna in a letter filled with news about her radio recordings, Buzz, and Tommy. "The Palestine question has kept me jumping but I think we are in the clear at last. . . . What did your first two weeks checks amount to? Is there any prospect of a sponsor?" she wanted to know.

On Thanksgiving Day she had time for a letter only to David, but cables to others.

Thanksgiving Day
Paris
Nov. 25th 1948

David dearest,

I must send you just a line before the day ends since one of the things I am most thankful for this year is the chance to know you better and count you as a friend from now on. I had the office and staff people for lunch but I missed home and my own family and friends.

Buzz is back from London and he enjoyed it tho' I don't think he saw a great deal! . . .

Franklin Jr. blew in for a day on a business trip and will be back for a few days on the 29th or 30th. His family affairs are very complicated and his description of everybody else's troubles makes me wonder whether the war or atomic radiation is not upsetting the human species!

. . .

I'm getting some side lights on French politics and have learned much in our fight over Palestine in the delegation. We do need psychiatrists to straighten out State Department policies.

My thoughts fly off to you so often dear. I hope life is not too difficult and you are well and the troubles will not be all encompassing. I look forward so much to seeing you, do you think you can find a little time to sit down and talk or will I have to be ill to get a glimpse of you?

Devotedly your friend
Eleanor Roosevelt

She organized a Thanksgiving dinner for sixteen members of the delegation including Ben Cohen and Sandifer as well as Buzz, Tommy, and Elinor Hendrick. "Mrs. Roosevelt carved the turkeys," Sandifer wrote his wife. "She asked the day before whether I could carve—I said yes, but I thought the guests would enjoy having turkey carved by her." She bought the two huge turkeys at the commissary and gave them to the Crillon kitchen to have them done. "The waiter came staggering in with both of them on one huge silver tray with their feet on," Sandifer commented. "I was rather startled by their appearance and then I realized their feet were still on sticking high in the air."

I had written her about an honorary degree that she received from Oxford.

Hotel Crillon
Nov. 27th.

Joe dearest,

A thousand thanks for your letter of the 14th & I'm sorry to disappoint you but hard times make Oxford scarlet robes impossible to obtain so they only loan you one for the occasion! It was impressive though!

This letter should reach you on your birthday & I hope you have received the cloth for your coat & like it. I enclose a small check to help you pay for making it up. . . .

Frankie is here & I took them all out to a little restaurant on the left bank for dinner. We had a long talk the first night & he told me all about Ethel & it does not sound very cheerful to me. I have to write her & I dread it.

I love your description of the Communist line on election results. I hope your studies lead you to an understanding which you can pass on to me. Pavlov [the Soviet delegate] put on a disgraceful scene in Com. 3 this p.m. & antagonized everyone I think. We are nearly through the Declaration & our other points should move fast.

. . .

Devotedly
E.R.

She encouraged Hick to do a book about women in journalism.

Hotel Crillon
Nov. 28th

Hick dearest,

I am so glad that you are in the little cottage & settled & enjoy it. . . .
Don't get an inferiority complex about your book, you've got lots to

tell that will help the young gal who wants to get into the newspaper business! It will be very interesting, much more interesting than Bess.*

I didn't think Truman could be re-elected & now that he is I have a terrible sense of responsibility. He made so many promises which can only be carried out if he gets good people around him & that he hasn't done successfully yet!

E.R.

As the session drew to an end she sometimes escaped the "wordy atmosphere," and the Soviet bloc fulminations "telling us what dogs we are." She left Sandifer in her place while she Christmas-shopped for sweaters, gloves, scarves, little girls' dresses, and toys.

[E.R. to Maude Gray:] [December 9, 1948]

I hope the last lap of my work on the Declaration of Human Rights will end tomorrow & that we get it through the General Assembly Plenary session with the required 2/3 vote. The Arabs & Soviets may balk— the Arabs for religious reasons, the Soviets for political ones. We will have trouble at home for it can't be a U.S. document & get by with 58 nations & at home that is hard to understand. On the whole I think it is good as a declaration of rights to which all men may aspire & which we should try to achieve. It has no legal value but should carry moral weight.

Despite her fears, the plenary adopted the Declaration the next day (December 10) and she wrote "long job finished." A weary but exultant Sandifer wrote his wife—

[Durward Sandifer to Irene Sandifer:] [December 12, 1948]

As you can see it is now 1 a.m. Sunday. I have just finished packing to go to the airport with Mrs. Roosevelt at 2 a.m. We had drinks and then dinner at the place whose card I am enclosing. . . .

We finished the vote on the Declaration at exactly midnight last night. . . .

Eleanor was pleased that she, a woman, had done indispensable work in the drafting and adoption of the Declaration, so much so that General Marshall had predicted the 1948 session would be remembered as the "Human Rights Assembly." And though at the time she doubted that the Declaration had legal force, "most international lawyers," according to John P. Humphrey, the Canadian director of the Human Rights Division who had prepared the "Secretariat Outline," as

* Bess Furman, Mrs. Robert B. Armstrong, took over from Hick for the Associated Press in 1933 when Mrs. Roosevelt moved to Washington. Mrs. Roosevelt had just read her meaty *Washington By-Line* in manuscript.

the first draft of the Declaration came to be known, "now think [this was 1972] however, that whatever the intentions of its authors may have been, the Universal Declaration of Human Rights is now binding on states as part of the customary law of nations."

She returned to New York on December 13. Her engagement book read, "Trude & Joe come in; 7:30 dine Elinor M."

It had been a hard year but the new note in her feelings was that of accomplishment and a satisfaction that she was willing to acknowledge.

XIV

"She's Just Made That Way"

NINETEEN FORTY-NINE WAS a peculiar year for Eleanor. Other former First Ladies had disappeared from view with their husbands' departures from the White House, but she had gone on to become a world celebrity. She took on with ease the duties that flowed from that status—intensive work at the United Nations; the reception, often at the State Department's request, of distinguished visitors; crowded schedules; the daily column for the syndicate; the monthly page of questions and answers for the *Ladies' Home Journal;* the finishing of *This I Remember,* the second volume of her autobiography; radio and television appearances; a never-ending correspondence. What was unusual about 1949, however, was the scarcity of personal letters to her friends. Fewer than five to David, equally few to Trude and me, one to Hick. There may have been many more. If so, few have survived. Since they were in longhand, there rarely were carbons.

Neither careless filing nor her busyness wholly explains the paucity of letters. Earl Miller's legal separation from Simone may have tempered her usual displays of affection. Simone had brought action against Earl in 1946 after they had had a row in which he had struck her. As she pressed her case, she accused Earl not only of striking her but of acts of adultery with Eleanor. Simone contended in court that Earl had a bedroom in Eleanor's Hyde Park cottage adjacent to her own and stayed with Eleanor in her Greenwich Village apartment, indeed had a key to it. She submitted a packet of Eleanor's letters to Earl that showed the "endearing" terms used by Eleanor, as Simone's lawyer put it.

Harry Hooker, an old friend and Franklin's former law partner, first represented Eleanor's interests behind the scenes. He later was joined by Franklin Jr.'s law firm. He had to know everything that had happened between them, Fjr. told her, if he was to represent her. Of course she had loved Earl, Eleanor answered, but "in the sense you mean there was nothing."* To the outside world, Eleanor seemed to take the proceedings serenely. Privately they devastated her, especially because of their possible impact on her children. In March 1947, when Simone began to raise the "sweetheart" business, as Earl had called it, in an effort, he claimed, "to extract more money from me," Eleanor had written Jimmy, "I was disturbed by John Boettiger's point of view that the situation would ruin the careers of all of you."

The judge granted Simone a legal separation and awarded her custody of the two children. The "endearing" letters were sealed. The newspaper reports were minimal. Nevertheless, it had been a sobering experience for Eleanor. It may temporarily have made her more cautious in writing.

Although there were few letters to friends, the letters to Anna continued undiminished. Of all the children, Anna seemed to have the greatest difficulties, and Eleanor's letters were full of encouragement. "I will do anything & everything to help you, my dear, & you can count on me," was characteristic. Anna was trying to make it on her own in Los Angeles, where she had moved after John had left her and the Phoenix paper.

The shadows left by her discovery of Anna's knowledge and silence about Mrs. Rutherfurd's presence at the White House did not diminish her loyalty to her daughter.

Early in January Eleanor flew down to Washington to see the President and give him her impressions of the Paris UN Assembly. Later that week she spent the night with Esther in Connecticut, and at the beginning of February she set out on a transcontinental lecture trip. She had misgivings about the fatigues of such a tour and insisted that her children on the coast not schedule public activities that might keep her from seeing them and the grandchildren.

---

* This is what Fjr. told me when I wrote *The Years Alone*. Many years later, James, in his second book, *My Parents: A Differing View*, written to correct Elliott's unpleasant portrait of his mother in *The Roosevelts of Hyde Park*, suggested that indeed there had been a physical as well as an emotional relationship between his mother and Earl. "I believe there may have been one real romance in mother's life outside marriage. Mother may have had an affair with Earl Miller. . . . Joseph Lash in his excellent book, *Eleanor and Franklin*, glosses over the relationship as though to protect her reputation, but I believe this is a disservice to her, a suggestion that because of her hang-ups she was never able to be a complete woman" (James Roosevelt, *My Parents: A Differing View* [Chicago, 1976], pps. 110–111). There may have been an affair. I have done my best to present all the evidence that has come my way.

February 11, 1949

Anna darling,

By this time you must have the schedule of my trip & my very belated letter making suggestions for the one evening I am free.

I do not want to make any other engagements. I might meet the Democratic women if they want to see me, for an hour one afternoon. I told the man for whom I am lecturing . . . that I would not go to a luncheon for him. . . .

I want to go to see Jimmy & Rommie's children & Johnny & Anne's children—go to one on one afternoon & the other the next day. Will you arrange for that at whatever time is convenient? Don't let the Democratic ladies interfere. I want to spend at least an hour with the children.

It is wiser for me to stay at the hotel, I think, because of the everlasting telephone & because there are people whom I will have to see. . . .

I was in St. Louis this week & I find that everywhere people talk about the program so I am sure we have a good audience. I am afraid it is fear of the name Roosevelt which worries the possible advertisers. Five times a week I think is right. I do believe people get into the habit of listening at the same hour every day & they do not like to have to remember that the program is on only three times a week.

. . . Do not get too tired because if you get sick or even get a cold which bothers your voice you will not be able to do the job. . . .

I have done altogether too much speaking since I came back from Paris & this lecture trip is really a foolish performance. If I find it too tiring I will decide never to do it again.

Ever since I heard Buzz on the March of Dimes I have been meaning to write to him. He sounded so natural & his voice was so good. Is he getting to like life as an undergraduate? I hope so because I think on the whole he was too old for his years & he was with older people too much.

Couldn't the radio cocktail party be *after* I see Jimmy's children?

The book is done, tho' of course there will be revising to do.

Devotedly,
Mother

A letter to Maude went into great detail about the troubles of her children.

[E.R. to Maude Gray:]   [February 13, 1949]

I'll see all the children on the West Coast which will be good. Jimmy was here & spent 24 hours at Hyde Park & things seem better with him & Rommie is improving but all is not yet clear sailing.—Ethel & Frankie seem to be moving toward a separation but I hope they may straighten out. Elliott is much better since he had his operation & Faye seems to be making a great effort. Johnny's store is doing well & all seems serene there. Anna still has no sponsor for the programme tho' all seem to like it & she's working hard on that & the magazine she's editing. John Boettiger still has no job he feels he can take & their personal relationship does not improve I fear.

Tommy has high blood sugar & she is not going on the lecture trip with me. . . .

Early in March she wrote Trude from Houston, Texas, where Dr. Homer P. Rainey, an old associate from American Youth Commission and International Student Service days, was president of the university.

March 11th [1949]

Trude dearest,

I hope to be back Wed. a.m. the 15th & if you & Joe can do come in at 5:30 for a drink & a chat but check with Tommy to make sure I get home! I asked David Gurewitsch to dine because he seems to want to talk something over with me.—Also is there a chance that you & Joe, with or without Jonathan, would like to come up for the weekend on Friday or Sat. It would be good to have you!

I've had a disagreeable time with George Bye & Bruce Gould & had to leave it to Tommy & Elliott to settle but I'll tell you about it later. . . .

Devotedly,
E.R.

Bruce Gould and his wife were the editors of the *Ladies' Home Journal,* and friends from the thirties when they had carried *This Is My Story* in their magazine, and George Bye was her longtime literary agent. Elliott's participation in the conference with the two men—along with Tommy, who was to receive half the proceeds from the serial rights to *This I Remember*—is a measure as much of his helpfulness to his mother as vice versa. He became her agent for the second volume of her autobiography, in effect firing Bye, and she permitted him to approach Otis Weise, the editor of *McCall's.* Gould's peremptory tone bothered Eleanor. Parts of the manuscript, he complained to Tommy, sounded as if they had been composed while riding a bicycle. "If Mrs. Roosevelt is willing to spend three months of intensive work on the mss & Mr. Gould is then satisfied, he would consider going as high as $150,000," Tommy's memo on her and Elliott's meeting with him read. Eleanor reacted bluntly: "In the first place I would have felt the book wasn't mine and in the second place I wouldn't have the time." Gould offended her. "So we told her to sell her book elsewhere if she wouldn't improve it, and her column, too," he later wrote, putting on a brave front for what proved to be a major publishing misjudgment.

McCall's gave her what she wanted for a manuscript that it bought sight unseen as well as a five-year contract for the monthly Q. and A. page, something

Gould had refused to consider. She wrote George Bye afterward, "I think I must tell you that I think we could have avoided this unpleasantness with Mr. Gould had you been a little more businesslike and worked for the price I wanted. . . . My relationship with the *Ladies' Home Journal* and Mr. and Mrs. Gould have been pleasant, but I think they had reached a point where they felt I would take whatever they cared to offer. That is always a bad point to reach in any human relationship. Perhaps you should have been the one to tell me that that point had been reached and that you were on the lookout for my interest." Graciousness did not mean sentimentality.

She handled that situation with dispatch, but the difficulties of her children, a constant worry that year, were less amenable to her efforts to hold them together as families. All but Johnny were having problems with their marriages. "Fjr & Ethel are getting a divorce & she goes to Reno in April," she wrote Anna. "Sad, but nothing can be done. Fjr is running for Congress if he gets the nomination."

She stayed in touch with John Boettiger, sending him his usual birthday check. He thanked his "dearest LL," as he continued to call her, and she replied—

[E.R. to John Boettiger:]   [April (?) 1949]

It was grand to hear from you and I'm so glad you have something in hand and are looking to the future hopefully.

I am back on the UN and after the General Assembly is ended the Human Rights Commission will meet so I will be in New York City during the week until the end of June. I do not like missing the spring in H.P. but as long as I am asked to serve on the UN I feel I must do it . . . Tommy joins me in much love.

Tammany did not want Franklin to succeed Representative Sol Bloom of the West Side of Manhattan who had died in midterm. It sought someone more amenable to its control. Although the district was considered a Tammany fief, the Liberal Party rallied to Franklin's candidacy and he won handsomely in an election that sent shock waves through the country. "Wasn't it a wonderful success," Eleanor said beamingly to reporters at Lake Success, "a fine beginning," and "he didn't have anything to do with Tammany." But privately she urged him to move slowly when he began to talk of going for the governorship of New York in 1950. He should stabilize his family situation first, establish a responsible record in Congress, and be sure that his law firm, whose partners had backed him enthusiastically, did not take on questionable clients, such as Nationalist China, which was being driven from the mainland.

For me personally the election was a turning point. I did not take part in Franklin's campaign. When Trude and I came to Hyde Park afterward Eleanor drew me aside to ask what had happened. When I said the episode had confirmed a realization that with my radical background I had to get out of politics, she did not demur, suggesting I was probably right.

Reception by Prime Minister Nehru at his house in New Delhi, 1952. At the right Mrs. Indira Gandhi, Nehru's daughter. (Courtesy Franklin D. Roosevelt Library. With permission of Press Information Bureau, Government of India.)

Mrs. Roosevelt dining with Marshal Tito on Brioni, July 1953. Maureen Corr, who succeeded Tommy, on Mrs. R.'s right. Dr. Gurewitsch on her left. (Courtesy of Mrs. A. David Gurewitsch. With permission of Yugoslavian Government.)

At the 1956 Chicago Democratic National Convention. "If I did not think you could win, it would not be worth doing a good job," she had written Adlai at a moment of discouragement. (Courtesy Franklin D. Roosevelt Library.)

Mrs. Roosevelt with boys from the Wiltwyck School. At her right is Mrs. Maria Gurewitsch, mother of David Gurewitsch. (© Photo by Dr. A. David Gurewitsch.)

With Prime Minister U Nu of Burma. (Courtesy Franklin D. Roosevelt Library. With permission of Leo Rosenthal.)

Mrs. Roosevelt loved giving picnics behind her cottage at Val-Kill. Here the group is the Institute of the Amalgamated Clothing Workers Union. Other groups that came often were the boys of Wiltwyck School, the Hudson Shore Training Institute for Women Workers in Industry, the Human Rights Commission. (Courtesy Franklin D. Roosevelt Library. With permission of Eleanor Roosevelt Memorial Foundation.)

In the Moscow Subway. (© Photo by Dr. A. David Gurewitsch.)

With her son Elliott. "If Elliott were not at Hyde Park I could not live there, in fact I would not want to." (Courtesy Franklin D. Roosevelt Library. With permission of Trans World Airlines.)

A television show that she did for Henry Morgenthau III, who sits at her left and was its producer. Dr. Clarence Cramer of Adelbert College is at the right. (Courtesy Franklin D. Roosevelt Library.)

Memorial Day, 1958. In the rose garden at Hyde Park where Franklin D. Roosevelt, Fala, and now Eleanor Roosevelt lie buried. Next to Mrs. Roosevelt is Franklin, Jr.; behind her John and to the left Barbara Forbes-Morgan, a cousin. (© Photo by Dr. A. David Gurewitsch.)

E.R. and Walter Reuther at Val-Kill. In the foreground Anna Roosevelt Halsted, in the rear Mrs. Roosevelt's grandson Haven. (© Photo by Dr. A. David Gurewitsch.)

"To Washington," her calendar for June 14 read, "Fjr sworn in—flew back to Lake Success." I remained on good terms with Franklin and, though I no longer worked with him, we talked politics whenever we got together. Trude, Jonathan, and I spent most of our June weekends at Hyde Park before we went to Martha's Vineyard. So did David. He had become a fixed point in Eleanor's life, as much as any of us, more, in fact, than we were willing to recognize. Sometime during that month she suggested to Elliott that he take me on as his assistant in editing F.D.R.'s letters during his years as Governor and President. As a result I spent most of the summer at Hyde Park, living in Eleanor's cottage and working at the Franklin D. Roosevelt Library. "When I came up on the train this afternoon," I wrote Trude, "I was really in rebellion. I felt I should be on the Vineyard plane instead. I didn't see how by putting in weekends at Hyde Park I was going to get the job done. Once I started to go through the files, however, I found the stuff fascinating and became somewhat reconciled to this exile from my family."

The plunge into Roosevelt's letters marked a shift in my personal life from politics into journalism and scholarship. I little realized that the path would bring me closer to the Roosevelt story and to telling that story to others.

Eleanor exchanged long letters with Anna about the latter's efforts to negotiate a new radio contract. ABC had grown less enthusiastic about the "Eleanor and Anna" show, as it came to be called, when potential sponsors avoided it. "I am happy it is ending! but sorry for Anna's sake we could not succeed," her note to Tommy read. She was reluctant to lend herself to some of the proposals Anna's West Coast agents now made.

[E.R. to Anna Boettiger:]   [June 17, 1949]
    I thought it over very carefully and for you I think it might be a valuable program, but in view of the fact that I am still on the UN and do have a certain responsibility to them and that I do not intend to give up working with the UN as yet, I decided it was unwise for me. I might get involved in all kinds of difficulties.
    Perhaps I am too fearful and I hate not doing anything which might eventually be helpful to you. Perhaps the inability to sell our program shows that something is fundamentally wrong. I have inquired around and find that some of the advertising people feel the program lacks appeal and if that is the case, then something should be done about it. I will have more time to work on it after this next week when the Human Rights Commission ends, and I will be in Hyde Park and more free. However, I do not really feel I am able to think up new ideas without direction.

    . . .

    I realize your feeling about staying in the west and I would not urge you for a minute to come east because I know how hard it would be to be further away from Sis and that both Buzz and Johnny really like that part of the world.

The letters from you and John make me very sad. In a way as long as you had to get a divorce I wish it had been possible to get it over with and he could get away since he has taken a new job. . . .

Anna explained that she, too, wished she could help John by starting divorce proceedings, but her lawyer was away and she did not know of any other. She was overcome by the sadness of it all, Eleanor replied. ". . . I gathered how you felt dear, from your letter to John. He telephoned & may phone again before going west. I wish things could have worked out for both of you as I don't think he'll be happy & I know you are not." The same letter told Anna, "Fjr has decided to announce his engagement to Sue Perrin around Aug. 1st & get married the latter part of Aug. if Congress is over & go to Campo for 2 or 3 weeks. . . ."

The fragment of a letter she sent David, whom she had been seeing frequently, sometimes with Nemone, more often with Grania, referred to the situation with John. "He will not hear of any help from a psychiatrist & insists all he needs is a more interesting job so he is going to try & find one. . . ." The melancholy saga with John played itself out. "Anna darling," she wrote on July 8, "I've been away for 2 nights staying with Esther Lape & no papers so till I got back yesterday I didn't see the divorce stories. I didn't like the way John did it but I suppose you planned it that way. Was Johnny prepared or did it upset him?" A month later (August 11) she wrote again, "I am glad the divorce is over. I hated it for all of you & what you tell me about John saddens me. There is no use trying to figure out something like this & it does no good & only brings more bitterness which hurts you. . . ."

She received an impersonal postcard from John in Indonesia: "Yesterday I had a most interesting visit with President Soekarno and several of his ministers. Today I hope to see the chief of the guerrilla fighters. I am beginning to see the picture more clearly. . . ." She sent him the news about "Sistie," who had had a baby, and added that Anna had been happy about the way Sistie had come through and that "Being a great grandmother when you haven't seen the great-grandchild does not seem to change one's feelings a great deal."

There was one letter to David and to me that summer. The first, typewritten from New York, had a postscript.

July 13, 1949

Dear Dr. Gurewitsch:

  . . .

Dear David,

The above is what Sheila [a secretary] thinks is the way you should be addressed. Thanks for telling me how to answer the would-be medical students. Do I bother you too much with these letters? I'll be in town for a few hours on the 21st and I'll call your office on the chance of being able to say "hello" and hear how you all are and what your final plans for arrival here may be. . . .

E.R.

The longhand letter to me was written from Hyde Park. I was beginning to write for the New York *Post,* edited by my old friend James Wechsler, and I had thanked her for having encouraged Elliott to employ me in the editing of F.D.R.'s letters:

July 13th [1949]

Dearest Joe,

. . .

You were a dear to write as you did. I've worried as to whether I'd done you more harm than good but I love you & Trude & Jonathan & where there is real affection & trust I feel the end result must be good.

I can never remember one day since we met that I haven't been glad that our friendship was growing warmer & deeper & having you near is always a joy.

Elliott is completely happy over working with you & asked me yesterday if I thought you were.

My love to you always,
E.R.

Most of that summer she spent at Hyde Park, David was in and out as was I. My own notes say nothing about him, although he usually expressed himself volubly. I may not have considered his political observations noteworthy, although Mrs. Roosevelt did. Whatever my surface cordiality, I was jealous. In any case, my notes dealt with the comings and goings of her children and chiefly with the explosive episode touched off by Cardinal Spellman's public letter of rebuke that ended, "I shall not again publicly acknowledge you." Eleanor's calm reply to the Cardinal in her column was, as Mayor William O'Dwyer, himself a Catholic, said, "devastating." It ended on a note that triggered the Cardinal's retreat. "I assure you," she wrote, "that I had no sense of being 'an unworthy American mother.' The final judgment, my dear Cardinal Spellman, of the worthiness of all human beings is in the hands of God."

From President Truman down, Americans in public life backed her. Edward J. Flynn, still the country's most influential politician of the Catholic faith, a longtime friend of Eleanor's as he had been of Franklin's, fearful among other things of a split in the country along religious lines and after a secret flight to the Vatican, arranged for a public reconciliation. It began with the Cardinal telephoning her at Hyde Park, led to the publication of letters by the two of them, and ended with the

Cardinal's "dropping in" on her at Hyde Park for a forty-five minute friendly chat. It left her, she wrote a young friend, "with a horrible feeling of insincerity . . . you would think I was one of his most cherished friends."

My diary entry for August 8 describes the exchange of letters with the Cardinal and the "reconciliation" engineered by Ed Flynn.

Ed Flynn had tracked her down at radio station and asked her to lunch with him. He was very upset and tired—said he was sick of politics—had had enough trouble with the O'Dwyer business, but the worst thing was the division that had set in. He had worked all his life against it. Would Mrs. R. be willing to talk with the Cardinal if he called her? He had talked with the Cardinal the night before and had a rough draft of a statement with him. Cardinal would like to get her approval before issuing it, Mrs. R. said of course she would be willing, that she would be back at Hyde Park by 6 p.m. Promptly at 6:30 the Cardinal called. He was gracious and extremely cordial—as if they were on the best of terms.

He said he had re-worked the statement and would send someone up next morning if Mrs. R. agreed with it generally. Promptly at 9:30 a monsignor appeared—to work with Mrs. R. on the statement. Mrs. R. wanted a specific paragraph included that the controversy had been unfortunate and that people had a right to differ. In her statement she wanted to include a paragraph also on what a federal aid to education bill should include. The monsignor begged her not to—said it would continue the controversy. She reluctantly agreed but told the monsignor he should tell the Cardinal that in a couple of weeks she would write such a column. Said she hoped the Cardinal would join her in sponsoring federal aid for child health. Monsignor said he would.

At five that afternoon (Friday) the Cardinal called again. Thanked her cordially. Asked whether she wouldn't have lunch with him at 50th Street the next week. Mrs. R. said she rarely went to New York. Could he, then, lunch with her at Hyde Park? "Of course," said Mrs. R. The Cardinal ended with "God bless you."

Herbert Lehman and his wife stopped by on their way down from the Adirondacks. He was prepared to run for the Senate but only if he were assured of the support of political leaders of the Catholic faith. August 13, 1949, my diary entry noted: "Mrs. R. told Dorothy Norman [a liberal columnist and one of Mayor O'Dwyer's confidantes] that she would be delighted to serve as honorary chairman of the O'Dwyer Committee [for reelection] if she were assured Lehman would be nominated and would have the *full* support of the Democratic high command."

The controversy with the Cardinal was much on her mind that summer, New York politics less so. Most of my diary entries as well as letters to Trude dealt with Eleanor's feelings about her children. In mid-July I had written Trude—

[Joseph P. Lash to Trude W. Lash:] [July 15, 1949]

The party for Faye broke up about 10:30 and Mrs. R. and I have sat talking until just now. I asked her about Anna and John and how much of their trouble was due to John's inability to find a slot for himself after the war. She thought it was rather that John had constantly to be bolstered up by Anna, involved her in great debts over the paper in Arizona, and then developed a blue funk about it. On the one hand he claimed the advantages that went with being FDR's son-in-law and on the other blamed his own difficulties on that same relationship. In any case it's become a pretty bitter business now. It's so sad because always when they were together they seemed to be so right for each other. Mrs. R. seemed quite stoical about it—even where Anna is concerned she doesn't seem to get her feelings deeply involved perhaps because she knows there's little she can do about it. Her approach and attitude towards all of us is very much like the attitude Tolstoy has to his characters and the stream of events in *Anna Karenina* and in *War and Peace*.

She's very worried about Frankie. . . . She feels he is unaware of the sense of insecurity he breeds in his two boys (when he doesn't appear when he promised) and that he now has to battle for their affections. . . . Mrs. R. feels we're the most happily married family she knows. . . .

Another letter to Trude reported the arrival of Franklin and Sue.

[Joseph P. Lash to Trude W. Lash:] [No date]

We had an uproarious time at dinner with Franklin and Elliott in their best teasing form. And both ganging up on their mother. They were upbraiding her for giving her imprimatur to an article some "Joe" had written about her. Why did she read such stuff before publication, they asked, and thereby take on some responsibility for the piece? She listened and then sweetly remarked "I need the publicity." You can imagine the roar that went up. "There are two Eskimos near the North Pole who haven't heard of Mrs. R." I said. . . . I have a problem—Elliott and Frank both try to line me up against the other and it makes me very uncomfortable . . .

When James and Romaine arrived on July 24, I wrote in my diary, he was chiefly concerned that Fjr. not interfere with his own political timetable in California politics:

Jimmy wanted to get agreement that Frank would not come in to California to speak on anything without prior agreement from Jimmy and he would reciprocate in New York. F. had been opposed to giving

such an agreement but when Jimmy left last night, he said he had it.
. . . Jimmy questioned me closely about F's timetable. What would be
the effect of two Roosevelts running at the same time for Governor?
Would it intensify feelings about a dynasty? Jimmy obviously is aiming at
the national picture—vice president in '52 and president in '56.

Eleanor had lent James $100,000. In addition, he was one of the executors of
F.D.R.'s will. So some of her letters to him dealt with money transactions between
them.

> Hyde Park
> Aug 13th

Dearest Jimmy,

Many thanks for the check which helps a great deal. I hope you kept
$5000. safely tucked away for illness! I don't intend to be ill but it is good
insurance. So far our investment has gone up!

Fjr. & Sue are here & we are celebrating his birthday as he'll be in
Washington the 17th. He expects to be married the 31st of August.

Very few guests now but busy just the same. Final proof reading on the
book is deadly.

My last bout with the Cardinal was breath taking. He called me, sent a
Monsignor up with his statement, put in my suggestion that people have
a right to differ & express themselves. Thanked me on the phone warmly
for my statement & blessed me! I'm asked to lunch or he'll come here!
I'll tell you the details when we meet.

I'm planning to be in Los Angeles Jan. 15th evening to Jan. 22d &
make no paid speeches while there so I can go to the university & other
small groups if they want me. I'll speak on way out & back for Colston
Leigh at regular lectures & go up west coast to spend a day in Portland &
see my new great grandchild!

I hope your boys are fine & Romaine not worn out by her return.

Much love to you & all.

> Devotedly,
> Mother

Anna's troubles—her debts, the collapse of her marriage and the newspaper in
Phoenix, her efforts to get a new job—were climaxed at the end of the summer by a
local doctor's diagnosis of a cough and fever as tuberculosis. He thought she would
have to be separated from young Johnny Boettiger and spend two or three years in
a sanatorium. At a birthday party in Hyde Park for Harry Hooker, Maude and
David Gray were there as were Trude and I. News had just come of the death of
Eleanor's old friend, Elinor Morgenthau. David Gurewitsch had telephoned to say
that doctors feared Anna's diagnosis of a "yeast" tuberculosis was an infection that

did not respond to any of the new drugs. Eleanor tried to be cheerful. We all sensed the effort she was making.

At the services for Elinor Morgenthau shortly afterward, Eleanor moved the closely knit Morgenthau family to tears with her sensitive remarks about Elinor's attentiveness to her family's needs, a devotion that she had combined with a steady interest in public affairs. A touching letter came from Henry Morgenthau III. He recalled a column Eleanor had written in 1938 which on rereading made him understand that the thoughts she had voiced in her tribute to his mother "had been planted deep in your life many years past" and since his mother shared the same philosophy it explained why their friendship had been so strong. He quoted the column, and since it dealt with parents' attitudes toward their children it bears quotation anew:

> So many people whom I know always are worrying about what they will leave their children. I feel quite convinced that it is more important to give your children all the advantages you can so that they may be useful in the world and may meet any conditions which might arise in their lives, than it is to worry about what you may leave them in dollars and cents. When you pass on, you will leave behind you a generation of well-equipped and useful citizens able to manage their own lives and cope with the world as their forefathers did.
>
> I am always proud and to a certain extent relieved when any of my children prove that they are entirely able to cope with life by themselves, for, after all, their own characters are the only absolutely sure thing we can count on in the future. As far as I myself am concerned, I am going to try to do what I can about today and let the next generation deal with tomorrow.

But that did not mean neglect of tradition and family piety, especially when the latter entailed no longer doing things for people one loves. Sometimes she spoke sharply to her children.

Sep. 22, 1949

Dearest Jimmy:

I am deeply hurt by your letter of the 16th and also frankly I was very angry. Through all the years Christmas at home was to me a joy and I had hoped I had given to you all the feeling that it was a time for thinking of others even if we were far apart. It is never a burden to me. If you and Rommie find the expense too great or the burden too great of thinking beyond each other and the children, I shall accept your decision. In fact now no presents from you would be acceptable but I think it strange that you want to deprive me and others of the pleasure of thinking and showing our thought of you and your children in a tangible way.

This is the kind of high-handed, pompous action which loosens family ties and does not bind them closer. When I was young and could only give little, I made things for family and friends but I gave and if I leave you and yours out of my Christmas thought and giving then I don't want to talk to you on Christmas Day.

Your letter does not sound like you. How could you have dictated it?

Also, how could you have sent it without a mention of Sis when you must know my deep anxiety and I hope are sharing it.

I have decided to send Rommie a copy of this letter. One must do things for people one loves or love dies and you are moving in the direction of narrowing your affections, one has less to give that way.

My love to you, dear
Mother

She liked her children to stand on their own feet, but when any of them were in trouble, she went to their help, as she now sought to rally the family to help a stricken Anna in Los Angeles.

Sept. 18th [1949]

Anna darling,

I am sorry for you to have this horrid attack but glad Johnny [Roosevelt] was there to make you behave & go to the hospital. You've driven yourself & been under a great strain for several years & you've suffered more than you would admit even to yourself I'm sure & it takes a toll physically.

I wish you'd come East & stay at Hyde Park & rest. Johnny could go to a boarding school in Dutchess Co. & Buzz could transfer to a college here in the East. I can swing the expense I'm sure! I'll write you a business letter tomorrow but this is just to tell you that I love you dearly & wish you were here now.

Devotedly,
Mother

The next day she wrote again.

Anna darling,

I wrote you a line last night but Tommy addressed [it] to your home address so I write again fearing the first may be lost.

I think of you & hope you won't worry. Johnny [Roosevelt] told me he would be here Friday & I can give him out of some money for serial rights in papers which has just come in money enough to pay all yr. bills & I'll send Buzz a gift too to cover what you would give him so don't worry about money.

The first day of briefing is over. By afternoon I cld hardly keep awake! There are lots of new people & they are slow at grasping what the advisers tell them! Tomorrow there will be the opening at Flushing.

Tommy and I have just been saying how we wished you were all here where we could take care of you! She sends her love.

A nice letter from Sistie today. She says she couldn't have managed without you. She sounds happy & competent & very pleased with "Nick"!

All my love darling
Mother

A quick note to David, who had been in touch with the doctors on the coast for her.

Sept. 29th (1949)

David dear,

Johnny talked to the Coast today & was told that the chest specialist was inclined to think it was not T.B. but this illness which is localized in the San Joachim Valley. It is like T.B. but shorter. One case has appeared in Santa Monica. It must continue to be [watched] however though some skin tests he said had been taken, only 1 showed any signs & it is on this he bases his idea that it may be this local disease. Perhaps when you call, the doctor will know more or tell you more. Johnny goes back Monday midnight if nothing changes his plans.

I am still happy over my time with you on Wednesday. I enjoy being with you & talking with you. Your mind is free & you have the courage to say what you think & so few people have!

Thank you & my love to you.

E.R.

Mme. Chiang sent me these little place cards & I thought Grania would like them.

A letter to Anna that same day reported the family's plans to help her out:

[E.R. to Anna Boettiger:]   [September 29, 1949]

Johnny tells me that the news was a bit encouraging from the specialist. He expects to go back Monday midnight so before long you will have your big, little brother close at hand again! Elliott, Fjr, & Johnny all met here this afternoon late & I was back from U.N. & we are sure that one way or another we have worked out the plans so you will have no financial worries until you are quite well again. Johnny will have $3000 to pay all the present bills on his return. He will give you details.

A warm, brotherly letter came from Elliott, and when Anna protested that their mother must not be permitted, because of her concern for her daughter, to accept questionable sponsors for her broadcasts because Anna might be the "packager," Elliott replied,

[Elliott Roosevelt to Anna Boettiger:]   [October 21, 1949]
First of all what Mother is doing she loves to do. It gives her a pride and feeling of really doing something worth while. It makes her feel closer to her own family, and she yearns for the affection and appreciation which you give her. . . . Mother would like to knit us all together as a family unit, united in good times as well as bad. . . .
The truth of the matter is that if Mother didn't do this for you she'd probably do it for someone else like a Lash or Gourevitch. She's just made that way.

Doubtless Elliott truly reflected Eleanor's approach to her children and her friends, yet I have a note in my diary, October 2, 1949, about a talk we had when I dropped by her Washington Square apartment during the UN General Assembly. We spoke mostly about Russia's more truculent behavior at the General Assembly since it had acquired the atom bomb, but her comments about Anna showed that, behind the fierce loyalty and mother-love that shaped her readiness to help her children, there was a tough old bird who saw all of them plainly. "Anna Boettiger has $4,000 in bank. All her income is attached in connection with law suit in progress. As she [Anna] has time in her illness to think things over, she begins to feel maybe John [Boettiger] was right. (He's supposed to have remarried in Java.) Maybe she did ride him too hard for lacking stamina—& took the lead in things he should have decided." That entry also said—and it causes me to shudder even as I reread it: "It was a little frightening to hear Mrs. R. say she did not think Russia had a stockpile of bombs as great as ours—so there was little danger of war, but it was well to be more on the alert than ever—to avoid another Pearl Harbor with atom bombs."
A big change in her personal life that autumn involved subletting her Washington Square apartment and moving to a small two-room suite in the Park Sheraton Hotel on 56th Street. The hotel, delighted to have so illustrious a tenant, agreed with Elliott to keep the costs minimal and to provide office space for Eleanor and Tommy as well as for Elliott. It caused Trude and me some pangs to have her leave the Village, but the reason probably was economic.

[E.R. to Anna Boettiger:]   [November 10, 1949]
. . . David Gurewitsch was very happy that his letter was helpful. He has a keen understanding of all you are going through & a great impatience with doctor's etiquette. . . .

I have no word from John Boettiger so I imagine he has decided that there will be less contact in the future. . . .

I am trying to rent this apartment furnished & take rooms with Elliott in a hotel. It is an experiment till next September but I think may be better & a little cheaper. I don't need a home & more to care for here. Just a place to sleep & see people & an office & no servant problems seems a wise arrangement, if we find we like it! If I don't I'll move back here in Sept. . . .

There was word from John Boettiger on December 15. He had returned from Indonesia. "I wanted to let you know that I am back in New York . . . and hope sometime I may run in to say hello to you." She did not invite him to come in but wrote what for her was a cool letter.

Dear John,

I am glad to hear that you are back and that you have had a successful time.

I read of your marriage and send you my good wishes for future happiness. [She then deleted that sentence and wrote instead] The whole month of January Tommy and I will be away as I am going to the West Coast on a lecture trip.

I read of your marriage and send you my good wishes for future happiness in which Tommy joins.

Affectionately,
E.R.

This I Remember came out in November. "Only a great woman could have written it," wrote Arthur Schlesinger, Jr., and reviews by writers like Elizabeth Janeway and Vincent Sheean were equally enthusiastic, Westbrook Pegler led the dissenters.

[E.R. to Anna Boettiger:]   [November 29, 1949]
Pegler is trying to dig up a story on Mrs. Rutherfurd & one of the boys came to see me today because Pegler has asked to see him! I told him to answer what he knew truthfully, & to say he didn't know where he didn't & not to volunteer anything & I hope he gets by. Mrs. Clapper's book seems to have started this search.

We move to the Park Sheraton Hotel, 7th Ave. & 55th St. on Dec. 1st. . . . I hope it will be easier & cheaper. I only need one home. . . . At one time the hotel had a bad reputation so they are making it respectable & that is why we get such a good price.

"Pegler is just writing as much nastiness as he can on it," she informed Maude and David Gray, writing about the reception of *This I Remember*, "& is now trying to dig up the Lucy Mercer story & chides me for not telling it." She should not allow Pegler to bother her, David Gray replied. "It would probably have been better for you to have mentioned Mrs. Rutherfurd at Warm Springs but it is not very important one way or another. I certainly wouldn't let it worry me." Anna's advice was the same. "Darling, I hated to have you bothered by that damn guy Pegler's nosiness. I can't imagine why Olive Clapper felt it necessary to go into this subject at all in her book. I had always understood that she was a pretty nice person, but now I have changed my mind." Olive Clapper, the widow of the columnist Raymond Clapper, had published some memoirs in 1946 called *Washington Tapestry*, which in a couple of paragraphs had told the Lucy Mercer story. Pegler, claiming he had overlooked the passage when the book had been published, used it now to hit at Eleanor for what she had not remembered.

At about the same time the work I was doing with Elliott in editing his father's correspondence came to the attention of anti-New Deal columnists such as John O'Donnell. They attacked Eleanor and Elliott's selection of me to help with the editing. My background in the radical youth movement, my attachment to the Roosevelts, meant that documents would be suppressed, the footnoting biased. Pegler linked Eleanor's alienation from Franklin because of the Lucy Mercer affair with her trip to the South Pacific in 1943, during which she was able to see me. In a depressed mood I suggested to Eleanor that perhaps I should withdraw from the editing project. Neither she nor Elliott would consider it, she insisted.

We talked about it over Thanksgiving when Trude, Jonathan, and I were at Hyde Park. She again voiced her indifference to such attacks and spoke of her attitude toward public and private affairs. "She mentioned Gerald K. Smith's attack, which I had not seen," my diary note for November 26 read, "saying openly what Pegler has only hinted at, that there was a 'romantic' attachment between the two of us. She said such 'dirt' didn't ruffle her at all as long as it didn't bother Trude and her children. Anyone who knew the difference in our ages would know how absurd it was. I said it distressed me because they were seeking to destroy what she and FDR symbolized. If people want to believe that sort of thing, she interrupted, there was nothing to be done. So far as she was concerned she was perfectly content to retire from public life to the country. She did the public things but the things that mattered were her personal relationships and they would continue."

Adding to her other worries was growing unhappiness about Elliott's judgments in personal and public affairs. Faye had divorced him in September. Mrs. Roosevelt had become quite fond of her, but she knew Faye had the quality that Shakespeare described when he spoke of women who approached men offering war rather than kneeling. "Elliott was so tired," she told Trude and me after she heard of Faye's divorce in September. "Elliott only feels a sense of relief at getting some rest. He does not realize at the moment how lonely it will be." She wished his business ventures would become stabilized. "He was too trusting," she went on, "and learns too late that people might want to do him injury."

"When we had dinner with Mrs. R. Wed. night," my journal for December 10 read, "she said she was 'scared' of the radio and television program Elliott had gotten for her. John Golden was adviser and on the program she would have people like Churchill, Vishinsky, Acheson! She didn't think she could get these people or know what to do with them. She sounded really desperate about it but felt reluctant to turn it down because the proceeds would go to Anna who needs money badly. She seemed to have decided to tell Elliott she was backing out and when she saw Trude on Thursday said she had 'scared' Elliott, but he finally prevailed. Today she talked as if she were going ahead. Tonight at the cottage* Elliott asked me to come in on the firm to do the preliminary work—who should be invited, briefing Mrs. R. on topics and questions. He wanted Churchill first, then Eva Peron paired with Helen Gahagan Douglas."

A note to Anna gave her holiday plans. The three Gurewitsches were coming for Christmas. Harry Hooker and his secretary and companion Nancy Halliday, and Tommy's companion Henry Osthagen also would be there. The Lashes were to come over New Year "& if the roads are passable we see the New Year in with Fjr in their new house."

By phone, letter, and messages through the boys Eleanor still pressed Anna to come east. Her daughter adamantly refused.

[Anna Boettiger to E.R.:] [December 14, 1949

Mummy, I hate to tell you but I'm still 100% sold on trying to work out a way of making my living out here, and therefore of not moving back East. Naturally I'm not going to be pigheaded, if, after I get entirely well and having made every effort out here, I cannot find any work. But I'm sure going to make the effort! And, of course, I'm going to try to get back on the air even if it's only on a Westcoastwise. Besides that I may do some other writing. But none of this can be decided definitely at the moment. When I go back on the air I'll try to compete adequately with you! . . . .

Eleanor yielded. In view of her own philosophy of instilling independence in one's children, she could scarcely do otherwise.

Dec. 29th, 1949

Anna darling,

. . .

As long as you want so much to stay West I hope that it will be possible for you to do so. I had hoped my radio programme could be

---

* The hilltop cottage a mile behind Eleanor's that F.D.R. had built as a retreat.

owned by you & Elliott but if you are not here to work on it we must think of something else. I don't like being in competition & when you go on again I will try to get off as soon as I can. Elliott says I cannot run out on my own contract. . . .

A world of love,
Mother

If she didn't do it for you, she'd do it for a Lash or Gurewitsch. "She's made that way," Elliott had written Anna. But there was an added distinction in her affections. There always had to be the "other." Seeking to elucidate the relationship of David Jackson to James Merrill's acclaimed poetry, Professor McClatchy of Yale quoted a line from Elinor Wylie: "The only engine which can fabricate language from spirit is the heart of each."* David Gurewitsch now was the one who spoke most directly to her heart. An undated note went to him on the Park Sheraton letterhead:

Tuesday night

David dearest,

    I am troubled about you, you seem not right, is it something I can help about? If so let me lunch with you Friday, if not just forget this note. I love you & felt unhappy about you tonight,

    Bless you & goodnight.

E.R.

* Shenandoah, vol. 30, no. 4, 1979.

XV

---

*An Invitation
to Campobello*

AT CHRISTMAS TIME in 1949 Eleanor received a sad but cordial note from Elliott's former wife, Faye. Their marriage had been hectic, but Faye missed, she wrote, "one of our celebrations." Then she added, "I shall always be grateful for the things you gave Scoop [Faye's son by a former marriage] and me—the privilege of knowing you and the happiness of being with you." Faye was a stormy petrel, but that was the effect Eleanor had on all.

Mrs. R. had been wary of Elliott's sense of relief at being freed of Faye's strenuous doings. He had not anticipated the unbearableness of being alone. He began to arrive at Hyde Park with a new girl every few weeks, intent on marrying each. They had names like Posey and Fifi—as if from the libretto of *Die Fledermaus*. He wanted all to be received and taken seriously by his mother. Trude and I were at Hyde Park early in the new year when one such lass arrived with her mother. She so clearly was on the make that she outraged Eleanor, who refused to go up to Elliott's top cottage while she was there. "If Elliott marries her I will move away," she declared. Her adamancy shook Elliott. Yet a year later, writing to Henry Morgenthau, the former Treasury Secretary, who sought to caution her about Elliott's business operations with the Hyde Park land, she wrote flatly, "If Elliott were not at Hyde Park I could not live there. In fact, I would not want to."

Some time after Eleanor moved to the Park Sheraton and I was in and out in connection with her television show for NBC, I was commiserating with Tommy.

She had complained about David Gurewitsch's ability to appeal to Mrs. Roosevelt's sympathetic nature and portray himself as the victimized soul in his marriage with Nemone. I chimed in, citing David's well-known dalliances with lovely ladies. Tommy was delighted to go to Mrs. R. and use what I had said to make a case against David. We both should have known better. Mrs. Roosevelt drew me aside one afternoon when I was at the Park Sheraton. She was deeply upset, telling me what Tommy had said to her. Did I not realize how many similar attacks had been made by friends and others who sought to protect her against her relationship with me? I had nothing to say for myself and could only fall back on Eleanor's forgiving nature. In any case she was in no mood to countenance such truths about David. She knew they were motivated by jealousy. David now was the one—*primus inter pares*—whom she loved. She was one of those lucky people fated always to fall in love, and the thought of her beloved enabled her to feel afresh the lines from Tennyson—

> *Now lies the earth all Danaë to the stars*
> *And all my heart lies open unto thee.*

A note from David as she left on another cross-country lecture trip.

1.10.50

Dearest Mrs. R.—
    You shall, I think, be off tomorrow. My thoughts are so much with you and I am missing you already before you have even left. I hope you will have an easy flight. I am sure it will be good to see Anna with your own eyes and to find out how she really is. . . .
    Nemone left for Florida today, tired but not too bad. A little depressed but not threateningly so. And I am trying to settle down and organize Grania. . . .

Your David.

She must have answered this, but these letters too, if they were written, have been lost. There were two letters to Trude and me. The first was from the Blackstone Hotel in Chicago, where during the war my visit with Eleanor had been bugged by Army Counterintelligence.

Sunday 1 a.m.

Dear Joe and Trude
    This is really just to send you both my love. . . . I do want to see all my children & grandchildren & great grandchild!
    Tommy is fine so far & 3 lectures are safely behind me. I enjoyed the time at Indiana State University. The President is fat & able & dynamic & has been advising in Germany on education.

We must go to the plane so goodnight & love to you both.

E.R.

The second was to Trude.

Los Angeles
Saturday Jan. 21st [1950]

Dearest Trude:

My time here is nearly over & tomorrow at dawn we leave for Portland. Anna goes today to Berkeley to rest for a month. . . .

The distances are so great here that I begin to understand why it is hard to meet! I wouldn't live here for anything in the world!

. . .

I picked up a bug here & was miserable for a few days. It was partly because I did so much I guess. I'm better again however but I dread my return schedule as it is very crowded, however it will probably work out better than I expect.

. . . My love to Joe. I hope Elliott is working more satisfactorily & not putting too much on Joe. A world of love to you.

E.R.

The Earl Miller business flared up again. Westbrook Pegler wrote three columns in February and March about it. Tommy wrote to Anna—

[Tommy to Anna Boettiger:] [March 20, 1950]

Did you see Pegler's columns about the Miller case? They were pretty bad & he stopped just short of naming names. The lawyer who represented Mrs. Miller gave him all the dope because what he wrote about me was pretty straight.* Miller got in a lather but it didn't bother your mother or me. . . .

Grace Tully was there and went into a long explanation of how she came to mention Mrs. Rutherford's [sic] name—she says Daisy Suckley told a newspaper man and she was queried by Pegler before she finished her book and hence included that item. She has sold to date about 20,000 copies of her book.

* Pegler's column, headed "An 'Unusual' Interest of FDR Clan in Earl Miller," among other things said, "Next, Gavin [John, Mrs. Miller's attorney] says, sometime in November [1946], Malvina Thompson, secretary to Mrs. Roosevelt, called on Mrs. Miller in Loudonville. Gavin says Miss Thompson scared Mrs. Miller and left the young wife in fear of trouble for pursuing her rights in court. Subsequently, Mrs. Miller switched lawyers and got a legal separation after a sensational hearing. She recently told me that she felt she didn't get a square deal in court."

Anna's son Curtis, who was not yet out of college, decided to get married.

April 7th [1950]

Anna darling,

I haven't quite recovered yet! Buzz seems young and I fear he doesn't realize what he's taking on. Jobs aren't plentiful & he has no college degree or special training. The girl may have a baby & then they'll have to live on Buzz's earnings. I'm afraid there are worries ahead for you & just now I'd like to be free from care for a while. You'll be lonely too for Johnny should stay in school & that leaves you alone. Oh! Well. I don't suppose one can make the young look on life with the eyes of experience!

Of course I'll come to the wedding & so will Tommy unless preparations to go abroad get her down. . . . What would they like as a wedding present? . . .

A world of love.

Mother

There was an unusual note here—"to be free from care for a while." It underscored how much her children's troubles weighed on her. She had had too many worries about her children. There was also her pleasure in David's companionship, which she wanted to savor.

[David Gurewitsch to E.R.:]   [April 11, 1950]

Tomorrow is the 12th. 5 years. I am sure that you cannot help but being affected. However much you will try to be philosophical about it. You will also be reminded from many sides. All I want to say is that I am thinking of you and that I am trying to use my imagination.

You have really showered us with presents. How you can make a day festive! And what radiation goes out from you. I do not get used to it and am experiencing it always anew. Thank you for it all.

And your invitation. . . .

The invitation was, it seems, to spend some time in Campobello, where she planned to be in August. It was a milestone in her relationship with David. A long diary note that I wrote in Hyde Park, May 21, a Sunday, dwelt on her ceaseless activity. Campobello was a respite from the outside world:

Mrs. R. didn't get here until 11:30 yesterday & there were 18 people for lunch—this is sort of thing that drives Tommy frantic & is real reason why Mrs. R. looks so exhausted. She has had very little time in the country this spring, particularly with the broadcasts on Sunday compelling her to leave at noon. But when I said to her that she had a right now to pick her spots & only do the things she liked to do she answered that nothing she did bored her. But she must be pretty tired as she called Anna in L.A. to find out whether she had to fly out tonight for Buzz's wedding. She returns to be in Washington on Wed. Then to Boston for speeches & meeting of trustees of Brandeis U. & finally back to N.Y. Sat.

She had her contradictions, I said to myself, when she asserted that nothing bored her. How often she had taken the view that all was vanity, and that the work she did was in large measure to overcome the emptiness of life. I suspected it was Franklin's death that was changing her—she no longer had to fight him and pretend to herself it was his life she was leading, not her own. Or it might have been the new excitement of David's entry into her life. Whatever it was, she now admitted to herself what she had so often denied, that she enjoyed the things she did. My journal entry went on:

> Frankie is closer to her now than ever before & called in the evening & talked on the phone for half an hour. Ethel didn't like Mrs. R. Frankie lives nearby. He respects his mother's judgment & he is worried about her. And he tells her all that is going on with him. Elliott was here for lunch with 6 friends. . . .
>
> In the evening there were just the four of us. Mrs. R. had agreed to go to a meeting of the local Dem. finance committee but when Trude & I showed no pleasure in it, was glad to have an excuse for begging off with a contribution.
>
> She was glancing at Gunther's book afterwards.* Said Gunther was wrong in saying that President's lack of deference to authority was because his father had never exercised authority over him—having died when Franklin was quite young. She said President's father was a strict disciplinarian & very authoritative and the Pres. knew him as such.
>
> She had glanced at the section where Gunther repeats Olive Clapper's story that during WWI Pres. had played around with a society dame & Mrs. R. had offered him his freedom, but old Mrs. R. had stepped in & stopped it. She hooted & said old Mrs. R. would never have been willing to admit such a thing existed & gotten herself to talk about it.†
>
> I asked about Pres.'s attachment to royalty during the war. Partly it was for political reasons, she said. Even Otto [Hapsburg of Austria] he said he couldn't be sure would not be useful after the war. Partly it gave him satisfaction to be able to patronize them & to put them at ease. Partly it was because they possessed power other people didn't. She said

---

* John Gunther's *Roosevelt in Retrospect* appeared in 1950.

† But Sara did talk about it to Eleanor's "Auntie Corinne," Mrs. Douglas Robinson. Insofar as we know what really went on, the vital confrontations were between Eleanor and her husband. Her daughter Anna said her mother's rebellion against Sara was so violent that she was unwilling to credit her with a role in the crisis.

Uncle Ted had the same ability: very democratic, loved the applause of the masses of people, very derisive of the pomp & foibles of royalty. At the same time he liked their company. He liked writing them letters. The President was the same.

The big event late that spring was Eleanor's trip to Norway at its invitation for the unveiling of a statue to F.D.R. In addition to Elliott and two of his children, Chandler and Tony, Tommy went.

It was Eleanor who wrote Ruth, Elliott's former wife, for permission.

[E.R. to Ruth:]   [April (?) 1950]

It seems to me that this would be a very interesting occasion for the children, and while I realize you may not wish to have them fly, it is the only way I can make it, and probably the way in which they would miss only a few days of school. . . . I think it is an experience they would remember in future life.

"This is my last night here," she wrote Anna from Hyde Park, "& I hate to go especially as my little dogs go to the kennel for the weekend & I feel sorry for them! I know the trip will be wonderful & once off I'll be interested but just now I'd like to stay home." A letter to Trude and me from Norway.

Skangina
Asker

[E.R. to Trude and Joseph P. Lash:]   Sunday June 4th 1950

It is hard to think that only two nights ago I said goodbye to you both! I don't like saying goodbye. I love you both & I like you to feel near & I hate to miss you at Hyde Park this month. Do have a good time.

The trip was smooth but not restful but we've been quiet today. Just lunched with the King & all are so kind that one feels comfortable. Being Sunday the roads were filled with bicycles, people going to the beaches with small children strapped on a seat behind. The houses are lovely & this house has a beautiful view, not unlike the coast around Campobello. The Germans were vandals but there is no damage from bombing to be seen here to any great extent & some building goes on but not enough they tell me.

The people look well & happy but Olaf says the occupation has made them understand the values of their democratic freedoms & cherish them.

Tomorrow a busy day so goodnight to you both & my love—

E.R.

Skangina
Asker
Sunday night June 4

David dear,

I cannot realize I was saying goodbye to you—and how I hated to do it —only yesterday morning! Our trip was good but *not* restful! We were met in Prestwick by the Provost, gold chain and all and a welcoming committee with flowers at 6 A.M.! Here, Olaf and Martha met us and seemed really glad to see us. [words indecipherable] but after lunch with the King and a walk around his garden we returned and had about 2 and a half hrs to write a column and rest so I am now rested! These homes and grounds are charming but not too grand and the view from this house is lovely and reminds me very much of Campobello. The King told me that he felt basically the USSR trouble lay in the fact that they were not Christians. Olaf follows our politics closely and is proud of the fact that he predicted to an American friend before the last election that Truman would win!

Tomorrow I have a press conference and make my speech. Josh White is coming in to sing after the Embassy dinner so that should help him as he will meet the Crown Prince and Princess.

Astrid and Chandler and Tony seem to get on well and the children are enjoying it. . . .

E.R.

American Embassy
Oslo
Tuesday June 6th

Dearest David,

The first big speech is over and seemed to go very well. I spoke from the balcony of the Lower Hall and many thousand people were in the square below and stood for over an hour and it was broadcast. There was applause and the car was mobbed afterwards for blocks. The Ambassador is happy. Now there are the ceremonies tomorrow where I must speak again and if the weather is good there will be a crowd. Tonight I spoke at 6 and work ends at 4 so all could come. It will be a bit earlier tomorrow— I hope it is a good job—

Elliott and the children seem to be enjoying it too. I hope the word comes tonight or tomorrow on his business and on James' primary—

. . . I'll finish tomorrow. Goodnight it is good to talk with you even on paper for a few minutes.

June 7

A great day here for 5 years ago the King and Crown Princess returned! The ceremonies are . . . and were short and dignified and the statue from the F. . . . . makes a good effect. It is seated and gives an appearance of strength and is done in granite. I spoke briefly and now find I must speak again tonight at a dinner given by the city in the new Town Hall. There is a reception this afternoon so this is a long day. I've just been to a crippled childrens home—many spastics muscular distrophy and few polio. I don't get the impression of as good care as kids would get at home. I must go and do the column.

What are you doing I wonder, may you have a happy weekend with Grania. My love to her and to you as

Always,

E.R.

There were more letters from Sweden.

June 10th

Dearest Trude & Joe,

We leave Sweden tomorrow for Finnish Lapland. . . . I've had some interesting talks with Ministers in power & opposition people in the parliament. The one unanimous feeling is fear & small wonder. . . .

. . .

All goes well & this Embassy too seems happy about the visit. Finnland [sic] is most ticklish so pray for me. From Holland on I'll relax.

Hope all is well at H.P. James won but none too decisively I fear. . . .

E.R.

Saturday June 10th

David dear,

The Swedish visit is nearly over. We leave for Finnish Lapland in the Embassy plane at noon tomorrow if weather is good.

Here all seems to have gone as well as in Norway. The King and I got on well and I like all the government officials. The women for whom I came to speak, my own Embassy people all seem happy and pleased about my visit. . . .

. . .

It seems to me that people are frightened over here and small wonder, but in Norway and here fundamentally they want the same things that we want. I've had some interesting talks with men in the government and will tell you about them when I get home.

Josh White is drinking, but gave a good concert last night, I'm told. I think I will have to be severe in Denmark when we meet again.

It was good to get your note written last Monday and to know you felt well and were thinking of us. . . .

Devotedly,
E.R.

"How do you feel about Jimmy's victory [in the California Democratic primary]?" she asked Anna the same day. "From the news bulletins it looks as though Warren must have polled a good many democratic votes which makes the next campaign [the November election] pretty tough. . . ."

Hick still was on the list of people to whom she wrote in longhand, although there were only three letters in 1950. "Here we are slowly progressing!" she wrote from Helsinki. "We haven't been gone two weeks & I feel we've been away for years because every moment has been packed with activity."

June 17
Copenhagen

David dear,

Your letter of the 12th was here on our arrival yesterday and I am glad that you had a quiet and pleasant weekend and this week you'll be with Grania. I'm happy too that she and Nemone are both well.

  . . .

This rapid trip leaves me most physically impressed with Finland! I'm astonished at the calm and cheerful desperation with which most of these people live. The Prime Minister asked to talk to me alone here and made a moving plea. I explained that I was a private citizen with no authority but agreed to tell the Secretary and the President his views but as coming from a collective group rather than from him alone! Have you heard the whole of the Danish scientist, Niels Bohr's letter to the U.N.? I'll bring home a copy in case our papers only print excerpts.

Last night we dined with the Magidoffs at the Montebello Sanitarium *[sic]* before going to see Hamlet.* It was really well acted by a company from the "Old Vic" and the setting was beautiful in the courtyard of the old Castle. I am fond of Nila Magidoff but I'm afraid what the doctor there said to me about her is true "Her soul is wrapped up in Mother Russia." That doesn't lead to much content.

Tommy was ill all last night and has looked badly all day. I fear I should not bring her on these trips. She never eats what she should and

---

* Nila Magidoff had spoken in the United States for Russian War Relief. A sparkling raconteur whose English was engagingly studded with Russianisms, she attracted Mrs. Roosevelt. Her first husband had died during Stalin's purges and she was married to Robert Magidoff, a Russian-born correspondent for NBC stationed in Moscow. In 1948 he was expelled for alleged spying activity. His arrest and charges, he said, were part of an "internal propaganda" campaign.

she gets worn out. I should probably stay at home like a well behaved old lady!

I am taking very good care of myself and am quite well, only I fear I shall get home too fat!

Are you eating regularly and sleeping well and am I going to see you soon after I get home? You are much in my thoughts and this takes you all my love.

E.R.

She began to formulate the thoughts she intended to pass on to President Truman and Secretary Acheson. From Copenhagen she wrote:

June 18th [1950]

Trude dearest,

I was glad to hear about the dogs & that your first weekend [at H.P.] was nice. When I get home you & Joe will be interested to hear about talks [word indecipherable] I have had here with the Prime Minister, a labor man social democrat & Professor Niels Bohr* who is coming this evening again. I want your advice & David's on European points of view & aspects but especially I want Joe's on our own situation in relation to all these. My feeling everywhere so far that people were valiantly living with fear is keener here but they have talked more openly here to me in high places. By the time I come back I'll have my thoughts pretty well sorted out but I want to talk to Joe before I go to Washington. Of course there is no complete unanimity here as to what course should be followed any more than at home but fear is unanimous! I have to spend my time explaining that I hold no position in government & have no influence!

Tommy is not really well. . . .

My love to you all & I hope Jonathan & the little Roosevelts have fun.

Devotedly
E.R.

Her next stop was Holland.

June 20th [1950]

Joe dearest,

. . .

We had a few nice hours in Amsterdam yesterday & I spent the night here. The others just had a drink & went on to the Hague. Today looks like rain but after I've had a talk with Princess Wilhelmina who is com-

---

* Eminent Danish physicist, Nobel Prize winner and a key figure on the losing side in efforts to bring about the international control of the A-bomb. His plan and views continued to enlist Mrs. Roosevelt's sympathies.

ing here at 9:30 I had a long talk with Juliana last night. At least in high places they seem less worried here & very pleased over the progress of integrating European interests.

Prince Bernhardt is charming but nice but I gather escapes at rather frequent intervals!

. . .

Devotedly
E.R.

Wherever they traveled, the crowds adored her. Would she have missed them if they did not turn out? She believed not and always protested the "fuss" she occasioned.

Rey Haag
June 21st

Dearest David,

I meant to tell you that I went to a most interesting Infantile Paralysis Institute in Copenhagen. . . .

I know one thing, I wouldn't put a man through what our Ambassadress' husband is going through!* I was uncomfortable for him all the time and I couldn't see how she could stand it for him or for his children.

This travel with me is pretty awful! We went to the island of Shoba today and practically the whole important Embassy Staff met us there and they had the whole little town out and all the Roosevelts from the area! I was interested in spite of the crowds but it was bad for all the others. I hope Paris is big enough to be lost for 4 days and the same I hope for in London. Anyway I've made no plans so Elliott and the kids will be free! Tommy frightened me by an attack which I hope was indigestion. She is better but she looks badly and I shall be glad to get her home.

I have got some side lights on European feelings on the trip that I want to ask you about for I can't tell whether I am right or wrong.

. . .

E.R.

I am as usual in good health! I attribute it to all your pills which I take regularly!

There was a fragment of a letter she sent him from Paris on a Crillon letterhead.

---

* Mrs. Eugenie Anderson of Minnesota, a supporter of Senator Hubert Humphrey and a staunch liberal in her own right, was the U.S. Ambassador to Denmark.

Sunday night

Back in Paris and more troubled about these meetings and yet there is a striving and idealism that has much good. I saw Bernhardt and he is troubled and so is the Lady-in-Waiting. It is mixed with a woman who has gained great influence over the Queen & predicts that the little blind daughter will be healed *if* the Queen has faith!*

Write to me how you are and believe that my thoughts and my love go to you.

E.R.

Paris is lovely and we had a good day, driving to Rheims, seeing the Cathedral, lunching with a lovely view before us, and good food. Then a stop to see the Monument at Château Thierry and have a bath after six. Dinner with Averell Harriman and some interesting talk.

I think Luxembourg is one of the loveliest corners of Europe, at our drive through the mountain countryside at least. We had a nice time but a little too advertised by Mme. Mesta. She was sent to us and I liked her and I don't like her. I suppose what I feel is that she might not always be nice!

There really was no incident with the King in Copenhagen, it was newspaper stuff! He didn't like what I wrote but he sent me a letter and his relations were most polite!†

I'm glad the weekend with Grania was so happy and sorry the problem with Nemone grows no lighter. I know it must be decided and I hope for the best and I don't want you to be hurt. I saw the Baroness de Bad in Brussels and she spoke of you.

My love to you. I do long to see you.

Devotedly,
E.R.

Her thoughts about what she had heard in the northern countries of Europe she crisply summed up for Anna.

---

* Although it was Prince Bernhardt who brought faith healer Greet Hofmans to Queen Juliana's attention in the hope she might cure Princess Maria Christina, who had been born partly blind in 1947, he now felt she exercised undue influence over the Queen. Miss Hofmans blamed the Prince's lack of faith for her failure in Maria Christina's case.

† King Frederick was not present when she was the honored luncheon guest at Christianbrook Castle. Newspapers hinted it was pique over Mrs. Roosevelt's critical references in her autobiography to his seeming unawareness of the worsening European situation when, as Crown Prince, he had visited Hyde Park in 1939. The King's heir apparent, Prince Knud, was at the luncheon, as was Niels Bohr, and Foreign Minister Rasmussen hailed her as "the American Queen of Democracy."

Hotel de Crillon
June 23d, 1950

Anna darling,

. . . I hope Buzz & Robin keep their feet on the ground but it isn't
easy you know when people try to use you & flatter you. . . .

Primarily all Europeans are afraid of Russia then secondarily they are
not sure of us. The two fears have "nuances"; Norway & Finland seem to
me to have the best spirit; Sweden & Denmark less secure. All countries
seem to be recovering very well & the contrast in the countries I saw two
or three years ago & now is enormous. Some countries may not be ready
to give up all aid in 1952 but some may & all will be far on their way to
be again on a competitive basis.

. . .

Mother

She wrote much the same to Trude that day, her letter ending, "Ten days & I
will be with you I hope."

A major event occurred: North Korea invaded the South, and the United
States rallied the United Nations to resist.

June 25th [1950]

David dear,

How I wish you were here! We had a lovely day yesterday and an even
lovelier one today and it would have been perfect if you had been with
us. All the glass is back in the Ste. Chapelle and it is a gem as always. We
dined at "Porquerelles" with champagne as usual on the house. We
lunched at Versailles and were shown rooms I've never seen before and
the clocks were played for us which delighted the children. We saw the
gardens in detail and I fell in love with the little cascade in the woods.
We saw the Petit Trianon too so it was a good day and cool and rainy
when we were indoors and blue sky and sunny as the fountains played!
Could the weather be kinder?

I finished Gunther's book on Franklin and the second part on the war
years is much better than the first. He knew something about it and he
had met Franklin so he is surer in his deductions.

The news today that Northern Korea has declared war on Southern
Korea might be serious and I am worried about it. Also the fall of the
government will just now sound very unfortunate.

. . .

This really says I just miss you and takes you my devoted love,

E.R.

A note from London to Trude, whose letter, she wrote, "brought me the news I really wanted. . . . The Korean situation is bad but I think we have done all we could do, at least that is how it looks here."

David envied her her stay in Paris. His thoughts would be with her when she flew over the Atlantic, but he would not be there to greet her on arrival. It was the long July 4 weekend and he was due in Wellfleet, but he would be in town the day after she arrived.

She was not much in Hyde Park that July. On Esther Lape's urging she had agreed in a letter from Oslo to speak at the Democratic convention in Connecticut. "Of course I realize that you cannot go around making Democratic State Convention speeches in every state," Esther wrote her, "or even in a few states. . . . I recall that when you and I were talking in your apartment in New York a few weeks ago, you, in deploring the small amount of available leadership, spoke hopefully of Bowles."

Cousin Susie died that summer. "I think from her point of view it was a blessed release," Eleanor wrote, and she was left the job of clearing out the house. She went down to Washington to give the President and Secretary Acheson her impressions of the European view of our policy. At Tanglewood she did the voice part in *Peter and the Wolf* for Serge Koussevitsky. She pressed David to join her in August for a rest at Campobello. She thought she had succeeded and reserved seats on the plane to Bangor for August 15, to return on either September 1 or 5. David begged off, saying he had to take his holiday on his own on Cape Cod. A letter from Eleanor dated only "Monday night" sought to explain her position.

> David dear,
>
>   I've wanted to talk to you but kept to my resolve not to pressure you! I think I should tell you why I wanted you so much to go to Campo and spend your 3 weeks with us. I've never felt sure that you enjoyed being with me enough so you would be willing to relax and be without other people and not be bored and when you accepted another offer with such alacrity I realized I had been right not to be sure and even though I saw your reasons were right and your instinct probably correct, I couldn't help being a little sad for as one gets older the joy of real companionableness is rarer and rarer especially with the young and one cares for fewer and fewer people. Most people are an effort and the hope of finding a mutual pleasure in enjoying any extended, quiet time together is not a hope often entertained. Then too I was not and am not sure that what you are doing will give you comfort and rest and no worry but I do hope so now with all my heart for I want you to be well and happy and return to the work you love fully refreshed.

There was nothing else on this letter as it was found in David's papers. She wrote him again on Park Sheraton letterhead, and of this letter too a page (or pages) is missing.

. . .

I used to love Campobello, the air, the woods and sea and sunsets, but people matter to me more than places. It would have been fun to show it to you and hope that it would give you some of the lift it used to give me. Tommy will enjoy it and I will try to give her a good time but our contacts are best in the field of work and not much good otherwise tho' we love each other dearly! She likes to play cards in the evening and I find it dull but perhaps little David [Roosevelt] will take my place and it won't hurt me if I have to play! I'll decide with Elliott on what needs to be done and get contracts and Elliott and David will leave us and I think we'll start home with Linaka on the 24th for nowadays unless I have someone I really want to be with up there it is not a good place to be. There are good and bad memories there but the bad get the better of me when I'm there alone. I'll read a lot and practice typing and the lamps aren't too good for night reading and there the night has a thousand eyes. So I'll be home the 25th or 26th.

God bless you! and my love to you

E.R.

She wrote him two letters from Campobello. The first was undated.

David dearest,

Your letter distresses me. I hate to think of you with a sore throat and a temperature sitting on an open porch at night. It does not sound to me like the right kind of care. Please take care of yourself and get all the rest and health and pleasure out of your vacation that you can. Of course if you say that my conclusions were not correct I will believe you probably because I want to hope you may someday be willing to try resting with me!

We drove in yesterday and the air had the tang of the sea and it was cool, but the fog has blown in and while it does not bother me I should be worried for you were you here. David and Scoop are blissful and have played Indians all day. It is the right terrain for that with pines all about and thick undergrowth all through the woods. Your Grania would love it for it is imaginative country.

Elliott and I have gone all over the house and the point we own on the other side of the island on the Bay of Fundy. If we put it in order he will try to use it for 6 weeks in summer, and I should do the same but I will not unless it can be really useful and give pleasure to some of those I love, so I don't live only on old memories here but build some new ones.

Elliott and the children leave Sunday morning and Tommy and I stay till Thursday morning and will be at Hyde Park Friday night of next week if all goes well. Tommy has not touched the typewriter today and I hope to improve daily.

Do you know yet whether Grania wants to spend your last week alone with you or whether you may come to Hyde Park? . . .

Devotedly,
E.R.

Aug. 20th

David dearest,

My typewritten letters still seem very impersonal to me and I know you are not happy and I am worried for fear you are not yet well and I would like to be near you and this scrawl is all I can do and it will take six days or more to reach you! If I knew your address I'd write to know how you are but I wouldn't ask because I thought you wanted not to be bothered and that you would give it to me if you wanted to write. Somehow I never thought you would be ill. I just thought of you as wanting to be free of all but new ties for a time. . . .

I've nearly finished half of the manuscript [F.D.R. *Letters]* Joe [Lash] and Elliott wanted me to read and it will be done in another two days. I find it interesting and hope it will have some success. The Korean news today sounded more encouraging. I hope it is good enough so all of us are willing to let the small nations try to mediate! War seems so senseless. At this remote distance I feel nothing could be worth even a quarrel.

You may not be able to read this but I feel closer to you and I hope it will give you too a little sense of nearness. I love you dearly David but try to remember to tell me that *you* want to be loved by me now and then because I don't want to be a duty or a bother!

Take care of yourself and rest and enjoy yourself dear. . . .

E.R.

A long letter to Anna explained among other matters why she was using the typewriter.

[E.R. to Anna Boettiger:]   [August 21, 1950]

My trembling is only bad in writing, it does not bother me in typing at all. Might not be so harmful as far as legibility goes if I had not written so carelessly for years so that I run all my words together. It is emotional in part at least for I notice if I am upset about something that is the way it shows up. Nevertheless I type so slowly that it is going to be hard to make it a habit as nothing seems important enough to put on paper this way, and I leave words out constantly because my thoughts outrun my fingers. . . .

Jimmy is discouraged I think. . . . It will be hard for any democrat to win this year, because of Korea. [Secretary of Defense] Louis Johnson, [General Douglas] MacArthur, and [Senator Joseph] McCarthy have won this campaign I fear for the Republicans. He insists that I come out to speak for him and for Helen [Gahagan Douglas], which seems a mistake to me but I have agreed to go on Sunday evening Sept. 10th to Los Angeles. . . .

. . . That business [cleaning out Cousin Susie's house] I hope to finish the week after I get back from here as far as taking out things goes, as the tax people from the government should be through. . . .

Back in Hyde Park she typed a long letter to David.

August 28th [1950]

Dearest David,

I have just read your letter of last Monday and talked to you on the telephone and I feel so happy to know that you are well and getting a real rest in a place you really enjoy. Do give Grania as much time with you and your friends as you can stay for once you come back you will plunge in to work and Nemone will arrive, and major decisions will have to be made, and Grania will have to start school and you will not be free to rest again for a while at least.

. . . There will always be room for you when you are back if you want to come up at any time and for Grania.

. . .

This little typewriter of mine is not very good and I apologize for the many mistakes.

[handwritten] My love to you, keep well and happy.

E.R.

Another long letter to David just before the Labor Day weekend. She liked his lecturing her to slow down even if she ignored his advice.

Sept. 1st [1950]

David dearest,

Your letter of the 30th came today which was a short time compared with the time it took in Campo and it does make you seem a bit nearer which I like.

. . .

You are right and both James and Helen would both rather have me later, but unfortunately I will be on the U.N. so I had to go now or not at all. I agree with you that trips like this are idiotic at my age, but six months ago I agreed to speak at a Kiwanis Club lunch here in N.Y. on the 13th. There is still work to be done in N.Y. at the Parish house and the evening of the 17th I come down to be ready for the General Assembly opening on the 19th. I just hope that when you do leave the Cape (and don't leave till you have to) that you will have a week and that you want to spend here or that you may be free some evening when I'm in town for dinner. Somehow this vacation must have clarified many things for you, and I would like to hear the result of all the thinking you have been able to do. I love you very much David dear, and I wish you were near to talk to now and then.

I am using my own little typewriter now that I took on the trip to the Pacific. It is so old that it does many queer things but I think I will soon learn to use it better.

. . .

I took all the little boys to see the Dutchess County Fair this morning and they enjoyed it and I saw a young pig we have bought to breed to the sows I got last spring.

The Sandifers come tomorrow from Washington and he brings me my first dose of position papers to digest, before I go to Washington for the briefing sessions[.] I'll take a late plane down to Washington so as not to leave here till about six P.M. & I'll get back on Friday in time for dinner I hope. . . .

I have just received almost as much galley proof [the F.D.R. *Letters]* as I read in Campo and I wonder how I am to find time to read it, but it is fascinating reading and I think on your winter vacation you will enjoy it.

Goodnight dear, God bless you, take good care of yourself.

[handwritten] My thoughts and love are with you,

E.R.

Trude and I were at Hyde Park the weekend that she had for Sunday dinner Ernest Bevin, the British Foreign Secretary, and Robert Schuman, the former French Premier and leader of the French delegation to the General Assembly. A diary note, September 25:

. . . A matter of protocol. Who should sit on Mrs. R's right, Bevin or Schuman, a former premier? Tommy called the State Dept. Answer came at 1:45—Mrs. R. had been right to give precedence to Bevin. . . .

Mrs. R. amusing on her birthday plans—one weekend ruled out because she can't have people she wants—another ruled out because she'll have people there she doesn't want.

Elliott's [Polish] Countess at his birthday party. George [Wenzel] saw her in Salzburg—a gay flyer.

Fjr and Sue went downstairs with Mrs. R. and picked from Mrs. Parish's silver, the best, I thought, in the lot. Elliott wouldn't go down at the same time. Insisted his mother go down with him later.

There was no birthday celebration. I sent her a note wishing her many happy years and received one in return.

[E.R. to Joseph P. Lash:]   [October 13, 1950]
I love you both & hate not seeing you more often. Perhaps you could both lunch with me next Tuesday. I don't think I'll have to go to the U.N. & I could meet you anywhere you both would like to go & find convenient.

She had little time for writing letters, she explained to Anna.

October 21, 1950
Anna darling,
I've been very bad about writing because I work night and day while the U.N. is on. I thrive on it, and get fun out of working with Elliott on the radio show. We do the whole thing now on recordings at night, but I will do some live once the U.N. is over. . . .

. . .

John Golden gave me the smallest and lightest typewriter for my birthday and I am just learning to use it and I think I am going to like it very much.

. . .

We lost our battle for a good permanent plan on the children's fund, but I still hope we may improve it in the plenary. Now we are on the covenant of Human Rights.

. . .

Mother

On October 31 she heard the dreadful news that John Boettiger, who had been working with a public relations firm and living in the Hotel Weylin in New York, had committed suicide by plunging from a seventh-floor window. He had been watched by a male nurse because his physician had sensed his determination to do away with himself and thought he had persuaded John to enter a psychiatric hospital. It was Elliott who was called by the police to identify the body at the morgue and who told his mother. She fell silent on hearing the news and only broke her silence to ask herself out loud, "Is there nothing I might have done to help poor John? What dreadful things can happen when people *fail* each other. I did try to offer him friendship, but what *good* did it do?" It was she who conveyed the news to Anna, telephoning her.

A diary note just before election, November 6, 1950:

At dinner last night at Park Sheraton—Mrs. R., Tommy, Doris Fleeson [newspaper columnist and friend of Mrs. R. from early New Deal years], Nemone and David, Henry Morgenthau III. At drinks in her rooms before going down to restaurant, Trude spoke rather caustically of Elliott's coming out for "Impy" [Vincent Impelliteri, who won an unexpected victory for mayor of New York against the organization candidate, Ferdinand Pecora]. There was nothing to the man and what did Elliott know about him? . . . . Mrs. R. made it clear that she was avoiding the mayoralty because she felt let down by O'Dwyer and was not going to make an endorsement in the future unless she had personal reason to believe in the character of the man.

I don't remember how it came up unless in reaction to my report on Drew Pearson's election predictions including victory for Helen [Gahagan Douglas] in Calif. but Mrs. R. suddenly stated with very great feeling that she had almost resigned from the UN a couple of days ago because of Truman's endorsement of Helen without an accompanying endorsement of Jimmy. She also was resentful that in his UN speech Truman had made no mention of FDR. But it was the Jimmy matter particularly that evoked the deep feeling. And she went on to say she would not accept reappointment to the UN. Edith Sampson [alternate delegate] was perfectly capable of handling the job. Everyone was stunned by her depth of feeling. Finally I said the UN matter and the California race were not related and that she was not a delegate to the UN as a favor to the President. Trude and Doris chimed in, "why punish us because of what the President did in California?" . . . I was considerably shaken. Mrs. R. does not separate her feelings for her children and her role as a public servant. Why should the Presidential prestige be committed in a gubernatorial race that seems almost hopeless? Helen can win and the question to the President was formulated in such a way as to help Helen and do the least possible hurt to Jimmy. Would it have been better for the President to have kept quiet? After all, Jimmy like many of us did support Eisenhower in '48 and Jimmy was the last holdout against Truman at the convention. . . .

What distresses me is that Mrs. R's work in the UN and her importance right now as a leader of liberalism in the US and the world should be so dependent on Truman's attitude toward the political fortunes of her children.

She did not go through with her threat to resign, but her loyalty to her children and her friends, and to her basic values, made her a unique figure in public life. Only rarely did they come into conflict.

> The Park Sheraton Hotel
> New York, N.Y.
> Wed. Nov 8th

Dear James & Romaine,

Just a line to tell you that I know what a let down you must feel after all the hard work for I remember how Father felt in 1920. Just check it up to experience, take a rest & then resume your normal lives! You had tremendous odds against you & Truman didn't help. If you had worked as a team in California you would all have done better.

I wish I could give you a hug! Tommy & Elliott & I have been talking about you a lot. I wish it were easier to *see* you!

Love to Romaine & the kids & a world of love to you.

> Mother

"Tommy is fine & seems very well & Hick has moved in at H.P. for her winter writing effort!" she wrote Anna. That exclamation point at the end of her reference to Hick spoke volumes. She continued to be helpful to Hick, but Hick's moving in at Hyde Park, as she had at the White House, was not as welcome as once it had been.

XVI

Playing with Fire

ALL ELEANOR'S LIFE she had fought loneliness. First there was the death of her parents, especially her father. Then there was the discovery of Franklin's inability to lead a life of shared intimacy, capped by his love for Lucy. And yet when Franklin died the pangs of loneliness became even sharper. She dreaded the return to Hyde Park, and only Elliott's decision to settle there made it possible for her to continue to live there. As disappointment grew with Elliott, she realized afresh how much Tommy meant to her. Her increasing resort to the portable typewriter she had taken with her to the South Pacific was meant to ease the burden on Tommy, who, alas, was beginning to fail. Tommy and the two scotties, elderly Fala and Tamas, were her sure standbys when she returned to Hyde Park.

To a writer who wanted to do a book about Fala, she wrote after the end of the 1950 General Assembly:

Fala is still living, he is eleven years old but extremely frisky. Just yesterday he ran away and was gone with his grandson for five hours. He has lived with me since my husband's death. For a while after that he used to lie in the doorway where he could watch all the doors, just as he did when my husband used to come over to this cottage to make sure he was not left behind.

I have always made it a practice to take him over to the big house and grave when there was any ceremony. If he heard the sirens he would stand stiffly on his four legs, with his ears up, knowing I am sure, that this had something to do with him and his master.

Fala is still very dignified and while he is happy here with me, I do not think he has ever accepted me as the one person whom he loved as he did my husband.

Whatever Fala's feelings for his dead master, he gave Eleanor relaxation and companionship, and the scottie's bonds with Franklin made him more precious to her. People were so contradictory, she sometimes said.

"I thought of you on Father's birthday," Anna wrote her on February 13, 1951, "and wondered if you wouldn't be going over to the grave, so it was good to know from you what you actually did that day and some of your thoughts."

Before flying to Geneva for a meeting of the Human Rights Commission she attended a concert at the Labor Temple in New York City where Nemone Balfour played and sang. Nemone, a tall handsome woman whose bearing and diction bespoke her wellborn English forebears, used her maiden name professionally. Mrs. R. was doing her best to bolster David's wife. Although she knew David was thinking of a divorce, she felt he wanted her to help Nemone. Moreover, that was her way with people. There may have been an added element. David, free of his marriage tie, might fall in love with someone who would exclude her. The endless discussions with him of his dilemmas of the heart, on which she thrived, might be ended, particularly if he should fall in love with some glamorous but essentially possessive woman. To share sympathetically in David's analyses of his difficulties with Nemone was a state not altogether unpleasant to the altruist in love.

The spring meeting in Geneva of the Human Rights Commission was scheduled to work on two covenants intended to give the force of law to the rights spelled out in the Declaration. She worked on them loyally, knowing, however, that the United States was unlikely to ratify them when adopted.

> Hotel des Bergues
> Geneva
> April 15th, 1951

Darling Anna,

Here we are safely settled in lovely rooms that face the lake & the snow capped mountains. Flowers bloom here but just a little way up in the hills the snow still lies on the ground. It is cold at night but the sun shone today & it felt warm.

Last night in London it was cold! We dined with Lady Reading & I did 2 1/2 hours of radio interviews in the afternoon. . . .

I think Tommy will be happy here, nearly everyone speaks English. We will take her to our office tomorrow & install her with girls who can translate so the work shouldn't be too hard. . . .

We are three weeks ahead on all the radio programmes & Elliott will be here about the 26th to do more. . . .

I wonder if you will see McArthur's *[sic]* reception?* The President did the only thing he could do I think but it is going to be stormy for a while. I don't know how long the other republican presidential aspirants will like McArthur however!

All my love to you & Johnnie
Mother

Letters to Hick and to Trude and me covered the same ground. She hoped that all was going well with Hick's initial writing projects and wanted all the news about Hyde Park. "The work hours are long for me," she wrote Trude and me—

[E.R. to the Lashes:]   [April 18, 1951]
  The difficulties of the work become more apparent every day. One feels far removed from the outer world & its troubles & all seems so peaceful & quiet that it does not seem so odd to stew over relatively distant questions in a covenant of Human Rights! I think of Joe & his immediate excitements & wonder if any of the people who bicycle past me on the street know about McArthur & the U.S. South!

"Yours was the first letter to come from home," she wrote Trude the next day, "& it told me what I most wanted to know. . . . The paper here says that McArthur's reception in San Francisco was colossal. . . . This whole day we are arguing procedure!" I wrote her about life at the UN, which I was covering for the New York *Post,* and she began a reply which, after a few introductory sentences, she put aside for several days.

[E.R. to Joseph P. Lash:]   [April 22, 1951]
  Continued in London April 22nd. There I stopped & since the 19th I have had no time for letter writing. I started to say the Swiss paper gave the gist of McArthur's speech & made the last a bit too dramatic as I surmised it was. Were you there?
  I took the Friday night train from Geneva & got to Paris early Sat. a.m. & had breakfast, lunch, tea & dinner with the Hendricks. . . . From 10–1 I worked on the film show, some outside silent shots & the interview with Schuman. It was five minutes & took over an hour to film! I got off for an hour & went & ordered a dress & a blouse. Jessup came to lunch & seems to take his interminable task calmly. From 3–6:15 we filmed Monnet & later Jessup. It was quite a performance & I wouldn't care to do it every week! Henry III [he produced the show] & I took the 10 p.m. plane & arrived in London at 11:40 p.m. This morning we did what I think, is a good kinescope show here. We were there from 11–1,

* The President had relieved General Douglas MacArthur for insubordination, and he had returned to the United States to what proved to be a short-lived triumphal tour.

then Henry & I went to a little restaurant in Soho. . . . I do an interview on the T.V. live from over here as a return for the use of their facilities. That is on from 8:15–8:30. Then I go dine with Arthur Murray,* now Lord Elibank & tomorrow at 11 back to Geneva so I'll miss one session.

Later. Of course here there is relief over McArthur's recall as you expect & will gather from the television interviews with Michael Foote & Brown, members of Parliament. I have just come back from a talk after dinner with Arthur Murray & shall dictate a memo on it & send you.

From Geneva, a note of commiseration to Hick, who was getting editors' rejections, preceded a letter to Trude, who had written her about MacArthur's reception.

[E.R. to Trude W. Lash:]   [May 2, 1952]
I love your list of McArthur's 3 first visits. I hope people will wake up & think they will but I wish the President was a better leader! Elliott's been making me state my ideas on him on radio & television so I told him he'd have to build me a bomb shelter to retire to when I get home. . . .

"Trude wrote me," she reported to Anna in the course of wishing her well on her birthday, "his [MacArthur's] first 3 calls in N.Y. were on the D.A.R., Herbert Hoover & Cardinal Spellman! Here feeling, as in England & France, is strong against widening the area of the [Korean] war. . . ."
A letter to David said that Elliott and his new wife, Minnewa Bell Ross, a friend of Johnny Roosevelt's and a woman of considerable charm and wealth, had come to Europe, Elliott to work with his mother on the television shows.

Hotel de Crillon
Paris
May 4, 1951

David dearest,
Here we are back in Paris for 2 nights and I have the stiffest and most enormous "salon" as a gift! My only consolation is that it faces the Place and tomorrow night we can watch the waters and it will all be lit up! We flew up from Geneva & it was lovely and clear.
We heard today that the film I spent so many hours over here with Schuman and Monnet is too poor to use as a whole. Elliott's trying to get them to use the BBC one this Sunday and then he'll see what he can

* A pillar of the Liberal Party, he had been private secretary to Sir Edward Grey, 1910–14. As assistant military attaché in Washington during the last year of World War I he became the friend of both F.D.R. and E.R. He often conveyed F.D.R.'s messages to Prime Minister Neville Chamberlain. He lost his seat in the House of Commons in 1923.

salvage of the French one. They leave Sunday and get home Monday morning. I think that we will do something on the Covenant and that it will be fairly good.

This is just a note to enclose Marty's letter to me which you will like to see. I told her not to bring too much furniture as I could only stay a few days at best and there would be many things I'd have to consider before I really took off. Among others I must see if it can be done quietly!

The chestnut trees are all out, I wish you could see them. I'd like to feel you were about to walk in!

I'd probably embarrass you by greeting you much too warmly because I feel a little lonely for the moment without any reason. Too much grandeur I suppose and Elliott and Minnewa want me to go to Maxim's for dinner and I don't really want to go there!

My love to you dear, take care of yourself and tell me how you are. I hope you miss me a little and will be glad to have me back to bother you now and then.

Devotedly
E.R.

How like a person in love. In Paris, amid all the broadcasting chores and the famous, she thinks fondly of the hours she had spent there with David and her present loneliness and she ventures even to ask whether he could not get himself to say that he loved her at least a little, even as David sends her "Marty's letter." It was from Martha Gellhorn, divorced wife of Ernest Hemingway, a writer in her own right, blond, spirited, and good-looking, whom David had met and fallen in love with, as he evidently had confided to Eleanor. Martha was an old friend of hers—from the time in the early thirties when, a lively graduate of Bryn Mawr, she had done investigative stories for Harry Hopkins and come to the attention of Hick, who had introduced her to Eleanor. And soon Hick was telling her of Martha's love affairs and Eleanor was offering counsel. Eleanor had long known Martha's mother, a society presence in St. Louis, where, after work in the suffrage movement, she had run the League of Women Voters and was a standby of the Women's Division of the Democratic Party and on the right side, at least so Eleanor saw it, of the issues that counted.

Martha's books had achieved a modest renown, and when she confided to Mrs. R. her love for Ernest Hemingway, Eleanor encouraged the romance, offering her cottage as a hideaway. Martha had gone to Spain with Ernest and together with him and Joris Ivens had made a film that Eleanor had shown at the White House so Franklin might see it. Later she and Ernest had married. But after several years the marriage had ended and Martha, an attractive woman in a way Eleanor never was, suddenly became David's love in a way she never could hope to be. Long experience with Earl and me had taught Eleanor to channel her feelings into altruistic wishes for her beloveds. Marty was living in Mexico and, seconded by

David, she invited Eleanor to come for a visit. David replied to Eleanor's letter, saying he, too, wished he might walk under the chestnut trees and go to little restaurants.

[David Gurewitsch to E.R.]   [May 9, 1951]
    Thank you for Martha's letters. I feel a little shy reading the adjectives she puts behind my name but it would be wonderful if we could go down there together?! if you could spend even a few days. The trip is really very simple. One night,—or shall I stop playing with fire?! Grania and Nemone are going to sail on the 31st of May. I plan to go to Mexico for part of my vacation. . . .

"Dearest Joe," Eleanor wrote me—

[E.R. to Joseph P. Lash:]   [May 6, 1951]
    I started this in Paris & then my pen gave out so forgive the pencil. I enjoyed the last Hersey article* as I am interested in what is being done to the White House & he managed to show some interesting sidelights & odd bits of Truman knowledge.
    Elliott, Minnewa & I flew up on Friday p.m. & went to Maxim's as that is the dressy [place]. I found it dull extravagance! We worked all morning & p.m. yesterday on recordings but lunched with the Hendricks & had a most interesting dinner with Jean Monet *[sic]* & his family in the country. I'll send you a digest of his ideas for background as when you go to Paris you should try to see him.
    . . .
    From over here McArthur's testimony seems awful but I wait to hear from the Chiefs of Staff. It looks as tho' it might be a duel between McArthur & Marshall. I hope Marshall wins.
    We are going to have a covenant I think but I don't think the U.S. will ratify, though we can honestly fight for it I think.
                                                                    E.R.

David's romance with Martha was much on her mind, but she buried references to it in other news.

                                                        [No date]
                                                        Hotel des Bergues
                                                        Geneve Suisse
Dearest David,
    It was good to find your 2 letters on getting back from London today. I

---

* A five-part profile of President Truman by John Hersey appeared in *The New Yorker* beginning April 7, 1951.

had worried a little for fear you were not feeling well—Now I quite understand [,] playing with fire is rather exciting, isn't it? Joking aside it must have been a nice change and I hope all the "papers" go well. [Evidently an additional reason for David's flight to Mexico was to read some medical papers.] Sometimes I'd like to hear you give one. I'm sure you make the dryest subject sound interesting!

Geneva is beautiful in Spring and I'm enjoying it, the lake and the flowers and the mountains, how could one do other than drink in the beauty. The hours of work are long and it is every bit as frustrating as I expected and the U.S. Senate will never ratify but so far we've not accepted anything we can't honestly fight for.

. . .

I hope you gave my love to Martha. If she is depressed you will help her. It helps to talk out one's troubles to an understanding and sympathetic person.

. . .

E.R.

A few days later she had a note from him on how busy he was. It was bad to be overburdened, she replied, but "perhaps it is good for you to be busy just now!" Geneva was beautiful in the spring, and Eleanor especially loved the lakeside. "I'd like to walk leisurely along with you and talk of an evening! As it is I work!" She spoke of her plans to return and her hopes they might be able to lunch together. "I count on you *all* for the following weekend." She did not want to pry. "I love you dearly and want you to be happy David dear, you know that, don't you? I'll be glad to hear anything you want to tell me, but always you can count on my love and understanding."

There were letters to Trude and me before she left Geneva.

May 13th [1951]

Dearest Trude,

A letter from both you & Joe started my day off well. . . .

At five (by special request) I was called for & taken out to see the ex-Queen of Italy. She lives in a lovely old house that belonged to the Conte de Savoie & she spends her time at home writing a history of the policies of the Contes de Savoie. These ex-royalties seem to be pathetic!

Tommy & I just dined with the Lehman's who leave tomorrow. Senator Nixon has just arrived but I doubt if I see him!

. . .

Here in Switzerland war does not hang over one but many are anxious. I judge McArthur is fading as Marshall's testimony is read.

. . .

E.R.

May 14th [1951]

Dearest Joe,

A thousand thanks for your letter & the interesting enclosures. I don't see how the President ever gets a speech written, it sounded as tho' so many people were in on it. The Times summary was excellent. I got a description today of the D.A.R. meeting McArthur addressed & it sounds fantastic. I was told the ladies wept & knelt in the aisles & corridors! Such hysteria must be embarrassing to him & frightening for sane human beings.

Herbert Lehman gave me his speech in the Senate & I'll save it for you in case you'd like to read it.

We went to tea with the Russians today & they had some fine photographs of buildings being constructed in Moscow. Marjorie Whiteman [one of her State Department advisers] had an interesting talk with the little NKVD man who speaks English well and Mr. Morosov & I had quite a talk. I should know in the next few days the results if any of mine!

I hope I can remember to tell you of some of these conversations. They may mean nothing but one must go on trying!

John Orton (remember him at Campo) came in for tea the other day with Mr. Roger Baldwin.* He is in Munich interviewing Russian refugees for a Harvard & air force project. He says their distorted idea of the world outside Russia is what surprised him most.

I think Marshall's testimony was [word indecipherable], at least all I've been able to read & the Tribune seems to have had good editorials.

E.R.

Her last letter went to David, who evidently had flown to Mexico again.

May 15th [1951]

David dear,

What a happy surprise to get a note from you this morning. You certainly are travelling and everything sounds well with you. Did you get in another weekend in Mexico?

What a nuisance that you still have to be careful of your tummy. I think it may be partly the strain of worry about Nemone and if she is well you will not be under a strain. . . .

. . .

Our work is not so good this last week but seen as a whole it may not be so bad.

* Roger Baldwin, conscientious objector in World War I, director (1920–50) of the American Civil Liberties Union, which he helped found, was now active at the UN on human rights and anticolonial issues.

. . .

. . . I'm going to listen for 1/2 hour today in the W.H.O. [World Health Organization] meeting. They should have a bigger budget but we have to support the status quo. Senator Lehman has gone and Sen. Nixon (who defeated Mrs. Douglas in California) has arrived. I doubt if he'll learn much but one never knows!

E.R.

Trude, I, and the four children wanted to travel that summer, to visit Trude's family, including her mother, in southern Germany, and to holiday on the Wolfgang See in Austria, which still was occupied. It required Mrs. Roosevelt's intervention at the State Department and a written deposition by me on my political history to get the Department to issue me a passport. We were much at Hyde Park during the month of June. Where David was I do not know.

June 12th

David dearest,

What a shame to have so much pain! I do hope it cleared and you could enjoy the beach and salt water swimming.

I came across a nice description today: "To see a face unfold to all its subtle shades of meaning and of softness, and to know one has moved that face to such expression, is to feel like God." Perhaps that is what doctors sometimes see in their patients. It might be what lovers feel, or friends who find a deep and enduring bond of understanding which does not run dry.

I've been reading the "Jungle Book" to the children from 5 to 6 every day that I am here and I am astonished at how much Jonathan understands and how long he will listen.

. . .

It was a joy to see your handwriting and to know that you are feeling physically better and without problems or conflicts. You sound as though you were glad to have me come and that makes me happy but the trip does not sound too pleasant in the rain. Perhaps the discontent goes deeper, well we will soon see! . . .

The State Department has asked me to go to India *after* the General Assembly but not *for* them. It strikes me it will be a long pull, do you think physically I can stand the Assembly and then the trip? That's one consideration, then I must be sure I can afford it and as I can't take Tommy I must find someone to go, I don't suppose you feel like going? Also I must find out what ABC and Elliott will feel. If I go the plans seem a bit involved. I can decide a little later however!

. . .

E.R.

Her reference to travel plans to see David are not wholly explained. Was David in Cuernavaca where Martha was living?

I had gone to work for the New York *Post* covering the UN, and all the while I was in Europe I feared that the explosion of events, especially in Korea, might make it impossible for me to stay on the Wolfgang See the whole month.

July 18th [1951]

Joe dearest,

I don't wonder the state of affairs today makes you uneasy. It troubles me much & the episode over your passport annoyed me more than I can say & I was thankful I could do something. Please never hesitate to "involve" me where I can help. I only hesitate when I fear I will do those I love more harm than good!

Dr. [Channing] Tobias [Negro leader] came to see me last week since the next week he is told will be on Negro leaders, Mrs. Bethune & he being among the first.* I said we must fight back, not in an organization but by standing together wherever we are sure of anyone.

I hope you are all having a wonderful time & I realize that before long you will be home tho' it doesn't look as though anything would be before the U.N. for a long time.

Anna & her Johnnie are here & staying till Aug 4th & Haven & Johnnie seem to be having much fun together.

Nothing very new seems to be occurring in the world situation but I feel we will get an armistice. What comes next heaven only knows! I don't see how whatever is done can help but be a help to the Communists.

My last T.V. show went off well last Sunday. Friday will be my last day of recording.

I'm beginning to think of swimming & reading & perhaps doing a short book Harper's wants.

I miss you all very much. You seemed nearer on the Vineyard. I don't love many people but you & Trude are close to my heart & I like to have you near!

My love to Trude & Jonathan & much to you dear.

E.R.

The next day she wrote Trude, "Elliott tells me the Linaka house [about two miles behind hers] is not sold. If you want it you can have it for $15,000, 10% down & rest of payments over ten years. . . . I write you because he wants to know if you want it as soon as possible. Perhaps Joe could decide on his return."

---

* Dr. Tobias was director of the Phelps-Stokes Fund and would be a member of the U.S. delegation to the 6th UN General Assembly. Mary McLeod Bethune, educator, founder of the Bethune-Cookman College, director of Negro affairs for the NYA and a friend of Mrs. Roosevelt's since White House days.

We had a family council and decided to buy if I thought well of the property. I left Austria at the end of July; Trude and the children stayed on.

July 30th [1951]

Dearest Joe,

Welcome home! It is good to have you back & we await you with open arms.

I'll try to phone you tomorrow. I have to see Anna off Sat. early but will be up with Buzz & Robin by noon & Tommy will be here Friday if you get up early. Bring your tennis racquet!

All my love
E.R.

Almost all the August weekends I spent at Hyde Park, but on arrival in New York I called David to give him the news of Nemone and Grania, who had spent some time with us on the Wolfgang See. On August 5 I reported to Trude, "It looks as if we have a country place. Yesterday afternoon I walked the boundary with Elliott and Mrs. R." After I told Mrs. R. I felt we wanted to buy the Linaka place, "she said it made her very happy. She said she had not wanted to indicate her feeling because she felt we should buy independently—so that if she died we would still want to be there." A week later I again reported to Trude.

[Joseph P. Lash to Trude W. Lash:]   [August , 1951]

Well, the weekend went off without any fireworks despite the simultaneous presence of David and myself. This morning at 6:45 we both had breakfast with Mrs. R. and she sent us off each with a kiss. I suggested that we depart at 5 minutes intervals so that we shouldn't try to race one another down and David willingly agreed.

I was foolish not to recognize and welcome for Mrs. Roosevelt's sake the strength of her feeling for David. She again had tried to persuade him to take his holiday in Campobello, but he had refused and afterward, when she was at Westbrook to spend the night with Esther, she sent him a letter on which she wrote, "For Dr. Gurewitsch only to read—Personal and private."

Thursday night

David dear,

Since our talk today I have thought much of what you plan and I am not happy. First to be worthy of you it seems to me 2 things must be considered—The decision must be clear with Nemone. Next, because a woman offers to go on a holiday with you and you want to find out if you can stop thinking of Nemone does not to me seem good enough. If you told me you were in love, the decision was taken between you and

Nemone, and you wanted to be sure for you and a new love if this was a real and deep love that would be clear, but going off for a three weeks holiday cannot be casual and if on your side there is no real love, well, one may forget a night now and then but 3 weeks of constant companionship either is very good or no good it seems to me.

Does there come into your plan any thought that you don't want to be beholden to me or to put me out? I think I will take Tommy to Campo in any case. I can leave the 15th or you and Tommy can go up ahead and stay after I leave or leave with me. I realize I cannot give you what a young woman can but till you are fairly sure of what you want, do you really want what you are now planning? It worries me for you and I think just now the care and love that it would be a joy to me to give might make you happier with yourself in making your final decision.

I do not want to interfere in your life for of course I have no right to do so but I do not want you to do something you regret. May God help and bless you.

E.R.

P.S. Perhaps one basic thing that bothers me is that you are letting an offer of this kind be made *to you* rather than making it yourself *to a woman* because you really love her. From all that you can tell me you have always been pursued and I think it is time for you to do the pursuing if any real good is to come to you. You are spoiled by pursuit and you are perhaps too sensitive to go out and get what you really want.

I imagine I am 20 or so years older than you are and I have lived many emotions and observed many and I am sure happy marriages develop when the man shows his desire to the woman and she responds fully and happily. Even at your age, tho' some physical satisfaction is essential, you must be even surer of mental interests and sympathetic understanding which will lead to complete and happy companionship.

E.R.

Extraordinary letter—or rather extraordinary woman. Strong-minded and tough though she was, she parted company with the feminists in her feelings about men and the relationships between men and women. Was it nature or nurture that caused her to admonish David that he had always been pursued by women and it was time for him to do the pursuing? "I cannot give you what a young woman can" —she was resigned to that, and she realized that "some physical satisfaction" was essential. She showered him with sage advice, with gifts, she brought him within the circle of her fame and power and invested all with her love. She pleaded with him to seek a woman who would be a companion and sympathize with his interests, but she underestimated the strength of the sexual drive. Or perhaps it was the inability of men to desire her sexually.

"How do you sleep with a woman you call Mrs. Roosevelt?" Earl Miller had exclaimed when I asked him about his relations with her. Earl's reply may have been intended to derail my inquiries. There was truth to it nonetheless. She carried an aura of greatness that set her apart. Neither Earl nor David nor I was able to call her "Eleanor." I have come to do so here only as a literary device in writing about her after her death. Partly it was the disparity in age between herself and the men she loved after Franklin. In 1951 she was sixty-seven and David forty-nine. That did not explain it. David was an old hand at paying court to older women. Yet he, too, wrote and spoke to her as "Mrs. Roosevelt." Her advice to David was sound, but the tragedy of her life was that, though she helped us all in our romances, for her there was no love "but borrowed love."

Although Nemone had visited us in Austria that summer, and left Grania with us for a while, neither Trude nor I fully realized what was happening to her marriage with David.

And much as I saw of Eleanor that August she never discussed him with me nor her despairing efforts to keep him from going off with Martha.

She always confronted the world with a brave cordiality.

Sept. 3d. [1951]

Trude dearest,

It seems sometime since I've written you but I've thought of you often & been happy Joe could come here as he was lonely. He is like a different person this week end, full of fun just in anticipation of having a family again.

This is just to welcome you home & tell you that I long to see you. I'll be in N.Y. this evening & if you feel like coming to dine I'd love to have you & Joe or any other members of the family you want to bring. I should be at the hotel by seven. I'll quite understand if you are tired in which case we'll talk on the phone & make a date.

I'm afraid I've got a full house the week ends of the 8th & 15th but won't you plan to come the 21st with Jonathan & if you want to drive up for the day any Sat. & Sunday before I'd love it.

All my love & I'll be giving you a big hug soon. I've missed you & I'm so happy to feel you will soon be here.

Devotedly
E.R.

There was a welcome letter also for David.

Sept. 3d [1951]

David Dear,

Just a line to welcome you home and tell you how good it is to know you are near. I'll be in town Wed. a.m. but have to take the 2 o'clock train home and will be here that night and will go to N.Y. Thursday after four as I hope to see Trude (who should fly in that morning) and meet Sisty and Van and the baby who arrive after midnight! Sometime I hope I'll see you and Marty. You can tell me what you decided about weekends. I'd love to have you for both but you might have more peace the 15th as Sisty flies that day and will probably go to N.Y. the 14th!

I hope you have gained at least 10 lbs. and have acquired all the calm and discipline which will make decisions easy.

My dear love to you. I've missed you and thought about you constantly.

E.R.

David's birthday was on October 31, when she would be on the high seas en route to the UN's sixth General Assembly in Paris. She wrote him before departure, marking on the envelope "to read now or on the 31st as you wish E.R."

David dearest,

This is a birthday letter whenever you read it. I fear it will not be a happy day this year but I will be thinking of you *every* day and wishing you greater happiness in the future than in the past. I shall be deeply sad when you go away but if you are happy I shall be glad for you. Remember always please that wherever I am open arms await you. My home *anywhere* is yours when you need it whether you are alone or whether you want to bring those you love. If you forget this I will never see you and that would leave me bereft. I cherish every moment we are together these last days that I am here for I realize that there may not be many more. You know I think that I would rather be with you than with anyone else, whether we are alone or whether I am just watching you from afar. I am grateful to have known you and hope that we may keep close even though you establish a new life far away.

God bless you and keep you and bring you satisfaction and happiness in your life, that is my daily prayer.

I wish I did not have to be away these coming weeks.

All my love David, dearest friend, and happy days to you always.

E.R.

There is an undercurrent of desperation in Eleanor's birthday letter. David was considering pulling up stakes and settling in Cuernavaca with Martha. Eleanor hated the thought that David, after establishing a good practice in New York and besting his illness, should abandon everything for a woman who, if she really loved him, would have left Mexico, she thought, to be with him where his work was. She was dubious about his venture but resigned.

XVII

"Things Inch Along"

A T THE END of October Mrs. Roosevelt sailed on the SS *America* along with other members of the U.S. delegation to the first part of the sixth UN General Assembly in Paris. She was the senior member of the delegation, enjoyed her work, and, as one newspaper put the results of a poll in Dallas, Texas, "completely dominated the field in the selection of the greatest living American woman." She stayed in Paris until mid-December, when she went home for the holidays, to return at the beginning of 1952 for the second part of the Assembly. At the end of it she planned to go to the Near East and India.*

Her letters to David continued to chronicle the progress of his romance with Martha Gellhorn. All her letters are suffused with compassion for the human condition. They illustrated the superiority of character over deed and a sense of right and wrong that enabled her to confront and disregard convention. Cloaked in outer dignity, there was an inner core of love and benevolence in all that she did.

[On board SS *America*]
Oct 25th [1951]

Anna darling,

Franklin jr. & Sue came to lunch the day I sailed & said Sis & Van were wonderful. They told him it would be grand to have you & Johnny over there & you could work in the E.C.A. [Economic Cooperation Administration]! Fjr is all set to ask Averill [Averell Harriman, director of

---

* For the period October 25 to December 12, the longhand letters available to me—and I believe I had most of them—were two to Anna, three to Hick, twelve to Trude and me, eight to David. I have used the letters as her journal for the period and her views on events great and small.

the newly formed Mutual Security Agency] to get you a job & wants me to speak to him. I don't think we should as if you want one I think you should write him yourself & ask about possible openings. I think I can swing a trip for you & Johnny to Paris next summer so start planning now! You'll have to go on this ship for I can get you better accommodations cheaper!

. . .

Mother

Her shipboard letter to Trude thanked her for a copy of Paul Tillich's sermons and took note of the easygoing lives of some of her colleagues.

Oct. 29th [1951]

Dearest Trude,

A thousand thanks for the book. I read it & understood a little but it is obscure!

We've had a smooth crossing & beautiful days—I've done some work with the advisers but the top people won't work! We might just as well have flown really, but you can't begrudge them a little rest & gaiety & they have had both!

Tommy & I have slept a great deal & eaten a great deal & I've walked around & around the upper deck & sat in my chair & looked out to the far horizon & thought much about all of you whom I love at home. . . .

E.R.

Back at the Hotel Crillon, her first letter went to Hick.

November 2, 1951

Hick dear,

What a joy your letter was today & now I can hardly wait to hear if you've lined up something nearby to bring in the $50 a week you need.

I expect you've been in Washington since last Sunday—are you with Marion Herron? I'll send this c/o Mary [Norton]. I also hope Nannine [Nannine Joseph, literary agent of Hick and of Eleanor, too] is better. Keep Mary well & finish before Xmas so you can come to Hyde Park! Give both Mary & Marion my love.

. . .

Work began today for me in the office & at the delegation meetings but the U.N. meets first on Tuesday p.m. We have a nice girl in the office, things are upset still but not as badly as at the U.N. There the buildings aren't finished & the telephones aren't connected today! The Congressmen on our delegation are such a contrast. Vorys of Ohio, a Republican, reminds me of Vandenberg. Basically in foreign affairs at least he's interested & liberal but every now & then he remembers Taft & his party & he pulls in his horns! Mansfield from Montana hardly ever speaks, is sometimes abrupt & gauche in manner but his face is intelligent & his expressions interesting to watch. Ask Mary about them & write me what she advises as the best approach.

Having Sis & Van here is grand & tomorrow we go & dine with them & I hope see Nicholas [their son]. They hoped to get an apartment in Paris today but are still sharing a house in a suburb.

Paris is subdued & soft in color. Not cold yet but rain today. Leaves are falling—it is a bit sad but people are better off.

Write when you can. Much, much love & keep well.

E.R.

Hotel de Crillon
November 4, 1951

Dearest Joe & Trude

This is written for your wedding anniversary & I wish I were home to tell you in person how much I love you & how much I hope the years will bring you contentment & greater happiness. The little gift enclosed you may want to spend together on something for the new house [at Hyde Park]. For me it is wonderful to have you up there & I think of it with joy.

. . . I have an attack of "trots" which Elinor Hendrick tells me is the result of eating lettuce. She sent me over a pill to take as we are going with them & Van & Sis to Chantilly this morning to see the Chateau & some fine old manuscripts which are on exhibition there.

Joe dear, I wish you were here but I don't see how we begin the session or rather continue it. The plenary hall is permanent but the new wings aren't finished, the telephones are not connected etc. The apartment & hotel situation is bad too but we are comfortable here in our [two wds indecipherable]. The offices are not bad either tho' a bit chilly. The Secretary's [Acheson] opening speech will be good but not as comprehensive as I hoped. Collier's made a sensation here & there is much adverse criticism among our allies.*

We are back from Chantilly & I've been with Sis & Van to a students club (International) filled & good questions. Now I shall bathe & go to bed early for I feel cold & weakish which means the germ is not yet dead.

All my love to you both
E.R.

* The entire October 27, 1951, issue of Collier's was devoted to fictitious articles and stories depicting the defeat and occupation of the USSR in World War III. The prevading theme was "The War We Did Not Want" and some outstanding American writers contributed the articles.

November 5, 1951

David dearest,

Your first letter just came and I hope the home birthday party was a happy one and the talk later with Nemone not too hard and that you can come to some decisions.

[Several sentences asking when he would be in his office so that she could telephone him] . . . I will have the joy of hearing your voice. It will be nice to feel you are not so far away even though the time is short.

Your pills saved me on Tuesday. I was cold and with a bad tummy upset, kept going all day, but by night I thought I really had a bug, but one pill and a long night and this a.m. I was cured. I can't be ill when you are not around!

I dragged Tommy through the early Italian paintings for an hour at the Louvre this afternoon but I think one has to begin young to really know and love them. I wished for Sisty who is interested and appreciative even if she knows little! . . . He [Secretary Acheson] is going to make a proposal but it is not what I hoped for though it may lead to something better. Ben Cohen, Channing Tobias [members of the delegation] and I are unhappy over the attitude we are apparently forced to take on Morocco.* The French are worried and to stick by them we are evidently going to help keep the question off the agenda.

I must go to bed, all my love to you and bless you.

E.R.

David and Nemone had finally decided on divorce. Eleanor touched on it and quickly moved on to describe the opening sessions of the Assembly.

November 8, 1951

David dearest,

I was so glad of "a visible sign" from you which came today. It was written Monday so it takes 4 days!

I am so sorry about Nemone and I wrote her a little note. It is hard and it must be a little worry to you both. Has she agreed to go ahead or are you waiting?

I wish you were here too, all the time. I begin to feel something may get done in this Assembly. The Secretary's speech went well today and Vishinsky made little impression. They still insist we started the war in Korea! They protest so much that I think they may be preparing to make a few concessions.

* Arab states had raised the issue of France's protectorate over Morocco. France argued that the matter was one of "internal jurisdiction" and with U.S. and British support kept the question off the agenda.

It is funny watching the top men in the U.K. delegation.* They've never been in the U.N. and it's all strange to them. Eden told Acheson he'd line the Dominions up on a policy of theirs and came back surprised and bothered to say South Africa was all he could line up!

The Latin Americans are getting grabby for places. They have the President of the Assembly and Com. 3 chairmanship but they wanted 2 more saying the Presidency had been the choice of outside delegations and they were putting a woman in Com. 3 and that of course couldn't count so they as a group had nothing!

This is all nonsense but it may make you smile and I like you to smile. Are you having good times with Grania?

I'm well but my tummy isn't quite straightened out yet. I'm not working hard enough so I don't sleep too well but it's enough. I've lovely roses in my room sent from the American Club where I spoke at lunch. We've begun going to work at 8:45 so goodnight and my deepest love to you.

E.R.

She wrote me the same day.

November 8, 1951

Dearest Joe,

I have wished all day for you. The Secretary delivered his speech well & it was good I thought. The enclosed was sent me by an old Belgian delegate wise in European ways who had told me the spirit was just right for Europe & in the afternoon as we neared the end of Vishinsky's 1 & 1/2 hrs of "rehash" he passed me this which Trude can translate for you. Keep it for me.

I am encouraged I think we may get something done in this Assembly. Certainly Europe needs it. The people here look better fed & somewhat better dressed but the spirit is not too good. At the top there is too much selfishness & at the bottom too little security.

Sisty is a joy to me so full of interest & enthusiasm & anxious to do everything & enjoying everything.

. . . Tonight I got Baroody to sit with us after dinner & he told us some wonderful tales about democracy, Saudi Arabia, Moslem style.† I found out his attitude on Com III items too. Last night I took Sec. & Mrs. Acheson & Ben Cohen & Sis & Van to "Les Porquerolles" for dinner & for the first time they unbent, relaxed & he told stories & seemed to enjoy himself.

* The Conservatives led by Churchill had regained power October 25, 1951, and Anthony Eden and Selwyn Lloyd headed the U.K. delegation.
† Jamail Baroody, born in Lebanon, was in effect the permanent representative of Saudi Arabia.

Does my column ever get into the World Telegram?

. . .

E.R.

November 9, 1951

Trude dearest,

. . .

Australia answered Vishinsky well in the Assembly today. Monday Eden will speak. I lunched with him today & he cannot get over Vishinsky's speech, feels they are so much worse than he realized.

Next Friday for the weekend I'll go to stay with Queen Juliana for her meeting to arouse spiritual leadership. I don't think Committee work will begin till the middle of next week, I feel as though I had been gone for ages & it was only 2 weeks yesterday!

Will you have Halley [Liberal Party candidate for Mayor] in N.Y.! Try to find out if *any* Democrat was elected in Hyde Park, & let me know?

. . .

E.R.

November 14, 1951

David dearest,

No word from you but I must send you a line just to say how much I have thought of you since Monday. I hope all went well with Nemone and the lump [?] was not serious. This will have been an extra worry and burden—How are *you* physically?

I have a sweet letter from Marty, giving me addresses of people in Israel so I can't send it till I answer it and copy the addresses. Will you go to Mexico for a long weekend or have you decided to wait?

I've had two 6:30 to 8 parties for Com. 3 members and today Pavlov and 2 other USSR delegates, 2 Poles and 1 Czech all came!

I've met Mr. Picot [new Under Secretary for Social Affairs] who has taken Laugier's place and I think I will like him better, tho' he hasn't M. Laugier's expansive enthusiasm.

A nice day and I'm quite well and if you were here doing some of the nice things with me Paris would be less sad and I would be very happy.

. . .

E.R.

When and where may I telephone?

There is no date but she sent David a note on whose envelope he wrote "1951 going to Mexico, 4 leaf clover."

David dear,

I must give you this little line to wish you luck and wisdom and ultimate happiness. I hate to have you go because I don't want you hurt and yet you can't be content unless you go so you must go. Remember dear marriages are two way streets and when they are happy women must be willing to adjust. *Both* must love.

My love to Marty and her mother.

My thoughts and my love will be with you and please wire when you leave. God bless and help you my dear.

E.R.

The weekend of the 14th she went to Holland. A letter to David dated only "Left for Holland" had an undercurrent of sadness. She had failed to stop him, as she must have learned when she tried to telephone him.

Dearest David,

So you left last night for Mexico and I never spoke to you. I should have tried to get you even tho' I wasn't sure of the best time. Now I feel sad because I deprived myself of a great pleasure! You will be gone 4 weeks and you will have your divorce on your return? Please go to the apartment in the hotel on your return so I find you settled there on my return for whatever time you spend in New York now or in the future alone.

I am glad all was well with Nemone. You say nothing of Grania? Does she know? I am glad you are no longer frantic, settled things are always easier than uncertainties. Marty will be alright now you are with her. Your plans for the fellowship in Mexico sound very good and I think it is wise to keep some ties to the hospital and your courses until all is settled and you are sure what you want to do.

Our committee met Friday morning and I left in the afternoon for Holland. Last evening and today I have been with the group. People largely from Holland but some English, French and Germans. . . . I think I understand the purpose of the meetings now. The Queen says there are no guidings, no organization is contemplated, each person who can achieve a sense of peace and relationship to God within themselves will be more open to guidance of a spiritual nature and ripples will go out from them to affect the world atmosphere. It will also be easier to live and carry your burdens because whatever happens is God's will and you must accept it and not strive for your own will. I can see that this may help her and she looks well and happy.

Needless to say [Prince] Bernhardt is not here. Her Mother [the former Queen Wilhelmina] is and told me her preoccupation now was with spiritual things and developing this sense of guidance. She felt Franklin had it. I think he did and it was a help and refuge but he would not sound as complicated as some of these people do! You would fit in here better than I do. Last night I talked to a doctor, 12 years general practice in a small place, imprisoned and escaped during the war and returned to his town. He said he gave people medicine but spiritual healing, the right words, at the same time. No illness was purely physical, and you must look at a person as a whole. I think you do that but you don't talk about it. I wonder if meetings like these are not really a search for escape from the problems Europeans have to carry today rather than a new avenue of acceptance and strength?

I go back tomorrow afternoon to Paris and now that I know you are in Mexico I will get Mr. Torres Bodet* to lunch and ask him to say a word for you. I'll mail this from Paris and add a word Monday. All my love and thoughts.

E.R.

David sent a postcard from Cuernavaca, Mexico, to Eleanor at the Hotel Crillon. It has no date and clearly Eleanor did not receive it until much later, but David's sentiments seem appropriate here:

Just my love. It *is* a wonderful rest from tension. Mexico at its very best just now. I'm trying not to think, at least for a short time. My love again and again and I hope you are well.

D.

She wrote him from Paris on her return from Holland.

November 23, 1951

David dearest,

I gather you did not leave N.Y. last Friday but on Tuesday so if you stay 4 weeks you will get to N.Y. the day before we do. Will you go to the apartment or back to Nemone and Grania? A letter from Nemone had told me you had not told either family or Grania and she told me her worries about Grania when she would know and her health. Are you getting the divorce? I have known what a hard time you were having and have been grateful for your notes. Of course I worried about you because I love you but I understood. These days in Mexico will not be too easy either but I hope you can get some rest.

The hospital office, the reorganization all sound as tho' work in New York might be possible to organize so it would be less strenuous and more rewarding. All of which makes the decision for you no easier I fear. I am so far away and feel I know so little so all I can do is pray every night for

---

* Mexican diplomat and at the time Director-General of UNESCO.

God's blessing to be with you and may you be given wisdom and strength.

I'm enclosing a letter from Queen Juliana just sent me from the man, a rather fanatical person I felt. He is a follower of the faith healer (a woman) who has promised to cure the blind child when God finds Juliana has proved her faith. The two I fear have a very unhealthy influence and yet with her it is the highest ideals to meet her personal burdens and her duties to her people. The man's letter seems to me many words and meaningless ones, about something which could and should be simple. I wrote 2 columns on the meeting and if I have copies I'll put them in tomorrow.

I had lunch alone with Mme. [Léon] Blum on Wed. and she told me a wonderful story. She and her husband were in a little house in Buchenwald and a factory was near so the bombs dropped often. One day they were [word indecipherable] and she pushed her husband against the wall and lay on him to protect him. They were cut and blood was flowing and she said "Now do you think that international organization for peace will ever come?" and he answered "Mais oui Jeanot et bientot"! She has an idea for international education for children which I am quite excited about and I'll be able to tell you more when I get home.

When you know write me what plans you want to make for Xmas. I want to make it as easy a time as possible. Do let me see you as much as possible when I am home. I've missed you so much and just to sit and look at you will be a great joy for me!

I do not think Nemone will have a depression and I certainly hope not for your sake.

I saw Mr. Bodet for a minute yesterday and he and Mme Bodet are coming to lunch this coming week.

Work has begun in earnest and there are endless people to see. I'm worried about the whole economic base here and in Italy. Their social security here is not built on a basis to build up the dignity of man! I wish I could talk to you about so much I am learning. I need so much more knowledge and understanding than I have. Pavlov made his first attack on the U S in our committee on Thursday. We are responsible for the lowering of living standards all over the world because we prepare for World [War] III. I answered extemporaneously. I hope temperably *[sic]* and with humor but he asked to answer my question and as I'd asked none I expect a long blast tomorrow.

Give Marty my love. My thoughts are with you constantly and I send my love always.

E.R.

I'm quite well and still hope to see something begin in this Assembly. How about your clothes? I'll be in London if all goes well December

15th and 16th. They could be sent to the Marchioness of Reading, 9 Smith Square, Westminster and I could bring them in.

Letters to Hick and to me were sharper about the faith healers around Queen Juliana and dwelt on the proceedings at the General Assembly, the problems with America's allies, and above all the Russians.

November 21, 1951

Dearest Hick,

A happy Thanksgiving to you, even if this will be late. I hope you are still in Washington & if so tell Mary I like Mansfield more & more. I think in fact I'm going to be very fond of him. I get on with Vorys but don't really care about him at all. I took Mansfield to dine in my favorite small restaurant with Sis & Van & Tommy & Dick Winslow* & he thawed no end.

I hope the book is done & Nannine feels happy about it. I hope too you get a job & sell some stories. You know there is always a period when all seems to go wrong & then a change comes & you are due for a change.

. . .

E.R.

To me she wrote—

November 21, 1951

Dearest Joe,

. . .

I wish so much that you were here for there is much to be learned at a session in Europe. The feeling of the people in France & Holland is disturbing. It is peace at any price at bottom though they get around saying it by looking at the daily round & not talking about the future. My 2 days in Holland were an example of another way to try to meet the difficulties. A spiritual way, of high idealism when honest, but capable of exploitation & dishonesty. I kept thinking of Rasputin though in the case of Queen Juliana it is a woman. I still am hopeful of things being done & do not mind the bluntness of Acheson because Vishinsky understands it. The dinner at the Élysée last night was a wonderful pageant but some significant things happened. They are cordial, the USSR people, to me & why? I wish we could find one thing on which we could cooperate & Mme Blum brought me an idea today I think might turn the trick so tomorrow I'll try it out on the State Dept. representatives here!

E.R.

* Richard S. Winslow, Secretary General of the U.S. delegation to the UN.

November 23, 1951

Dearest Trude,

I love the poem & it expresses what I feel here, somehow something must be done & I grasp at every straw! We talk about the economic & social conditions of underdeveloped countries, just now I feel I must talk about Europe. There is no sound economic basis here & from my point of view there is no social security. If we pull out it is communist or fascist at once & no will to fight for freedom because the people have nothing to fight for. I'm talking to Averill tomorrow & I lunch with Auriol [Socialist President of France] on Tuesday & will see what they say. Schuman just said "You are right, but I could never get a vote." The rich industrialist here is blind & selfish & does not want to see where it leads. All tell me Italy is the same or worse. I wish Joe were here to talk over so many things, tho' heaven knows I talk to enough people!

Work has begun in earnest, 2 sessions Wed. & Thursday & in between yesterday I went to a students house Reid Hall & had Thanksgiving lunch with them & spoke. Sis & Van & Tommy were asked too & Miss Strauss so it was nice. I had to go to a UNESCO cocktail party & in the evening we had 40 for dinner here. Some of the minor lights of the delegation & the girls who work in our offices. Sis & Tommy did all the work & found a pumpkin, fruit & vegetables for the table and 5 men carved the smallish French turkeys & Tommy got them stuffed! The Morgenthaus arrived & came & Marcelle does her hair better & looked sweet & seemed at ease at last. The Hendricks & Amb. Wood & Betty & John Hight were my other outside guests. Everyone seemed to have a good time so I was happy & I called & talked to the children which was a joy. Minnewa wrote me too you were stopping in tomorrow for tea. They all seem happy & busy & interested. Johnny will get his knee done & there is more than enough for both to be very busy I understand.

If you go to Otto Berg* & tell him I am away & can't tell you how to finish the pine but I knew he could. I feel sure he will. He lives in East Park, stone house on the left just as you get to the corner.

It seems a long way off to promise a Sunday in May. The Human Rights Commission will be in session & I'll only have weekends free but I can stay down if Wiltwyck really needs the money. They can choose & let me know.

I hope you will be settled in your house April 5th. I have to get home April 3d & Tommy has to have everything arranged for tentatively Juliana & Bernhardt are spending that weekend & going to Kingston (probably Saturday) for their celebration. It will be the high point of their period of celebration so I hope it comes off.

* He had been the chief craftsman at Val-Kill Industries and was given much of the machinery and the "stain" formulas when the factory was discontinued.

I hope you had a wonderful Thanksgiving in Putney [School]. . . .

I'm sorry for Nemone & David. Neither of them are clear in themselves & both worry about Grania.

Where you & Joe both try hard I'm sure there will some day come smooth sailing for you both.

Today I had no meetings but saw, 2 Moroccan students, Care's representatives, a woman from Washington who has formed a league of women against war & wants fool things but is so full of good intentions! Had Jimmy Yen* to lunch, UNESCO has called on him as a consultant on mass education. Did a 2-minute Pathe newsreel—went out to the new Quaker center to talk with a French priest who belongs to the World Congress for Peace. He's been to all the Communist peace meetings & he was interesting. Got home & had the boy at the head of the World Youth Assembly to tea. Did 2 columns, dined & now for letters. I really am not idle, am I? All my love to Joe, Jonathan & you.

E.R.

Tommy sends love. I don't think she loves Europe!

November 25, 1951

Dearest Joe,

This is a birthday letter & takes you my love. . . .

I know these last months have not been easy but I hope you begin to see light ahead. I hate not to have you here but I feel you may be getting a firmer place in the paper by working as you have. Your all around usefulness & your acceptance of a difficult situation will I'm sure not go unnoticed & unappreciated.

The Morgenthaus are here & lunched with me today, also the Torres Bodet's and Mme Pandit. I've just had a visit from the son of an old English school friend & Dr. Cook & his son. The latter a Howard University graduate & professor of French literature is here on a Fullbright scholarship & our cultural attaché says he's been most helpful in making speeches in French. Good for our Embassy to have a Negro to cooperate with! The son is at Polytechnic which is one of the best political science schools.

. . .

I saw Averill yesterday & got a broader picture of economic problems & then from Admiral Badger a military picture with his economic slant which is remarkably good, but the fundamentals are still as bleak & grim as I first envisaged them. Averill told me to talk to Auriol & to David

---

* James Yen, educator, active in Chinese-American affairs and president of the International Mass Education Movement.

Bruce* but I can't see the latter till he gets back from Rome on Thursday.

My devoted love as always. I'm so glad you were born on that Dec 2d, how many years ago?

E.R.

November 28, 1951

Dearest Joe,

How nice to get your letter today & to hear about Thanksgiving at Putney which must have been fun. The drive down sounds nice too. Did you stop at Hyde Park? I gather not, but the things you bought seem destined to reside there!

Your review of Taft's book is grand! I too prefer Harriman to Vinson but agree that Eisenhower would win over them. I quite understand your Boss' [Jimmy Wechsler] column.† It is an understandable feeling & I'm sure had I gone I'd have felt the same! I sent nothing to the sale except those flag plates which Johnny refused to keep & I couldn't house or use. I did write a letter, not about infantile, but just to say these things were genuine & belonged to us. All of them were Elliott's & I don't believe he wanted to sell but I think he felt he had to do so. Anyway he had a right I felt to do what he wanted with things he took.

Poor Nemone & David, he wrote me you & Trude had been so helpful.

I saw Louis Ruppel‡ tonight & told him the Colliers number had not had a good effect here but he won't see it!

Went to hear a French correspondent back from 4 weeks in America lecture & thought he observed & understood a great deal. Some Senators would have had fits over his remarks on our capitalistic system which he feels is the nearest thing to pure communism!

Henry Morgenthau & Marcelle came in to say goodbye & leave tomorrow for Israel & will be here when I return in Jan.

Amb. Austin is ill & I am senior delegate which means you do the dirty work like telling the Latin Americans you can't vote for their choice for the Court at the Hague! French Sécurité wants to follow me but I refused & got away with it!

My love to Trude & Johnny & a heartful to you.

Devotedly
E.R.

---

* David Bruce, U.S. Ambassador to France.

† Elliott through the Hammer Galleries sold off a considerable collection of Franklin D. Roosevelt items —miniature books, caricatures and sketches of him, selected china, silver and glass. Roosevelt loyalists, including James Wechsler, editor of the New York *Post*, were outraged that the late President's memory should be commercially exploited.

‡ Louis Ruppel was editor of *Collier's Weekly*. He had handled Mrs. Roosevelt's column for United Features. A *Collier's* article had depicted a western victory over USSR in a World War III. He had abetted Russian charges at the UN that the United States planned war.

A letter from David arrived in response to the one she had written mostly while she was in Holland. He thought "the dangers for a big scale conflagration is continuously becoming smaller, in favour of many smaller wars," and then he went on with the family news that may have interested her more.

No Grania does not know and I am having nightmares about it. I am still not thinking and I am much less relieved than I expected, still. It is beautiful here and vacation spirit, in spite of a little work and beginning lectures. And I still cannot write. . . . Cannot commit myself to an expression of how I feel, not even to you—I imagine this is because I do not know myself. Martha understands that her gift and her inclination to make plans have to be held back just a little at the moment.

My love to you—and many thoughts.

Your David

November 29th, 1951

David dear,

How hard it is, torn apart, and so much to decide which affects others. I say little prayers for you, nothing specific, just that you may be given wisdom and strength. It is so hard to know what will make one best able to live with oneself at long last.

I fear Grania does guess and that is one reason for her feeling ill. I hope she gets better soon and that Nemone does not have a depression. Of course I understood how you could not write and did not want to talk and I really don't expect you to make plans. Just know that whether you decide at the last minute, if it makes life easier for you [it] is right with me. I only hope to see as much of you as possible. I'll write your office and make a date to be given all the necessary shots!

It will be no trouble to pick up your suit if I get to London and I'll let the tailor know.

I'm glad you were named to Blythedale* even if you give it up for it is a satisfaction I'm sure. Ambassador Austin is ill and I fear it is a stroke, the doctors say a slight cerebral hemorrhage which at his age does not usually mean a return to full activity—they want him to go home when he's well enough to leave the hospital. For me this means being the senior delegate. . . . I'm sending the travel bureau 2 itineraries, I'll enclose both so you can see what I'm doing. If you can go to India and want to return to Palestine O.K. Mrs. Pandit said March would be warm but not bad, just wear thin clothes and she'd plan for the north the latter part of the time and Bombay and Madras first.

I've seen Mr. Bodet twice and can ask him anything you want so when

* A Westchester hospital that pioneered in the education and treatment of the handicapped child.

you know what you would like to know write me. I gather you are not getting the divorce this trip.

I have the speeches made in Holland but want to reread and then I'll send them to you.

Tommy seems well and I am quite well and only moderately busy. I'm sad but I couldn't tell you why, worried about things here and no one to talk [to]. You and the whole of humanity seem to be so defenseless in the grip of forces they cannot control.

I'm glad Martha is happy and easy, that is the way she can help you best. God bless and keep you and goodnight my dear. I love you always.

E.R.

She answered his earlier note.

December 1, 1951

David dearest,

Just a line to thank you for your little line written last Sunday.

You and I have come to the same conclusion in spite of your source of information being a Mexican paper. I feel every day puts the big conflagration farther away but the USSR will try to foment all the little difficulties possible and conquer from within. Changes must come in Europe or she will succeed. I have much to tell you on this scene [?] that I have not the time to write.

I have endless conferences now with members of our own delegation, with others from other groups. The Korean troops are honored tomorrow and I have to make Ambassador Austin's speech in the Assembly. The Latin Americans are behaving like naughty children because we can't vote for the candidate of theirs for the international court. We've gone with them on all other candidates but they want 100 per cent and threaten to vote for Byelo Russia for the Security Council if we don't do as they wish! I really grieve that I can only have 8 days at home. I want all the time I can have with you!

I hope your lecture and work goes well and that the beauty and vacation spirit rests you physically. Poor dear, it is for those one loves one always suffers most in this world. I know you do not yet know how you feel that is why I pray for wisdom and strength for you. God bless and keep you. You are constantly in my thoughts and I love you.

E.R.

My love to Martha.

He had two patients in Cuernavaca, David reported, "and the lectures were coming off," but he felt a deep apprehension, "an apprehension against starting life here. . . . Marty is well and she is in no hurry."

December 4th, 1951

David dearest,

Your note of the 28th was a happy surprise. I'm glad you have 2 patients and the lectures are coming off, but I'm sorry about the digestive upset. I hope you don't let it run on this time. It is of course in part because of the way you feel in spirit and not all because of physical reasons.

You must have more letters from me soon after you wrote, at least I hope so. I note too, you had good news from Grania, it must have been hard to leave her when she felt so low.

Tommy is mailing you my speech given at the ceremonies for the boys from Korea. They all seem to like it.

I am going to speak at a memorial meeting for Léon Blum in French next week and I am much worried about it.* I'd like to do it well, on account of Mme Blum for whom I have a great admiration.

I spent an hour with 7 members of Congress today discussing France and I hope helped them to understand a little the problems.

The gala performance at the opera for the UN last night was a real pageant, "Jeanne au Buchet" I had never seen before. It is modern but I found it moving. I sat next to Mr. Vishinsky!

Mr. and Mrs. Pendar† invited Tommy and me to dine tonight with some very nice French people from Morocco. All are deeply worried about France's shortcomings there and I'm worried about our own position! Mr. Pendar asked after you and I told him nothing!

Everything I do here makes me wish for you, to talk and consult with, to enjoy things and feel them with you would add a great deal. I wonder if we will take a trip together! Bless you and take care of yourself. My love to you.

E.R.

Tommy mailed you the speeches given at the Holland conference.

Her becoming head of the delegation meant she had to stay until the 22nd, she informed Trude, "& will come to your Xmas party unless you have it on Saturday." There was news about the UN and she ended, "I went to the Sainte Chapelle this afternoon & even tho' the sun was not shining the marvellous colors were a joy. Anything lovely like that soothes the soul!"

A week later there was a note of comfort for Hick and a fuller letter for Trude. She entered the lives of her friends with painstaking solicitude. She did not wholly agree with Hick about the political situation at home. "I'm sure the Democratic party has been in power too long but the alternative of Taft is even worse!"

* Léon Blum had died in March 1950.
† Maurice Pendar, an American, might be called an "old Morocco hand."

Dec. 7th, 1951

Dearest Trude,

I was happy to get your letter of the 1st & Joe's of the 3d both on the same day. The picture of Elliott & Minnewa & Rexie [Minnewa's son by a previous marriage] sounded peaceful & relaxed & I'm so glad you & Joe felt at last you might make friends. Elliott's inner worries & tensions is what has made him so difficult for so long & I hope they may gradually grow less.

I am interested in what you said about Nemone & David & sorry Grania had not yet improved. I think she is disturbed because she feels something threatens her world. I don't think David is sure of where his heart can be at peace.

Poor Jonathan! I don't wonder he hates the penicillin injections. I hope the bug was conquered fast. I'm glad you'll have Vera home so long & the saving project sounds wonderful. Will you stay with me over New Year (only I'll have to leave the 31st) or will you be in your own house?

. . .

E.R.

Dec. 8th, 1951

Dearest Joe,

I loved your letter of the 3d as I am enjoying sitting down to write you today. I spent the morning in Com. 3 listening to all those who oppose 2 covenants with 2 exceptions. Most of those speaking came from the Near East or Asia (Afghanistan, Pakistan, Iraq, Syria, etc.) all of them were enraged by some paragraphs in Belgium's speech which implied that they read us lessons but that those who did shld look to their qualifications. It takes maturity to take criticism & these few words of de Housses' [Fernand Dehousse] may well cost us the thing we (& he) want to achieve!

. . .

I am getting more & more suspicious of Churchill & his policy as regards Russia. He is I think going to play the conciliator, the wise, calm statesman who forgets grudges & we are to be cast in the role of the young, hard & unforgiving, inexperienced people who really threaten the USSR & in so doing threaten the peace of all Europe which only can be kept by Churchill's skillful handling! I often wish you were here to help evaluate people & what they say. Every word counts & one dreads saying too much or too little!

. . .

E.R.

Although she did "little" Christmas shopping, as she put it, she tried determinedly to preserve her holiday traditions.

Dec. 12th, 1951

Trude dearest,

I am so happy your party will be the 23d & now we'll keep our fingers crossed & hope the weather will let me get in. . . .

Life is busy, things inch along. We must learn to be patient & still work, a hard lesson! I don't know whether I do well or not but I realize things could run even without me & am not deluded to thinking I have any importance.

I spoke at a meeting in memory of Leon Blum last night & it was an impressive occasion. There was a high ideal[ism] in the men who spoke, a fire for great things.

. . .

I liked to hear the last papers on the house were signed & I wish I'd been there!

. . .

E.R.

A weekend trip to London was meant to introduce Sis and Van to its historic charms as she saw them.

A letter to David that he misdated "Le 12 March 1951" from the Crillon she probably wrote December 12. It shows his courtship of Martha was reaching some resolution.

Dearest David,

I gather from your letter of last Saturday which has just come that you will go to the Park Sheraton this coming Sunday and have cabled you that is fine. I told the hotel before I left & you have a key so I hope they will let you in and Miss [Maureen] Corr* will expect you whenever you appear! I fear next week will be very grim for Grania will have to be told. Poor David! I wish I could be near you.

---

* A new secretary whom Tommy had obtained through an employment agency, Irish-born and of the Roman Catholic faith. She was efficient, quiet-spoken and conscientious. The less Tommy was able to do the more Maureen took on, and she soon became one of Mrs. Roosevelt's standbys. A note Tommy left for Maureen in the fall of 1951, six months after she had been employed, read:
"Miss Corr:
"While we are gone you can answer all letters as definitely as possible. If they want information about the UN, refer it to the US Mission. If you feel the letter should be acknowledged, say that Mrs. R. has left and she will be so busy no mail is being forwarded.
"If requests come in for Mrs. R. to speak or accept citations, etc., say that Mrs. R's plans after the GA is over about Feb. 15th, are too vague to make any commitments as she may stay abroad to accept some of the invitations to visit various countries to which she has been invited. After she returns, which may be about April 15, she will almost immediately have to attend meetings of the HR Commission which means she cannot make engagements away from NYC.
"I know there will be such a variety of requests that no form will answer them all, but you use your own good judgment in answering them. However you did extremely well while we were in Geneva last Spring so I leave it to your auspices."

Being head of the delegation is just nominal and they wouldn't think of putting me in Austin's place. Mr. [Ernest] Gross will be moved up or some other well known man will be named. It just can't be done now because Austin hopes to get back and he hasn't been told he has to rest 6 months, so they have to put me in while we are here.

Martha did not write me what I was to do with Torres Bodet but when I return I can take it up with him.

I gather your decision on some things at least is made. . . .

E.R.

What is one to make of Eleanor's falling in love with men whose romances with other women she abetted?

After an all-night flight from Paris she took sundry children and grandchildren to lunch and proceeded to Hyde Park. Was her ceaseless energy fed by the oblique loves which could not be played out? Her letter to David gave her precise time of arrival, which I have omitted. Was she half hoping David might meet her, yet did not dare to say so? She knew he was involved in his own life, so she poured herself into "duty-pleasures" (a phrase suggested by Merloyd Lawrence as was much of this paragraph) as grandmother, mother, ambassadress, devoted friend of many.

Martha Gellhorn in her oral history remarks recorded by the FDRL in February 1980 has her explanation:

> . . . He [F.D.R.] was really a brilliant politician, and politicians are power, and she was love.
>
> And she wasn't a bit interested in success; she wasn't against it but it didn't mean anything to her. What meant something to her was people doing something. I suppose, really, she *had* to help, so that as soon as anybody got beyond needing her help, then they were more less dismissed, as it were. . . .
>
> She never envied any human being. She was *all* generosity; she was without vanity, too.
>
> And then she took up with her doctor, Gurewitsch (I can't remember his first name, which I certainly ought to)—David. It was wonderful because *there* was somebody [on whom] she could lavish her devotion, her care. She could worry about his not eating enough, and being overworked, and all the rest of it, and having a luncheon engagement with him in New York and [his] being kept by a patient and keeping her waiting three-quarters of an hour or an hour. And it was just *wonderful* because it was like having a son for a change who was also devoted to her. And wait—somebody will write a book about *that* and suggest that *that* was a love affair, in which case I'll go and find them and *choke* them! But it was a chance, as always with her, to look after somebody.
>
> . . . She ran errands for David; she did any old thing. I wouldn't have

been surprised if she knitted socks for David. Well, of course, David adored her but then so would anybody love his mother if his mother was that nice to him. So that would seem rational to her. But I don't know if he'd been named head of whatever you can be named head of, the eighth biggest hospital in New York, then she probably would have drifted away because that was how she was.

One does not wholly quarrel with this diagnosis, but the explanation of Eleanor's behavior lies deeper. She had learned the processes of sublimation by which sexual desires were subtly transformed into a concern for all creatures great and small. "Things inch along," she had written Trude at the end of the General Assembly. "We must learn to be patient and still work, a hard lesson!" She had learned that lesson in her private life, and the realization went much beyond her love for any of us. "A spark disturbs our clod," Robert Browning wrote in "Rabbi Ben Ezra," and keeping love alive was to nurture that vital spark. Sometimes she imagined being swept off her feet and the world well lost for love. One cannot escape, however, her talent for loving men who proved to be—and she encouraged them to be—inaccessible.

XVIII

Eisenhower's Dislike of Mrs. Roosevelt

A WOMAN who loves a younger man, especially as she approaches old age, accepts signs of reciprocity a younger woman might shrug off. Such receptiveness was especially true of Eleanor, whose love for people was suffused with benevolence and solicitude. She had always had doubts about Martha's commitment to David, so it was with relief that she learned during the Christmas recess between the two parts of the General Assembly that David was having second thoughts about settling down in Mexico—indeed, about his compatibility with Martha. Although her glamour and physical attractiveness pulled him, she had a willfulness that comes from having been desired by many men, which, added to a native high-spiritedness, would inevitably make life with her stormy. So David realized.

Eleanor, in planning her trip to the Middle East and India after the General Assembly, had originally sounded out Anna on accompanying her. Anna had declined, however, so she was delighted Christmas week to find that although matters between Nemone and David and David and Martha were as unsettled as ever, he was happy to join her. David gave her some of the shots she needed for the trip, recommended a doctor in Paris to whom she might go for the remainder, and they discussed visas and tickets.

At the beginning of the year she returned to the Crillon in Paris and promptly talked with Forbes Amory, who handled her travel arrangements when the State Department did not take care of them.

January 1, 1952

Dearest David,

My first letter in this New Year to you, so it takes you all good wishes for a better and happier year and all my love always—

Forbes Amory walked in and had lunch with me today but he'll be back in the U.S. next week. He says it is better for you to get your passport visas there but Mrs. [Ruth] Shipley will not do it as the Consul officers in N.Y. can do it. I'll get ours done here and inquire whether yours could be done here. I straightened out with Forbes your going direct to Israel but your departure date from the U.S. you must still arrange with him.

Somehow you still seem near, the flight was short and smooth and non stop so we landed here 11:30 a.m., only a few minutes over 12 hrs actual flying time. Beautiful day so the 3 Seagraves, Miss Corr and I drove to the Bois and walked a bit this afternoon. Then I saw the Morgenthaus and had the Sandifers and Dick Winslow to dine so I'm caught up on work and ready to start in a new office tomorrow morning.

I think of you so much and feel very useless so I pray that courage and wisdom may be yours and I love you and trust you. Bless you.

E.R.

Her decision to leave Tommy at home had been a wrench for both women but Tommy realized she no longer was able to cope with travel abroad. She equipped Maureen Corr with all sorts of knowledge, including a tipping schedule, and her memorandum ended:

Mrs. R. will make you the custodian of the money and will expect to draw from your fund. The cashier in the hotel there will give you small money for large bills. I try to keep a supply of 50 and 100 franc notes on hand for tips. Here the legal rate is 250 francs to the dollar, so 50 or 100 francs does not amount to much.

I doubt Mrs. R. will give any large parties, but if she does, tip the waiters on a 15 percent basis.

Back alone in Paris was a low moment for Mrs. Roosevelt.

Jan. 5th, 1952

David dearest,

How wonderful of you to write so soon and such a warm letter. It made me happy for if I can bring you any happiness it makes me very happy. Let us hope this New Year will bring *all* those I love greater contentment and happiness, then I will be happy too!

. . .

I feel very low in my mind about the Russians and all our U.N. work at the moment, probably because I am forced to argue the refugee question again and with a new difficulty since the Syrians like their—the U.S.S.R.['s]—emphasis on repatriation and are willing to insist on it because of the Palestinian Arabs. Ah! well, one must do one's best that is all one can do!

I love you dear, and I know how hard these days are for you and my thoughts are with you much of the time. God bless you.

E.R.

". . . if you do," the same letter said about David's joining her. She feared that the needs of David's practice, unsettled domestic problems, Martha's attractions, any one or all might keep him on the other side of the ocean. Also she was superstitious: she couldn't quite believe her good fortune to have David accompany her.

A letter to Trude dwelt on Dwight Eisenhower's announcement that he would be a candidate for the Republican nomination for President.

Jan. 7th, 1952

Dearest Trude,

. . .

Work goes on here, not too well but slowly in the right direction. Eisenhower made an announcement today & I wonder what the reaction at home in the Republican party will be.

It looks as though the Korean question would go to a special session. I'm not too busy but discouraged now & then, which one should never be! Congressman Mansfield may come back I hear today & that would be a good thing for us I think.

Tell Joe I hope if Eisenhower runs he is with him in the campaign as I want to know what he is really for. Fjr. will have a hard time! No word about Sue & the baby. How unpredictable first babies are!

I must go to bed, but I just wanted to send you all my love.

Devotedly,
E.R.

She suspected Eisenhower was unbeatable and her concern for Fjr. arose from his involvement in Averell Harriman's campaign for the Democratic nomination.

A letter on January 10 to David, projecting possible dates for the Assembly's ending, showed the narrow line she walked between wanting him and not pressing him.

David dearest,

. . .

Please, what do I give you for vaccines? I'd like to send a check before you leave.

I think I can arrange to come in thro' Jerusalem so you will meet me there.

We are all invited, as I feared, to stay and be the guests of the top people in Pakistan but I've written you wanted to make a study of present day medicine and I've said what I wanted to see. You won't have to do any parties or meetings that I do unless you find them interesting. They do too let us go a way into the Khyber Pass and I've always thought that would be beautiful.

Be sure to let me know the day you get here so I have your room and can meet you at the airport or if I have meetings can send car.

Your letter makes me feel you are really coming and yet I can't help worrying about all your uncertainties. Not to have Martha come and not to see her, not to have anything definite with Nemone, you must feel sad and in some ways lost. I feel happy at the thought of seeing you and yet I want you to do what will bring you real happiness in the long run. I hope Nemone is not resentful against you or me when she is less unhappy. I wrote her and I hope I said the right thing. I wrote Marty too and thanked her for her Xmas wire and said little else.

I am very busy too but I keep evenings free from the first days of Feb. tho' I may be in Luxembourg from the 1st–3rd but even if you get here the 2d I know you'd want to see old friends probably, nevertheless if I *know* you are coming I will probably stay here as I long to see you and won't be able to wait a day if I know you are really here!

Take care of yourself and keep well. I know these weeks are a strain and you suffer in many ways. I wish I could really help but I love you and when you come I hope I can make you feel what it means to me to have you near.

Bless you,
E.R.

Hick sent her new leaves for her engagement book, a service she had lovingly performed for Eleanor since the early Thirties. Eleanor urged her to come in from Long Island to stay with Tommy in New York.

Jan. 22d, 1952

Dearest Hick,

. . .

Life here has been busy beyond belief & the work has been exasperat-

ing . . . I'm glad you got the check for your article & do let me know
what you hear on the book.

Sisty & Nicholas came to tea today because I had no afternoon meeting . . . Last Sunday we went to Lannoy but it should have been Mama
& FDR they would have loved all the family stuff & I felt a little lost!

Tommy sounds busy & is getting rested I think tho' she is lonely. Miss
Corr is good & seems interested but I don't know how she will work out
when we get on the road!

Much love dear
E.R.

She explained to Trude why work made letter-writing almost impossible and
went on:

Jan. 23d, 1952

. . . I feel as you do that there is nothing any of us can do for David
& Nemone on the central question of whether they want to make a life
together or apart. Either way it is going to be difficult for both.

I'm interested in your decision on drinks & your reasons for not having
them for a few months. I think it is easy to slip into just having a little
too much & that does cloud one's judgment & self control & make one
emotional. . . .

Our work is dragged out by Mr. Pavlov [of the USSR] & sometimes I
am discouraged but I suppose we will end! Some good things have been
done & I do not feel the threat of war so close. What you feel about
people is a natural letdown after a long strain, don't push too hard.

. . .

E.R.

The next day she wrote me.

Jan. 24th, 1952

Dearest Joe,

. . . I'm not surprised at the reactions you heard on Eisenhower. It
will be a sad day for him, & in a way for the country, if he runs for
President. He will win but as a hero he will be tarnished & it will get
worse & worse. We need our heroes & we need him here & I doubt if we
need him more as President. I'd rather see Truman back if he'd really
clean house!

. . .

People here say Churchill can't work more than 3 hours a day & I shall
be interested to hear what Mr. B. has to say about his visit. They must

have financial aid from us & they know we can't let them go under. I'm sure Mr. B. gave financial advice.

I'm glad you saw Franklin jr. He needs to feel he is being watched & intelligently criticized & supported. He seems delighted with the baby & I'm so glad all went well for I was getting worried. Fjr. has his Father's buoyancy & courage & perhaps he'll gain in wisdom.

. . .

Com. 3 behaves too horribly but I take it calmly now! I am told we will close the 5th & I plan to leave on the 8th. I'll send you an itinerary in a few days. Good things are emerging slowly. Nations are free that could not exist without the U.N. & strong powers are held in check by this organization. There is much intrigue, greed, dishonesty, but in spite of it all we move forward. I am a bit weary & will be glad to get off as the calls to do this & that increase everyday. All my love to you & Trude & Johnny.

E.R.

A quick letter to David before he flew to Paris.

Jan. 29th, 1952

David dearest,

This will be the last letter that I can send before you leave so here are good wishes for the trip and happy landings. I shall be awaiting you anxiously and your room is reserved here. Should anything hold me at the U.N. look for my car outside. I have to dine out with the Society France Amerique on the 6th but I've asked Dr. and Mrs. Debat to lunch on the 7th as I think you'd enjoy meeting him and do plan to go out with me to dine that night as Miss Corr and I leave around 1 on the 8th. I think it would be fun if we could go to Les Porquerolles for dinner on the 7th, don't you? Sis and Van will want to go too as it is the last night. I hope this is going to be a happy and interesting trip for you and I look forward to our meeting in Israel. Everything will be made easy for you in Israel, and everywhere I am assured.

I am glad you are here doing some pleasant things and that life at home has gone smoothly and I shall wait to hear [from] Marty. Evidently she won't be here in the spring so why don't you go home with me. I think it will be a hard trip and it would be fun. You can always change your ticket here, so do think about it! . . .

The work goes better and I am well so take care of yourself and all my love to you love to Nemone and Grania.

E.R.

Martha sent her a startling letter from Cuernavaca. She not only was unwilling to go with Mrs. Roosevelt and David to Israel and the Middle East but her romance with David was finished. David had everything in the world at the moment except Martha, the letter said, nor did the writer think that was a great cause for sorrow because Martha judged David wanted her less and less. He was fine, better off than when he had first met her, and Mrs. Roosevelt should not let him think otherwise. It was not going to work between David and her, though she hoped they would always stay friends. Evidently Mrs. Roosevelt was as relieved by this news as David, and though she remained fond of Martha, she was content to see the relationship remain at a distance.

She said nothing about this matter to any of us. She did not mind writing to Trude and me about Tommy—even about David and Nemone. She was discreet but informative, especially when she trusted the recipients, who had learned to read her letters for their exclamation points and, when they were with her, for the signs around the mouth and eyes that added to what she was saying.

Jan. 30th, 1952

Dearest Trude,

. . .

I know Tommy is lost without me but I surmise that in spite of mail she is relaxing & getting the only kind of rest she will ever take & she sees some people & goes out quite a bit on her own, all of which is good for her. She is better off in N.Y. than in H.P. because she doesn't walk a step on the snow & ice!

I'm glad you enjoyed a concert with Nemone & David. Nemone does have a love for music & wonderful taste & knowledge. I hope David enjoys his trip, being with me won't add to his joys but it may give him opportunities to see more of the things he wants to see. I rather imagine I'll have to do some women's affairs & speeches & I'm sure they will plan for him to see medical things for I wrote that was his interest. He's worried that we'll have to see too much but of course he won't have to go anywhere he doesn't want to go.

We are nearing the end of our work & tonight after dinner I sent Sis & Van & Miss Corr to listen to Channing Tobias speak on the Oatis case. [William Oatis, an Associated Press correspondent in Prague, had been jailed by the Czech Communist government.] There will be a row & as the State Dept. did not feel I should sit "behind" anyone I couldn't go & I want to hear about it! I go back in the chair after the one point is argued. There is a delegation meeting tomorrow & Friday & it will be recorded on the air as a sort of discussion by the delegation of the results of the Assembly. . . .

E.R.

Feb. 6th, 1952

Dearest Trude,

. . .

David arrived today & had not minded the trip. . . .

We ended the session today & now I have reports to write & formal goodbye visits to pay on Pres. Auriol & Mr. Robert Schuman & much other work.

Tomorrow afternoon at 5 I have what is left of the delegation in at 5 for a drink & go to a France-Amerique dinner in the evening. I forgot to say I have Mrs. [Perle] Mesta for lunch so you see I am not idle!

. . .

We will draw up 2 Covenants of Human Rights but our vote in the plenary was a majority of 4. I think on the whole this session may have *begun* a number of good things. . . .

Devotedly
E.R.

I'm sure you'll give me a better garden than I've ever had & I'll be so grateful.

The next day, as the Assembly ended, she wrote Anna, Hick, and me. The Arab-Israel confrontation was much on her mind, the more so because she soon would be on her way to Lebanon, Syria, and Jordan.

Feb. 7th, 1952

Anna darling,

I get off with Miss Corr for Beirut at 1:45 on Saturday the 9th, & I'll send you P.C.'s even if I can't write for a little while. They seem to be arranging a very tight schedule! . . .

My work is really done but I still have to go to the office tomorrow morning & sign mail. My reports are written but I have 2 columns to write & I still want to rewrite the 1st chapter I wrote of the book & write the 2d! I'm loaded with information & all kinds of people are prepared to show me things so if I don't learn something on this trip I just can't learn! I'll be walking on eggs in the Arab countries because they know I believe in Israel but so far with the Arab press I've got by!

David arrived Tuesday & is busy as can be & enjoying Paris to the full. He'll go to Israel Sunday night & we will meet in Jerusalem on the 15th.

. . .

Devotedly
Mother

She crisply summed up the Assembly for Hick.

Feb. 7th, 1952

Dearest Hick,

. . .

I wrote my report & picked out the Arab situation as one of the
explosive problems that needed attention. Then our own colored situation & the distribution of truthful facts about us & the need to move
forward on disarmament . . .

E.R.

Her letter to me also dwelt on the Arab-Israel situation.

Feb. 7th, 1952

Dearest Joe,

. . .

I read the Secretary's speech carefully & agree with you but the Near
East Arab situation is pretty explosive I fear & cannot be treated only by
long range economic development plans. What else must be done is the
difficult thing to decide. Perhaps I'll have some more ideas to write you
later but judging from my schedule I'll have little time to write until I
reach India the 27th!

. . .

I think Adlai Stevenson would make a good President but I doubt if he
can get the nomination.

E.R.

Her reference to the need to distribute "truthful" facts about the United
States reflected a realization that the propaganda barrages of Vishinsky and Pavlov
were having an effect upon European opinion, even more on the undeveloped
countries. She had repeatedly cautioned the President and Secretary Acheson
about this. At the suggestion of the Voice of America she had done a weekly
fifteen-minute broadcast in French over the facilities of French radio that was also
carried over the Belgian and Swiss networks, in which she presented the American
viewpoint, speaking simply as a woman to women.

Her experience in the Middle East fortified her belief that the United States
had to pay more attention in deeds as well as words to the "developing East." She
foresaw the conflicts ahead for the Arabs and Israelis.

Karachi
Pakistan
Feb. 22d [1952]

Dearest Trude,

. . .

For a rapid review! The Arab countries are awakening but oh! so slowly

& painfully! The refugees were a horror & it is the Arab govts who keep them stirred up to go home with a little help from the communists! It is like being in another world even in Lebanon & that is the most progressive but the new rubs shoulders with the old everywhere. Jerusalem, the Dead Sea & the Jordan were from the religious historic point of view the most interesting. The feeling between Arabs & Jews was most painful & because of my reputation I was guarded in the Arab countries everywhere by 6 soldiers at least! However I think I left with a little better feeling & still never hid! I never thought of it, but I think they thought I had personally shown courage! Israel is like a breath of fresh air after the Arab countries. Horrible problems, but wonderful leaders & such able assistants. I will have much to tell you & Joe but it is too long to write. I felt at home with the people of Israel.

Here you step back again but efforts are being made, leaders are good but *no* helpers. They want help & should get it I think. So far I've worked on an unbelievable schedule. It was printed & when I leave I'll mail it to Tommy & make her show it to you. David has been oppressed & depressed by it tho' he has been able to get off on his own most of the time. Every place has had a schedule as heavy as the one I will mail home from here! Miss Corr has rested here & is better. I'm thankful I didn't bring Tommy. . . . I feel far away as I've had no mail here.

Devotedly
E.R.

Governor's House
Lahore [Pakistan]
Feb. 25th, 1952

Anna darling,

You must wonder what has happened to me but I've lived on such a close schedule that I've had a hard time to write the column & letters have been few & far between.

. . . The Arab states were hostile as I expected tho' their officials tried to be friendly & I hope I left them more friendly. Israel was a great experience & if only there could be better feeling & those refugees could be resettled, Israel could enormously help the Arab countries & get some much needed food stuffs & other commercial advantages in return. Their collective communities are most interesting but it is the quality & ideals of all government people that is so impressive. If it can be preserved I think it must be a great nation some day.

Here problems are staggering but top people are able & fine but such a mass of ignorance to carry! Everyone has been very kind but I feel there is so much to be done & will I have time & strength just to set the ball rolling. Who knows? No one may listen after I get home!

We go to one of their big development projects tomorrow, all except David who has had bad sinus & hopes to stay home & flirt with some lovely ladies! The next day we leave for India & I hope from there on for a somewhat lighter schedule on lunches & dinners at least!

I hope all is well with you & I long to hear. My love to Johnny & much, much to you darling.

Mother

A note to Anna after ten days in India.

Lalitha Mahal
Mysore [India]
March 6th, 1952

Anna darling,

. . . We've seen a good bit of village life & the level in the village & city slum is far below anything we know. The spirit, religious life & dignity of these people is also something astounding however. . . .

We've seen a princely State, we've of course been a government guest so there have been endless schedules & every meal official & speeches without end. So far I've had a good press & I don't think I've made any bad mistakes. I've cut . . . my programme & that may mean hard feeling but I didn't think it wise to take 2 long flights they had planned. The State Dept. & [U.S. Ambassador] Chester Bowles I hope will feel that on the whole I've done my job & been helpful.

No letters from home so I feel rather lonely & far away.

All my love
Mother

Eleanor had some deeply ingrained moods and attitudes that she had learned to conceal but that nonetheless devastated her. At the time of Austin's illness when she became acting chairman of the delegation, Trude had suggested she should be made permanent chairman. That position the men reserved for themselves, Eleanor had replied. Scarcely less deep-seated than the conviction that it was a man's world was an inability to acknowledge her own merit. The huge crowds that turned out to greet her in Pakistan and India, people kneeling in the streets as her car passed, brought the comment, "I hadn't realized how they cared about Franklin." This was a felt tribute to Roosevelt's greatness as well as a manifestation of genuine modesty. But there was also the sense that had begun with her mother's calling her "granny" of how little she had to offer others. When in the thirties she had commiserated, almost fatalistically, with Hick's lament that she was always treated as Eleanor's surrogate instead of being appreciated for herself, her sympathy reflected her own situation, as she saw it, of living in Franklin's shadow.

In India her "breakneck" schedules, which involved huge numbers of people and long distances, endless receptions, dinners and speeches, turned David rebellious, as she had feared. That, coupled with the obvious expectations of Indians and Pakistanis that she might get U.S. help for them which she was powerless to deliver, produced a depression that came to a head in one of her old "Griselda" moods. Her mouth tightened, she became elusive and silent. Her depression in South Asia crystallized midway during her stay in India when David announced that he had had enough and, instead of accompanying her to another reception and dinner, would find his food elsewhere. David's account of what happened as he told it to the Sandifers the following summer stressed her fatigue. In any case she announced to him

> she could take no more, that she was going home tomorrow. . . . He [David] told her that she was not ill, that her problem was that she was suffering from fatigue and persuaded her to take a few day's rest and continue. He told her she could not quit and turn back and said, "What would your children think of you?"*

But some years later, after Mrs. Roosevelt's death, when I interviewed David for *The Years Alone*, his account of the episode had a different emphasis. The morning after the dinner from which David stayed away she appeared with telegrams she had composed to Nehru, Acheson, and Cass Canfield of Harpers canceling her trip. David remembered her telling him, "I represent the United States and they expect all these things from the United States and think I have the power to deliver them what they need." That was what she said, "but the real thing was that she was hurt," David went on, "and had fallen into one of her 'what am I living for' moods. . . . The whole day was impossible. You couldn't get a word out of her." She was fatigued. Her inability to promise Pakistan and India help in the absence of power to deliver did her credit. But would they have triggered one of her "Griselda" moods if she had not feared David's alienation? The following day she had recovered her poise and serenity. "I do not know how many more official welcomes, lunches and dinners I can stand," she wrote Acheson, and instead of canceling the rest of the trip went on, "but I will do the best I can." Part of her strong reaction, Maureen Corr felt, "was that David not only went off on the town, but there were girls involved."

"Her trip to India and Pakistan was a great success," Acheson briefed the President when she reported to the latter on her return. An unexpected accolade, in addition to the sessions with Representatives and Senators, as well as the Defense Department people headed by Secretary Robert Lovett, was an invitation from the chief of the CIA to brief his people. Together with the book that she wrote, *India and the Awakening East,* she did a great deal toward alerting America to what later became known as the Third World. She probably would have perse-

* *Mrs. Roosevelt as We Knew Her,* by Irene Sandifer, privately printed, 1975, p. 98.

vered even if David had not been with her, but his presence added a personal zest that she found indispensable.

Fala was a victim of old age. She buried him in the rose garden near his dead master. Elliott, who accompanied her to the interment of the little dog, wrote later, "She had not wept at Father's burial, but the tears came this day. I had never seen her openly give way to grief before. . . . In lamenting the end of the scottie, Mother wept for his master."

The Human Rights Commission worked away on the two Covenants that spring, and she persevered even though she knew that Republican support for the Bricker amendment* made Senate approval unlikely. She had been in politics long enough to realize that the public mood changed and in international affairs perseverance and patience were indispensable. Involvement in Human Rights meetings, moreover, made reasonable her avoidance of support for any of the candidates bidding for the Democratic nomination. They included Harriman, Estes Kefauver, and Adlai Stevenson. Fjr. was working for the first, Jimmy for the second, and Stevenson interested her. Elliott privately and Johnny publicly favored Eisenhower, so she was glad to have a legitimate excuse to keep hands off.

It took a special plea from President Truman to get her to make a speech on the UN to the Democratic convention in July. She doubted anyone's ability to make the convention delegates listen but she would do her best.

July 26th [1952]

Dearest Hick,

It was wonderful to get your letter. I kept thinking of '40 during the few hours I was there & wishing you were there. I had dreaded the assignment for I couldn't imagine a convention stopping to listen to such a speech & yet I felt the Republicans had done so badly we must do something . . .

. . .

Now to business. Harper's wants a primer for women on politics. I can't do it alone, but if you'll do it, I'll help & work with you & both our names can go on as coauthors. Please consider it, it is needed, but I can't give the time to consultations with them, research & basic writing—I'll discuss with you & write some parts & go over all of it & we'll have fun I hope. They'll give you an advance.

. . .

E.R.

The writing of *India and the Awakening East* did not go as easily as she had hoped, she wrote Trude and me on Martha's Vineyard:

---

* The proposed amendment by Senator John W. Bricker (R.-Ohio) would have shifted the treaty-making power from the President to Congress, even to the forty-eight states. The Senate rejected it in 1954.

Aug. 9th [1952]

Dearest Trude & Joe,

. . .

Harper's still feels I've written too much of a travelogue & their suggestions will come thro in a few weeks so I hope to be thro' with that before Sept. is out. It won't be out till Jan.

I hear Jimmy Wechsler & Joe are to be dissected by the Journal-American in Sept. or Oct. I hope they get their answers & evidence all ready as this may give them both a full chance of reply which they have never had. I'm a bit suspicious that it is aimed at me too & if so I will be glad to take any part possible short of answering Pegler!

. . .

E.R.

David spent much of that summer at Hyde Park.

August 11 [1952]

David dear,

Your telegram came. . . . I miss your voice and presence and I wish you would feel this was home and you would always come and go as you chose. This includes those you love, of course, and want to have with you.

If you could lunch with me next Wednesday let me know and I'll make no other engagement for I'll take a 2:30 train back. Anyway I'll telephone you. Somehow I don't like you to be back in town, in the heat, at work and yet I know you long to be on the "polio" cases. I dread the chance of infection for you just now and I will be saying prayers for you as I do for my own children. Does that make you laugh?

. . .

E.R.

She was not wholly sold on Stevenson at the time.

August 21st [1952]

Dearest Joe,

. . . Of course I miss you all. . . .

. . .

Eisenhower does not seem to me to be saying much. I'm anxious to see Stevenson develop his theories. He told Averell he was critical of F.D.R. in his handling of Congress & his inability to get along. It isn't really possible under our system I fear, for the Executive & the Legislature to get along well.

My dear love to Trude & to you & Jonathan,

Devotedly
E.R.

Hick, as Eleanor hoped, met with the publisher of the proposed book on women and politics and a contract was drawn up.

[E.R. to Lorena Hickok:] [August 22, 1952]
I was delighted when your letter came & the contracts followed & I signed & returned them. Now the outline is here—Doris Fleeson is coming this p.m. & I'll try my hand at an interview even tho' you sent me no questions. Send me my list of interviews. I go to Washington in September.

As she wrote to Anna, "I am on the delegation to the G.A. [UN General Assembly] & trying to do a little for Stevenson around here & so busy I hardly have time to breathe. The finishing touches on the book seem impossible to do!" She and Tommy intended to fly out to Los Angeles for Anna's wedding to Dr. James Halsted. Two of Johnny and Anne's children, she added, had polio, "& David who was with us knew at once." A note on October 23 grieved over the death of her aunt Maude Gray.

[E.R. to Anna Boettiger:] [October 23, 1952]
David [Gray] is here & quite wonderful. It seems impossible that Maude is gone. We met so little of late & I'm so busy that I can't mean much to anyone, but she is the last person I have known as long as I can remember. I love the young about me, but I remember all about them & they can't know anything of my past so with Maude that particular tie is gone forever.
I don't look forward to the Chile trip but if I live thro' this coming weekend, I should live thro' anything! . . .
I wonder what you think Stevenson's chances are? I never saw a campaign in which the regular organization seems to have done so little & the amateurs & volunteers seem to have run the show. . . .

She made a few campaign speeches but one in Harlem must have stung Eisenhower. She reproached him—the words were soft but deadly—for not having defended General Marshall against Republican Senator Jenner's scurrilous remarks.

I know that it must have been terrible to face yourself—to realize that you have been persuaded that you must go out and stand beside men who have said things about someone who had been your best friend, someone who had really given you the opportunity to rise to great position.
Yet he [Eisenhower] stood by the side of [Sen. William E.] Jenner, who said that General Marshall's life was a living lie.
How General Eisenhower could do that I cannot understand. I cannot

understand how he could give a mark of approval to Senator McCarthy. . . .

The speech had no effect on the Eisenhower landslide but it may have seared him personally. After his election Eleanor promptly submitted her resignation. Career diplomats at the State Department who had worked with her hoped the General would rise above partisanship and in the American interest prevail upon Mrs. Roosevelt to remain. Bernard Baruch, who had supported Eisenhower against Stevenson, inquired and learned that Eisenhower had told Dulles, who would be his Secretary of State, that he did not want her reappointed. Muriel Sandifer, the wife of Mrs. Roosevelt's chief State Department adviser, wrote in her memoir: "Mr. Baruch told her that President Eisenhower had been told by Mrs. Mesta, the U.S. Ambassador in Luxemburg, that Mrs. Roosevelt had said that Mamie [Mrs. Eisenhower] was an alcoholic. One of the members of her family was in the group and said, 'Did you?' Mrs. Roosevelt replied, 'I only asked if it were true. It was going all around Paris that winter.' "

That was Eisenhower's reason for accepting her resignation as Eleanor understood it. A fatalist in regard to things that she really wanted, she had been preparing herself for the likelihood that a Republican President would not want to continue her at the UN. She did not expect to be reappointed, she told the world. But David remembered how "upset she was at the acceptance of her resignation. Somehow she had expected to be treated differently."

There was more to the new President's decision than the remark she had been rumored to have made about Mrs. Eisenhower. Professor Athan Theoharis, who has tenaciously pressed for documents under the Freedom of Information Act on what has come to be called the "Lash-Mrs. Roosevelt matter," was sent a batch of material from FBI Director Louis Nichols's file that included a memorandum of January 8, 1953, on his meeting with Eisenhower confidantes James L. Murphy and Francis Alstock in which the incoming President's plans were discussed. Nichols reported to J. Edgar Hoover:

> The General has a thorough distrust, distaste and dislike for Eleanor and told Dulles [the incoming Secretary of State] several times to get her out of the picture. Overtures were made to the Eisenhower Headquarters by John Roosevelt to keep her in the picture. Alstack [*sic*] reasoned that as long as Eleanor was in the picture, she would not become the subject of any Congressional investigation, but that sooner or later there was going to be an investigation of her affair with Joe Lash.

Professor Theoharis,* who passed this memorandum along to me, commented, "I am struck by the extent of the bitter animus felt by conservatives for Mrs. Roosevelt, in great part I am sure because of their bitter hatred for FDR."

* He is researching a book on *Liberty and Security: Intelligence in a Democratic Society.*

Both in her private and public life there were considerable changes. For the first time in twenty years the country was governed by Republicans rather than Democrats. She promptly went to work for the United Nations Association, a nongovernmental organization to build support for the UN among the American people.

Friday night Dec. 19th

Anna Darling,

I have been a wretch about writing but today we had our last Com. meeting & tomorrow our work will go thro' the plenary so I feel care free, with plenty of time on my hands! In one way it is sad to leave the U.N. officially but working with the U.N. Ass. will be a challenge & seems to me very necessary. I may fail but it is worth a try. . . .

I haven't got any radio or T.V. yet, the advertisers think I'm too controversial! . . . The best of New Years to all & a big hug to you.

Mother

There were changes at Hyde Park. The John Roosevelts had settled in the stone cottage. There were rows "like Kilkenny cats" between Elliott and Minnewa on one side and John and Anne on the other. Elliott moved away, despite Eleanor's efforts to patch things up. One morning Eleanor awakened to read in the New York *Times* that the top cottage built by the President had been sold by Elliott. Eleanor's friends had the impression of a deep disappointment framed in an overall sadness. Yet she never stopped loving Elliott and pleading with him to remain at Hyde Park. In Elliott's book, *Mother R,** he printed his mother's letter to him after the sale of the top cottage.

Darling Elliott: I have been sick at heart all day for I hurt you and that is not what I ever want to do. I know what you spent on the place and what a millstone the debt has been and I know when you sold the Top Cottage it was the only thing you could do. I never said a word about it tho' I felt badly for you and for myself for I knew I would miss you sadly and I wanted above all to have your love and keep your home there. . . . I hoped you would all come back and be with me often and perhaps in the end you and Minnewa would live in my house if Johnny stayed. . . . If Johnny wanted to stay, I'd gladly hand my house over to you any time and build a cabin. . . . If you don't want to come back to Hyde Park, perhaps you'd better sell it all. Tell Johnny quickly before he puts money into it and we'll all go our own ways. I can live much more cheaply in other countries. . . . I have never been "disturbed, angry and disappointed" in you. I've always loved you dearly, wanted you near and been

* New York, 1977, p. 202.

proud of the fine things you have done. . . . You have weaknesses and I know them, but I never loved you less because I understand so well. I know you have tried to do the right thing and you have never failed me! Living at Hyde Park itself means little to me. Keeping it for you and Johnny would have had a meaning. . . .

It was a rough year for the woman to whom success in private functioning was far more important than the "public things."

An episode that David told me about resulted in a long talk between the two of them about suicide. John and Elliott had nearly come to blows, the former quite drunk and Elliott at his most outrageous. Their scrapping with each other at her dinner table ended with both turning their accusations against her. She talked with David afterward about doing away with herself. "My children would be much better off if I were not here," she said to David. "I'm overshadowing them."

The sadness with her children—perhaps that was another service her friends performed. We kept her from sinking too far.

XIX

The Root of the Matter

IN JANUARY 1953 Mrs. Roosevelt left the now-familiar offices of the U.S. Mission to the United Nations and entered those of the American Association for the United Nations, an organization that was committed, as its name indicated, to rally popular support for the international agency. All she wanted, she told its officials, was a cubicle, into which she walked, wrote New York *Times* correspondent A. M. Rosenthal, "as if it were the Gold Room of the White House." Her Oyster Bay kin said of leaders strong enough to face harsh realities that they had the "root of the matter" in them. That was true of Eleanor. As time went on that winter and the Eisenhower administration yielded to its Republican right wing on human rights, what had been a hunch with her became settled conviction that she never would have been able to represent the administration's position. But she also knew its passivity would be changed only by work at the grass roots. In the twenties she had toured New York State tirelessly to build the women's division of the Democratic Party; now she began to tour the nation for the AAUN.

She was changed in appearance from the twenties. Gone were the heavy tweeds, the sensible oxfords, and hair nets of that period. She sought to look attractive, younger, interesting. She had changed in that respect in the White House years. There was an added element. Now fighting off loneliness, she wanted to look as young as she felt. She made great efforts to slim down. She tried different hair styles, once cutting her hair short, another time frizzing it. She returned from Europe with striking clothes. The famous Roosevelt protruding teeth had been replaced after her automobile accident outside New York City in 1946. Martha Gellhorn spoke of Eleanor's solicitude for David as motherly in character. It also had a romantic element, and like older women generally who are interested in younger men, she wanted him to see her as bright and appealing rather than dowdy.

Martha gradually was fading from the picture, as confused about David as the latter was about her. Having refused to marry him when he was in Mexico, she had second thoughts and turned up in New York in 1953, but by then David, to Eleanor's satisfaction, had turned cautious and did not revive his offer to marry.

As Tommy became more of an invalid, Eleanor's fear of being alone at Hyde Park intensified. "If Johnny [Roosevelt] moves now," she wrote Elliott after he and Minnewa had moved away, "I would not stay at Hyde Park as I cannot undertake to run the place and be there alone."

She flew down to Sarasota, Florida, to spend some time with David Gray. On the same trip she spoke for Israel Bonds in Miami, saw Earl, who was living in retirement near Fort Lauderdale, and made appearances for the AAUN. Her letters to David chronicled the trip.

Miami
[no date]

David dearest,

It was nice to hear your voice yesterday morning and I loved your thought.

Our trip down was bumpy and we were an hour late, however all went well at the press conference and Bonds for Israel meeting. Dr. Dov Joseph and his wife came too for the meeting. He is Minister of State for Israel, was Military Governor of Jerusalem and his speech was good. I had a talk with his wife about the loss of their youngest daughter in the army during the war, one of those curious talks when you feel a sudden bond of understanding with a perfect stranger. I imagine that happens often to you.

Two of my speeches are made, this morning at the university it seemed to go well. There have been full houses but it remains to be seen what happens tonight and on Sunday in Sarasota.

I hope you feel well, take care of yourself and enjoy Grania.

My love to her and to you. Devotedly.

E.R.

David had a delicacy of understanding of people that was almost psychic in nature, inherited perhaps from his mother, a physician who was even more psychic in her approach to healing people, going as far as "laying on of hands" in her practice. Eleanor believed his intuitive understanding was what made him such a good physician.

> Sarasota
> March 16th

David dearest,

Tomorrow we leave for Daytona and Wednesday afternoon for home so I will hope to call you Thursday morning at home. I do hope you have been well and not too busy to enjoy Grania.

. . .

Last night's Israel Bond meeting was a great success. $50,000.00 bought which they said was good for this place.

I marvel at the people who seem to be able to spend months in Florida. I would not like it! My love and thoughts go to you.

> E.R.

Back at Hyde Park.

> Easter Sunday

David dearest,

Somehow Easter is the day when everything is born again or rather we are reminded of it. The hopeful time of year and so on this day I wanted to wish you joy and happiness but I couldn't get you this morning. I called at 9:45 and 10:15 and then realized the day was lovely and you had probably found youth and beauty and gone to enjoy the day! Instead I write you these lines just to tell you my love and best wishes for you. You mean more than you know to me.

Bless you take care of yourself and I look forward to Friday and next weekend.

> E.R.

Tommy, who had been with her on the trip to Florida, was paralyzed by a stroke soon after their return.

> April 6, 1953

Dear Trude and Joe:

It was so nice of you to send the beautiful flowers to Tommy and I know if she could see them she would enjoy them very much. Unfortunately she is still unconscious with no change today. All we can do is hope for the best.

> Much love,
> E.R.

Stalin died early in March and the whole world speculated over what the shift to Malenkov might mean. Mrs. Roosevelt was cautious. The Soviets will not be educated to a "live and let live" policy for a long time, she wrote in her column, but if they were disposed to allow armistice talks in Korea, she hoped the United States responded with statesmanship.

April 9th

Joe dearest,

I loved your note, I concede the policies were Truman's & I should not have given this Administration any credit! I read your articles every night & they are grand. I'm very proud of you.

Tommy seemed a shade better today but it is hard to know what to hope. You & Trude are a real help in your constant love & thoughtfulness. Bless you dear.

E.R.

On April 12, the anniversary of F.D.R.'s death, Tommy died. "I went to H.P. at 4:45 this morning," she wrote Elliott, "but as soon as the people who came to lunch after laying a wreath at Father's grave had gone, Joe and Trude drove me to town and straight to the hospital." Tommy died just as she got there. She wired the news to James and asked him to tell Anna and Elliott. Her letter to James continued—

[E.R. to James Roosevelt:]   [April 12, 1953]

I've thought these past twelve days of every possible adjustment that might have to be made, and it isn't a shock, but we are all going to miss Tommy a great deal. She was loyal and loved us all very deeply. I hope she was happy and I think she had the kind of life she wanted.

Her letter to Anna added, "So far I've found no will. . . ." "I know there is no use dwelling on how much you (& we 5, & Sis & Buzz & some of the other older grandchildren) will miss her," replied Anna, "but still, not having her around is going to be hellishly hard to take."

A note to Hick before she flew out to the West Coast to speak for the AAUN and to visit Jimmy, Elliott and Anna, and Tiny: "Hick dearest, How sweet of you to write & how nice to get it today before going off. You will miss Tommy, as we all will daily for she did so much for those she loved."

On her return from the Coast, on David's urging she made what later proved to be a premonitory visit to the hospital.

April 23d [1953]

David dear,

I never thanked you for the flowers you sent Tommy but there was and always is so much to thank you for. You have been such a dear and understanding friend, and I have been and am endlessly grateful.

I'll be at Harkness on the 29th at 5 P.M. Meantime try to get here by 7:30 for dinner upstairs on Monday. The theatre is near but goes in early.

My love and thanks to you. Some day I may be able I hope to do some little things for you. Devotedly

E.R.

A journal entry that I made in May just before she left for Japan explained her visit to the hospital.

Also on Monday Mrs. R. had innumerable stitches taken out of her wrist where the week before the doctors at Columbia Presbyterian had taken a sampling of her tissues because of worry over a finger that was tending to become immobile. David said the 3 guesses in order had been, leprosy, cancer, tb, but on opening up it was none of these only some minor disorder, but there had to be a great many stitches. It did not slow her up one whit and simply forced her to cancel one UJA meeting the night she spent at the hospital.

The same journal entry recorded some of the events that attended her departure for Japan. She was accompanied on that trip by Maureen and Minnewa. It was underwritten by the U.S. Committee on Intellectual Exchange, which was administered by Dean Harry J. Carman of Columbia University. Afterward she intended to meet David in Athens and from Greece go to Yugoslavia.

She had asked Secretary of State Dulles whether he preferred to have a Republican woman go to Japan and he had loftily replied that it did not matter since she would not be representing the United States and had pointedly ignored her offer to come to Washington to be briefed by the department.

Tokyo
May 26th evening

David dear,

I shall mail you the reports I write to Dean Carman as I couldn't write so much long hand. I miss not having Tommy at home to send me news of family and friends! . . .

Some papers at home must have created an "incident" out of a simple little situation. A group of communist women waited for me at the Labor Ministry crying "Go home Yankee, we know war and don't want it." They were led by a high strange, fanatic Anna Rosenberg (the woman

whose record they tried to hang on Anna Rosenberg!).* I simply said we
did not want war either and drove away and that was all!

. . .

My love to Grania and so much to you.

E.R.

Minnewa is valiantly learning.

She wrote much the same to Trude and me, adding, "I made my first speech
yesterday p.m. at the Tokyo Women's Club, mostly foreigners stationed here. . . .
This is a fascinating experience & I like so many people here." She was meeting
more Japanese than she had Indians in India, she wrote Anna. "We did get a
glimpse of Fuji on Sunday, snow-capped with clouds floating about the base. . . .
Tokyo was so badly destroyed that much of it looks like flimsy slums. . . . Sunday
we go to Kyoto, the old capital, untouched in the war, very beautiful they tell me.
. . . How I hate translated speeches!"

"Everyone has talked to me," she wrote Hick, "& I should understand Japanese thinking in many varied groups since my hosts tell me no one has so successfully drawn people out. As usual the problems are great."

[E.R. to Joseph P. Lash:]   [June 3, 1953]
    . . . All young people here are Marxist or nearly all! It is theory how-
ever not based on reality. . . . The [British] Coronation topped all news
here. Two Senators have been here but haven't made much of a splash.
. . . These people don't want to rearm! I think they'd prefer to let the
Soviets walk in than to fight. They don't like us deep down but it is
because they think we'll force them to rearm to fight Asians! Economic
conditions are a staggering problem.

On the way to the industrial city of Osaka, she stopped at Nara.

Nara Hotel
June 7 (1953)

Dearest David,
    This temple and these carvings date back to 600 A.D. and are [the]
oldest *wooden* structures in [the] world. I have a beautiful picture of this
Buddha which is the loveliest I have seen. This hotel is beautifully situ-
ated. We are about to go to the park and see 200 deer fed and then
another temple. This afternoon on the way to Osaka a communal farm
community somewhat like a kibbutz will be visited.
    These are good farming areas but next week we'll see some where

* An American who had married a Japanese and was named Mrs. Anna Rosenberg Fujikawa.

poverty is so great that the father will sell his daughter to the tea house city procurer for 10,000–30,000 yen according to her beauty.

I'll finish this in Osaka.

Sunday evening

We were warned of a typhoon so did not see the communal village but in pouring rain went thro' an Etu village. Somewhat like untouchables in India and under a new constitution made legally equal. . . . Reminded me of bad Indian villages at home or mining areas in the depression! People were friendly and glad to see me. Girls from here go to cities and get picked up at station and become prostitutes. The conditions around our camps are shocking and of course narcotics enters into the picture especially where Negro troops are concentrated. Too long a tale to write and the military make light of it but I fear it is rather serious.

Grania may like the P.C.'s if she hasn't left. Give her my love.

[E.R.]

The transcript of the next letter was marked by David "(Last page of a letter; first page(s) missing)."

Hotel Osaka

Should you want to move into my apartment after Grania goes and be there in August and have Grania there in September no one will be there and I would love to have you use it. I'm really going to look for a house when I get back! It seems a long time since I said goodbye to you on May 19th and it is still more than 3 weeks till I can look at you again. My little photograph does not take the place of the reality and I will be very happy to see you.

This is a wonderful experience however. . . . I dictated the first draft tonight of an article on one subject everyone brings up. The students and young people, labor and the professors and women don't want to rearm but the students are most vociferous. Some of it is engineered by the communists but they play on responsive chords. The next article should be on the change in women's position. I'll see the Emperor and Empress on the 24th.

. . .

We go to Hiroshima tomorrow and Tuesday and Wednesday are bad days. . . .

I always thought Japanese art was a poor copy of Chinese art but they do some beautiful things.

Bless you, David dear, stay well and be happy when we *both* reach Athens!

My love to you dear always.

E.R.

Her letter to Anna from Osaka, which she called "the Chicago of Japan," although she admitted to aches and pains, was still indicative of a readiness to try something new. She was growing old, perhaps that was why she did not dwell on such symptoms when writing to the rest of us. To Anna, too, she confessed doubts about U.S. policy toward Germany as well as Japan.

Osaka
June 4th [1953]

Anna darling,

. . . Two things I find difficult here. I cannot flop on my knees gracefully, sit back on my heels for an hour or two without moving & rise without effort! Nor did I bring shoes that I can walk in thro' mud, slip off when I go indoors or thro' a temple & put on again easily without sitting down! I'm really not sold on Japanese food either, tho' I never miss trying a new thing. It is a little like having a whole meal of hors d'oeuvres, an endless variety of bites is put before you, rice is all you get in any quantity! I do like the idea of doing your guest honor by the flower arrangement & the particular art objects you bring out on display for the occasion. The houses with their matting or even wood floors are spotless because no dirt comes in on shoes!

. . . The economic situation is basic to establishing a democracy & making them feel free & not *driven* by us is basic to good will between us. Sometimes I wonder whether we wouldn't be safer with Germany & Japan unarmed. It would at least show what we hoped for in the world & if we do arm them, we or the U.N. will have to really defend them, they can't be trusted to do it alone. Many of these people just don't want war again, period & if Russia invades[,] well, it may not be worse than present conditions is their feeling. Freedom & democracy are so new & so hard for the masses to understand & the communist ideal is easier to grasp & they know nothing of the reality!

. . .

I'm really not tired yet & I do find it interesting. Minnewa has been a good soldier, gone to nearly every meeting, been nice to everyone & very helpful. She & Miss Corr are out shopping right now. . . .

Mother

A week later, back in Tokyo after travels that included Hiroshima—

June 12th [1953]

Trude dearest, It was wonderful to find your letter here when we got back from our long trip in southern Japan. I enjoyed all of it except Hiroshima which was a great strain. Human misery is hard to see, no matter where the blame lies.

I saw none of the coronation but it was celebrated here, as it was all over the world. The British know how to emphasize their unity.

. . .

I'm sure Adolph Miller* expected to outlive his wife. Men never see themselves dying first. I'm sorry for Mary but she has money of her own, & if she didn't live in that big house I really think she'd be less lonely.

I've argued the American point of view in so many groups on this trip because a lot of people are theoretical Marxists & anti-American. Russia wants peace & we want war, they say. I think our position would be better if we went home but I can't be sure they won't go communist. I'll send Joe my report to Dean Carman tomorrow.

All my love dear to you & Joe & Johnny & I'll think of you on your birthday.

Devotedly
E.R.

Her letter to me the next day described the situation among the Democratic-Socialists.

Tokyo
June 13th [1953]

Dearest Joe,

Here is the report I wrote yesterday. During the day I had some rather interesting talks with leaders of the left & right wing Democratic-Socialist parties. Latter oppose re-armament but in majority of ways resemble our democrats. Left wing is very Marxian. No one among the intellectuals is a communist but many are Marxist & refuse to recognize the realities of modern communism. Economic problems are so difficult & the people very poor. Population is so great & the average farm is only 1-1/2 acres. Thought the enclosed might amuse you. One feels big & clumsy here. Women are small & graceful & few men are big. Our chief companions Professor Takagi & Mr. & Mrs. Matzumoto are fine people & I like the interpreters & secretaries too.

E.R.

A letter to Jim Halsted, her new son-in-law, repeated that "Hiroshima was painful" and the schedule was beginning to be a strain. "Yesterday for example was a long tough day, 2 hrs. in the morning answering questions from some 30 men, members of the Civil Liberties Union, 2 hrs & a half standing, speaking & answering questions & going to a reception . . . & 2 hrs in the evening on a panel

* The Adolph Millers—he was an economist and Federal Reserve appointee under Woodrow Wilson—were members of the Sunday "Club" that met regularly, usually at the Roosevelt house, during the Wilson years.

discussing the status of women in Japan! Today however is easier." She drank everything in, the way East and West met in every household—a dining-room table while a grandmother sat on a mat on the floor—and she was fascinated by the country's political future.

Tokyo
June 17th [1953]

Dearest Joe,

. . .

I don't believe the international situation is going to become less interesting for a long while. If a truce comes [in Korea] & we really sit down & settle terms for Asia our troubles really begin. Japan *must* trade with communist China. I'm breakfasting Monday with Mr. Joe Robinson, who came out to break up the big combines of business here & has stayed on to advise them how to operate. I want to hear how he sees the future shaping up. He seems very hopeful but I want to get the basis of his optimism. We dined with the Pan Am people tonight & tomorrow I speak at lunch to the American Chamber of Commerce. I've seen so many Japanese that this is giving me the other side of the "medal."

The Japanese newspaper men want me to go to one of our big bases & see the shocking goings on, but I have Father Ford's report & have seen enough in smaller areas to know & I think it wiser not to make a story for them. I wouldn't think it wise to publish the truth about it at home but I mean to talk about it where I might do good.

. . .

N.Y. City [Democratic] leaders sound too dumb for words but I'm glad F)r. is not running for Mayor. I think Anna Rosenberg would make a good Mayor but I don't think she could get enough backing.

I hope I've done a good job here. . . .

E.R.

She was satisfied as she left Japan with her impact on the Japanese people but worded her admission obliquely.

[E.R. to the Lashes:] [June 22, 1953]
. . . I've nearly ended & was pleased to have Mr. Griffith, a business man more than 26 years in the Orient, tell me tonight he thought I had made no mistakes & done much good for the U.S. I hope he is right. The people become more friendly everywhere I go.

On the way to Athens she stopped in Hong Kong, for "I want to learn about the British point of view *out here* on China (communist) I mean," she wrote Anna. Four days later she reached Greece and her long-anticipated rendezvous with

David. "I've been adamant about engagements here but on the 1st I must lunch with the King & Queen & all of us dine at the Embassy." A letter to me said, "David arrived Monday night after two gay days in Paris. He seems well & I'm hoping will enjoy himself." She was full of the glories of Athens.

[E.R. to Joseph P. Lash:]   [July 1, 1953]
We all three spent yesterday morning on the Acropolis with Miss Tracy, an American archeologist working on the American excavations here & we went back in the late afternoon. It is all most interesting but much more beautiful in the sunset light. Then the Parthenon is over-whelming.

She sent a firm motherly admonition to James.

July 10th
Sarajevo

Dearest Jimmy,
A letter from Anna tells me you are trying to get Rommie's consent to go back into politics. Are you sure that you are enough out of debt to do that? You know if I were to die tho' I'm leaving a request to my trustees that you be not pressed they might feel you had to pay back over a definite period. For me of course you are my best investment but trustees are different & you must consider this!
Certainly Romaine sounds difficult beyond words & I'm glad you have Anna to help you.
This is an interesting country. Everyone agrees vast changes have oc-curred in the past year & I do not feel the secret police though I know they exist & a "bourgeois" is not in a comfortable position. This particu-lar city is a mixture of races & cultures. The Turks were here 500 years, then the Austrians, now there is a Yugoslavia, but each Republic is jealous of its rights. Everyone is a politician & I get asked about McCarthy & our freedoms by a peasant! Haven't yet got my letter of credit but hope it will reach me in Zagreb. Luckily I don't need it!
All my love
Mother

She sent Trude and me three letters from Yugoslavia.

July 11th
Kotor, Yugoslavia

Dearest Joe & Trude,
. . . I hate Joe not to get a real holiday but with this latest news about

Beria* he must be run ragged. Every one here is excited about it & say Malenkov is a "little" Stalin. They expect that Molotov may have a "heart attack" some day soon but concede it might be Malenkov instead!

We've not seen a paper since July 3d no English ones or anything but Yugoslav ones penetrate these areas! They tell us air mail letters to the U.S. take *12* days!

David has collected much interesting hospital & health data for me & I've seen & checked & rechecked on many things told me in Belgrade. Economically, if no war comes I think these people are the best fed in Europe. There is great poverty still & clothes are scarce, poor materials & sky high in price but food & shoes are down, tho' of poor quality & there is little variety in food. I never took a more beautiful drive than we took today from Titograd here, such mountain roads but such views! If David's pictures all come out you will enjoy seeing them.

. . .

E.R.

If David were here I am sure he'd send his love.

From Brioni, Tito's hideout on the Adriatic, she wrote—

July 18th

Dearest Joe,

. . .

I've spent the better part of yesterday & today with Tito. The interview was fascinating to me but I haven't seen Stevenson's & can't tell about duplications. He believes no Soviet moves mean a permanent change of policy, just a response to internal situations. He warns against the West pushing them too hard so they can incite their people in the belief the West will attack them or the satellites. He thinks we should make [Syngman] Rhee give in.

I like Tito & his wife. David & I have discussed him at length. He has charm, a great personality & intelligence, but he is a doer & practical & I think honest. He claims he is no dictator & that communism exists nowhere, least of all in the Soviets. What is being developed here is socialism & he is a social democrat. A step towards communism which however is a long ways off. He insists that each country must develop according to its own needs. Everything is nationalized here & all live on what they earn.

* Lavrentia Beria, former chief of the secret police, was expelled from the post-Stalin collective leadership, accused of treason and trying to seize power, and later executed. V. M. Molotov reappeared beside Malenkov in the ruling Presidium, but power already was moving toward Nikita Khrushchev.

Dubrovnik was such an interesting & delightful place, someday I wish
we could all see it together.

I am trying to finish my Tito article, at least the first draft before I
leave tomorrow afternoon.

I think I get in late Aug 2d, if so I'll call to see if you are in town.

My dear love to you & Trude & Johnny.

Devotedly
E.R.

Her last letter, July 21, from Zagreb to Trude, summarized her Yugoslav visit.
"This has been a most interesting trip. I've been writing letters to Johnny so his girl
could copy & send them to the children & to you so I hope you have had them.
The article has been written & will go off to Nannine Joseph today. The interview
with the Emperor & Empress of Japan went off from Greece & I hope she found a
buyer." The letter ended with an impersonal reference to Martha Gellhorn, who,
she said, "turned up for a night at our last stop." The coolness of the reference may
have cloaked the strength of her feelings. Mrs. Roosevelt was "irritated," Edna,
whom David later married, remembered his telling her. Maureen's recollection was
harsher. Martha had written Mrs. Roosevelt asking when they planned to be in
Yugoslavia and Mrs. R. felt she was asking because she wanted to see David again.
"Maureen told me only recently how angry Mrs. R. was at the time," Edna remarked in 1983.

To judge by the letter Martha sent Mrs. Roosevelt after their encounter in
Yugoslavia, she sensed a chilliness in Mrs. Roosevelt's attitude and feared it reflected a feeling that Martha had hurt David willfully and casually. She had, in
fact, been terrified at the prospect of seeing David again and had almost lost her
nerve. But it was better for both David and herself that she had not, for the
meeting had left both of them with the realization that it was over. If they were
meant to be together it would happen just by itself.

I am on tricky grounds here. In the course of writing about Mrs. Roosevelt, I
have learned that she did not share the judgments of people around her, even of so
valued a collaborator as Tommy. She neither shared Tommy's caustic evaluations of
many of her friends nor allowed herself to be prejudiced against them. She did not
want David to marry Marty, but a few months after the Yugoslav encounter she
was writing "Dearest Marty" a four-page typewritten letter that she signed "affectionately" and that brimmed with news.

[E.R. to Martha Gellhorn:]   [November 2, 1953]

It was lovely to get your letter and I am ashamed to see the date is
September 17th and here it is November 2nd but I was very busy getting
into my little duplex which I am really enjoying. . . .

I saw your mother briefly when I was in St. Louis for a regional meeting of the AAUN. . . .

Planning one's life, my dear, is an exhausting thing and I am not sure anyone ever succeeds very well.

I never thought you were careless or that you willingly hurt anyone and I am glad you can be content and passive.

. . .

I think Stevenson has a difficult position. He must not give the impression that we are a divided country on most issues but he must disagree enough with the administration to have some points of difference in the campaign. I don't think he is in full swing as the leader of the party and I hope he gets there soon.

. . .

I haven't the remotest idea where to send this so I am sending it to your mother and asking her to forward it to you.

By the middle of December I will be much less busy and hope to write more often.

"Be our joys three-parts pain!" Robert Browning's Rabbi Ben Ezra says. Months before, Mrs. Roosevelt had had a letter from Martha saying her romance with David was finished, and she was glad for David's sake and, one suspects, her own. "Sometimes I wish I were as above and beyond all emotions as I try to make myself sound!" Eleanor later wrote to David in connection with a visit to Elliott. The pain was there, but somehow she transformed it into strength and composure.

Esther had been searching for an apartment for her. Eleanor thought she might interest David, who was on the point of a divorce from Nemone, in sharing a house with her. "When I get to Athens on June 29th," she had written Esther from Japan, "I will talk to David and see whether he would consider going into the house perhaps with me, since you suggest it may be a good idea to get someone to share a house with me. He is the only one I can think of who is looking for house quarters and possibly office quarters at the same time." Perhaps David was not interested or both realized that, with the status of David's marriage so uncertain, sharing a house was not a good idea.

From Zagreb Mrs. R. went to Vienna, where she summed up her feelings about the trip in a letter to Hick, typed by Maureen. It began with a few restrained comments on Hick's draft chapter on Mary Lord, Mrs. Roosevelt's successor on the Human Rights Commission, for *Ladies of Courage*. She predicted that Esther Lape might not be too helpful for the chapter Hick was doing on Mrs. Roosevelt. Esther's view of Hick might have been influenced by Tommy, although Mrs. Roosevelt did not say this.

She had seen Hick, Esther had written her. "I told her I did not feel I could" give her material not available elsewhere, but Esther had urged that Steb Bowles, Chester Bowles's wife, be included as representative of a "woman functioning politically and effectively *as wife* of the office holder." In Eleanor's case "the manner of your functioning as a wife developed so firmly and fully into functioning on your own and as yourself only. It is wonderful that it occurred; I think better of the organization of the world because it did; but even if it had not come to pass the original contribution would have still been tremendous."

Back at Hyde Park Mrs. Roosevelt began to plan her move from the Park Sheraton Hotel. Esther had found an apartment, and by Labor Day she hoped to be settled in at 211 East 62nd Street, a duplex. It had a garden so at last she was able to bring her Scottie, Tamas, to town. David as always had a room at Hyde Park. Blythedale, of which he was medical director, was in Westchester on the way to Dutchess County. Eleanor sought to interest Bernard Baruch in Blythedale's rehabilitation work for children.

Hyde Park
August 7th

David dear,

Mr. Baruch telephoned today that on account of a wedding he'd rather postpone our dining with him till he gets back from the West. Do you want to dine with me just the same? I'd love it, but I want you to feel free if something turns up you'd rather do. I hate to go down Tuesday but if for any reason you can't make dinner with me let me know, as I'd go down later.

Hope all has gone well this week and you are not tired. I understand well your feeling of not wanting to make plans ahead and being as free as air. It is a grand feeling! . . .

E.R.

August 19th

Hick dearest,

At last tonight I've finished reading your material & it is simply swell I think. Much more interesting than I thought it could possibly be made.

I have the India book for you when you come to town.

I have been snowed under ever since I arrived by mail, appointments & things I'd promised to do. . . .

The Russians censor in Vienna & I mailed my Tito article in Vienna. The British & the U.S. also censor so every letter is held up at least 3 days!

When I catch up on work I'll be glad I'm back[,] just now I feel a bit burdened. I'd love to see you so come up soon. What has happened with the W.H.C. *[Women's Home Companion]?* . . .

All my love & your work is fine.

E.R.

The seven previous autumns she had been busy with the UN General Assembly. The early weeks of this September were spent in moving and fixing up her new apartment.

> 211 East 62nd Street
> New York City
> September 14, 1953

Hick dear,

I think the chapter is fine and I can certainly appreciate your difficulties during the hot spell but that didn't prevent you from doing a really good job.

Our moving days fell during the heat wave and we suffered from the two evils. However we are getting slowly settled and the apartment is taking shape. It takes me a little while to get used to new quarters but now I am beginning to feel at home. At least the furniture is not in heaps and piles and in all the wrong places.

. . .

> E.R.

She enjoyed entertaining. At the White House she had freely invited people to lunch, to tea, to dinner, a hospitality that she had continued, although with more limited numbers, as a member of the Human Rights Commission and delegate to the General Assembly. The Park Sheraton Hotel had cramped her style, and now that she had an apartment again having people in gave her much pleasure. David, if he was available, was a fixture of such occasions.

> Sept. 23d

Dearest David,

As long as you have to come here on the 29th to help entertain the Wan's* I think it would be too much of a burden for you to have to come the 27th. So I won't expect you to dine that night and I send you these tickets on the chance that you want to go, if not give them to nice Mrs Daniels [his secretary].

Don't bother to telephone Saturday, I don't want to add to your burdens and a long distance call is a nuisance and I might not be in. I'll hope it is good news and if it should happen to be not so good you know that I will just wait to be told how I can help.

I'm trying to find something amusing to go with the Thais on Wednesday the 28th and if I do we will have to dine at 7:15. I'll let you know. My love to you.

> E.R.

* Prince Wan Waithayakon of Thailand, later president of the General Assembly.

There were guests and friends who invited her in return and she enjoyed having David escort her, although she was perfectly ready to arrive on her own, driven usually by "Tubby" Curnan, a local Hyde Park man whose shape was correctly indicated by his nickname. There were some, like Hick, who did not live in town for whom she was always doing things and who were unable to reciprocate. "I'm away a lot & if you come when I'm off you can sleep in my room—I'd like to see you though," she wrote Hick on October 20 and, getting no reply, wrote again, "I'm sending as my usual Xmas gift the money for your coal as you must want to put it in soon. . . . Travelling pretty steadily but here in snatches, Maureen knows you may come." A few weeks later, "Just back from Boston. Go to Syracuse Wed. I hope Tubby can take you to Albany, go on to Syracuse & pick you up on the way back."

She remembered the birthdays of all her children and her friends, and those of us who were married received notes on our wedding anniversaries, sometimes even as the recipients themselves had begun to let the date fade. "Dearest Joe & Trude," she wrote us in an undated note, probably in early November,

> As the years roll on, you have struggled & I hope you find life easier & better. This day should remind you to recapture the first days of your love now & then & as you go on the daily incidents will build a strengthening wall about you both. I love you both so dearly & wish you love & happiness with all my heart. Bless you, spend this gift for something you want.
>
> E.R.

Conversation at her dinner table was brisk. She brought up serious matters, usually voicing her own opinions. A diary entry I made October 28:

> Last night at dinner at Mrs. R's the Rosenmans, [David] Levys, Harry Hooker and myself and Trude. Much talk about Wagner's candidacy and twitting of Mrs. R for her lukewarm endorsement of Bob. Adele summed it up as vote for him as the lesser evil. When Adele said later she would see Bob today with a check, Sam quipped, "Some of the root of all evil for the least of all evils." Sam amused us with story of how they gathered elder statesmen, Lehman, Rosenman, Harriman at Wagner hdqtrs. They suggested Bob not enter name-slinging contest but stick to the issues. A brash young man promptly told them that might have worked 20 and 30 years ago, but it was different today and they were dismissed.
>
> Talk turned to mediocre quality of leadership today. Mrs. R. asked who of today's leaders could stand up to and deal with people of calibre of F.D.R., Churchill and Stalin. Mrs. R. thought Tito. Stevenson might after he developed more self-confidence. Sam demurred about latter. He had great reservations about Stevenson's lack of political instinct. Said he had run into Cardinal Spellman who asked him to get Stevenson to speak

at Al Smith dinner this year—that Stevenson had turned them down year before. When Sam saw Stevenson, latter said he had two invites— one from Al Smith dinner, other from Woodrow Wilson Foundation— wasn't sure which he would accept. Sam said, "You have to make up your mind whether you want to be a statesman or politician."

As always we spoke about deterioration in relations since 1945 with Russia. Sam and Mrs. R. both felt that break could have been prevented had F.D.R. remained alive—at least Sam said this firmly. He thought [James] Byrnes had been a very bad and evil influence and practically acted as president at Potsdam.

Mrs. R. said she understood why Truman did not want to meet with Stalin, that he did not have confidence he could deal with him. Different with Eisenhower and she was greatly disappointed at his holding back and failure to make imaginative use of breaks like Tito's. Sam said he thought even Truman should have gone to meet Stalin.

She said there had been no original idea in foreign policy since Atlantic Charter and UN.

I demurred on whether F.D.R. could have gotten Russians to cooperate in post-war period. Soviet policy was pretty well set in late 1944, I asserted, and seemed to be influenced by other considerations—domestic and internal security—rather than those that governed our thinking. That Churchill's installment on Warsaw uprising showed that handwriting was on the wall in 1944. However, I agreed with Sam that we couldn't do much other than we did at Yalta.

She loved her friends, as she did her children, but her strongest feelings were for David.

Sunday night
[December 1953?]

David dearest,

I thought you might like to know just who will be here Wednesday for dinner:—

Amb. Krishna Menon [of India]
Amb. Comay and Mrs. C. if here [of Israel]
Mr. and Mrs. Eichelberger [of the AAUN]
Mr. and Mrs. Ed Murrow
Dr. Heidelberger
Franklin Jr.

We will not eat till 8:15 as the Murrows can't get here.

Irene's* daughter is alright, but they took the baby at 2 a.m. last night as it was dead. Irene will stop for your wash Tuesday evening as she insisted on coming back then.

Maxeda von Hesse† says you were wonderful to her. She seems to have had a bad time.

Henry [Morgenthau] III will be in N.Y. Hospital all this week but he says he feels fine.

. . .

If you are free on the 14th I think Elliott and Minnewa will be here and we'd love to have you drop in to dine but don't feel it is a date, you can say "yes" or "no" at the last minute.

Don't let anything I ask you to do make you feel hounded. I understand your schedule and never want you to feel you *must* do something I ask. I only want you to enjoy yourself and get relaxation.

I suppose Jimmy's plane will be late and I'll have to wait up for him! I must be up at 6 a.m. so I hope it isn't too late!

. . .

E.R.

[no date]

David dearest,

I want you to have something from me on Xmas eve when you are alone just so you will know how my thoughts are always with you. It is a gift you do not need but I saw them in Japan and thought they'd be attractive with a tuxedo.‡

My Xmas will begin when you arrive on Xmas day. I am so happy you will be with me and hope you will act as though you were in your own home and do just what you want to do and nothing else. Just get a rest and enjoy Grania.

I want you to get over your sinus. I hate to have you suffering.

Do you mind if I tell you now and then how much you mean to me? I love you dearly and respect and admire you deeply but the loving is the most important because that will be there no matter what you do. Goodnight and bless you.

E.R.

* Irene served as Mrs. Roosevelt's cook and housekeeper in town. She entered her employ on the recommendation of David, for whom she had worked. Conscientious and a hard worker, she was not a good cook but that did not trouble Mrs. R.
† Maxeda von Hesse had given voice lessons to Mrs. Roosevelt in the thirties and taught her to bring her high-pitched voice under control, so much so that she had become an outstanding public speaker.
‡ Pearl studs.

1954 was the year in which she would celebrate her seventieth birthday. Its beginning was shadowed by the explosion of James's domestic troubles into the headlines. His marriage with Romelle had had its ups and downs. They focused on James's deep involvement in politics, money matters, and his flirtations. The births of three children had eased the tensions between them only intermittently and finally, at the end of January, the attorneys of Romelle, who sued for divorce, released to the press photostats of a letter James had written Romelle, while on wartime leave from the Marine Corps, that among other things named nine women with whom he had had extramarital attachments.

Eleanor grieved over the impact on Jimmy's children and over the hurt to F.D.R.'s name and the liberal cause. How could Jimmy have given such a letter to Romelle, she asked herself. It was not the way a gentleman behaved. Nevertheless, she considered flying out to the West Coast to lend Jimmy moral support. Esther strengthened that impulse.

[Esther Lape to E.R.:]   [No date]

After a night's reflection: isn't there somebody not too old, vigorous, objective, devoted, in the wide circle of those that loved Franklin who would go out to Jimmy now, confer with him and give him the sound advice he so obviously needs?

I do believe that the presence now with Jimmy of a capable friend, legally and psychologically adept, would give him the support that would not only encourage him to hold onto life (the threat is obvious that he might not) but would also help him to work out wisely the case that could undoubtedly be made for him.

The urge Eleanor had to fly out to James was strongly opposed by her other children. They rightly feared her presence would only fuel the headlines. Jimmy, moreover, had no wish to do away with himself. Instead he decided to run for Congress and vindicate himself that way. She counseled Jimmy against that, telegraphing him—

FEEL IT IMPERATIVE FOR SAKE OF YOUR CHILDREN THAT YOU AN-
NOUNCE IMMEDIATELY RETIREMENT FROM PRESENT CANDIDACY FOR
PUBLIC OFFICE BEFORE ANY COURT HEARING STOP THIS REMOVES
ONE WEAPON AGAINST YOU STOP THOSE WHO PUSH YOUR CANDIDACY
NOW DO YOU A DISSERVICE LOVE

                                                                    MOTHER

A few days later she telegraphed him again:

PLEASE DO NOT ACCEPT ANY POLITICAL COMMITMENT UNTIL YOU
RECEIVE LETTER FROM ME LOVE MOTHER

The letter she sent Jimmy is closed at Hyde Park, but parts of it are printed in
Elliott's *Mother R.*

[E.R. to James Roosevelt:]   [No date]
    No matter what Rommie may agree to or what may happen in the
next few days, I am convinced that you should not go into politics for
several years. . . . I have talked with a great many people, Democrats
and friends, and there is not one dissenting voice. They all feel it would
be a great burden on the Party, on your running mates if you were to try
to run, and that it would bring on you much censure and keep alive a
great deal of feeling which, if you go to work and devote yourself to
business and your children, will die down. You want to get out of publicity, not stay in, for the next few years. If you do the right thing, I don't
think you need be afraid that you will never have other opportunities.
Opportunities always come to people when they are honestly doing their
jobs well. You will be opposed by Democrats from the top down if you go
into political life at the present time, and what is more I would oppose
you and feel that you were doing something that the family was justified
in opposing both in your interest as well as the public interest.
    I want to help you in every way possible to do right, but I cannot help
you do what I consider is wrong. I hope you will show this letter to your
lawyers. Much love,
                                                                    Mother

    Her sternness toward Jimmy was reflected in a letter to David from Fayette-
ville, Arkansas, where she was lecturing as part of a stint that had been arranged by
her lecture agent, Colston Leigh. "Elliott telephoned me last night after the second day of hearings on the money settlement in court and all he reported was
disquieting. It is sad that Jimmy can't be honest with himself." Neither her advice
nor that of the rest of the family changed James's view. Eleanor saw him on a
lecture trip to the West Coast in April.

                                                         Cleveland 15 Ohio
                                                         April 5th
David dear,
    It was nice to hear from Maureen that she talked to you. . . .
    Half my trip and the most strenuous part is over and I think went well.
The papers were quite decent in Los Angeles and I had an afternoon and
evening with all the children and a long visit with Jimmy alone. . . .
    Please don't go till I go away again the night of the 18th. I'll be back

the early a.m. of 24th and that is the day I am holding to go to Blythdale with Mr. Baruch so I suppose you would have to be back too. I'll be gone from the afternoon of the 25th–30th also and then May 2–6 and that ends my long trips, thank heaven! I long to see you this coming Sunday at 7:30 so please come. I miss you. I like to be in the same place even if I see you rarely! I love you very dearly, take care of yourself. How about the checkup?

Your devoted
E.R.

A settlement between Romelle and James was reached. His confidence that he would be able to win the Democratic congressional nomination was vindicated in June by his massive victory. That was one kind of rehabilitation, but it needs to be said that his mother's feelings about the wrongness of his behavior did not change.

Trude and I decided to sell our house at Hyde Park, a few miles from Mrs. Roosevelt's cottage, and build on some land we had bought years earlier on Martha's Vineyard. Although she was not happy over our decision, she made no effort to stop us. "I hate not having seen you," she wrote Trude and me after calling us, only to learn we had gone to the Vineyard, "but I hope you love your new house."

Ever since Franklin's death she had contemplated a trip to Russia, only to be dissuaded either by the President or his Secretary of State, as well as by her own recognition that the time might not be right. But now with Nikita Khrushchev emerging as the dominant figure in the post-Stalin leadership, she agreed to go for *Look* magazine, providing the Soviet Union permitted her to bring her own translator. She talked with all of us about her trip, and when I urged her to stay in the Embassy in Moscow lest the Russians used her failure to do so to buttress their propaganda that neither Truman nor Eisenhower had carried on the policies of F.D.R., she replied—

Friday night

Dearest Joe,

. . .

I haven't been asked to stay at the Embassy & I can't ask myself. The Bohlens may be afraid to have me. I'm more afraid of what I'll do if the Russians ask me to be their guest & I'm going to put that up to Washington thro' Gardner Cowles [*Look's* publisher] when I see him on Monday! No one in the State Dept. seems interested to tell me anything, at least they've made no sign! You couldn't be too cautious, I feel I'll need every bit of your caution.

Would you & Trude like to dine here Monday night with the Walter

Whites, Mark McCloskey's & Dr. [Lawrence] Kubie* at 7:45. I'd love it
if you could.

Devotedly
E.R.

The Russians vacillated about giving a visa to any of the persons whom Mrs.
R. wanted to bring, so she canceled the trip. As she wrote to David, who was on his
way to Europe for a summer holiday—

June 28th at night

David dearest,
    I will not mail this to Mme Vienot for it could not arrive. Before I left
New York I telephoned and you had not yet left but they assured me you
would leave and I hope you did.
    I do not know yet if I go but I sent a wire to the Soviet Embassy
tonight saying "If I do not hear that Mr. B. [Whitman Bassow] can
accompany me by Wednesday I must regret that I will be forced to
postpone my trip." My hunch is that I won't go.
    We had a nice day at Hyde Park Sunday with Franklin Jr and Johnny
and their families in church and Buzz as well for the dedication of the
modest little plaque to Franklin's mother. I think Ellie Elliott [her niece]
did a lovely job on the lettering and I like its simplicity and only hope
that my mother-in-law if she knows about it is pleased. Trude says she
will talk to the Putney people about Grania.

. . .

    Franklin was interesting at lunch and seemed hopeful that the British
would help calm our [word indecipherable] people but tonights paper
says they got nowhere on an Asian agreement.

. . .

E.R.

July 1, 1954

David dearest,
    As you see I am here and not on my way to Russia! No visa came
through for Atwood [William Attwood] or the other man Look offered
tho' I warned twice, so this morning at 10 I had a press conference in
Look's office and explained why reluctantly I had to give up the trip. At
3:25 the Soviet Embassy phoned the second man could have a visa and if
he could not get it in Washington he could get it in Paris! Everything
was cancelled and we decided not to go later. I will not be meeting you in

---

* Walter White, longtime director of the NAACP and associate of Eleanor Roosevelt. Mark A. McCloskey, educator active in public welfare and education fields. Dr. Lawrence S. Kubie, neurologist, psycho-
analyst, researcher in nervous and mental diseases.

Paris and coming home with you. Shall I tell . . . [?] to put you back on Sabena?

I'm sorry not to go but I shall enjoy a free month. I'll be in New York August 1st but I know you've arranged to be East (?) so if you don't want to be bothered with me I'd like to go out and get a glimpse of you and then I'll leave you! Perhaps you will dine with me that first night unless you have other obligations and I'll hope that you will come up here in August for as many long weekends as you can and over Labor Day I hope. I shall miss you so much this whole month that I'll be longing to see all I can of you on your return.

. . .

Undoing things is almost as hard as preparing to go away, but I'll get much done here that should be done. President Truman is better. The British visit did good I think.

. . .

E.R.

Eleanor's letters to David during his month's holiday in Europe are solicitous about his relationship with Grania and rarely mention Nemone, from whom he was separated and about to be divorced. Nemone went to Reno to make it legal. Both by this time appeared to be ready for it, and arrangements for Grania were settled without rancor.

"David dearest," Mrs. Roosevelt wrote him on the eve of his departure,

This just to wish for you and Grania the happiest of holidays. My thoughts, prayers and love will be with you every day. You know I love you dearly and that everything which troubles you is of deep interest to me so take care of yourself and may the summer bring you all that you hope for. Bless you. My love

E.R.

David's holiday started in Paris, where he had two long-time friends, Mme. Viénot ("Andrée") and Lady Mendl ("Yvonne").* Both were socially well connected, Lady Mendl a figure in international high society. He was their doctor, intermittently, and also their friend. When Eleanor spoke of his having a flirtatious time in Paris she had in mind ladies like Mme. Viénot and Lady Mendl. The longer and more serious connection was with Andrée. Grania remembers her as "a booming, monumental lady—but a kiss like a tender feather." She adds, however, about her father's relationship with Mme. Viénot, "I'd be willing to bet it was platonic."

* Andrée and Pierre Viénot were socialists who moved in the highest circles in French society and politics. She was the daughter of a Czech munitions manufacturer. It was at the fabled estate of the latter in Luxembourg that David met André Gide and kindred folk.

Hotel Edelweiss, Sils-Maria
July 4, 1954

Dearest Mrs. R.

Yesterday I wrote you a post card to the Hotel National [in Moscow] and found out later that the papers had published that you are not going. I was very sad. How frustrating. After all the preparations. I am sure that you had a good reason and that you really would not have been sufficiently free. But it is sad. And now you are not going to come at all! Stay in Hyde Park? I imagine your children had something to do with your decision.—Thank you for Stevenson's speech and Grania's pencil.

Andrée was far less belligerent than I had expected. From here Guatemala seems an awful blunder and a good propaganda for the Communists.* The English and French papers gave a much different story from what I would read out of Time and the Times. Quite a shock to me to find out to what point reporting has been falsified.

. . .

Love and many thoughts and wishes that you may enjoy the sudden free time that you got.

David

July 6

David dearest,

Your letter of the 28th reached me today and I'm so glad I was here to get it! It must have been lovely with Mme. Vienot and it made it just right that you found her relaxed and free. By now you may be near St. Moritz and settled for your long vacation. The mountains are beautiful and I hope you are relaxed and resting and enjoying every day.

Over the weekend it was cold, we had fires each day! It rained but cleared long enough so every day I've had a swim. I've had to begin the work of weeding out books as Anne wanted the space for her own books in their cottage. It is fun but work too! I found a wonderful book on photography which I shall take to N.Y. for you as you may find it useful. Going over books means I spend much time reading bits of a strange variety.

. . . That afternoon I'll fly to Colorado and spend 5 days with Elliott and Minnewa. I'll write you later what I do after that but on the 7th I'll be in N.Y. by evening to find out about your plans and tho' I know you will be regretful at getting back you won't mind if just for myself I am very happy?

. . .

E.R.

* The left-oriented regime of Arbenz Guzmán in Guatemala had been overthrown in June 1954 by a U.S. CIA-supported invasion of exiles from Honduras.

Sils-Maria
Tuesday July 6th

Dearest Mrs. R.

. . .

I wonder how you are? And wonder whether you may not like to come over and spend the last 2 weeks with us. But it would seem a little abrupt and short. So far all is well with Grania but not very intimate.

I wonder though, whether it will become more so in the coming weeks. Therefore I become dubious of my need for subjugating everything to that end.

My love and many thoughts—

David

Monday night July 12th

David dearest,

. . .

Mary Lasker* came to lunch today and she and Anna Rosenberg and another lady go to Europe on the 24th. I am glad I am not going with them! She was very interesting about the state of our mental institutions however and she is going to send me some material to pass on to Franklin Jr. How I hope we keep out of war if not, no improvements can be made anywhere.

Mr. Vanderbilt's† "letter" written in [word indecipherable] Germany gives me the creeps. He insists everywhere in Europe war preparations advance and his quotes from European papers are not reassuring. You spoke of being shocked at their antagonism to us but do you feel they expect and prepare for war?

Mrs. Lewis Thompson was here over the weekend, as full of her institutions and her preparations for the prison conference as ever. It is wonderful at 82 to enjoy life so much and have such enthusiasm.

This is just to say goodnight to you and I love you. I'll finish later *Tuesday July 13th.* I had a note from Nemone today and she says you and Grania report good weather and sun so I hope it has improved since you wrote and that you are in Switzerland and having a wonderful time. Thank her. I have no address for her.

The man who's writing the 6 vol. life of F.D.R. [Frank Freidel] came to lunch today and seemed so young we couldn't realize he was a full professor at Stanford. I also went over to the Library to meet a large group of social workers from India and liked them very much. There were some very fine faces among them.

. . .

* Wealthy art connoisseur and supporter of medical research and public health, and also of Adlai Stevenson.
† Cornelius Vanderbilt, author, lecturer, movie maker, man-about-town.

Dulles has gone to Paris. I hope he goes to Geneva. I wonder what you find the Swiss feeling is. I was glad they refused to let U.S. [investigate] employees of the U.N. there, even if they are U.S. citizens.

My love to you.

E.R.

July 9
Morning

Dearest David,

I went to town again today for a meeting of the A.A.U.N. and saw Maureen, who starts her holiday tomorrow and to my joy found 2 letters from you.

It really wasn't frustrating not to go because I had decided unless a visa came through for Look's man it wasn't fair to them to go. I could see no way of safeguarding them if they had no one they trusted along. No one of the children said a word and they were disappointed I think. There was a box in The World Telegram saying "Pegler Should Sue Mrs R for canceling her trip to Russia."

A thousand thanks for thinking of asking me to come over and join you but this is your time with Grania and by now I'm sure the intimacy is growing. Give it every chance. You want to build something which can't change even when you are not together, so that whatever she does and feels she instinctively wants to share with you. Then she is safe and you have a relationship which will bring you happiness all your life. I would love to be with you but try to keep as many weekends in August and perhaps over Labor Day as you can. I have always loved the trips together and shall miss [a] longish, consecutive time together but I feel you and Grania should have it and probably it is important to have it alone especially this summer.

Guatemala seems to be coming out fairly well—Churchill and Eden did well but now Knowland made a bad statement which the President and Dulles toned down. I will tell you many sidelights when you get back but frankly Radford and Knowland and his followers are frightening I think—*

. . .

E.R.

David and Grania moved on to Venice and he wrote Mrs. Roosevelt, "Grania is growing into this being together. She is warming up to Venice and I can relax a

---

* William Knowland (R-Cal.), Senate majority leader, said on July 1 that if China were admitted to UN membership he would resign his leadership and "devote my full efforts" to getting the United States out of the UN. Admiral Arthur Radford, chairman of the Joint Chiefs of Staff, had advocated heavy bombing raids, including possibly nuclear weapons, to relieve the French at Dien Bien Phu.

little more. Still not much intimacy, but it is better." He complained that the mail had stopped.

On her way to Elliott's ranch in Colorado, she wrote David from Denver.

July 16th, 1954 night

David dearest,

I think it will be safer from now on to write to Paris so this will go there. . . .

I brought Irene down for her holiday. . . . She looks forward she says to putting you in order and she insists the apartment needs her care though Anna [Polenz] is coming in twice a week for half a day to clean!

. . . New York has taken on none of that less crowded look that made you say last summer you wished August conditions could always prevail in the streets. It still seems crowded everywhere! . . .

Franklin Jr. made a speech on our foreign policy which I am saving for you. Nothing satisfactory seems to happen in Indo-China and Russia gets her way more and more. Nothing at all happens in Korea. The papers are unhappy reading.

They have drought here, no sage for the cattle, men on farms going bankrupt, it is not a happy place even to land for a night as I have done. I'm anxious to hear what Elliott has to say on his conditions.

Trude and Joe are finally in their new house on the Vineyard and Joe is getting all of next week as a holiday. Trude will go up to Maine with me on the 27th and I think it may be restful for her to get away.

Nothing to tell you dear except that I think of you always and love you.

E.R.

From Elliott's "Rolling R Ranch" in Meeker, Colorado—

July 20, 1954

David dearest,

I hope I find happy news of you and Grania when I go through N.Y. on Thursday for it seems to me a long time since your letter of July 6th. I hope however that silence means you are enjoying yourself too much to write!

It is such beautiful country here. The ranch itself is not beautiful but very comfortable. Elliott says he wishes you and Grania would come next summer. There is fishing, and riding. Some nice people and many native "characters" whom you would find interesting but you have hours of leisure with no one. Beautiful walks and climbs in the mountains to the lake on foot or on horseback and great peace and freedom. I hope I have straightened out with Elliott a number of problems that bothered me and I am glad I came, though on the way out I felt it was a long journey! . . .

I write this with the sound of the rushing river in my ears and otherwise all is quiet.

Bless you dear, may you be rested and not too sad on your return. All my love.

E.R.

My love to Grania if you write before you return.

"Grania does not like sights—but still we manage," David wrote on the 21st. "Nemone is in St. Vigilio on the Garda Lake. She will probably come here to fetch Grania and I shall go from here to Paris." Eleanor wrote in anticipation of his arrival in Paris.

July 22d

Dearest David,

Your letter of the 14th was here when I arrived and I was so glad to get it. Too bad you had to leave Switzerland but you sound as though Venice had proved rewarding. What a lovely pantomime that must have been on the Island. I wish I had been there.

I'm so glad the relationship has grown with Grania. I'm not surprised you are a bit lonely. I think it was something you had to do this once for her but it won't be necessary again till she is older and you feel you both need it again. . . . I met so many human problems in the days in Colorado, I hope wisely—human beings young and old are a fascinating study —Sometimes I wish I were as above and beyond all emotions as I try to make myself sound!

I got back this a.m. to a mountain of work and Trude phoned they were not in their house so I am staying here, with great relief till Sunday a.m. and will drive through to Portland that day and Trude will join me there on Monday evening. I'll be here Sunday afternoon August 1st to meet you the next morning. Just ten days more, they seem long to wait because when you are far away I feel somehow suspended in space and time is so long, but it passes, only I have a great desire to hold you very close and not to let you go.

All my love to you

E.R.

That was her final letter, though David wrote from Paris, "I am happy to see them, [the Mendls] but somehow I am in a hurry to be off. It will be lovely to step out of that airplane in New York and find you, I hope, and go back to normal life again." He had spent the last day in Venice with Nemone, who had come to get Grania. The latter was "not the least emotional. . . . Nemone was a little tense, but I think she too relaxed."

The summer ended with visits to Westbrook to Esther and to Martha's Vineyard to see our new house and a quick trip to Canada for Colston Leigh.

August 30, 1954

Dearest Trude:

I hope you and Joe will be able to have dinner with me at the apartment in New York on Wednesday, September 8th. I have invited Porter McKeever [he had been press officer of the U.S. Mission to the UN during her years there] and his wife and Harry Hooker.

My love to you,
Eleanor Roosevelt

[She added a postscript in longhand to the letter Maureen had typed:]

The above was dictated but I meant to write long ago & thank you & Joe both for a wonderful visit. I loved every minute with you & still think of the lovely view. Henry III lunched here on Sunday & said how much he liked the house.

I'll be glad when you are home & I'm planning the changes in the playroom [where we would be able to stay] now! . . . The Queen Mother of England comes to lunch on election day, Nov. 2d do you think you & Joe could plan to get off & be here?

E.R.

A poignant, loving letter to David.

Wednesday evening
[September 1954]

David dearest

Two warm days here and I hope you have not been too hot for comfort in Washington. I thought of you giving your paper yesterday and hoped it went very well and that on the whole you were enjoying this week. I wish I could have heard you and I would love to be there and to go see the Adams Memorial and the Lincoln statue at night with the light on Lincoln.

New York is lonely without you, but you know I always want you wherever I am.

I've been busy and tomorrow I leave for Montreal. I find I can get off the train Sunday a.m. in Poughkeepsie and I shall hope to leave there about 3 p.m. so if you are in town telephone. I can have supper as late as you like, if you are here and want to drop in just to eat. I know you will have work to catch up on. Please bring me your paper to read.

. . .

Take care of yourself and have a good time. God bless you. My love always.

E.R.

David did not want to make plans and she encouraged him to be "free as air." She, in turn, tried to accommodate herself to his wanderings. A lopsided relationship, but perhaps typical.

The big event that autumn was her seventieth birthday. As on previous birthdays she was reluctant to have it celebrated but yielded to the entreaties of some of the groups she worked with, especially the AAUN, to mark it in a way that enabled them to show their appreciation of her and also to raise some money for their organizations. So the Wiltwyck boys serenaded her and the AAUN gave a formal dinner at the Waldorf-Astoria. She had allowed her hair to gray and her figure had thickened. She no longer rode, although while on Elliott's ranch she had resolved to try again. "No, I have not slackened my pace," she firmly told Emma Bugbee, who had covered her for the *Herald Tribune* since White House days and had come to interview her again. "At least, not yet. I probably shall. Everybody does." Although no member of the Eisenhower-appointed U.S. Mission to the UN came, Dag Hammarskjold, the Secretary General, did, accompanied by his predecessor, Trygve Lie, and Ralph Bunche. So did Andrei Vishinsky, who had informed the organizers of the evening he would be "very glad to sit anywhere."

Despite her criticism of the Eisenhower-Dulles policy toward human rights, her faith in the United Nations did not waver. The UN remained the "hammer blow on the head," as Zola once had described the original Napoleonic ideal. It colored every ambition, undertaking, decision. In permitting the AAUN to pay her homage and celebrate her birthday, she showed that the UN had tempered even her basic stoicism.

> As for accomplishments, I just did what I had to do as things came along. I got the most satisfaction from my work in the UN. There I was part of the second great experiment to bring countries together and to get them to work for a peaceful atmosphere in the world, and I still feel it important to strengthen this organization in every way.*

Her final words on that occasion were for her family. Her four sons and daughter were there and several of her nineteen grandchildren—she also by then had four great grandchildren. More than achievements, "I treasure the love of my children, the respect of my children, and I would never want my children or my grandchildren to feel that I had failed them."

"I really enjoyed Monday night," she wrote Hick afterward, "though I really dreaded it. It went much better than I had dared hope. Now it is over & I hope the AAUN can pay some bills! David's pills stopped my cold as they always do & I am quite alright. . . . Have you got the money for coal or do you want it for Xmas & how much?"

Yet fate still had some surprises for her that year. James, whom she had urged

---

* Eleanor Roosevelt at her seventieth birthday dinner, New York *Times*, Oct. 8, 1954.

to withdraw from politics for a time, was overwhelmingly elected on November 4, while Fjr., a successful Congressman for five years, handsome and strapping, the proven vote-getter, lost a bid for election as attorney general of New York State. She knew Fjr.'s shortcomings but also his abilities and helped him as best she could. She had sat with him and Sue in the rear of the armory where the Democratic state convention had been held and the bosses engineered his defeat for the gubernatorial nomination, which they gave instead to Averell Harriman. Earlier Fjr. had told her that Carmine De Sapio, the leader of Tammany and the key Democratic political leader in the state, had advised him to come to the convention as the upstate candidate. She had warned, "Don't ever trust him." And when the leaders came to him, after denying him the top spot on the ticket, to urge him to run for attorney general because they knew his vote-getting ability, she alone cautioned he might lose. But she also had agreed he had to accept: "They may never forgive you if you don't run." On election day, however, he was the only Democrat on the ticket to lose. "Fjr. was defeated because they [the Republicans] put a *very good* Jew [Jacob K. Javits] against him," she explained to Uncle David. "Ordinarily he has the Jewish vote but much of it had to vote for a good Jew. Then De Sapio & Buckley in Manhattan & the Bronx cut him in the Italian & Irish votes."

Politics were fickle. She had always been the one to remind family and friends of the ever-present possibility of defeat. But having seen her husband surmount the devastating blow of polio, she was sure Fjr. had the chance to do the same, and though she was sad for him to lose what he had wanted so badly, she sought to steady him with her faith in him.

"Goodbye David dear," she wrote in an updated letter,

> It is 3:30 a.m. and I see on T.V. F Jr. has conceded so I'm going to bed.
>
> . . .
>
> I've just written F Jr. I'm afraid it will be hard but losing if you take it well does no harm. James just called but I can't be so happy over his victory tho' I'll try to be.

Asked at her birthday about her general philosophy, she had crisply replied (for she knew what she thought), "Life has got to be lived—that's all there is to it. At seventy, I would say the advantage is that you take life more calmly. You know that 'this, too, shall pass.'"

XX

"I Get Tougher with Age"

NINETEEN FIFTY-FIVE BEGAN inauspiciously for Mrs. Roosevelt. During the Christmas holidays at Hyde Park she sat on a radiator and scalded her backside. She tried to make light of it, as she always did of her physical ailments. This time there was the added embarrassment of being unable to sit. A fatalist note always present began to sound more audibly in her letters. The prescription as usual was work. Bravely she insisted on fulfilling a lecture schedule in the Southwest.

While in Dallas she wrote Anna about her mishap.

Jan 9th [1955]

Darling Anna.

. . . I haven't written because I've been so uncomfortable I didn't want to do anything I didn't have to do! Tuesday a.m. after Xmas I sat minus clothes on a *very* hot radiator in my bed room in H.P. thinking no heat was on & burned my behind painfully. Thought it was nothing & found I was wrong & have suffered discomfort ever since & probably will for ten days more I'm told. This trip has been successful but not comfortable!

. . .

It will be good to have you near again.

Devotedly
Mother

She kept David up to date on her condition.

Jan 9th

Dearest David,

. . .

This has been very successful from the work point of view, but pretty uncomfortable from a personal viewpoint. Thank heavens I get interested and forget when I have to speak! Friday night a young doctor changed the dressing in New Orleans and said it was coming on fine but I couldn't expect to be over it for 10 days. I should be grateful all is well! All my love

E.R.

She did not want anyone as her doctor except David, but he, too, found her a perverse patient. "When she burned herself unmercifully on the hind side," Maureen later said, "who did the ministrations? I did. I begged David to look at the burns, but she insisted David give her ointments and I applied them. Even now I have tears in my eyes when I think of the pain she was under. She wouldn't admit to frailty."

At the end of January she was ready for a second lecture trip. "The burn has healed & I'm fine," she assured Hick.

Knoxville Tennessee
Feb. 18th

David dear,

. . . Dear, dear, nothing seems to suit me does it? Least of all do I like being where I can't easily get in touch with you without feeling that I'm being too great a pest!

This has been an easy trip and on the whole interesting. Today and tomorrow I'll see Oak Ridge and T.V.A. and both will be interesting. The whole area has changed and grown so much more prosperous. If as someone said the other day TVA is "socialism and communism" then the combination seems to stimulate private enterprise in a most desirable way.

I'm enclosing a letter which just came from Addis Ababa and I wrote politely saying we had to change our plans but hoped it was just a postponement. I have some thoughts we might discuss for a later time if I don't grow too decrepit.

. . .

E.R.

A note from Gary, Indiana, informed Hick that "Helen Douglas & Nannine have accepted and I am sure our party will be gay. . . . Please don't feel I am going to any trouble about the party. You know I love doing it." Shortly afterward she left for Israel accompanied by Trude and Maureen. At the last minute Trude almost decided not to go when Mrs. Roosevelt hinted David might like to come along. That angered me for I would have liked to have gone except for duties at the newspaper. Trude told Mrs. R. that if David went she would not be needed and Mrs. R. did not press the matter.

> en route by clipper
> March 7, 1955

David dearest,

I think you know how much I hated to leave you, tho' I know full well you do not need me. Please take care of yourself, my thoughts will be with you constantly and I will be hoping that the holiday with Grania will be restful and full of happiness for you and for her.

I will try to do a good job and have something worthwhile to show for the trip. We are making good time and are now out over the ocean and making a non-stop flight to London. It is a bit bumpy but the plane is not crowded and we should have a good night after the usual sumptuous meal!

God bless you dear, it is always hard for me to say goodbye to you but it grows harder each time and somehow this time I could hardly bear it.

All my love to you and God bless you and keep you always.

> E.R.

They stayed at Claridge's in London in an enormous suite, wrote Trude, with spring flowers and an open fireplace. Lady Reading took them in tow; they had tea with Madame Pandit, India's representative in London, and went to the English Speaking Union to listen to Chester Bowles, who had been the U.S. ambassador to India and had just visited Africa as well as India.

[E.R. to Joseph P. Lash:]   [March 8, 1954]

We had a good flight & were very comfortable. It is a good time of year because there are few people travelling. How I wish you were with us! I know Trude hated to say goodbye to you & Jonathan yesterday & so did I!

We went to the American Embassy this p.m. Much too plush!

"I dragged Mrs. R. on a walk to Grosvenor Square to see the President's statue," wrote Trude. "It is a good one but Churchill is right—he should be sitting down. . . . I think Mrs. R. enjoyed herself tremendously today. She obviously loves a charged political atmosphere, loves to take part in highest level discussions."

March 10th
evening

David dearest,

At a Youth Aliyah* meeting which Trude and I attended this after-noon a Miss Warburg asked warmly for you, hoped you were here and wanted me to send you her love. You were once in love with Ingrid, I'm told, but when I knew her she did not seem to me someone who would hold your love—but she had probably changed.

I saw Anthony Eden this morning and he made a good statement to Parliament on the Asian trip. I lunched with the Churchill's and he has aged so much that in spite of his very excellent speech on defense† which I will send you, I feel he should resign and let Eden take over. I dined with Arthur Murray and had a long and excellent lesson on China! In fact I have learned much about the situation here. . . .

Trude has done all she wanted to do and is happy and Maureen has had a good time with cousins so all is well.

. . .

E.R.

What have you done about your office, apartment etc.?

It is tempting to read into Mrs. Roosevelt's letters to David at this time particularly affectionate feelings, stimulated perhaps by David's divorce finally from Nemone, even more by his absence on this trip. The "Miss Warburg" that she met in London was Ingrid Warburg Spinelli's sister. She was active in Youth Aliyah and had settled in Israel. Both were daughters of the German Warburg banking house. Mrs. Roosevelt came to know Ingrid in the late 1930s when she was active with the German underground group, New Beginnings, one of whose members was a young-ster named Willy Brandt. David had courted Ingrid in the midthirties before he was attracted by Nemone Balfour. Why Mrs. Roosevelt thought Ingrid an unlikely candidate for David's affections is unclear.

A quick, impersonal note to me.

March 11th

Joe dearest,

I got a fairly good political picture yesterday, while Trude studied social conditions. They don't want war here over Quemoy or even over Formosa!

* An Israel organization responsible for the transfer of refugee Jewish children in 1955 mostly from Africa to Israel and their rehabilitation. It and Hadassah were the sponsors of Mrs. Roosevelt's and Trude's trip.
† Churchill addressing Parliament March 1, 1955 called Russia's H-bomb power limited and said Britain's decision to contribute to the making of the H-bomb was the "only policy" and for the West it meant a "defense through deterrents."

All of us are cold which is not unusual!

. . .

My love
E.R.

"The Labor Party here is split and papers are full of the news about the expulsion of Aneurin Bevan, leader of the leftist group," she wrote in her column. Trude wrote me about Mrs. Roosevelt's talk with Anthony Eden.

[Trude W. Lash to Joseph P. Lash:]   [March 10, 1955]
She told him she liked his speech on Formosa and he asked her, please, to tell Sir Winston that she did. She had lunch with the Churchills a little later and tried twice to tell him—without success. She thinks he has changed greatly and should resign. Arthur Murray, who is now in the House of Lords, told her that all the Tories felt that. The main subject of Mrs. R's (and my) political discussions is, of course, China. And it seems clear that the English people don't want to fight for the off-shore islands or even for Formosa.*

They spent a night in Paris at the Crillon, time for a quick note to David.

March 12th, 1955

David dearest,
I called Lady Mendl but she was away till tomorrow morning and leaving then at once for what sounded like Balmain to spend a month recuperating. I did talk to Sir Charles who told me the above and after he finally took in my name warmly invited me to go and see him!
Sorry I can do no better than write Yvonne a note. Perhaps she can call me on my way back.
Paris is lovely and warmer than London. I had interesting talks there and one with Sir Anthony Nutting on Israel which amused but saddened me. Abba Schwartz has spent the day with us. This is a lovely city. All my love to you.

E.R.

They had encountered the Nuttings† at dinner at the Kensington house of the Douglas Fairbankses, where, in addition to trying on saris brought by Madame Pandit, they had talked about the Middle East. "Apparently Nutting got hold of

* Senator Knowland had declared that a Communist Chinese attack on Quemoy and Matsu would mean "a military opposition on our part."
† He was British Minister of State for Foreign Affairs and leader of the British delegation to the UN General Assembly 1954–56.

her," Trude wrote, "and tried to instruct her as to Israel. He says they are getting too cocky, don't even say they are sorry.* And there is an agreement that there will be sanctions for warlike acts. I do not think that he moved Mrs. R. one way or the other." They drove from Paris to the south of France to Cambous, a camp run by the Joint Distribution Committee, with 1,500 African Jews "of all ages, all cultural levels, and from all ages. . . . Some looked like Bedouins in white burnouses, others like Biblical characters in black robes and hats. . . . What a task for Israel," wrote Trude. After a trip along the Riviera during which Mrs. Roosevelt "slept all the way" from Marseilles to Nice "or nine tenths of the way," said Trude, she was ready to face the music in Rome.

[Trude W. Lash to Joseph P. Lash:]   [March 14, 1955]

We were greeted at the Rome airport by more press and television than ever before, also by Embassy representatives, and Mrs. R. chose this particular time to be difficult. The charge d'affaires Claire Luce sent was very nice, as a matter of fact he was Liz Eagan's friend Durbrow. He offered his services, an embassy car, etc. But Mrs. R. felt stubborn, and finally I had to get into the discussion, Result: we have an embassy car and Mrs. R. became very much interested in hearing Durbrow's report. (He is economic counsellor.)

Hotel Hassler
Rome
March 16 evening

Dearest David,

. . .

Poor Nemone and poor you for I know you will worry about her. It will be good however if you have to take a few days more holiday with Grania. . . .

We had an interesting time at F.A.O. [Food and Agricultural Organization] this morning and I have 2 reports from the Embassy on the economic situation and social security here. This p.m. we did some sightseeing with an interesting woman archeologist [Countess Lelli] and this evening I spoke for the UN Association and dined with a group. Have just done 2 columns and soon to bed.

Thanks again for writing dear, my thoughts and love go with you.

E.R.

Love to Grania

* It was just after Israel's reprisal raid into the Gaza Strip, then controlled by Nasser's Egypt.

Mrs. Roosevelt was anxious to get on to Israel and to find out, wrote Trude, what had happened since she had been there, whether the promises of three years ago were being kept. But there were things to be done in Rome.

[Trude W. Lash to Joseph P. Lash:]   [March 17, 1955]
    Mrs. Luce [the U.S. Ambassador] was at her most charming at luncheon yesterday. Her residence is fabulous. . . . The food was excellent. There were about 50 people. After luncheon she asked Mrs. R. to speak and Mrs. R. responded with an enthusiasm I have rarely seen. For an hour she spoke and answered questions, obviously enjoying herself tremendously, I've noticed that several times on this trip, that she does not seem really happy unless she explains something to a crowd of people. . . . She worries me because she does seem so tired.

Their final night they had dinner with friends of ours living in Rome, Charles and Braddy Boni, at Il Bucca's, "a sweet place near Piazza Santa Ignazion," Braddy wrote me and Jonathan.

[Margaret Boni to Joseph P. Lash:]   [March 18, 1955]
    We arrived unannounced but trailed by the Italian police at the ungodly hour of seven. Il Bucca was in a state because nothing was ready. No one in Italy eats dinner before nine. They were in even more of a state when they recognized Mrs. R. and the entire staff and family, even the little old Italian mother who usually stays in the kitchen and cooks, would come every few minutes to peep at the door, stare at Mrs. R. (who fortunately was completely unconscious of this) nod solemnly in approval, then steal away. Charlie and Trude went into a huddle and ordered us a fine meal, Mrs. R. was suddenly not tired but gay and talkative and interesting, and altogether it was an evening which I shall not soon forget.

Israel had indeed changed in the three years since Mrs. Roosevelt had been there. An "enormous amount of building," she told Trude. The landscape had changed, too—"there are many new orange groves." But she had also changed. "People who know her here are a little shocked. . . . It is noticeable when she is bored or tired. But she is all fire when she is really interested. Ben Gurion interested her and the meeting at Jakov Herzog's house. She made Mrs. [Chaim] Weizman who had been to Russia last year tell about her experiences there. That interested her." They were in Israel nine days. Their schedules were packed even by Mrs. Roosevelt's standards. She managed a postcard to David.

March 22d

David dear

I've thought of you so much today and our trip here and our time here, but it is [word indecipherable] in April. Everyone asks after you. There is no food shortage now but it is very expensive. We spent last night at [Kibbutz] Degania.

My love
E.R.

She appended a note to me to Trude's letter.

Dearest Joe,

Your wife does her duty nobly & will know all there is to know on her return if she's still alive! Seriously, she loves it & is very interested. I've got the material I need & am ready to start for home but it is a wonderful country!

Much love,
E.R.

Back in the Hassler in Rome they did little but have hot baths and catch their breaths before going on to Paris the next afternoon, except that Trude reported that Claire Sterling, who was a contributor to Max Ascoli's *Reporter* magazine, and Martha Gellhorn were coming in for lunch. "She [Martha] sent me to a fabulous podiatrist," Trude recalled. Mrs. Roosevelt made no reference to Martha in her letter to David.

March 28th

David dearest,

I feel very far away from you so I don't know when or where you and Grania finally went or when you return. I've reread your letter of the 12th over and over but it told me no plans. Not even if you decided to buy a house or move your office! I know you haven't had time to write and I hope so much you've had a real rest and enjoyed every minute of your time but—I can't help feeling lonely!

The trip to Israel kept me working from 7 a.m. to midnight but I saw and learned all I needed to know. Trude went off for several days and has served Youth Aliyah well.

Dr. Shiba reported the woman in charge felt she could not use your mother because her treatments were not orthodox. A friend of your Mother's arrived the day before I left and felt she could bring more pressure so I asked Dr. Shiba to send her your mother's papers.

I'll send Lady Mendl some flowers on Tuesday if I don't manage to see her.

I've done my last columns on Israel and all of us are so completely exhausted tonight that I think we will go to bed. I hope this reaches you before I arrive and I pray all is well with you.

My love always,

E.R.

"I've done so many speeches since I got back I've had no time to write & I must do some of it soon." So she wrote Hick on May 11, adding that she wasn't free till June 1 "but if you are coming in do lunch with me that day." She was worried, as always, about Hick's finances.

May 19th

Dearest Hick,

Here's a little check Nannine sent me but I don't want it for you did *all* the work on the book so use it for odds & ends. Let me know if you are really short of money. How nearly are you nearing the end of the book? The ideal way for you to do would be to turn out short stories, lurid ones, to live on & do them fast & then write the books slowly. . . .

E.R.

The World Federation of United Nations Associations was scheduled to meet in Bangkok in August. The AAUN wanted her to be a delegate and David also, since he found he could accompany her. They planned to go by way of Japan and the Philippines with a long stop in Bali.

Saturday night
June 4th, 1955

David dearest,

What do you think? I've been going over boxes stored here [Hyde Park] and rereading all your letters to me of '48 and '49. It seems incredible all the personal things we have lived through in less than eight years as the world changes. So short a time and I feel now that life with out you *near* simply would not be life to me. You are part of my daily thought and so deep in my heart that I feel whatever makes you glad or sad affects me too. Have the years brought you the same feeling? I do hope so.

David Gray, Marie and the children came yesterday. Mrs. Thompson and Peter today. The dinner at Mrs. [Tracy] Dows was pleasant and brought me an invitation from Roland Redmond to go over the Metropolitan Museum with him just to see the best of the last acquisitions. Would you like to go someday?*

My heart failed me when I talked to Forbes Amory and I told him

* Geraldine (Mrs. Lewis) Thompson, a former Dutchess County neighbor, one of the three Morgan sisters of Staatsburgh and now a New Jersey Republican and active in prison reform.

when the itinerary was complete, I'd let him get my ticket. It evidently means so much to him and I'll just take your itinerary complete with flights hotels etc. and he says he can get me the same and just say I am with you and want to be near you on planes and at hotels etc. I know you will think I'm an idiot to take the trouble but he sounded so sad!

. . .

E.R.

She was beginning to tire more frequently and nod off, as Trude had found on their trip to Israel. More and more she thought of death and being prepared for it.

June 20th [1955]

Anna darling,

. . . This last week was hard for me. I spent Friday in Fall River [Massachusetts] for Mrs. Louis Howe's funeral. She had 2 strokes & death was merciful. Sunday I came down for John Golden's funeral. I shall miss him very much for he was a dear & thoughtful friend always, but he had suffered very much of late & so death was probably merciful in his case too. After 40 we all live on borrowed time & there should really be no cause for grief in the passing of one's contemporaries. Just a few more holes in this life to warn us to be prepared! I've tidied up much in the house this year but this summer I must see that all the papers I can get rid of are destroyed & the rest properly filed! . . .

Mother

The tenth anniversary celebration of the UN was held in San Francisco, and the New York *Post* sent me out to cover it. Trude wrote she had had dinner with Mrs. Roosevelt at Charles Restaurant, one of our favorite places in the Village.

[Trude W. Lash to Joseph P. Lash:] [June 1955]

We talked about many things: about John Golden and his insistence that no Jewish rabbi read his funeral service because he wanted it to be gentile. About the fact that Anne and Johnny don't understand that it is because of them that Mrs. R. stays more and more away from Hyde Park; about her annoyance at Marie who every night says good night to Mrs. R. and tells her she is tired and then spends the rest of the night over at Johnny's. How vulnerable she is. And I guess we all hurt her, even if we don't mean to.

Mrs. Tracy Dows was matriarchal head of the Hudson River clan of that name, the mother of Olin Dows, the painter. Roland Redmond, president of the Metropolitan Museum, was another Hudson River neighbor.

Evidently remembering my previous meeting in 1943 with Mrs. R. in San Francisco on the eve of being shipped out, I wrote her a depressed letter. Her sympathy immediately was aroused.

Saturday night

Joe dearest,

Your letter of the 23d came today & I understand your wave of depression. These times come in all our lives & I wish I had been in San Francisco to dine with you again in the same place & talk it out. I see these past years of yours so differently from the way you do. You have made such strides in conquering yourself. I loved you dearly then as I do now but you are a bigger more disciplined person today. I've read your articles daily, they are good, you have a job & are doing it well. You & Trude have grown & Jonathan is a boy to be proud of, moody, as you were at times, but you will know how to help him there. I think your gains far exceed your losses. The drive & sense of success we had in youth seldom remains but it is replaced by steadier action & clearer thinking. I am grateful to you for telling me your thoughts & I'd like to be more useful to you if I can help. Perhaps you might like to make the effort to lunch with me now & then? I always managed to lunch with John Golden once a week if I was not really far away & I'd like to do it with you if & when you feel like it.

. . . You are right dear I don't enjoy many people but a few are very important to me & you are among the few—

E.R.

On her way to the Pacific she, David, and Maureen stopped at Elliott's Rolling R Ranch in Meeker, Colorado. Hick had to give up her house in Moriches, Long Island, and was much on her mind. She urged her, if unable to find a place to stay, to use the Hyde Park cottage during the winter and write.

The stay at Elliott's ranch, the trip to Bali, reflected an avidity for new experiences that age had not ended. They included a determination to ride again, "the kind of riding even old ladies could do," she said in her column. A week later she responded to the horse Elliott had given her, "I like all his gaits except his canter. I find this rather pounding though I know perfectly well it is partly my fault." How characteristic, the blame was hers even though she knew the horse had "a hard canter."

[E.R. to Lorena Hickok:]   [August 9, 1955]

I was glad to get your letter & to know that Tubby had been adequate & you & Muffin were all right in the apartment.

Of course you will forget the bad time at the end & eventually think only of the pleasant memories. Life is like that, with ends which have to be forgotten.

Maureen returned east, and Eleanor and David went on to Los Angeles, where she saw Jimmy, and then they were off. The week she spent in Japan revisiting people and places she had seen in 1953 reassured her that Japan was settling into democratic ways. She also remembered to take a pair of shoes that she could easily slip off when entering a house, a relief because she did not have to bend over to untie the laces each time. "This display of Buddhas is quite impressive with a fine central figure. There were our soldiers & sailors in this temple & I couldn't help wondering how much they enjoyed it!" she wrote us.

From Hong Kong on the way to Indonesia she reported to Anna that she was losing weight so effectively that clothes and girdles were beginning to hang on her. Hong Kong's contrast with Japan was instructive, the overcrowding was such that "Harlem is luxury." The letter ended, "Have you found work?"

As a listening post next to Red China, Hong Kong with its newsmen and diplomats fascinated her.

August 24th

Dearest Joe,

. . . Yesterday we lunched with the Gov. Gen. (same one as last time I was here) & I had a chance to talk with a young British diplomat just going home after 2 yrs in Peking.

He said he never felt watched but there was a constant feeling of restraint. He felt the poorer classes might be a little better off but the middle class was wiped out & the rich were poor & all were under some constraint & fear.

The standard of living is appaling *[sic]*. I saw one new refugee housing area & it may be better than living in huts on the sidewalk or on the hills but I will never compare Harlem or our N.Y. Porto Rican area to this. I suppose it does more harm at home because we know what decent standards are.

David is off this afternoon with the Gov. Gen. & then the Police Commissioner & later I go to the U.N. Ass.

I hope you are having a grand holiday.

Much love
E.R.

"David," she wrote Trude that same day, "drank some water yesterday & is upset today but I hope he will be over it soon but it shows how careful one has to be. I am as usual in rude health."

Her stay on Bali began as the guest in the Rajah's compound with a one-room cottage of her own from whose ceiling she could see through the mosquito netting myriads of lizards suspended. The Rajah had an orchestra of his own and the island's life was dancing. "I never saw so many dancers or so much dancing." She enjoyed her visit, but by the time she and David left for Bangkok "I felt I had seen enough dancing to last me the rest of my life." "All the people dance," she wrote Anna, "but only little girls" were professionals. "When you are married (at thirteen) you are too old & no longer a virgin so you can't dance!" An elegiac note. "A special hug to you & thanks for writing. Being away makes one realize how easily one could slip out of life & not have it even noticed."

As Mrs. Roosevelt may have anticipated, Hick at her urging ended up at Hyde Park in Tommy's kitchen and bedroom.

They were greeted on arrival in Bangkok by the Prime Minister, Field Marshal Pibul Songgram, and his wife. The World Federation sessions were not too interesting, but she and David made a trip to Angkor Wat in Cambodia, which contained "the most impressive monuments" she had ever seen. At the meeting, she wrote us, "I was troubled because our chairman Mr. Marbury is naïve politically & the iron curtain countries certainly used the meeting. We were badly organized & prepared & I don't even feel happy about the Federation Secretariat, so I feel my report will be very unpopular." The Thais had been "especially kind" to her. "I'm quite fond of having large lizards crawl up & down the wall!"

> On way to Geneva
> Sept. 12th

Dearest Anna,

. . . I'll be glad to have David in a more invigorating climate after tomorrow. I have not been ill a minute & have found I could manage the column easily & never give up doing anything, I really do get tougher with age!

This year I'm not going to celebrate my birthday, last year shld last till I'm 75 & we can forget it till then. No gifts for I need nothing & now I should give & not receive. . . .

> Devotedly
> Mother

> Geneva
> Sept. 15th

Dearest Trude & Joe,

. . . I hate not to get news from the few people whom I love & I imagine all kinds of things may have happened! I can't think what happened to the itinerary I told Helen to send you.

. . . As long as it relieves you of some strain I'm glad you sold the H.P. house. I am really less & less there myself & may turn it over to Elliott soon with the privilege of renting the months I want to be there. . . .

I'm not as thin as you picture but I've made a beginning & will continue the good work!

Tell Joe I was horrified at Stassen's rainbow chasing.* . . .

To Hick in Hyde Park—

Sept. 21st

Dearest Hick,

I think we are spared the hurricane but I was glad to know all preparations were made!

I thought I wrote that when I'm home I hope you will have *all* meals including breakfast with me except when that happens there will be no need to use Tommy's kitchen for cocktails. . . .

E.R.

Thursday,
[October 6, 1955]

Dearest Hick,

Many thanks for your letter about Tamas. Irene thought she was to blame which is nonsense. Sooner or later death comes to all & it sometimes is pleasanter than life. Let us hope in his heaven Tamas finds it happy. He was a sweet dog & we will miss him. I want no more dogs. I'm away too much & when I find the right person I will give Duffy to them. Meantime we'll keep him & hope he will be as well & happy as possible. He was never personally tied to anyone like Tamas.

Here is a note you must answer at once.

Much love
E.R.

She did not celebrate her birthday, but a few people came in for dinner. David sent her a birthday note.

Oct. 11, 1955

Dearest Mrs. R.—

In spite of you wanting to forget about it let me wish you a happy birthday. Let me tell you that I love you. Let me wish you happiness for the years to come.—I am not very articulate saying thank you for the

* It is unclear what particular "rainbow" Mrs. Roosevelt had in mind. At the time Stassen was predicting an Eisenhower-Nixon ticket in 1956, a Harriman-G. Mennen Williams ticket for the Democrats, and that the USSR would eventually agree to Eisenhower's "open skies" plan of mutual aerial inspection. Stassen's usual "rainbow chasing" was for a place himself on the presidential ticket of the Republicans.

warmth and the spoiling you give me—but I do thank you and I do feel spoiled.—Just my love and God bless you.—

David

on way to Minneapolis
October 13, 1955

Dearest David,

I never really thanked you for your note, it is a precious possession and I did not tell you either how useful the gloves will be. I have no new pair. The bag is so beautiful that I will probably not be able to wait to use it, tho' I have such an affection for the old one that I can't bear to give it up though I have to acknowledge that it begins to be a bit worn! I have so much to thank you for and all I can do is say "thank you." Most of all I'm grateful for the time you give me. I enjoy things more if you enjoy them with me.

You had sinus last night and I felt you were relieved at not going to Putney* and that troubled me for it means that you are tired again. Do get some rest over this weekend since you are not going away, unless of course you go to the country in which case I hope it will be a restful place.

. . .

I love you always and thank you for being you.

E.R.

For his birthday on October 31 she left him a note.

David dearest,

I would like to telephone you Wednesday morning but I may not have time between train and plane so I leave this as a greeting on your birthday morning. May it be a happy day from beginning to end and may you have many, many more. I am thankful every day that you were born and I pray for your health and happiness daily.

You know, without my telling you that I love you as I love and have never loved anyone else, and I am grateful for the privilege of loving you and thankful for every chance to be of help. God bless you and keep you and give you joy and every wish now and always.

E.R.

She wrote Trude and me for our wedding anniversary, "I pray that as each anniversary comes it will be happier than the last & life will be good to you both. Ellie Elliott [Hall's daughter] wrote me the other day 'Oh—it's just fine. The very

---

* Grania was at school there.

real struggle of two people seeking to live happily together—is so worthwhile if they can somehow doggedly—get over a few increasingly insurmountable obstacles!' "

Her family was ever present in her plans.

November 21, 1955

Dearest James:

I am sure you won't be East but I wanted to tell you that Anna and Jim will be in Hyde Park on the weekend of December 17th and Elliott and Minnewa will be with me also. It would be lovely to have as many of the family as possible together on that weekend and this is just in case you happen to be in this part of the world.

Much love,
Mother

[in longhand] I'm having the party for the people on the place early as they like to see Anna.

She sent David her Christmas schedule, indicating where she hoped he would fit in.

Dec 11th

David dearest,

I was sorry to give up lunch Wed. but found I had made a date so Major Golan [of Israel] says he will come to dine on Monday next the 17th. So do come if you feel like it and bring Grania if you want. Peter Casson of Geneva will be lunching here Wed. the 19th at 1 if you care to drop in.

On the 20th for Nehru, dinner will be at 7 would you like Grania to come at 8:15 and go to the meeting? I'm sure Elliott and Minnewa would love to have her for dinner and bring her over. I will have a Carey car that night for me then and Elliott and Minnewa.

May Grania and I have your permission to fix your tree on Friday, December 21st at about 3 p.m.!

Grania said she would like, if carol singing were not interfered with to come up with you on 24th. So you would have 2 nights at Hyde Park. I enclose a time table so you can let me know about trains. If you come Xmas we don't worry about Grania's stocking. I will have all that is needed for you to fill it. The Lash's come on 24th.

December 26th

Cocktail party for Grania 7–8 and I count on you. I have 4 tickets for the Foreign Press Association dinner dance that night at 8. Would you like to go? I'd like to ask Joe and Trude if you think you'd find people to dance with, otherwise you can ask two people. I have to go for a time. I can't go to film on 21st. Shall I get you tickets that night or would you and Grania go December 28th or 29th when I can go?

December 30th

4 seats for Handel's Messiah Leonard Bernstein conducting. Would you like to bring your mother and Grania and lunch here first?

December 31st

Joe and Trude and Jonathan are dining here and going to the New York City Ballet coming back afterwards to see the New Year in. I've told them to ask anyone they like. I hope you and Grania will dine and go with us and come back and ask anyone you wish. If any of my children are in town they will come in.

Don't feel tied by any of this. I only tell you so you can do what you want. Needless to say I want you always for everything, and I love to have Grania but I know I must not be selfish and you have many others who want you also.

Off tonight for Seattle and then Los Angeles. I'll be home Monday a.m. the 17th by 1:30 if all goes well.

Take care of yourself darling, have a good time and God bless you.

Devotedly

E.R.

We all served her, but David had her heart in a way the rest of us did not. Still the old pattern was at work. Her love poured forth but as in the past it was love for a man who was inaccessible—it was love for a man whose basic unavailability enabled her to do the work she had to do. If she were a religious figure, the world would know how to evaluate her and her friends. But in a secular age, as her passionate attachments have become known, the historian and biographer have groped to place her in categories of profane love which she had long transcended.

XXI

The Private and the Public

S HE HAD NOT TAKEN an active part in the 1948 and 1952 presidential
campaigns because of her responsibilities in the UN. Insofar as it lay in her
power she wanted to keep America's relationship to the world organization
above partisan politics. No such compulsion existed in 1956. Her increasing dis-
enchantment with Eisenhower's leadership was matched by her growing esteem for
Adlai Stevenson. He had been her candidate in 1952, and his pronouncements and
urbane political style since then had fulfilled her hopes. "I hope you enjoyed your
dinner at the Harrimans," she wrote Anna at the end of 1955. "I fear he isn't
happy that I am for Stevenson openly & tho' Fjr. I suppose will say nothing I think
he is also for Stevenson." She did not thrust herself forward into the political wars,
yet before 1956 was over she had been instrumental in overcoming Stevenson's
hesitations about running again, argued successfully with black leaders to moderate
their desegregation stand, single-handedly stalled former President Truman's convention drive for Harriman, helped gain the nomination for Stevenson, and delivered a convention speech that the seasoned political observer Edward R. Murrow
called "the greatest convention speech I ever heard." Though in the end
Eisenhower's grip on the electorate proved unbreakable, she had succeeded, in the
1956 campaign at least, in giving the Democratic Party a lift and a vision in an
unusual show of political astuteness and authority. In the midst of it she took off
for a three-week holiday tour to show the sights of Europe that she loved to two of

her grandsons, John's Haven and Anna's John Boettiger, and to Grania Gurewitsch and David, as if to demonstrate how private affection intermingled with public efforts.

By 1956, David, a divorced man, had become a fixture in her daily life. The paths of psychic energy are unchartable, especially the exchange between libidinal desire and good works. Her campaign to help Stevenson win the presidency reflected her feelings for the human condition. It paralleled her solicitude for David, and though we do not understand how it happens, the latter fed the former. She talked of slowing down, but she continued to be as involved with life as if she were a young person.

> January 2d
> 1956

David dearest,

Welcome home, it is good to have you back and I do hope the few days off have given physical, mental and emotional rest and much pleasure. I doubt if you have had time to think out all your problems but you may have been able to decide what are your most important desires!

. . .

I had called you New Year's Eve but afterwards I learned you also called me. . . .

Bless you and don't catch cold, remember this is winter even if you have been in Florida!

Call me when you have a chance. I'll be in except from 2:45 to 5:00 when I must be in the office.

. . .

> E.R.

She was unable to have enough of David's company.

> Jan. 7th
> 1956

David dear,

. . . My plane from Boston gets in at 7:10 on the 18th if all goes well, so perhaps if you eat something in the afternoon, dinner at 8:15 might be possible? On the other hand weather is so unpredictable that I hate to tie you down to a date and then perhaps not get home! You will be at Mrs. Lasker's party on the 20th and you will dine with me on the 21st, the night before I leave again. If you'd like me to I could try to get Mr. and Mrs. Misle on the 21st from Look to see your pictures [of Bali and Angkor Wat], just tell Mrs. Daniels to tell Helen if you'd like them asked and she'll do it. Maureen will be away this trip with me as it is a lecture trip and not A.A.U.N.

. . .

E.R.

Jan 21st ['56]

David dearest,

I meant to give you these to read. I hope you like the statement.*

You were so good to come tonight and I loved having you and look forward to the 28th, only a week from tonight!

I love you dearly and I feel something is going on inside of you these days, not unhappy exactly, and yet not perhaps quite happy either. Am I imagining? Anyway be happy for that makes me happy!

Good night, your devoted

E.R.

These letters of a woman in love with a younger man were followed by two that showed the depth of her attachment. Perhaps she was willing to let herself go in this manner because David for the moment was without marital ties; perhaps the basic motive was the loneliness of a life at Hyde Park. She showered attentions on David. Few were better than she at making another—man or woman—feel close. "I don't say that he ate up flattery," said Grania years later, "but he did like to be appreciated." Eleanor, out of an admixture of loneliness and erotic feeling, gave him that appreciation. But Grania also said, "He was accustomed to strong women and I didn't think Mrs. R. more extraordinary than my grandmother or my Aunt Mum, or Andrée Vienot."

Feb. 8th

David my dearest,

I've been sitting here thinking of you tonight and wondering why I make you feel shy. I want you to feel at home with me as you would with a member of your family and I can't achieve it! Something wrong with me! I'd love to hear you call me by my first name but you can't. Perhaps it is my age! I do love you and you are always in my thoughts and if that bothers you I could hide it. I'm good at that.

You read me a lecture† and I thought you really cared and so I'm being very careful, but it is a good deal of bother, anyway I'll see if I can go on for a while. In the meantime love me a little and show it if you can and

---

* A statement critical of U.S. policy toward Israel, drafted by Judge Polier, transmitted to Mrs. Roosevelt by me, and endorsed by former President Truman and Walter Reuther.

† About her health.

remember to take care of yourself for you are the most precious person in the world. All my love.

E.R.

Then in March—the letter has no date—her endearments and solicitude became their tenderest.

David dear,

This is a little note to beg you to get rested. You do so much for others and of course a doctor has to live a life dedicated to others. There are deep satisfactions I know but you deserve and should have more care and help than you are allowing yourself. Of course I don't know how much you allow others who love you to do but judging by how little you let me do I fear you are always giving and not getting the things which any of us who love you would so gladly give. Unless I bother you please let me do *useful* things more often. I have more free time already since I've begun to keep myself freer and when I get home March 31st I'm going to be here all the time and much freer!

I know you don't believe what I told you, but if you should have to rest again, I could not see you go away alone. I'd try not to be a nuisance but I would want to be near always. Perhaps this is such a dreadful threat to you that you will determine to take better care of yourself!

I am not stupid dear and I never forget that twenty years lie between you and me but I love you deeply, and long for closeness and the chance to be of service to you. I know you love youth and beauty and independence and I would not want to keep you from these joys but I would be so happy and so grateful if there were ways when you wanted me to do something for you and were happy and relaxed in using me and anything I could offer. What I have, in the few years I have left, is yours before it is anyone else's.

My whole heart is yours and I shall worry till you have your check up so please *wire* me the results. God bless you and keep you and my love to you.

E.R.

In 1971, nine years after Mrs. Roosevelt's death, David showed Mrs. Roosevelt's letters to him to Eleanor's old friend, Esther Lape, asking whether he should publish them. Esther appreciated their meaning.

[Esther Lape to David Gurewitsch:]   [1971]

   . . . You were dearer to her, as she not infrequently said, than anyone else in the world. Yes, she not only loved you, she was in love with you. You loved her and were not in love with her. But this is a story of a truly great love that confers nothing but honor upon you and upon her. Yes, she was a lonely "unfulfilled" woman. But not unfulfilled in the derogatory sense that use of the word carries. I am impressed by how frequently her belief in your work appears, forming a basic substructure in her love for you. The truth of this is, to me, very important. . . .

But Esther counseled him against publication, at least at that time.

Women perhaps should not confess that they are in love. There is a special pathos when a great person admits to a love that is unrequited, as it appears to have been in this case. Not that David did not love her. He did, but not erotically. So she redoubled her work in public things, and this episode gives a clue to the underground springs that fed her public life. She had to love—that was structured into her nature—but the beloved seemed fated to be fundamentally unavailable.

The dominant public matter that concerned her that year was the presidential election. She expressed her feelings to an old family friend, Lord Elibank, formerly Arthur Murray.

[E.R. to Lord Elibank:]   [January 20, 1956]
    I don't know what is going to happen in the next nine months but I am doing what I can to get Mr. Stevenson the nomination. Many of my friends tell me that there is no question but that Eisenhower [he had been sidelined by a heart attack for two months] will be nominated and Nixon will be Vice President. If that is the case the Democrats will have to work harder than ever because I doubt if Eisenhower can stand a second term and I doubt if the country can stand Nixon as President.

She lectured as usual that winter and spring for the AAUN and for Colston Leigh. She also campaigned for Stevenson in the primaries, helped him raise funds, and heartened him against the discouragement to which he was occasionally prone. That was particularly the case after his defeat in the Minnesota primary, which was carried by Senator Estes Kefauver of Tennessee. The only congressional districts Kefauver did not carry were the two in which she had campaigned.

At the same time that she served as one of Stevenson's main protagonists, she planned a holiday excursion at the end of the summer with two grandsons and the Gurewitsches. "I tried 'sounding out' Johnny about your tentative plan to take him and Haven to Europe from Aug. 17 to Sept. 9, but his immediate reaction was so spontaneously a thrilled 'yes! how wonderful' that I had to tell him all you'd written, emphasizing, of course, that it was all still indefinite." So Anna wrote in a letter that thanked her mother for helping to turn her birthday party into a family celebration. ". . . No more now—but *thanks* for being the amazingly thoughtful person you are, in so darn many ways."

A note in my diary, June 17, 1956:

Mrs. R. told us that on Thursday before travelling up to Connecticut for a women's conference, a Nigerian woman was in to see her to tell her about work she intended to do. Friday she went up to an African Students Conference at International House. Her escort was "a beautiful girl" from South Africa—rather light-skinned so Mrs. R. thought her father might be white. The girl said her friends were urging her to stay here, but she felt her duty was back in Capetown. What a difficult decision it must be, thought Mrs. R. When she got to Hyde Park Friday evening, there was a group from Morocco, including the Sultan's aide. Before they went over to FDR's grave to lay a wreath, the aide shooed the others out in order to give her a message from the Sultan—that it would be all right on the American bases in Morocco, not to worry, it would be done in memory of FDR. Mrs. R. told it to Johnny. He might want to pass it on to the White House or State Department. Friday night, also, 80-year-old Hasegawa arrived with an interpreter. It was too late to go over to the grave so he stayed the night. . . . He has been called Japan's Veblen. Apologized because his kimono was not the most formal one—as if we knew the difference. Ate food smacking his lips so his interpreter, a teacher at Columbia, explained to Marie [Morgan] that he was being polite and showing how much he liked his food. . . .

Mrs. R. could be our most potent force in our relations with the uncommitted countries, but the Administration refuses to use her.

On the way over to Peter Pratt's [Trude's son] wedding in Connecticut with Trude and me, she jested about Pegler's columns suggesting an illicit amour with me. Even some people who should know better, she said, would seem puzzled when Mrs. R. spoke about all the things she did with Trude—as if to ask with their eyes—didn't Trude mind her relationship with me?

At Peter's wedding part of the service consisted of readings from Gibran's *Prophet.* * When we got home Mrs. R. pulled out some of his books and began to read to us from them. She also read Countee Cullen's —"to make a man black and bid him sing."

Said she was going down to Washington at the invitation of Paul Butler, the Democratic National Chairman, to a key meeting before the convention on a civil rights plank. The only Negro leader she really trusted was Ralph Bunche. She was disappointed in Channing Tobias because he accepted all of Roy Wilkins's positions. . . .

She had proven her worth to Stevenson in several critical primaries, including the last and most important in California, "running around so madly speaking for Adlai that I had forgotten I was a grandmother, and a great grandmother at that!"

---

* Khalil Gibran, Lebanese poet and mystic. He lived in New York after 1910, Countee Cullen, popular black poet. Roy Wilkins succeeded Walter White as executive director of the NAACP.

she wrote a young friend, after Stevenson's two-to-one victory in California, a victory in which the local leaders reported that her stay there had been "the most helpful thing that happened during the campaign."

The Negro vote had gone overwhelmingly to Stevenson, and Harriman, Stevenson's real rival for the nomination, hoped to wean it away from him by picturing him as the spokesman for "moderation," which Roy Wilkins, the newly elected leader of the NAACP, said meant no progress at all. There was justice in his stand, and Mrs. Roosevelt herself acknowledged there might be no way to hold the party together and live up to one's convictions, but she was determined to try, and especially to try to hold it together for Adlai, going so far as to criticize Wilkins for his "hotheaded statement" about Stevenson's plea for moderation. She had faith that Stevenson would do the right thing at the right time on the civil rights issues, and she was willing to underwrite that faith with her own considerable prestige among Negroes.

A journal note, July 4, 1956:

> Mrs. R. said she had written Butler, after tentatively agreeing to speak on the 16th at the Convention, to say "no,"—that she would come if Adlai wanted her to do something specific and it would have to be early in the Convention as she flew to Europe on the 17th.
>
> I argued with her that if the segregation issue left wounds, she might be just the person to heal them—as she had in the Wallace nomination in 1940. No, she wasn't needed. She would meet with the Committee on Platform and discuss the segregation plank with people like Bunche.
>
> [Congressman Adam Clayton Powell from Harlem at the time was forcing a vote on his rider to a school construction bill that would deny federal funds to the states that refused to comply with the Supreme Court's school desegregation decision. The vote on it was difficult for Democratic politicians, especially the liberals.]
>
> Later in the evening Jimmy called to tell her of Rivers* attack on her and the family in connection with Powell Amendment vote (she did not favor Powell Amendment!) and he too urged her to go. He said she should make the same speech she did in Los Angeles. "How could he say that?" she asked quizzically, when "he hadn't heard me speak?" Fjr. called. He is leaving today on a 2-week holiday. What were Stevenson's 2d ballot plans? Lyndon Johnson and Sam Rayburn would move for him. Fjr. felt it was important that the move should come from the north not the south, and were there plans for polling the N.Y. delegation? Mrs. R. replied she would discuss it with Finletter and Anna [Rosenberg].
>
> Mary [Lasker] and Anna had heard that she had booked herself in the fall for AAUN and Colston Leigh and were appalled. Adlai called to beg

---

* Rep. Mendel Rivers (D–S.Car.) was chairman of the House Armed Services Committee. He had attacked her for her support of the Powell amendment.

her to keep herself available for the campaign. She couldn't see why, she protested, but did proceed to get out of as many engagements as possible. Told Leigh all lectures were off except those for which contracts actually signed.

I said teasingly she should also keep herself free in January to go back to the UN. She did not like that and said, a little irritated, she was not going back to the UN. But she wants very much to go back to the UN and that's why I shouldn't have joked about it. She left us at 10:30 to work on mail and we argued merrily until 12:15.

Toward the end of July David flew to Europe. She would not get there for another month.

David dearest,   July 21st
My heart and thoughts will be with you as you fly out today and there will be no day I will not think of you till we meet. I'm hoping you will get a real rest and find pleasant people to enjoy and more interest than you anticipate.

My life will be very busy and full of people whom I will try to make happy. Jimmy and Irene come tonight just for tomorrow and Sisty and her three kids on Monday or Tuesday, which will mean 7 children in the house! Nevertheless when you are far away there is an empty feeling in my heart, and I seem to miss the sound of your voice and the glimpse of you now and then.

God watch over you and keep you. My love goes with you.
                                                                        E.R.

David on the way to Paris wrote her, "Just my love. It was wonderful to get off this way, with your warmth and care and help. It felt like on wings. . . ." That same day, she wrote him again.

David dearest,   July 22nd
No news so you must have landed safely in Paris and I fear the day will have been hard and left you sad and I know it will be hard to leave Yvonne [Lady Mendl, who was near death]. I only hope you found her better.

I went to your apartment and picked up Irene and she had everything pretty well done and plans to finish tomorrow when she goes down to N.Y. for her day off. It was nice to be in your rooms for a few minutes and feel your presence.

Then we went to 211 so I could sign mail and came on here [H.P.] arrived about five. Little things to do here like putting linen away, seeing

At the Washington Conference of the National Advisory Committee on Farm Labor of the United Automobile Workers Union. Behind E.R. is Helen Gahagan Douglas, next to her A. Philip Randolph. Seated at Mrs. Roosevelt's right Dr. Frank Graham and at her left Secretary of Labor James Mitchell. (Courtesy Franklin D. Roosevelt Library. Nate Fine Photo with permission.)

Mrs. Roosevelt with special glasses that included a hearing aid. (© Photo by Dr. A. David Gurewitsch.)

With son Jimmy at Val-Kill. (© Photo by Dr. A. David Gurewitsch.)

Mrs. Roosevelt in Iran in 1959 to visit daughter Anna and her husband, Dr. Halsted. With the Shah in Teheran. (Courtesy Franklin D. Roosevelt Library.)

Lyndon B. Johnson, then Senate majority leader, was invited by Rep. James Roosevelt, standing behind his mother, to speak at the Memorial Day exercises in the rose garden at Hyde Park, 1959. The Reverend Gordon Kidd of the St. James Episcopal Church is delivering a blessing at the planting of the tree in front of the Roosevelt Library. (© Photo by Dr. A. David Gurewitsch.)

Nikita Khrushchev and his wife Nina at Val-Kill without time for the picnic lunch Mrs. Roosevelt had prepared for them. At top left, Soviet Foreign Minister Gromyko. (Ed Clark, *Life* magazine © Time Inc.)

When presidential candidate John F. Kennedy visited her at Hyde Park in August, 1960. "It's the raft at Tilsit," Kennedy told William Walton, the artist, referring to the meeting between Napoleon and the czar, "and I want an ally with me." (© Photo by Dr. A. David Gurewitsch.)

Welcoming Queen Beatrix of The Netherlands at Val-Kill. John Roosevelt at the left. (© Photo by Dr. A. David Gurewitsch.)

Lorena Hickok when she lived in Hyde Park Village. (Courtesy Franklin D. Roosevelt Library.)

Mrs. Roosevelt with Edna and David Gurewitsch. Maureen Corr took the photograph. (© Photo by Dr. A. David Gurewitsch.)

Mrs. Roosevelt's bedside at the time of her death. (© Photo by Dr. A. David Gurewitsch.)

Jimmy and Irene's room was ready and there were flowers and then they arrived. . . .

I lay in bed last night and again early this morning thinking how lucky I am to have met you 11 years ago and how grateful I am that you have allowed me to be your friend when youth and beauty and more interesting people are constantly at hand and claiming what little time you have to give. I never cease being surprised and grateful but I love you very much and I hope you know it and you give me all my real happiness.

Bless you and my love.

E.R.

She wrote us on the Vineyard on July 22, "I went to Washington Friday for a meeting on the Civil Rights plank & it isn't going to be possible to meet what the colored leaders have drafted but the 2 Southerners seemed reasonable & I was surprised that they agreed to what seems to me pretty good wording on both the planks on education & civil rights. It won't be strong enough for Harriman, but I think it says all that needs to be said & would allow for any action one could take & still I think it won't divide the party."

She had eleven children in the house at the end of July, mostly Sisty's and Ellie's. "I have to do much planning and directing," she wrote David, "but it is a change of occupation!" The letter went on—

[E.R. to David Gurewitsch:]   [July 26, 1956]

What a shame you were so late on your flight. . . .

You gave me wise advice in your letter "enjoy it don't just cope with it"—I'll certainly try. This has been a full and interesting day but some difficult problems which I'll write you about later. The Victor Hammers came to dine, just back.* The Russian son was all they hoped for and the reunion a great success.

I miss you and send my love.

July 28th

Dearest David,

Just a few minutes here before going to the 4:45 train to H.P. I took our 7:55 plane to Washington and caught the one o'clock back. We've come to the best agreement we could on the wording on Education and Civil Rights but the crux of course the Southerners won't touch. We should pledge a limit on the filibuster and a modification on the seniority rule to have the Platform mean anything.

Yesterday Justine Polier came to see me about the 7,000 Jews who have

---

* Victor Hammer, the distinguished art dealer, was born in Russia and was the father of a son who had grown up and still lived there. Mrs. Roosevelt liked the Hammers and helped bring about the "reunion."

not been allowed to leave the camps in Morocco in spite of many promises and I'm trying to write a letter to the Sultan.

I also had the question put up to me yesterday of giving the membership list in Alabama of the N.A.A.C.P. under court order. We're fined $10,000 if we don't by Monday and $100,000 after. We face reprisal for them if we give them and I voted not to give them.

. . .

H.P. Monday morning early—

A busy Sunday. Geno Herrick spent the night. She is my old friend whose husband died of cancer last spring and who had one cataract operation later and will have a second one in November. It is wonderful to see a human being with great courage and a zest for living in spite of such ordeals.

We dined, all the grown ups with Fjr and Sue and he looks better but still too fat!

. . .

E.R.

A letter three days later about her family and friends added: "I also saw Ralph Bunche and Roy Wilkins and both said they'd accept the wording we worked out for the Civil Rights plank, now let's see how much gets thro' the platform committee." She chided David for telling her "nothing about Paris nor your daily life, *please do.*" She reported that Justine Polier had approved her letter to the Sultan of Morocco and ended that she missed him, "but I'm too busy to think, so I just send you snatches of blessings now and then!"

David worried about her physical condition, including her heart, but she replied there was little she could do about easing off until after Election Day.

[E.R. to David Gurewitsch:]   [August 9, 1956]

I worried you unnecessarily, my heart is O.K. I can swim and dive and walk as well as usual. I was mentally tired more than physically. Running a house for so many, means constant thought and active chores, tho' it doesn't seem so and I enjoy it. Then there has been endless telephoning and reporters and everyone has needed to talk to me alone, not always easy to manage, but after Chicago this will all be over. Adding a visit to Dr. Bruenn [the heart specialist who had treated F.D.R.] to my present schedule would be very difficult even if he is in town which I doubt. I love you dear, but if you were here you would know this is not necessary. I know I should live more reasonably but I can't till after Nov. 6th. So let's concentrate on doing the best I can and not worrying. I'm sorry I wrote you as I did in my last letter for my sense of strain is going and I am quite all right and even my neck is a little better, so I won't die just yet, and I can't live forever you know!

. . .

P.S. Mr. Truman is lunching with me Sunday in Chicago. I have a note from Marty's husband, saying he will be there and would like to see me so I'll try to get in touch with him. There is to be a press conference at noon.

Nasser of Egypt had seized the Suez Canal. The British and French pressed for firm retaliatory action, the United States sought to hold them back. "Suez is bad," she wrote us.

[E.R. to the Lashes:]   [August 4, 1956]
    I wish all these trade waterways were under U.N. We raised $75,000 at the Stevenson dinner last Wed. night with 135 people present but the Kefauver announcement* sparked the optimism everyone felt. Mr. S. came here for a couple of hours to discuss Civil Rights & he wants *much* more specifically said in the platform which I would love to see done but doubt if he can get by the Southerners.

All the time that she was straining at the leash to get off to Europe she was proving herself a politician of a "formidable toughness" on behalf of the Stevenson candidacy, and never more so than at the Democratic convention in Chicago, to which she flew in a plane together with Stevenson, the Finletters, Jane (Mrs. Edison) Dick, and Elliott. The latter privately thought Stevenson was a lightweight and was himself for Eisenhower. No sooner had their plane landed than she was whisked off by Stevenson's managers to a press conference where they hoped she might be able to undo the damage caused by former President Truman's announcement the day before, for Harriman. She did not like the assignment because she was grateful to Truman and appreciative of his having given her an opportunity to serve at the UN, but she had no alternative. So facing "more reporters and cameramen than I had ever seen before," she proceeded to deflate the Truman boom for Harriman. Years of press conference repartee enabled her to be every whit the deft performer that her husband had been. She ended her forty-five minutes with a forthright defense of a civil rights plank that was under attack by Negro leaders. It was doubtful, wrote several columnists, that any other northern Democratic leader could have said the things she did and survived politically. Both she and Mr. Truman were old, she observed gently, and it was time a younger generation was permitted to take over. "It was an adroit and ruthless performance," said Arthur Schlesinger, Jr., one of Stevenson's top aides.

    Delegates streamed into her rooms to see her. She appeared at state caucuses

* He withdrew from the race.

with Stevenson and topped it all off with a speech to the convention that sounded again the question that she had so often asked Franklin, "What did he want the victory to mean?" She gave her own answer, "There are new problems. They must be met in new ways." The party needed a "vision," and she recalled her husband's "one-third of a nation ill-housed, ill-clothed, ill-fed." "Twenty percent today is the figure they give us. Could we have the vision of doing away in this great country with poverty?" She said nothing about her support of Stevenson, but her dress sported a large "Adlai" button.

Afterward some politicians congratulated her on the role she had played in gaining the nomination for Stevenson. Others were pleased that she had urged the Democrats to stake out new ground, and one old Washington hand, Helen Hill Miller, wrote: "It isn't very often that a person who has been at the very center of one period in the life of a political party has the forward-lookingness and the resilience to note the transition to a new time, much less bring it forcefully to the attention of the current members of the party." But she thought she had made a bad speech.

> Chicago, the Sheraton Blackstone Hotel
> Monday night
> August 13th, 1956

David dearest,

This goes to you in Paris. . . .

I left to come here at 1 a.m. Sunday and it has been hectic as it always is. Truman's decision to support Harriman threw Adlai's people into gloom but I'm not sure (the ball pen just gave out) it is all bad. He himself knows now that if he wins he is free and owes no allegiance to Truman. The latter is using all his influence and much Harriman money to defeat Stevenson but it does not seem hopeless to me. They are making me stay over till Tuesday evening but I hope I can get away then. I enclose an account of my press conference which went well. My speech tonight was *very* bad.

I hope your time in the south of France has been wonderful. Good-night dear, and bless you. My love to you.

> E.R.

After she left the convention and was on the plane bound for Europe, she wrote him in pencil.

> August 17th, 1956

Dearest,

. . .

I had a hope, I didn't dare even acknowledge that you might be at the airport tomorrow morning but I know now that you won't be and I am somehow sad. I wanted just a glimpse of you more than I realized I guess!

Well, Stevenson was nominated and they've just told us Kefauver wants the vice presidency. They'll make a good team for the campaign but I'm not so sure how they will work together afterwards. I think they can win but it will be a hard fight. I've brought some clippings, too personal to me to give you much idea of what went on, but it may give you a little. It was all exciting and I wished for you so often. This would have been a most interesting convention for you to see and so often I wanted to know what your judgment would be. I may have been very wrong in my statement on the platform and I still want to talk to you about it. You, forgiving soul that you are, would like Stevenson's attitude on Truman.* I'll tell you the whole story when we meet, if our young ones give us any time to talk! You won't consider coming with us on the 5-day motor trip in France, will you?

. . .

There has been little sleep for the past nights and ever since I left Chicago I've been hours on the telephone. (I dread to see my telephone bill next month!) I am completely drained, but well and not especially tired, just glad it is over.

Bless you and all my love. I need you.

E.R.

She wrote few letters while she was with her grandsons, mostly postcards, except for a longish letter to Stevenson in which she offered "certain observations," provided he would disregard anything he considered invalid.

"Everyone I talked to feels that the crucial point in the election is to show that prosperity will not come to an end if the Republicans are defeated." She planned to be back in New York by September 12 and hoped to talk with him about the campaign. "Since the Republican convention I feel more certain than ever that you can win. They seem to me empty and void of imagination or content."

Hotel Des Indes
[The Netherlands]
Monday eve. Aug. 20th

Anna darling,

. . . Your Johnny is a joy to travel with. So interested & the year

---

* At the end of the convention Truman called Stevenson to ask whether he could come down to his suite. "No, no, Mr. President, I'll come up." The brief talk, cordial on the surface, seems to have been perfunctory. Afterward, back in Independence, Missouri, Truman wrote Stevenson, "I wouldn't blame you if you'd never speak to me again. . . ." Stevenson, intent on closing ranks, acknowledged he had been disappointed by Truman's behavior at the convention but said he would "take full advantage" of his "generous proffer of help."

between Haven & himself seems to mean much more maturity. It is hard
to tell what the impact of all the new experiences are but he will tell you
& in any case I think both boys are having a good time . . . The 2 hrs
in museums in the p.m. may have seemed long but they apparently saw a
great deal in spite of crowds. It is a wonderful collection of Rembrandts.
. . . Today we've visited the Queen . . . seen a publishing house & a
small Dutch home & now to bed & tomorrow to Copenhagen . . .

Devotedly,
Mother

Copenhagen
August 21st

David dearest,

. . .

I can hardly wait to see you and feel it is a long time till Friday. Don't
forget if things are possible I have tickets for you both for Versailles the
night of the 14th and reservations out there for dinner. I do hope you can
both go. All my love and sympathy to you dear and to Grania.

E.R.

Hotel de Crillon
26th August 1956

Anna darling,

. . . Yesterday p.m. we went back to see . . . Marie Antoinette's
farm village & walked up thro' the Versailles gardens just as the fountains
came on which was lovely. . . . One other piece of luck. We heard the
liberation day commemoration service in Notre Dame, just a little of it
but the music was lovely & one so rarely hears music in that cathedral
. . . thanks for letting me have Johnny. I love him.

Devotedly
Mother

Hotel de Crillon
27th August 1956

Dearest Trude & Joe,

Here we are in Paris. Grania has joined us. David is with us when he
can be but Lady Mendl is very ill. He is both sad & worried. As apparently she must die one can only hope she will be spared pain & it will not
last too long.

The three young ones seem gay & happy together & I hope are having
a good time. Somehow one never knows at least I never do! How much

should one plan & how much should be left to them to work out & plan? I try not to be quick & decisive but you know I'm not too good at that!

We dined with Henry & Marcelle [Morgenthau] last night & they came here with me afterwards to ask about politics. He wanted Truman & Harriman as a ticket & thinks Stevenson can't win but I feel more hopeful since some clippings came with the San Francisco convention [of the Republicans]. Just as at home the rich Americans & French want Eisenhower & are sure he can win!

I saw Juliana in Holland & remind me to tell you her view on New Guinea. I was very much interested in the Danish garden plot places for factory workers & think it might be adapted to help the juvenile delinquency problem.

. . .

E.R.

She returned to the United States to campaign for Stevenson in two of the most hectic months of her life. They began with an appearance on "Meet the Press" in which she scorched the Eisenhower-Nixon ticket, "the wisest, most gracious and convincing performance in my recollection," a grateful Stevenson wired her. Trude and I were at dinner a few days later, my journal records:

Mrs. R. is showing rare gusto these days—it's primarily because she has become so needed in Stevenson's campaign. Maureen told Trude that in Europe she was bored really at showing children the sights— museums that she had visited a dozen times before, and though she loved the children she only perked up when she got to Geneva where she was sought out for advice and was basically at the center of activities.

She told us last night that she was frightened at the way the Stevenson people had come to rely on her to perform magic. If you go here, they told her, still you have to be in Harlem with Adlai on the 4th, even though it means flying back from Michigan in the afternoon and out to Wisconsin the next morning. Anna Rosenberg told her Stevenson's speech in Harrisburg was a waste of money. The only thing that made up for it was Mrs. R's appearance on "Meet the Press." . . . She was amused by Nixon's efforts to be chivalrous and his insistence that he had never called Helen Gahagan Douglas a communist didn't disturb her one bit. That was the burden of his attack on Helen, she said.

We were having dinner because at the last moment she had bowed out of the Danish ballet, David having come to the studio to say he did not have a ticket even though it was a benefit for his hospital. I tried to prevail upon her to use my ticket, saying I did not like ballet and that it would be hard on the audience not to have her there, but she insisted she didn't like ballet either and that no one knew she was coming. I said I would much prefer going to the movies. She said she would go to the movies with me on Tuesday.

. . .

The Johns are moving back to the city leaving to Mrs. R. the burden of whole Hyde Park expense. Tubby [her chauffeur] asked whether he could use her as a reference for a permit to carry pistol. She said yes indicating she still had a pistol herself. Later in the evening, when we were talking about fear of coming into a dark house, she said she no longer was afraid. If they wanted to steal she'd let them do so and she thought she was too old for an intruder to be interested in anything else. Publishers want her to expand her convention speech into a book.

"I live in a mad rush but it will end some day," she wrote Hick at the end of September. Amid it all she sent a note to David to enable him to fit his schedule with hers when she was in New York.

Note

October 22 Tuesday

We are dining with Joe and Trude and you go with me to the "West Side Story."

October 24 Thursday

Have 2 tickets concert at UN. Will you dine and go?

October 26 Saturday

Anna and Jim, Sisty and Van, Buzz and Ruth and 2 of Jim's Czecho-slovak friends dine here and we hope you'll dine and show your pictures and if you want to ask anyone for dinner or afterwards please do so (they leave Sunday am)

October 27 Monday

2 seats for Romanoff and Juliet

October 29 Thursday

Dine at home

October 31 Thursday

Your birthday free and will do anything you wish or you can forget about me as you wish but I want a glimpse of you sometime that day at the office if nothing else is possible.

November 5 Tuesday Election Day

Free home for dinner

November 7 Thursday

House of Detention at 6. Dine there or here as you wish. I will phone Com.[missioner] Kross.

Oct. 31st
Evening

Dearest David,

A happy, happy birthday to you! May your day be full of satisfactins and God bless you now and always. Many, many happy returns of the day is my prayer for you.

I did not want to wake you or disturb you in the morning so I am putting this in your mail box so you will know my thoughts are with you bright and early and always—

My love—
E.R.

To the very end of the campaign she kept to the arduous schedules the Stevenson managers had prepared for her. They provoked disbelief in newspaper city rooms. One of them assigned a reporter to stay with her just to see whether she did. She campaigned until weary of her own voice, flying back to New York in time to get to Hyde Park to vote—"the last if not least important thing I could do in behalf of Governor Stevenson." She was inured to disappointment in politics, she said, and writing about the election afterward concluded it was difficult to defeat an incumbent administration when the public had no great or compelling reason to make a change, and to Adlai she wrote, "No one could have done more but the love affair between President Eisenhower and the American people is too acute at present for any changes to occur."

A birthday note to me on the relationship of the public to the private.

Dec. 1st 1956

Joe dearest,

Many, many happy returns of the day & may each year be happier. I love you very dearly & to see you interested & content inwardly means much to me.

These are bad times in the world [Russia had used troops to overthrow the Nagy Government and Britain, France and Israel had invaded Egypt] & therefore more than usually difficult for people who care about the world & its poor people. Just because of this anxiety I think the value of all really warm & deep personal relationships is heightened. My thoughts are therefore constantly with you & my love is deep.

Bless you,
E.R.

Toward the end of 1956, a disturbing new presence appeared, Edna Perkel. "He didn't first bring me to Eleanor Roosevelt," Edna, who later became David's wife, said, correcting my question, "he brought Eleanor Roosevelt to me." Edna and David met in September at a Museum of Modern Art opening, where some Canadian friends they had in common introduced them. She was pretty, nubile, young, very much involved in the art world. She impressed him. A week later, when she and David went to Toronto for an art show as guests of the same patrons who had introduced them, David saved the seat beside him in the plane for her. He had been smitten by this competent young woman, who radiated beauty and health and, though he did not tell Mrs. Roosevelt, already had it in his mind that he might marry her, indeed had told Edna she was the kind of woman one married and had children with. As Edna recounts:

I met Mrs. Roosevelt for the first time on October 11, 1956. David, to whom I recently had been introduced brought her to an evening art review that I had helped to arrange. They had come from the theater. It was Mrs. Roosevelt's birthday. They looked very distinguished, Mrs. Roosevelt in a long evening dress topped by an embroidered Japanese coat, and David, tall, graceful, very handsome, a small yellow rose in his lapel.

Mrs. Roosevelt did not need to be told. She knew something was up, must have realized it even more when David appeared at a Stevenson rally with Edna, and though he did not see Edna for several months after that, Mrs. Roosevelt steeled herself to meet with grace and kindness a presence that for a time must have been unwelcome.

XXII

To Russia with David

> . . . the active character of love can be described by stating that love is primarily *giving* not receiving.
>
> Erich Fromm, *The Art of Loving*

EVER ADVENTUROUS, ever the activist in whom love was an energizing force, Eleanor thrust aside advice to slow down. She was seventy-two, but she neither wished nor believed the way to retain health was to retire from life. She overrode the protests of her aging body, and it was a blessing to have David, a sympathetic physician as well as beloved friend, to turn to no matter how crowded his schedule. She sent him hers at the beginning of January 1957, hoping he would be free to dine and escort her to the Philharmonic, go to an American-Hungarian Medical Society dinner and concert, come to lunch and/or dinner on her free Sundays, and she ended: "Madame Pandit will lunch with me here on Saturday, January 19th. Would you care to come? Mrs. Lasker and Mrs. Lasvogle will probably come, and I have also invited Mr. Baruch."

She did two lecture trips in January and February, the latter to the West Coast, even though she was not feeling well. "I am still travelling too much," she wrote Anna's husband, a physician, in December, "but it seems inevitable." Some might have canceled. "This has been a trip!" she postscripted to Hick in late January. "I've been fighting the 'grip'." It was more than that, she indicated to Anna, with whom she communicated more frankly than almost anyone else.

[E.R. to Anna Halsted:]   [February 6, 1957]
    . . . I guess I was more tired than I knew & that was probably why I

was so hard hit by whatever bug I had on my last trip. David says I had pneumonia & a near pleurisy but I'm back & more rested than I have been in a long time . . .

David had flown to Paris to help the ailing Madame Viénot. Saloniste, former Socialist minister, wealthy, indisputably charming, she asserted rights with David he willingly granted.

Modesto, California
evening Feb. 13th

David dearest,

I thought of you last night flying back to New York and I hope so much that you were able to help the poor lady and also have a little real vacation and pleasure, seeing other friends as well.

Three speeches are done, in all cases to rather poor audiences. The first two in small college communities and sponsored by a student organization so I worry as to whether they will be in a hole. Tonight it was the Lions Club and they can probably afford it. Four more remain to be done. We've had much trouble with our connections, landslides and fog, and we are completely familiar with the San Francisco airport and all its facilities!

I'm feeling perfectly well and keeping rested, could you make an effort to do the same?

I've got about 3000 words done of the 10,000 that must be done on this trip but it is going easily tho' I suppose before it is finished it will have to be changed in many ways.

. . .

E.R.

The hazards of winter traveling figured even more strongly in a letter to Trude. It sounded a tiny peal of triumph over difficulties conquered. She had not missed an engagement and with Maureen to take her dictation had managed to get a start on the two articles she had promised the *Saturday Evening Post* to finish by March 1.*

Modesto, California
Feb. 13th 1957

Trude dearest,

. . .

The trip is going well, though we've had many trials over connections, what with landslides & fogs. We know the San Francisco airport inside

* They were not published until 1958.

out & we've spent hours there! We've made all our destinations before the lecture time however. Rather poor audiences, largely Republican communities which may be a reason, tho' this town was one of three in California that Stevenson carried! I've had to eat too much on this trip & I'm sure I gained back some weight but I mean to keep on losing more slowly but steadily & I feel perfectly well. I've done 3000 of the 10000 words that have to be done for the Sat. Eve. Post before we return but of course it will have to be changed before it is finally done. It is going easily though. . . . My dear love to you both.

E.R.

In a way, despite the bug, she was glad to meet exacting schedules. It took her mind off worry about David and also Stevenson's defeat. She had given the presidential race so much of herself and she did not want to brood over the outcome. "I had quite a talk with Adlai the other day," she informed Anna, "& readjustments are hard for men but I think he's going back to law & trying to do largely international work which should be good." That was only part of what the two had talked about when Stevenson had come to her apartment. As he wrote his friend Agnes Meyer the same day Eleanor wrote Anna, "Homeward bound after satisfactory visit to N.Y. . . . Also good talk with Eleanor . . . P.S. Eleanor admonished me to do nothing impetuous romantically,* & I guess there is no likelihood anyway. But she was a dear and so very, very wise and comforting."

Her lecture trips over, she prepared for a trip to Morocco. Sultan Mohammed V's representative had invited her the previous year when he had visited Hyde Park to lay a wreath at F.D.R.'s grave. David and Grania decided to join her. So did Elliott and Minnewa and three of their friends. Hick should use her apartment while she was away, she wrote. "Everything is o.k. with my health again."

Fez
March 22d 1957

My dearest Joe & Trude,

You know already that this is a fascinating country but we are seeing a little more than Trude could in her few days. We are a little like a Cook's tour but we all adjust a bit & get to know each other & I think all will go well.

. . . This is an interesting place & I'm glad that we decided to come here & give up [word indecipherable]. The narrow streets can only be seen on foot, or with a donkey, no other mode of transportation is possible. We saw the Jewish community yesterday. Because of last year's repri-

---

* Several strong women were devoted to Stevenson and he to them. There was a rumor at the moment he might marry Mary Lasker, widow of Albert Lasker. She often entertained him and was a heavy contributor to his campaigns.

sals on the French in Meknes, which we brushed on our way here, the whole Jewish community is jittery. The Sultan, I think honestly, wants no trouble & fairness & good will for the people of all races living here but in small far away places in the south communities are on the move into the better established ones out of fear & they bring problems of added unemployment, & disease in the bigger cities like this one & Rabat & Casablanca. The Jewish Community thanks to American money & the well organized "Joint" [Joint Distribution Committee] has better organized schools & social services than the rest of the community. The rich & able have a great sense of responsibility to their whole community as they have anywhere in the world. None of the Jews are getting visas to leave as families & that makes them very anxious. . . .

. . .

French papers do not give one much news, so I feel cut off from the world but as far as I can tell, decisions hang in space while negotiations seem to go on.*

I have succeeded I think in losing some real weight, if I can just hold it but we are given endless Moroccan meals & they are [word indecipherable] & very rich. We have all learned to eat with our fingers out of a dish in the middle of the table & it saves much washing up of dishes & cutlery!

Much, much love to you both,

Devotedly
E.R.

Hope you can come & dine April 1st.

Eleanor's letter to Trude and me said nothing about the tensions that had developed in the little group between on the one side Elliott and his friends, who settled happily into Morocco's gay life, and on the other side Eleanor's interest, supported by David and Grania, in seeing the country's realities. Grania was sixteen at the time of the visit to Morocco. "They embarrassed me," she said of Elliott and his friends. "We were in Fez and the tension blew up and I heard Mrs. R. say in a tiny voice [to Elliott], 'I want to go home.' There was this grand lady and this tiny voice. It passed." That was the way, Grania thought, with Mrs. Roosevelt's depressions. Eleanor wrote Anna lightly four days later, "It turned out a bit as I feared, too big a party but Elliott has been interested. I have enjoyed it, but I'm very tired & I'll be glad to get home on the 1st. This is a beautiful spot & I have Churchill's suite! The Sultan is charming but I haven't Father's gift of making interviews valuable!"

* Over the withdrawal from Suez.

Marrakech
Tuesday, March 26th

Dearest Trude & Joe,

. . . A good place to rest & vacation & so we decided to stay here & take excursions out. Yesterday we went to a very small old town, 10th century, they said, in the foothills of the mountains. They were told beforehand & prepared a touching welcome, but the enormous Arab feasts we are given each day are wearing me down! I succeeded in losing pounds however so all my clothes have to be taken in on my return!

We go to Paris from Casablanca on Thursday night so David can have three days there. . . .

Elliott has gathered much information & so has David, but I shall try to get Elliott a chance to speak with some people in Washington because time seems to me to be of the essence here. If we help in the right way here we may build up a balance in N. Africa against Nasser's power. The papers give one little news of the outer world but I saw last night the Suez Canal question might soon be settled.

. . .

E.R.

Eleanor felt as concerned with Grania as with her own grandchildren. Grania was a spirited and willful teenager, and in Paris, while David was off seeing his patients, Eleanor watched over Grania with the strict standards that reflected her own Victorian upbringing.

Paris
[March 30 (?)]

Dearest Hick,

. . .

It has been an interesting two weeks & these two days in Paris will be pleasant I think. David went off as soon as we reached . . . and Grania went out with a boy . . . to show her student night life in the Latin Quarter. She is only 16 & I am a bit worried so I saw her off & after Dr. Nussbaum [a one-man Amnesty International], who sat with me through dinner, tho' he was fasting (because of the murder of some 7th Day Adventists in Colombia) left, I came up to finish work. It is now 12:40 & I am doing my usual worrying & wishing I'd set a time for her to be home. . . .

E.R.

"I went to a ball in Paris. On the way back in the limousine, I was kissed for the first time. I got into the Crillon at 5 a.m.," recalled Grania. "There was Mrs. R.

writing letters. She startled me by asking me to help her undo her corset. It was such a touching womanly request. 'I used to love you for your dear father's sake,' she later wrote me, 'but now I love you on your own.' I was so touched at her letting me do this."

Eleanor as usual managed to combine holiday with a cause. American-Jewish groups were eager to talk with her on her return, and Trude hesitantly wrote Mrs. R. asking for a date for them and apologizing. "You are never presumptuous," she replied from Marrakech—

[E.R. to Trude W. Lash:]   [March 27, 1957]
& in this case everyone is trying to arrange a meeting too. I'll telephone you when I get back on Monday & I told Maureen to ask you & Joe to dinner either Monday or Tuesday or *both* nights. . . .

I am glad to hear at last Joe can get away from his 5 a.m. stint & hope it means you can both have some good times. I'm going to be freer in April so let's be busy together!

We had an interesting day in the mountains yesterday. I think David is resting at last & he & Grania are having a good time. He has served notice on me that in Paris he has nothing to do with me but I hope he will see Grania now & then & feel sure he will want to see her & show her off! I did not want 3 days in Paris but I find Joe Alsop is there & I think I can manage to have a good time!

This is an interesting country & if we are going to save them, the economic problems have to be met soon.

I am delighted you saw Sue & she was gay & happy. I'm going to get her to help me at H.P. too.*

The first few days back in the United States were busy with reporting what she had heard and learned in Morocco, whose huts as well as palaces and parched fields she had sought to see with "understanding eyes." "I have been busy as usual since my return!" she wrote Hick, who was at Hyde Park helping with research on *On My Own*. Eleanor hoped that American leadership might encourage Morocco and Algeria to serve as a counterbalance to Nasser in Egypt. The United States under Eisenhower and Dulles supported Dag Hammarskjold's moves to get Britain, France, and Israel to withdraw from the Suez. No sooner had the latter done so than Nasser asserted Egypt's, rather than the UN's, control of Gaza. I was back at my dawn-to-dusk stints at the New York *Post*.

> Minneapolis
> April 12th

Dearest Joe,

　. . .

* Sue Roosevelt had taken classes in landscape gardening and would help us with our plantings around our house in Martha's Vineyard.

It looks as tho' your hopes for a rest had not materialized. I felt the Egyptians might do just this. Our reaction as reported here doesn't please me! They say, we hope it just means their administration will sit with the U.N. commander. I wonder if we will ever stand up to Egypt?

E.R.

David had resumed seeing Edna Perkel. Eleanor knew. Part of her wanted David to marry; part of her didn't. The intimacy of two would become that of three. He could hurt her and she was vulnerable, as an undated letter written in pencil indicated.

David darling,

I am writing this because I may not have the courage to say it all. I love you so dearly that you can hurt me more than anyone else. I should be past all emotions I know but I am not. The lesson you taught me the other night was one I knew before but it suddenly hurt, probably because I had been worried & frightened. To me seeing you when I had not seen you for 11 days was a matter of joyful anticipation, as the hour got later I thought of emergency care or accidents or your having forgotten. I called your apartment from 11 p.m. several times & your message service to be told they heard from you at 10:42 but did not know how to reach you. I sat & waited in the hall. At midnight I went back to my desk & tried to work & then you called, you had taken a lady home & not even bothered to call me to say you would be late, you were alright. I was relieved & hurt. I've always known I couldn't mean much to you but suddenly I had to face how little I meant to you. I was crushed and rejected [?] & ashamed, & for two days it was hard to concentrate on anyone but you. That was because I was trying to hurt you. Love must be given freely & not look for any return. It is only pride that makes one crave a return. I apologize & I give you my word not to make you feel tied down nor to ask you to do unreasonable things again. If you can find it in your heart now & then to want me a little & to ask for my presence it would help my self respect. Otherwise I do all the asking, a beggar wanting & asking too much & therefore feeling ashamed.

Forgive me, for your mere presence, a look, the sound of your voice means so much to me, it is ironic,

E.R.

"As long as there is hurt, there is expectation," commented a friend who saw this, the most painful of all the letters to David. "Here her strength and resilience seem to falter. It makes one question Fromm, and ask to what extent love can be pure giving."

Who the lady was, this writer does not know. David told me there was a woman he had been seeing before he committed himself to Edna. Once when he had dined with Mrs R. he mentioned that his laundry was still sitting in his apartment, unpacked. She immediately said she would go up and put away the finished laundry. At the top of the pile of articles when they came in, David went on, was one of this woman's undergarments. "Mrs. R. put it aside and never said a word." She was determined not to make her love a burden.

At the beginning of May she flew to England to be a guest of the Nottingham Roosevelt Scholars, fellowships which had been established by the town of Nottingham in F.D.R.'s memory.

She reported the hostility she encountered in England to Dulles, whose policies toward Nasser had precipitated the Suez crisis. She hoped to be able to see Sarah and Kate, James Roosevelt's eldest daughters. They had been adopted by Jock Whitney, who had married their mother, Betsy Cushing, Jimmy's first wife. Whitney was then U.S. Ambassador to the Court of St. James.

> Scarborough Manor
> May 3d

David dearest,

Spring is lovely anywhere but it does make London a riot of color. They have had no rain here for nineteen days but the grass is green and the flowers lovely. There is lovely blue forget-me-not under my window and I nearly sent you a spray.

I had flowers and a nice card from Betsy but nothing more so I doubt if I will be able to do anything about the girls and Jimmy.

The way people talk about Dulles here is bad and today they published a very bad picture of him with Selwyn Lloyd [British Foreign Secretary]. The Queen Mother told me rather naively that of course one should go through the Nile but they felt something had to be done but she hoped relations would improve with us.

. . .

. . . I'll add to this before I leave on Monday.

Sat. Late p.m.

You would have enjoyed this day. Grey skies and cold but [word indecipherable] air and I've been so lazy. Had breakfast in bed and read till 10:30 then walked a bit before lunch and wrote letters. We drove to Brighton and walked again and now I write looking out at the garden with a fire and tea awaiting us in a lovely room that I think you would enjoy. Part of the house is Georgian and lovely things and so comfortable! . . .

> Devotedly
> E.R.

Her next letter to David had a cordial reference to Martha, who was now remarried, living in London, and no longer a threat to her.

> The Central Hotel
> Glasgow, C 1
> May 8th

David dearest,

Rain today but we cannot complain for so far all has gone well and my hosts are pleased with my money raising! . . . Marty and her husband came to dinner and we had a long talk. She can only talk of you. She looks very well however, better than she has in years, and gives the credit to a hospital in Rome. . . .

> E.R.

Her letter to Trude and me the next day said nothing of one of her hopes on this trip to see Jimmy's daughters, Sarah and Kate, much as a possible meeting with them was on her mind.

> On train to London
> from Nottingham
> May 9th 1957

Dearest Trude & Joe,

All my speeches are over & I am carefree but last night a wire came saying the Hungarians [exiles who had fled Hungary after the Soviet takeover] in Salzburg were so angry that they were not leaving for the U.S., that they were putting on a hunger strike in anticipation of my visit. We wired the High Commissioner as I don't want to create trouble tho' I will hate it if I can't go & see Vera [Trude's daughter, who was studying in Vienna]. You may not even get this before I see you Sunday!

I'll be glad to see you both & I think I've helped Youth Aliyah. Mr. Kol* has been here & he looks forward to seeing you & Joe in Israel. . . .

It has been an interesting visit & I go to see the Queen on getting back to London today but I've not seen the Churchills. You can't read this so all my love till Sunday.

> E.R.

I made some scrappy notes about dinner that Sunday with her after she returned:

* Moshe Kol, Zionist, leader of the Progressive Party, Youth Aliyah, member of the Knesset, government minister.

Madame Pandit deeply concerned at Krishna Menon's* hold over her brother. He was more than defense minister. He will come back to the UN. He was putting his people into all departments. She wondered whether he might not be Nehru's successor. If he were he would deliver India to the Communists.

Betsy [the former wife of James Roosevelt, now married to Jock Whitney] sent flowers as did she. The press kept asking whether she would see Sarah and Kate. Betsy cut off all communications. Not even her gifts were acknowledged since she would not go to the Embassy. Ambassador sent word suggesting she come to the Embassy.

A diary note, June 12, 1957:

Last Wed. night dined alone with Mrs. R. before going over to UJA [United Jewish Appeal] dinner for Stanley Lowell.† Mrs. R. sent Hick out! We talked about religion. Mrs. R. said she went to church because Roosevelt family had occupied a certain place in the parish, she was speaking of the President and his mother, and she felt she should give the Rector and his family support. She liked many parts of the Service, but she could read them just as meaningfully sitting out on her lawn. She had no conception of afterlife and there was no point in worrying about it. Those like Uncle David who assumed one, picked up earth's relationships in heaven. She did not contradict them, but thought it might be somewhat confusing. While she had no sense of God sitting on the clouds, she did have a sense of a divine presence. At times she appealed for divine help. Often she got up to speak without any notion of what she should say. She prayed for help to enable her to say something meaningful to the people in front of her and the prayers were answered.

She was led to this train of thought when I mentioned how, when I thought I could no longer go on, I visited my father's grave and came away peaceful and stronger. She thought her sense of a divine presence might not be dissimilar.

At the beginning of the year the Scripps-Howard papers did not renew their contract for her "My Day" column. Since its New York outlet, the *World-Telegram*, had been omitting it with increasing frequency, she was happy to have the New York *Post* take it over. Soon the latter's publisher, Dorothy Schiff, came to her with a proposition to visit Red China, perhaps Russia. She wrote David.

* Krishna Menon, head of India's delegation at the UN, where he was spokesman for the Afro-Asian bloc and hospitable toward the Soviet bloc, a waspy, supple diplomat.
† Stanley Lowell, reform politician, lawyer, deputy mayor, active in efforts to aid Soviet Jewry.

P.S. I would like to talk with you on something which has been suggested to me by the N.Y. Post yesterday. I tried to phone this a.m. but you were not there. I will call when I get in Sunday evening on the chance that you will be home or if not I'll try Monday morning—

I'll be home after 11 pm tonight but I expect you'll be out.

E.R.

Dulles turned down her request for permission to travel in Red China. The State Department pleaded its inability to protect her. But U.S. passports did not ban travel to the Soviet Union, and the Russians, eager to have her come, were ready to give her a visa. A long unrewarding experience of trying to deal with the Russians in the United Nations had not changed her view that we had to learn to live together if we were not to die together.

Trude and I with two of Trude's children, Vera and Roger Pratt, went to Israel and Yugoslavia that summer, Jonathan went to Camp Treetops near Lake Placid, Grania stayed with Mrs. R. at Hyde Park, working in the summer stock theater, opposite the Vanderbilt mansion. David came up occasionally, his courtship of the comely Edna having resumed in earnest. Edna was surprised to have him call, she remarked, sometime in the spring after not having heard from him in several months. "Why didn't you call me?" she asked him at Longchamps restaurant, where he had invited her. "It was hard," he replied, looking diffident although the words were bold, "because you are the kind of woman one marries and I had to be sure if I called you again, that I was ready for a marriage and babies."

They began to see each other regularly. "He told me he was a non-stop talker and also about his ladies, some of whom I subsequently met. He asked me to tell Mrs. Roosevelt about paintings." He invited her to Mrs. Roosevelt's apartment for dinner, "just the three of us around a small table. Later I told her I was too awed to swallow. 'That was foolish, dear,' she commented. 'You are much too thin.'" David told Edna he was a "non-jealous person." She asserted the same.

There was nothing about Edna in her letters to us.

> Val-Kill Cottage
> Sunday night, June 30th

Dearest Trude & Joe,

I hated to say goodbye on Friday but I'm really glad you are off & I hope you will be much à deux & enjoy it very much.

I telephoned your Johnny this morning, he sounded well, happy, pleased & said he was having a very good time. It was nice to hear his voice!

David came up with me Friday & we got home about 11 p.m. He found Grania asleep & his mother well & cheerful. I think they all had a nice weekend. David & his mother went down with Tubby after dinner tonight. He is not returning until Grania wants him. She said she wanted to be on her own. Tomorrow she starts & I wonder how it will go. Charles Pursell [a young actor friend] & Maureen come up tomorrow & I go down Tuesday at 10 & return early Wednesday p.m. & then have to leave Friday morning to get out to Kansas City & return Sat. night late to N.Y. & back here on Sunday. The Walter Reuthers get here for dinner that night I hope.

Franklin jr. & Sue came to dinner last night & both were in good form. He got talking about his ships in the war & Grania looked much interested. Needless to say I have no real news to tell you but I like to feel that you know, you & yours are constantly in my thoughts.

Give Vera & Mickey my love & a world of love to you dear Joe & Trude.

Devotedly
E.R.

Her thoughts were mainly on her forthcoming trip to Russia.

Val-Kill Cottage
July 9th

Dearest David,

Would you like to see this man at lunch with me at the apt. one day? He wrote saying he'd like to tell me about his recent trip to Russia. I saw him before and I'm told he does know a good deal.

Walter Reuther is sending me his suggestions for travel!* Next week, I'll try to see Jimmy Wechsler [editor of the New York *Post*] if he's home.

. . .

Grania is tired of the theatre experiment and I think they are doing a poor job so she is getting hard work and no real teaching. I shall be sorry to see her go as I have enjoyed having her here, but I think you did not expect it would last long so you will not be really disappointed I hope.

My love to you.

E.R.

Tubby will look for a convertible he thinks good.

An amusing letter about her trip to Kansas City for the dedication of the Truman Library.

Val-Kill Cottage
July 9th 1957

Dearest Trude & Joe

Your trip in Israel will be over when this reaches you. I hope to both of

---

* He had spent two years working in the Soviet Union in the early thirties. He was now head of the United Automobile Workers and the Congress of Industrial Organizations.

you it brought real joy & understanding. I had a letter from the Mayor of Haifa saying he looked forward to seeing you & I hope the city looked well, tho' I fear its greatest beauty, the roses were over. . . .

. . . I was away quite a bit last week, in N.Y. & then out to Kansas City Friday for the dedication of the Truman Library. A highly non-partisan affair with Knowland making a speech for Lyndon Johnson & himself as the Senator from Texas had to leave early for Washington. Mr. Hoover was most affable but much older I thought. Mr. Truman beamed all day & we were *most* friendly. The Chief Justice made a very nice dedication speech & was nice all day. I returned on a plane filled with Senators & Governors & drove on up getting here at 4:20 a.m. on Sunday morning. The Walter Reuthers came on Sunday evening & left today & I found him as always stimulating. She is sweet too.

. . .

E.R.

Val-Kill Cottage
July 16th
evening

Dearest Trude & Joe,

I read last night a wonderful piece by Joe in the Post on the present Israeli situation. . . . When Ellie & I came home from Bard where I went to speak to the Co-op group tonight, I found Grania had gone back to the theatre & left word the apprentices were having supper together afterwards & the boy would bring her home so I thought I'd write awhile & make sure she got in safely! She told me today she was staying into August tho' last week she was leaving at once! I only hope that on the whole it proves a good & helpful summer for her.

. . .

. . . What Joe said about the UN being partial to the Arabs I have felt often. I do feel the Administration has done well, if it is responsible for the Jordan & Lebanon attitudes but I'm not sure we have really done anything to bring this attitude about. Walter Lippmann praises the Administration highly for this achievement in today's column however.

I haven't called Johnny again as I thought he'd rather not be called too often but I may do so next Sunday! Shall I send him a birthday cake or will you want to celebrate when you all get together again?

I think *my* Russian visa is coming through but nothing on Maureen & David. Jimmy Wechsler said tonight he thought we might still go to China! I called him to find out if I should do anything more.

Maureen postponed her vacation a week & we finished the Saturday Eve. Post articles, now it remains to be seen if they take them. When she

gets back in August I must do the book, meantime I'm reading & sorting
letters. . . .

E.R.

Val-Kill Cottage
July 24th

Trude dearest,

. . .

The Sat. Eve. Post has taken the articles but wants to do some re-
arranging & I'll go over them the 5th & 6th with their man.

The visas have come for Russia so I'll leave Aug. 30th. There still
seems a hope for China.

I saw Irwin Ross the other day.* He's doing some articles on Cardinal
Spellman & finding it hard to collect his material.

. . .

We had an AAUN board meeting, (endless!) last night & I came back
this a.m.

Grania [her divorced mother was abroad] has settled down & seems
happy but does keep late hours which I'd like to avoid! I love having her
but when the children go I fear she will be lonely. David does not come
at all, but then I doubt if he would come in any case & it is probably as
good for the child to be here as anywhere else. She has such great possibilities I hope she will bring her Father the happiness he has never had
some day & be happy herself.

Charles Pursell has done a fine job on books & I can find all I want
now!

. . .

E.R.

It was touching that she should conceive of a daughter's relationship to her
father in terms of the happiness she might bring him rather than the other way
around. Was she correct though in assuming Grania's father had never had happiness? She was thinking, perhaps, of her own father's tragedy-ridden existence and
her sadness.

Trude returned to the United States as I flew on to Austria and Poland for the
Post.

Val-Kill Cottage
August 8th

Dearest Joe,

I meant to write you in Poland & thank you for your good letter of the

---

* A well-known journalist who had gotten to know Mrs. Roosevelt in 1941 when he arrived from
Harvard to edit *Threshold*, the magazine of the International Student Service. At this time, he was
writing feature series for the New York *Post.*

2d from Vienna but I realize it is too late to reach you there & so it must go to Bonn.

I think I have read all your pieces & they are fine. The paper gave you cover notice on the first from Yugoslavia.

. . .

Your Jonathan wrote me a very sweet letter. He says he likes camp & the sunsets are lovely but he liked hearing my voice!

Adlai Stevenson came to see me Tuesday, the day he landed & looked & seemed well. The trip has convinced him that we have to move on civil rights—I met Lady Reading at the steamer Tuesday, at least Tubby & Maureen did, & she had tea & dinner with me & it was a joy to see her.

Dore Schary read us his play on F's polio years Tuesday night & Jimmy & Fjr, the only boys there liked it— . . .

E.R.

At the end of August she, David, and Maureen flew to Frankfurt en route to the Soviet Union. "I hope I do a good job & don't get fooled & don't see only through prejudice!" she wrote Hick. "Remember to come here if you want to. I hope the book [about Helen Keller] comes on well."

From Frankfurt they went to Berlin and then to Copenhagen.

Hotel Codan
Copenhagen

Anna darling,

We've had wonderful flights & 2 nights in Berlin. The days were full of interest in Frankfurt & Berlin. I can't write of the refugee work [East Germans were streaming to the West before the Berlin wall stopped them] till I get home & even then I will have to be careful for much must be secret.

Tonight we spent in "Tivoli" that incomparable spot in which to be frivolous. I really like Denmark & it was fun to come in & be greeted by . . . our very Republican new Ambassador, Mr. Peterson. I hope he'll do well here for his parents came from here . . .

Well, day after tomorrow I'll know what I'll be able to do in the Soviets. We leave at 10:15 & get there at 6:35, so there isn't much we can do but see a ballet or something tomorrow night. All my love

Mother

Hotel National
Moscow
Friday, Sept 6th 1957

Dearest Trude & Joe,

I have temporarily (I hope) lost both my ball pens & am reduced to a

pencil. This is an interesting & challenging trip but at first it seemed slow
in getting started. We arrived in the evening, had dinner & then drove
around a bit—At ten the next morning Wed. a visit to the Ambassador,*
very kind & wanting to be helpful, regretful that as an ambassador or
diplomat he was unable to do some things which tourists could do. He
gave a reception to some diplomats & foreign press at 6 p.m. on Thursday. I met the Israeli Ambassador & had an interesting talk. Sunday
morning I shall try to see the big synagogue & head Rabbi & the Baptist
Minister. Maureen & I visited a state farm Thursday morning. This is
now more favored as the pattern for agriculture than the collective. Then
we went to Zagorsk, really lovely 15th Cent. Church & a most amusing
midday meal at the Greek Orthodox divinity school! They are stout these
gentlemen & eat & drink well. We were plied with champagne & I was
glad of my agreement to drink only water. Maureen found her line—
taking one glass—looked upon with incredulity & not accepted!

I have had interviews with to date, & Joe can pass this on to Jimmy if
he likes, the Minister of Education, the Minister or sub Minister of
Social Welfare, the Minister or acting Minister of Health. At all interviews the heads of all Depts. are present. I have been impressed by all
these people as earnest & devoted. The Minister of Health impressed me
as the quickest but he understood English & also had a very good protocol officer to do the translation in fluent English. The young man had
seen much of Kate [Roosevelt] & said he would like to lunch with me.
We will see! I was asked to submit my questions for Khrushchev & they
went to him with a note this morning. If Gromyko is in town I shall ask
to see him as he heads the Foreign Office & deals with exit visas for
foreigners but also for Russians wishing to visit or emigrate outside the
USSR.

Today, whether as a result of my visit to the State Farm or for some
other reason the Minister of Agriculture asked me to go & see him & set
Monday about 11 a.m.

I have cut down on travel plans feeling I did get more by interviews &
seeing things here but Monday night we go to Tashkent & return here
early Sat. a.m. the 14th.

David saw two hospitals today & wants to return to both. He feels this
a big challenge, is interested but always torn as to what he wants to do
most! We have been to a circus, a ballet, & a huge & beautiful amuse-
ment park in the evenings!

Our time is fully occupied & I am glad I write only 2 columns a week.
I make them longer but there is so much to see I find it hard to allocate

* Llewellyn Thompson had succeeded Charles Bohlen in April.

the time. The evaluation is a long process. The welcome in spots almost embarrassing. . . .

E.R.

Tashkent
Thursday Sept. 12th
1957

Dearest Joe & Trude,

We came here by jet plane on Monday night 3-1/2 hrs for over 2000 miles! This trip was on time & all was done casually but they tell you a jet plane is not noisy on the inside & I think it far noisier than the others. I am glad we chose to come here. It is so completely different & yet the central plans are carried out. On Monday at lunch we had met at the Embassy a group under Parran* of our public health affairs & one man from Harvard who spoke Russian fluently. They told us sanitation & public health were worse here than in any other Central Asia place they had visited but David finds this is good from his point of view & I think from maternal care & children is good. Much more emphasis on prevention of illness & keeping well. I have come to the conclusion that one has to divide one's thinking here. The political & ideological side concerns a few important people at the top but the essential things to improve the life of the people seem to go on at a separate level & they are very good. I surmise there is not much corruption, in many cases the people in charge seem dedicated. Security exists materially—The lower paid workers find life hard but shelter & food is available. Clothes are poor, glamorous women well dressed & groomed, don't exist & yet the elder women dye their hair!

Reliable statistics are hard to get at but when you see things it is not "plush" but very good. The newest educational feature is "boarding schools." I visited one yesterday—We heard all the theories in Moscow & here in this distant area we are seeing how things are done. You will both be interested I think. I met Ludmilla with the Russian women's group. The 2 boys came thro' the war too but are in far away areas. They asked to be remembered to you & Joe thro' Ludmilla.†

Tomorrow we go to Samarkand for the day & Sat we leave the airport at 7 a.m. & because of change in time arrive Moscow at 8 a.m. We have an interesting day today, a collective farm & a textile factory, then David will visit homes with a nurse.

All my love,

* Dr. Thomas Parran, U.S. Surgeon General, 1938–48.
† The three constituted the Soviet delegation to the International Student Assembly in September 1942. Ludmilla Pavlichenko, Red Army sharpshooter; Nikolai Krasavchenko, head of Moscow's Komsomol; Lt. Pavel Tchelintsev.

Devotedly
E.R.

Russia's deliberate distortions of America's reality never ceased to amaze her and confirmed her conviction of the need to counter its propaganda.

[Moscow]
Sept. 16th, 1957

Dearest Anna,

Back here just for part of a day yesterday as we were half a day late in leaving Tashkent because of fog here in Moscow. Went with the Indian Ambassador . . . to see a touching Russian war film just finished & some scenes about a Russian traveller in India in the 15th Century which is being done in collaboration with Russia.

The days in Central Asia were fascinating, not the least interesting is the contrasts of 50 yrs ago & now. The life of the people is enormously improved & most of them don't worry about politics. On every hand "peace" is preached & we are depicted as the one danger to peace. They have no news that is truthful about the outside world so they believe & are grateful for all the improvements at home. A strange "Alice in Wonderland" world. . . .

A world of love
Mother

August 17th [she meant Sept.]
Sochi USSR

Dearest Joe & Trude,

Samarkand was an interesting day from the sightseeing point of view & Tamerlane became quite real & not just a myth. They have there too a T.B. bone hospital, which serves a large area. There were some 260 children's beds, all out of doors, & such good children! These institutions are good, primitive in facilities according to our standards but the results are good & treatments modern.

Our day in Moscow was cut short by a delayed flight, but we met one of our delegation from World Fed. of U.N. Ass. who said all went well at their meeting. In the evening we went with the Indian Amb. & Mrs. Menon to see a new Soviet film, a private showing. It is a war film, well done & touching. They showed us too some scenes from a film they are doing with the Soviet film producer, good but dragged a bit! We had supper afterwards & I had a chance to check some of my impressions with the Ambassador & get his feeling. Santha Rama Rau* is in Moscow with her husband & boy gathering material for a book.

Up at 5:15 a.m. again to catch a 7:35 plane for this health resort. There are over 50 sanitoria in Sochi alone. We are in the one belonging to the Ministry of Health, almost the Palace of Versailles! Every trade union has one but there are hotels & we hear Aneurin Bevan† is here with his wife. I'd like to see him if it can be arranged, just to get his ideas. David has gone to see the Research Institute & all the different treatments. I doubt if there is much for me to do here but try to think out my articles & sit in the sun as I foolishly brought no bathing suit.

The mountains come right down into the Black Sea, the water is warm, the sea & sky a deep blue. The beaches are [word indecipherable] round pebbles, no sand, the sun is hot & the nights cool.

Sue wrote me she had plans for your Martha's Vineyard cottage which she thought were good & hoped you liked.

We leave here the 19th & have the 20th, 21st & part of 22d in Leningrad. Maureen & I leave there at noon for Kiev but David takes the midnight train to Moscow. We will only have a day in Kiev & that will give us an idea of an old city. Then I'll have four days in Moscow & finish up my interviews. I know just what I want but have no assurance even from Khrushchev. They love to keep you waiting but they hate you to deviate from a plan for one minute!

. . .

E.R.

Leningrad
Sept. 20th

Dearest Joe & Trude,

This will be the last note I will send you for the last letter to reach me in Moscow last night was dated Sept. 6th so I may get home *before* you get this.

What a lovely city this is! far lovelier than Moscow but they tell me cheerfully that it rains every day except in summer & summer is over & even then it rains now & then! They were badly bombed by the Germans but rebuilding has gone on fast & the scars are almost hidden but 900 days of siege are still much in the minds of people.

Getting app. to see "services" & not just museums is very difficult. No one does anything till you arrive & then "Intourist" is a reluctant agent. I hope my appointments, including Khrushchev, are arranged for my last four days in Moscow. I've learned a lot though, even if it is trying not to get what you want. Tell Joe if Jimmy Wechsler is in town I'd love to see

---

* She was married to Faubion Bowers and wrote on Indian themes.
† British Labour MP, Minister of Health and leader of the left in the party.

him the 29th either for lunch or tea so he might ask him for me. I hope all goes well with you & yours. I never felt more cut off [.] Letters received were marked Sept 6th & no world news in any Soviet paper & nothing else is to be had!

Much love to Joe & to you & Jonathan.

E.R.

Three days before they were to depart for home she received word that Khrushchev would receive her the following day in Yalta, where he and his family were on holiday. Accompanied by David and her interpreter, Anna Lavrova, who also had interpreted at the Yalta Conference, they drove in Khrushchev's car from the palace in which the Big Three had held their conference to his dacha that looked toward the city of Yalta. He met them, a short, stocky man, in the loose white Russian blouse beloved by the Russians, this one handsomely embroidered on the fringes. For several hours they went at each other with gusto on most of the issues that divided the two countries—disarmament, the origins of the Cold War, the Near East, who threatened peace. At the end of this spirited exchange they were joined for a few minutes by Mrs. Khrushchev, her daughter and son-in-law.

"Can I tell our papers that we had a friendly conversation?" Khrushchev asked as he saw them to the car.

"You can say," Mrs. Roosevelt replied, "that we had a friendly conversation but that we differ."

"Now!" he exclaimed smiling. "At least we didn't shoot at each other."

Her visit to the Soviet Union would make the final four chapters of *On My Own,* and though she had sought to understand what was happening in Russia "by looking at the country through Russian eyes," she also had to say, "I think I should die if I had to live in Soviet Russia."

A letter to Hick, ten days after her return to the United States, about her birthday: "I've made no plans for I don't intend to celebrate till I'm 75." She was "desperately busy," she added, relieved, no doubt, that it should be so.

David dearest,

You are coming to meet the press Friday and Maureen will let you know place and time you must be there. . . .

I'm going to be in N.Y. only going out for the day until Nov. 1st and I'll be at H.P. Nov. 1st to a.m. of the 5th in case you can be induced to come for the weekend?

On Nov. 8th I leave for speeches and won't return till noon on the 17th and then I go out again Nov. 22d and get home noon on 23d and am gone 24th until the night,

Since you are the person I'd rather have with me than anyone else I give you my free times and the nights when I have tickets. Come as often as you can and as you wish to, just check so I know. If you want to change at the last minute you always may do so so don't feel you are to be shut in!

. . .

My dearest love, Take care of yourself and if I can help you or Miss Percale [Edna Perkel] on anything when you move let me know.

E.R.

XXIII

David Marries Edna

JANUARY 1958 meant another lecture trip to the West Coast. Why did she do it? She was seventy-three. She might well have stayed at home or found a spot in Florida to finish the third volume of her autobiography, *On My Own*. She gave the answer in that book. Her attitude as she left the White House was:

> I did not want to cease trying to be useful in some way. I did not want to feel old—and I seldom have. . . . As time went on, the fact that I kept myself well occupied made my loneliness less acute.

Robert Browning spoke of "two soul-sides" in large-minded people, one with which to face the world, the other "to show a woman when he loves her!" In Eleanor the two were linked. One fed the other and both were nourished by an unflagging love and trust in people. Hick was ailing and increasingly a burden. Before Eleanor left for the West Coast, however, she saw her settled in an apartment in Hyde Park. Hick no longer drove and had to be fetched when they met. That did not matter. "I hope you will take it," she wrote after looking at the apartment, "as I feel you will be better off in the village [Hyde Park]. I think I can find enough furniture & buy essential kitchen things if an ice box & stove are in?"

Her first wish at New Year's was for David, who often talked with her about the pros and cons of marrying Edna. He was, as usual, conflicted in regard to women. "May you know what you want and then I know you will achieve it and may those who love you be helpful and give you what you want." Edna later said, "David was not the marrying kind. He was afraid of being tied down." Eleanor knew that side of him. She knew too she could never satisfy his need for a wife and home. But she did not want to lose him in the course of finding one.

David flew to Paris primarily to see Madame Viénot, the old and close friend whom he would have wanted to apprise of his maturing decision to marry Edna. Eleanor hoped to meet him at the airport on his return but, in case she was unable to manage it, had a note and flowers for him.

n.d.
[1958]

Darling,

Just in case I miss you at the airport, for you should be gone before I arrive, these flowers will brighten up the apartment and tell you how happy I am to have you home. It is good to have you near! A thousand welcomes and I can hardly wait to see you tonight.

Your mother and 2 friends went with me Sunday pm to the French lecture on the "Mime." Too long, but she loved the demonstration and admired his body control and wanted you to see him!

The [Kenneth] Pendars were here tonight to go to Washington Tuesday and return in Feb. They leave the 8th so could you dine here with them the 6th for a farewell? That would mean being here 2 nights in succession but please come the 7th. . . .

I have kept free time the days I am here in case you have any important news for which you want quick arrangements made!

. . .

E.R.

A thank-you note from David.

1/31/58

Dearest Mrs. R.

Just a word to thank you for the wonderful welcome home from Paris —You sitting there—having come all the way out so early! And then your letter and the flowers.—I so often receive without acknowledging my joy! Thank you again and again. I just must improve. Last night was a deep impression to live these days and years with you being there was strange and moving.

Just my love. And my thoughts and my thanks.

David.

The "important news" Eleanor had mentioned in her letter related probably to his self-examination as to whether he should marry Edna. He wanted the steadying influence of a home run by an attractive and competent woman, as Edna was, but he also liked the life of a free spirit and basked in the adulation of cultivated ladies. Eleanor sent him a postcard from "The Arizona Inn" in Tucson.

> Sunday eve [February 9, 1958]
>
> First speech over and successful. Here it is lovely and you might enjoy
> it as a rest. This is a place of memories for me tied to Isabella Greenway.*
> Between a tea and the lecture I dined with 2 of her children in her old
> house. A good time with Elliott and Minnewa. I hope all is well with you.
>
> E.R.

Her next letter was from Los Angeles. "2 lectures are over and successful I think. . . . I'll probably call Thursday a.m. from here if I wake or Friday at your office in early afternoon."

The next day she heard the news about Edna. Maureen, who was with her, said she blanched.

> Wed. night
> [February 12, 1958]
>
> David dearest,
>
> It was so good to hear your voice today and you sounded happy and I
> hope it is because you are fully satisfied with your decision.
>
> I am free till 3 p.m. on Sunday the 23rd [when he and Edna were to be
> married] if you need me later than that, wire me St. Francis Hotel, San
> Francisco and I'll get out of the afternoon and evening dates.
>
> . . .
>
> E.R.

Three days later she wrote from the St. Francis Hotel.

> Sat. Feb 15th
>
> David dearest,
>
> I hope this will await you Monday and I think of you with Grania and
> hope the pictures and lecture were a great success. I'm sure they were!
> Perhaps Edna went with you which would give you a pleasanter trip.
> Give her my love.
>
> Life was hectic in Los Angeles but it is worse here! However, all went

---

* "It seems strange that she should have died," she wrote Hick about Isabella's death, "& I should still be flourishing!"

well at Stanford yesterday and will pray all goes well here and my plane is on time going back.

I'll call you Tuesday p m and I'm all prepared to do anything you wish the 23rd. Wouldn't you like a buffet lunch? I hope for you the deepest and most satisfying happiness. My thoughts and love go to you.

E.R.

Chandler Roosevelt, Elliott's daughter, was married while Eleanor and Maureen were on the coast, and Eleanor's letter to David reflected her tempered hopes for marriage. "She was a lovely bride and the boy seems nice. God grant they may be loving and patient enough to grow into the kind of happiness that can bear life's inevitable burdens and sorrows. It was amusing in ways with two sets of parents on *both* sides."

I was in Israel gathering material for a series of articles to be published in the *Post* on that country's tenth anniversary. Eleanor wrote me from San Francisco.

Saturday
Feb 15th
1958

Dearest Joe

I cannot be in San Francisco & not write you a line because I never forget the last night spent here before you left for the Pacific. What a deal we have all lived through since then. I hope as you look back you feel the rewards outweigh the penalties.

. . .

Here I'm busy every minute but Stanford went well yesterday. . . .

Much love always
E.R.

David and Edna agreed to have their wedding and reception in her apartment, and Edna wrote appreciatively.

February 21, 1958

Dear Mrs. Roosevelt,

I am writing you from a very full heart trying to find words which will give you some idea of my feelings.

I am most grateful to you for the wedding tomorrow which I know will be beautiful. And I must thank you very, very much for what you have done to make the wedding possible. I know how much you mean to David and what your feelings and opinions mean to him. I can repay you in part only by doing all I can to make David happy. I shall try very hard.

I have admired you so much all my life and to this I add my love and deepest gratitude.

Edna

Eleanor heaped gifts upon them.

Edna—At your wedding you should wear
    Something old and something new,
    Something borrowed and something blue,
    So I give you a little blue bird who brings happiness
    May you be happy and you will then make the man you love
        happy.

To David went two wood figures, standing in a canoe, paddling, and the card said—

> *These little figures may be a symbol*
> *May they take you on smooth seas*
> *Where the storms are few*
> *May you have the understanding*
> *   which gives kindness*
> *And may you both give and*
> *   receive the warmth of love*
> *Which will bring you both*
> *   happiness.*

Another gift for David—

David dearest,

    This is *part* of your wedding present and I thought it might be useful towards buying a new car. I feel you really need one and I'd like to give you something you would be using constantly. This is a rather selfish pleasure to give you something because I will enjoy having you use it!

    Perhaps you can add enough to get a Buick which I know is what you want and do have power steering!

    . . .

E.R.

And on the day of their wedding, another gift—

David dearest,

    I have no wedding present for you and Edna but I think what will bring you the greatest pleasure is the gift of your next real trip whether it is to Russia China or Timbucktwo *[sic]*, so I hereby promise you 2 tickets for the next real trip you want to take! Sometime when I find something you could use and enjoy in your home I will get it as a *post* wedding gift.

You know you have all my love and may this day bring you the perfect relationship you have dreamed of and a home you can fully enjoy.

God bless you always

E.R.

"She met us at the door," recalled Edna. "She was very pale. She stood with a small leather box in her hand and said to me, 'This is a necklace for you. It is not valuable, but it is something that has always been close to me.' "

"The wedding could not have been easy for her," Edna commented in the same article in *American Heritage,* and later recalled to me how "tense she was at the wedding." Maureen stated it more bluntly. "One of her most difficult moments was when David married Edna. She carried it off in style, having the reception in her apartment, but afterwards she was spent, completely, and looked terrible."

"I believe she thought she would lose him," said Edna. "She needn't have worried. I loved her, and he respected her confidences. The relationship changed but remained close differently."

The day after the wedding, Eleanor wrote Edna.

Monday night
Feb. 24th, 1958

Edna dear,

Your lovely roses are giving everyone who comes in a joyful welcome and as I go in and out I think of you. Many thanks but above all my thanks for your sweet note.

I loved having the wedding here, as I have always loved doing anything I could for David and now I shall love doing anything I can for you and for you both. I never want to be a burden, but it is a great joy to me to feel close to the few people I really love and to be able to do anything for them. I need you both very much, but don't let me be a nuisance for David and you both need time alone in your own home.

Will you let me know if you are going to the concert on the 26th? I can't get there till 9:30 so I won't go unless I find you there!

My thanks and love to you.
E.R.

She sent me in Israel a spare account of the wedding that was sandwiched in among other matters, including Trude's being snowed in at Oakland, New Jersey, where we had rented a cottage during the winter.

Sunday Feb 23d

Joe dearest, I think of you so often & feel sure the time in Israel has been rewarding.

Trude & Jonathan must have had an adventure last weekend. . . . Since I got back from the West Coast last Tuesday I've been very busy. Catching up & going to some new place to speak each evening. Today I had Edna & David's wedding here, just with the two families. I like her very much & hope it will bring both happiness. She grows on you so you & Trude may like her too as time goes on.

C.R. Smith [head of American Airlines] took me in the afternoon on my annual trek to speak to the cadets at West Point. This time on Russia. They seemed interested & asked good questions. Dan Shore [Schorr, formerly the CBS correspondent in Moscow] came to lunch the other day & says he's had much interest on Russia too.

I can't get in from a lecture trip in time to meet you on the 5th but I want to hear all about your ideas while they are fresh so I suggested to Trude you come to dine that night & bring any & all the family you want to come. I miss feeling you are in town!

My love to you & best wishes
E.R.

When Trude saw her the next day she had the withdrawn look that appeared when she was depressed. It did not go easily at first between her and Edna. The latter recalls a luncheon of the two alone. "I got shyer and she grew deafer." Like "a bolt out of the blue," remembered Edna, "she remarked, 'Don't worry. He will give you everything you want.' It left me very uncomfortable, as though she had not gotten everything she wanted." Misgivings about David's remarriage were submerged in work, as reflected in a letter to me.

Feb. 25th

Dearest Joe,

What a joy it was to get your letter from Jerusalem of Feb. 15th yesterday. Your first sentence was a tribute to the joys of travel with your family & I'm glad you found you could enjoy Israel & be interested even tho' it was lonely. You sound as though every minute had been made to count & I can hardly wait to read your articles & to talk with you.

I've just come back from speaking in your part of town for the Independent Democrats (old Stevenson group). They had a panel, Ernie Gross, Dr. Counts* & myself on "reappraisal of situation today between USSR & ourselves." It was a good group I thought.

* Ernest Gross, distinguished lawyer and one of the leaders of the U.S. delegation at the UN 1949–53 with the rank of ambassador. Dr. George Counts, outstanding professor at Teachers College, Columbia University, author, and head of New York's Liberal Party 1955–57.

Soboleff [Arkady Sobolev, permanent representative of the Soviet Union at the UN and former Assistant Secretary General] & [name indecipherable] came to lunch today with Mr. Eichelberger & me. We talked about W.F.U.N.A. & the possibility of our exchanging some of their members & ours to see how we all work. Then he & I talked about our countries future possibilities of preserving peace & it was interesting —I shall ask him again sometime.

The last two days have seemed as tho' spring were near but of course March will bring us more storms.

Trude & I are going to Dorothy Norman's* show tomorrow & then at four to the meeting for Aubrey Williams to talk about the Southern Conference. I hope many people come but I feel they won't—Saturday I will be off again till the 5th & you will be home when I get back. How good it will be to see you. I hope you've kept well & on the whole enjoyed your trip. Everyone here has missed you. Much, much love

E.R.

Self-effacing and considerate, Eleanor soon made Edna feel included in all her thoughts of David. "You were good to share so much of your short holiday with me," she wrote the two of them at Easter, "and I appreciate it very deeply." In late April David's mother, an independent soul, on her way to visit a patient, collapsed at a crossing, almost as if a passing bus. had backed into her, and was dead. A small woman, she was robust of spirit and gifted with extrasensory perception that she applied in her practice and that always interested Mrs. Roosevelt, for David seemed to have some of the same intuitive quality.

Edna accompanied David to the police station when the latter received the news. "He went in to examine his mother and came out with shining eyes. She had not been touched and had died of heart failure. David said, 'It's wonderful to die with your boots on.' She was a divine woman," Edna added, "of a special breed who felt that fifty cents of every dollar she earned belonged to society." Eleanor was not a mystic, certainly not a believer in faith healing, but both David's and his mother's intuitive powers fascinated her.

[early May 1958]

David dearest,

I will love having your Mother's scarf and I will try to be worthy of her and of your dear thought. My warm thanks.

I'm delighted about the car, as much because of the self-assurance as because of your very evident pleasure. You need never have had a bad

---

* Dorothy Norman, civic worker, columnist, friend of Steiglitz. Her home was a mecca for intellectuals in the forties and fifties as well as for the leaders of India including Nehru, his sister, Madame Pandit, and his daughter, Indira.

conscience about your Mother, she loved you deeply and had great pride in you.

Edna will help you grow in strength, she loves you and I am deeply happy about it. Bless you both and my love.

E.R.

She dwelt on his relationship with Edna again at the end of May.

May 27th

David dearest,

Such a dear letter as you wrote for the A.D.A. Journal! It made me happy and I thank you.

I want also to tell you that Anna [Halsted] said she had such a lovely letter from you. I hope the hard letters are nearly all written but you have been wonderful and I admired your selflessness and thought of others. Sorrow is given us, I believe to help us to greater understanding and sympathy for others, but you never needed it for you had all the sensitivity and ability to give.

I want you to know how happy I am to see and feel your happiness with Edna and hers with you. I fully expected that our relationship would have to change but I think Edna is so lovely that I can mean something to you both and not hurt the happiness and closeness between you. It is good, so good, to see you well cared for and happy and to feel that I can keep and share and perhaps contribute a little to both of you. It is a great happiness to me.

My thanks again dear for what you wrote and my love to Edna and always deep love and gratitude to you.

Devotedly,
E.R.

The ADA also had asked me to send a letter* on Mrs. Roosevelt's services to liberalism for its convention journal, which was dedicated to her.

* David Gurewitsch's letter read: "It is difficult to put into words one's feelings about someone to whom one is close. I imagine, as Mrs. Roosevelt's physician, I should say something about her prodigious energy; however, medicine can take no credit for her vitality. She owes it to her constitution and to her ability to organize and to relax. In addition, she possesses a self-discipline and a sense of duty with which she can drive herself beyond the endurance of most people.

"Mrs. Roosevelt has retained an unusual ability to feel, to learn, and to absorb. These are attributes of youth. At the same time, this very same ability to retain, to digest, and to continue to use her many and varied experiences give her the wisdom of age. She is therefore young and old at the same time.

"Time and again I have marveled at Mrs. Roosevelt's modesty and her conviction that her arrival in a new place would not arouse particular interest. All this in the face of continued and abundant proof to the contrary.

"One afternoon in 1952, we were approaching Karachi coming from Jerusalem. The day had started at 3:30 a.m. and we were looking forward to our arrival and a little rest. As the plane was touching the ground I saw in the distance a huge and colorful crowd. Somewhat apprehensively, I pointed this out to

May 27th

Dearest Joe,

I have just read your letter for the ADA journal & I thank you more than I can say. I deeply appreciate it, it is such a lovely letter & means so much to me coming from you. You know dear, that I've always loved you deeply & as the years go by I not only love but admire trust & respect you & you are among the few people I hope never to have really disapprove of anything I think or do.

All my love & thanks,

E.R.

Involved as Eleanor was with David and Edna and other close friends, her solicitude for her children never flagged. A journal entry I made in Hyde Park dramatically reflected that involvement.

May 29, 1958

After dinner Mrs. R. and Johnny left us. They went upstairs for "a talk," Mrs. R. explained. The Roosevelts are so outgoing and so accustomed to discussing all kinds of problems in front of their guests that I concluded something really troublesome was up.

Trude and I remained behind with Geno Herrick, Hick and Nannine Joseph. They started to reminisce about old Mrs. James R., arguing that "Sunrise at Campobello" had not done her an injustice. Hick spoke of

---

Mrs. Roosevelt. With the most genuine conviction she remarked, 'Somebody important must be arriving, this crowd has nothing to do with us.' It turned out that besides many hours of receptions which had been prepared for Mrs. Roosevelt, all school children, and tens of thousands were on hand to greet her at the airport, with a chorus shouting in unison, *'ROOSEVELT SINGABAT'*—*'MRS. ROOSEVELT HAIL.'*"

—Dr. A. D. Gurewitsch
Mrs. Roosevelt's physician

Mine read: "Mrs. Roosevelt frequently laments her lack of college education. But her example proves that heart and character are better foundations for a sustained liberalism than ideology or learning. I came to know Mrs. Roosevelt at the end of the Thirties and to understand the depth of her sympathy for the problems of youth, the sharecropper, and the Negro in the depression.

"Today, many of her fellow workers of those days have yielded to age, disillusionment, conformity and comfort, but she remains as much the tribune of the dispossessed and the keeper of the country's conscience as she was before the war.

"There were frequent criticisms then of her efforts inside of the government and out to help people. 'We never elected her,' was the opposition's cry. Would that today the one-fifth of a nation that remains ill-housed, ill-clothed, ill-fed, had as brave and selfless a friend at court!

"Once during a visit to a National Youth Administration project the Negro chef there presented her with a huge cake and bid her cut it. Obediently she started to comply.

" 'Am I doing it right?' she asked.

" 'Anything you do is right,' he answered.

"I believe that is the way the whole country has come to feel about this very special woman."

—Joseph P. Lash
*UN Correspondent for
the New York Post*

steering clear of her and only making the grade when Mrs. James temporarily and mistakenly associated a Navy commander with her. They also, but not Nannine, complained of Mrs. R's style of writing. They wished she went at it a little more professionally, not dashing it off. I said Mrs. R. was first a personality, a writer incidentally, while the two of them were pros. Major Henry Hooker also here but had gone up to bed with a book about the Mayo Clinic. . . .

When Mrs. R. came down she explained the "mystery" to Trude and me after the others had gone to bed. Anne had twice tried to commit suicide—the first time while drinking she tried to jump out of a window. John caught her and her remark was "where would your political career have been then?" The second time was this week when she swallowed a whole bottle of sleeping pills. . . .

Johnny obviously quite scared. Feels it essential Anne stop drinking and is prepared to go "on the wagon" with her, but Mrs. R. can't suggest it, nor should David who reached the hospital afterwards. She thought it best if it came from their Dr. Solley. Mrs. R. quite stern with Johnny. She told him he was basically a sensitive boy but had covered it with a veneer of hardness, first in business, then in politics, and even in the family, shouting at his children. He had her tendency in such situations of going icy, but he should think of his father's example. He was always able to be sympathetic and understanding of their problems. He, Johnny, would have to be able to thaw out to Anne. . . . Mrs. R. kept coming back to the two drinking escapades and her own horror of getting into situations where she was not in control of herself and confessed to an inability to understand others who did get into such messes. . . . Mrs. R. seemed to me to take it all in her stride.

There was a new dimension about Eleanor. Beyond the thickets of worldly cares in which she was always the ministering presence, there was the desire to see the permanent realities of things. It was as if she looked at us with the eyes of a master novelist. The effort to ameliorate the human condition remained strong as she grew older, but there was now a detachment, a spiritual distance, even with the closest of us.

A big change in her style of life resulted when her landlord proposed to raise her rent sharply at the end of her lease. She decided that she and the Gurewitsches should buy a house together and Edna undertook to scout the possibilities. She would have to have a considerable mortgage and hoped that her estate would guarantee it for her. That needed the consent of Anna.

August 12, 1958

Dearest Anna:

. . .

I hope you will be willing to agree to this arrangement because I would like, as I grow older, to be in a house with someone I know, though I want to live alone and be entirely independent. The house we are hopefully planning on will give me more room and will mean I will have a permanent home in New York City. I am going to give up my present apartment on the day I leave for Brussels because they want to raise the rent by $150 a month which seems to me ridiculous.

Much love,
Mother

At the end of August she and the Gurewitsches traveled to Moscow by way of Brussels, which was the site of the Worlds Fair and a gathering of World Federation of United Nations Associations delegates.

Hotel Metropole
Bruxelles
August 31st 1958

Dearest Trude,

You were a dear to come down last Wednesday & I enjoyed so much our evening together.

We had a smooth & easy flight & arrived about on time. A few hours later we were at the fair & decided at once that our grounds & buildings are delightful & imaginative & original. Foreigners like our building & it is a pleasant contrast to the Russian which is filled with heavy machinery, sputnik, & Lenin! They have an automobile almost as big as ours on exhibition!

. . .

We've heard the Menotti opera in our theatre the night we arrived. It was nice but the audience small & the fair seems to die about 9 p.m. I think it is so far out & the people are tired & come back to town for dinner & just stay. The Russians give their ballet (same as N.Y.) in a theatre in town. We went last night & it was filled to capacity.

Our first meeting comes tonight at 9, so I'm glad we've seen a good deal of the fair already tho' there is much more to see.

. . .

E.R.

Her son-in-law Jim Halsted had been awarded a Fulbright Fellowship to teach medicine and do research in Iran for a year. Jim "jumped at" the chance, Anna less so.

Bruxelles
August 31, 1958

Anna darling,

I shall be thinking of you both as you start off soon after this reaches you. I hate to have you so far away but after you get there let me know your telephone number & I'll try to reach you at Xmas. No place in the world is really far away nowadays so remember if you need me any day I can come! This is one advantage of being footloose & fancy free!

The fair is interesting, not as gay as some others I have seen. . . .

Devotedly
Mother

"We all leave tomorrow a.m. for Moscow in spite of the rather ominous news from China,"* she wrote Hick. "Good luck with whatever you are writing."

In Leningrad she dwelt on the beauties of that city, although it lacked the "dynamic drive" of Moscow. A letter to Anna gave her philosophy of promoting contacts with the Communist world.

Sept. 12th, 1958

Dearest Anna,

. . .

It is difficult to assess the value of contact unless you accept the need of our recognition of realities. If we accept Mr. Dulles theory that men want to be free so communism can't last, then there is no value in what we did as a delegation or are now doing as individuals. If, however we believe that communism is here to stay awhile & that we must live together & very slowly changes may be coming in both our systems which will make co-existence possible, then I think intercourse has value. Now, we talk, but we don't mean the same things & we dare not try to clarify unless we manage to talk alone with one individual. We need some realistic thinking in high places I think about the USSR & China.

. . .

Mother

Moscow
Sept. 17th

Dearest Trude,

. . .

You sound happy about your Mother. If you can spend Oct 4th & 5th in Hyde Park with me won't you bring her? I plan to arrange the little apartment upstairs for you & she could have the little room. It will be

---

* There were few Western reporters in China and they were allowed to see little, but rumors of "rectification purges" and battles against "regional nationalism" suggested disintegration.

quieter there & there is a desk so Joe could write & Jonathan if he had work can use the desk in the cross room. Do come & it will be a joy to really see your Mother.

  . . .

I spent 2 hours in a school in a newly built area of town & learned much I wanted to know this morning. Gradually I'm getting the answers to many things I wanted to know. I also am sure that often we don't see what we want because they can't comprehend what we want. David has had a harder time than I have but he saw his mother's brother yesterday & was very pleased.

  . . .

E.R.

A last letter to Anna during her stay in Russia she sent to Shiraz in Iran, hoping it might welcome Anna on arrival there. "They," she said of David and Edna, "will probably be back many times but I imagine this is my last trip for I feel my time is limited & I should see new things or stay at home!"

One purpose of their stay in Paris was to enable David to introduce Edna to his longtime friend Madame Viénot. The ladies were not without jealousy. Edna's account of the visit follows.

" 'Edna, I'm going to Andrée's at 11:30 and prepare the way for you,' he said. 'You come at 12. At 1 we'll go to lunch.'

"I was ready to go on my morning rounds. Mrs. R. was ready to go on hers in the car the Embassy made available to her. 'What are you doing for lunch?' I asked. 'Nothing,' was her answer. 'Then come with us.' 'No,' she protested, 'I'm not invited.' She added something to the effect that she and Andrée did not get on. I refused to accept her refusal. 'They will speak in French and I won't have anyone to talk to.' With that she said all right.

"Later I told David that Mrs. R. was joining us for lunch. From 12:45 on he kept jumping up to see if she was arriving. Andrée Viénot was as annoyed as all hell.

"We had lunch and afterwards when we deposited Andrée at her house David went out to help her. 'Come up for a few minutes,' Andrée urged him. 'I have something to say to you,' and David went. 'We'll come back,' Mrs. R. said. As we drove to the hotel, I remarked, 'I've had it with that woman.'

"Mrs. R. was very firm. 'She must now see David as a couple. I loved

David and I have loved you because of him, and now I love you for your own sake.' "*

Eleanor's acceptance of Edna made the idea of sharing a house with David and her ever more attractive. The house still had to be found. In the meantime she returned to the Park Sheraton Hotel. "I'm settled comfortably here," she wrote Anna, "but the cooking facilities are *very* poor. We will survive but I hope we find a house soon! I've been very busy ever since I got home, speeches, people & much mail & some writing but after the next two weeks I ought to be freer."

A house was located on East 74th Street.

> Hyde Park
> Sunday, Dec 28th, '58

Darling Anna,

 . . . The financing of the house was difficult too because we have, since Mr. Hackett died, a bank as our trustee & finally I gave up borrowing from them & David & I have a 1st & 2d mortgage & each put in an equal amount of cash. Luckily I had invested a little income each year so I had a little capital of my own & so had David. I am surprised I ever was wise enough to do it for I never expected that I would want to buy anything! Now I have to live to be 84 at least to pay off the mortgages! For 2 years I may have to live on one floor unless a present tenant whose lease runs to '61 in Sept. moves out voluntarily but I'll be at least as comfortably established as in 62d St. & it will be everything I want when I get the 2 floors. The address is 55 East 74th St. & I hope the sale goes through tomorrow or next day. I can't move in till next Sept. however. David & Edna can get their floors very soon, so I can profit by watching any changes they make. . . .

> Devotedly
> Mother

---

* Mrs. Gurewitsch, who read in manuscript the chapters dealing with David, agrees that Mme. Viénot was a "strong personality" but believes I exaggerate her importance in David's life. Others gave me a different impression. Mme. Viénot and her husband were people of great wealth, but public-spirited and leaders in the French socialist movement. André Viénot had been Under Secretary of Foreign Affairs in Leon Blum's 1937 cabinet, had been imprisoned with Georges Mandel in a Vichy fortress, and when in 1944 he died in London of angina pectoris General de Gaulle said, "France has lost a great servant and England a faithful friend." His widow thereafter called herself Andrée Pierre Viénot as testimony to how extraordinary she thought her husband had been. "Andrée was just one of several interesting people in my father's life," said Grania.

"David never had a flirtatious time with Andrée Viénot," Edna said. "She was one of the least feminine ladies one could meet. A smug G-R-E-A-T intellectual, bossy and aggressive, short gray hair, body built like a tank and never walked, only marched. Mme. Viénot threatened Mrs. R.—but differently, by her aggressive demands on David's time in Paris. She assumed loyalty to her by 'entitlement.' I was not jealous of her. I did not like her. And she wasn't jealous of me. She was a super-busy and self-satisfied person. She was more of a pest than anything else. Mrs. R. took her seriously because she could be rude to Mrs. R. She and David did not even correspond very much.—Do as you please with this information."

She had finished writing *On My Own* before she went to Russia the second time, but the second visit did not alter her views.

> The only thing that frightened me in Russia was that we might be apathetic and complacent in the face of this challenge. I can well understand why the Russian people welcome the good that has come to them. But I cannot understand or believe that anything that has to be preserved by fear will stand permanently against a system which offers love and trust among peoples and removes fear so that all feel free to think and express their ideas.
>
> It seems to me that we must have the courage to face ourselves in this crisis. We must regain a vision of ourselves as leaders of the world. We must join in an effort to use all knowledge for the good of all human beings.

That was her public life. Her private life was reflected in the dedication page of the book:

> Now that I near the end of my active life, I would like to dedicate this book to all those who have worked with me, one of whom is no longer living, except as she lives in my memory. I am grateful to them and to my children for allowing me to live freely, and to my close friends. I list them here below in the hope that this book will bring them a few interesting hours:
>
> Malvina Thompson
> Maureen Corr
> Anna Roosevelt Halsted
> James Roosevelt
> Elliott Roosevelt
> Franklin D. Roosevelt, Jr.
> John A. Roosevelt
> David and Edna Gurewitsch
> Joe and Trude Lash

XXIV

" . . . *The Wise Never Grow Old . . .* "

HER ATTITUDE TOWARD Adlai Stevenson was undergoing a change and it was a measure of the political stature she had attained. A few of us around her sensed the change. It was not that she no longer admired this witty, cultivated man more than any other public figure in America. She still considered his qualifications for the presidency superior to all others mentioned among the Democrats. But she recognized that the defeats of 1952 and 1956 had exacted a toll on the man's appetite for the job, even more on the electorate's readiness to have him run again. Those were factors. Even more troubling to her was his inability to identify with the aspirations of the black man, the worker, the average American citizen who made up the country in a bewildering variety of backgrounds, life styles, and tastes. She had begun to realize it in 1956 when she accompanied Adlai to a rally in Harlem. On the way up he had turned to her in the car, David was with them, and in some anguish asked her what he should say to the blacks whom he would be addressing. She made some reassuring remarks, but privately she realized that if this brilliant man did not know what had to be said,

despite his sparkle and engaging modesty, there was little to be done to educate
him that late in the day.

She herself knew that compassion, care, and empathy had to be practiced not
to dry up. She had made special efforts to make friends of black political colleagues
like Mary McLeod Bethune, Pauli Murray, and Walter White, traveled often to
black areas and institutions, and fought for civil rights in New Deal days when the
term was not even known, one of the few in Washington ready to do so. Befriend-
ing the people she worked with was part of her way of getting to know them. It had
always been her approach to people, but her education had begun in earnest in the
1920s when, as Franklin's surrogate, she had traveled repeatedly all over New York
State in her runabout. Together with Nancy Cook, Marion Dickerman, and Elinor
Morgenthau, she had set up and nurtured local Democratic clubs of women. Those
intineraries had become national in her White House days. She knew America and
Americans at first hand, and in postwar days her solicitude had extended to the
world's peoples.

Gandhi on his return from South Africa, a relatively young man of forty-five
but the hero of Indian nonviolent-resistance to the British there, told Indian National Congress leaders he had to take time away from the centers of power to
reacquaint himself with the India of the countryside and mills. For almost two
years he traveled barefoot, third class on trains, and along dusty roads with the
poor. Even in South Africa he had given up everything he owned and treated all
people as part of his family. He applied the same principles in India, getting to
know it again in the process in a way no other Indian leader did.

Such a *Wanderjahr* of identification with people from different walks of life
represented in Eleanor's eyes indispensable apprenticeship in politics, especially for
cultivated, upper-class Americans who aspired to democratic leadership. She had
urged Adlai to forget comfort and elegance and travel about America in a jalopy.
When he said it was not his style she accepted that, but had remembered. In 1956
she had been happy to be an instrument of his purposes. In 1960 he would become
an instrument of hers.

The November 1958 elections resulted in larger Democratic majorities in
both House and Senate. I have several journal entries touching on Adlai's possibilities in 1960 as reflected in Eleanor's household talk during the time.

October 20, 1958, Mrs. R. improves with age. Last night at dinner,
William Aitken, M.P., nephew of Lord Beaverbrook, there. He was recommended to Mrs. R. by "Uncle David" [Gray]. Aitken's wife spent
time with the Grays in Dublin during WWII when they were bombed
out in London. Aitken was in the hospital, smashed up, and she had been
about to have a baby. Minnewa's mother also there, slim, remarkably well
preserved for 81, but a little "dotty," kept on breaking in with irrelevant
memories from McGuffey's Fifth Reader, including lines from Tennyson's "Charge of the Light Brigade." Her memory was bad, she admit-

ted, but it didn't matter. You could add all the figures in a column and it
was the sum that mattered. Mrs. R. answered her seriously. She said it
was not so, that materials of the past took on different shades and meanings at different times. She made a similar comment Friday night at the
Overseas Press Club [where she had spoken in connection with
Steinberg's newly published *Mrs. R.]* when she had noted the difference
between what is written as history and what actually happened. Even in
her own books the same episodes looked different at different times.
Were she writing the books now, she would write some parts differently.
Which? I wondered.

Mrs. R. told us about her trip to Kansas. She had gone out for a
dinner, flying there Saturday afternoon and back late Saturday night,
arriving in NY 6 a.m. Sunday. She had been unable to remember on the
way out why she had agreed to go, and only caught on when her hosts
said how happy they were she had come to the first FDR dinner. The
Democratic National Committeeman was there and at dinner began to
speak up for Gov. Mennen Williams of Michigan. Mrs. R. politely said
he was one of the good younger men. That didn't satisfy the committeeman. He said Stevenson didn't get across to people. In reporting this
Mrs. R. seemed to agree with the criticism. She replied she would insist
on one thing—that whoever was the Democratic candidate pledge to
make Stevenson Secretary of State. Aitken liked that. From Europe's
point of view that would be wonderful, he said. The Democratic committeeman also said that Truman's candidate seemed to be Stuart Symington [Senator from Missouri.] Mrs. R. surmised that was what Truman in
Washington was interested in telling her when he said he wanted to
come and see her when he was in New York. She had told him her view
of China's readiness, almost eagerness for war. The Chinese reasoning—
had she heard it from the Russians?—was that it had 600 million people.
Three hundred million would survive even a nuclear holocaust and China
would then be top dog. He wanted to talk to her about that too, Truman
said.

Mrs. R. then said she hoped she would not again have a candidate, as
she did in 1956, whom she wanted so badly to win that she felt she had
to campaign for him night and day. Edna and David tried to talk up a
Bill Douglas [Justice of the Supreme Court] boom with her. Friday night
at the Overseas Press Club Abba Schwartz who had sponsored the Steinberg book, said Douglas was not a candidate. Douglas was a close adviser
of Jack Kennedy. The relationship went back to the Securities and Exchange Commission which then was headed by Jack's father, Joe Kennedy. Bob Kennedy went with Douglas to Russia. Abba is one of those
who are trying to pave the way for Jack Kennedy with Mrs. R. He wants
Trude and me to meet with Jack Kennedy and talk foreign policy with

him. Trude and I were tempted, but knowing Mrs. R.'s views about the Senator thought it better to decline. Other efforts have been made to ease Mrs. R's opposition to the Senator. I think Jimmy [Roosevelt] has talked to her about the McCarthy episode and Buzz has tried to do something.

Mrs. R. said the Philip Morris people wanted to do a film about her but she's reluctant. Turned it over to Frankie. Maybe an episode. She again talked about "Sunrise at Campobello." Made the point she did at Overseas Press Club—that Elliott in the picture was not at all like the young Elliott who had been a thin, sickly child. Dore Schary said the play needed Elliott to be the way he was in the play rather than in life. Ralph Bellamy was evocative of FDR, she felt, and Louis Howe's wit in the film was like the real Louis Howe, but that the character on stage was much cleaner and less cadaverous than the real Louis. Unfair to the President's mother who was a great personality, never petty. . . .

Aitken said his son Jonathan at Eton, 15, had to debate the topic—a falling balloon with the following on it, Churchill, Ike, Billy Graham, Harold Macmillan—who should be dumped first? Mrs. R. liked that. She made a strong point that it was wrong to equate democracy with capitalism, India would have to do it otherwise. . . .

Mrs. R. loved the talk and when we arose at 9:45 to leave wanted us to stay on which we did for a while. She goes to New London to see Esther, tonight to the meeting of Trude's Citizens Committee for Children and tomorrow to Des Moines. She was in fine humor at the Overseas Press Club, emphasized her lack of formal education and how little she knew when she first went to Washington in 1913. She was told by her Aunt, Mrs. Cowles, what her duties were as the wife of the Assistant Secretary of the Navy. Her account had everyone rolling with laughter. She was to call on everyone—Monday, the Justices of the Supreme Court, Tuesdays, the members of the Cabinet, Wednesdays, the Representatives, Thursdays, the Senators, Fridays, officers of the Navy, Saturdays, you had to yourself and your children.

When Steinberg reminded her of Senator Tom Connally's praise of her, she imitated Connally in London at the UN Assembly, saying that in the Senate a point was argued and then finished, but at the Assembly the same point had to be made day after day with the Russians. He had argued the same point for the last time, he once told her. Mrs. R. predicted the Russians would persist and he would have to go over it again. He would not, he insisted. He did, she remarked. She thought Dulles and Vandenburg praised her so highly because they had expected the worst. That had reminded her of Louis Howe's advice—don't show yourself as knowing it all. Appear stupid, then when you vouchsafe some information or knowledge everyone will say, "how brilliant."

She spoke of how little she had known in the early days of Committee III at the UN, not even enough to raise her hand to vote. Sandifer [her Chief State Department adviser] once whispered desperately, " 'Raise your hand Mrs. Roosevelt. Other countries are waiting to see how we will vote.' I was waiting to see how the others would vote."

Then she turned serious. Her current theme—Russia and China are here to stay. We should not make the same error with Red China that we had with Russia. A small incident showed how much influence the Chinese had over the Russians. Khrushchev had the Chinese Ambassador go over his note to President Eisenhower. The tail may be trying to wag the dog and the Russians may be more disposed to deal with us. We are living in a dream world. . . .

The subject of Red China and the presidential race came up a few weeks later at Mrs. David Levy's (she was a member of the Rosenwald clan), where we were having dinner.

Nov. 11, 1958 . . . Mrs. R. said she was minded to support Bill Douglas in '60 because he was the only one willing to speak to Americans frankly on China. Anna Rosenberg said he was untrustworthy. . . . On Adlai Mrs. R. came back to her fear that he did not communicate with people. She wanted him as Secretary of State. Anna said he was unable to make decisions. She told of going to him in 1956 along with Mrs. R. and Tom Finletter and Stevenson explained to them that he stayed up until 3 and 4 a.m. polishing his speeches. Mrs. R. counselled him gently, "Governor, not every speech has to be a Gettysburg address. It is more important what you say." Mrs. R. repeated that Truman was for Symington. Anna doubted it. Truman hated him for having run and defeated his candidate for the Senate from Missouri. Truman had said in 1956 that he was for Symington, but really had worked for Harriman. Anna thought he was playing the same game.

There was more talk about presidential politics during the Christmas holidays when we were in and out of Hyde Park, but it was chiefly a time of personal rejoicing for her and lavishing love on others. When at our family Christmas party, which we held two days before Christmas, I toasted family, country, and sharing our good fortune with the other peoples of the world, Eleanor, who continued the tradition of celebrating with us before going up to Hyde Park, published the toast in her column, for she always was reminding us of our responsibilities in the world. "I called Sisty Xmas day," she wrote Anna in Iran. "I tried to get her tied in to talk to you but couldn't arrange it. I'd like to pay you for the call so please let me know whether to send you a check or add it to your check here. . . ."

She seemed happy in the happiness she made for others, but always we had the sense of a lonely woman unable to count on coming first with anyone. The emotional security that had vanished with the death of her parents and that had been rebuilt in the early years of her marriage to Franklin never returned. And we younger ones were all helpless.

Notes went to David and me on New Year's Eve.

> 202 56th Street West
> New York 19 N.Y.
> New Years Eve

Dearest David,

First so many thanks for coming at Xmas and for all you gave me and for all the time you let me enjoy with you and yours.

The new year will soon be here and tonight I will be happy drinking a toast to you. All I can wish for you is that the coming year will bring you as much happiness as the past year brought you. I feel somehow that every married year will be better than the one before. I only hope that I may contribute a little to your health and happiness.

As always my deep love, admiration and gratitude go to you and my pride in you grows with every year that our friendship deepens.

God bless you and keep you.

> E.R.

> New Year's Eve

Joe dearest,

Just a word of thanks for my many & wonderful Xmas presents but above all for letting me be with you & for coming to me. It makes all the difference in my Xmas.

We'll have a toast tonight but I won't say all the love & gratitude that is in my heart for gift of your friendship.

> Devotedly
> E.R.

Thank Jonathan please for his many & useful gifts.

She planned to visit Anna in Iran that spring, taking Nina, John's daughter, along and stopping in Israel en route home.

> 202 Fifty-sixth Street West
> New York 19, N.Y.
> Jan 4th

Sis darling,

. . . Of course I am coming unofficially dear, the State Dept & the President [Eisenhower] wouldn't send me anywhere & I have no official position! . . . I would like a stenographer as I plan to do my own column & notes on the trip & . . . to have someone take dictation at the start & finish of my visit would be wonderful. . . .

Much, much love
Mother

Hick resided in Hyde Park Village. She, too, was in and out while Mrs. Roosevelt was at the cottage, but had to be fetched. What did Hick need? she was constantly asking her old friend, often adding such mollifying sentiments as "I'm waiting for your outburst of fury."

"Someone brought me these as a Valentine and I leave them at your door with love," she wrote in pencil to David and Edna and soon afterward sent further notes to Edna in connection with her birthday, "To one of the people I love best in the world and may she make more birthdays for all of us to enjoy," and another gift on which she wrote, "You are very dear to me and I love you even more because you make David so happy and have given Grania so much that she does not yet realize is deeply important and valuable." She went to Washington, spent a night with Jimmy, who was then in Congress, and his wife Irene. Fjr. and Sue came over for dinner and "we had a real Roosevelt discussion evening." Then Trude, Jonathan, and I joined her and we motored down to Williamsburg and Monticello. The week before she had been to the coast to do a broadcast, a project which her agent, Thomas Stix, justified by pointing out all the good she might be able to do with the large fee.

Feb. 19th, 1959

Anna darling,

. . .

I went on Frank Sinatra's show in Hollywood (the pay for 5 minutes was fantastic & my part rather nice) but I'm not very good at "entertainment." I never had so many compliments however & I found watching the mechanics amusing! . . .

I started to fly to Pittsburgh last Sunday a.m. for 2 speeches & we couldn't land so had to go to Columbus, Ohio. They sent us back in a greyhound bus that got in a ten mile tie up on the West Va. road & we took 12 hrs to reach our destination & I just got a night train at midnight for N.Y.! I'm so glad you are coming home & do get here for Johnny's [Boettiger] wedding. All my love

Mother

In March with Nina she flew to Iran. During a stopover at Orly airport in Paris, a postcard to David and Edna was evocative of her reliance on them. "How dear you were to see me off and how I hated to leave you. I hope we go on long trips together in the future." Later that day in Rome she wrote each of them.

March 12, 1959

David dearest,

How I hated to say goodbye and how I miss not having you and Edna
with me! I'm never lonely when I'm with you and even when I know you
are somewhere not too far away!

We had a good trip but were late here and got no sightseeing in but it
is all set for three hours with Countess Lelli tomorrow a.m. . . .

This line is to tell you David, that I'm glad that agreement [to purchase a house on East 74th Street] got signed because now you can go
ahead and turn it into a partnership, and do it *fast* so you will get the tax
break on income taxes. Remember I pay for the roof. I think we need no
written agreements but I want you protected if I die. As long as I live I
only want it to be made easy for you wherever I can help and what you
want I will always want. Through the years that I have known you that
has always been so.

My love always,
E.R.

She wrote much the same to Edna. "Do remember to push the roof . . . a
month goes fast. I know you will both be busy and I surmise I will be too!"

Shiraz
Iran
Sunday, March 15th, '59

Dearest David and Edna,

We are 5000 feet up here, the sky is a deep blue and the atmosphere
has a clarity that matches the sky. You are cut off from the world the
moment the plane which brought you leaves. No newspaper, very bad
radio now and then and letters which come about three times a week are
your only connection with the outside. Jim is very happy and Anna is
happy because Jim is. He is challenged by the enormity of the problems.
They are working to bring the University and the Hospital closer. . . .

. . . On the plane to Teheran the head of the Turkish Army was
coming on an official visit so at 6:30 a.m. having left at 1:00 a.m. we got
off to be greeted by a guard of honor for the general and a band! The
Ambassador and wife and Henry [Morgenthau] and Marcelle were there
and saw us off at 7 a.m. with the air force attaché in a military plane. It
was Nina's first 2 1/2 hrs in bucket seats and we were both weary but they
took her for an hour into the cockpit and once here at 9:30 we had some
breakfast, a bath and 2 hours sleep and both of us felt better! After one
hospital inspection at 4 p.m. we went to see a rather nice Persian garden
and a very grand house, now empty and government-owned because the
people wouldn't pay taxes! A tribal family in disgrace!

. . . Anna and Jim go on the 22d for one week to India, New Delhi and Agra. I'll keep this letter open till they tell me it can be mailed! *Later.* Henry Morgenthau looked in. They had been to Saigon, Bangkok, etc. Marcelle said the trip was "enough." In other words they were uncomfortable. They will be home April 3d.

I think of you both often and wish you were here to listen to this country's problems. So much to be done, money spent by the U.N. U.S. and gov't and so little benefit to the people.

We've just visited a woman who heads one of the tribes—50,000 people under her and on the move all year. The government wants them to settle but she says, show us that we would be better off in a village and then we will do so but not now. The tribes are strong and healthy, the village people sick and poor! I think how much Israel administrators could help. They are friendly to the government of Israel but dislike their own Jewish communities.

I hope you've had a peaceful Sunday and seen Grania this weekend. Nina seems interested in everything and there are no heart complications pulling her homeward as yet, it is a good age to travel!

All my love to you both.

E.R.

P.S. Jim showed us his slides last night and I think so often what wonderful light this would be for you to get pictures in David dear, from the women to the heavily laden donkeys you would enjoy yourself.

Shiraz, Iran
March 16th

Dearest Trude & Joe,

This is cutoff from the world! No radio to speak of, no papers for days, mail about 3 times a week but quite irregular!

It is wonderful to see Anna & Jim. He is fascinated by the enormity of the problems & Anna more frustrated & I think with more yen to be home! It is all interesting & the people are nice but they lack security in themselves & live in the glories of the past. It is a rich country potentially but the mass of the people are poor & disease ridden. T.B. is a scourge.

I go to the Jewish Community tomorrow morning & we leave at 1:30 for Esfahan. Nina is a good traveller & I enjoy watching her.

I miss you all very much & think of you often. All my love.

Devotedly
E.R.

In Teheran she found a letter from Edna and immediately replied, repeating much that she had already written, adding, "Don't be nervous about the moves.

Marie and I can help! You are giving David the confidence and love he needs and minor things don't matter. Thank you for saying we are a nice team but you are the important part. . . ."

The day before she and Nina left Iran for Israel, she wrote David and Edna from the embassy in Teheran, where they were staying.

March 21st

Dearest David and Edna,

Ten days of the trip are over and I think very successfully. Nina seems happy and I'm trying to remember to treat her as tho' she were grown up in the way you treated Grania. That last is meant for David when he let Grania at 16 go to a ball in Paris! I'm letting Nina go with Mary Bingham (much older) and 2 Iranian gentlemen to the movies and I won't be happy till she's home! . . .

I learned much yesterday about U.N. projects here and by tonight I'll know much about Point 4 projects. We lunched with the Shah yesterday. Nice but dull tho' the marble palace was something to see. There are beautiful things here and then the most horrible taste right next to beauty.

. . . David dear, I've got to give you a little time to try to improve my left leg if I'm to move about easily and quickly. So we'll see.

I've begun to read Dr. Zhivago and like it but it is sad from the start. . . .

I must lie down now as I try to rest an hour each day. Tonight all the top people of the staff come to dinner and then ask me questions.

E.R.

Eleanor tried hard to understand the greater freedom many parents now allowed young daughters. But she was always shocked. When Anna had allowed Sisty to go off campus on a weekend unchaperoned, she had been startled and weakly protested. Though she thought of Grania's night at a ball in Paris as the beginning of forebearance, Grania remembered that when she came in at dawn there was Mrs. R. writing letters waiting for her. So it was now with Nina. "Grandmère says I have to be in at twelve," she complained to her aunt, who was also staying at the embassy. "Suppose I can't be home by twelve?" "Oh, she will be asleep," Anna comforted her. But that was no protection, Nina replied. Her grandmother had told her to come in and kiss her good-night when she came in. Nina did so and the next morning told her aunt it had been "terrible." Grandmère had awakened, "But Nina, it's two o'clock." Anna went to her mother. " 'Mummy dear, please realize times have changed. Nina is with a group of people selected by the Ambassador. Nothing will happen to her. She shouldn't be under restrictions and have to check in with you.' Mother was annoyed. 'Oh, very well, if that's the way it has to be, I'll tell her.' " Yet as the letter to David and Edna showed, she was trying to learn. Still, it was difficult to shake some of the habits she had learned in her youth.

A message from Tel Aviv to David reported he had been asked for when they had lunched at Degania, the oldest kibbutz in Israel. "I still hope some day you and Edna and Grania may let me come back with you. The advances are great."

A letter from the Negev detailed some of the advances she found.

March 25th

Dearest Edna and David,

We left Tel Aviv this a.m. and flew to Elath and it is astounding to see how the port is growing and the place itself increased in population. We visited a kibbutz 7 miles away where 80 young people (60 boys and 20 girls) are literally reclaiming the desert and making it bloom. They grow iris and gladiolas, tomatoes, onions, feed for beef and milk cows and large numbers of poultry.

I can't help wondering how many of our young people would do this hard work. They seemed healthy and happy.

This place Beer-Sheva, is unbelievable in its growth and the mayor is a remarkable man. They now have 42,000 people and 5 industries and 48% of their budget goes for education. Dubinsky's Union [the International Ladies Garment Workers Union] has given $1,000,000 towards their new hospital and they have 2 swimming pools!

Will be in Jerusalem tomorrow. . . .

I do hope Edna dear you and Maureen prodded Mr Karplus [architect for the East 74th Street house] to good effect on the roof and that you got the discussions for the cedar closet in the right spot before Maureen left. I hate you not to move the kitchen *now*. Wouldn't you let me pay for it and do it now, so you'll have a good place to work in and you won't have to tear up the apartment later. It won't cost more than $3000 and I'd love to give it to you or if you want make it your Easter and Xmas present and birthday for the next year? Please do. I agree David's office should come first but I'd like to give *you* this. The record player is really a present to David.

I fear the Anne Frank movie is bad. Trude wrote that she hated it but she has had a bad time with an infected jaw and everything looked black, so I hope it isn't as bad as she said.

I'm glad you miss me. I [like] to have you with me when things are nice and when I'm miserable I long to talk to you! . . . I spoke tonight at the opening of the Youth Aliyah meeting. It is tiring but Nina is wonderful, she is fascinated with Israel and listens to everyone. I am amazed and delighted.

. . .

E.R.

A postcard to Hick from the King David Hotel in Jerusalem was eloquent about the city's colors. They "are true. It is beautiful to look from our windows at sunrise or sunset, across no-man's land to the old City." She wrote Hick at greater length the same day, having forgotten to send her a monthly check.

"There are wise leaders here," she interpolated. She was amused and slightly aghast at Nina's efforts, abetted by Abba Schwartz, to buy a camel from the Bedouins. "I'm keeping my hands off. I won't even contribute to buying it. She cabled her Father but no reply. Mr. & Mrs. Ben Gurion are entertained by her project!" She wrote Trude, "We've just come from tea with Mr. Ben Gurion. He looks wonderful & young & she was herself & a character as usual. Lots of others there including Edward G. Robinson." Change and growth were everywhere. "We came here in the late afternoon and the light on the city was beautiful," she wrote David. "Much building of homes is going on and the 'new settler shacks' are slowly disappearing. Their problem seems to be to make new settlers like to live on the land instead of crowding into the cities." Before the trip she had talked with David and Edna about going to China but now had to write them, "It doesn't look as tho' we'd get to China. Nannine got no favorable replies from any magazine." There was more about Nina's camel. It was "creating a sensation and I begin to fear she may really get him home free with Abba's help." Her dominant reaction to Israel in 1959 was the quality of its leaders. "I think Israel will survive because of her leaders," her letter to David and Edna stated. "On the whole she has more greatness than any other people in her leaders. We dine with Golda Meir tonight." The next day they would cross to the Jordan side, but she was not allowed to walk, "They are afraid of a demonstration against me!"

In Paris back at the Crillon, she wrote Edna, "I am glad to have Maureen, who arrived this morning. . . . Nina has been a wonderful companion however, and I think she has enjoyed it." To David she added, "Driving in from the airport last night I thought how excited you always are by arriving in Paris. . . . It looks as though Nina would really bring back [the] camel but what Johnny will do with him I wonder!"

There were letters to Trude and me from the Crillon.

March 31st

Dearest Joe,

. . . The two suggested 1960 tickets don't thrill me & so it will be easy to keep out of the campaign for me, but you younger people will have to be active.

. . . Now that I have Barbara [Morgan] to compare Nina with, I am feeling that to an astonishing degree Nina is mature with qualities of mind & heart that make her capable of understanding conditions of people in a way which is unusual for her age.

My door just blew shut & the wind is cold!

. . . I'm trying to evaluate what makes the real difference between Iran & Israel & it isn't easy to explain.*

Mr. [Thomas] Stix [her radio and television agent] writes he has some offers for me to consider on my return. I hope one will be good.

E.R.

March 31st

Trude dearest,

. . . It is far from spring like here, really cold & I went to buy a spring hat & hated them so decided to wait & get one from Sally Victor even tho' my one brown one looks a bit worn!

. . .

We did get to Jordan for the Easter Service tho' a small group of [Arab] newspaper reporters protested my being allowed into Jordan! Esther Herlitz† gave me a very funny book on Israel which you & Joe will enjoy. The Israelis really seem to have a sense of humor about themselves which is a saving grace.

. . .

E.R.

March 31st

Edna dearest,

. . . I love all you said about David, remember as a young man he made a fair fortune in business before he became a doctor. He's a very versatile person but when all is said, you are right I think, he is a grand doctor, he loves to heal and he can heal, souls and bodies. He is coming into his own now because you've made him happy and secure, if you didn't understand and appreciate him he wouldn't be so sure with others. To some degree people take you at your own evaluation and as you make him secure and happy, he passes on his feeling of power. . . .

* As she flew out of Israel her column sought to explain the differences between the atmosphere in Israel and the Arab East. Part of the explanation echoed what F.D.R. had felt strongly was the key to Near East revival.

"Basically, I think in any country the loss of the fertility of the soil and the forests which once clothed the mountains is the key to basic economic instability. Physically this is demonstrated in bare mountains devoid of soil and in deserts. The mass of the people have become poorer and poorer. The health of the people has deteriorated. . . .

"There is a different atmosphere in Israel. Its young people are partly responsible for it. They are excited by the dream of building a country. . . . Above everything else I think Israel's good fortune lies in its top leaders. Ben Gurion knows how to capture the imagination of the young, how to make them willing to leave well established easy living in an old Kibbutz or a good job and give themselves to establishing a new kibbutz, and the incredible hardships in the Negev, or to move to a new and growing town which is still raw and in formation and give their knowledge of organization and administration. You cannot look at Ben Gurion with his snapping eyes and think of age in connection with him. He is young with his country and with the young people whom he expects to build it."

† A member of Israel's Foreign Ministry.

I hope Mrs. McK is ready to move when I get home so I can get work underway and move in soon! Please consider my longing to have you switch the kitchen and bathroom *now* so you don't have to be messy again in a few years. I can *easily* do it, no matter what the cost, and *would* love to, so please do it *now*.

I fear we won't get to China this summer, but try to think up something you both want to do in your vacation and let me join you!

E.R.

March 31st

David dearest,

Today came your letter of the 26th and 1 from Edna too and I feel rich. I think you are becoming very knowledgeable about plans and building, what with your own and the Medical Center and Blythdale, Edna says you are better than the architect but of course she might be prejudiced. I am a bit too, for I think you are coming into your own. I've always known what you were, but now because you are happy and secure you can show it to others and they are recognizing it too.

I'm glad you'd rather have me in town and near enough to call you out of your bath every morning! Just hearing your voice starts my day better.

My legs hold up but I guess I should pay them a little more attention! Well, we'll talk about it, but there seems little to tell, just how can I grow old and still feel as young as possible, that sums it up I imagine. . . .

E.R.

The next day she had disquieting news to report.

April 1st

Dearest David,

Nina came in tonight complaining of her left leg and her back. I think she needs rest and so she went to bed before dinner. She wanted to see you before going back to school, so could you give her an appointment the afternoon on the 10th? . . .

April 2d. Nina seems alright today but I still want her to see you. . . .

A note to Trude ended the story of Nina's camel. "We have just heard that the camel cannot go to the U.S. as it originates in a hoof & mouth disease area! I felt this or something similar would save the situation & I'm sure John is relieved! Anyway Nina's camel has enlivened the trip & kept both Abba & Nina amused." They arrived in London on April 3d and had the "grandest rooms" at Claridge's, she reported to David and Edna.

[E.R. to the Gurewitsches:]   [April 3, 1959]

Tomorrow Nina and I go to Lady Reading for the night and the others come to lunch on Sunday and we'll drive back with them. Lady R. has organized all sightseeing and tho' Maureen is tried by her I'm rather glad she does it or they wouldn't see so much. David would sympathize with Maureen however, and I guess I'm just lazy and glad to have someone else organize!

A postcard to Hick that showed Lady Reading's country house had the added news, "I dined with Marty & her nice husband tonight."

A journal entry, April 12, 1959, recorded Mrs. R's first weekend at Hyde Park after her return as I saw it.

This was a rather extraordinary weekend at H.P. for changes, or so I think, in relationships. Anne & Johnny were obviously pleased as punch at Nina's having accompanied her grandmother & having done such a good job and given her grandmother so much pleasure. Mrs. R., in turn, seems to have been much taken with the child, her openness both to her example and to their experiences—in Iran, Israel, London. As Trude says, Nina may be the answer to her feeling, sometimes verging almost on desperation, of not *really* mattering to anyone.

David upset her terribly by not being willing to come to H.P. where he could examine Nina's foot—the one that was injured because of a slight bout with polio several years ago & which bothered her on the trip. David made all sorts of excuses—like needing a rest, busyness at the hospital, etc. which Mrs. R. might have been willing to accept for herself, even though it was odd that David did not plan to be at H.P. the first weekend after her return from abroad, but it angered Mrs. R. that he made them despite her evident concern for Nina. He called Sunday morning & it was clear from Mrs. R's unwillingness to be pinned down as to when she would be free, that she was annoyed. David sensed it, & while Mrs. R. was at church called again & told Marge [Entrup, her housekeeper] to keep it a secret because he & Edna wanted to surprise Mrs. R., but they would come for lunch. When we got back from the Big House where Mrs. R., the Pa. Democratic Women, the ADA, & the Rev. Bill Levy and his mother had laid wreaths, she sensed that lunch was being held up & wanted to know why. She counted the places at the table and saw there were 22 instead of 20. Why? she asked Marge. Poor Marge was caught in the middle. Finally she explained. Mrs. R. who had thought it was Fjr & Sue & said even with them she didn't like surprises, was furious & turned on Trude who said she had no part in it, had not answered the phone & that she shouldn't blame Marge either.

When David arrived he promptly withdrew with Nina to examine her, but Mrs. R. was not to be placated—if anything the point had been proven. Instead of showering the usual special attentions on him she dealt with everyone evenly & then as we drove off was going over to the garden with Johnny to discuss spring planting.

I feel sorry for Mrs. R. I have felt all along that she turned to David because Trude and I were so often unavailable when she needed us in the postwar years or when she felt we ought to be there. While she recognized how hard her children made it for us, she resented our building our own lives, especially the Vineyard—which is why she would never visit us there. So I understood her need for someone like David, but I must say that being thrust aside for David was one of the hardest things to bear these past ten years . . . All the special things she did for us were stopped and done for David, often, of course, in our presence. . . .

Poor Mrs. R. Poor Mrs. R's children who have had to put up with all of us!*

If the episode caused any permanent change in her feelings toward David it was not apparent to us. Nor is it reflected in her letters. A week later she was writing Anna.

> 202 Fifty-sixth Street West
> New York 19, N.Y.
> April 19th, 1959

Dearest Anna,

. . .

I'm dieting hard so I should be sylph like when you arrive! I'm also working on my neck & feet so my body is taking up much time & thought. I'm as busy as I can well be.

David & Edna moved into the house last Tuesday but have only one floor so far. My lady hasn't moved yet but all the preliminaries are getting done so work can get under way on my floor as soon as she goes. . . .

> Devotedly
> Mother

A typed letter went to Edna.

> April 28th, 1959

Dearest Edna:

I am asking Buddy [Bertram Perkel, Edna's brother] and your father

---

* Mrs. Gurewitsch disagrees with this interpretation of the incident. She has no recollection of it, but comments, "David never made haphazard excuses to Mrs. R." and she doubted Mrs. R. "would expect David to drive to H.P. to examine Nina's foot and be angry if he would not."

and mother and Mr Silberman* if they would care to drive up for lunch at 12:00 noon on Memorial Day as Mr Truman is going to give the address this year and I thought they might like to come. Of course it may not be of any interest to them, so this is just to let you know about it and to tell you if they don't want to come they must not make an effort to do so, but I would love to have them. I would be happy to have Buddy stay over Sunday and if you and David care to come I would love to have you. As you know, your room is always ready but I am not going to burden you because I know you both have so many things to do, particularly with the excitement that comes towards the end of the school year in getting Grania into a job. You will want to be around here [N.Y.] as much as you can then, so I don't want to urge you to do anything you don't really feel would be pleasant.

Much love,
E.R.

Of course Grania is always invited too.

On the anniversary of the death of David's mother, Eleanor wrote him a tender note.

David dear,

This time is sad for you but I hope it also brings you happy memories for that is as your mother would want it to be. She would want you to feel her love and her protective presence and would rejoice in your growth. You probably do not realize it but you have grown in personal strength and power in this past year. Edna is doing much for you but you are doing much for her and through what you give you are able to give more to others.

I love you dearly and I am so proud of what you are making of your life that on this day I want to bring you some happy thoughts. The 28th must have some feeling of loss but this note and flowers are to bring you a message of love and remembrance of your Mother and gratitude to her for what she was, and above all her gift of you for you bring happiness to so many. All my love

E.R.

In May she was off on another lecture trip, and she wrote them from the Sheraton-Blackstone in Chicago, "Many thanks for taking me to the airport, it

---

* Abris Silberman, owner of the art gallery at which Edna had been employed.

made the coming week less long to get a glimpse of you yesterday and now I look forward to next Sunday evening." At the end of the summer they took a holiday together in Puerto Rico.

> Sept. 3d
> Dorado Beach Hotel
>
> Dearest Trude & Joe,
>
>   . . .
>
>   I haven't written sooner because there was so little to say. This is a beautiful place & one can have complete privacy & do nothing but eat (very good food, sleep & good beds) sit in the sun swim in the pool or ocean & read. I haven't read so much at one sitting in years. It is hot in the sun but there is nearly always a breeze from the ocean.
>
>   Yesterday afternoon we went into San Juan & everyone will get Xmas gifts from Puerto Rico! The town is becoming a miniature Miami. To-morrow I will go over the mountains to Ponce & the next day to the northeast part of the Island to see Adrian Dornbush's* new land. It is nice to see him again & he is a charming person. . . .
>
>   E.R.

On the eve of their return to the mainland, she sent an affectionate note to David.

> Dorado Beach Hotel
>
> David dearest,
>
>   Since this has been such a happy week, please may it be part of my birthday present to you. You and Edna have given me such a happy time that it is really a gift to myself. May we all be here together again or may we have many more happy birthdays and holidays together. I love you both very much.
>
>   E.R.

Her seventy-fifth birthday passed without any real celebration, but she told the Democratic Advisory Committee that it could describe its fund-raising dinner in December as in honor of her on her seventy-fifth birthday. I sat next to her at an AAUN luncheon where an award was given to the High Commissioner for Refugees.

> She said the boys were "calm" about Jimmy's book *[Affectionately, F.D.R.]* despite all the advance rumblings of suits, etc. . . . She said that requests she would like to get out of if they related to books she

---

* Adrian Dornbush had been head of the WPA's Technical Services Laboratory.

sends them to Nannine Joseph, speeches to Colston Leigh and radio and tv to Tom Stix. She was getting pretty good at saying "no," she claimed. Edna and David late. I went out to call them at 1:30 because Mrs. R. anxious. Edna showed up first with mother and friend and David at about 1:45. He had to stop in to see a patient, he said. . . .

Her love for David was unbudgeable.

> 202 Fifty-sixth Street West
> Oct. 31st

David dearest,

I have nothing you will really like for your birthday in the way of things. So I'll try to put into words a little that is in my heart and just give you that.

I'm grateful for the day you were born and for all you've given me and taught me. Watching you I've learned that the more one gives love, the more one has to give. You have the power to forgive and forget which I can never emulate but admire deeply. Every year you grow and are a fairer, more understanding, bigger person. God bless you and keep you. May the coming year bring you only happiness, this I wish with all my heart.

> All my love
> E.R.

"The apartment begins to look as tho' someday I'd move in—but not till Nov. 27th!" she wrote me in Israel where I had gone to cover the elections for the *Post.* She moved from the Sheraton and had her first dinner with David and Edna as guests.

> 55 East 74th Street
> Thursday

Dearest David,

I loved your note and I hope the evening was as pleasant as you anticipated! You know I always love to be with you and to do anything with you at all times. . . .

> E.R.

Don't ever be humble. You give much more than anyone could give you!

David realized how blessed he was to have her of all people in the world say what she said of him in her postscript. For humility and caring marked her life above all. As Adlai said at the Democratic dinner honoring her a few days later, "her compassion encompasses the globe, she has walked with the less fortunate, and devoted her enormous talents and energies to working for justice, happiness and harmony for all humanity."

The dinner at the Waldorf turned into a major political event, at least among Democrats. Seven potential Democratic candidates for president spoke, each introduced by former President Truman. But the highlight of the evening was the public dispute between the former President and the former First Lady on the principles that should guide the Democratic Party. It focused on the role of "liberals" in the party. Mr. Truman would not exclude but subordinate them to the practical politicians. His distaste was for the "hothouse" liberal, the "self-appointed guardian of liberal thinking" who often "paved the way for reaction." The way to implement liberalism, he insisted, was "a united Democratic party. . . ." He beamed as he sat down to the considerable applause of the diners. Mrs. Roosevelt surmised he was speaking for the Democratic political establishment who wanted to head off liberals like herself and Stevenson.

Mrs. Roosevelt had the final word. She rose, a queenly presence as always. A hush fell over the hall. It was a replay of the conflict between the two at the 1956 Democratic Convention and there was a sense among the guests that the fight was really over the soul of the Democratic Party. "I'm going to differ with him a little bit tonight. He doesn't like certain kinds of liberalism. I welcome every kind of liberal that begins to learn by coming into our party what it is to work on being a liberal." Older people in the party—she and Mr. Truman were seventy-five years old—"have something to learn from liberals that are younger . . . because they may be conscious of new things that we have to learn."

She believed in the Democratic Party and hoped a Democrat would be elected in 1960 who would be able to guide the country so that it would "bring to the people of the world the thing which they wish for most, which is peace and an opportunity to make life better over the whole area of the world. . . . I want unity, but above everything else, I want a party that will fight for the things that are known to be right at home and abroad."

Stevenson's graceful tribute earlier, many in the audience felt, had spoken rightly. Women occasionally had had an impact on their times, he remarked. "How blessed we are that our beloved guest of honor is the representative by whom we are proudest to have posterity judge us—whether we deserve it or not!"

The *Times* devoted a full page, including the text of her speech, to the debate. The dinner set the stage for the 1960 Democratic presidential campaign. She passed it off with a paragraph in a letter to Anna.

> At the dinner the Dem. Advisory Com. gave for me, Mr. Truman & I had a "little difference" again. I thought I was gentle but the papers played it up. Adlai's speech seemed much more mature than any of the candidates. . . .

XXV

A Final Canter

NINETEEN SIXTY WAS a presidential year. Mrs. Roosevelt was approaching seventy-six years of age, but while she often protested that it was time to take a backseat, she was unable to resist trying to place her special imprint of compassion-cum-practicality on the Democratic side of the campaign. She liked Adlai. They were political associates, good friends, but she had her own purposes, among them a fear of John Kennedy's candidacy, and they were not necessarily Stevenson's. For the sake of the country as well as Adlai she dearly wanted him to be Secretary of State if a Democrat were elected, but, as is recounted later, her own moves as the chief of Stevenson's supporters made it more difficult, if not impossible.

She described her personal circumstances, including her new living arrangements in town, to Anna at the end of 1959. She had finished the mail and yet was awake enough to write.

[E.R. to Anna Halsted:]   [December 17th, 1959]
  The mail has increased to appalling proportions & being 75 was of no help.
  I love my apartment. . . . In a year & a half "he" [the tenant with a lease] will have to move & then it will be perfect. Now I sleep on a couch in the dining room & dress in one bathroom & the kitchen is fine very modern, but our office is tiny! Someday it will just house the maid! . . . I'll need to do very little downstairs, only add a guest bathroom. . . .

Could Hick lunch with her on March 4? She would "invite all your usual people. . . . Is there anything you want for your birthday? Please let me know as I shall otherwise give you something you don't want!" She advised Anna's husband, Jim Halsted, ". . . I don't think Nixon unbeatable but I haven't found the candidate yet among those running I think can surely do it!" Stevenson's position at the beginning of the year was that he was not a candidate. He was determined to keep out of the primaries but would not refuse a request to serve. As draft movements sprang up around the country, managed by Stevenson loyalists, he stoutly maintained his noncandidate status, and Eleanor at the time was content to accept it at face value.

In February Stevenson left on a two-month trip through Latin America. Just before he did so he asked to come and see her alone. She immediately invited David and Edna. She did not want a private session where he might ask her advice on whether to run for President. "[H]e's really coming," she told Edna, "in the hope that I will persuade him to run for President. I will not persuade him. I believe that anyone who needs to be urged should not run." The main movers in the unofficial draft-Stevenson movement were in touch with her, but she was not sure whether a fight should be made to draft him, whether Stevenson wanted a fight made, or how much she wanted to become involved. James and Fjr. were actively for Kennedy. Moreover, Anna was pressing David, and he agreed, to get her to cut down on her activities.

An entry in my journal, February 21, 1960.

> I lunched with Mrs. R. Mickey [Pratt, Trude's third child, a senior at Amherst] came along. . . . Amazed at the number of people who came up to her and said they had seen her on the Frank Sinatra show— everyone on American Airlines—showed what people watched. (I didn't like it one bit but she hasn't asked my opinion. Trude skirts around it by saying how wonderful Mrs. R. looked.)
>
> She didn't stop off in Washington on the way back from the coast in order to talk with Lyndon Johnson [Senate majority leader] because it was Lincoln's birthday and everyone was out of town speaking. Instead she sent him a letter. She says she does not share Mary Lasker's view that he is a secret liberal who will push hard for Mary's bill. He will do just what he thinks the traffic will bear.
>
> Chester Bowles came in to see her. He professed that he had nothing on his mind, but in the end the purpose of his visit came out. He was for [Senator] Humphrey and would not do a thing to injure Hubert, but the Connecticut organization was solidly for Kennedy and he could not be out of step. There had been no promise of Secretary of State nor was he trying to beat Adlai for it. He was much interested, however, in Mrs. R.'s suggestion of 2 secretaries—one a travelling negotiator, the other in Washington.

A few days later another entry about lunch with Mrs. Roosevelt.

> Mrs. R. had a letter from Joe Rauh [Washington lawyer, a leader of Americans for Democratic Action and battler for civil rights]. He was worried over the possibility that Senator [Wayne] Morse would use the fact that he was speaking at the Young Democratic Club in Washington together with Mrs. R. in order to harm Hubert [Humphrey]. Morse was saying that Hubert was a front for Johnson. Mrs. R. troubled but did not see how she could back out of her commitment to appear. If Morse said anything to indicate she was supporting him, or attacked Hubert, she would reply. She did not believe Hubert was fronting for Johnson, but knew he was quite close to him and could well understand why, after ten ballots or so, he might throw his support to Johnson. She did not seem to think that so heinous. . . .

In March Adele Rosenwald Levy died and at the small funeral service Eleanor spoke feelingly about Adele's championship of liberal causes and her great generosity. It was "a sad group that gathered with the family in a service of love for this lovely woman," she wrote afterward. Moved perhaps by the services at the Campbell Funeral Chapel, she talked later of the bomb threats when she visited "Uncle David" in Sarasota, Florida; the police had searched for explosives in a hall where she spoke. The editor of the local paper told her his old mother had come back from that speech saying if she had to be blown up, there was nobody she would prefer to be blown up with than Mrs. Roosevelt. She returned to the subject of final things the next day.

> . . . She had seen Ben-Gurion [Israel's Prime Minister] who told her he thought Israel will get the arms it needed. So Secretary of State Christian Herter had assured him. I mentioned Ben-Gurion's interest in longevity. She wasn't, she said. There were a few things she still wanted to do and would do them this summer. They involved her grandchildren. Otherwise it was interesting to do things, saying to yourself, "this is the last time I will do them." It was an excuse to do a great many things you might not feel free to do otherwise.
>
> She said she had kept a memo for Frankie and Harry Hooker, her executors, on her funeral and burial. She wanted a plain wooden coffin, no embalming, except her veins cut because she did not want to wake up with piles of earth on top of her. When you are not embalmed you have to be buried quickly. All this necrological talk, I observed, [she made] in very good humor.

"I had only one cold all winter & David found the right pills & I wasn't even in bed," she wrote happily to Anna, pleased also that her once-a-month TV series,

"Prospects of Mankind," produced by Henry Morgenthau III and sponsored by Brandeis University and Boston Educational TV, would appear again the following year.

To a few of her friends she acknowledged occasional thoughts of death, but to the world she was still a miracle of energy. Stevenson, writing from Latin America to his good friend Agnes Meyer, urged her to rest when she was in Florida: ". . . take care—you're *good* but no Eleanor Roosevelt!! I agree that she's past any understanding; and she breaks *my* heart too. But her power isn't from abstinence; I'm sure it's from God, because she seldom does anything for *herself.* 'My country is the world. My countrymen are all mankind.' "

Rarely was her ability to bridge the difference between private pain and public brightness better illustrated than when a youth who happened to be black carelessly backed his car into her, knocking her down as she was on the way to François, her hairdresser. She told the young man to leave quickly, refused to summon aid, limped to her destination, and despite the pain made her speech. Later, after first chasing Maureen and David out, she allowed David to tape up her leg and, despite torn ligaments, went through the rest of the day's schedule, ending up at the Waldorf-Astoria, where she apologized for speaking while seated on a high pillow. Though she had to use a cane to walk, she insisted to a New York *Times* reporter that she was "too busy to think much about the injury. She did not know the name of the motorist," she said. To Anna she wrote a week later—

[E.R. to Anna Halsted:]   [April 10, 1960]
. . . Now, I must tell you that I stood back of an automobile on 8th St. last Sunday & got myself backed into & knocked down! I was up at once & no crowd gathered & & walked away but I found my right foot functioned less & less well. I opened the cancer benefit I was going to, & luckily Joe & Trude were picking me up to bring me home & I greeted & fed a group of some 24 kids 8–10 with their chaperones on arrival here, & then I called David because I had to speak at a cloak & suit Industry dinner for Brandeis & I was finding my foot less & less use! David did all he could & I got thro' the evening but Monday a.m. David insisted on an x-ray at the medical center & their best surgeon to see me. Nothing was broken just torn ligaments but under the instep so the foot would bear no weight. They told me if I didn't be still & keep it up *all* the time it would bother me for weeks whereas a week might cure it with complete rest. So I've been here a week but far from alone & not too restful. Whenever it was possible my activities were just brought here! Yesterday at least 40 reform N.Y. City candidates were photographed here with Sen. Lehman & me! I've done 3 recordings, tons of mail each day & seen *all* the people who intended to see me here or elsewhere!

   . . .

We (Maureen, David & Edna & I) are going to H.P. Wednesday night to stay till Monday morning after Easter because I feel David & Edna need a rest! I have felt for sometime that this might be so therefore I'm going to cut out a number of things & say the foot has to be rested! . . .

She was unable to admit to herself that she was taking things more easily. She had to ascribe it to David and Edna's need of a rest. Her exclamation point, however, hints that she realized she was telling herself a white lie. The letter to Anna had other information about her health. "I'm going to use the foot as an excuse to cut out a number of things because David found some signs that my heart was overstrained a bit. He's making me go for a checkup . . . next Thursday." Six days later she wrote Anna again.

> Val-Kill Cottage
> Saturday, April 16th
>
> . . . My ankle progresses steadily but slowly. I can use it, but then I have to lie up & rest it. I had a partial checkup. Found I was aneamic (how do you spell it?) which might account for the heart skip. In itself the heart is nothing, just a warning & I am slowing up in earnest! So, nothing to worry about where I'm concerned.
>
> Mother

In April several "draft Stevenson" movements emerged. They were the work of Stevenson's friends and followers and inevitably inspired speculation as to his position. By failing to stop them, it was argued, he passively encouraged them. In particular his employment of William Attwood, a first-rate political writer and friend who secured a leave of absence from *Look* to do speech-writing and other political chores for him, excited speculation. The Stevenson headquarters that were opened in Washington were headed by Senator Mike Monroney, Jr., and included a former Stevenson law partner, George Ball. While Stevenson steadfastly maintained he was not seeking the nomination, he left himself one out—he would not refuse to serve if asked. He returned from his two-month trip through Latin America at the beginning of April and summoned Bill Attwood to Barbados where he worked on a major speech, "Jefferson and Our National Leadership," that he delivered at the University of Virginia on April 12.

Journal entry, April 12, 1960.

> Mrs. R. said Stevenson had called her on the way to Charlottesville and said he wanted to talk with her on way back to Chicago via New York on Wednesday. This will be her first day back at the AAUN office and both will try to fit it in! He said he didn't quite know what Bill Attwood was supposed to be doing for him. No one wrote his speeches, perhaps he could help with research.

The relationship with Attwood reflected the thin line Stevenson was trying to walk between an active and a passive candidacy. When Attwood let slip that "I wrote half that speech, [Julian] Boyd the other half . . . ," Stevenson was shocked. Attwood had violated the "conventions" between speech-writers and principals, he thought, "So please don't write or draft anything more for me." But a footnote in Walter Johnson's seventh volume of the Stevenson letters states, "Mr. Attwood writes that shortly thereafter, Stevenson changed his mind and resumed their 'editorial' relationship."

Another journal entry, April 12, 1960.

Trude & I had dinner with Mrs. R. alone after she came down from H.P. Bill Levy & his mother had driven her up. [It was the date of F.D.R.'s death and she always appeared at his graveside.] Sam & Dorothy Rosenman, the Morgenthaus, [Isidore] Lubins & Averell Harriman there. Brought them all back for lunch. They tried to smoke her out on a presidential candidate, she said. Averell began it. On the way up to H.P., he said, he and the Rosenmans came to the conclusion that Humphrey came closest to what they believed in and should be supported. What did she think? She refused to be drawn out. Dorothy Rosenman then said that women stuck to Adlai—they either wanted to marry or protect him. Wasn't Mrs. R.'s attitude the protective one? No, she replied. He did not interest her at all as a woman, that it was his mind that interested her. Averell confided to her that he did not agree with Truman and Acheson on foreign policy, which Mrs. R. interpreted to mean Averell is pushing to become Sec State.

Mrs. R. confessed to being shocked by President Eisenhower's setting April 12 aside as polio vaccination day without any reference to FDR. She felt a sense for his own place in history would have led him to treat FDR's place with greater respect and dignity.

Although he was not a declared candidate, the pro-Stevenson network was widespread.

Journal entry, April 23, 1960, Hyde Park.

. . . Mrs. R. said Walter Reuther had been in for breakfast and assured her that it was getting better every day for Stevenson. He thought he could swing James Carey for him at the right time. George Meany was for Symington or Johnson. Reuther asked her to call Hubert which she did. . . . She wanted to tell him of a column she was writing, she said, against the injection of the religious issue into the West Virginia primary. . . . Humphrey is angry with Walter for not supporting him in Wisconsin and not listening to Joe Rauh and others even though they were worried about his tactics in West Virginia.

At the meeting of the civil rights subcommittee, someone who had spent considerable time with Mr. Truman brought her a message that he was grateful she had not spanked him for his remarks about sit-down strikes being communist inspired. She explained to the Michalowskis [he was the Polish representative at the UN] that Truman came from the south-inclined part of Missouri, so had grown up in an environment where Negroes were deferential. He never had sat down and really thought through his position. As a result whenever he acted from anger, he did wrong things. She said Negroes were much influenced by developments in Africa. When they saw Africans standing up for their own rights and fighting back, they too from inside of themselves decided they would no longer let whites fight for their rights, but do so themselves. . . .

In May the *Post* sent me to Paris to cover the "summit" meeting of Eisenhower, Khrushchev, Macmillan, and de Gaulle. It collapsed when Khrushchev announced that the USSR had shot down a U-2 reconnaissance plane over Russia and withdrew his invitation to President Eisenhower to visit his country after the summit conference. I wrote her about these events from Paris, hoping to hear in return about the politics of the looming Democratic convention.

May 13th 1960

Joe dearest,

It was good to have your letter on my return from Washington yesterday [to address Democratic women and dine with Doris Fleeson and other newspaperwomen]. I've been "on the way" for about ten days & all has gone well with the foot.

You sound as tho' you were seeing & observing much & I imagine the "Summit" will need all your abilities. What a mess we have made of this plane business, but Khrushchev behaves very badly!

I go to H.P. tomorrow with 2 Russian ladies, next week I hope Trude can go up with me . . .

. . .

E.R.

I came back to this country briefly after the collapse of the summit. Eleanor's fear of Kennedy's winning the nomination, as well as her worries over the summit collapse, made her more receptive to proposals of the draft-Stevenson forces to try to hold liberals in line. She had written both Walter Reuther and Governor G. Mennen Williams of Michigan to urge them to wait until the convention and find out what Stevenson's chances were before coming out for Kennedy. A Stevenson-Kennedy ticket, she suggested, was "the strongest" the Democrats could muster. At Hyde Park the Memorial Day weekend liberal Representative Richard Bolling, who was the speaker, was a Kennedy supporter. The talk at the cottage before going over to the rose garden inevitably was about presidential politics. She apologized for seeming to visit the sins of the fathers upon the sons, she said, but she was unable to forget Joe Kennedy's defeatism in 1940, nor was she able to overlook John Kennedy's vacillation on the McCarthy issue.

I left after Memorial Day weekend to return to Europe to research a book on Dag Hammarskjold.

May 29, 1960

Dearest Mrs. R.,

I do not feel completely easy in my mind at having urged you to go to Los Angeles. From some of the things Dick Bolling said, it may well be that Jack Kennedy will have it all sewed up by the time the Convention begins or that the crucial decision will be to throw Stevenson support to Kennedy to keep Johnson from getting the nomination. From things you have said I doubt whether a Convention revolving around such issues would be very interesting to you. That is why I write this note.

I hope you do go out: a) because you speak for the soul and conscience of the party, b) because Stevenson may need you, and c) because your counsel and advice may be even more important if Kennedy is the nominee. Kennedy has grown and I have recently begun to wonder whether Stevenson might not be more effective in the field of foreign affairs as Secretary of State in a Kennedy administration than as President of a bitterly divided country.

I write also because the conversation between you and Dick on the subject of Stevenson's inability to communicate left me highly insecure about his electability. There, I feel better having said these things. Much love. I shall be thinking of you.

She liked my candor, but already she was moving toward a decision to press Stevenson more openly. On June 1 she wrote Mary Lasker, the philanthropist who together with Agnes Meyer was footing Bill Attwood's salary, that "If there is a chance that Adlai might be nominated and that I could help on that, I will certainly come at once." A few days later she was called by Anna Rosenberg, Mary's closest adviser and good friend.

June 7th

Joe dearest,

I did appreciate your note very much. I decided not to go & today Anna Rosenberg called me & reasoned with me! She said I couldn't interfere with the boys if I didn't come till Wednesday. Paul Butler wanted me to speak towards the end if we had trouble on the platform & I could help on that. I cd leave on Friday p.m. so this I will do.

I don't know whether Stevenson *or* Kennedy can be elected. S. *&* K. can, I believe, but Paul Hoffman said tonight "the Democrats have a genius for defeating themselves"! He thinks it will be Nixon *&* Rockefeller.

. . .

The last programme was done on Sunday so I'm not sure it is good! Adlai, Prof. Hatta* & Kissinger were good but the subject was too big & we should have brought it up.

. . .

E.R.

A cable from Trude to me in Oslo: ER WANTS YOU INFORMED SHE COMING OUT FOR STEVENSON-KENNEDY FRIDAY STOP EAGER HAVE YOU CHECK EXCITING RELEASE ALL LOVE   TRUDE.

Theodore White, author of *The Making of a President,* was visiting Stevenson in Libertyville about this time. Their conversation was interrupted by "a lengthy phone call from New York. Stevenson was told Eleanor Roosevelt was about to insist that he declare publicly whether he sought the nomination." White went on, "For an hour there in the sun he tried to resolve these turbulent thoughts into some clear answer that Eleanor Roosevelt could make public; and the telephone rang from Washington and again from New York, and one had the sense of a distant clamor calling for executive leadership. Yet he would not act. He would wait."

On June 10, in a statement inspired by the organizers of the draft movement, she said forthrightly—

I am about to exercise the prerogative of a woman and change my mind. Up to this time I have been firmly saying I would come out for no one as the Democratic nominee for the Presidency until the Convention, and now I am going to join some of my friends in a plea to the Convention delegates to nominate as the standard bearer of the Democratic Party Adlai E. Stevenson. He is not a declared candidate. . . .

Stevenson wrote her the same day that her statement had left him "a little shaken" but, though he doubted whether he would become involved in Los Angeles, he had heard from Mary Lasker that Eleanor did not plan to go to the convention. He hoped she would reconsider: "I would think as a Democrat that your presence is important, symbolically and actually." The matter of Stevenson's status remained unsettled, and the contretemps between Eleanor and Adlai continued. The next day (June 11) she called on him to clarify his position. He replied on June 12 that he would not lift a finger to get the nomination, but "I think I have made it

* of Indonesia

clear in my public life, however, that I will serve my country and party whenever called upon."

That was enough for Mrs. R. "From this statement I think you will find it clear that Mr. Stevenson is a candidate," she wrote in her column. The New York *Times* headline on the story was "Stevenson: Not a Candidate. Mrs. Roosevelt: Yes, He Is." Political commentator and old friend Doris Fleeson wrote, "Mrs. Roosevelt came through for her friends again. The best working politician in the trade secured from Adlai Stevenson the 'will serve' statement about his candidacy he was unwilling to give anyone else." To the *Times* reporter who called Stevenson he repeated that he was not seeking the nomination, "Therefore, I am not a candidate." When the reporter read his statement of noncandidacy back to him, he murmured, "Oh, dear, I suppose this will get me into trouble with Eleanor, won't it?"

Privately Mrs. R. was not happy over Adlai's allowing his friends to proceed with the draft movement while insisting that he was not seeking the nomination. Politics in a democracy deserved plainer answers, she felt. Among notes she had prepared for herself during the 1956 campaign, the first one read—and it indicated its importance to her—that Stevenson was no longer the reluctant candidate he had been in 1952. Better than anyone else she appreciated how Franklin had been a master of timing and keeping his real objectives hidden when that served his purposes. Adlai's cat-and-mouse game in 1960 was not unlike Franklin's sphinxlike attitude toward the various efforts to draft him for a third term. There was a big difference. Franklin had enjoyed power, Stevenson seemed to shun it. She credited it to a genuine humility, a quality that she shared, but sometimes she wondered whether the indecision did not mask an inability to grasp power and use it. She was not unwilling to have Stevenson's friends use her to pull him forward. She put the best possible face on his conflicted behavior. Walter Johnson reports a lengthy conversation with Stevenson at Libertyville on June 14, 1960.* Attwood was a participant. The latter's memorandum on his conversation with John Kennedy was at the top of their agenda. Johnson described Eleanor Roosevelt's press conference.

> I explained to him how beautifully she handled the question of why you weren't a candidate. She explained to the press that you had the experience, the brains, the wisdom, and then she paused and said the humility to be President. She then said, you see, he is not a candidate in the ordinary sense because being a man of humility, he doesn't think he is the only person who can save the world. Then she added, in her own inimitable way with the charm of a great lady but with the devastating knife she can put in, that the others who were so avidly campaigning

---

* Professor Walter Johnson had been cochairman of the 1952 Draft Stevenson Committee and was editor of the eight-volume *The Papers of Adlai E. Stevenson.* Stevenson's farm and home were in Libertyville, Illinois, on some seventy acres.

lacked—and then she paused and then said—shall we say they lack sensitivity. Adlai was very pleased about this report.

June 15

Dearest Joe,

    . . .

    I did my 2 commencement addresses last week & Walter Reuther & family spent Sat. & Sun. in H.P. even tho' I was gone to Amherst all Sunday. Frankie came up to dine Sat. night & I wished for you. Walter feels we are lost unless Stevenson & Kennedy agree before the convention that whichever one can't win will throw his votes to the other, which means that if Kennedy starts a band wagon he'll win. Walter's argument is that unless they are agreed they will elect the Republicans as Johnson will swing his disciplined votes & Symington's to Adlai to stop Kennedy & that means no Catholic & no Negro vote for Adlai & a Rep. victory. Petitions are being circulated in every state for Adlai. Finally I've agreed to go out Monday a.m. July 11th & if I have to I'll stay till Friday . . .

                                                                            E.R.

Trude had joined Jonathan and me in Oslo.

June 17th

Trude dearest,

    How I miss your cheery voice every morning! I thought of you on your birthday & I suggest that you & Joe & Jonathan dine here with me & we have a delayed celebration Monday, July 18th & we ask in for coffee at 9 the Gurewitsches & any others you like & Joe report on the trip! How will that suit you?

    . . .

    There is no letup in activity. People all the time! I'm not tired however, I'm sure thanks to the pills I take! . . . Tony wired that they had a little girl born the other day, so now there are 13 great grandchildren!

                                                                            E.R.

"Politics are very active," she wrote Anna, "because I decided to come out for Stevenson & now I have to go out to the convention."

June 19th

Dearest Joe & Trude,

    I think of you so much as the political struggle gets hotter here. Agnes Meyer & Mike Monroney called me tonight on a point of strategy. Would you think Joe, that Adlai's name should be presented on the first ballot to the convention? He would make a poor showing, the galleries

even are controlled as Paul Butler has given seats to $1000 contributors &
seen to it that most of them are for Kennedy. It probably must run 4 or
five ballots before much change, so should Stevenson's name wait to be
presented? . . .

I have some family worries but it will be time enough when you get
home to tell you about them!

. . .

E.R.

"[T]here are some worrisome things about the boys & wives again," she wrote
Anna.

I wrote Mrs. Roosevelt from Constance in southern Germany, where we were
visiting Trude's mother. "It does seem to me that unless an early entry of Stevenson's name is necessary in order to keep votes from drifting to Kennedy, that it
would be more consistent with the image of Stevenson that the world has, not to
rush his name in but wait until Kennedy has had his run."

"I came to the same conclusion on Stevenson's nomination that you did & so
did Sen. Monroney," she wrote us in reply.

Her next letter mingled the mundane with the more momentous. Trude and I
should let her know the flight number and time our plane would arrive at Idlewild
(subsequently renamed Kennedy) airport so she could meet us and give her the
names of friends whom we wanted to have in for the party she intended to give us.

[E.R. to the Lashes:]   [July 5, 1960]
I go to Oyster Bay for a speech tomorrow a.m. & then to Wash. for a
Stevenson rally in the p.m. We all listened to Truman's press conference
in which he charged the convention was rigged for Kennedy & resigned
as a delegate. I got a feeling he wouldn't mind having it rigged for
Lyndon Johnson & he listed 10 possible candidates & never mentioned
Adlai! Yesterday Kennedy answered in a press conference. He did very
well. Firm about not giving up but most courteous to Pres. T. I have a
feeling he did himself good but H.S.T. did himself harm.

David accompanied her to Los Angeles to the convention. Though the Stevenson forces put on a considerable show, Kennedy had the delegates and the best
organization at the convention. She held a press conference, but the delegates
wanted a winner and feared Stevenson was fated to lose. People loved her but
disregarded her message. Her press conference was no blockbuster, nor did her
appearance before state caucuses do much for Stevenson even as it reminded delegates of a quality of leadership that had disappeared from the party. When she
came into the convention hall, delegates gave her a standing ovation. She refused
to acknowledge it. "Why?" a nonplussed David asked her, "Why?" "It is impolite
to the speaker," she replied.

But it was more than that. She was unhappy with her performance. Perhaps she had hurt Stevenson's chances of becoming Secretary of State. She did not like to oppose her sons, all of whom except Johnny were working for Kennedy. And just as she had noted how Truman had harmed himself with his press conference attack on Kennedy, she realized she had diminished her own influence by having so obviously misjudged Stevenson's possibilities.

David later talked with me about the convention and the events of that summer. She placed pressure on Stevenson to be a candidate, he thought, less because she wanted him than because she opposed Jack Kennedy. When I asked what he thought were the sources of her fear of Kennedy, he replied, "because of McCarthy, of Catholicism, his father." Yet he was unable to understand her unwillingness to move quickly to support the Democratic candidate after the convention, especially when "tricky Dicky" was the Republican candidate. For weeks she refused to have anything to do with Kennedy. "How reluctantly she agreed. 'Oh, all right, I'll see him.'"

"July 17, 1960, Hyde Park," I wrote in my Journal.

When Kennedy & Stevenson got together on Thursday (after Kennedy's victory) they tried to reach Mrs. R. She & David had already checked out of the hotel, but Kennedy reached her at the airport. Kennedy & Stevenson both talked to her. She told Kennedy he did not have to bother about her——that he had more important things to worry about, like organizing his campaign. They didn't have to talk together. Any messages he wanted to send her he could do through Fjr. & she the same with him. When I talked with her early Friday a.m. her voice sounded listless & tired. At the Friday night stadium rally Jimmy R. read a "message" from Mrs. R but she told us on the way up to H.P. Sat. she had sent no message of any kind & knew nothing about it. But she didn't appear angry. I urged her to campaign for the ticket. Said she was willing to make a few TV appearances but she did not know whether Kennedy would like what she would have to say——that the election of Nixon was the greater evil. I said I hoped she would be able to get herself to say something nice about Kennedy as well as the platform. And at dinner Sat. p.m. she told Fjr. she would give him a list of dates when she would be available for speeches. The Kennedy people, judging from Fjr., are quite worried about New York. I asked Mrs. R. whether she knew that Stevenson wanted people like herself to go ahead & make the fight or was embarrassed by it. Said at first she never really knew, and thought that his attitude was as it appeared——that he couldn't lift a finger for it, but if it came he would accept any task party asked of him. But she did tell us of an episode during the convention when Reuther came to her & said if Stevenson came out for Kennedy it would clinch the Sec State for him & keep the Johnson forces from slipping in. It was not up to her, she answered. Reuther made a plausible case, but it was up to Stevenson & they would continue to fight until Stevenson himself gave up. Walter said he would go to Stevenson, as she said he should, & she heard nothing further. She concluded that Walter had not persuaded Stevenson.

Fjr said last night the Kennedy forces were furious with Stevenson because of his failure to stop the draft movement. They kept getting messages he was embarrassed by the whole thing, that he knew Kennedy had it but couldn't let his devoted following down. He would, however, try to do something. (Even Fjr could see, as he himself pointed out, that Stevenson could not kill off the draft-Stevenson movement in order to get Sec State job.)

Apparently the Stevenson movement—telegrams, demonstrations, etc. caused great nervousness in Kennedy camp Tuesday night. Fjr doubted Stevenson would be made Sec State, thought he would be fobbed off with UN job. Said something about Johnson being made chief international negotiator for the United States and Bowles SecState.

Fjr alive again politically.

The weariness I had sensed in Mrs. Roosevelt on our return from abroad registered the advance of an illness that had begun to worry David. The latter pulled me aside at Hyde Park the following weekend.

July 25, 1960. Diagnosis still "goodish." The fear of cancer had been eliminated but there still was a chance of a slowly developing leukemia or some kind of blood disease. Her white cell count which had been 2000, now was up to 3400 but some of the cells were not as they should be. They could do a definitive test, but if the results were positive there was nothing that could be done and she would have to be told why they wanted a sample of her marrow. Now she was reassured by the information that her blood count was up and there was no cancer. Jim Halsted agrees . . . no hurry on a definitive test.

She withheld a decision to join Herbert Lehman as honorary chairman of the New York Kennedy Committee until she spoke with Kennedy and found out how closely he intended to work with Stevenson and Bowles, especially in the foreign affairs field.

She sent David and Edna to meet Kennedy at the Dutchess County airport. She met alone with him but allowed David afterward to photograph the two of them, and his many shots of the occasion included one that caught the look of wariness in the eyes of both.

Afterward she described the meeting to a few friends, including Stevenson's closest supporters. "I had my talk with Senator Kennedy. . . . Now, I have no promises from the Senator, but I have the distinct feeling that he is planning on working closely with Adlai. I also had the feeling that here was a man who could learn . . . he seemed so little cocksure and I think he has a mind that is open to new ideas."

The meeting was shadowed by the death the previous day of John Roosevelt's daughter Sally, who had been killed in a riding accident. Kennedy had offered to cancel the meeting but she told him to come. Her sorrow, however, over the child's death was deep.

Aug 16th

My dearest Joe,

Your dear letter warmed my heart. I know both of you would come if there was anything you could do but there is nothing when fate strikes its blows except the knowledge of love & that I feel & it gives strength.

Anne & Johnny will love hearing from you. They have been wonderful but I know it will be a long time before they stop expecting to see Sally at every turn. I can hardly realize that I'll never see her run into the house or ride by again. Let us hope that beyond this life there is joy always for the young.

. . .

E.R.

Aug. 17th

Dearest Anna & Jim,

. . . You'll never know how glad I am you were home & with us this week end. It meant so much to Johnny & Anne. I find it hard to realize even now that I'll never see that child running thro' my house again.

David has just been in to tell me today's results & I suggest he stop worrying & we forget about it. I'll take my pills & pay a fortune for these tests from time to time to satisfy him but I assure you both I *feel* quite *well!*

My love to you both.

Mother

At the end of August she went to England with Maureen, to join up later with Edna, David, and Grania in the Swiss Alps.

Aug. 31st 1960
Flims-Waldhaus
[Switzerland]

Dearest Hick,

I meant to write from Paris & was kept so busy that I never did. Maureen & I enjoyed our day in London & then she had a day & a half in Paris & I had two. Henry [Morgenthau] III met us in London & we had fun & got everything set for the recordings the 12th & 13th & we saw a part of the Picasso exhibit. In Paris I saw the UNESCO building at last & Maureen joined me for lunch with the acting director & we met Prince Aly Khan which amused Maureen I think. After she left for Ireland I saw 2 newly decorated Louis XIV rooms in the Louvre & the Salle d'Apollon & in both London & Paris I did much Xmas shopping!

The 26th in the late p.m. I joined David, Edna & Grania here & it is a beautiful & restful spot. On the 4th we leave for Warsaw & then the 11th it is London, Paris & home the evening of the 14th.

I hope [name indecipherable] is completely recovered & that all goes well with you. By the way what do you want for Xmas? Could I get it over here, a new sweater or gloves?

I feel fine & Gabriele is sending no mail so I'm very free & I sleep much more than at home but I wake so often thinking of Sally. It still seems hard to believe.

Much, much love

E.R.

Mrs. Roosevelt wanted to buy some sheets and pillow cases of Irish linen. She asked Maureen to find out the cost and sizes. Maureen did and Mrs. R. told her to "buy." She sent her a blank check which she had signed and told Maureen to fill in the amount. "But don't spend more than £75 because I need money for other things."

Flims
Switzerland
Sept. 2d

Dearest Trude & Joe,

. . .

We've done little here but eat, sleep & read & I'm over half way through Schlesinger's last book *[The Politics of Upheaval,* vol. 3 of *The Age of Roosevelt]*. I find it deeply interesting for it explains much that I only half understood at the time. How enraging Franklin must have been at times to his co-workers!

I see that Khrushchev is coming over as head of the USSR delegation in Sept. That will mean Mr. Herter will have to attend, won't it? This may mean all top people must come!

. . .

E.R.

In the Swiss Alps they traveled up a mountainside in a "telecabine" and David, an inveterate mountain climber, proposed that they climb the rest of the way. Edna demurred and stayed behind. Ten minutes later Mrs. Roosevelt returned, saying she did not want to leave Edna alone, but Edna suspected she did not want to climb. There were others about, recalled Edna, "but no one seemed surprised to spot her at the top of that mountain."

They went to Poland as part of a delegation of the World Federation of UN Associations. "Sightseeing in Krakow," recalled Edna, to illustrate how angry Mrs. Roosevelt could get, "we entered an old castle that had a forbiddingly steep, long staircase. My husband took aside a member of the official party and quietly suggested that we all climb the stairs slowly. Mrs. Roosevelt was instantly suspicious as we began the slow ascent and asked the official, 'Why are we going so slowly'? The poor man answered, 'Because your doctor said we should.' With that, in a rage, she shook off everyone and ran up the stairs leaving the rest of us behind. It cost her a great deal of energy to do that. She stayed angry the whole morning."

Edna also recalled that the government had placed a car and driver at their disposal and the Polish equivalent of an Intourist guide. They were driven about Warsaw the first day, but not to the site of the Jewish ghetto that the Nazis had razed, although David had asked that they go there. Finally they told the guide, "If you don't take us there, we want to get out." Reluctantly they were taken there. "We were alone. As we walked over the gravel paths, Mrs. Roosevelt remarked, 'it was awful,' the way the government maintained the place, no trees, a housing development all around." Afterward the WFUNA delegates attended a commemoration arranged by the government at Paderewski's house. "Why not also at the ghetto?" David suggested to Mrs. R. The government agreed, and she asked David to get some white and blue flowers—Israel's colors—which she placed at the foot of the ghetto monument.

October 22, 1960

Dearest Joe:

      . . .

Thank you so much for looking up the Thanksgiving Day words of F.D.R. They are exactly what I wanted. I agree with you that he was large minded and I grieve at the smallness of our usual speakers.

E.R.

October 31, 1960

David dear,

A happy birthday and my love. Cold nights this might be nice as you read in bed.

E.R.

Anna and Jim Halsted shortly after their return from Iran in August 1960 settled in Lexington, Kentucky, where he became assistant dean of the new medical school. A distressed David called them with the news that Mrs. Roosevelt's aplastic anemia might really be leukemia and he thought she was going to die.

Anna and Jim suggested to David that since he had been trained in "rehabilitative" medicine that he get a good internist familiar with the ailments Mrs. Roosevelt was said to have to take charge. "He handled this," Dr. Halsted told Bernard Asbell,* "by going to Mrs. Roosevelt and saying, 'Well, Jim and Anna don't think I can take care of you properly. They want me to turn you over to Dr. So-and-so.' She said, 'Well, David, if you don't want to take care of me, I won't have *any* doctor.'

"In the long run," said Jim, "it probably wouldn't have made much difference —probably didn't make any difference. Nevertheless, it was the proper thing to do. He shouldn't have taken care of her."†

Neither Jim Halsted nor Anna liked David. Nor did David have high regard for Jim as a doctor. But the dates of their clashes are unclear. David wrote Jim giving him the results of tests made by Dr. George Hyman, a specialist in blood diseases.

October 31st, 1960.

Dear Jim:

Our patient has had the symptoms of an infection without, however, any localizing symptoms. For over ten days she was having chills, feeling cold at night, with bouts of perspiration at night. All of this has now improved, though it has not completely disappeared. We did another blood count on October 26th. It was done by George Hyman and here are the figures:

Hemoglobin	10.0	
RBC	3.80	
WBC	5,800	
Differential	-	
Neutrophiles	64	(0-20-44)
Eosinophiles	2	
Lymphocytes	30	
Nonocytes	4	
Platelets	120,000	
Reticulocytes	0.7%	

He is not ready to take back his initial diagnosis, but so far so good. To me it is very encouraging that her hemoglobin has gone up. If this were a relative leucocytosis she would have predominantly one element, but the rise in white cells seemingly was quite uniform. Again an encouraging sign.

She is over doing these days by any standard, and is very tired in the

* Bernard Asbell: *Mother & Daughter* (New York, 1982) p. 344.
† "David *did* have an internist monitoring Mrs. R's case. He came often—made house calls," Edna Gurewitsch commented.

evening, having at times really to drag herself. I imagine until Election Day this will have to continue.

> Affectionately,
> [ADG]

David sent me a note at the same time.

> October 31st, 1960.

Dear Joe:

Translated into non medical terms, the last blood count was very encouraging, and even leading one to hope that the initial diagnosis may not be correct. However, discussing it with the hematologist it seems that it does not rule out our present diagnosis. However, the news is good and I wanted to let you know.

> Sincerely,
> David

"I have seen the videotape you did with Mrs. Roosevelt on campaign and election night reminiscences," Henry Morgenthau III wrote me. "I think it turned out extremely well and you were great." On election night, together with the Gurewitsches and other friends, we were with her to receive the election returns. It was a heady evening and as it became clear that Kennedy was winning she turned to David and me and asked whether we were interested in working for the new administration. I begged off; what David said I do not know.

[Anna Halsted to E.R.:]   [November 8, 1960]
. . . I'm so hoping that after today you will cut down drastically on your schedule. You have done yeoman's work for the ticket. People in Miami told me they'd seen you on the Jack Parr [Paar] *and* the Dave Garraway [Garroway] shows—not the most desirable hours for you to be working—but they said you were wonderful! Has your virus bug disappeared completely?

And two weeks later, expressing relief that it was Kennedy and not Nixon, Anna inquired eagerly, "Do you think that because of you we might be invited to the inauguration in Washington?"

Mrs. Roosevelt had just turned seventy-six. She continued to astonish everyone.

Nov. 19, 1960. At dinner Thursday night at Mrs. R.'s she told us of her weekend in Boston and Brandeis. She had finished late and when she got out to Logan [airport] discovered it was fogged in. She took a cab to the South Street railroad station. A sleeper would have gotten her in too late to make a plane at Idlewild for the midwest the next morning, so she took the coach and sat up all the way down to New York.

She said the President-elect had called her before he left for Florida and said he would come to see her on his return. No, no, she insisted, she would go to see him . . .

December 4th, 1960

Dearest Hick,

I'll have the party for people on the place on Sat. Dec. 17th from 5–6:30. I think you like to come so suppose Tubby picks you up at 4:30? Please just stay on for dinner. Don't bother to write. I'll know you will come if I hear nothing.

I got home from Boston late last night & Maureen & I leave at 7 a.m. tomorrow for Ogden Utah then L.A., Palm Springs, L.A. again & home Friday a.m. Next week end back to Boston. My long trips will all be over however.

Hope book goes well & you feel well.

Much, much love
E.R.

Val-Kill Cottage
Monday night

David dearest,

All is quiet and the house is empty, I'd like it even better if you and Edna were here. I love you both very dearly and I hope the new baby [it would be born June 27, 1961] whom we are all going to love so much is just like you, with a few little touches of Edna to add to his or her perfection.

Thank you a thousand times for all the lovely presents but above all for your thought and closeness. It is good to know you are near and even a glimpse or the sound of your voice starts my day better. I don't mean to be selfish but I am afraid I am[,] for when I have free time I always want to spend some of it with you.

Bless you for all you are and do, and God be good to you and all your loved ones is my daily prayer.

All my love
E.R.

She also wrote Edna the same evening.

[E.R. to Edna Gurewitsch:]   [December 26, 1960]

. . . I have been reading and thinking of you and David. You mean everything to me, so much devotion and love and a sense of closeness. I love you so much! I love all my presents from you both because they come from you and I enjoy them and because you in yourselves are a great gift. I love Xmas because it is an excuse for giving but even more because the story of Christ is one of love. Every new baby is a gift from God and I hope we will have many Xmas days together *with* a child to add to the joy.

My love to you and thanks.

Trude and I dined with Mrs. Roosevelt at La Toque Blanche, a restaurant near the United Nations patronized by Dag Hammarskjold. I scratched a few notes on a sheet of paper.

Dec. 28, 1960

Mrs. R. at La Toque Blanche said she had heard from Jimmy & Abba Schwartz why Fdr Jr. was passed over for SecNavy by McNamara [Secretary-designate of Defense]. Neither told Fjr. so she felt she had to. . . .

Kennedy wanted Mrs. R. to take part in the Inauguration. She turned him down including invitation to sit in the Presidential box.

At Edna and David's urging she agreed to take a holiday in Arizona after the Inauguration.

[January 14, 1961]

David dearest,

These are your Xmas present and Anniversary present from me. I could think of nothing you needed or wanted at Xmas and thought the vacation trip would be less of a burden if your only loss was the earning!

Let's rest and have fun. Without you two I wouldn't be going but with you two it will be nice.

All my love.

E.R.

"I have seats for the inaugural ball & parade for you," she advised Anna, "& I hope you have your own invitation by now to the ceremonies. . . . I'll be going to Frankie's house to dress. . . ."

Perhaps Kennedy's failure to appoint Stevenson Secretary of State figured in her refusal to sit in the presidential box. She gave as her reason her preference for sitting down below where she could see better. So on the crystalline, frosty day that graced Kennedy's Inaugural she sat among the benches below, wrapped in a mink coat and an army blanket. David and Edna were on one side, Trude's daughter Vera and I on the other, as well as Maureen and Abba Schwartz. Behind her sat Agnes Meyer, an ally in the campaign to draft Adlai.

"I think we will have a good President," she had advised friends just before election day, and now as she heard his flat Boston-tinged tones proclaim that "the torch has been passed to a new generation of Americans . . . Let us begin anew," she was surer of her prediction.

She left Washington for Tucson, Arizona, with David and Edna, and, said Edna, "a real vacation. . . . It was very peaceful there. We played croquet." Still they were surprised to be the only ones in the well-filled hotel to watch Kennedy's first press conference.

Her reactions to the Inauguration and to the semienforced holiday were suggested in her letters to Hick and to Trude and me.

Arizona Inn
Jan. 23d 1961

Dearest Hick,

Here we are, yesterday we had sun but today it is rainy & not at all like summer.

The snow last Thursday really played havoc with Washington. Traffic was snarled, cars ran out of gas or their batteries gave out, & they were abandoned in midstreet adding to the chaos. I tried to get to the gala performance but sat 4 hrs. in a traffic snarl & when a break came I went home! Inauguration Day itself was cold & beautiful & the streets were clear & the ceremonies impressive. I thought the speech magnificent, didn't you? I have reread it twice.

. . .

E.R.

Arizona Inn
Jan 24th 1961

Dearest Trude & Joe,

What an awful hour you left Washington & I fear you were held up in N.Y. for we waited four hours for our ten a.m. plane to get out of New York & reach Washington. The trip down seemed endless & Edna & David could hardly speak from fatigue when we arrived but one day of sun revived them. Now we've had two days of rain & I can only say it is preferable to your snow & cold which we read about. It is enforced quiet & I have enjoyed it & slept hours on end but for the sake of the others I hope it clears tomorrow.

I know you are both working hard & I feel guilty to be so lazy. . . .

E.R.

She still viewed a holiday as an interruption in life's real rhythms. It was something that had to be forced on her, yet she also knew a regular job with the U.S. Mission was beyond her physical capabilities. She told Adlai, who had been appointed our ambassador to the UN, so and in one of his preinaugural talks with the President Elect their conversation went as follows:

> S. May I ask about Mrs. Roosevelt—member of the delegation—adjourned session of the G.A. in March?
> K. Fine, if she would.
> S. Not full time, but I think she would be flattered to be invited to be a delegate—would make a good impression on Africans & Asians.
> K. Right.

But with Mrs. Roosevelt's acquiescence Kennedy did not reappoint her the U.S. representative to the UN Human Rights Commission. Stevenson urged that the beauteous and public-spirited Marietta Tree be named, and Kennedy left it up to him. Mrs. Roosevelt, now stooped, slower of movement, and her hair almost white, felt it had to be so. Too many men in important positions considered themselves indispensable. She had always feared becoming a victim of that quality but still was grateful when she was needed.

A book that she published in 1960, *You Learn by Living*, was subtitled *A Distillation of Mrs. Roosevelt's Life Experience*. It was suggested by her literary agent, Nannine Joseph, and she wrote it in collaboration with Mrs. Elinore Denniston. Aphoristic and wise, the book's subtitle was genuinely descriptive, it was a *distillation*, and among other matters sought to answer a question with which she had grappled almost all of her life, "the most important requirements" for happiness. She listed three: "a feeling that you have been honest with yourself and those around you; a feeling that you have done the best you could both in your personal life and in your work; and the ability to love others." That had usually been her answer, she wrote, now she added another: "the feeling that you are, in some way, useful." She felt that strongly. "Usefulness, whatever form it may take, is the price we should pay for the air we breathe and the food we eat and the privilege of being alive."

She recognized that age imposed impediments, but she was determined to remain useful as long as it was possible. She remembered her "Aunty Bye," who "was, in spite of crippling handicaps, a happy woman." She had models aplenty even as she was in the course of becoming one herself. She may even have been happy.

XXVI

"One Has to Work"

THERE WERE a few handwritten letters in 1961. The reason may have
been weariness from her illness, which at the time was thought to be
aplastic anemia—the signs of which included lowered resistance to infection, bleeding, and a persistent fatigue. Often, especially at high altitudes, she
dozed off. The disease manifested itself fitfully with pains and fevers that she
shrugged off as a "bug" or the "flu." They were white-lie belittlements with which
we were willing to fall in, although David had apprised us about his real anxieties.
When Jim and Anna Halsted returned from Iran at the end of the summer of
1960, Jim had said to his wife, "You have to realize this is going to shorten her life.
You will get to transfusions and broken down veins."

Eleanor was determined to remain useful. "When you cease to make a contribution you begin to die," she had written in her seventy-fifth year. She continued
to live by that tenet in the face of increasing ailments. At the resumed session of
the General Assembly in March she was again a part of a U.S. delegation headed
now by Adlai, but as it came to a close, after illness had kept her away from most of
the meetings, she wrote President Kennedy, "I don't think I have been very useful
but I think I accomplished what Adlai wanted in just appearing at the UN."

A note to Adlai was more descriptive. "To all intents and purposes I am
marooned at H.P. with the 'flu. Actually I don't have the 'flu but phlebitis. I didn't
want to talk about it and thought the 'flu a good excuse." She would try to get to

the delegation meeting "but I think I should probably be at home with my two old legs in the air!" She signed "affectionately," her feeling for Adlai unmistakably warm, but firmly declined to accept a position or title unless she was able to do the job. She took her responsibilities seriously and gently poked fun at the nabobs, usually men, who played while others worked.

A cheery note in her private life was the acquisition at last of the second floor of the duplex in the house she shared with Edna and David. There was still pleasure in furnishing it, and to have adequate space for work and guests was a minor felicity. "My warm thanks for the typewriter," a scrawled note greeted David. "That and the new apartment should lighten Maureen's burdens by April or May! Let me know if it costs more." Maureen revealed to Anna that her mother had said, "I don't want to live to be old. I don't want to live to when people will not be coming to me to talk about their problems." Immured at home, she welcomed people coming to her and she liked to be called on the phone.

With the President, however, she insisted she should come to him. "Even after a brief visit with the President," recalled Edna, "she would call me and tell me of her pleasure in the interview. Once at the end of a ten-minute interview which she had requested she arose to go, saying 'my time is up.' 'Don't rush,' the President importuned her." At the young President's request she joined Walter Reuther in heading up the "Tractors for Freedom Committee" after the Bay of Pigs fiasco and later in the year brought him a three-page list that Trude helped her assemble of women he might consider for positions in his administration. She agreed to preside over a Commission on the Status of Women.

A sad letter of resignation, despair, love, and waning strength went to all of her children, who had gotten into violent arguments during one of their "reunions." It was written in longhand on an American Airlines flight from Los Angeles to New York.

Monday, June 12 [1961]

Dearest Anna,

I am copying for you a letter I am sending F. Jr. and John. Much of the responsibility may fall on you in the future.

Dearest ———

I was deeply troubled by Sunday evening at Hyde Park. I never want to assess blame, it is such a wasteful occupation, for being mortals the blame for situations is usually rarely all one sided. One thing I want to say to you, and I am writing a similar note to (F or J) and to Anna. I believe good relationships and affection and help of each other within a family, are a great strength. One has to work for whatever one really wants in this world. Such conditions don't just grow, much thought, many acts of unselfish devotion are required day by day, but without it family ties deteriorate and are weakened and the nation suffers as well.

I think this responsibility is hard for the next generation to face when one member of the older generation lives on beyond the allotted span. I have determined therefore to hold no more "reunions." I will make every effort to go and see each one of you as often as I can, and I hope after the New Year to arrange my own activities on a more limited basis.

I love you all very much and I am proud of you when you are your best selves. I know your virtues and your weaknesses and love has nothing to do with your success or failures. Love is unchangeable. You can, however, make me unhappy and it affects me more deeply when things go wrong among you than when it touches the relationship with me. You are, I hope, going to live and work together for many years to come. My time, I hope, is limited.

God bless you and my love always,

Mother

Anna darling, you are character-wise the strongest, there is little weakness today in you and I think you will have great influence with your brothers as you have with your own children. You have learned more and are wiser than I am. My love and God's blessing on you and all this large family through the generations.

Devotedly,
Mother

A big event in her personal life was the birth in June of a baby to the Gurewitsches. She sent Edna two baby pillows.

Edna dearest,

These are really for when you want to show the baby off. With 1 of your plain covers you can use as extras when you need them before the infant appears! Love

E.R.

A note went with two bedjackets and a nightgown that Eleanor had worn after her first child was born.

[June 12, 1961]

Edna dear,

Could you use these in bed after the baby comes? The nightgown wld have to be shortened.

They were mine years ago but are now much too small and they are pretty I think. Love

E.R.

The baby, named Maria Anna after David's mother, was born June 27. A month later she was writing Anna and Jim from Hyde Park that it was "fun watching Edna & David's baby grow! They come next Saturday for a week & I look forward to it. . . ."

August 23, 1961

Dear Edna,

I find I can pay all of my share for the furnace. So here it is. Much love,

E.R.

Her handwriting was becoming more scratchy. Even to her closest friends she dictated replies to Maureen, interspersed, when she was able to manage it, with longhand notes.

55 East 74th
Tuesday Sept 12th

Dearest Hick,

You were a dear but you shouldn't write letters when you are so busy.

Nannine is very happy with all you sent her & I hope the publishers are! That was a nice check! [Uncle] David is [word undecipherable] & I'm sure he was pleased.

I'm glad he's not been lonely.

. . .

E.R.

55 East 74th Street
Oct 14th

Dearest Hick,

Thanks ever so much for your letter & the birthday wishes. I am so glad the book is done & now perhaps if I pick you up Thursday at 1:15 you'll have lunch with me? I'll stop by on my way & you can tell Marge [Entrup, her H.P. housekeeper].

Sorry if she was upset, but I didn't want a birthday cake & didn't even know if she got home. . . .

I ought to say you can quote anything you like but you do have to get Harper's permission.

I'm supposed to be in L.A. but my flight was cancelled!

A world of love & thanks
E.R.

Oct 14th

Joe dearest,

I felt the night of the 10th was the only birthday celebration I would have, but you know birthday or not anytime you can come in I'd love it & don't ever hesitate again. I love your birthday wish & I certainly hope I'll be with you for sometime to come.

. . .

E.R.

55 East 74th Street
October 28

David dear,

On your birthday on the 31st you will be surrounded by family and friends who love and admire you and I will be happy among them. This is just a little pre-birthday note as I thought you would rather have your gifts tonight. The enclosed is *not* for the foundation tho' I hope I can give to that later, this please put in a car fund not to be used till you have to get a new car! I like to feel I have a little something which you can use so constantly.

. . .

E.R.

A sure measure of her ebbing strength was her absence from the U.S. delegation to the sixteenth session of the General Assembly, which opened in September. Although she had nominally served at the five-day emergency session in August convened to hear Tunisia's complaint against France's armed presence in Bizerte, she no longer felt up to a regular assignment. She kept abreast of the issues, wrote the President, dined with Stevenson, but did not participate.

She was listed as a "special advisor" to the delegation. Adlai had asked her:

September 8, 1961

Dear Eleanor,

Do you have any objection to our listing you as a Special Advisor to the United States Delegation to the General Assembly?

I recall that during our last talk you seemed willing to be included as an advisor on my assurances that the duties will be in your discretion. I hope this is still the case.

I have your letter about Eddie Roddan* and will do what I can.

Affectionately,
Adlai

* Edward L. Roddan covered the White House for the International News Service in F.D.R. days. He worked for the Democratic National Committee in the 1936 campaign.

Kennedy spoke at the General Assembly, and she sat among the seats reserved for his family, behind Jacqueline, and afterward wrote: "A change has come over the President. I don't think anyone in looking at him thinks first nowadays 'This is a young man' . . . I was delighted that the emphasis of his speech was on disarmament. . . ."

Having declined to serve on the delegation because of lack of strength, she proceeded to move about the country characteristically, flying to Newfoundland at the President's request, making speeches for Colston Leigh and the AAUN on the West Coast, in the Rockies, the Midwest, and the South. Had she secretly hoped Adlai would insist she serve on the delegation?

It was a troubled autumn internationally. The Soviet Union, after unilateral abandonment of the U.S.-USSR moratorium on nuclear tests, exploded superbombs, one of fifty megatons, the next one even larger—an "act of intimidation," Mrs. Roosevelt called it—and followed these terror-inspiring acts with the erection of the Berlin wall. Then, when Dag Hammarskjold died mysteriously in a plane crash in the Congo, shock waves jolted the U.S. government. As usual the practical men who insisted on an answer in kind were confronted by the more visionary, whose suggestions were denounced as appeasement. Although she was on the sidelines she pleaded with Kennedy not to abandon efforts to negotiate with the Soviet Union, especially to resist "the usual pressures being put on the government by certain scientists, by the Pentagon" and others who opposed a treaty to end nuclear tests. "Negotiations must go on, and that means give and take, and we had better be preparing our people not to look upon anything which pleases both sides as appeasement on our part."

The President replied ambiguously. The problem of nuclear tests had his close personal attention and he had little use for those who equated negotiation with appeasement, he assured her.

She intervened, also, in regard to Vietnam. After the Taylor-Rostow report to the President, which recommended the dispatch of military "advisers" to Vietnam, a worried Ben Cohen came to the AAUN's executive board to urge that the issue be taken to the UN. The board decided to send a delegation to the President to urge such a course of action. She joined the delegation. The group, which also included Ben Cohen, Clark Eichelberger, Norman Cousins, and Oscar de Lima, was referred by the White House to the State Department. There it was informed that the department had considered going to the United Nations but after talking with Dag Hammarskjold had concluded that the United States could not get the action there it wanted. "They decided they could handle the situation better alone," commented Ben Cohen on the episode eight years later. "Had they gone to the United Nations I am sure they would not have gotten what they wanted. But the American people might have had time and opportunity to learn into what a tragic pit they were being asked to leap."

"Mrs. R. in jolly form," my notes read on New Year's Eve. Fjr. and Sue were there full of tales about the Kennedy White House. Stevenson had spent several hours with President Kennedy and Jacqueline at Glen Ora outside Washington. When Adlai told the President about the offers to him to run for the Senate from Illinois, Kennedy said, "I told him we needed him in the UN and that I counted on him to stay on." At Hyde Park, just before the champagne was offered around at midnight—

> Mrs. R. asked how the President and Stevenson got on. Jackie was there when the President told Adlai he wanted him at the UN. Fjr. asked her how the chemistry was between the two. Jackie had replied Jack can't bear being in the same room with him.

One way to see the people she had come to know in her many years of public and private involvement—she was now seventy-seven—was to have them in groups. A luncheon with the "cousins" was a regular and long-standing event. So was the gathering of the newspaperwomen who had covered her. Fortunately, she had the ability—it was a Roosevelt trait—to immerse herself in the concerns of the person she was with, even if it was only for a few minutes, and the impact of her personality was such that the encounter became a vivid event in the lives of the people she met.

A letter from Anna to her mother, who had gone to Israel, showed that getting onto Mrs. Roosevelt's calendar had its difficulties.

Feb. 18, 1962

Mummy darling,
    I hope this meets you in Israel . . .

    . . .

    We drove Dorothy Roosevelt [Eleanor's former sister-in-law] to the ADA [Americans for Democratic Action] Roosevelt Dinner this last Saturday evening and she asked if she could drive you to the airport from our house the morning of March 30. She pointedly said this was the only way she'd get a chance to talk to you. With this last I agree because I'm going to be selfish enough not to invite her over the afternoon before nor for breakfast the next morning—unless you insist! . . .

Anna

Before she went abroad in February she went to Washington three times—on an AAUN mission, to a meeting of advisers to the Peace Corps, and to sessions of the Status of Women Commission. On her return from the latter she flew with Maureen to Paris and London, where they were joined by Edna for a visit to Israel. An undated letter to David showed what a difficult patient she might be.

Hyde Park
Wed night

Dearest David,

As you see Jim [Halsted] asks I send you the enclosed.

I was quite well before when I came through those areas. I am glad to have you ask anything for yourself but I hate to have people bothered about me. I should stay home if I can't travel like anyone else and please don't do this kind of thing again for me.

Much love dear,

E.R.

There was the usual vigilant attention to her friends' concerns.

Hotel Crillon
February 15th [1962]

Dearest Edna and David,

I think of you much and hope all goes well with you and that this Sat and Sunday will be fairly free so that you can enjoy each other and little Maria.

I was tired on the first day here and I worked hard so today is the first day I begin to feel normal. We worked all morning on the second show and both are I think good. This p.m. I had several people for tea and the Mochs' wanted to be remembered to you and invite us to tea on our return.

I dined with the Finletters tonight and spent an hour before with a man who will interview me for the Jewish radio tomorrow a.m.

. . .

E.R.

David was to meet them in St. Moritz on their return from Israel.

Claridge's
Sunday, Feb 18th

Dearest Joe & Trude,

The days in Paris are over. We saw no disturbance tho' they talk of plastic bomb explosions, we saw none, but soldiers stood outside the T.V. studio where we spent much of our time. Henry was a dear, but we worked hard & I did nothing else but rest! One day some people came to tea, otherwise those of us who worked together ate in different good, little French restaurants & enjoyed the food.

Maureen enjoyed Paris I think but knows no one here & will find it lonely & dull I fear. Lady Reading met us & I am lunching with her today & dining with Lord Elibank so she is all alone.

Trude dear, I read the memo & have sent it off with a letter to Ribicoff.* I know this is another way to cut the budget so I told him if he did not want to speak to the President to send it back & I would ask him if he really felt the small amount of money saved would compensate for the loss. Teaching people to live "our way" may not be such a good idea either. I don't know how much Stevenson has to do with foreign aid tho' he must know about it. There is no harm in sending it to him however.

Joe dear, do tell me what happens to the Post.

. . .

E.R.

A welcome note for Edna, who arrived on February 19.

Claridge's

Edna dearest,

You may be here before I get home. Just use the sitting room and I'll be here soon. You are so welcome. I can hardly wait to see you.

My love
E.R.

Claridge's
Feb. 21st

Dearest Trude,

. . .

Tell Joe I hope this raising money doesn't last long for he & Jimmy must find it hard to run a paper.

On the end of this week or next[,] one of the recordings done in Paris will be on & I'd love to know if you think it good. Henry [Morgenthau] III said you would get a postcard. I dined with Lady Reading last night to meet 6 ladies in policy making government positions & today I lunched with her in the House of Lords & met [words indecipherable]. I hope they come to the U.S. before I forget them! Louis [Morley Cochrane] & her husband came to tea yesterday & asked warmly after you both.

. . .

E.R.

A cable to David: THINKING OF YOU 23RD EDNA WELL LEAVING FOR ISRAEL LOVE ROOSEVELT.

In Israel there was time only for postcards on the dynamism of that little country.

* Abraham Ribicoff, Secretary of HEW.

St. Moritz
Sunday March 4th

Dearest Joe,

Many thanks for your letter. It seems to me that you might speak to Fjr. about the President & ask him to ask the President. Lamsdell Christie should be back from Arizona now, if you & Jimmy can't reach him sooner & still want to see him on my return I can ask him to lunch.

What I read of the student pilgrimage* sounded worth while & I will be interested to hear your Johnny's reactions.

I hope you do the article Boland wants. What magazine would you do it for?

All I've learned about Europe's reaction to Moscow is meagre. Mme. Tabouis thinks the meeting there on March 5th or 6th will ratify Khrushchev's attitude or condemn & a soft or hard policy will follow. Ben Gurion was optimistic about everything. I can tell you about more conversations but whether any have much value I don't know.

. . .

Devotedly
E.R.

Kulm Hotel
St. Moritz
Tuesday March 6th, '62

Anna darling,

. . . This is no longer considered "the season" & many are leaving but I find it very pleasant & have never had such a good rest. I believe the same could be had in places at home & probably no more expensive! The air does give you a lift & no one has colds tho' they are wet every day. . . .

Needless to say I have endless begging letters in German which Maureen can't read & when I'm stumped we have to get David to decipher but I'm being hard hearted for the number of rich, arrogant Germans I've seen in this place makes one feel they are simply able to take care of their own.

There is much speculation about the meeting in Russia these 2 days & whether Khrushev's [sic] milder policy will be approved or whether China's position will be upheld in which case I suppose we can expect more & more difficulties. . . .

Mother

* Students from secondary schools and colleges, mostly in the Northeast, joined black children of Birmingham, Alabama, who were boycotting classes in support of Martin Luther King, Jr. Jonathan and a friend, juniors at Putney, a progressive school in southern Vermont, went.

Easter was another occasion for an exchange of presents, especially with the Gurewitsches.

> 55 East 74th Street
> [Easter 1962]

Edna dearest,

As Bonnier tells me they are discontinuing their china I got their extra plates for you and David for Easter. The bag is for you & I hope you'll like to use it this Spring. The bunny is obviously for Maria and give her a kiss for me.

I shall miss you this weekend but for David I know it is more restful to be here unless he can have at least 3 or 4 nights. Thanks again for my lovely gifts and I hope I catch a glimpse of you all (as I pass) Tuesday p.m. I should get here 4:30 and we leave 5:45.

A world of love to you and David and Maria,

> E.R.

On her return her engagement book for March had read "dine Esther" and "Edna & David party" and two trips to Washington for the day. She was back in Washington twice in April for meetings of the Commission on the Status of Women, the second time "Recording with President for Status of Women," lecture trips to California and Kansas, yet she was always adjuring her friends not to work too hard. "I seem to be swamping you with letters," she wrote to Adlai, forwarding an appeal from the South Moluccas, "& I apologize for taking your time. . . ."

My mother, living at "a guest house for the elderly" in Long Beach, Long Island, amused Trude, who told the story to Mrs. R. She claimed she was eighty-six, four years more than she was. "Why?" my sister asked her. "So the men will not bother me," she said mischievously. She died May 15, and I wrote Mrs. Roosevelt to explain why I had not asked her to come to the funeral services before burial. They were in Rockville Centre, Long Island, a long haul.

> 55 East 74th Street
> Sunday

Joe dearest,

You did not have to write. I understood as I always have with you. I would have been glad just to be near & hold your hand for a minute—but perhaps for the rest of your family it was better not to have me there. It may have given them more comfort to be with you & have a sense of unity. I think you did all you could for your Mother & to go as she did was for her merciful.

My thoughts are with you & my love always. I look forward to Thursday evening.

Devotedly
E.R.

The death of parents always touched her own deepest memories of the death of her mother when she was eight and of her adored father when she was ten. These memories enabled her to come closer to those around her who went through comparable experiences. But the process also worked in reverse. Present sympathies kept her own memories fresh. She made the lives of others—whether they were Hudson River gentry or Jews, blacks, Puerto Ricans—her own and her own theirs, and experienced the true meaning of kinship. In a discussion of friendship, the philosopher Immanuel Kant wrote, "It is not man's way to embrace the whole world in his good will; he prefers to restrict it to a small circle." Yet Kant also insists, wrote the philosopher Robert G. Hazo, that "any tendency to close the heart to all but a selected few is detrimental to true spiritual goodness, which reaches out after a good-will of universal scope."

Perhaps those who, on the assumption they were helping her husband her strength, did not call on her for help did her a disservice, for she was part of that "small minority" who were able "to find happiness along the path of love."

XXVII

"All Goodbyes Are Poignant Now"

A T THE END of June David went to serve on the hospital ship *Hope* in Trujillo, Peru. He was there for three weeks. In case her illness flared up she was to go to Dr. George Hyman, a specialist in blood diseases. Her letters to David were tender and solicitous for him and his family—not for herself. She had wanted him to go. She was ill enough at this time to require a blood transfusion at Dr. Hyman's, yet also kept active especially where tradition was involved.

Mrs. Roosevelt wrote on envelope to this letter: "David—To Be Read On The Plane *Not Before.*"

> 55 East 74th Street
> Thursday night

David dearest,

I've just seen you for the last time I surmise till you come home so I write you these lines which I hope you will read when you are on the plane and all the hurry and worry is over. You will begin then to enjoy and savour the adventure of the trip and I hope it proves to be all you hope for and that you return refreshed in spirit and less fundamentally weary physically than you are and have been.

To me all goodbyes are more poignant now, I like less and less to be

long separated from those few whom I deeply love. Above all others you
are the one to whom my heart is tied and I shall miss you every moment
till we meet again and I shall come down with Edna and Maria to greet
you on your return. I will do all I can to help Edna, for I know this
separation will be hard for her to bear.

On your side will you try to think out how to lighten your week a little?
A woman needs companionship and a little more leisure than you have
been able to find this past winter. We are all selfish when we love someone and want the one we love to give to us personally part of the time.

And now an end to preaching! I know what drives you have, and I am
deeply appreciative and admiring of the standards and values you set for
yourself. God bless you and keep you wherever you are, my prayers and
thoughts will be with you constantly. Au revoir, and my love always.

                                                                E.R.

Enjoy life and take care of yourself.

                                                        [Hyde Park]
                                                        July 3rd, 1962

Dearest David,

There is nothing for me to tell you as life here you know is uneventful.
Edna and the baby are a joy.

It was wonderful to get your cable and Edna got a letter this morning
and looks very happy. Her days are filled by the baby with some reading
and sleep. She is eating a little better. The baby seems to like the crib and
I think has had no bad nights. She eats well and seems happy.

David [Gray] is well but looks a little frailer to me. He is as alert and
keen as ever and seems to enjoy guests.

I know Edna misses you and I can only hope that we can give her some
distraction to help her bear the five weeks!

Never did I feel stronger or better so you have no worries where I am
concerned.

My love to you always and enjoy your work.

                                                                E.R.

                                    from the Hope Ship, Trujillo, Peru
                                    Wednesday 7/4/62

Dearest Mrs. R.—

Thank you for your good letter. Yesterday it came, the first mail since I
left. There is more and more pressure of work, what for I am not quite
clear about. A daily clinic of proportion and kind you have seen in India
or Karachi or Marakesh. Only they come from far away to see the "famous specialist". Each time one opens the door there is a fight to get in

and for us to keep the many mothers with Polio babies out, except for one. Much, much polio. I have 18 prospective therapists to teach 2 hours every day and medical students and where will it lead once I am gone? . . .

Just my love.

I hear that by now you had your transfusion—I hope.

I also hope Anna is better. I was so dead tired when I saw her that I could barely speak.

Give my love to Edna and to Uncle David,

Your
David

And my love to Maureen.

On July 4 there was a picnic lunch at the pool outside the stone cottage that she, Nan, and Marion had built in the twenties and that now belonged to the John Roosevelts. There were various grandchildren about, "Uncle" David, then ninety-two, Edna Gurewitsch and the Lashes, the Soviet cultural attaché and his wife. As usual the Declaration of Independence was read, at the end of which for the benefit of the younger ones she enumerated the signatories who were among their ancestors. Suddenly "Uncle" David was heard accusing her of trying to "indoctrinate" the Russians.

"You should put fingers in your ears," he said to the somewhat embarrassed Soviet couple.

"No, no, David," she demurred. "I was only trying to indoctrinate my grandchildren."

Friday July 6th [1962]

Dearest David,

Edna is very happy with your letters and only afraid that now that you are on the Ship, they may take longer to reach her. She had dreaded this first week and thought it would seem very long but she tells me it has gone more quickly than she dared anticipate. The baby is sleeping well and eating well and seems her happy self.

. . .

I went in and had the type blood taken and on Monday the 9th at 10 A.M. they will do the transfusion at the office and let me go at 12 so I hope to leave the house on the return drive at 2:30.

The Wiltwyck picnic has just come to an end and was a great success I think. Mr. Stix got a magician to come and perform for them but so many asked for the story, that I've promised to go over some afternoon later and read and provide ice cream and cake so it will be like another party!*

. . .

I think Edna is really getting rested. I couldn't feel better. Tell me how you are. Much love

E.R.

July 10
[1962]

David dearest,

Edna reported that all goes well but you are not too luxurious. I only hope it is comfortable enough so you can sleep and that the food is fairly good.

Edna looks and feels better and the baby is adorable but I wish she'd learn to let Edna sleep til 7:30, just now she's taken to getting up at 5:30.

I had the transfusion last Monday, 2 full bags, so I should need nothing more for a long time. Anna reports a little improvement. Helen Robinson† died last Sunday but because her daughters were cruising in Greece the funeral will not be till Thursday. A long time to wait. I've left directions for burial the next day, Maureen suggested that it's awkward if there is a gravediggers strike, so we must hope to avoid that calamity!

. . .

We've been having a bad time over Elliott again, but I left it to the boys and they are coping quite successfully, I think, tho' I don't believe Patty or Elliott enjoy it.

. . .

E.R.

July 14th [1962]

David dearest,

Edna says mail has been slow in reaching you and two weeks are now over. I hope Edna's father and mother will be up this coming week.

I shall go to Westbrook to visit with Esther Lape on Monday and spend the night in N.Y. and return Tuesday.

. . .

I am trying to lose a few pounds and told Dr. Hyman the diet I would follow and he thought it would be o.k.

---

* A school for troubled boys, mostly black, then located across the river. The entire school came to picnic at the outdoor fireplace behind her cottage and the boys loved to hear her read "How the Elephant Got His Trunk" from Rudyard Kipling's *Just So Stories*. Thomas Stix was her agent for television and radio.

† She was the daughter of Franklin's half brother, "Rosy" Roosevelt, and had married Theodore Douglas Robinson, a son of "Aunty" Corinne. She lived in Hyde Park in a house overlooking the Hudson just south of the big house.

Dr. and Mrs. Bunche and their son are here for the night. Uncle David is asking Dr. B. all kinds of questions that he doesn't think I know how to answer.

. . .

E.R.

July 18
1962

David dearest,

. . . Your letter to me seemed to indicate an impossible amount of work. I'm afraid that having left exhausted you will return even more exhausted. This can't be good for you. Your baby needs you and is so extraordinary but she has many years in which your guidance is essential. I realize more every day how much Edna needs and depends on you. I do not find her very strong, she hasn't half the endurance I had at her age. You are essential to this small family and I surmise no less important to Grania in the next few years, though she would probably not acknowledge it.

. . .

I work with Miss Denniston* off and on and the book goes forward, not as well as I would like but it moves.

I stayed in N.Y. Monday night to dine at Mary Lasker's with Congressman Rooney and I asked him if he thought Representative Gross and the 124 Congressmen really understood that they had given the Communists what they could never have won for themselves, and his answer was "the fools, of course not." That is rather discouraging, isn't it? . . .

E.R.

On July 22 Trude and I received the last longhand letter from her. The effort to use a pen had become too much for the woman whom her son Fjr. described as "the writingest lady of our times."

55 East 74th Street
July 22d

Dearest Joe,

Here is my check for Jonathan's [school] next year. I am so happy to have a small share in his education & am very proud of him.

I think he will do well & be of use to the world because you & Trude are his parents!

All my love
E.R.

---

* She was helping with the book *Tomorrow Is Now,* published posthumously.

A typed letter to Trude, who was on Martha's Vineyard.

55 East 74th Street
July 26, 1962

Dearest Trude:

It was lovely to get the nice long letter from you today and I am particularly glad to think of Jonathan arriving on Saturday for a week with Joe. . . .

From all we can hear from the State Department, things in Peru on missions like the Hope ship are safe and Edna is reassured, though she will be enormously relieved to have David home.

I don't know when anything has pleased me so much as to think of you and Joe being alone in your house on the Island and having time to do things together.

. . .

The Island always seems to attract interesting people and you sound as though you were all having a good time . . .

Fr. [Father] Ford [a Catholic priest of liberal views] has been here for a couple of days and Mr. Christie and his family have just been here for lunch. On the whole, life goes along rather peacefully. I have to go down for the Democratic Voters tomorrow but will be back on Friday.

Maria has really grown a lot and I think really looks very well for her time here.

With much love to you and Joe,

Devotedly,
E.R.

She went to New York to campaign for the reform group, the Committee for Democratic Voters. Her strength was ebbing but her philosophy was that if she did not do it who would, and if she did not perform these little chores of helpfulness it would be a form of death. So she went, delighted that her coming meant something to people.

She visited Dr. Hyman's office on July 31. "Home to bed," her engagement book read. Five days later, "Sat. Aug. 4 'ER Hospital,' " Maureen had written in it. I have two journal entries about what had happened.

August 6, 1962. . . . Maureen called me about 4 yesterday and said that Mrs. R. had called, that her temperature was up again and she didn't feel up to seeing me. She had strength enough only to do the column. When I talk with Maureen later she doubted Mrs. R. would get home today, but she was after F jr. about having a station wagon available in which to go home. When I went in to see her Sunday she was almost in sparkling spirits. She kept me there chatting about the Vineyard, Representative Rooney, her car bills, her hospital bills for things done to her which she hated. She said she had had a transfusion after David had left and that it was supposed to take the place of injections. Three weeks ago when she began to feel badly, she thought she could shake it off; it was a trial, moreover, to get in touch with a doctor who was not her regular one. It finally got to the point where if she saw a chair, she couldn't keep herself out of it, she felt so badly. Her first transfusion in town last week was a disaster and produced the terrible reaction that came to a climax after David's return when her fever went up to 105½ and David took her to the hospital in a stretcher and ambulance.

When Trude saw her last week she was very depressed and somehow tied her illness together with Elliott and his new wife Patricia. She described her dream—Elliott and Hall were combined into one and were piled upon her. She repeatedly said she no longer wanted to go on living. Patty had called and said she and Elliott would need $1500 a month and it was up to the family to find it. . . . Mrs. R. turned over to the three other boys the job of getting Elliott out of his jam. It was, she said, an admission of defeat. The result of their settling in Hyde Park, David said, would be that Mrs. R. would stop going there. She could scarcely wait until they left her apartment when they were East.

Two days after this entry I saw Mrs. Roosevelt again.

August 8, 1962. Maureen called last night. Said Mrs. R. was in better spirits. She had been allowed up and out of bed for half an hour. But she still "looks very spent" and her fever during the day hovered between normal and 102. David said something about her "sedimentation rate" being ten times more than it should and Maureen didn't know what that meant. But she was well enough to argue with Maureen causing the latter to tease her, "listen, you're feeling better." "Joe must think I'm terrible," she remarked, "but I'll be well enough to be civil tomorrow." . . .

When I saw her this afternoon, she said she was much better, but clearly was weaker and wearier than when I saw her Sunday. She is planning on going to Campo [for the dedication of the F.D.R. Memorial Bridge connecting the island with the mainland] and Tubby has already left. But I cannot see how she will be strong enough. . . . She talked again about the course of her illness. She hadn't been well all month but did not go to Dr. Hyman's until she came down last week for the education meeting. She then went to see the doctor. She needed a transfusion, he said. Could she come for it the next day? "You go right home and go to bed," were his final words. She was never happier than to get home and have to get into bed and not feel the next morning she would have to dress. Then she had the transfusion which had such a bad reaction. She had not wanted it. Her first reaction had been that David was coming home Sunday and couldn't she wait until then? she asked the doctor. It was at that point he firmly told her to go home and get into bed.

She balked the night she was taken to the hospital but David insisted. When the two large men came in to carry her down to the ambulance she was so delirious she did not recognize Jimmy who notified by Maureen had come right up. The tests that morning had been very disagreeable but she had only one more. . . .

She hoped to be home by Friday and off to Campo by Saturday. Her constitution no longer was able to take the punishment she normally meted out to it, she would have to ease up. Adlai had wanted her to go out to Wisconsin for Gaylord Nelson [for the Senate] but she had had to cancel and was cancelling a lot. . . .

She would drive down from Campo with Trude, but David had taken plane seats for her and him and Edna. David does not find motoring restful and I do, she explained. She should have remembered the trouble these virus pneumonia had given her in the past.*

A longhand note on the letterhead of The Towers in the Waldorf-Astoria where the government maintained an apartment for the head of the U.S. Mission:

Please get out of there quickly! And *please, please* let me know if there is anything I can do.

Adlai

P.S. I'm hoping you can come to dinner with Martha Gellhorn and Tom Matthews on the 12th,

AES

August 12, 1962 [typed]

Dearest Trude:

I got your sweet letter the morning I returned from the hospital and I want to thank you for all your kind thoughts.

We got off easily and I did not get over tired. Campobello is lovely and I count on your coming over next weekend and driving down with me to Boston on Monday.

Joe came to the hospital and I loved seeing him.

Devotedly,
E.R.

Let us know flight to Bangor & Tubby will meet you there.

* Mrs. Gurewitsch: "David enjoyed motoring. . . . He took plane reservations on this occasion to make the trip to Campo as quick for Mrs. R. as possible."

Campobello
August 13, 1962 [typed]

Dearest Sis:

I am sure you are anxious to know how the trip went. Everything went smoothly and while I am feeling stronger all the time I imagine it will be quite a while before I feel entirely normal.

. . . I look forward more than I can say to seeing you and Jim on the 23rd [at Hyde Park]. Come as early as you can . . .

Much love,
Mother

Trude later wrote Paul Tillich, who had married us, about Mrs. Roosevelt at Campobello.

For the first time that morning she walked up and down in front of the Campo house "so that I can manage the steps of the Scarlett house" [Bishop Scarlett of the Methodist Episcopal Church was living in retirement at Castine, Maine], she said. She was terribly frail and complained that she had forgotten how to take a deep breath and had to learn again. She said that she learned that Friday night (when she had 105.6 temperature) how easy it was to die. She was just slipping away without regret or pain, and she was pleading with David to let her go.

We drove down the Maine coast to do once more the things she always loved to do. We visited Bishop Scarlett and his wife, Leah. We met an old friend, Molly Dewson. . . . Then we went to a place called Perry's Nuthouse where Mrs. R., Joe and I used to stop to buy wild strawberry preserves. She was too weak to get out of the car, and when we came back, having purchased what she wanted us to get, was only vaguely aware of what was going on.

On the long drive to Boston she hardly spoke and when she did it was so faint we could hardly understand her. In Boston Henry III came in. From Boston on the way to Hyde Park she stopped for a visit with Esther Lape, one of her oldest friends, and then she went on to Val-Kill, where she had a few days where she even worked—but after Labor Day the fevers and the chills and the blood transfusions and endless injections took over and the lonely descent began.

She was in New York at the end of August determined to tour Queens, as she had promised the Committee of Democratic Voters, for a number of reform candidates. "I must have picked up a bug of some kind," she explained to the young law student who came to chauffeur her around. "My head is heavy, and if I go you'll have to steady me when I get out of the car." At the end of the evening she confided to the reform Democrats that she hoped the next morning to go to Hyde Park and beat her illness by remaining in bed. She preferred that to seeing a doctor, she explained.

Anna and Jim were living on the outskirts of Detroit and Jim was the chief of medicine at the Metropolitan Hospital. "You sounded so wonderfully chipper on the phone last Monday evening," Anna wrote her mother after the Labor Day weekend, "that you made us both feel happy—happy in the knowledge that you really are getting stronger all the time." That was the impression she first made on Trude and me the next weekend when we stopped at Hyde Park on the way back to New York from Putney School.

September 9, 1982. Arrived Friday evening, Sept. 7 around 7 p.m. We were going to Johnny and Anne's, Maureen informed us. Mrs. R. came down around 7:30 and said that while we were waiting for Uncle David we might as well have drinks at her house. She asked for her usual dubonnet. She seemed in good shape, quite vigorous of voice but slow and deliberate in her movements and we did not like the flush and pallor of her cheeks. She had had a good day, gone to New York, met with Nannine and Uncle David about revisions of his book, and with a publisher about Ellie's [her niece] doing drawings for a book and with Tom Stix about her television show. She was remarkably untired after such a day.

At Johnny and Anne's . . . Johnny, who is heading up the Nationalities Division for Nelson Rockefeller, said Bob [Morgenthau, who had stepped down as U.S. attorney to run against Rockefeller for Governor] had been promised a judgeship. Mrs. R. said no but that the Attorney General had indicated that if Bob did run, President wanted him back as U.S. Attorney if he lost. . . .

Marge [Entrup, Mrs. R.'s housekeeper] told Trude that after Mrs. R. had a bad spell she announced there would be no more big parties and that Marge would be glad to hear that. She then added casually there would be 14 for breakfast. In Mrs. R.'s book, Trude explained, that wasn't a big party.

Breakfast Saturday morning was awful. She came down breathing with difficulty and when she sat down at the table trembled violently. She couldn't hold a fork or lift the cup of tea which might have helped her. She would lean over the cup, try to sip and not allow any of us to help. She blamed it on sleeping on the porch for it had been a cool night. Finally Trude insisted on bringing her a shawl and we persuaded her to go into Tommy's room and sit by the fire. She hadn't allowed Lester [Entrup] to turn on the heat before then. David later explained she hated deferring to her illness. . . .

David and family arrived at 11:30. By then Mrs. R. in living room at work with Mrs. Denniston on Tomorrow Is Now. She would not allow David to take her temperature. Poor Mrs. Denniston became more and more uncomfortable and left at 12:15 instead of 1. She then submitted to the thermometer which showed 101. . . . Mrs. R. said she would not sleep on the porch again. As so often when she says these things we had the feeling she was saying a final goodbye to another of the things she loved to do. . . .

I had a long talk with David Gu. about Mrs. R. He said that all they could do was try to control the situation with cortisone. They were unable to cure it. Basically there was something wrong with her blood-producing mechanism—aplastic anemia—which showed itself by the swelling of lymph gland, at the moment in the lung which was why she had such difficulty breathing. Just before they left for Campo Fjr. came and told David he was taking charge and would transmit any messages to the rest of the family, including Jimmy. The only helpful one had been Jimmy, he said.

Jim Halsted, in David's view, perhaps a good administrator and researcher, but ignorant of medical advances that were common knowledge in the medical profession. He was glad Jim wasn't around. (Jim thinks David not too hot either!) . . .

When Trude called to tell Mrs. R. that her mother had died, she said that she didn't want to go on, that it was so easy to pass on, but Uncle David said Mrs. R. had told him she had regained her will to live. Had she said that, I wondered, because it would have been too difficult for David otherwise. . . .

After lunch she went up to nap and when she came down for Charley Curnan's surprise party, she was normal again.

After the party we sat in Tommy's living room before dinner. Mrs. R. worked at her check book (the night before after we had returned from Johnny's she had happily discovered how to reconcile a $1600 discrepancy between her check book and bank statement). There was a call from Congressman Manny Celler's aide. He wanted to tell her that Celler on T.V. was going to propose her as the Democratic candidate for the Senate. "Under no circumstances would I run," she commented firmly. "I don't believe in old people running."

Walter and May Reuther came by after dinner. They were on their way back from Putney. Mrs. R. said she wanted to use Walter's idea— that economic aid not military was the way to stiffen the borderlands against the communists. Could she use the idea and credit it to him?

. . . Walter interested Mrs. R. He is stimulating and thinks in large terms and we didn't break up until 11.

Her decline was evident, even to those who saw her daily. The Reuthers were deeply upset, and though the conversation with Walter kept her going, her inability to rise to it was a measure of her descent.

XXVIII

Unafraid of Death

ANNA HAD RESIGNED her job at the Metropolitan Hospital in Detroit. Though Eleanor was almost seventy-eight and Anna fifty-six, their roles toward each other never shifted. Eleanor was still advising, cheering up her daughter.

A letter to Anna, her last.

> 55 East 74th Street
> September 12, 1962

Darling Anna,

I will be calling you some time soon. But as you could not read if I wrote I am just dictating this to say your letter reached me with all its changes [in jobs]. I am not sure that in the long run these will not be beneficial. I am sure there is more interesting work to do.

I am looking forward to seeing you both on October 7 and you will let me know later the flight Tubby is to meet.

> Much love,
> Mother

> 55 East 74th Street
> September 14, 1962 [typed]

Dearest Hick,

I was glad to get your letter and I do hope the blood sugar leveled off a little bit lower and you don't have to take more Insulin. I'm happy if talking to Walter Reuther was helpful. I'll be back on Monday.

Love,
E.R.

Hick was doing a book about Reuther and as with so many of Hick's projects it was Eleanor who seemed to make it possible. Through all the pain of her final illness, Eleanor approached people always with the guiding impulse of how to be of help. My notes September 20, 1962:

One evening last week we were at Mrs. R's for dinner. Lady Reading who was staying with her came in toward the end of the evening. She told us about lunch with old Mrs. [Geraldine] Thompson, a former Dutchess County neighbor, now an eminent New Jersey Republican. She arrived with a bagful of projects she wanted Mrs. R. to undertake in the child care field, but Mrs. R. gently turned them away, one after the other. In desperation she finally asked Mrs. R. "and what do you do for the Audubon Society?" Mrs. R. had been out that day with Tubby, but found it difficult to leave the station wagon. She wanted to buy some sturdy chairs for the dining room, because, she said, Uncle David when he came down would find it difficult to sit on the rather frail ones she had. So she went to Kaltman's [a dealer in antique furniture] and told Tubby to go inside and send out Mr. Kaltman. She explained what she wanted and he brought chairs out to the sidewalk for her to inspect. . . .

We were up again Sunday for dinner before she went to the AAUN reception for the U.S. delegation to the 17th General Assembly. . . . David and Edna went to the AAUN with her. She sat on the dais for 2 hours and was miserable throughout.

We were there again for dinner Tuesday night and she was terribly listless and discouraged because the fever which she thought was gradually being brought under control was going up again. . . . When we left instead of saying goodnight, as we did, she said "goodbye." We were terribly depressed and Trude collapsed in the vestibule downstairs. She did not mean to give things up and stay in bed, she had told us, for fear that if she stopped it would be difficult to do them again afterwards but it had taken her one and a half hours to dress, she whispered in explanation.
. . .

When we got home Johnny [Roosevelt] called. He had seen his mother that afternoon and was terribly worried. Should he notify the other children? I didn't know what to say. He and Trude both felt that perhaps another doctor should be brought in. I said that was silly. David was consulting others and doing everything possible. Irene [her city housekeeper] was so unhappy that even she had begged Mrs. R. to let her doctor come to her. Why should she diet? she had asked us.

There were occasional moments of relief, more, perhaps, for those of us who came in and out than for her. A journal entry toward the end of September:

Last Sunday (Sept. 23) an Israeli delegation was due to go to Hyde Park —a pilgrimage to FDR's grave and lunch afterwards at Mrs. R's cottage. Mrs. R. suddenly remembered with horror she had some fresh pork in the freezer and Marge might serve it to the Israelis. She called Marge to learn she was planning on chicken.

She went back to Columbia Presbyterian hospital on September 26. On hearing the ill-omened news, Stevenson dashed up there.

September 30, 1962 [longhand]
Dearest Eleanor
     I have been getting regular bulletins from Maureen and *pray* it won't be long before I can come to see you—and what a long deferred visit it will be! How I wish that preparations for the General Assembly and all these trips to Washington had not interfered with the visit to Hyde Park we had planned before I went abroad! . . .
     The General Assembly is off to a better start than usual. . . .
     I love you dearly—and so does the whole world! But they can't *all* come to see you and perhaps I can when David gives me permission.
                                             Devotedly—
                                             Adlai

Jim and Anna came east and stayed at Mrs. Roosevelt's apartment. A team of specialists met regularly at the hospital to study the results of tests, but she was considered David's patient. It was he who had told Stevenson when he had come up to the hospital that she was not up to receiving visitors. Privately he told me she had not wanted to see him.

Oct. 5. David asked me to come up and talk with him at his office. He said he was not able to talk with members of the family about it—not even Jim Halsted. He outlined how Mrs. R's illness was developing. Several times his face sank into his hands. He got to the most recent episode. Her fever went up and stayed up, instead of the usual up and down pattern. He took her back to the hospital. In the middle of the night the thought came to him the rise in fever might have been caused by having taken her off streptomycin. They had done so because the side effects of the latter were affecting her sight and hearing. He decided on his own to put her back on streptomycin. The other doctors, including Jim, were opposed. Her fever came down but a cloud showed up in her lungs—he didn't know what it was—might be miliary TB.

. . . [H]e was against further tests. If they showed an ulcer or cancer they were unable to operate anyway. His problem was whether to decide on his own to have her taken home where she would be more comfortable. Other doctors on the panel had a professional bias against permitting a patient to go home as long as their illness remained undiagnosed. That was the way with professors. But even if the diagnosis was successful, it would not show anything they could do anything about.

When Trude saw Mrs. R on Sunday Mrs. R whispered to her there were so few people she really cared about—so few. But she was trying to interest herself in things. When I saw her Monday I tried to do most of the talking because she was so hot. She said Bob Morgenthau's press people [he was the Democratic candidate for Governor of New York] should be getting out stories to humanize him and he should be getting around town and really interest himself in how people lived.

Her condition was worsening, but the struggle went on between interest in life and readiness for death. No one dared mention her birthday, but she did, by being hostess, although absent, to a children's party given in her apartment. She asked Edna to bring Maria, aged sixteen months, and Trude's daughter-in-law, Elaine, to bring Christopher, aged five years, and Ann and Timothy Pratt to East 74th Street, where her housekeeper Irene had little birthday cakes, favors, and ice cream for them and two of her grandsons, Curtis and Johnny Boettiger, and their wives joined the group later for birthday toasts. Reverence for life and acceptance of death.

Journal notes made October 29:

I saw her at the hospital, October 15. Anna and Jim were in the lounge outside her room, conferring with two of the specialists on her case. When I went in Mrs. R said bitterly of the doctors, "they have me where they want me. They can do with me what they want, not what I want." She had told her nurse earlier, "I don't want to be disturbed for anything," and said to me when I came in, "I have the strangest kind of sleeping sickness, I just manage to read the papers." For the first time she was incoherent. . . .

She wants the tests over and to go home. "I am going to ask David to let me rejoin the human race."

They brought her home on the 18th. There were awful pictures in the newspapers. I went up to 74th Street on the 19th and talked with Anna who was quite hostile towards David. She said he had gone to pieces when he saw the photographers and reporters outside the house on the

way down from the hospital and had carried on in front of Mrs. R,
shouting and trying to order them away until she [Anna] went out and
took command. . . . She, Jim and David had heated arguments about
bringing another doctor in. When they insisted on it David stalked out,
"I'm *not* the doctor in charge," he exclaimed, and made himself inaccessible to them.

"You know when they wanted David off the case?" Edna asked when I interviewed her about these events. "At the very end when Mrs. Roosevelt was coma-
tose. Anna wanted her husband to be Mrs. Roosevelt's doctor. The week before she
died David came upstairs (at 55 East 74th Street) and started to shave. He looked
as if he had been punched in the stomach. 'They want me off the case,' he finally
said in explanation of his looks. 'What will you do?' I asked. 'Mrs. Roosevelt took
me on as her doctor. Only she can dismiss me.' "

Edna also described the course of Mrs. Roosevelt's final illness in some notes
she made at the time and which David gave me to read in 1971.

Wednesday, Oct. 17, 1962, 6:30 p.m.
David brought Mrs. Roosevelt home from the Medical Center today
at 12:45 p.m. David had originally proposed to Mrs. Roosevelt that she
come home tonight, when onlookers and press might not be around. But
she was so eager to return here that she insisted on early in the day. Last
night at 11, her nurse telephoned David on Mrs. Roosevelt's instructions,
saying Mrs. R. did not want to make the trip via ambulance, but wanted
to drive in her Jaguar (small), lifted by Tubby into the house. This was an
impossible idea as Mrs. Roosevelt cannot sit up for any length of time,
certainly not for the 30 minute drive. But dear David wanted very much
to accede as much as possible to Mrs. Roosevelt's wishes, so last night he
arranged [for] an "ambulette" . . .
David made endless preparations for her homecoming. It meant so
much to her. And he had given his word to her weeks ago, that she would
not die in the hospital.
Among David's preparation this morning were his efforts to protect
her from photographers. . . . David said she very much enjoyed the ride
home. It was a lovely autumn day. She mentioned, en route, that in the
following days, she would have Tubby (her impossible chauffeur) take her
for drives. This is not possible. But David said she "must rest" for a few
days . . .
When I returned from Abris's [Silberman], where I had gone this
afternoon, I was received by the startling but happy news that Mrs.
Roosevelt was inviting us to dinner tonight. Instant, automatic responses
pressed to mind—the fascinating, cozy dinners we have had in this house
as her guests. I was ill-prepared for the dying lady I saw tonight. A small

table was set in her bedroom. I kissed her. She was too weak to respond but soon gathered her strength to ask if I had any recent news of Grania. It was obvious she could not care about a reply, though I told her a sentence or two on the subject. David had arranged that all courses should be served at once as we should stay only 15 minutes. It was difficult for me to keep my control. Mrs. Roosevelt tried to manage her small meal on a bedtray by herself as best she could. She was so weak. Irene fed her dessert. . . . She has always hated to eat alone, and now that she is at home, invited David and me "to dine with her." . . .

As I left I heard Mrs. Roosevelt say clearly and well to David, "Tell Edna this is my first night [at home]. I shall be better tomorrow."

October 19. I spent the afternoon helping Maureen open and sort the countless birthday messages and get well letters which arrived for Mrs. Roosevelt. . . . Maureen showed me a lovely letter President Kennedy had written Mrs. Roosevelt on her birthday, October 11. . . . The President's letter was written by hand and delivered by a representative of his to the hospital.

Mr. Colston Leigh, Mrs. Roosevelt's lecture agent called for Elliott's number as he would like Elliott to take over some of Mrs. R's speaking engagements. . . .

Trude was there early in the day. Also Joe. Elliott will come for the weekend, and Franklin returns from a 5-day stay in London tomorrow. He just telephoned David. Maureen sent him daily night letters about his mother's condition.

Anna is as cold and efficient as the well-known cucumber. Not an ounce of sentiment is apparent.

I heard Mrs. R. tell Curtis that she has to start doing things for herself again. She dozed most of the day. There are three round-the-clock nurses. . . .

My own journal notes that I made on October 29 read:

When I saw Mrs. R. on Saturday, the 20th, (the day before she had not recognized me and talked mostly about how much she had slept) she was lucid and asked me "what day is today?" Anna said a heavy dosage of anti-biotics had brought her temperature down. Immediately she wanted to sit up, sign checks—sometimes she signed ROSEVELT—. . . . She was so glad to be home that her will to live has revived. Anna said David was playing "footsie" with them yesterday and this morning. He said he had to go to the hospital. Anna followed him up to his apartment. "We have to ask you some questions," she insisted. . . .

Jim Halsted got up the statement which Maureen read to the AP and

UP in which Mrs. R's condition is described fairly candidly. They issued it because so many people have assumed that Mrs. R's departure from the hospital meant she was getting well. . . .

October 21. A call from David out of the blue. "Mrs. R's situation 'unchanged.' Sometimes she is aware, but most of the time only a quarter there, thinking it's evening when it's morning and most of the time unaware where she is. She doesn't complain. Sometimes she says there's plaster on her legs, 'What are you doing with my legs?' she asks. She had a transfusion yesterday. I wasn't happy with it. It didn't help and gave her a fever as well as allergic reactions. A tough time for me because Jim Halsted insists somebody else should be in charge. I was willing to accede but then decided nobody could discharge me but Mrs. R. I owe it to her. I cannot bow out of it, especially at this stage of such extremis. There were always other people in on the case. Jim said I was too close that I was practically a member of the family. I said why didn't you think of this a year and a half ago. This is not the time to switch horses. I started to agree but then thought this would be a disloyal act. The one she trusts is me. I would have to transmit their orders in any case. I can only be dismissed by her." When I asked about Trude's and my visiting her, he said we should go for short visits.

October 22. When I saw Anna she said, "David came in yesterday and finally agreed to remain on the case out of loyalty to mother." Jim is staying on as liaison between Dr. H. and David. Dr. B. refused to come in—pleaded that he was too old, also that he had problems with David. A long time ago they had wanted David to bring someone else in. He had gone to Mrs. R. and she had said either David or no one. . . . I had wondered to myself what I would do if I had the responsibility for euthanasia. I felt that someone like Mrs. R who has always been in command of her destiny should not lose control of her fate because she is in the hands of the doctors. . . . Anna had talked with Jim about it. Nature must be allowed to take its course with the patient kept as comfortable as possible.

Edna's notes:

October 22. Mrs. Roosevelt is still the same. The house grows more oppressive. . . . There are great comings and goings of family members and Trude and Joe. Elliott came to New York. Franklin Jr. arrived from London and returned to Washington after having visited his mother. He will be back in N.Y. today. Franklin came up to our bedroom around noon yesterday to talk to David. He cried. He spoke of how appreciative

he and others are to David. He keeps the President informed about his
mother. . . .

The atmosphere in Mrs. Roosevelt's home has changed greatly besides
her heartbreaking illness. Anna Halsted has taken command of it, and
poor Maureen has had her feeling of contribution and years of carrying
responsibility taken away from her. . . . She is told firmly what to do.

There was another little drama of the doctors being played out behind the
scenes. I learned of it when I was doing interviews for *The Years Alone* and talked
with David Gurewitsch:

I made the diagnosis of TB and I was furthest away from my specialty in
doing so. Then after a week it showed up in the X-rays and still they [the
specialists] disagreed with me. But one girl, an X-ray specialist, said, "I
have seen this once before," and dug out the picture. Still they disagreed.
Only when her bone marrow culture came back three weeks later and
showed TB was everyone convinced. Autopsy showed TB but even autopsy said terminal TB involved the whole body—not finally TB of the
bone marrow but TB of the whole body.

But the TB diagnosis had first been suggested, David told me some nine
months later, by Dr. Moses Suzman of South Africa.

The second time Mrs. Roosevelt went to the hospital, David said, all
the doctors would meet at the hospital at 7 p.m. That particular day after
the doctors finished, he left the room feeling that Mrs. R. was being
given up as a dying woman. He then went to his dinner date. He was
seated between the guest of honor, Helen Suzman, the noted liberal
M.P. of South Africa, to whom he paid no attention because Ellie Gug-
genheimer on the other side was so diverting.

After dinner he was introduced to Dr. Suzman, a grouchy, rather
disagreeable man, who turned out to be a hemotologist. After a few
moments he asked Dr. Suzman whether he might describe the condition
of a patient of his and get his diagnosis. He did, and Suzman asked
whether they had taken a culture of the bone marrow. David said no. He
should, Suzman urged, because he had had seven cases with the symptoms described by David which turned out to be TB of the bone marrow.
He went home, said David, and was unable to fall asleep. Then he had a
vision of Mrs. R's chart during her first stay at the hospital when she had
arrived with a 106 temperature and after administration of a whole bat-
tery of drugs, the temperature had gone down dramatically and they all
had concluded that the drop had been due to cortisone.

But now David reasoned that night, one of the drugs had been streptomycin, and perhaps that had been the agent that brought Mrs. R's temperature down. He got out of bed and searched through his medical books but could find nothing. He was at the hospital early and went through its medical books and then ordered that Mrs. R. be placed on streptomycin and related drugs. Later he called Suzman and told him. But do you have a bone marrow culture? Suzman asked. Not yet, said David. Then stop the anti-biotics or they may mask the picture in the bone marrow culture. David did, but when he took it up at the doctors' conference and said it might be TB of the bone marrow, they all scoffed at him. It's a typical a-leukemia leukemia, said the blood specialist. It's a typical cancer, said the cancer man. It's not TB, said the TB man. He had had some political experience as a lobbyist working for WFUNA, David noted, so he went to work, beginning with the bacteriologist, and then Dr. B. swung over, saying Mrs. R. was, after all, David's patient. Later the bacteriologist called him. "Sit down, David," he said over the phone. The results of the culture had come in and they showed a positive for TB.

But as the autopsy showed, it was all too late. TB was so generalized through her system that it could not be stopped. One final element. Suzman had found out who David's patient was and called and said he should be permitted to see her. The family was violently opposed but he felt obligated to allow Suzman to come. But when he did, Mrs. R. was in a semi-coma and he left without any recommendations.

Lash journal:

October 23. Anna said Mrs. R. several times had said "I want to go now." David was wonderful. Told her mother "We are treating you for only one thing, the possibility it is tuberculosis. We are easing off on all other medications." She was doing her best to keep all the boys away. F.jr., Elliott, and especially [Elliott's wife] Paddy . . . As I went in to Mrs. R. Anna said to me, "We don't want her to talk. Tell that to Trude too. Just go in and wave your hand." Jim went in with me. Mrs. R. was taking oxygen. She recognized me and said "hello, Joe." When we went out Jim reported this to Anna.

Edna's notes:

October 25. . . . Mrs. R. had a good night. When David returned from Mrs. R this morning to have his breakfast, he said he told her about the Cuba blockade. We should try to interest Mrs. R in the world again, as she is very depressed, he said. Anna picked up this new idea to talk to her mother on subjects other than her mother's illness. Maureen will do the same. David promised Mrs. R. to send Joe over today "to tell her about the world." I called Trude to give the message. One dare not get too elated about a possible recovery. But one's heart *is* lighter.

Lash journal:

October 25. Trude called. Edna and Anna had both called. Mrs. R. had perked up, was quite lucid, even said at one point about something "this is utter nonsense." David said she had a chance. According to Edna, Mrs. R. wants me to come and brief her on the world situation. I got there at one. Anna was upstairs with Jimmy who had flown in and F jr. I went in. Mrs. R. talked but she wandered and I didn't know when she was talking about the world or herself. "Hello, Joe," she greeted me, and then said, "not anybody makes any sense" and followed that with "it'll never come together." Was she talking about the world, I wondered, for I had tried to describe the showdown over Cuba, or about her head and her difficulty in focussing. She stirred restlessly and unhappily, "All I want," she began and I thought she was going to say, was for them to get together. Instead she said "is to be turned over."

October 26. When I stopped in yesterday at 4 F jr. there and Anna. They showed me message phoned in by David that lab tests had shown the presence of TB bacilli in her marrow. Her chances had gone up "5000 percent," he asserted. He talked the same way with the newspapers. Anna agreed with the analysis Trude and I had made of what was happening. David must have promised Mrs. R. that when it was hopeless and she was helpless he would give her a knockout pill, but now that it was happening and with the kids and others objecting, he couldn't do it. So he squared it with himself by making himself believe there was a chance. When we went in to her bedroom, Anna asked me to try to rouse Mrs. R. who had been out all day. I shouted in her ear. She roused enough to say "hello, dear" without opening her eyes. Fjr. went over and tenderly kissed her and we went out.

October 29. Maureen said today that Mrs. R's only response to David when he told her she had TB and could be treated for it, was "I want to die." Maureen believes Mrs. R knows what's going on but has decided to withdraw and lies there breathing heavily and if she opens her eyes, gives no sign of recognition. . . . Maureen thought Anna should have handled Paddy more diplomatically. . . . Edna came in bristling over story Anna gave the *Post* yesterday which described Mrs. R's condition as it really is. The family was appalled at David's giving the *Herald Tribune* story about "cheering" news. . . . Maureen in tears several times.

When Trude offered to sit at her desk until Anna returned, she replied tartly, "I'm under orders now from the family."

October 30. When Trude came back from Mrs. R's she said her eyes had been open but she wouldn't talk. Trude also is convinced she is aware of what is going on, but deliberately has withdrawn into herself. She will no longer take pills or eat and when she learned pills were being secreted in applesauce, she refused to touch the applesauce from then on.

Nurse Waldron works on her crossword puzzles. She told me Mrs. Roosevelt opens her eyes but will not speak except to say no, to the doctors she says she wants to die. She may be incoherent, confused, but she remains clear and iron-willed on that. She will not eat or drink, thrusts it aside. Nurse Waldron said it was sad a woman of such great force could not go quickly. She believes Mrs. R. has been going downhill for two years now and seriously since April. Anna describes her determination to die with the phrase "she clenches her teeth" and will allow nothing to enter her mouth. . . . Once Nurse Waldron got into her mouth and found it padded with white pills which she had secreted but refused to swallow. At the hospital, Anna said, before she and Jim had decided to bring her home, she had threatened several times to jump out of the window. There is a glucose, potassium drip. . . .

October 31. In yesterday's battle of the communiqués, Maureen gave out a line on the basis of what David told her that was more hopeful than the weekend one. Buzz called her (his mother Anna was in Detroit) and rebuked her and said a member of the family should be the spokesman.

Mrs. R. was taking a little food today and awake. When I went in her eyes were open and she was propped up on pillows as the nurse fed her some milky syrup. She didn't recognize me and kept saying in a raspy voice to the nurse while pushing her hand, "go away." I shouted in her ear how wonderful it was to see her eating and she should finish. She did allow the nurse to finish ladleing out the stuff and then said something about "let the ceremony begin . . . let the ceremony begin."

All the doctors except David have agreed she should be given another transfusion. Maureen is afraid it will kill her. David thinks she is responding to the anti-biotics directed at TB and is more hopeful than ever that he is on the right track . . .

Johnny Bott [my city editor at the *Post*] called me to read me a *World-Telegram* story that quoted Jimmy Roosevelt as saying Mrs. R. had asked to see Stevenson and that he had left the UN in midst of the Cuban crisis and gone up to East 74th Street to see her. "I didn't know anything about it," I replied and called Maureen who said Mrs. R. was "pretty good, pretty good. The transfusion had gone pretty well. They tried to knock her out for it, but she's so strong, it didn't wholly take." "No," she did not know about the Stevenson visit, but here is Mrs. Halsted, "I'll let you talk to her."

Anna—"my only reason for doing this [letting Stevenson come] was that David had been so terribly rude to Adlai. There were such hurt feelings. The boys felt he should be allowed to come and to wave at her. He had left a rather pathetic note for her at the hospital. I called him to bring him up to date. He sounded like a rather irate gentleman who felt he had been close enough to mother and should have been treated better. Come if you would like to, I said, but I don't think she will recognize you. He dropped everything and came within the hour. I warned him not to tell anybody and I also warned the boys. . . ."

When I went up to 74th Street at 4, Maureen's version was that Mrs. R. had tried six or seven times to see Stevenson and he wasn't able to find the time. When it was disclosed she had gone to the hospital, it must have bothered his conscience and he came up to the hospital and ran into David who wouldn't let him see her. He went away furious and has been repeating the story around New York. . . . She would not have wanted Stevenson to come. She doesn't do these things by the "importance" of the people involved.

Edna disagrees with Anna's account of what happened with Stevenson. "David was not rude to Adlai, but loyal to Mrs. R. *She did not want to be seen by Adlai as she was—ill and old—*as well as by others not close to her. And David left orders accordingly. David was dealing with his *patient.* Adlai came because Anna called him. Simple. He fled with embarrassment."

Edna's notes:

November 5, 1962. This afternoon David brought in a doctor from South Africa whom he happened to meet, to see Mrs. Roosevelt. The doctor knows a good deal about TB of the bone marrow. Earlier, David had taken him to the office of Dr. Hyman, the blood specialist David had brought in on Mrs. R's case. This evening, Jim Halsted, Anna's husband, came to see David to ask him to let Dr. Hyman take over Mrs. R's case, instead of David being in charge. That is a ridiculous request, which David turned down, as he, David, always had to persuade Mrs. R. in the past to see Dr. Hyman for even 10 minutes. She would never want Dr. Hyman to be her doctor. But Halsted and his wife feel with Hyman in charge, Mrs. Roosevelt will be allowed to die, whereas David is not giving up, leaving no stone unturned to try to save her.

Lash journal:

November 5. This past weekend Jim Halsted here and met with the consulting doctors. Should Mrs. R's sufferings be prolonged? Dr. A. believes the TB cannot be treated, it is spreading. Anna said that when her mother's temperature goes down, her pulse goes up and vice versa. Was it right under these conditions to keep her alive? . . . Trude says that on Sunday there was the look of a frightened animal in her eyes. . . . When I was there I saw that Mrs. R's jaw had gone slack. I went upstairs to say hello to Elliott and had a drink with him and Anna. He couldn't face up to going in to see his mother. When he went out of the room Anna told me she had not told him about her mother's stroke or F jr. either. . . . I gathered that as a result of the doctors' conference all they are doing now is trying to keep her as comfortable as possible, some antibiotics, otherwise she would burn up.

Anna and Elliott agreed that this prolonged suffering was exactly the way their mother did not want to go. Elliott wondered if someone two years earlier had explained to her that in view of her low hemoglobin count, it was essential she take things easy but Anna and I replied nothing would have slowed her up. As long as she had the energy to do something she would do it.

Anna said David had cornered her on the stairway that morning. He wanted to countermand yesterday's decision and try something else. But then he gave up and said to Anna, "I've known for 10 days it was hopeless." Nurses have been told David was not permitted to alter treatments without orders from Dr. Hyman.

Edna's notes:

Tuesday, November 6. Mrs. Roosevelt had a stroke last night around 11 p.m. From what I can gather her right side is paralyzed. It makes no difference. She is in a coma. David says she had possibly small strokes in these past 3 days. It is hopeless. We shall lose her. . . .

The Halsteds told David this morning that Mrs. Roosevelt felt David was another son. But it was more than that. They resent David. It is understandable but still despicable. They had to swallow all these years that only David could influence their mother. Now, in death they are claiming her. . . .

Lash journal:

November 6. David called this morning at 10:30. . . . Mrs. R. had a severe stroke. . . . It's altogether hopeless now. Her pulse is not so good. It could happen this weekend, could be within a day. Could I help? I asked. "Later on," he replied. "We can help each other. I have trouble with Anna and Jim. They were determined for some time she should go. I felt she was savable. We could have had the same diagnosis (I assume for TB) a year ago. The people in Boston would have done it and she could have been saved. It was left for me to make that diagnosis 40 days ago. Others should have made it, especially the hemotoligist . . . The dirty linen will come out. . . ." I sought to stop him. "Later, later, David," I said. . . .

November 7. At 7:30 Trude called me. Mrs. R. had died. Maureen had called to tell her. Trude had been at 74th Street at 6. Anna had pushed her out. . . . At 11:30 we went up. Anna read me the notice they had sent out.

November 8. Went up end of the day. F jr. told me the funeral arrangements. The children would have dinner Friday evening at his house to talk business, the grandchildren at Johnny's, the rest of us at Mrs. R's. They were going up that night to seal the coffin . . . David and Edna wanted us to have dinner, but I couldn't face an evening with David using me as a wailing wall and we did not know when Jonathan would get in from Putney.

Edna's notes.

November 8. Our dear Mrs. Roosevelt died last evening. . . . Around a quarter of nine, I saw from my bedroom window, the simple casket leaving the house, it being placed into the hearse and Mrs. Roosevelt alone with David driving away from 74th Street for the last time. I called out many goodbyes from the window.

David stayed with her. An autopsy was performed. . . .

We leave for Hyde Park tomorrow. We go together with the Lashes.

We traveled in separate cars but met for dinner at a restaurant on the way up. "Would we ever go to the cottage again?" I wondered out loud. Johnny had invited them, Edna replied, but she was against doing so. David demurred. He would go, he said. "Then it poured out," my notes read, "first from Edna, then David. The children, when Mrs. Roosevelt was brought home from the hospital, were resigned to her death—ready for it—preparing for it, and the big fight with David arose because he wanted to save her." But at breakfast the next morning in Mrs. R's cottage Anna, who was sitting at the head of the table with Jim opposite, said to me, "If my mother had been told in 1960 she had a blood disease and would have to cut down on her activities, she would have done it. . . . Had she done so she could have been saved for three or four years."

A month later, David wrote me about the results of the autopsy.

December 15, 1962.

Dear Joe:

This is one o'clock in the morning. Fifteen hours ago we had a clinical pathological conference including the final results of the autopsy of Mrs. Roosevelt. I thought you would like to know.

I have been rushing the whole day. But now that I have some peace, an enormous sense of relaxation has come over me as a result of this conference. The pathological findings show without any question that Mrs. Roosevelt had a primary disease of the bone marrow, in which the bone marrow, to a very high extent, lost the capacity to form blood. Therefore, the anemia. We know no treatment for this condition. It is really a miracle that she was able to carry on as actively as she did for as long as she did. The trip this spring to Israel was on borrowed time alright. No medical knowledge is available which could have saved her even theoretically. The organism, however strong it had been, had been depleted of all reserves to such an extent that in the end, I mean about three months before the actual end, an old otherwise utterly innocuous tuberculosis gland, could spread tuberculosis infection into the bone marrow and in virtually all other organs of the human body other than the central nervous system. The resistance of the body had been weakened to such an extent that not the slightest resistance could be seen of the body to the infection. This is very rare. Even in the most advanced case of tuberculosis we see body resistance, attempts at encapsulating, localizing the infection. Here was none. Nothing could have been done to save her.

Incidentally, the man who examined her brain made this statement: that she had the brain of a young person. I thought you would like to know that too.

Just my love.

David.

Several years later in researches for *The Years Alone,* a letter Dr. Halsted sent to James Roosevelt, then serving on the U.S. Mission to the United Nations, also described the course of Mrs. Roosevelt's last illness.

March 25, 1966

Dear Jim,

. . .

The facts are as follows in respect to the sequence of events:

She had aplastic anemia (also known as bone marrow failure) which was diagnosed in 1960. The cause of aplastic anemia is usually unknown and this was the case with your Mother. Approximately six months before her death she was given steroids because the course of the anemia indicated that she might begin to develop internal bleeding and steroids are an effective remedy for that in aplastic anemia. Unfortunately she had an old tuberculosis lesion dating back to 1919, the scars of which were shown in the x-rays of her chest. Steroid treatments of many illnesses "light up" inactive and healed tuberculosis if carried out over several weeks or more. This is what happened in your Mother's case. The tuberculosis which was activated by steroid treatment spread rapidly and widely throughout her body and was resistant to all kinds of anti-tuberculosis treatment. This was the cause of her death.

    . . .

> Affectionately,
> Jim

"There was only suffering for Mrs. Roosevelt," Trude wrote Paul Tillich, "from the first day in July when she was taken to the hospital for the first time. There was no moment of serenity. There was only anger, helpless anger at the doctors and nurses and the world who tried to keep her alive." She felt "betrayed and persecuted by all of us," Trude went on.

> She was not afraid of death at all. She welcomed it. She was so weary and so infinitely exhausted, it seemed as though she had to suffer every human indignity, every weakness, every failure that she had resisted and conquered so daringly during her whole life—as though she were being punished for being too strong and powerful and disciplined and almost immune to human frailty.

Later, when I began work on *Eleanor and Franklin*, I found in Mrs. Roosevelt's "file of special papers" a poem written by Amelia Earhart the year in which she made the flight into the Pacific on which she disappeared, along with Walter Lippmann's tribute at the time. "Courage," Miss Earhart wrote, "is the price that life exacts for granting peace/The soul that knows it not knows no release/From little things . . . How can life grant us boon of living . . ./Unless we dare/The soul's dominion? Each time we make a choice, we pay/With courage to behold resistless day/And count it fair." Miss Earhart and people like her, Lippmann wrote, "No pre-conceived theory fits them. No material purpose actuates them. They do the useless, brave, noble, the divinely foolish and the very wisest things that are done by man."

Mrs. Roosevelt kept such papers about people who did things worth doing in a special file not because she thought she exemplified them but to move in the same direction. When she was asked toward the end of her life on Edward R. Murrow's program, "This I Believe," whether she believed in a future life, her spontaneous answer ended:

I think I am pretty much of a fatalist. You have to accept whatever comes and the only important thing is that you meet it with courage and with the best that you have to give.

Appendix

S EVERAL YEARS LATER I met Dr. Moses M. Suzman, an animated, no-
nonsense, agreeable man. The late Allard Lowenstein, also a friend of Eleanor Roosevelt, had encountered him in South Africa during a mission that
took Al to Johannesburg. He brought us together at lunch when Dr. Suzman was in
the United States. The story Dr. Suzman told of his involvement in Mrs.
Roosevelt's terminal illness coincided with what David had told me except in some
critical respects. My books about Eleanor Roosevelt, however, were written. David
was dead. I had no wish to second guess or adjudicate doctors' decisions and
disputes. I let the matter rest.

But when I came to review these times in connection with this book I did not
trust my memory and wrote Dr. Suzman in Johannesburg. Just before the manuscript went to press I received a sixteen-page vivid account of his involvement. I
leave it to him whether he wishes to give it to a medical journal. I can only use it
sparingly.

Dr. Suzman is an internist with special interests including "disorders of the
blood." His competence is attested to by the work he has done in the United States
with doctors who were "famous names in Haemotology." At a dinner party at the
end of September 1962 the hostess had seated him at the same table with David,
who proceeded to give him a patient's case history without naming the patient. Dr.
Suzman immediately voiced disagreement with the diagnosis of leukemia made by
the doctors in attendance, believing rather that David's patient "almost certainly
was suffering from tuberculosis with invasion of the bone marrow, the effect of
which was to cause both profound anaemia and a leukomoid reaction." The latter
is a blood disorder, writes Dr. Suzman, that resembles leukemia or aplastic anemia.

Dr. Suzman's diagnosis startled David, who found it sufficiently persuasive to tell him the name of his patient and to ask "whether I would be prepared to discuss the matter with his colleagues and perhaps see his patient as well." When Dr. Suzman replied he was prepared to do both, David undertook to arrange matters subject to the concurrence of the family and his medical colleagues, who were meeting regularly on the case.

But there was no agreement among the doctors. Except for Dr. Suzman who believed that with anti-tuberculous treatments "a satisfactory response might just possibly have been achieved," the other doctors insisted that the tuberculous infection was "superimposed on a primary blood disorder, be it leukemia or aplastic anaemia."

This is a disagreement beyond the province of a layman to judge. Even doctors, without access to Mrs. Roosevelt's charts, which were placed at the Franklin D. Roosevelt Library under seal until 1990, may find it difficult to reach a judgment.

Index

Catalog

If you are interested in a list of fine **Paperback**
books, covering a wide range of subjects
and interests, send your name and address,
requesting your free catalog, to:

McGraw-Hill Paperbacks
1221 Avenue of Americas
New York, N.Y. 10020